WILD BILL WELLMAN

Hollywood Rebel

WILLIAM WELLMAN, JR.

The photographs found on pages 485, 489, and 493 are courtesy of
George Eastman House International Museum of Photography and Film.
All other photographs are from the personal collections of William Wellman, Jr.

Library of Congress Cataloging-in-Publication Data
Wellman, William A., [date]
Wild Bill Wellman : Hollywood rebel / William A. Wellman, Jr.
pages   cm
Includes bibliographical references and index.
ISBN 978-0-307-37770-8 (hardcover : alk. paper). ISBN 978-1-101-87028-0 (eBook).
1. Wellman, William A., 1896–1975.   2. Motion picture producers
and directors—United States—Biography.   I. Title.
PN1998.3.W454W48 2015   791.4302'33092—dc23   [B]   2014028021

www.pantheonbooks.com

Jacket photograph: Collection of William Wellman, Jr.
Jacket design by Kelly Blair

Printed in the United States of America
First Edition

9 8 7 6 5 4 3 2 1

To my lovely and devoted wife, Flossie, who makes every day worthwhile; my kids, Teresa, Cathy, Mark, and Chris; my grandchildren, Emma Grace and Jackson William; my brothers, Tim and Mike; my sisters, Pat, Kitty, Cissy, and Maggie; and all the extended Wellman family and close friends near and far.

To my wonderful mother and father: her love for her children and her Bill was always on display and never diminished. His enduring love and support for his family was lifelong.

Of all the great stars and filmmakers that he knew and worked with, his favorite people were fliers. Beginning with those chivalrous knights of the First World War, he continued to see their reflections in any living person who ever took to the skies in an aircraft. This kind of steadfast devotion spilled over onto his Dottie and their family.

CONTENTS

INTRODUCTION
WILD BILL WELLMAN

I n France, during the First World War, they called him "Wild Bill." When he came to Hollywood, William A. Wellman kept the nickname. As a fighter pilot, he fought the enemy in the air and on the ground. As a movie director, he fought the producers and the great moguls—some with his fists—for the right to make his films his way.

My father lived a life more adventurous, more confrontational, more unpredictable than anything in his movies. His childhood was packed with conflict. He left home and hearth to fight in a war that his country wanted no part of. He told his family that his reason for leaving was because it was either war or jail.

He was a member of the vaunted French Foreign Legion before attaining his aviator's wings in the Lafayette Flying Corps. For his valor, he received one of France's highest honors, the Croix de Guerre with two Palms—each Palm is like another Croix de Guerre. He survived many combat missions and six major air crashes. He was seriously wounded and sent home before joining the U.S. Air Service. He finished the war as a flight instructor at Rockwell Field in San Diego, California, where he married a movie star and entered the world of the cinema.

He fought his way up the Hollywood ladder, finally attaining the rank of director. He brought with him his passionate personality, roguish behavior, fierce determination, driving ambition, and a trunkful of life experiences. For his movies, my father was always searching for a different story, a different point of view, something unusual and not like the films he had already made. It was never about the accolades or the money he would make; it was always about the making of the movies. He directed seventy-six of them and there were powerhouse gangster films like *The Public Enemy* (1931), making a star of James Cagney, and *The Hatchet*

Man (1932) with Edward G. Robinson; fast-moving adventure pictures like *Wild Boys of the Road* (1933), *The Call of the Wild* (1935) starring Clark Gable and Loretta Young, and *Beau Geste* (1939) with Gary Cooper and Ray Milland.

There were Westerns like *Yellow Sky* (1948) with Gregory Peck, Richard Widmark, and Anne Baxter; *Westward the Women* (1951) starring Robert Taylor; and the classic *The Ox-Bow Incident* (1943) with Henry Fonda and Dana Andrews. There were war stories such as *Battleground* (1949) and *The Story of G.I. Joe* (1945), which made a star of Robert Mitchum, who received his only Academy Award nomination. The picture remains, perhaps, the greatest fictional tribute to the American soldier.

There were comedies, too—movies like *Nothing Sacred* (1937) starring Carole Lombard and Fredric March, and *Roxie Hart* (1942) toplining Ginger Rogers; along with hard-hitting melodramas such as *Beggars of Life* (1928) starring Wallace Beery and Louise Brooks, *Safe in Hell* (1931), *Heroes for Sale* (1933), *The Light That Failed* (1939) starring Ronald Colman, and his Academy Award–winning *A Star Is Born* (the original 1937 film) with Fredric March and Janet Gaynor. He even made a semi-musical, *Lady of Burlesque* (1943) starring Barbara Stanwyck.

Throughout my father's thirty-five years as a director, he continually returned to the skies for his love of aviation adventure. He never forgot those courageous young Americans that he met and flew beside, who fought so bravely in a foreign land, flying French planes, sacrificing their lives in the pursuit of life and liberty. Even when his movie heroes were not airborne, they brought a similar grace and gallantry to other adventurous tasks.

Beginning with his monumental *Wings* (1927), the first film to depict the Great War fought in the air and winner of the first Best Picture, there would be ten more aviation pictures, including *Island in the Sky* (1953) and *The High and the Mighty* (1954), both starring John Wayne.

His eleventh and final aviation film was to be called *C'est la Guerre* (It's the War). The picture was his tribute to the young fliers of that long-ago war. It had taken almost three decades to get the green light, and in the end, retitled *Lafayette Escadrille* (1958), the film was so dismantled by Warner Bros. mogul Jack Warner that my father, heartbroken, retired from the industry he had helped to create—an industry that had provided him with a résumé of over a hundred pictures, seventy-six directed films winning thirty-two Academy Award nominations and seven Oscars. He received only three Academy nominations for directing—*A Star Is Born, Battleground*, and *The High and the Mighty*—but never won. Academy recognition did not come his way for other classic films, like *Wings*, even though it won for Best Picture, *The Public Enemy*, *Beau Geste*, *The Ox-Bow Incident*, *The Story of G.I. Joe*. His only personal Oscar came from the writing of *A Star Is Born*.

Although his trophy case was only half full, the Directors Guild of America bestowed upon him their Lifetime Achievement Award in 1973. Personal awards, however, meant little to him. What counted most was his forty-two-year marriage to his devoted Dottie, his seven children, twenty-two grandchildren, and eleven great-grandchildren.

In his retirement, he wrote two books, *A Short Time for Insanity* (1974) and *Growing Old Disgracefully* (unpublished). Dad enjoyed his expanding family for as long as he could. Many times he had battled and defeated near-death encounters, but he could not conquer the cancer that stole his life two months shy of his eightieth birthday. He left those of us who loved him a grand treasure chest of memories. To the world of cinema, he left a great legacy of film. William A. Wellman took giant steps across the pages of history, but more important are the footprints he left behind.

WILD BILL WELLMAN

1

THE REBEL

It was late afternoon and we knew the time was fast approaching. I stood beside my father's bed fighting back tears but losing the battle. He was lying on his back staring at the ceiling. He turned his head to me and said, "Bill, goddammit, don't feel sorry for me. I've lived the life of a hundred men." Soon he was gone.

He left a great legacy with his more than forty-year career and over a hundred films. There were screen classics among his seventy-six directorial achievements that produced thirty-two Academy Award nominations and seven Oscars. And yet, he and his body of work are decidedly underappreciated.

"Wellman was a true Jack London character," said film scholar and Oscar winner Kevin Brownlow. "Colorful, vivid, and fascinating, he suggests an authentic figure of the Old West, tall and lean with a tough, weather-beaten face and a voice exactly like John Wayne's."

"He was a bully. He was a smartass. He was a poet, a ruffian, an artist, a brawler, a soft-hearted sap," wrote author and film historian Frank Thompson.

"He used to stand outside the front office and yell obscenities up at the executives," said Wellman assistant director Arthur Jacobson.

"Bill was born a rebel," said Frank Capra. "As a director, he fought many a battle, some with his fists, for the right to make his films the way he thought he should make them."

"He didn't waste a lot of time on useless, silly sentimentality," said Robert Mitchum. "You know . . . he wore no man's collar. I was very, very fond of him, and he tolerated me."

"The eternal rebel, trying something new. Perhaps to do something he hadn't done or been allowed to do before," said Clint Eastwood.

"He has humor and guts. But most of all . . . heart," said James Stewart.

"Bill Wellman was a man's director, but he was also very much a woman's director," said Gregory Peck.

"He could be very intimidating," said Nancy Davis Reagan, "but underneath that he was a pussycat . . . I loved him."

"A slim, handsome young man . . . an intricate man . . . bewitched by his own success in Hollywood. So fascinated was I by a quiet sadism practiced by Billy behind the camera, especially in his direction of women," wrote Louise Brooks.

"You were always my favorite director, but you were a hard taskmaster," wrote Clara Bow in a letter to Wellman.

"I miss you, Bill Wellman. I love you," wrote Barbara Stanwyck in a letter to him.

William A. Wellman had built a rather large résumé by the time he was thirty years old: he had been a juvenile delinquent; a professional ice hockey star; a decorated fighter pilot in World War I; married three of his five wives, including a Hollywood movie star and a *Ziegfeld Follies* showgirl; and directed eleven films including *Wings* (1927), the winner of the first Academy Award for Best Picture.

On February 29, 1896, a leap year, William Augustus Wellman was born in the four-poster bed of his mother, Celia McCarthy. Mother, father, Arthur Gouverneur, and sixteen-month-old brother, Arthur Ogden, lived in a middle-class neighborhood in Brookline, Massachusetts. Celia, less than five feet tall with flaming red hair, had sailed to America in 1872 with her mother, Cecilia Lee Guinness, and father, Charles P. McCarthy.

Cecilia Lee was a member of the renowned Guinness Stout family of Ireland. Her great-grandfather, Arthur Guinness, founded the Dublin Brewery in 1759. He boasted of twenty-one offspring. The family included royalty—Lord and Lady Iveagh. Lord Iveagh descended through two brothers who were sons of Arthur Guinness and his wife, Olivia Whitmore.

When the young Cecilia declared her intention to marry Charles McCarthy, a Protestant minister, her family was shaken. Although the Guinness family were pillars of the Protestant Church of Ireland, they also protested this union with vigor. Cecilia, however, would not back down and the wedding took place. Her family refused to attend and Cecilia was disinherited. The newlyweds left Ireland, settling in Chel-

Mother Celia and son William, December 1896

Brother Arch, mother Celia, William Wellman, 1903

tenham, England. On August 12, 1869, Cecilia gave birth to a daughter, whom she also named Cecilia but called Celia. Three years later, the McCarthy family set sail for America, settling in New York City where Cecilia earned money as a singing teacher. One of her pupils, daughter Celia, made her debut in vaudeville as a singer and actress. Cecilia gave birth to another daughter, Grace. When Charles took the position as minister of the First Unitarian Church of Providence, the family moved to Rhode Island and later to Boston. Before Celia celebrated her twenty-third birthday, she caught the eye of a personable Englishman, Arthur Gouverneur Wellman.

Arthur's parents, William Augustus and Matilda (Ogden) Gouverneur, were married and settled in Boston. The father was a prominent banker and one of the founders of Brookline. Arthur was born April 8, 1858, in Brookline. He had a sister, Mary Fairlie, and two brothers, Joseph and Francis L. The three brothers attended the Massachusetts Institute of Technology. Arthur was the only one not to graduate, choosing to accept a position in an insurance brokerage in his hometown.

Arthur never gained the respect or success of his brothers, sister, and father. Francis L., born July 29, 1860, also attended Harvard University before becoming a celebrated attorney and wrote several popular books on law: *The Art of Cross-Examination* (1904, 1920), *Day in Court* (1912), *Gentleman of the Jury* (1924), and *Luck and Opportunity* (1938). Arthur's sister, Mary F., married Samuel Williston, an eminent lawyer, on September 12, 1889. He was the dean of Harvard Law School (1909), the first gold-medal winner of the American Bar Association, in 1929, and authored numerous articles and books on legal subjects, including *The Law of Sale* (1909, 1924) and *The Law of Contracts* (1920).

After a brief courtship, the Englishman and the Irish girl tied the knot in Boston, August 2, 1892. In 1843, Arthur's father had built a Greek Revival–style house in Brookline and later moved it to a better location in the same neighborhood at 4 Perry Street. It was an elegant interpretation of a popular style in Brookline. There were four pilasters which extended across the principal facade in the Corinthian order. The house was symmetrical with matching windows. The porch extended around both sides with columns every four or five feet.

On the property stood a carriage barn that was converted into a home for the bridal pair. Later, the carriage house was given the address of 20 Linden Place. This is where Celia gave birth to her two sons. Arthur Ogden, named after his grandmother, was nicknamed "Arch," while William Augustus, named after his grandfather, answered to "Billy." Since

Celia and Arthur honeymooning, Boston, 1892

Billy's grandpa had passed away before his grandson's birth, no Junior or II was attached to the newborn.

For the next eight years, the family enjoyed the good life of Brookline. The carriage home was large enough to be comfortable, and the picturesque neighborhood, with its lovely parks and rows of bright-hued trees, served as a fine playground for the growing boys. There was an abundance of young children as playmates and congenial neighbors. Knowing Billy was born on February 29, in a leap year, the neighbors all said that he would either be a wonder or a fool, so that in any case, having covered possibilities so thoroughly, they could say, I told you so.

Celia was the all-caring mother and devoted wife. She often took the boys to the Boston Common and Public Garden, which contained walking paths, open green spaces, a swan pond where boats could be rented, and a fountain frequented by children on hot steaming days. The family played along the banks of the Charles River, and south to the beaches at Hull and Nantasket. These towns boasted an exciting amusement park, and they could stay overnight at "Aunt" Fanny Randall's Inn. She wasn't their real aunt, but she treated them like family with free rooms and clambakes at the shore.

Celia and the boys entered the large doorway to the Museum of Fine Arts. The original MFA opened its doors on July 4, 1876, the nation's centennial, and was home to 5,600 works of art. In 1909, the museum moved to nearby Huntington Avenue. The family traveled to Paul Revere's house and the Old North Church, built in 1723. In 1775, this was the church where two lanterns in its steeple signaled that the British were coming, and Paul Revere leaped on his horse, carrying the warning across the countryside to Lexington. Celia and her boys loved the view of Boston Harbor as they watched the sailing ships come and go to all parts of the world.

Arthur had provided a good life for his family. He was caring and attentive to Celia and the boys. On weekends, he involved himself with his sons. There was baseball, boating, and beach time in the summer; sledding, ice skating, and snowball fights in the winter; croquet in their own yard. Arthur taught the boys the finer points of this most popular sport.

By 1904, Arthur was forty-six years old, had developed an acute drinking problem, and was replaced by a younger man at the brokerage firm. The family was forced to sell their home and move to a rented one in the neighboring town of Newton. This moving to rented homes would become, just like Arthur's drinking, a continuing habit. Newton became the place where Billy and his brother, Arch, would finish grammar school and attend Newton High School.

Crystal Lake was a block from their new home. They cut ice there in the winter and stored it in the big icehouse on the other side of the lake. The railroad track ran alongside and they spent many hours watching the freight trains come and go. "In the winter we skated, in the summer we swam, in the fall we gathered chestnuts that fell from the big proud trees that lined the lake," remembered Wellman. "Have you ever tasted roasted chestnuts? Not the big ones. The medium size. Not the ones you get in New York. The Boston chestnuts. You've heard the expression 'sweet as a nut'? Could well have been 'sweet as a Crystal Lake chestnut.'"

Wellman recalled with mouthwatering relish, "Boston baked beans, fish balls—not cakes—steamed clams, and chestnuts. Steaks and chops and roast beef you get anywhere, and they're good anywhere, but nowhere can you get these savorous four—the beans, the balls, the clams, and the nuts—except in Boston, and they're very inexpensive dishes. You can feast on them if you're broke, which by the way, we were a great deal of the time."

Wellman wrote about his dad as an inner and outer. One month they would eat the beans and the balls and the nuts most nights, sometimes every night until you got full of them and wanted something different. But the boys never got sick of them. Then when the old boy would come home with his pockets bulging and his breath an alcoholic haze, they would have the best on the dinner table until his luck suddenly vanished and they went back to beans, balls, clams, and nuts.

Soon after the move to Newton, Billy and Arch received a special Christmas present from their mother—a dog of their own. He was a round, black-and-white, furry mongrel; a little Spitz, a dash of Eskimo, a touch of Border collie. He wasn't young and he wasn't old, just a friendly pet with the name of

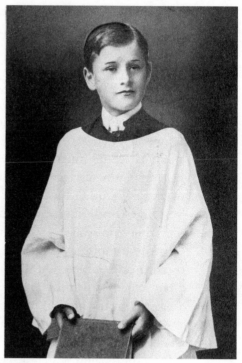

The choirboy, Billy Wellman, twelve years old, 1908

Taffy, after the current President Taft. Taffy even liked beans.

Arch loved to tinker with hammers, saws, nails, and such out in the shed in the backyard. Using his father's jigsaw, he made all sorts of things out of wood and other materials. Billy spent his time out of doors; ice skating in the winter, tapping the maple trees for their sweet syrup, baseball and swimming in the spring and summer, football in the fall. Wherever Billy went, Taffy was next to him. The two pals were inseparable. Soon everyone referred to Taffy as Billy's dog. The next Christmas, Arch's present to his brother was his half of the dog.

As Arthur's work and liquid diet problems worsened, Celia began to look for a job. This, however, was not at all proper. The right to vote, equal education, and work opportunities for women had not arrived. Women were expected to be at home running the household, preparing the meals, raising the children, dedicated to the husband.

Celia cared about all these matters in addition to women's suffrage and equality with men, but her boys needed to be clothed and fed. She didn't want to go through any more frigid winters having to burn pages of books in the fireplace for warmth. Arthur's brother-in-law, the esteemed lawyer Samuel Williston, happened by one winter's day finding Celia tearing off encyclopedia pages, throwing them into the fire. The love of her family, the frustrations and embarrassments of her poverty-repeating existence, gave her strength to find a solution.

Celia always enjoyed the company of her son's friends. She encouraged the boys to bring their schoolmates home, and the friends loved her company. They wanted to be near her, to listen to her stories. Since she attended school functions and sporting events, she met many of them. Her door was always open, and it wasn't surprising to find fifteen or twenty boys around the house. On Sundays, Celia took groups to the St. Paul's Trinity Episcopal Church in Newton Highlands, and later to the Trinity Episcopal Church in Newton Center. She urged the boys to sing in the choirs, even started a boys' choir. Arch had no ear for music, couldn't carry a tune. On the other hand, Billy had a beautiful voice and often soloed. When there was extra money, he took private lessons from a prominent teacher in Boston.

As a way of keeping the boys active and out of trouble, Celia started a baseball team in the summer months. Of course, girls were not allowed to play sports with boys, especially such rough-and-tumble games where bats were used—they might get dirty, tear their dresses, or hurt themselves. At Newton High School, the boys played football, baseball, ice hockey and field hockey, tennis, golf, track, basketball, and fencing. The girls were engaged with two all-girl sports, field hockey and basketball. Their uniforms included dresses.

Boys began to ask Celia for advice. Parents brought their troubled youth to see her. She called them her "wayward boys." She contacted city officials and, in her most persuasive manner, asked for employment as a kind of truant officer. They gave her the job. The only problem for Celia, there was no pay attached to the position. She pressed the issue, eventually creating a new post as a probation officer. There already was a probation official for men but not for women and children. The pay was minimal but of great help to her struggling family.

In grammar school, both Billy and Arch were active in sports and school events. Arch excelled in his scholastics, Billy did not. When the boys entered Newton High School, nothing had changed. Arch tried to help his brother, who was far more interested in extracurricular activities than books. Fortunately, Billy succeeded in other endeavors—even as an actor.

Beginning in grammar school and continuing through high school,

Celia wrote and produced plays, enlisting the aid of her two boys. Arch preferred duties behind the scenes—building sets, handling finances, costuming, and makeup. He even gave haircuts to the wigs and the players. The cast members were all boys; no girls were allowed on the stage. Arch got so good at cutting hair, parents paid him to cut their son's locks.

At first, Celia created minstrel shows. Covered in blackface, the boys sang and danced to the delight of the parents and teachers. Later, Celia wrote dramas. Since all the players were boys, they had to play the female roles as well. Billy excelled at this. Boston's *Morning Telegraph*, Sunday, July 21, 1918, reported that Wellman [Billy] "made the best stage lady in command of the boys' theatrical club. And he strode the boards as Bessie McCoy or as Lillian Russell, or even Bernhardt [Sarah], with as much eclat as Joe March, Miss Alcott's immortal heroine, donned the red boots and played the villain with a muffled curse on his lips."

Another play, produced in 1915, *In Dreamland*, was a musical presented

Newton High School baseball team: Billy and his dog, Taffy; coach Dickinson over them; brother Arch top left, 1914

by St. Paul's Boys Club, Newton Highlands. Billy was a featured player portraying the role of Celestia, the Goddess. He sang a solo, a song titled "Little Grey Home in the West." Billy also switched genders and performed a specialty song-and-dance number with another player.

Billy's first sexual encounter—"My first call of the wild, sex," he said—happened during his freshman year. She was much older and taught dancing to the mothers and fathers of Newton High's students. "She met and liked me, I liked her, she invited me to her home the next day, two miles away, then kissed me. I froze from heat. I had never been kissed like that, sure I had been kissed by Marion, Vera, Peggy but they were giggly embarrassed pecks but this, wow, I get weak, shook all over."

Wellman couldn't sleep all night long, just kept turning over and over. Taffy, his dog, who always slept with him, got tired of going to sleep and getting awakened, going to sleep again, and being snapped out of it. "He gave up," said Wellman. "He jumped off the bed, crawled under it where he thought he could get some rest, but it didn't work, my constant turning and flopping was just as annoying under the bed as on top, so he sneaked over to the farthest corner, flopped down on the hard floor, with an unhappy grunt went sound to sleep—he must have thought I had worms.

"I ran the two miles as fast as I could, never stopping, never changing my pace, just running my ass off—it was a hell of a fast run, a sex run and there she was on the porch waiting for me. I put on the brakes, tried to act nonchalant but my heavy breathing gave me away. I excused myself leaving her standing there and walked slowly around her house.

"When I arrived in front of her again, I was breathing as quietly as if in church—she liked this, smiled, asked me to come in, my breathing was natural but I was scared to death." They didn't sit down to talk. She started petting Billy, running her fingers through his hair, over his face, down his arms, waist, and legs, unbuttoned his pants and lay down, pulling up her dress. "Her legs were pretty—she pulled me down on top of her, it happened. I lost my breath again, my heart was pounding like a trip hammer, my head was muzzy, I was terrified, I got up, ran out of the house, and kept running the two miles back home. Taffy was waiting, he jumped all over me as we flew up the stairs two at a time and charged into my room." Billy locked the door, and lay down on the bed, panting. "Taffy jumped up, lay down beside me—put his head on my chest, and just stared at me, his tail was wagging softly. I swear there was a proud smile on his face, kind of made me feel good—I smiled back, patted his head—I felt great, I was a man."

Jesseppi Shinicerella, the fruit man's daughter, was Billy's first girl. "She taught me how to fight," said Wellman. "Because the kids could think up and yell so many dirty verbal acrobatics with her name, but to end this bloody mess it did something to me, whoever's blood it was, it changed a questionable personality into a lousy one."

High school brought no changes in Billy's world of hostilities. The Wellmans lived in a neighborhood composed of various ethnic families— none in the majority. However, in order for Billy and Arch to venture out of their domain, even going to school, they had to cross neighborhoods where insiders ruled over outsiders. Wellman said, "I have fought with Irishers who lived on the other side of the aqueduct, for robbing our pails of nectar from the maple trees in the winter. From the Irishers who lived in Kerry Cross through which we had to pass to and from high school. The 'we' being me and my brother, a very handy man to have around."

It seemed that if there was a scuffle somewhere in Newton, Billy was a part of it. Celia was having trouble controlling her younger son. His studies were down and his rumbles were up. The number of angry parents of the boys Billy fought with was increasing. Even the law came knocking and not just about fisticuffs. In a rage, Billy had thrown a rock through a school bully's window. Feeling guilt-ridden, he returned to the scene of the crime and owned up, said he would pay the damages. The unappreciative parents contacted the authorities and the arm of the law fisted the Wellman's door. Celia explained that Billy wasn't a bad boy, just a kid going through a silly stage of his life, and he wouldn't be doing it again. They bought her story but left a warning. Celia grounded her boy, Arthur gave him the strap.

Times were difficult at the Wellman house. Arthur was drinking more and coming home less, Celia's job required much of her time, and Arch was left to bring it all together. When neighbors saw Arch, they whispered, "There goes the good boy!" Arch became the family mediator. Barely into his teens, he tried to supervise his brother's affairs, temper his father's alcoholism, and retain some semblance of family unity. Even though Billy had a high regard for his brother and his opinions, having another authority figure in the household didn't sit well with him. On nights when dad didn't come home, Arch was committed to finding him at his favorite watering holes and leading him back. Celia was there for support but Arch became the man of the house. Little did he know that this role would last for many years. Beginning with their high school days, the brothers' relationship became strained, but their respect for one another would last a lifetime.

When it was just Billy and Arch together, they protected each other with passion. In sports, they were very competitive against one another, but also able to play well as a team. Both the boys were three-lettermen at Newton High School—football, baseball, and hockey. Although Arch was a fine athlete, Billy was extraordinary. The *Boston Sunday Post*, February 24, 1918, recalled, "In his school days, he was acclaimed the best quarterback that Newton High School ever boasted of. . . . As an athlete William Wellman had few equals in Boston schoolboy events. He was not only a football star, but excelled in hockey, basketball and baseball."

The Morning Telegraph, Sunday, July 21, 1918, also recalled, "And they will tell you out there that he was the best quarterback they ever had on the high school team; he was captain of the hockey team, and played second base with considerable success." In the 1914 *Newtownian*, Newton High School's yearbook, the hockey team was honored for winning the league championship. Only a freshman, Billy was singled out: "Wellman topped the list for making goals, having a string of nine to his credit. His playing throughout the whole season was fast and full of 'pep.'"

Before the hockey season began for his junior year, he was offered a position on the Arena Seven—a semiprofessional team in Boston. Because of being chosen captain again of the Newton High team, he declined the offer. He felt a responsibility to his teammates, his school, and his mother's wish for him to graduate.

The *Boston Herald, Post,* and *Morning Telegraph* of 1914 and 1915 were filled with stories of Wellman's exploits on the athletic field. Nineteen fifteen, however, proved to be the end of Billy's sports fame in the newspapers and at Newton High. He and a friend, Stafford Brown, were barred from playing hockey for the remainder of the season. The headmaster had caught the boys cutting classes, thus leading to the disciplinary action. The newspapers neglected to mention one additional infraction—they were caught dangling an arrogant schoolmate by his heels from a second-story window.

Being booted off the team was a serious blow to the team and to Billy. With problems mounting in and outside the classroom, deteriorating conditions at home, sports had been his salvation. This setback was also a slap at Celia and her philosophy with Billy. She was always attempting to calm him down, teach him right from wrong, give him confidence and faith, keeping him involved with activities such as school plays, church choir, and sports.

Billy wanted to change. He wanted to please his family, especially Celia. He wanted to do the right thing—but on his terms. He did not want to become a victim like his father; he wanted to be a winner like his mother.

When Billy reached his teens, he had moved from certainty to doubt, from devotion to rebellion. He found society alien and authority figures oppressive. His spirit had become independent and defiant. He was driven by momentary impulses, an impatient temper, and a constant striving to attain some unknown fulfillment that was often unsatisfactory and fleeting. His abundant energies kept him searching for answers, but driving in the wrong direction, down the road to delinquency. He couldn't slow down or change direction.

Both Celia and Arthur believed that summer camp was the place for Billy. There were multiple activities and . . . sports. It would be an educational experience and a learning process getting along with other boys. After all, they would live together tent-style. Most importantly, there would be camp counselors to supervise the activities and Arch would be there looking after his brother's well-being. They thought camp would be just perfect but, of course, it was not.

Billy wasn't against his parents' wishes to attend camp; as a matter of fact, he rather liked the idea of a new adventure . . . and getting out of town. The initial problem was finances. Fortunately, there was no financial difficulty the first year, as Arthur had a good business streak going and was able to afford the tariff for both his sons.

One sunny summer morning, Arch, Billy, and Taffy were off to Camp Passaconaway, located on Bear Island on Lake Winnipesaukee in central New Hampshire. Nicknamed "Winnie," it is one of the largest natural lakes in the United States. Driving distance around is sixty-three miles. Bear Island is three miles long and three-quarters of a mile wide. The nearest community, half a mile away, is Meredith.

The head of the camp and the counselors were quite surprised to meet Billy's dog. Pets were not allowed. Since the Wellmans had already arrived and were first-timers, Taffy was accepted but with reservations: the dog would have to be with Billy at all times, even in his tent.

For a time, Billy followed the camp curriculum and did not break any rules. He was happy playing baseball, swimming, tennis, fishing, barbecues, camp games and he had his dog. There was only one thing missing—girls.

Campers were not allowed to take boats out unless accompanied by a counselor. However, a small group with a leader would leave Bear Island for Meredith every so often for food and supplies. Billy made sure he and Taffy were part of the group. While the team was shopping, Billy and pal would sneak away to search for girls. Billy found one and she was pretty and willing. This Billy-plan worked well but the durations were too short and the trips not frequent enough. Billy got another idea. At night, he would go to bed with his swimming trunks on. When the camp was asleep, he and Taffy would creep from the tent, run to the lake, and swim the half mile to Meredith. Now the courtship could last longer, as long as the bad boys were back at camp, in bed before sunrise.

On the next crossing, Billy asked his Meredith sweetheart to find a partner for his dog—about the same size and in heat. She liked Taffy and wanted to keep Billy's attention, so the search was on. When the boys hit the drink again, a smart-looking collie was waiting at the other shore. While Billy and girlfriend were enjoying each other's company, Taffy and Miss Collie were doing the same. Later that evening, the swim back to camp was more satisfying.

Arch, Billy, and Taffy looked forward to next year's summer camp but, when it arrived, Arthur's piggy bank was empty. He didn't have money to pay for Arch's graduation class ring much less summer camp. Celia solved the ring problem by writing and selling a story titled "The Tale of a Pup." It was published in February of 1913 by the Canton Magazine Company, Canton, Ohio. She received the sum of $25. Arch solved the camp problem by getting a job as a counselor and making sure that his brother was also hired. Even though Taffy had conducted himself properly, as far as the camp leaders knew, he was not invited back.

Celia and Arthur were well pleased with Arch; the boys could attend camp, it wouldn't cost them anything, their sons would bring home some needed funds, and Billy would learn more responsibility. For Billy, this was different than being captain of a sports team. He would be responsible for a large group of boys around the clock. The question was whether or not he, as an authority figure, could get along with the others. As it turned out, he couldn't. He showed some leadership qualities and excelled in camp activities, but had difficulty dealing with the multiple personalities of the campers, the authority of the older counselors, and head of the camp.

"There was a big fat guy in camp," said Wellman, "who hated me as I did him. I had bloodied his nose so many times it began to look as if it belonged to someone else. I could and did handle him on the ground, but in the water he was too much for me—he was a water buffalo." Whenever the camp had their hours in the lake, Billy had to be on guard at all times, staying out of his range and near the safety of the shore. The "Buffalo," who outweighed Billy by some fifty pounds, kept watching and waiting for that golden opportunity.

This perpetual distraction was driving Billy mad and ruining every camp water period. He devised a plan in case he was captured and, as expected, the seizing happened. After a backflip off the diving board, Billy swam to the surface, right into the Buffalo's fleshy, powerful arms. "He caught me," remembered Wellman. "I could hold my breath for a long time under water (my voice training) and faked a lousy struggle which maneuvered me into the position I wanted with my hands just even with his balls, these I gathered in a very tight, strong fistful, a death grip so-called, and damn near testiclized him. I hung on all the time he pulled me to shore, yelling like a Banshee Indian in excruciating pain. I released my hold on his elongated privates and kicked the hell out of him legitimately, never hitting him on the nose, as I had been warned not to do again by the gentleman who ran the camp." Thereafter, Billy had no more trouble during the swimming sessions at camp.

When camp closed for the summer, Arch was invited to return as a counselor for the following year. He was instructed not to bring his brother. Arch responded that he would return only on the condition that Billy was with him. Arch did not repeat as a counselor at Camp Passaconaway. He graduated from Newton High but there was no money for college. It was time to seek employment. It didn't take him long to get started. He had a friend who had a connection at a popular gum company, Beeman's Pepsin Chewing Gum. Arch and his pal got jobs and became salesmen. Arch realized his potential in sales, and when he tired of chewing gum, he moved on to the wool business as a merchant.

Billy's senior year at Newton High was jam-packed with trials and tribulations. Arch was working and not always around to help Billy out of his predicaments, although Arch did stay in the Boston area to help out at home. Due to Billy's history at school, he was under scrutiny by the faculty and headmaster. For a while, he followed the straight and narrow, but his wildness worked against him. Before the school year ended, the headmaster told him that he was no longer eligible for team sports, school plays, or any other school activities. In order to graduate, he would have to report after school and work on his studies. Billy found this all too painful and, in his mind, totally unfair. So, in front of students and faculty alike, he struck back at the number one authority figure at the school. From the second-story window of his after-school classroom, he dropped a stink bomb on the bald head of the headmaster. The name

William Augustus Wellman did not appear on a graduation diploma from Newton High School.

Celia and Arthur demanded that their son get a job, try to make something of himself. With much of his childhood crowded with chaos, how could such a nonconformist conform to a structured work life? How could this teenage hellion learn to take orders from an executive figure? Only time could tell. In addition to his penchant for finding trouble, Billy did possess qualities of leadership, as well as good looks, charm, enthusiasm, and raw talent. These qualities and maybe a few others were on display when he interviewed for jobs. Not knowing where his strengths would lie or what choices were available, he jumped in with both feet and succeeded at landing one sales job after another. But the old problems kept surfacing. He had trouble sticking to any one thing, despised taking orders, got tired of selling and being civil to people just so they would buy his wares.

Finally, he found something he liked and was good at—the lumber business. "I didn't have to use my brain," said Wellman, "and I didn't have to be nice and polite to some druggist or mill superintendent, hoping the son of a bitch would buy a couple of boxes of Green Seal chocolates or a few pounds of wool."

Billy was a piler at the Butterick Lumber Company. He worked hard, was well behaved, and got along with the other lumbermen. The yard boss was called Fleming. He had a habit of strutting through the yard, yelling at anyone he could find to holler at. "His yells were of the four-letter variety," said Wellman. "In fact, he was one of those guys that couldn't speak a sentence without saying shit or Christ or son of a bitch. He was my height, but much stockier, about one hundred eighty on the hoof. He had the evilest face I have ever seen, with a broken nose that was his own brand of toughness."

The old-timers ignored Fleming's tirades, but obeyed him. The younger men were all scared of him—with the exception of the piler. One day, Fleming bawled out a new kid for resting after a hard day's work—just taking a smoke break for a few minutes. He called him every dirty name he could think of. Billy watched the scene from the top of a large pile of lumber. "Nobody was ever blasted as was he . . . and when Fleming ran out of four-letter words aimed at the kid, he changed directions and aimed his profanity at the kid's father and eventually, without losing a breath, at his mother."

The poor kid was shaking in his boots and the piler had heard enough. He called down to Fleming, "Knock it off. Leave the kid alone." The yard boss yelled up at him, "Keep your mouth shut, you dirty son of a bitch." Billy began to climb down. "He stood there waiting for me, but wasn't saying anything. . . . Everyone in the yard was watching. Guys on high, in trucks, in freight cars, on the ground, from the bleachers to the box seats."

The moment had arrived and Billy beat the hell out of Fleming. The next day, Billy was promoted to tallyman—evidently, the people of the Butterick Lumber Company didn't like Fleming's voice either. Wellman later wrote: "They say fighting is not the way to settle things, that nobody ever wins. I wonder."

Soon, Billy's career in wood ended. The atmosphere around the lumberyard had changed. His job as tallyman was less physical and more yard boss, and the lumbermen became jealous, hostile, or overly friendly to the pugilist victor. Billy wanted no relationship with these sorts.

Billy's passion was ice hockey. When once before he had spurned an offer to skate on a semiprofessional team, now he accepted and began a sporting career in the Boston Arena—where the frozen playing surface was not expected to cool his hot temper. He became a standout player. One evening, a visiting celebrity was in the stands and took a liking to this aggressive young player nicknamed "Spider"—because of his ability to attack and engulf his prey, the opposing skaters.

Douglas Fairbanks, popular star of stage performing in the nearby Colonial Theatre, and on his way to becoming a Hollywood film icon, was a fan and wanted to meet the penalty-prone athlete. In hockey, a violation of the playing rules causes penalties to the guilty player, taking him off the ice and into the penalty box. Depending on the severity of the infraction, he sits and waits a period of time until allowed back into the game. While he is gone, the team must continue a player short. Fairbanks appreciated Spider's style of fast, hard-nosed play and his extended time in the box. After introducing himself, a friendship developed over several get-togethers.

The star even invited Billy backstage during several of his performances. Fairbanks told Billy, "If you ever need a job, come out to Hollywood and look me up."

On another day at the Boston Arena, Spider met a man whose occupation was exciting to him. Earle Ovington, one of aviation's earliest pioneer fliers, invited Billy to visit his workplace—an airfield in Woburn, Massachusetts. Ten miles northwest of Boston, Woburn was primarily agricultural until the nineteenth century. By 1885, it was the leading leather producer in the area and the city retained this lead well into the

Douglas Fairbanks as "the Black Pirate," 1926

twentieth century. First settled in 1640, historic Woburn is one of the oldest communities in New England.

Billy's acquaintance with Ovington led to meeting other pilots, taking aerial rides, and just being a presence around the field. Billy became thoroughly fascinated with flight. He read about Wilbur and Orville Wright and the first powered Wright Flyer at Kitty Hawk, North Carolina, December 17, 1903. He listened to the pilots talk about America's Glenn Curtiss and Alexander Graham Bell, who had joined forces in October 1907 and built planes called Drome 1, 2, and 3. Number 3, called the June Bug, made the first all-public flight in America on July 4, 1908. Curtiss flew over a mile in front of several hundred enthusiastic people at Hammondsport, New York. In 1910, Curtiss started flying schools in the West, the Wright brothers did the same in the East. On May 29, 1910, Curtiss was awarded $10,000 for flying from Albany to New York City. It took him two hours and fifty-one minutes to navigate the 143-mile trip with two stops for gas and repairs.

Aeroplanes were already sneaking into nickelodeons, newsreels, and the movies. Barnstorming air shows were touring the country. William H. Pickens, a famed promoter, rounded up many of America's best pilots and was touring fairs from coast to coast. As James H. Farmer describes in his *Celluloid Wings*, "By 1914 and the beginning of the Great War in Europe, Pickens' flying circuses boasted an air force larger than the combined American services. They comprised 60 fliers—men and women—54 aeroplanes and 6 flying boats." Billy was entranced with the development of the war plane. At the air show in Reims, France, in August 1908, no plane could fly faster than 50 mph or climb higher than 500 feet. Within seven years, airplanes could fly 120 mph, climbing to 20,000 feet, while engaging in dogfights in the war-torn skies over France and Germany.

Celia, Arthur, and Arch did not see ice hockey as a career for Billy. As good as he was, there was little money to be made in ice hockey in 1915. Arch used his influence to gain employment for his brother with Coffin and Gilmore, Boston wholesale wool merchants. Billy was back in sales, but his dreams were in the sky. On the ground, the enforcers of the legal system came calling again. Billy and his friend Stafford Brown, known as Staff, had an unusual habit. Since neither of them could afford a car or had the use of a family vehicle, at night they would find an automobile, hot-wire it, then drive off for an evening on the town. Before going home, they would return the car where they found it, sometimes refilling the gas tank. One dark evening, the merrymakers were tardy with their return and the long arm of the law was on time, depositing them in the Newton County jail. Later they stood before the judge. Celia, heartbroken, Arthur and Arch, disgusted, were in attendance watching the proceedings. Billy pleaded not guilty, explaining to the magistrate that they were not stealing the car, just borrowing it for a few hours, then returning it. The judge, however, refused to see the difference between "stealing" and "borrowing" in this case, and the boys were found guilty.

Before sentencing, the judge noticed that Billy's record showed previous reprimands for vandalism and fighting with other boys. Billy apologized for not controlling his temper better, but about the fighting, he explained that he and his brother were just trying to get to school. His Honor scolded and warned him about future violations of the law. If he and his friend did not change their ways, they would end up in juvenile detention camp. The judge considered Billy's record, his age, his apology, and reasons for the infractions before sentencing both boys to a six-month probation. They would have to report every week to the probation

Celia, age forty-nine, dressed for Congress

officer of the city of Newton. The judge became somewhat puzzled when he saw the name of the probation official—Celia McCarthy Wellman. Once a week, Billy reported to his mother. He was remorseful, felt defeated, and didn't want any more trouble with the law.

Celia was so successful in her work with "wayward boys" that, some years later, she was requested by Congress to speak on the subject of juvenile delinquency. She told them that of all the thousands of boys she had worked with, the only one she couldn't control was her own son.

Throughout the fall of 1916 and the winter of 1917, Billy persevered in the wool business but his efforts produced only meager results. His thoughts were somewhere else. He was successful at staying clear of the law and finished his six-month probation. He dreamed and often spoke of his love of flight and the escalating war in Europe—a horrific conflict that France was losing in the trenches and in the air. The bloodshed from this so-called war to end all wars had already accounted for the lives of millions of young men with the final count estimated at over ten million dead. The newspapers were filled with war news and the need for pilots in the U.S. Air Service—in case America entered the conflict. Billy was frustrated at not having the money for flying lessons. All he could do was dream and talk and read the newspapers.

American president Woodrow Wilson had campaigned for reelection on the slogan "He kept us out of war." But Germany's proclamation of unrestricted submarine warfare caused him to go before Congress on February 3, 1917, and ask to sever diplomatic relations. On April 2, he again addressed Congress, asking for a declaration of war, which Congress approved on April 6. However, the country and its services—army, navy, and air force—had not prepared for war and, if war was declared, the buildup would take some time.

Billy volunteered his services. When his own country rejected his application for enlistment—primarily due to lack of education—he signed with the French. For an American citizen to fly for France it would require a considerable connection with a strong sponsorship. Billy had two powerful lawyer uncles who had written celebrated books. Francis Wellman and Samuel Williston carried much influence in the New England area.

Several of Billy's friends, David Putnam and David Judd, had already enlisted with proper sponsors and joined the ambulance corps. Once overseas, there were two choices: stay in the ambulance corps or join the French Foreign Legion for basic training, then transfer into the French Air Service (Lafayette Flying Corps or Lafayette Escadrille). With help from Uncles Francis and Sam, Billy suited up with the Norton-Harjes Ambulance Corps in April 1917.

Even with Billy's papers in order, Celia, Arthur, and Arch were still disappointed with his decision. "Why go off to war?" "Now that you have a good thing going, why not stay in business with Coffin and Gilmore?" "France is losing the war, all their young men are being killed." "We need you here at home, we're your family." "You could die in France like millions of others." Billy had grown tired of arguing his position. His final answer to his mother, father, and brother was: "For me, it's either war or jail."

2

THE RECRUIT

As Billy's departure date for France was getting closer, he consulted his employers, Coffin and Gilmore. Even though he was not one of their top salesmen, they had appreciated his enthusiasm and effort. They understood that he was trying to change from his troubled past, and accepted his path for the future as a combat pilot fighting for liberty and justice. Billy neglected to mention his primary reasons for going to war were not so honorable—to get the hell out of Boston and learn to fly. The C&G bosses believed that it was high time for America to stop Germany's aggression. They promised financial assistance to Billy and his job back upon his return.

On May 19, Billy and his family sat down to their last dinner together before his leaving for New York the next morning. He had requested his favorite meal: beans, fish balls, clams, and chestnuts. Taffy, sitting at Billy's feet as usual, enjoyed his favorite meal, which included a portion of Boston baked beans. There was less conversation than usual; Celia, Arthur, and Arch finally resigned themselves to this life-threatening event. Billy said his final goodbyes to his father and brother that evening. Since Celia would be boarding the train for New York with her son, her farewell would come later. As Billy's roommate, Taffy's adios would wait until morning.

Taffy was getting old and a veterinarian said he had a touch of rheumatism. "I lay down on the bed and called him up, he ran and jumped, barely made it. I put my arm around his black old head and I thought for the first time that perhaps my pal might not be here, if and when I got out of whatever I was getting into. We sort of just lay there for a little while, the way we had countless numbers of times in the long ago. Taffy looked at me, I looked at him and, believe it or not, we were both trying not to cry. It was getting rugged so I patted his head, kissed him and left the room, never looking back. The last sound I heard was Taffy whining, so softly."

On May 20, Celia and her son whistle-chugged into New York City, staying at the Wolcott Hotel, 31st Street by Fifth Avenue. The French ocean liner *Rochambeau* was set to sail at 10:30 the next morning. Billy told his mother not to go to the pier with him, but to stay at the hotel. While her son slept, she wrote him a letter and placed it in an envelope with instructions not to open it until his ship was plowing its way to France. The next evening, on board ship as promised, Billy opened and read her letter:

My beloved son -
I cannot tell you what is in my heart for you—No one in all the world
can ever love you as I have always done, ever since God gave you to me.
Remember this, dear, when you think of me, and how hard it has been
for me to see you go. I know you are going to help and no one can
do that better than you. Don't forget your prayers, and even through
all the suffering and vice and things that you will see, remember our
heavenly Father watches over us all. I give you into His keeping and
every breath will be a prayer that you will come home safely to us.
    God bless and keep you always.
                                                Your loving
                                                Mother

Billy suddenly felt heartsick. What a cruel thing he had done by not allowing his loving mother to see him off because he was afraid she would stand on the pier covered with tears and embarrass him in front of the other young adventurers as they climbed aboard the *Rochambeau*. She had never done anything to embarrass either of her sons. She had been the strong one, never losing her temper, always consoling, always loving. Despite Billy's turbulent behavior or her alcoholic and sometimes wandering husband, she loved them no matter what. Yes, she would cry over her younger son's departure to join the war, but it would happen in her lonely hotel room, maybe in the taxicab to the South Station and on board the train back to her empty-feeling home. Every tear would be a prayer to keep Billy safe and bring him back home to her.

This letter would become Billy's good-luck piece, and it would be placed in a thin flat wallet his mother had given him with his initials

Wellman and new pal, Reginald "Duke"
Sinclaire, 1917

emblazoned on a small gold strip. The wallet would rest in the pocket of
whatever uniform or outfit he was wearing, wherever he would travel, on
the ground or in the air.

The *Rochambeau* was built in 1911 and named after the French general
Jean-Baptiste Donatien de Vimeur, comte de Rochambeau, who fought
beside George Washington in the American Revolution. By the end of
the ninteenth century, the Golden Age of ocean liners had commenced.
Sails gave way to steam engines, and nationalism bloomed around the
world. These giant vessels became great symbols for their nations. Shipping companies placed new emphasis on the size, comfort, and speed of
their ships.

In World War I, the large ocean liners were also used as troopships
and hospital ships. During Germany's unrestricted submarine warfare,
the ocean liners were easy prey. German U-boats sank a number of these,
including the British *Lusitania*. She had departed New York, May 1, 1915,
for Liverpool, and was the fastest ship afloat. An enemy submarine hunted

her down and its torpedo finished the job. Within twenty minutes, the giant ship slipped beneath the surface drowning 1,198 passengers—114 were Americans.

The *Rochambeau* was not going to be easy prey. When she arrived in New York Harbor, March 9, 1917, guns were mounted fore and aft—90mm on the bow about sixty feet in front of the bridge. This sight sent shock waves through the gathering crowd.

Billy's trip would be a ten-day, three-thousand-mile voyage to Europe and France—some of those miles would pass through enemy waters. On board were other young adventurers on their way to join the French Air Service. Like Wellman, some had enlisted with other branches of service and would have to transfer into the Lafayette Escadrille or the Lafayette Flying Corps. France's Lafayette Escadrille had attracted widespread attention in America. It was composed of volunteer Americans only. Originally named the Franco-American Flying Corps, it then became the Escadrille Américaine, and finally the Lafayette Escadrille. The new name became official April 20, 1916.

With so many American adventure seekers joining up, there was no longer any accommodation available in the Lafayette Escadrille, and the fliers were assigned to other French squadrons or escadrilles. American industrialist William K. Vanderbilt came to the rescue, forming the Lafayette Flying Corps. In this way, even when an American pilot joined a French escadrille, he retained his American identity in the Lafayette Flying Corps—an offshoot of the Lafayette Escadrille. Vanderbilt, who strongly opposed America's neutrality, became the guiding light in furnishing funds to over a hundred fliers as well as establishing a rest house in Paris for the fighting men of France. On October 9, 1918, the French government conferred upon William Vanderbilt the Cross of the Legion of Honor, the citation stating: "The Government of the Republic is happy to express its appreciation and gratitude to one of the citizens of America, who, from the very first hour, has been a warm and valued friend to France."

Wellman was in fine company on that voyage. There were several friends from the Boston area, including David Judd, a Brookline neighbor; and Reginald "Duke" Sinclaire, from Corning, New York, became an instant buddy. The threesome would stay together through flight school. There was great passion and camaraderie among all the young Americans. They had arrived with differing reasons; some filled with patriotism, others looking for adventure, still others escaping from the life they had known.

Nonetheless they had one common motive: they wanted to fly and were willing to gamble their lives in its pursuit.

The first eight days of the crossing were uneventful. The last two were another matter. When the liner entered the danger zone, a U-boat was sighted and the captain ordered all lifeboats to be swung out, all bulkhead doors to be closed, lookouts to be doubled, and steam pressure to be kept high to give the ship maximum speed. Fortunately, nightfall was arriving and the *Rochambeau* would be more difficult for the submarine to chase. The captain signaled a staggered course for his ship, and commanded that all passengers be dressed and come to the upper decks where they would remain until reaching France. The precautions proved successful and the passenger liner dropped anchor at its French port, June 1, 1917.

Three days after his arrival in France, Billy wrote the first of eighty-two pen-and-ink letters to his mother, father, and brother. This author has selected some of these, and their excerpts, to appear in the early pages of the book. The selections here record a history of the Great War through the eyes of a volunteer American fighter pilot. The accounts written by this young rebel, without a high school diploma, are included in their original form with grammatical errors and all, no editing of any kind.

JUNE 4, 1917
HOTEL DE BAYONNE
BORDEAUX

Dear Mother:

Had an eventful trip. Rough as blazes and I am beginning to believe me a real sailor, having passed without once getting sick. The last two days we spent looking for u-boats as the Rochambeau has been the boat to successfully evade these water-devils. They were laying for us and we zig-zaged in our course and did many other tricks. The last two nights we were not permitted to go below and were forced to remain dressed on deck or in the saloon. Gambling was the big amusement on board, at which I fortunately stayed clear. Many of the boys lost all their money shooting craps. Arch would have had a beautiful time.

There were several stage folk on board so we were not at all bored. Two bully little girls, both French, with their governess, acted the teacher to me and I learned quit a little french. The meals were typically french. Two courses of meat and fancy cakes and all varieties of cheese. Believe me I prefer the good old American meals every time.

I met a great crowd of fellows, most of them from the west. Older fellows but the real open hearted, happy-go-lucky type. Unfortunately but few of them are in the Harjis-Norton Ambulance Corps. Most of them are in the American Ambulance Corps. However there should be good chances to see them in the days to come.

France is certainly beautiful. It is just like a picture book, with its wonderful chateaus and marvellously cultivated fields, its cobble-stones and odd buggies rattling over them. Everything is wonderful but I suppose the reason is because of its freshness and all the novelties that one sees. Paris tomorrow and then the real test. This red tape is hard and I am very anxious to become started. Not only because of the work but also the money one has to spend. New money, new language, new acquaintances, new experiences. That is a combination that sounds very, very, good to me.

The uniform we wear is a wonder. It costs $135 so should be worthy of a king. Bully Kakki and cut in the latest English style. Some little dishes.

I hope Dad is coming along in business every day. He deserves it. Arch no doubt is doing well. He will be wealthier than I, but believe me so far I wouldn't swap for the world. Take good care of yourself, Mother and remember that there are just two letters that I have with me, Yours and Dads.

Love
Billy

Unfortunately, no letter from Billy's father exists. This author believes that it included remarks about his son's health, welfare, happiness, and behavior. Billy's future letters would show a new address as the family made another move to an apartment at Riverbank Court Hotel, Cambridge, Massachusetts.

Wellman and the other Americans spent much of their first month in France taking physicals, doing paperwork, and waiting for their enlistment documents to come through.

JUNE 8, 1917

FRIDAY P.M.

HOTEL DU PATAIS

28, COURS-LA-REINE, PARIS

CHAMPS—ELYSEES

————————————

ADRESSE TELGRAPHIQUE:

PALATEL, PARIS

TELEPHONE PASSN 60-82

Dear Mother:

Rather than cable and so resort to only a few words, for my money is scarce, I am writing to tell you what I have done and the reasons for so doing. I have passed my physical and mental tests for the Franco-American Flying Corps. otherwise known as the Lafayette squad. My term is for the duration of the war and I am happy to say I have done the right thing. This ambulance job is considered really a joke. A good job for conscription shirkers or bums who want an excuse to come to Paris and raise h—l. Why Mother, we don't realize the seriousness of this war. France is practically wiped out. They are playing on their nerve. All their wonderful men and boys are gone. England has just started to do a little, and many claim that if we had not come to the rescue when we did, the Germans would have won the war inside of six months. Their ability and cruelty can't be deciphered. They are devils and believe me, unless all appearances are false those Germans will be able to hold out for a long time. America realizes a little bit, but not the public. The government will in all probability take over these Red Cross Units and then the ones will get put wherever Uncle Sam sees fit. That branch of the service is a good job for fellows like Francis Sketton not for real red blooded boys. This service used to be good, when Dave Douglas was here, but conditions have changed thus lowering the standard. Now, Mother, the casualty list is greatly exaggerated and a man with a clear head and a good training can get by O.K.

There should be nothing in the world that our country wouldn't at this time, do for France. They have sent a big fleet and we have General Perching and 9,000 in troops here, but what is that number compared to those really needed? I feel sure that you and Dad will think I have done the right thing, the only thing, after having chosen a brand of the service that appeals to me and at which I believe I can show the best service. There are so many (ambuscaders) as the french call them, men who by some pull have chosen a brand of the service in which there is practically no danger, that not for the world would I be classed with them. Arch should be getting busy. He will have to do so in a short time.

The hard part of this, is waiting for my papers to be vised by the French government. I will have to live here for two or three weeks doing nothing, just waiting for the word, and spending my precious little gold bag. Now Mother, write me just what you think and address the letter Lafayette Flying Corps, Avord, France. If you want to get ahold of me before the three weeks is up I will be here but I don't believe you will receive the letter until well into that period. I surely hope Dad is having grand success, I know that you are Mother. Now don't worry for I have had a queer presentiment that all will turn out fine and that I will return safe and well to you, the most wonderful little woman in this world.

Lovingly,
Bill

The Allied dream that soon there would be massive army divisions on the ground and the skies would be filled with American fighting planes didn't happen, and nothing close to the dream would take place for many months. America had not prepared for war, and time was needed for the training and buildup of troops, machinery, pilots, and planes. For the time being, the only Americans fighting in France would be the volunteer fliers of the Lafayette Escadrille and Lafayette Flying Corps.

Ten weeks after the declaration of war, General John J. "Black Jack" Pershing, commander-in-chief of the American Expeditionary Forces, arrived in Paris. Wellman was in the City of Light at the time, and reported, "The reception given Pershing and his staff was remarkable. Paris virtually went wild. God only knows every day is a wild day here, but on his arrival they just about doubled in enthusiasm and believe me Paris went crazy. Flowers were showered on the boys and all through the crowds strong men were crying, for they realized that America will in all probability win this terrible war. With Pershing would be seen Old Marshall Joffre. He is a wonder and a fine example of a true military man. I understand the object of Pershing's visit is to determine the number of men required and then our boys will be immediately sent across. It sure does seem as if America was awakening at last."

Before receiving his final enlistment papers and transfer orders from the ambulance corps to the Foreign Legion to the Lafayette Flying Corps, Billy wrote several more letters home. At twenty-one years of age, never having been further from home than Lake Winnipesaukee, trying to adjust and conform to a new country, new people, new language, new money, new everything, it was important that his family be behind him supporting in every way possible. In a letter dated Monday, June 18, he wrote.

Tell Dad I have safely come through the temptations he so much feared for me. Also tell him I have seen more fellows who never knew what hell meant in the United States, go there on arriving here in Paris that I dare mention. It is a good place to stay away from unless you are lucky as blazes or possess the gift Arch has shown. . . . Keep in touch with me often Mother. Letters from home are like a gift from heaven. By George things as they are, make me appreciate beyond compare, luxuries and opportunities that I had in America. I will do my best in writing you, but my chances will not be as good as yours. Tell Dad to keep fighting. It would be wonderful to have the war end as it should and to come home safe to see Dad on top. He will get there I firmly believe. . . . Lovingly, Bill.

For the next week, Wellman spent time in the American Hospital of Paris with a case of blood poisoning from an infected cut in his toe. He was frustrated at having to delay his trip to camp for the French Foreign Legion's version of basic training. When he left the hospital, June 25, he was feeling fit as a fiddle and thankful for the fine treatment he had received. He knew that soon he would be missing the good food and sleeping in soft clean sheets. As he left the hospital, he began walking next to the Seine on his way to his room at the Hôtel France et Choiseul on the Rue St. Honoré. "Suddenly," said Wellman, "I saw a blackclothed conductress poised at the top of a bridge, she took that long welcome jump into eternity which during the war had become a tragic habit."

Billy stripped off his boots and flying jacket, dove into the river, and started swimming to where he had seen her disappear. He hit the mark as her bobbing head appeared in the current; it went under and he dove after her. He came to the surface with her in his arms, and started to swim to the pier where the riverboats pick up their passengers. "She never stopped struggling. I thought she was trying to get away from me. I was a fine swimmer, had been taught how to save a person under these conditions, so I cold-cocked her, she became limp and I was able to get her to the pier and pull her up on it."

Two French policemen came running down the boardwalk to the pier. They both were talking in a hopeless sort of way. Billy couldn't understand one word, but by their bored tone and relaxed actions, he knew it was just another one of those poor miserable heartbroken women. "I took a long look at this pathetic black uniformed not too young girl, lying on her back, soaking wet, with outstretched arms as if crucified, a voice tremulous with sobs, looking up at me with a frozen hatred on her

Wellman, fourth from right, at Avord with his instructor to his right and mechanics in front of a Blériot trainer

glassy face—a look I will never forget. . . . Why didn't you mind your own business, instead of being an unwelcome idiotic hero? That long struggling swim through a river of shit is exactly what you deserved."

On the morning of June 27, Billy rode the rails to Camp d'Avord in the south of France. Avord was large, comprising dozens of barracks, thousands of men, and hundreds of aeroplanes. There were some ninety Americans who had enlisted in the Foreign Legion on their way to membership in the air service. Other Legionnaires included Algerians, Chinese, Russians, and French. Among these was a smattering of hardened criminals and other assorted thugs. Thefts and fights were common, the barracks were infested with rats, lice and graybacks burrowed in their navels. Due to the absence of toilet paper, there were finger-drawn feces paintings around the latrines that had to be whitewashed weekly. Due to the lack of clean fresh food, the recruits suffered from boils and dysentery. Their uniforms were filthy and ill-fitting . . . and the pay was three and a half cents a day.

Wellman's circle of friends would begin to grow. In addition to fellow Brookline native David Putnam, already there or soon to be were Frank L. Baylies, New Bedford, Massachusetts; William Meeker, New York City; Wellman's Newton High buddy Staff Brown; Sidney Rankin Drew, Jr., New York City; Thomas Hitchcock, Jr., Westbury, New York; and, still together, Judd and Sinclaire. The fledgling fliers were trained under adverse conditions. The instructors, known as monitors, speaking only French, ordered them to exercise maneuvers and pilot the various aircraft. Then, the students would take to the air and try to perform. The monitors would never get into a plane with a recruit.

There were five basic steps in the flight school. The planes used were called Blériots, named after their inventor, Louis Blériot. They resembled prehistoric birds. The first Blériot was called a "Penguin" because it could not fly with its shortened wings. The students were only able to taxi on the ground, and the slightest crosswind made even that journey almost unmanageable. However, the recruits were able to learn to handle the aircraft, with its three-cylinder Anzani engine, on the ground. The next craft was called a "roller." It was a type of Blériot with larger wings and an engine fitted with six cylinders that, at full speed, could rise twenty-five feet off the ground. The recruits graduated from the roller to a full-scale Blériot monoplane—a model of the type first flown by Blériot across the English Channel in 1909. This step was called *tour de piste,* or following a set course. The students would take off, fly around the airfield at an altitude of five hundred meters, perform specified maneuvers, and then land. They learned to use the elementary controls of rudder and ailerons, making simple turns and gaining confidence. Crashes seldom resulted in serious injury.

For the final two steps, the recruits graduated from Blériots to Caudrons. Caudrons resembled flying bathtubs but were powered with an 80 hp Le Rhône rotary engine. The students would fly at altitude, do the turns and maneuvers they were instructed to perform until passed by their monitors. Then came the final step—the big trips. The recruits were to complete two triangular cross-country flights of approximately 150 miles each. The route flown was from Avord to Châteauroux to Romorantin. The next day, they would reverse the order. The countryside was pleasing to the eye, but became a graveyard for more than fifty students, many of them American volunteers, who crashed due to bad weather, engine trouble, or simply becoming lost.

Those who survived the flights but failed the Blériot or Caudron training were assigned to Bomber School, where the training and flying were simpler and less hazardous. The men who graduated from Camp d'Avord became the cream of the fliers, piloting *avions de chasse,* that is, pursuit planes.

Quite often, there were training delays due to high winds or bad weather. All flying would cease and the men would return to their barracks. While waiting for the weather to clear, poilu (French soldier) food—horsemeat and lentils—was available and gambling was the pre-ferred recreation. For a while, the men were subjected to close order drill. The free-hearted Americans did not like to march and, since only a few spoke French, they all pretended not to understand and performed the opposite of the commands. Eventually the instructors considered them mentally defective and stopped the drills.

JULY 24, 1917
ECOLE D'AVIATION MILITAIRE
AVORD (CHER)
FRANCE

Dear Dad:

Just a man's letter, Don't let it get beyond you, for as you will see there are things in it that I would rather not let Mother read.

Life here is damn hard. Hours, food, work, lice and consequently all kinds of sickness. So far I have been very lucky although I have had a pretty bad cough. Not an uncommon ailment in France for the first two or three months. I have been advanced two classes now thus putting me just a bit nearer the front. Then comes the real test. Nerves, ability, skill, and last but not least, luck. Believe me Dad, a fellow does a lot of deep, sensible thinking down here. Home is just about the next dearest word to Mother.

Write me honestly just how Mother is. I have been writing at least twice a week and sometimes more. With luck you should get most of the letters. News is so hard to get. Has Arch been chosen? I hope he has not, for one from the family is enough. Keep him there as long as possible. I am not crawling, for I would do the same thing over again, however, Arch has always been a success in those things of life that count, and consequently he deserves the best, and that cannot be gotten here at present.

We are waiting developements on the U.S. Government taking us over. This is good in some ways, bad in others. Financially, it will help a lot, and that is a help. On the other hand, if we have to use our inferior American machines rather than the French, God help us.

Dad, you can't realize what a play of luck comes in there. Yesterday, one of the boys took a nose dive into the roof of one of the nearby houses. Didn't scratch himself, but smashed his "Nieuport" all to pieces. Right after this another of the boys broke his leg just turning the propelier. God give me strength to get too the front without any of these mishaps.

Keep writing often and get after the business, I have a feeling that things must improve. It sure would be fine to come home with the Huns beaten and find everything as it should be. Mother deserves so much that she has never had.

All my love. I think of you often Dad.

Lovingly,
Bill.

JULY 26, 1917

ELEVÉ PILOTE

CAMP D'AVORD

CHER, FRANCE

Dear Little Mother:

Your bully letter of July third on hand. By George it certainly was a wonder. So glad to hear that you do agree with me on aviation, However, Mother, you are wrong, absolutely wrong on the "embuscis" part of driving an ambulance, This refers of course, only to those within the conscription age. When Pershing arrived some of the drivers of the Paris Ambulance Corp. made up of Americans, he asked how many of the fellows would volunteer for the various branches of the real service. Six boys out of one hundred and sixty stepped out of the ranks, and this was before a great crowd. Why, it is the laughing incident of Paris, and this is only one instance of how the ambulance drivers stand in the estimation of the French.

My changing from these Norton people was O.K. In fact they congratulated me on my choice. Another point, Mother . . .

Billy for Dad. Dear old Taffy, I sure could make use of him here as a good companion. I know that I shall see him again and sincerely hope that he won't forget me. In all my life I have never loved any four legged animal the way I did Taffy. He should have a wonderful summer, and I have written Mr. Dickenson asking him to take the best of care in keeping him down to shape. They might easily spoil him, Taffy is so dog-gone clever at begging. Those beautiful brown eyes of his just about used to talk . . .

Last night, coming home from flying at about ten o'clock, I went

With a letter to Celia from Avord during
training

over to the lower end of the camp and witnessed an Arabian dance.
Done by real Arabs, for we have many of them here at camp. The
dance is typically oriental, done by men who take off the women for
they are not here. Such a crazy thing I have never seen. They all get
under the influence of some herb they smoke and the fun starts. It sure
is a rough house often ending up with a fight and those boys with
knives. We also have Russians, all kinds of French, Annamites,
Arabians, Spaniards and many others here. Such a conglomoration.
Good experience being mixed up with such a crowd.

Keep writing often Mother, and I will do my best to answer. Your
letters are all so wonderful. A good teacher, may I be an apt pupil. Love
to Arch and Dad.

Lovingly,
Billy

AUGUST 6, 1917
ELEVÉ PILOTE
CAMP D'AVORD
CHER, FRANCE

Dear Old Dad:

So glad to hear of Arch's good fortune. It is fortune not luck, for he deserved it all. Arch has always been a splendid example for me. I have always been such a fool in not taking advantage of it. May I be the success over here that he is in the States. Then I will be satisfied and will return to make good in something.

And your business Dad, those $200 dollar weeks certainly should be a help. I have all kinds of confidence in you Dad. We three should all be huge successes for we have something to really work for, little Mother. She is such a little power in urging us on. May she have all kinds of comforts and luxuries that have been denied her before. She truly is a Queen among Gods people.

Dad, I have really become quite proud of myself. Down here at camp I have not once taken a drink or had anything to do with the many drunks the boys pull off on days of repose. I have become a "Lone God" as I realize that to get through this, one has got to have all his faculties at his instant command. Hence vis on the liquor and the wild women.

When you receive this Dad, I should be just about through my training. Another month and things will look so different. Yesterday, I had two runs in the air. It is some experience, but terribly tiring, such a test on ones nerves. Good luck to you Dad. I write often.

Lovingly,
Your Son.

AUGUST 20, 1917

Dear Arch:

To-day Arch, I finished the Bleriot school and will start on my last leg of training within a few more days. Between times I am going to take a short 48 hour leave to Paris. George the city will look good after being tied up here for such a long period. So far during my training I have not missed a single morning or night. Quite some record but it tires one. No more mono-planes [Blériots] for me. Finished my spiral and Serpentine [elementary turns in the air] from 3500 feet in the air and at that height those little planes are very uneasy. Am going to Paris with Reginald Sinclaire, a fellow from N.Y. He is a peach of a boy and a whale of a pilote. We are trying to go through this school together and as far are succeeding very well. He is somewhat older than I am, perhaps six years, (has a wife and two kids, very wealthy but somewhat unhappy and consequently is doing his duty.)

Many of the boys here Arch are gradually dwindling off. Some for incompetancy, others for sickness. Lots of the latter kind. It sure is a big problem to keep ones self in grand shape here. Unless he has money with which to eat as he desires, the ordinary 'poilu' food is all that can be had. Sometimes, it is very hard to get away with it. Damn fine of you Arch to send on that locket. By George I hope I get it. One place for Mother and Dad . . . and you. With that combination I should come through any kind of scrape in grand style. Send on Arch, a picture of yourself, one that will fit in the locket. Also of Dad. I have one of Mother. Remember me to everybody.

Faithfully

Bill

Arch Wellman, young businessman, age twenty-three, 1917

ON ACTIVE SERVICE
WITH THE
AMERICAN EXPEDITIONARY FORCE
SEPTEMBER 5, 1917
AMERICAN
Y.M.C.A.

Dear Little Mother:

Just received your bully letter of Aug. 6th. First to answer the questions, My letters probably have not been censored because there are so many coming through that it takes a lot of needless time. They also realize, this letter coming from an aviation camp in Avord, that as a rule there would not possibly be anything to censor. Way south of everything. Nothing doing but flying sleeping and eating when you can stand the food. News is a rarity, in fact to write to anyone but those most dear to you is almost an impossible task.

The U.S. has not taken us over yet. If I had money they would not get me, I would stick to the French. They know the game from A - Z and I have changed my mind and now would like to stay where I am for two or three months and then if conditions warrant it, change to the U.S. However this will be impossible so here goes.

Your letters Mother, are marvelous. I am saving each and every one of them. They all, without exception, cheer me up, and in this day of fighting and lack of joys, little things count for so much. How often have I thought of Arch's riding around in his own car. Does he realize how lucky he is, and does he appreciate it all? Then the chance to swim and play tennis and sing and play the piano. Well I will get them all once more and then believe me look out.

Am tickled to death to hear that Dad's business is coming along. May it keep up and may Dad prosper. After all, a man who is a real success, is the one who gets it late and still holds the love of his wife and family, and deservingly, as Dad does. We will all be running around in cars, and perhaps I will have my "plane" just to amuse the folks with.

I will not go to Pau for some time Mother. Perhaps another two or three months. We are getting perfectionné in many kinds of machines and they all take time but make one such a good pilot.

Change is a great thing, you appreciate your own home so much more when you return. If, of course, you really don't care to accept different invitations that is another matter, but for the love of heaven Mother, for once think of yourself just a wee bit. Over here I will honestly say that it is an "all for yourself" game. You have to keep that attitude or you won't pull through.

Have never forgotten my prayers Mother. Will promise you that I never will. Several times however, I have been so deadly tired that everything is just of no account. In fact one night I slept on the ground of the hangar in my clothes. Had been flying alone for around five hours during the day and being new at the game it tired me out.

Love to all and so glad to hear that Aunt Sarah is staying at the Ruretash. She is a dear.

Billy.

ON ACTIVE SERVICE

WITH THE

AMERICAN EXPEDITIONARY FORCE

OCT. 2, 1917

AMERICAN

Y.M.C.A.

Dearest Little Mother:

All your plans of my coming back. They must be wonderful, may I have the fortune to take advantage of them. Your growing old, absurd, you will forever be my Mother, young and beautiful. To me old age is sacred. I really feel more as if life was worth living after seeing some grand old couple go by, two who have lived through life and conquored. Just as some day I will see my own Mother and Dad. Then is the time I will have my share of proudness on seeing the sweetest little Mother, old perhaps in age, but still so youthful and fine. Soon we will be able to take a real fishing trip. Just a regular good but close warming time. Under Gods earth, and a peaceful earth. After this I don't ever want to fight again. Not that I have lost all my fight, but at least the ever looked for opportunity will be dismissed from my mind. That pain I have used at least a dozen times. It is great and just the kind I know you would pick out . . .

Have started my work on "Nieuport". Wonderful machine, so fast. Next Pau and the real fun starts. No need of you worrying, so many of the boys get by, why not little Willie . . .

All for now. God Bless you Mother

Lovingly
Billy.

OCTOBER II, 1917

Dear Little Mother:

Yours of Sept. 20th on hand. Along with it three packages. One of my final suit of underwear. Great stuff, warm and just what I need. In the other two packages were two pairs of bully socks and one woolen helmut. Certainly is bully getting these different gifts from home . . . As to my smoking pipe tobacco is of course perferable, but oh so scarse and expensive. Very seldom have I had the pleasure of lighting my two pipes. I smoke cigarettes. As to their making me nervous, that may be so but as yet I have failed to notice it. One either looses his nerve here entirely, or gets an over-abundant supply of them . . . I am very anxious to get away from Avord. That word is like a nightmare to me . . . I should finish in a week or two. Then "Pau" and, I trust, better treatment . . .

Lovingly
Bill.

During Wellman's final days at Avord, he was working with the same type of pursuit plane that he would be flying in combat—the French Nieuport. He was also schooled with the Vickers machine gun. On October 18, he wrote home, "To-day I had my first machine-gun conference. We took apart the 'Vicker' Machine gun, the one we will in all probability use on our machines. They are wonderful, shooting five-hundred and fifty shots per minute and through the revolving propeller of a plane. That is some stunt for the propeller of a 'chase' machine revolves about twelve hundred times a minute. Just think how the gun has to be timed to do its work successfully."

On September 29, 1917, Wellman completed his brevet class at Avord. His primary training had comprised takeoffs and landings, short and long solo flights in Blériots, Caudrons, and Nieuports. He had mastered maneuvers or turns in the air called serpentines and spirals, as well as other elementary acrobatics, and passed gunnery training. Now he received his license and was considered a full-fledged *pilote,* or military aviator. On his tailored uniform, he wore a single golden wing on either side of his collar, corporal chevrons, and two wreath wings, one of silver the other of gold, on either side of his uniform jackets just above the pockets. After seven days' furlough to Paris, he reported to Pau for advanced fighter school in acrobatics and gunnery. The food and accommodations were improved. He would also be flying all the combat planes used in the war.

Before the war, Pau, located in the Basses-Pyrénées area of southwestern France, was a popular destination for well-to-do travelers, especially the British. The town boasted the first golf course in mainland Europe, steeplechasing, fox hunting, and a mild climate with many fine English-style villas. Pau was considered the most elegant of the towns and cities that overlook the Pyrénées. From its high bluffs, parallel with the mountain range, the view is breathtaking.

During Wellman's time there in late fall and early winter, the slopes and peaks of the Pyrénées would give off a kaleidoscope of colors from dark purple, red, and blue to gold, green, and snowy white. "This is the most beautiful spot," Wellman said in a letter home. "The place is but fifty miles from Spain. We are separated only by the pyrannes which at this time of the year are snow-covered. The view from the ground is wonderful but from the air it is awe-inspiring. The marvellous sunsets and sunrises. Seems as if life really was worth while living. Palms are everywhere. This is the famous English resort in the winter. Since the war it has died down considerably but lots of life still. In Pau itself there are two suburb Hotels and the shops are snazzy. Someday I hope to return here when the war is a thing of the past."

Some of Wellman's Avord pals made it to Pau, and took the short train ride out of town to the training camp. Sinclaire, Judd, Putnam, Baylies, and Hitchcock were still together with Wellman. Sidney Drew had been a late arrival at Avord, and by the time he appeared at Pau, the others had left for Le Plessis-Belleville, the final training ground before being sent into action. Staff Brown, also a later arrival at Avord, never went to Pau. When the French stopped the Blériot training, he was sent to a camp for a different type of aviation school. The first casualty among Wellman's closer friends was Billy Meeker, killed in a training accident at Pau on September 11, 1917. Wellman's "pal in misery" was doing a vertical spiral in an 18-meter Nieuport when he fell into a wing slip and failed to pull out of it before crashing. Meeker's death was devastating to Wellman and it set the stage for the loss of friends and volunteer Americans in the war-torn skies of France.

OCTOBER 31, 1917
ECOLE D'AVIATION MILITAIRE
PAU P.B.

Dear Arch:
Here I am at Pau the acrobatic school. Believe me I will be able to run a machine if I ever get out of here. So far I have done the first leg of my

acrobatics successfully. Am now in "vol de group" flying. Everything is
done in little fifteen and thirteen meter machines. They go anywhere
from one hundred to one hundred and twenty miles an hour. The
landing speed is terrific. They have rotary "Rhone" motors, 80 H.P,
and 110 H.P. and 120 H.P. God, will they climb. Two thousand meters
in five minutes. Everything is O.K. with my eye now. It was pretty
bad for a while but after I had the thing cut and a little piece of bone
taken out, it felt much better. That is the reason for my cable for aside
from the fifty francs Mrs. Aund sent me long ago, I have had no other
money but my French pay, six dollars per month. Hope to hear soon of
your success with Coffin & Gillmore. They should stick to their word
and I think will, but it is hard to do business from across the waters.
The hundred francs Mother sent me has not as yet turned up. Perhaps
it will later. I hope so. Be sure and use my latest address, Morgan,
Harjis Co. Paris. They will reach me at all times for my address from
now on is liable to change considerably. Take care of yourself and don't
break your neck in the new Hudson.

Faithfully

Bill

At Pau, the pilots were flying real fighting machines of various sizes
and speeds. Wellman started out in 13- and 15-meter Nieuports. While
in the cockpit of an 18-meter machine, with an 80 hp Gnome rotary
engine, he climbed to 5,500 feet and executed right turns, left turns, serpentines, dives, corkscrews, spirals, and all the other acrobatics required.
His first class was in *vol de groupe,* or follow-the-leader stunting. Some of
his maneuvers were: *virages,* or quick reversals of direction; and *vrilles,* or
spinning nosedives with the engine turned off. Wellman got a good taste
of the spinning vrille instruction to keep one's head inside the cockpit
with eyes glued to the altimeter when he watched a Russian pilot stick his
head out during his vrille and die in the resulting crash.

Wellman and the other pilots learned to land their planes inside a
twenty-foot white circle painted on the landing field. The next step was
to do the same trick in a dead-stick landing. In other words, cutting the
engine at the proper time, ending up at least close to that white circle.
Other acrobatic stunts included the "Russian Mountain," a power dive
followed by cutting your engine before leveling off, then switching on the
engine to full power and executing a power zoom upward and looping
the loop; the *renversement,* a change in direction after starting upward in
a loop, at the top cutting off the motor, and by tilting the side ailerons

going into a wing-slip and continuing in this fashion in a semicircle until your machine has turned over and resumed its original horizontal direction . . . in the opposite direction from which the maneuver was started.

One bright and sunny day, Wellman, Sinclaire, and Judd decided to do their own brand of follow-the-leader. They each took turns trying to outdo the others. Sinclaire started as leader and noticed a bridge across a large river. One at a time they all flew under the bridge. Next, Sinclaire pulled up his Nieuport and went into a loop, then down under the bridge. Not to be outdone, Judd followed in the same fashion, as did Wellman. After several hours of various types of stunting, they returned to the airfield. Complaints began pouring into headquarters. The captain called the threesome on the carpet. The boys expected punishments but, instead, they received congratulations!

After that incident, the boys did every kind of flying imaginable. They chased cars, trains, anything and everything they could find. "We would fly any crazy formation or scheme that our French instructors could dream up," said Wellman. "They were a very sensible lot. Their attitude was one of Oh, what the hell. . . . If you crazy Americans are going to get killed, you might as well get killed now than later on." During the last week at Pau, Wellman received his graduation papers from the school. The commandant wrote on his certificate: "A born pilot—but crazy!" At first, Wellman thought this was a compliment, but the French officer told him it was not. No matter, Wellman liked what was also written on the certificate. He was recommended to be trained on Spads and to report to Plessis-Belleville for assignment to a frontline fighting escadrille.

ON ACTIVE SERVICE
WITH THE
AMERICAN EXPEDITIONARY FORCE
NOVEMBER 14, 1917
AMERICAN
Y.M.C.A.

Dear Little Mother:
Mother the only things that one could wear as a mark of having a son in the aviation is a pair of wings with the propeller between them. They of course cannot be gotten in the U.S. but I have been waiting for a more favorable time in which to get you one and then send it by someone who is returning. Just be patient and you shall get it, believe me.

Arch is a wonder, I have written him my thanks. I couldn't get on without his help for at the front we have to buy our own share of good food. Everything costs. I am trying to save for another uniform. The French insist on you looking well in case of being taken prisoner by the Borch.

Aunt Sarah is a peach sending me those bundles and you. May I have the luck to get them for my Xmas is going to be very lonesome. Thank God I have such good times to look back at. Former Xmases and that could help to pass the day. My Xmas without a doubt will be spent somewhere at the front. Some outlook.

Plessis-Bellville to-morrow morning. There to stay until the front. Just getting used to "Spads." Thank the stars I passed "Pau" in good enough shape to get a "monoplane recommendation".

Am very tired Mother dear so will close. Of you my last thoughts.

Billy.

The finished pilots were sent from Pau to the troupe des Divisions d'Entraînement (G.D.E.), the Pilots' Pool or clearing station for all aviators destined for the front. G.D.E. was located at Plessis-Belleville in the Zone des Armées of northern France, about thirty miles from Paris. At Plessis there were fields that provided every type of war-front plane: Voisins, Breguets, Sopwiths, twin-engined Caudrons, Letords, Morane Parasols, and Nieuports. The average time the fully trained pilot spent at Plessis-Belleville before his active-service orders came through was about three weeks.

"I had finished my acrobatics at Pau," said Wellman, "and was on my way to Le Plessis Belleville via one unforgettable night in Paris. That was all they allowed you. It was here at this rather picturesque sounding little village that you waited until some pilot, in the 64-odd pursuit escadrilles scattered the length of the front, got killed or crash-landed for devious reasons in enemy territory." The pilot who was next in line became the replacement.

"Your time in Plessis," said Wellman, "was spent drilling, listening to lectures you didn't understand a word of, unless there was an American buddy with you who spoke French. Then came the very few sorties you had, flying a Spad with a fixed Hispano-Suiza motor. After flying the Nieuports with their rotary motors, the Spad made them look and act as if they had been built and flown by Father Time. At this stage of the game there were some escadrilles flying the Spads, the majority were still using

MR. WELLMAN'S COMMISSION AS AVIATOR IN THE
FRENCH ARMY

Wellman received his commission as an aviator
in the service of France on September 29, 1917,
and was ready for combat.

the Nieuports. They [the French] kept secret what position you held in
the rat race of extinction . . . you knew you could be number one, and
your great hope was that the pilot whom you were replacing had received
his good-bye baby in a Spad."

It was at Plessis that Wellman experienced two monumental firsts: surviving a critical plane crash and falling head over heels in love. Although
he had fractured a bone above the eye while turning over a Nieuport at
Avord, he had never been exposed to a severe air crash.

On a cold, wintry afternoon with thick dark clouds hanging over the
airfield, Wellman took off in his Spad for a last run of the day. As he powered upward through a blanket of fog, the ground disappeared behind
him. There were two guidepost railroad stations to help pilots find the
airfield. Wellman couldn't see them, and as he dove through the overcast
he suddenly came in contact with a field that was littered with old barbed
wire entanglements built by the Germans during the First Battle of the
Marne in 1914. When he tried to level out, he was too close to the ground

and crashed headlong into the maze of wire, each strand extracting its piece of the disintegrating aircraft. A short time later, he was spotted by a search party, sitting and waiting patiently next to the fragmented fuselage of a once proud Spad.

NOVEMBER 22

To the boys:
Good luck to both of you Arch and Dad. Get after the old man joy. He is the chap that can bring you through anything. Believe in Douglas Fairbanks and this world will be brighter. Believe me when I say that through all the wild planes I have been in the last six months old Doug and his book "Laugh and Live" have been a wonderful inspiration. Just two days ago I had motor trouble out in this country. I was in a "Spad" Machine that is used at the front. Two hundred horse power "Espano-Suiza" fixed motor. Imagine the speed. I decended in a field and hit the barb wire trenches, for this country once belonged to friend "Boche" Little Willie was not scratched but was cold for fifty minutes and the first thing I thought of when I was found, was of "Laugh and Live" and I am just as O.K. as usual. I have gotten to pretty near worship that Chap just on account of his view on life. Eat lots of turkey for me and remember somewhere over here I am eating just as much only perhaps of the wrangler variety.
                                          Lovingly,
                                          Bill.

Wellman's second shining new experience was his first true love affair. He had enjoyed teenage romances, but this was one of a kind and star-crossed. Many of the American pilots roomed at the Hôtel de la Bonne Rencontre located near the railroad station of Plessis. It was old and rickety but charming. The furniture was heavy antique, the wallpaper ostentatious, the rooms were not large but the service was personable and the place had an enchanting magnetism. The Plessis barracks were overcrowded and Wellman could not afford a regular hotel room, but he talked his way into having one of the storage rooms converted to a hotel room. It had white walls, one small window, a single bed with a trunk for clothes at the foot of it, a slender chair at a small desk, and the bathroom was at the end of the hall—but still, it was private and sure "beat hell outta" the Avord barracks! Even the bugs were smaller and less intrusive, and Wellman was allowed to pay whenever he could.

Near the hotel was a bakery. On a cool, blustery morning, when no flying was scheduled, Wellman was walking toward the bakery. A young woman, dressed in dark clothes with a wool scarf wrapped around her head, was scurrying from the opposite direction to open the store. As she keyed the door, Wellman arrived and gallantly opened the door for her. She pulled off the scarf and thanked him, "Merci." He bowed as she entered but didn't close the door behind her. She stopped and looked back at this attractive young American pilot, standing outside still holding the door. Wellman was mesmerized by her natural beauty. For a brief moment in time, they locked stares, then shyly she turned slightly and said, in broken English, "You are American?" Wellman answered, "Yeah . . . I mean, yes." She giggled and said, "Close the door or come inside." He closed the door and came inside.

The next few weeks, Billy and Renee saw as much of each other as possible, and their romance blossomed. Renee's mother had died when she was very young; her father was killed in an air raid at the beginning of the war. Renee had a pregnant sister, married to a French soldier and living in Paris. After the death of her father, Renee allowed a Plessis family to help run and be co-owners of the bakery. This gave her time to spend with her sister in Paris and pursue a career in painting.

On December 3, 1917, Wellman's name hit the top of the list and he was assigned to Escadrille N. (Nieuport) 87, stationed at Lunéville in the Alsace-Lorraine sector of eastern France. This date marked the end of his training period. He had spent 118 days at Avord—delayed by weather, crowded conditions at camp, and the scarcity of instructors. In only twelve days at Pau, he had received a crash course in advanced aviation— primarily acrobatics and gunnery. He completed the training cycle at Plessis-Belleville in only three weeks—the time it took for enough combat pilots to lose their lives and have Wellman's name reach the top of the list.

By December 12, most of Wellman's Avord pals had been sent to the front. Frank Baylies joined Escadrille Spad 73 on November 17; David Judd joined Baylies at Spad 73 on December 1; Reggie Sinclaire became a member of Spad 68 on December 4; Tommy Hitchcock would join Wellman at N. 87 on December 10; David Putnam was sent to Spad 94 on December 12; Sidney Drew joined Spad 31 on March 25, 1918. Staff Brown, Wellman's Newton High partner in crime, never joined a fighting escadrille and never saw action, as he was released from service on September 12, 1917, for disciplinary reasons.

Wellman in foreground (second from right) in front of his Nieuport at Escadrille N. 87

Wellman's departure from Plessis-Belleville was a mixed blessing. He was red-hot eager to finally be getting into action, but would sorely miss his Renee. The lovers made a pact that while he was getting settled in Lunéville, she would arrange for the Plessis family to take over the bakery, and she would join him as soon as possible.

3

THE PILOT

After a long, slow ride on a crowded troop train, Corporal Wellman made his entrance into World War I. Lunéville was half a ghost town. The only civilians remaining were those caring for the fighting men. Many of the houses and stores were vacant, and few vehicles were seen on the streets. The town was located only ten miles behind the first-line trenches. As Wellman reported to headquarters, he could hear the distant pounding of the artillery guns. Escadrille N. 87, Les Chats Noir, the Black Cats, was a famed group of French fliers. Fifteen pilots comprised the escadrille. N. 87 had recently lost one and Wellman was the replacement. He was the first American to join them. Many of the French airmen had never seen an American, much less lived with one.

The pilots lived in a time-worn but comfortable château across a dirt road from the airfield. For Wellman, it was a big step up from the arachnid-infested barracks at Avord, the second-rate hotel at Pau, or the converted storage room at Plessis. For him, it was a palace. The three-story château was built of stone and wood with a ten-foot-high brick wall surrounding it. The entrance gate was large, made of iron and rusty to the core. It screeched when Wellman opened it on his way up the narrow, pebble path to the tall, double wooden door of his new business address. Patches of snow covered the yard, which claimed a rock-covered fountain surrounded by leafless trees.

There were not enough bedrooms for all fifteen pilots to have their own room. In the pecking order, the aces and senior fliers had private rooms, the rest doubled up. Since the Frenchmen weren't sure what to expect from the oddball American, Wellman was given his own room. The majority of bedrooms were minus a bathroom, but Wellman was used to trekking down the hall for his comfort station. The château contained a big kitchen on the ground floor next to a spacious living room that also served as the dining room. The considerable dining room table, made of oak, was capable of seating all fifteen aviators at one time. The walls of the room were painted gray, the ceilings were high, and no pictures hung down. Other smaller tables and chairs, a few sofas, filled out the room. Near the twelve-foot-high eighteenth-century limestone fireplace stood an upright piano—these French aviators had an ear for music.

The pilots of N. 87 had built an outstanding record with several aces among them. For an aviator to receive the distinction of ace, he must shoot down five enemy planes and have the kills or victories confirmed, meaning they must be witnessed by a minimum of two other fliers from the same squadron, or be seen from the ground by military observers, or be witnessed from the air by observation balloonists; or the pilot must land his plane, tear off the black cross insignia from the downed aircraft, and return it to his escadrille. Since many of the air battles took place over enemy territory, there were no friendly military observers on the ground or in the air, and in a dogfight the pilots are concentrating on the enemy, not their compatriot's victories. To think that in the heat of battle an aviator is going to stop the war, dive down, and land his plane—possibly in enemy territory—run over to extract the black cross emblem, then run back to his plane, take off, and resume the war . . . well, let's just say that it is easy to imagine that few fliers received all the credits they deserved.

Early on the morning of December 4, Wellman and the fourteen French fliers began crossing the dirt road from the château to the *pilotage,* or headquarters, for their briefing. The building was attached to one of four hangars and each hangar was capable of holding ten airplanes. Wellman had already met his commandant, Captain Azire, at the train station. Azire was short in stature but long on experience. He was flamboyant, wore a pointed black mustache, and spoke English for Wellman's benefit during his remarks about the weather and flight plans. Azire explained the rules to N. 87's new arrival: patrols took place twice a day, early morning and late afternoon when the wind was calmer. When the wind was strong and the weather harsh, you waited until it improved. Then Azire discussed a brand-new idea. Since it was normal to send up a patrol of five or six planes, he believed that one pilot, flying low to the ground and under the eyes of the balloon observers, could surprise the enemy with a speedy strafing and bombing attack, and return to base before they could counter. When the commandant asked for a volunteer, no hands were raised, as the aviators believed the idea was suicidal.

Then, murmuring among the Frenchmen began as one hand reached upward—it belonged to the lone American. Wellman's response to his commandant for volunteering was quite simple . . . he wanted to get into the action as soon as possible.

Wellman was assigned a new ship: a Nieuport 27 camouflaged with blotches of green and reddish brown. Because the colors were dark, a white cat was painted for better visibility and escadrille identification. Later, Nieuports had a natural linen finish and the black cat with a white collar was used. Wellman's mechanic, François, pushed his Nieuport out to the runway and the American prepared for takeoff. Captain Azire and his second officer watched the one-plane dawn patrol leave the ground as the sunrise was peeking over the nearby mountain range.

Depending on the surprise factor, Wellman had been instructed to make one or, at the most, two passes at the enemy airfield, which was almost an hour away. Because of the distance, further passes would consume too much gas and Wellman might run out before making it home. Extra passes would also allow the enemy time to overwhelm the single plane with ground fire and a counterpatrol of their own. Wellman's Nieuport traveled at over 100 mph, hedgehopping across fields, over low hills, and down steep valleys. As the German airfield came into view, Wellman could see a dozen planes, Fokkers and Albatroses, parked on the runway with mechanics working on them while a group of pilots stood outside one of the hangars. It was a complete surprise. Wellman's plane dropped down just above the ground and his tracer bullets sprayed the planes, mechanics, and pilots. Bedlam ensued as German pilots and mechanics ran in all directions, several planes burst into flames, and structures were being torn apart. On Wellman's second pass, he noticed several mechanics and pilots lying on the runway. Ground troops raced for positions to return fire while a few pilots were running to their planes to take off. Wellman released all six of his 10-kilo bombs, and opened fire at everything he could see including the hangars containing other planes in the hopes of causing a fire or an explosion. Now the German soldiers were returning fire with pistols and rifles while two other soldiers were in position to fire their antiaircraft gun.

The sky around Wellman's plane came alive with puffs of black smoke from the antiaircraft gun and bullets whizzed by his head, some striking the Nieuport. Wellman surveyed the damage below, considering making one more pass. At least, he thought, why not stop the planes from taking off? He made the third pass.

Back at N. 87, standing on the tarmac, Captain Azire checked his watch and frowned, knowing the time for Wellman to stay airborne was running out. François stood nearby as Azire looked skyward. Suddenly, the two men focused their attention in the same direction, on a speck in the sky growing larger. It was Wellman's Nieuport gliding over the nearby hills, the gentle winds pushing the plane down almost touching the treetops at the end of the runway—completely out of gas. François began shouting and clapping and running toward the aircraft as it floated down to a bumpy but safe landing. Other mechanics joined the celebration and several pilots came out of the pilotage to view the scene. The overjoyed François helped his pilot from the cockpit, kissed him on both cheeks in the French style, shook his hand with gusto while heaping praise. As Wellman walked over to his commandant, he removed his goggles and helmet. He saluted Azire and gave his report. The captain complimented him and offered three days' leave. For the second time in only a few hours, the American surprised his commandant by choosing Plessis-Belleville over the more tantalizing choice of Paris. Of course, the captain knew nothing of his pilot's lover. Nothing in Wellman's report mentioned anything about the number of passes the American had made at the enemy airfield. From this day forward, Captain Azire referred to Corporal Wellman as . . . "Wild Bill!"

That evening, the American sat down to dinner with all fourteen French pilots. During the cocktail period, Wellman received a mixed reception from the aviators. Sergeant Miot, a cherubic, talkative ace, showed respect and admiration for Wellman's heroic dawn patrol. He welcomed the new arrival with the escadrille's favorite cocktail—equal parts champagne and brandy. It was smooth going down but provided quite a kick once there. Several other Frenchmen smiled at Wellman but viewed the young American with suspicion. Still others disliked Wellman's volunteer-into-action mode and stayed away from him. Sergeant Jeannot was one of these. He was tall, athletic, a leader, and always in the company of two or three followers. Before the war, Jeannot had been a *savateur*—he practiced *savate,* a martial art popularized in France utilizing stiff-legged kicks and sharp, straight punches. Wellman was the replacement for Jeannot's friend, who was killed in combat.

When the dinner was ready for serving, Miot motioned for Wellman to sit in the empty chair, the one that had belonged to the slain aviator. Even though Wellman didn't know their customs, didn't speak their language, he wanted to fit in, to be one of them . . . but not in that chair. He tried to explain his superstition, but it fell on deaf ears. The American pulled up a smaller chair from a nearby table and sat down. The meal was served. Wellman felt self-conscious, out of place, but he sure liked what was in front of him: a large serving dish piled high with steaks, fresh green beans, roasted potatoes, a variety of cheeses, and fresh baked breads. Half a dozen bottles of red wine were placed around the table.

DECEMBER 4

W. A. WELLMAN

PILOTE AIRATEUR AMERICAIN

ESCADRILLE N. 87

SECTEUR 44

Dear Little Mother:

Things are going smoothly enough. The front is very different than anything I have ever even dreamed of. A life of thrills and luck and I feel sure I have both in my favor. I am not permited to say much. . . . When I have had about fifty hours over the lines I will be made a sergeant than things will be much easier. Am depending on Xmas for a new uniform and shoes . . . One more thing, will you send me a lot of music. Old and new stuff for we have a piano here and with music I can amuse.

DECEMBER 6

Dear Arch:

Well we are in the real thing now, To start with, my writing will have to be careful for not much gets by . . . Dad writes me you are going into aviation. That is up to you. I have not and never would advise it. The time you spend in training is perhaps the most dangerous so if you do start flying take care and go easy. Let the other fellows get the name of dare-devil. Just plod along and when you get to the front, then you can show them. Often times getting Germans is not the sign of a wonderful flyer. A man may be in the war for years, do his work every day and still not have any fabulous number of "Boche" to his credit. As an example "Thaw" the Americain with the Lafayette Escadrille since the start. He is one of the best in the game yet, in pretty near three years has only one boche to his credit . . . These are just a few of my ideas Arch but the big one is for you to keep out of it. You have to much ahead of you. In my case it was different. I am not brilliant in business as it is very evident you are. If anything should happen to Dad I could not take care of Mother in the proper way. All these things you could do . . . In my notes that my Captain heard of my work at all the schools, I was pronounced a "bon pilote" but crazy. I had luck, but am sorry for that last word on my notes.

Faithfully

Bill

The weather forecast for the next few days looked menacing and no patrols were scheduled. Regardless, Wellman decided to take his three-day pass to Plessis-Belleville. Renee met him at the station. It had not been long since they were separated, but they acted as if it had been a few years. For the next day and a half, their biggest separation was a matter of feet.

Renee's co-ownership in the bakery was not worth much money, and the Plessis family could not buy her out. At best, the bakery afforded a basic day-to-day existence. Wellman was torn between her business and their togetherness. He didn't want her to lose her livelihood at his expense. After all, he was struggling to make ends meet for himself and couldn't support her. She made it clear that nothing mattered more than the two of them being together.

The afternoon that Wellman and Renee returned to Lunéville was cloudy with patches of blue sky. The morning patrol of six planes returned home with only five Nieuports making their landing. Another pilot had given his life to the cause of freedom. A replacement would be arriving soon. It didn't take Renee long to find employment in a small bakery near the airfield, and a place to live with a local family. During the inclement winter weather, when no flying was scheduled, their romance continued to bloom. Wellman wanted to keep his love affair a secret. The name of Renee would never appear in any of his letters, and she was never brought to the airfield or the pilots' château. The lovers would meet at the bakery, somewhere private in town, or at the small farmhouse where Renee occupied a room. "She was older than I," said Wellman, "but beautiful beyond compare, not only in appearance, in every other way imaginable—she was one of the great number of women who, despite each and every known handicap, persisted in being close to the one and only man that meant everything to them. No matter where they had to go, wherever the war was that their man was a part of, that was where they went, living on the outskirts, cold and hungry, but existing for the few heavenly dwarfisms of time they were able to get together. She was that way with me at Lunéville, working in a bakery shop."

Wellman was happiest in the air. His love of flight was all-consuming and a constant inspiration. While on patrol, his only concern was the enemy. On the ground, it was another matter. His first priority was Renee and her happiness. Although they were in ecstasy when together, he felt guilty at not being able to care for her properly. His relationship with the other pilots was less than satisfactory. He had made only one friend, Sergeant Miot. The other fliers only tolerated him or stayed clear of him. When in the company of the American, Sergeant Jeannot continued a steady diet of whisper, snickering, and innuendo. Wellman kept his cool, minded his own business, but his patience was wearing thin.

It was standard procedure for pilots to place a name, symbol, or some other designation as a sign of good luck on the fuselage of their plane. Wellman's choice was *Celia,* after his mother. François took it upon himself to paint a *I* after *Celia.* François's number addition would prove to be prophetic. Wellman's first patrol in *Celia I* was far from successful. Four N. 87 Nieuports took off at sunrise. The air was chilly and their destination nearly an hour away. No enemy activity was sighted. During the return, the cold and boredom caused Wellman to leave the formation and dive to a lower altitude where the weather was warmer. The other three pilots continued on their course. Wellman spotted a camouflaged two-seater machine, an Aviatik, returning from a photographic mission. Wellman had been trained never to dive on a two-place machine from above, as the gunner, in the second seat, operates a swivel machine gun that can fire in all directions except downward. Instead of coming from underneath, Wellman, in a fit of fury, dove from above. Fortunately for the reckless American, the enemy gunner was a poor shot. As it turned out, Wellman wasn't any better, as he fired many rounds without a single hit. On his next pass, his gun jammed just as the Aviatik gunner was reloading his weapon. The two combatants stared at each other as Wellman sped away in a hasty retreat.

The disappointed American met with another critical event at his own airfield. He was so elated to be back, he forgot another training mandate. During his landing, he neglected to pull his control stick back to bring the aircraft parallel to the ground. He crashed headfirst into the ground, causing his $6,000 Nieuport to separate into fragments. This brought the demise of *Celia I,* but only the wounding of its pilot's self-esteem. Next up . . . *Celia II.*

That evening, Celia—not Wellman's plane but his mother—became indirectly involved in the conversation between her son and Jeannot. The

The remains of Wellman's plane, *Celia I,* crashed on his own airfield, 1917

pilots were gathered in the château before dinner. It was normal for mail to be delivered before their evening meal. On this occasion, Wellman received the last piece of mail—a letter from his mother. Jeannot whistled, snickered, and said, "Une lettre de Maman?" Wellman quickly responded, "What'd you say?" After some more chuckling with two of his friends, the sergeant, in broken, sarcastic English, repeated for the American, "Letter . . . from . . . Mommy?" Wellman calmly tucked the letter in the upper left pocket of his jacket before speaking. "Leave me alone." Under his breath, but loud enough to be heard, Jeannot replied, "Connard d'Américain." Wellman recognized a few French swear words; *connard* meant asshole. No more words were uttered. The American corporal walked over to the French sergeant and his quick right fist deposited Jeannot onto the floor. The Frenchman got up and the fight was on.

The battle resembled a choreographed dance with Jeannot displaying his savate technique, and Wellman a boxer's crouching, advancing style. The Frenchman moved gracefully around the room, never knocking into tables and chairs, always slipping between and around the furniture, while striking the shorter American with sharp punches and stiff-legged kicks. Jeannot was able to land blows from various angles, even with his back turned to the aggressive American. Wellman always moving forward, pressing the fight with jabs, hooks, and counterpunches but missing the target. The corporal was taking a serious beating as blood flowed from his mouth, nose, and a cut above the right eye. The other pilots watched the proceedings from a safe distance. However, as Wellman began to throw lamps, small tables, and chairs out of the way to get at Jeannot, no place was safe from flying furniture and the airmen backed into the hallways and against the walls. Realizing that his style was futile against the Frenchman's savate, Wellman stopped and pretended to quit, while taking a few moments to think it over. Miot stepped forward to stop the slaughter, but was pushed back by the other fliers.

The door of the château burst open and in walked Captain Azire and the second officer. They stopped near the doorway to size up the situation. Resolving disputes by fisticuffs was a way of life at Lunéville and other escadrilles. As long as no flier was seriously injured, the combat was allowed to run its course. Now, a new strategy came to Wellman and he moved slowly forward after Jeannot. His crouching, attacking style gave way to a more cautious bob and weave, becoming a more difficult target for the sharpshooting adversary.

Wellman began closing the distance between Jeannot and himself. Instead of attempting to hit the Frenchman's stomach and head, the American began striking Jeannot's legs and thighs. This course of action slowed the sergeant's foot speed and brought down his guard. Now Wellman was able to connect a solid punch on Jeannot's jaw, dropping him to the floor. The Frenchman got up quickly as Wellman rushed in on the attack.

Azire didn't like what he was seeing. His American pilot, Wild Bill, bathed in blood and continuing the fight. It seemed obvious that more blood would be shed, increasing the possibilities of serious injury to one or both of his fliers. The commandant stepped forward ordering a halt to the brawl. The second officer grabbed Wellman from behind and Miot stepped in front of Jeannot. Azire took a position between the fighters. The captain spoke in both French and English. He wanted to know who started the fight. The other aviators said that Wellman threw the first punch. When Azire addressed the question to the American, the answer was, "I did." Sergeant Jeannot said nothing. The commandant explained to N. 87's newest pilot that fights among the fliers were common and allowed to finish—as long as no critical injury resulted and the morale of the escadrille was not diminished.

After viewing the destruction in the room, the captain exclaimed, "Chairs can be replaced. Good pilots are more difficult." Looking straight at Wild Bill, Azire remarked, "You are the first American at N. 87, others will follow. You are setting a bad example. Do you have anything to say for yourself?" Wellman answered, "No, sir." Before exiting the room, the commandant told his American corporal, "I have sent men to the stockade, I put you on probation. Attend to your wounds. Dismissed."

Wellman waved off any help from the other pilots. Renee would be his nurse.

As a result of this encounter, a significant change took place between the American pilot and the French airmen. One by one— even Sergeant Jeannot—they began to treat Wellman with more respect, even friendship. In their minds, he had fought a courageous battle and taken the responsibility for it. As time marched on, his comradeship and chivalry in the air became more valuable to them and their escadrille.

On December 10, the replacement for the slain aviator arrived at Lunéville. Wellman was ecstatic to see his Avord buddy, Tommy Hitchcock, walking into the pilots' château. Thomas Hitchcock, Jr., of Westbury, New York, from a distinguished family, excelled as a sailor and horseman, particularly in the sport of polo. In Hall and Nordhoff's *The Lafayette Flying Corps*, this description of Hitchcock was given:

Thomas Hitchcock, pilot and polo player

It was said by the instructors at Avord that Hitchcock was one of the most remarkable Blériot pilots the school had ever turned out. Absolutely at home in the air, he possessed a love of flying, a sureness of touch, and a keen eye that made his landings perfect and his air work a pleasure to watch . . . In spite of his antiquated machine [at N. 87] . . . Hitchcock distinguished himself in a very short time by bringing down two German biplanes. He was always in the air, alone or with Wellman, searching far and wide for Germans. Once he found an enemy he never left him, attacking again and again, until the plane went down or until his ammunition was exhausted.

Hitchcock and Wellman roomed together and often flew as a team. They were called the "A-team" and the "Wild Bunch." During the next three months, the A-team was credited with five confirmed kills and received multiple medals and citations, including one of France's highest honors, the Croix de Guerre with Palms. Each Palm was like getting another Croix de Guerre.

For the next two weeks, the weather became turbulent, and the no-fly days outnumbered the fly days. Wellman was excited to introduce Tommy to Renee. Of Wellman's friends and fliers, Hitchcock was the only person to know the beautiful French girl. Renee happily befriended her lover's best pal, and they enjoyed each other's company. As Renee had become close to her live-in Lunéville family, she was able to host small dinner gatherings at the farm. These diversions from war were readily appreciated. Since Wellman was scheduled for patrol duty on Christmas Day, they celebrated on Christmas Eve. There was an exchange of simple gifts. Wellman's gift to Renee was not so simple. Tommy had given his buddy a family keepsake, and Wellman placed the thin, gold wedding ring on Renee's slender finger. The merry group raised their glasses in toast to the formal engagement of Renee and her American pilot. Renee's gift to Wellman was a four-by-six-inch painting, depicting a sunset over a small village in wintertime. High up in one corner, a biplane flies toward

Wellman in front of his Nieuport fighter, Lunéville airfield, 1917

the setting sun. The colors are dark except for some golden lines refracting off the sinking rim of the sun, reaching out to touch the plane.

Darkness drifted away from the sun's morning light, snow sparkled on the ground and roofs of the buildings in Lunéville—a picture-book Christmas morning. Captain Azire acknowledged a quick "Merry Christmas," and it was back to work—war knew no holidays. Wellman would be protecting a three-place machine, a Letord, on a photographic mission. He wore his winter wardrobe: three suits of underwear, three pairs of woolen socks, and a heavy winter uniform. This was supplemented with a fur-lined flying combination and helmet, fur-lined boots, a sweater, and a muffler wrapped about his neck, ears, and forehead. It took two mechanics to hoist him into the cockpit and strap him in place. Santa Claus never looked like this. In the six pockets of the combination suit were placed small boxes, covered on the outside with velvet, and containing a slab of charcoal that could be ignited at the last moment by a fuse at one end. They glowed and shed some heat for a while.

Six escorting Nieuports came on line and followed the cumbersome Letord as it taxied across the snowy field and slowly floated into the crisp air. The mission was to photograph troop movements over the town of Saarburg, about an hour away. As soon as the squadron crossed over into enemy territory, the sky became alive with the black puffs of antiaircraft explosions—a "Merry Christmas" from the enemy.

After completion of the picture taking, the group turned for home. There were no enemy planes in the sky as it turned dark and deadly with rain, hail, and wind. Before they had gone halfway back, snow began to fall. Icy particles covered the glass windshields and the pilots' faces. One by one the planes lost sight of each other. Wellman's motor began to misfire and he struggled to keep *Celia II* in the air and on course for home. He was able to follow a bare outline of the Vosges mountain range and later the Forêt de Parroy, which runs some three miles from French territory crossing the front lines into Germany. Still working to keep his engine alive, he spotted a bright light in the black storm coming from burning gasoline on the airfield for the returning airmen.

The windstorm buffeted Wellman's small aircraft as it neared the snow-covered ground. The slender wheels sank into the snow, sending the machine over and over in three complete somersaults. When the plane stopped rolling, it was smashed to bits, with the back end of the fuselage bent around until it almost touched the front, both its wings separated from the fuselage. Wellman was amazed to still be alive and able to walk away from the final gasp of *Celia II*.

DECEMBER 27, 1917
W.A. WELLMAN
PILOTE AIRATEUR AMERICAIN
ESCADRILLE N.87
SECTEUR 44

Dear Little Mother:

When I finish this note to you I will write one to Arch having received news of his joining the U.S. aviation. Will give him all the dope I know and let him profit by it if it is any good to him. Am waiting for another bunch of letters and of course there will be those from you and they are the first to be opened being the most valuable to me. Weather terrible. Snow very deep and consequently our landings have to be made with a great deal of care. Christmas was spent over Germany as I have already written you. Believe me Mother it was cold, very cold, in fact I never before knew what cold really was. Am just waiting for this winter to get over, then the summer and perhaps a permission home. If I still am satisfied in all probability I will stay here through the summer and take my permission along about September. This will enable me to have a longer stay at home perhaps six or eight weeks. Then we can talk all things over and if I do not change to the U.S. will try and get out of the thing all to-gether.

My health is wonderfull. Feel like a "fighting cock" all the day. If I do well and get any kind of a record with each promotion more money will be given me. Then, very soon, I hope, I can stop depending on Arch. He has been a wonder to do what he is. Will his firm take care of him in the way mine did? I guess not for he is to good a man to loose. Am waiting for the music. Those old tunes so good and the new ones. A little now and then on the piano will help so much. Tell me in your next letter just how Dad's business is, truthfully. I have had and still have heaps of confidence in Dad.

Lovingly
Bill.

Arch Whitehouse, in his *Legion of the Lafayette*, gives this account:

On one occasion Hitchcock and Wellman came upon a German two-seater and began a relentless chase, each one taking turns darting in from tight angles to taunt the gunner. Still, the biplane stayed in the air and started to glide for its field near Nancy. Wellman and Hitchcock tried every trick in the bag to torch them, but the rugged two-seater crew hung on, so the two Nieuport pilots turned their attention to the field itself. They shot up aircraft standing on the line, then dove on hangar after hangar trying to hit something inflammable that would start a good fire. The defense machine guns tried to drive them off, but Tommy and Bill forked the gun teams out of their pits, and when they had driven everyone to cover, pulled out and raced back for their own lines. By the time they returned to their field neither one had a round of ammunition left. They heard later that one of them had killed the German observer in the two-seater.

Wellman and Hitchcock patrolled together on many occasions. Even when they were attached to a larger group, there were times when they split off by themselves. As long as their maverick style didn't endanger the other airmen or the mission, Captain Azire made no mention of it. However, there were times when the commandant was forced to administer reprimands to the Wild Bunch.

The A-team was part of a five-plane patrol returning from a photographic mission that encountered no enemy activity. Boredom set in. Halfway home, Hitchcock decided to springboard from their low excitement level to a rip-roaring high—with a new and slightly peculiar mission. It would be just for the two of them. Tommy flew closer to Wellman's plane and, smiling and pantomiming, pointed toward the Vosges. Wellman, remembering their conversation of the previous evening, understood immediately:

> Tom had the answer that might possibly stir things up. He had noticed on one of our flights a small town close to the mountains that had a wide straight roadway that ended on a church with a good-sized belfry with a very good-sized church bell. He wanted to ring that bell by flying up the street and just before he had to fly up and over the belfry, to let go with as many shots as he could, cut his motor and hear if he had rung the bell.
>
> I was to circle to one side and above and cut my motor at the same time, continuing my circling, and perhaps I would hear the church bell rung. I bet him I would hear them and the only bells ringing for him would be those that were constantly ringing in his head. When he finished we were going to change positions and give me a chance to be a bell ringer. It sounded like fun so off we went to awaken a sleepy little town.

The two prankster pilots arrived at their destination, Tom flying down the outside of the town preparing for a fast turn and a swift flight up the main street, full power, while Wellman lazily circled above and close to the belfry. "Here he came," said Wellman, "just a few feet above the street, people ducking into doorways, full motor with one hand on the gun ready to pull the trigger and the other doing the flying with the thumb on the coupe contact button, to stop and start the motor and listen."

Tom did a great job hitting the bell with a cluster of shots and just clearing the top of the church tower as he started the motor again. Meanwhile, Wellman lost altitude as he circled with his motor shut off. He heard the sharp pings of the bullets as they glanced off the bell. He gave it full motor and went the same way Tom had done. "I did it exactly the same speed," he said, "cut the motor as he did, and Tom duplicated my previous maneuver. He heard, as I did, I heard as Tom did, nothing but the rotation of my motor even before giving it full power to get me over the tower.

"You can hear a church bell ring," said Wellman, "without pulling on a rope, and incidentally scare the hell out of a group of quiet homey townspeople. They must have held a meeting to try to decide what two enemy planes were doing, not shooting at anybody or anything except the church bell, maybe they were heathens and that was a warning, or an odd way to defame God, or perhaps it was just a couple of young crazy fliers playing games. Which it was."

On January 19, 1918, Hitchcock and Wellman were members of a six-plane patrol, again flying protection for a Letord on a photographic mission. Wellman was comfortable in his brand-new Nieuport 27. It was painted in the basic camouflage scheme of green and brown blotches. The white cat on the fuselage stood out as did the large lettering of *Celia III* on the side of the fuselage, near the cockpit.

The mission was successful and the squadron had encountered no enemy fighters on the return trip. As they neared Lunéville, Wellman noticed a series of black puffs in the air below him. He recognized that it was coming from a French battery, and figured they were firing at an enemy plane. He broke away from the squadron to have a look-see. Another Nieuport went with him. Wellman could plainly see the number "7" painted on the fuselage of Miot's machine. As the two pals dove down to the area of activity, Wellman spotted a two-place machine, a Rumpler. Wellman turned to signal Miot, but was surprised to find that the daring ace had already seen the plane, and was diving directly at the enemy ship—in the same manner as Wellman's ill-fated attack on the Aviatik in early December. In an attempt to keep out of the enemy gunner's sights, Wellman peeled off and around to get underneath the Rumpler. Before

Wellman could make his attack, Miot was hit by a fusillade of machine gun bullets. The top port wing of Miot's Nieuport crumpled up, the strain from the dive causing both wings to tear loose, and the wingless machine plummeted to earth. Wellman watched in horror as his friend's ship entered a spinning nosedive, crashing to the ground with explosive force.

Wellman turned back to the action with the two-seater, and coming up from underneath the enemy plane, opened fire. His bullets riddled the undercarriage of the Rumpler.

In Wellman's letter to his father on January 19, he added this to the account:

> Well, by this time Tommy Hitchcock, the other American with me here, had arrived on the scene and together we tackled the "Bosche." First, Tommy diving from above and coming up underneath him and then shooting when as near as possible, then I would repeat the performance. He, the "Bosche", was descending all the time (now in enemy territory) and finally at two thousand meters his engine must have given out for his propellor stopped. The rest of the way he had to vol-o-plane and believe me Dad we gave it to him in great style. Also they were a couple of gamsters for they were shooting at us all the time. The pilot when his machine was in a good position and the gunner, the man behind, all the time, to make a long story short, the Bosche smashed just between the trenches and as Tommy and I had followed him down to the ground, we started a lot of fun in the trenches. We were just twenty yards above the trenches and they gave us hell from their rifles.
>
> Although we were not touched the machines were pretty badly. One wing has to be changed and the other is well patched up with cloth coverings over which an iron cross is painted. This Dad, is the whole story and is the first experience of my new machine, the "Celia III." May I have as much luck always and be able to add a few more palms on my "Croix de Guerre" for I will now have that medal with one palm, a citation from the Army of France.
>
> Love
>
> Bill

Celia III was patched up and out she went on another patrol, this time, a two-plane excursion with Tommy Hitchcock. The A-team headed for Nancy, a few miles to the north. They spotted a two-place machine taking pictures of the once pretty city, now ravaged. The pilot saw them coming and took off for Mamy, their home base, some eighteen miles behind their lines. The battle raged all the way to Mamy, with Hitchcock and Wellman diving, coming up from underneath, strafing the plane; the enemy gunner and pilot firing furiously at the attacking Americans. The Wild Bunch continued a prolonged assault on the aircraft all the way down to its landing. Wellman killed the pilot as he ran from the plane for cover. Hitchcock got the gunner, who, until he died, kept firing his machine gun from the second seat of the motionless plane.

Billy and Tommy, with motors going at full speed, now turned their attention to the airfield. They poured bullets into the open ends of the hangars and everything else in sight. The A-team attack had been so swift, so unexpected, that the Germans were paralyzed. When they recovered, fireworks commenced. Soldiers raced onto the field and into protected positions. They began firing with pistols, rifles, machine guns, and antiaircraft weapons. With shells bursting and bullets whizzing around them—some finding their marks in the Nieuports—the Americans pulled up and headed back to their airfield as fast as possible.

Much of the conflict was seen and heard by Allied military observers on the ground. Captain Azire received a report before his A-team arrived back at N. 87. The Americans were greeted by their commandant, other officers, pilots, and mechanics. François and several mechanics helped Wellman and Hitchcock from the cockpits of their battered planes. After their report, they were congratulated by all. François counted eighteen holes of varying sizes in the wings and fuselage of Wellman's plane. There was also one large piece of shrapnel lodged in Wellman's cockpit seat. *Celia III* was sent to the rear for extensive material repairs—next up, *Celia IV*.

Billy and Renee entered a time and space often described by words like despair, dejection, dispiritedness . . . depression. For Wellman, the cause was threefold: the recent demise of his French pal Miot; the staggering loss of pilots in the war; his predicament with his lover. The tragic death of Sergeant Miot—before his own eyes—would never be erased from his mind. The eternal rest given scores of combat fliers made Wellman wonder if his number might be coming up soon. The possibility of losing Renee was unthinkable, and even if he survived the war, how could he take care of her in a proper manner? These things were prominent in Wellman's thoughts and prayers.

For Renee, her melancholy was twofold: the strong possibility of losing her lover, and the plight of her pregnant sister, Lorraine. Renee had

GLOIRE A NOS HÉROS

CROIX DE GUERRE

Pour citation à
l'ordre de l'Armée

ABOVE (LEFT AND RIGHT): Wellman
wins the Croix de Guerre. BELOW:
Wellman in the German two-seater that he
and Hitchcock shot down (1918)

lost interest in her painting, and did not share any of Wellman's love of flight. Flight was fright to her. It was torment with the endless hours of hoping, praying, waiting to see if her pilot would return from so many missions. From the nearby bakery, she could hear the thunderous engines of the Nieuports as they took flight, and the high-pitched whine of the Rhône engines when they returned from their battlefields in the sky. If she gazed out the window of the bakery, she could see the messengers of war as they rose above the airfield hangars on their rendezvous with the enemy. If she dared watch for their return, she could count their number and know who had triumphed and who had perished. Then she would wait for the front door of the bakery to swing open, and there would stand her American pilot. She dreaded the shadowy thoughts that swam through her mind, telling her that when the door opened, she would see only space and emptiness.

Adding to this funereal period, Renee received word that Lorraine's husband was missing in action. Lorraine had not heard from him in almost two weeks. Renee told her sister not to give up hope, news traveled slowly in wartime; however, Lorraine's spirits were badly shaken and her baby was due soon. Renee would have to leave Lunéville for Paris. She would become a nurse again.

Billy and Renee consoled each other. They prayed, talked by the hour about their togetherness, their future, the war and its hoped-for ending. One thing was crystal clear, the only future that they could count on was the here and now . . . this moment in time.

Tommy Hitchcock served as best man at the wedding ceremony. The marriage took place in a small church on the outskirts of Paris. The two fliers were dressed in their best blue uniforms, complete with matching Croix de Guerres and Palms. Lorraine, the matron of honor, wore a light blue dress, which didn't conceal her expanded baby section. The bride looked simply gorgeous in her sister's white wedding dress, with tiny pink flowers in her dark hair. A gray-bearded minister presided over the nuptials. The groom slipped Hitchcock's family heirloom, the gold ring, on Renee's delicate finger. The church organ played softly, and in the distance, the organ of war was playing its tune of insanity.

Mr. and Mrs. William Wellman shared only one night of enchantment before the A-team returned to the war. Different from Renee's wishes, Wellman wanted to keep their marriage a secret from his family, until they could all be together—one complete family. She disagreed, but understood and accepted her husband's decision.

When Hitchcock and Wellman checked in at the pilotage, they were greeted by a smiling commandant in very high spirits. Azire had a special invitation for the Wild Bunch—to drop President Woodrow Wilson's messages to Congress and the American people over enemy territory. While the Americans were away in Paris, the captain had received orders to get rid of some of the hundreds of pounds of propaganda leaflets and pamphlets that were building up in the war zones. Much of it concerned America's entrance into the conflict. When Azire asked his French pilots to drop the bundles from their planes, they were unimpressed with the notion. Rather than paper, the pilots were far more interested in dropping bombs. After thinking the problem over, the commandant settled on the idea of offering the job to Hitchcock and Wellman. Those crazy, daredevil Americans might jump at the chance to taunt the enemy with their president's words, translated into German and French. The captain's choice proved absolutely correct; however, the A-team's exhilaration became slightly diminished when trying to figure out the process for delivery.

François and another mechanic pushed Wellman's and Hitchcock's Nieuports into position for takeoff. *Celia IV* was freshly painted onto the cockpit of Wellman's plane. As they so often did, the two fliers waved a salute to each other before leaving the ground. Salutes were also per-

Wellman's Nieuport 23, *Celia IV,* Lunéville airfield, 1918

formed by Captain Azire and the officers, pilots, and mechanics lined up on the runway.

The weather was less than desirable, with gray, low-hanging clouds and strong winds. As the Americans neared German territory, they experimented with the propaganda drop. The packages were small rolled-up bundles tied loosely with twine; however, simply dropping or tossing them overboard at over a hundred miles an hour caused an entanglement with the wings and fuselage. Also, the strings would break or slip off in midair, and the pamphlets would go fluttering down in a mass of confetti. The fliers tried a number of unsuccessful bundle drops before Hitchcock got a better idea. He motioned for Wellman to watch. He executed a vertical virage (a turn in the air), tossed two bundles over while flying perpendicular, and at the same time kicked the machine around sharply so that its tail would not hit them. Now the plane could pass before the parcels had dropped a foot and the strings remained intact on the way down.

Once in enemy territory, the planes separated so that their sectors could be covered in half the time. Flying at low altitudes for several miles at a time, over heavily populated trenches, would cause quite a stir and bring about a hailstorm of bullets and shrapnel. These acrobatic stunts would have to be quick, hit-and-run operations. Surprise was on their side as they powered their way across this field of madness, laughing as they witnessed the soldiers dropping their rifles and running after the messages fluttering down.

Hitchcock completed his bundle drops first. He waved a salute to Wellman and sped for home, thinking his buddy would follow right along. Wild Bill had another idea. He still had one more package to deliver. Instead of the virage, he sped upward for several hundred feet, turned, and dove vertically at the enemy in their trenches. Just before crashing into the earth, he performed a renversement—turning the plane up, flipping it over on its back, tossing out the bundle, then pulling up so that he came out in exactly the same line in which he had started. He sped upward in a loop, and at the top of the loop, his motor died. The magneto had broken, leaving him in an upside-down position just a few hundred yards above the ground without any power. Bullets filled the air around him, some hitting the plane, as Wellman turned the machine on its side and coasted with the wind away from the enemy.

When Wellman took off from N. 87, the heavy wind was considered a possible problem. Now it was a godsend or, in Wellman's vernacular, a turn of luck. The wind was strong enough to carry the Nieuport back over no-man's-land and the first-line French trenches. As Wild Bill passed over the heads of the poilus, they shouted encouragement. Wellman was able to land *Celia IV* in a large shell hole. Before he could unhook his harness and gather up his compass, maps, and a few personal items, the poilus began yelling at him. Even though he didn't understand their language, he soon got their drift. The Germans began their voice of a different kind of encouragement, the encouragement to leave—the reverberating sound of an artillery shell passing overhead and landing some twenty-five yards beyond, exploding with an ear-shattering blast and shower of dirt and rocks. Wellman jumped out of his cockpit and, leaving everything behind, raced to the nearest trench, diving headlong into it. The shelling, in his honor, continued for a long while; when it ceased, *Celia IV* was obliterated.

Luck was always on Wellman's mind. He believed in it. He talked, wrote, and thought about it constantly. Ever since he arrived in France, good luck had been his constant companion. They walked together as friends. As a good-luck charm, Wellman kept his mother's goodbye letter with him at all times. For good luck, he had her name, Celia, painted on all his combat planes. Wild Bill had survived the French Foreign Legion, flight training, and many types of risky aircraft. He had lived through minor and major air crashes. He had been shot at by hundreds of enemy soldiers without serious injury . . . and through it all, his pal, Good Luck, was standing beside him. But when Renee sent word that Lorraine's husband had died in the trenches, and the baby was ready to be delivered, Good Luck walked away from him for a long while.

It started to rain in Lunéville. The weather reports said the rain would continue for days. Wellman asked for and received permission to go to Paris. Renee met him at the train station and escorted him to her small apartment. The concierge brought word that Lorraine was about to deliver. Renee kissed her husband, told him that the maternity hospital was nearby, and that she would return soon. She gave him directions to a café around the corner where he could enjoy a light dinner. They walked downstairs together, then separated. He stood there for a moment, watching her walk toward a narrow cobblestone street. She stopped, turned back to him, and blew a kiss. He acted as if he caught the kiss in his hands, then put it in his upper uniform pocket, next to his mother's letter. He saluted a goodbye to his lovely wife, executed a military right face, and marched to the corner of the street. She giggled, smiled, and watched him disappear around the corner, then turned and hustled up the narrow street.

Just as Wellman began eating his meal in the café, he heard the distant explosions of cannon shells. These were followed by another louder interruption, the wail of the alert siren. Wellman lost his appetite as the cannon detonations came closer and closer. He knew about the Paris Gun, as it was called, a 210mm weapon designed and operated by the German navy in 1918. Seven of these guns were produced, and they could fire on Paris from 131 kilometers away. Their base was the forest of Coucy. It took 170 seconds for a shell to reach the city. Over time, 367 shells were fired; casualties numbered 256 dead, 620 wounded. Their aim was often wild, but the damage was considerable.

The shelling by the Paris Gun lasted only a short time. When the Alert siren blared out its final all-clear, Wellman ran from the café to Renee's apartment building and the narrow cobblestone street where he had last seen her. There were no pedestrians, and Renee's building was untouched by the shelling. Half running, Wellman started up the narrow street. The skyline ahead of him was alight with flames from the explosion of a gas reservoir. His pace quickened. He entered a scene of devastation; many of the apartment buildings on the block were afire, some starting to collapse. A group of citizens were huddled together outside one of the burning buildings, sobbing and moaning as Wellman approached. He asked where the maternity hospital was located. Several of them pointed up the street, said something in French, then returned to their grieving.

Wellman continued running up the street and around the first corner. There he found another crowd gathering, many of whom, in every stage of dress, had rushed from neighboring homes and apartments. This group was far more agonized and verbal in their anguish. They were shouting out, shrieking, falling to their knees in prayer and pain. Wellman's pace slowed to a walk, and he entered the group. Two words passed from lip to lip that he understood . . . "l'Hôpital" and "Infirmerie." Wellman pushed his way through the crowd to see the building that was their focus of attention. He could read two words on a smoldering sign above the entrance, "l'Hôpital" and "Maternité." The wild aim of the Paris Gun had made a direct hit. The small hospital was in complete ruin. Gendarmes had just arrived and were digging for survivors, but finding only bits and pieces of dead mothers and their babies. A nurse and some local citizenry sifted through the destruction. They coughed and vomited. The smell of burned flesh filled the air.

Wellman charged madly into the still-burning rubble, an anger encompassing him, driving him berserk, as he dug into the smoldering debris, finding nothing but blackened bits and parts of human beings. A man nearby pulled up an arm and leg, then fainted into the smoking remains. More rubble searchers arrived. After a few moments of digging, several of them started crying and screaming, while others ran away. Wellman reached down and came up with something—a charred finger and some of its hand. There was no fingernail joint, just part of the finger connected to what was left of the hand . . . and on the finger, Hitchcock's gold wedding ring. Wellman stopped digging, for this was all that was left of his beautiful Renee. He got sick to his stomach and threw up. He staggered out of the holocaust, and dropped the ring and remains into a pile of burning wood—a funeral pyre for his beloved.

Wellman returned to Lunéville as soon as possible. There was only one person he could talk to about this horrifying tragedy, Tommy Hitchcock. With the exception of his best pal, Wellman would never tell another human being about the life or death of Renee. She was, and would remain, his first true love, his beloved French girl, his enchanting first wife, his angel from heaven. For the next fifty-five years, he placed the entire chapter somewhere in the deep recesses of his mind, away from any light, in a sealed sanctuary. Not until he reached the age of seventy-seven did he relent and unseal that solitary asylum, allowing the light to penetrate and bring to the surface the story of his dark-haired angel from the long-ago.

At Wellman's next meeting with Captain Azire, he asked for more patrol duty, even as a single. After what the American had been through, one can only imagine his state of mind. How much, if anything, did the captain know about this French girl who had worked at a nearby bakery for many weeks? No records support Azire's knowledge of Renee, but he gave Wellman permission to fly more often, even as a one-man patrol.

Wellman's former friend, Good Luck, continued to abandon him on March 6, 1918. While Wellman was assigned to a five-plane morning patrol, Hitchcock went out solo a short time later. Wellman's patrol returned without incident, Hitchcock never came back. No report on Hitchcock was received by N. 87. All that Wellman knew was that Tommy went out on solo patrol, observing troop movements in the surrounding sectors. Wild Bill considered going after him, but didn't know where to start or how far his buddy had ranged. He went anyway, flying some of the sectors Hitchcock likely had covered until his gas ran low, forcing him back. Then Wellman waited on the tarmac at the airfield well into the night. Hitchcock didn't return. His name was added to the missing-in-action list. Wellman would not know if his pal was alive or dead until after the war. From Arch Whitehouse's *Legion of the Lafayette* comes this account:

While flying alone on March 6, 1918, Hitchcock came upon a large flock of Albatros fighters and attacked them boldly, but after his first pass he found himself well trapped by this swarm, and although he made a brave effort to get clear, a German bullet creased his back and another cut an aileron control wire that deprived him of much maneuverability. The Albatros pilots moved in closer and closer until he was finally forced to the ground in German territory. Tommy's wound was not serious and after a short time in a German hospital he was imprisoned at a compound at Lechfeld. From the minute he was put behind barred gates, he planned an escape.

After repeated attempts to break out of the prison camp, and over five months of imprisonment, on August 28, 1918, Hitchcock made his escape. He was traveling at night during a prisoner transfer aboard a train with German soldiers, when he stole maps and money from his guard and leaped from the speeding train. Under the cover of darkness, through heavily wooded terrain, dodging enemy patrols, he eventually crossed the German border into Switzerland and freedom.

Hitchcock and Wellman, they were inseparable. They were the A-team, the Wild Bunch, Billy and Tommy, as close as brothers. They trained together, flew together, shot up enemy airfields together, shot down enemy planes together, delivered President Wilson's message together, lived together, went to Paris together. Tommy was best man at Wellman's wedding, and the best friend anyone could ever have . . . and now he was gone. Wellman felt as if he was the one missing in action. What was left to lift his spirits, to end that long-lost emotion, to quiet the maddening sensation inside him? Only his fervor for flight. He would throw himself completely into flying and the resulting combats.

On March 9, Wellman was called into the commandant's office to receive orders for the next patrol, with America's Rainbow Division. It proved to be monumental in the annals of the war. This date would be their beginning, their first "over the top" attack on the German lines, and William Wellman was to be the only American pilot in the air flying support.

The Rainbow Division was the 42nd Infantry, formed within months of America's entry into the conflict. Individual states competed with each other for the honor to be the first to send their National Guard units to fight in the battlefields of Europe.

The government created a division composed of handpicked units from twenty-six states and the District of Columbia. The 42nd Infantry was born and then trained at Camp Mills, Long Island. Their chief of staff, Brigadier General Douglas MacArthur, said, "The 42nd Division stretches like a Rainbow from one end of America to the other." The division arrived in France in November 1917 and entered the front line in March 1918. They joined the 117th Engineers and the French 167e Régiment d'Infanterie. The 42nd remained in constant contact with the enemy for 174 days, which included six major campaigns. They endured many bloody battles and great victories until the Germans were finally defeated.

Captain Azire explained the historic day to his pilots, elaborating on the element of surprise in the coming offensive. Wellman remembered his orders: "Under no conditions will you allow an enemy's machine to fly over the French and American lines! If they attack, and your machine gun jams, ram your opponent!"

Wellman was chosen to be the leader of the lowest patrol at one thousand meters. Eight other planes would follow, with a second patrol just above. There would be patrols from all the flying groups of the sector at various altitudes up to six thousand meters.

Celia V took to the air with the other pursuit ships of N. 87 close behind. Their sector was a three-mile corridor to be patrolled back and forth over the Allied lines. Wild Bill searched the skies for the enemy, but all he saw was a cloudless pale blue crowded with the circling hawks of the French patrols.

Below, he could make out the battle-scarred fields of France and the narrow, snaking roads through war-torn and desolate villages. He could see the first-, second-, and third-line trenches extending north and south like thin dark ribbons; the network of barbed wire; the soldiers, like tiny insects, waiting in their trench-homes; the snowcapped Vosges Mountains on one side and the way distant parallel lines of black—the German trenches.

Wellman could not distinguish between the American and French soldiers, but he knew the Rainbow Division was in the center with the poilus flanking them on either side. The trench soldiers were silent; there were no flashes from the concealed guns; no explosions; no enemy planes in the sky. It seemed there was no war at all, just the French flying machines in the air, circling and watching.

Suddenly, the wait was over, the silence ended. Flashes of flame belched forth from the camouflaged weapons in the ruined villages and network of trenches. Over the roar of his engine, Wellman could hear the crashing detonations from the barrage below. Soon, the tiny soldiers leaped from their trench-prisons and raced across no-man's-land to their targets.

Random thoughts permeated Wellman's mind. He wished Tommy Hitchcock was flying next to him, ready to fight as the A-team had done so many times before. He thought about how strange it was to be the only American serving as air guard for so many Americans being battle-tested on the ground. The sole American pilot in a French machine, wearing a French uniform and fighting under the Tricolor instead of the Stars and Stripes!

The unordered thoughts transpired as the distant blue sky came alive with black specks, like a swarm of flies growing larger and larger. As the enemy squadrons arrived, Wellman rocked *Celia V* from side to side, signaling the attack. Wild Bill dove at the enemy leader in a Rumpler. His vertical dive was too fast for the German gunner in the second seat. Wellman executed a sharp Russian Mountain and powered up underneath the ship, firing streams of steel into the belly of the Rumpler. As he sped past, he could see the gunner drop, dangling over the side of the cockpit. The Rumpler began to smoke, losing altitude and going into a spinning nose-dive. Another Nieuport from N. 87 dove in to finish the enemy pilot as he was trying to control the spin. The German airship burst into flames and its wings separated from the fuselage.

Before the dogfight ended, Wild Bill had escaped the clutches of two Albatros fighters, shooting down one of them. The enemy plane crashed near the American first line of trenches. Before long, America's Rainbow fighters and their brave French allies were on their way across the German lines, forcing the retreating German army back where they came from. The land battle had been won. The crippled German air fleet had hightailed it back to lick their wounds, while the Nieuports of N. 87 and their comrades from the other escadrilles were on their way home—their job had been accomplished.

Military observers had reported the results to Captain Azire. In that report, a Nieuport bearing a Black Cat and numbered "10" had brought down two machines during the combat. Number 10 was named *Celia V.* As a result of this achievement, Sergeant William Wellman received another Gold Palm Leaf on his Croix de Guerre.

On March 21, 1918, just nine days after the triumphant Rainbow Division victory, and only fifteen days after Hitchcock's disappearance, Wellman took off on a one-man patrol. His mission was reconnaissance. He was not to engage the enemy, just observe troop movements over the region of Toul. The weather was clear but chilly with a strong wind blowing the fighter plane from side to side. Wellman, in *Celia V*, was flying at an altitude of a thousand meters, checking the map on his lap. The clouds below him formed a kind of atmospheric lake with holes dotted across its surface. He put aside the map and dove down through one of the holes to two hundred meters. Dead ahead was a small, picturesque French village that had been taken over by the enemy. There were no townspeople in sight, only German soldiers. It was a relaxed atmosphere. Soldiers were sitting in chairs, on benches in the town square, and walking casually down the one main street. The German flag waved from its pole in the center of the village. Several large cannons stood guard and two bunkers housed the antiaircraft weapons.

Wellman dropped down even lower and opened fire, raking the surprised soldiers, who scurried to their trenches like rabbits to their holes. In his overcharged emotional state, he made pass after pass over the small village. The German flag had been peppered and fallen to the ground in a heap. Half a dozen soldiers were lying dead in the street. An ammunition dump had exploded, causing a huge fire. Several other buildings were in flames. The soldiers were taking positions in the bunkers and trenches, returning fire with rifles, pistols, and machine guns.

Celia V had received many hits and the Rhône was sputtering. After a last look, Wellman turned and headed for home. He would never make it back to N. 87. An antiaircraft shell found its mark. A blinding flash in Wellman's face, a crashing detonation in his ears. Half stunned, he closed his eyes, then opened them, realizing that his plane was losing power and falling to earth. With blood dripping from his ears and nose, Wellman pulled back on the control stick, working to pull the plane out of its spinning dive. The damaged Nieuport continued to rush earthward, headfirst and whirling. Wellman looked around and up at the tail of his fuselage. Part of the canvas was flapping violently, the control wires shot away, the rear ailerons out of commission. He was completely helpless. He looked down, seeing the earth rising toward him with appalling speed.

Suddenly, a strong current of air changed the spinning nosedive into a sweeping spiral, slowing the downward plunge and pushing the nose of the plane up, and the spiral became a side wing-slip. The wounded flier was riding the wind into a thick forest. At the instant the Nieuport hit the treetops, Wellman banged his fist against the fastening belt of his harness and it released. The force of the impact threw him out of the plane and into the trees. On the way down to the ground, Wellman grabbed on to branches and limbs, which shattered and broke. He was finally able to catch hold of the bough of a big fir tree. Stunned and filled with pain, he half slid, half scrambled down the life-saving tree, ending up on the ground next to the crumpled remains of *Celia V.*

Wellman woke up in a French hospital. Poilus had found him and brought him there in an unconscious state. The American was partially paralyzed, suffering from moments of blackout. There was internal bleeding. His back was broken in two places. The control stick of his plane had been forced through the roof of his mouth, and a piece of shrapnel was embedded in his nose, an eighth of an inch from his eye. But his former friend, Good Luck, had returned and lay beside him, for Wild Bill had escaped death. French doctors removed the shrapnel, and a silver plate was inserted into his skull. He was fitted for a full back brace, and there was some question as to whether he would ever walk again. At the very least, he would be modeling the brace for many weeks.

Wellman at Lunéville, Escadrille N. 87, 1918

William Wellman's days as a fighter pilot had come to an end—but a better end than that of most of his American buddies:

The determined and patriotic New Yorker Billy Meeker died in a training accident at Pau, September 11, 1917.

The gentle-mannered Sidney Drew, already an accomplished actor, screenwriter, and playwright in New York, made the supreme sacrifice in his first air battle, May 19, 1918.

Frank Baylies, New Bedford, Massachusetts, charming and modest, became one of the best American fliers, with twelve confirmed victories before his death, June 17, 1918.

David Putnam, Brookline, Massachusetts, a Harvard man and fervent patriot, scored thirteen official victories before being killed, September 13, 1918.

Wellman's high school buddy Staff Brown was released from service for disciplinary reasons, September 12, 1917.

Wellman's best pal, Thomas Hitchcock, missing in action on March 6, 1918, imprisoned for over five months before escaping, became a world-renowned, ten-goal polo player before being killed testing an air force plane prior to World War II.

Of Wellman's closest friends, David Judd, Brookline, and Reginald Sinclaire, Corning, New York, also survived the wars. Juddy, as Wellman called him, built a fine record at the front with the Royal Air Force, as well as the French. Duke Sinclaire, known as Reggie, received the Croix de Guerre with three Palms for his outstanding service in the Lafayette Flying Corps.

On March 29, 1918, Sergeant William Augustus Wellman received his honorable discharge from the French army and Lafayette Flying Corps.

Decorations: Croix de Guerre, with two Palms
French Grande Guerre (War medal)
Verdun Commemorative Medal
Citations: A L'Ordre de L'Armée
Le Pilote Américain, Marshall de Logis
Final Rank: Sergeant

Wild Bill's Croix de Guerre and the first Palm came with two confirmed victories. There were four official victories from air battles, three unconfirmed kills while flying alone and in enemy territory, and countless enemy planes destroyed on their airfields and in hangars from strafing and bombing.

Two hundred ten Americans saw combat duty with the French. Sixty-five were shot down or killed in accidents. Thirty-five were wounded or taken prisoner. There were one hundred casualties. Seventy-two pilots were credited with official victories. The Americans accounted for 199 confirmed victories, with hundreds unconfirmed.

These patriotic volunteer Americans, from all walks of life, wearing a tapestry of heroism, were not swashbuckling braggarts but mild-mannered idealists. They all triumphed and their spirit will always be up there with the roar of engines in the clouds of heaven.

4

THE WAR HERO

The French ocean liner *Espagne*, built in 1910, began service to New York in 1912. It was advertised as "the fastest way to Paris." On May 2, 1918, the luxury liner carried 183 passengers past the symbol of freedom, the Statue of Liberty, into New York Harbor. There were war veterans on board, including those in the United States Army, the U.S. Air Service, the ambulance corps., and one injured flier from the Lafayette Flying Corps. Dressed in his best uniform, wearing his medals and full back brace, Sergeant William A. Wellman watched from the railing of the upper deck as the *Espagne* was greeted by hundreds of well-wishers crowded on the dock. The multitudes shouted and cheered, the bands played, camera bulbs flashed, reporters talked, and confetti filled the air. Wellman's family was not among the jubilant assemblage.

During Wellman's rehab period in France, he notified the family that he had been injured, but that it was not serious. He later wired that he would be coming home soon. They did not hear from him again until the passenger liner dropped anchor in the Empire State. The reasons for his lack of information to the family were twofold: he didn't want them to worry about his injuries, and, for the time being, he didn't want them to know about his intense desire to return to combat. He had underestimated his country's nationalist frenzy. He never imagined how much attention would be heaped on him and his war experiences. Reporters at the dock converged on him. They wanted to hear stories of air combats; how many Huns did he kill; how many Boche planes did he shoot down; how were other Americans faring in battle—all manner of stories that could fill a rousing article to satisfy the people's voracious appetite for upbeat war news.

Even before Wellman left for France, the country was swept up in a tide of patriotism, the call to arms, America's young volunteers fighting for the cause of liberty and justice in a foreign land against the imperialism and aggression of Kaiser Wilhelm's war machine. A wounded and decorated twenty-two-year-old American airman was just what was needed to help fuel the headlines that sold newspapers and magazines throughout the country. Even a book, *Go, Get 'Em!* (1918), was written from Wellman's war experiences.

Consider these banner headlines that appeared May 3, 1918, the morning after Wellman's arrival:

SERGEANT WILLIAM WELLMAN ARRIVES WITH COVETED CROIX DE GUERRE (*New York Tribune*)

MODEST AIR HERO BACK FROM FRANCE (*Boston Evening Telegraph*)

Boston Herald Rotogravure Section, 1918. Wellman wrote twenty-two for his age.

WOUNDED FLIER GLAD TO SEE NEW YORK AGAIN BUT HEARS CALL OF BATTLEFRONT (*Boston Globe*)

EAGER TO GET BACK IN FIGHT (*Boston Globe*)

WOUNDED HERO OF THE AIR WHO HAS BROUGHT DOWN FOUR HUN FLIERS (*Boston Globe*)

The accompanying stories covered multiple columns in each paper.

Before returning home to Cambridge, Sergeant Wellman entered a recruiting station in New York. He ditched his back brace, suppressed the pain, and walked in tall without the limp. He interviewed and filled out an application for service in the RAF. Dressed in his best blue uniform, adorned with golden wings on either side of his collar, sergeant stripes on his sleeves, a silver wreath wing over his right pocket, and left pocket

ABOVE: Taffy, on doorstep, waits for his master's return.

RIGHT: Celia and Arther waiting for their wounded son after ten months abroad

BELOW: Arthur, age twenty-four, a lieutenant in the U.S. Air Service, 1918

medals including the Croix de Guerre with Palms, what a sight he must have been, standing next to other young hopefuls dressed in their street garb.

Wellman explained to Colonel Lord Wellesley of the British and Canadian Recruiting mission that even though he had been released by the French, his wounds had healed and he was ready to return to active duty. Billy mentioned his desire to join his Brookline pal, David Judd, with the RAF. The colonel said that his case would be reviewed by Provost Marshal General Crowder in Washington. If accepted, he would be required to take a full physical. Wellman assured the officer that he could pass any physical—which, of course, he could not.

Before going home, Billy had one more mission to accomplish. He arrived at the home of Major and Mrs. Thomas Hitchcock. With him were two articles from Tommy's personal effects—his diary and his Croix de Guerre. It wasn't much but it represented tangible belongings from their son, who was still missing in action. Like Wellman, the Hitchcocks reasoned that after two months without word it was likely that Tommy had perished in the line of duty. Who better to talk about their boy than his A-team partner, who had loved him like a brother. The Croix de Guerre would find a special display place for all visitors to the Hitchcock residence, and being able to read their son's diary would fill another void.

Now it was time to take the train to Boston. Celia and Arthur would be waiting at the station. Upon arrival, Billy limped into the waiting arms of his mother, and a strong hug from his father. (Arch was down in West Point, Mississippi, going through flight training in the U.S. Air Service.) Celia had trouble releasing her son from her arms. She could not stop hugging and kissing him. She could feel his back brace and wanted to know all about his injuries. On the taxi ride to Cambridge, across the Howard Bridge, over the edge of the Charles River, they discussed a great many subjects. Billy made light of his physical problems, explaining that everything had healed, and the back problem was much improved. Of course, one of Billy's first questions concerned his dog.

> Taffy was there just waiting. My Dad had to go to the office, so Mother and I took the elevator up to the floor we were living on. Mother unlocked the door and pushed me gently into the living room. There, sound asleep before the fire, lay my dog. His head wasn't black, it was black and white. I called softly to him, "Taffy." He didn't hear, he was partially deaf. I called again louder, "Taffy!" This he heard, snapped his

old head up, saw me, struggled to his feet and we both started running to each other.

Taffy tried to jump, he made it about six inches off the floor, with the heavy brace I tried to catch him, and some way or other he landed in my arms, with his bleary old eyes searching—for one fleeting moment he seemed to bring them in focus and he got a clear view of me, he licked my face, closed his eyes and with a long, wavering, satisfied sigh, Taffy said good-bye.

The loss of friends and loved ones had become a way of life for Billy. Even at such a young age, he had already learned that these heart-piercing tragedies not only happen, but their accompanying pain does not disappear soon. The stabbing pain may ease over time, but it will never be completely gone or forgotten. His mother had taught him to accept the heartbreak as a part of life, make the best adjustment possible, and, with God's help, continue on. Billy would always remember his valiant comrades in arms, his cherished wife, Renee, his treasured dog, Taffy— they were only gone from his sight, never from his heart. That first evening home, Billy gathered his thoughts away from Taffy's passing, and sat down to dinner with his mother and father. Celia served his favorite: Boston baked beans, fish balls, steamed clams, and roasted chestnuts. The conversation was relaxed and Billy continued to play down his war wounds with no mention of his eagerness to return to the battlefield. Little did he know that the morning newspapers would bring a torrent of attention, excitement, and activity to the Wellman's low-key Cambridge world.

After dinner, Arthur excused himself and his son from the table. He told Celia that a father-and-son walk around the neighborhood was in order. During the walk, Arthur asked his boy about his plans. Did he want to work in sales or in management? Arthur thought he could persuade one of his patriotic business contacts to hire Billy. Maybe Billy should give Coffin and Gilmore another chance. Billy told his father that C&G was definitely out—they had gone back on their word and they would be the last place he would ever go. Billy said that he needed some time away from it all and give things some serious thought.

Soon, the two walkers came upon one of Arthur's favorite watering holes. Arthur suggested a welcome-home drink before retiring. When Arthur pushed open the door to the gin mill, a surprise party was awaiting. The tavern was not only crowded with Arthur's drinking buddies, but with local citizenry who had gotten word of Billy's homecoming. Arthur stepped aside to allow his son the full stage. Standing just inside the doorway, still in his uniform, Sergeant Wellman listened to the clamor, the applause, and the songs of the throng, many well into their cups. The pickled group offered their renditions of "Over there, over there, the Yanks are coming, the Yanks are coming, the Yanks are coming everywhere . . ." and "How 'ya gonna keep 'em down on the farm, after they've seen Paree?" and the like.

Realizing his son was uncomfortable, Arthur stepped in, put his arm around Billy's shoulder, and ushered him over to the bar. The crowd gathered around the two Wellmans, shoving drink after drink in their direction, asking question after question about Billy's war exploits and the success of American pilots in the skies over Europe. Until Billy had knocked a few back, he was having difficulty answering this raucous crowd. Even after feeling no pain, Billy was reluctant to answer many of the questions. Soon it became toasting time. The merrymakers raised their glasses, mugs, and bottles to the volunteer American fliers, the war effort, the end of the kaiser, the end of the war to end all wars. They drank to Billy's safe return, his war hero efforts, his future, and thank God for John Barleycorn. By now the pack was becoming unruly, as some of the revelers were three or four sheets to the wind. Many of those who could still stand and talk left. A few fights broke out, but didn't last long—the fisticuffers couldn't remember why they were fighting.

Arthur entered the chug-a-lug arena by interrupting the hubbub to toast his son's improving health, and early departure of his unsightly back brace. The ballyhoo started up again, and Arthur urged Billy to take off the "goddamn" thing, throw it across the bar, and never wear it again. In Billy's swacked state, he thought it sounded like a fine idea. With help from his fuddled father, they removed the French uniform jacket and shirt. This brought about a thunderous applause, some thinking it was strip time. With great difficulty, the two Wellmans unlaced the leather and steel-ribbed brace. More hoorays and clapping from the pub crawlers before Billy grabbed hold of the brace, flinging it across the top of the bar, taking glasses, bottles, and dishes with it before crashing to the floor. When the evening finally came to a pulsating, head-throbbing finish, Billy had retained just enough sense to retrieve the brace and drag it and his father home.

The morning after. When Billy awoke, he couldn't tell which hurt more, his head or his back. He fumbled around looking for his brace. He found the goddamn thing, strapped it on, laced it up, and staggered a wobbly course toward his morning coffee. On the way to the kitchen, he passed through the living room. Celia and Arthur were there, holding court with several neighbors, two reporters, and one photographer. When the newsmen saw Billy, they stood up and addressed him by name. He stopped, blinked at them, did an about-face, and returned to his bedroom. This was just the beginning of a period that Wellman would later label "a time best forgotten."

With the morning headlines and related stories of heroic deeds and all came the seemingly endless stream of phone calls and drop-by visitors. The guests, many uninvited, included the press, dignitaries and politicians, neighbors, old friends, new friends, and those pretending to be friends. The interest in seeing, interviewing, photographing, talking to Billy was overwhelming. Celia began to keep a record of names and their interests. There were invitations to all sorts of events and functions. There was no way for Billy to have time for himself and reflection or, for that matter, his family.

Billy was happy to be home and with family. He was proud of his service in the war, and delighted to discuss his comrades and their heroism. But he did not like talking about himself, and he certainly did not like the notoriety. A dark cloud was forming. It was called . . . the future. Billy had no idea of where his place would be in it. All he could think about was returning to flying.

Newton mayor Edwin O. Childs appeared on the scene. Without asking or even meeting with Billy, Childs organized a hometown parade in the war hero's honor. The proud parents accepted for their son, and Billy sat in the backseat of a convertible, waving to the roisterous crowd. A parade was not the mayor's only interest. Childs had received a call from James M. Curley, Boston's mayor, and together they invited, or better said, told the decorated flier that it was his duty to speak at a war bond rally. Celia and Arthur proudly accepted for their son. Reluctantly, Billy allowed the plans to go forward. He had no experience speaking to a crowd, but he did believe in helping the war effort, and in aiding his compatriots in France.

On the morning of May 13, 1918, Mayor Curley sent a car to take the three Wellmans to the Pilgrim Publicity Association Thrift Stamp rally. The rally took place at the Common Garden, where Billy and his brother had enjoyed many hours during their childhood. *The Boston Post,* May 14, 1918, reported the event. Headline: "BUY THRIFT STAMPS TO WIN WAR, SAYS AIRMAN WELLMAN" (above photograph of huge crowd). Caption under photograph: "Big crowd that heard aviator

Wellman tell of his experiences fighting Hun airmen." Caption above photo of Wellman speaking at rally: "Young Wellman yesterday at the Pilgrim Publicity Association Thrift Stamp rally on the Common urged his hearers to buy stamps to aid the boys in France." Some of Wellman's quotes in the long article: "Don't idolize the airmen. Theirs is the spectacular part. Buy Thrift Stamps for the boys in the trenches. That is where the trial is" . . . "If the war lasts two years longer bombardments and air raids will be upon us" . . . "It is America that must win the war and they will do it if they ever get airplanes enough. Buy Thrift Stamps" . . . "Give and save Boston." The article went on to say Wellman "was the idol of the throng and they listened eagerly and responded generously to his 'Give and save Boston.'" . . . "The young flier's speech resulted in more individual sales of Thrift Stamps and War Savings Certificates than have been recorded for any previous day."

Wellman's success at the war bond rally led to a grand dinner in his honor in Newton. On May 18, 1918, Mayor Childs and other VIPs hosted the event. Boston's *Morning Telegraph*, Sunday, July 21, 1918, carried the story:

> In Newton they appear to have a French love for the heroes who came home. On May 18, this year, a hundred citizens, including Mayor, Senators, Congressmen, and business men who had known him all his life, gave him a dinner. On this particular evening his father brought over the silver plate engraved: "Presented to Marshall de Logis, Escadrille N. 87, by the citizens of Newton in recognition of his valor and high achievements as a volunteer in the service of France for the cause of Liberty." It was then that Senator Weeks said that such an honor had never been paid any citizen of Newton before, and that Bill Wellman was a boy's boy and had always been, and that he was the most beloved youth in the village because he had always helped the down-fellow.

How interesting to hear that Senator Weeks, who purported to have known the flier since childhood, said that Billy was the most beloved youth in the village. For many of Billy's former years, he was considered the terror of the village. How quickly things change when politics rears its head.

For the next several months, Wellman's calendar was filled with the activities of a celebrity. When called upon to speak, he continued to exclaim, "We airmen are not the heroes that we are acclaimed. I say it now. Flying is safe, under ordinary conditions, and under extraordinary ones it is nine-tenths luck—and the other tenth is foolishness. It is the men in the trenches who are the real heroes of this war, for theirs is the hardest work; theirs the most horrible conditions. All honor to them." It was soon after this speech that the RAF rejected Wellman's application, citing health issues. Billy was upset by this setback. He was growing increasingly tired of this life as a war hero. He didn't feel like a hero; rather, he felt like a broken-down ex–pursuit pilot who had lost his wife, his buddies, even his dog, and had no future prospects that he cared to pursue. He began to turn down invitations and the media. There was one invitation he couldn't refuse—from Teddy Roosevelt.

The former president of the United States had retired from public life, and was spending his time at home in Oyster Bay, Long Island. He was nearly sixty years old and felt wholly forgotten. As Alice and John Durant write, "Theodore Roosevelt had been the youngest man to become president, the wealthiest (up to this time), the most popular since Andrew Jackson, and by far the most athletic, dynamic, colorful and adventurous. No shrinking violet was our twenty-sixth president." After his years as president, he took time off, but returned when his Republican Party fell into disorder. He formed a new organization called the Bull Moose Party. During an election speech, he was shot by a crazed assassin. He recovered but lost a close election to Woodrow Wilson, the Democratic candidate. When the war with Germany began, Roosevelt offered to organize and train a troop division, in case the United States entered the conflict. He was rejected by Wilson and this ended his political and military career.

Wellman figured that the former president was interested in more than his aviation service. Roosevelt was the father of twenty-year-old First Lieutenant Quentin Roosevelt, the youngest child by his second marriage. Quentin was a sophomore at Harvard and engaged to Flora Payne

Theodore Roosevelt during his presidency (1901–1909)

Whitney when the war broke out. He enlisted in the U.S. Air Service and was sent to France. It was painful being separated from his Flora, and she was denied permission to go to France to marry Quentin. Like Wellman, Quentin trained at Avord, but was later assigned to the 95th Bomber Squadron. On July 14, 1918, Quentin was shot down by two German fighters, crashing behind enemy lines. His body was recovered and buried in France. His grave was later moved to rest beside his brother, Ted, in the U.S. Military Cemetery in Colville, France.

In 1919, the French government would posthumously award Quentin the Croix de Guerre. To illustrate the cruelties of prison camp, a returning pilot told about morbid photos of dead fliers being shown to prisoners in the camps. One postcard displayed the photo of Quentin's mangled body beside his crashed plane. By 1918, it was being rumored that Teddy Roosevelt was having difficulty recovering from the death of his youngest son.

Roosevelt sent a driver to pick up Wellman and take him to Long Island. "His home was in Oyster Bay," said Wellman, "not far from the Hitchcocks, so I was driven there to meet a great man. It's funny, but I don't remember meeting anybody else. I must have, but he was such a titan that it is only he that I can remember. I can't even remember eating lunch, if we ate at all, just sitting on the porch of a spacious home in Long Island and listening to a man that I felt sorry for."

The two veterans talked about the war, flying, Tommy Hitchcock— still missing in action—then Roosevelt came to the reason for this meeting. "He asked me how well I knew his son," said Wellman. "I told him I didn't know him at all, just met him once for a few minutes, with Tommy, and that was it. He looked away off as if trying to remember something. He had a strong powerful face, but there was a sadness in it. He thought of something, and it made him smile, the sadness disappeared."

Roosevelt turned to Wellman and said, "You know all my kids and their friends were known as the White House Gang. I used to play around with them once in a while, and one day I got word that the gang were preparing an attack on the White House. I sent a message to the kids through the War Department, ordering them to call it off. An armistice was declared." "He looked off again," said Wellman, "into that way-off world of his, and then he said very quietly that you two wild indians would have had a lot of fun together. I didn't say anything. There just didn't seem to be anything to say."

"How do you feel, boy?" the former president asked. Wellman told him he felt all right. A little backache once in a while, didn't bother him too much. "Don't let it ever bother you," said Roosevelt, "won't do any good if you do, and if you don't, chances are you'll forget it. That may sound a little foolish, but it isn't. I've always had trouble on my left side. I'm blind in my left eye and deaf in the left ear. People all knew about my deafness, I couldn't hide my ear, but nobody knew about my eye because I wore glasses, and I never said anything about it. I learned to see with one eye as well as a lot of people could with two. It's like a game, doing something better than the other fellow who has more to do it with than you. [President] Wilson had too much more. I can't understand that man. In 1914—Germany, a ruthless, militaristic country, and he wouldn't even start getting ready, just in case; and then finally after we are in it, I ask permission to raise a division of troops to fight in France, and he said no. So I sit here alone. It's peaceful and quiet, but the whole world is so noisy." Wellman later said, "Theodore Roosevelt died January 6, 1919, of a broken heart."

A short time later, another invitation seized Wellman's full attention. Captain H. Clyde Balsley called from Washington. Wellman had last seen him at Plessis-Belleville, waiting for his transfer papers into the U.S. Air Service as a captain in the Pursuit Division in Washington. Balsley was well known to the American volunteers as one of the original members of the Escadrille Américaine, later known as the Lafayette Escadrille. He was also the first American to be severely wounded in the early days of the war. Although from San Antonio, he was not the typical Texan. He was polished, well groomed, and wore a trimmed military mustache. Balsley started out as an ambulance driver, then transferred into French aviation on September 16, 1915. He received his wings on January 2, 1916, and was attached to Escadrille V. 97 and flew with the Paris Air Guard until May 26, 1916. He went to the front with the Escadrille Américaine on May 29. He was shot down near Verdun by two enemy planes on June 18, 1916.

Seriously wounded, shot in the hip by an exploding bullet that left a gruesome wound, he was found by French soldiers and taken to the French hospital at Vadelaincourt. His condition was critical. He was later transferred to the American hospital at Neuilly. He received six operations in an attempt to remove small and large bullet fragments from his body. On one of Wellman's stopovers at the hospital, he and Balsley met and developed a friendship. After nearly a year and a half from the time of Clyde's ill-fated combat, and although permanently crippled, he was sent back to America.

Captain Balsley had heard and read about Wellman's homecoming. He was calling to offer the ex-flier a job. "Can you still fly?" he asked.

"You're goddamned right I can. What's up?" "I'm working in the Pursuit Division, United States Air Service," said Balsley, "and we need a couple of veterans to teach combat, one at Mineola and one at North Island in San Diego, California. Which one do you want?" "I'll take California," said Wellman. "Good," said the captain. "You get First Lieutenant." Wellman said goodbye to his mother, father, brother, the engulfing press, and was on his way to D.C. He would be adding another pair of wings to the French and Lafayette. If commissioned, he would receive respect, fine accommodations, a good starting salary, far better than his three and a half cents a day as a second-class soldier in the Foreign Legion. Wild Bill made his landing in Captain Clyde Balsley's office. They exchanged pleasantries and stories of the old days. Clyde chuckled when he showed Billy the French aviation report from Pau that stated, "A born flier but," the captain added, "a little crazy." Wellman told him to erase the "a little" and add "completely."

For the first time in quite a while, Billy felt comfortable and happy; however, he did not tell the captain the whole story of his back problem. When Clyde explained the orientation schedule, and the physical, Wellman's smile began to fade, for he knew he could not pass any physical. Balsley finished his little speech with, "Don't worry about the physical, we have our own system here." In an attempt to look and act in perfect condition, Billy took off his brace and reported to the doctor's office in another building. He was not smiling when he stood before the attending physician, a stern-faced lieutenant colonel.

LT. WILLIAM WELLMAN, TWENTY-THREE YEARS OLD. ENLISTED LAFAYETTE ESCADRILLE, 1917. GIVEN RANK OF MARSCHAL DE LOGIA. AWARDED CROIX DE GUERRE WITH TWO PALMS. ONLY AMERICAN AVIATOR FLYING OVER RAINBOW DIVISION WHEN IT FIRST WENT OVER THE TOP. WOUNDED AND HONORABLY DISCHARGED FROM FRENCH ARMY. ENLISTED IN U. S. ARMY WITH COMMISSION OF LIEUTENANT. IN CHARGE OF U. S. AVIATION FIELD AT SAN DIEGO.
(Photograph by Bachrach.)

"He told me to strip," said Wellman, "which I did, and then the comicality started. They pounded me, rubber-fingered me, deep throated me, looked at everything I had, including a very bored penis, at last came the moment of truth, a long white line down which I must tight rope walk without a stutter." Unfortunately, Wellman had not listened to Clyde

Wellman's First Lieutenant Appointment document,
September 16, 1918

and did not keep his brace on until the last minute. His back was sore and tired when he made the walk like a drunk.

The charming lieutenant colonel chimed in with a dilly, "You haven't had anything to drink, have you?" "Not this early in the morning," said Wellman. "Get dressed and come into my office." "A comforting invitation. This I did, and my nonflying pal got right to the point and said I could never be a flyer, and his advice to me was to join the Signal Corps. That, to a flyer is a third-rated insult, you can't sink any lower, so I left his office saying nothing, you can see I was growing up. I could have said go fuck yourself, but that would have been so untidy."

Wellman figured the whole deal was blown. He strapped on his brace and returned to Balsley's office, carrying a frown in place of the earlier smile. When Clyde came into the room, he was carrying a brand-new U.S. Air Service uniform . . . in Wellman's size. Balsley's system had worked and First Lieutenant William Wellman was on his way to Rockwell Field, in San Diego, California. Wellman wrote, "I changed uniforms and became an officer in the U.S. Army Air Service . . . I now had three pairs of wings." Wellman had the only Spad, while his pupils were flying Thomas Morse Scouts, "monstrosities," said the instructor, "supposed to resemble the French Nieuport. Thomas Morse Scouts against a Spad was like a Nieuport fighting a Fokker D.VII; of course, in San Diego we were shooting at each other with camera guns. You could get your picture taken, but where I came from, you could get your brains blown out and splashed right back in your dead face."

Being back in the air again brought a big boost to Wellman's spirits. He even mothballed the back brace. For weeks, he enjoyed that old feeling, the excitement of flying, the doing of what he loved. It was comforting to be an officer with salary, respect, admiration

Rising movie star Helene Chadwick

from peers and pupils. He could tolerate being a war hero who flies, rather than one who gives speeches and interviews. But something was missing. Instead of searching the skies for the enemy, he was looking for good camera angles. Instead of the thrilling dogfights with his comrades, it was the execution of test scores for his pupils in the classroom. There was no life-or-death combat, just a teacher and his students. Boredom was creeping into his world, and that dreaded lost feeling with the affiliated black cloud. How long could the war last? What would he do when it ended? Who would he spend the future with? These were the questions that haunted him, but where were the answers? Then, like a bolt out of the blue, like a Spad diving on a Fokker, came renewed exhilaration and . . . some answers.

"Good-looking tailored uniform with decorations, three wings, and a slight limp," said Wellman. "If she was a real pretty little thing, the limp became more pronounced. It stepped up their mother instinct. I always remembered to be humble—above everything, be humble. I learned how to be great by inference. Always told of the exploits of Tommy Hitchcock or Duke Sinclair, Dave Putnam, or [Frank] Jules Baylies . . . but I always threw me in as the guy who was there. Made sure that I told them of the deal that Tom and I made. One day he would be the leader, the next was my turn; and no matter where we led one another, we stuck together. Then I'd describe a dogfight, but always from Tom's or some Frenchman's point of view. I might throw in a 'I didn't see it all because I was a pretty busy guy myself' just to remind them that I wasn't up there on a sight-seeing tour."

The Wellman method received a serious challenge one night at a Del Coronado Hotel dinner party given in his honor by French film producer, Louis Gasnier. He was producing the popular Pearl White serials starring Tony Moreno and a beautiful ingenue, Helene Chadwick. "This was my introduction to a new wonder world," said Wellman, "the land of the cinema. There were a lot of strange new people there, actors and actresses, and they liked me and the uniform, and the medals; and I was very humble, and my limp was eye-catching.

"Then I met her. The ingénue. She was lovely, and her voice was low and much older than she. I forgot to limp, and my humbleness began to leak. I was like an airplane trying to get into a fogged-in airport."

A beautiful girl, a crazy flier, youth, and desire—an unbeatable combination. But all good things must come to an end: Wellman met her mother. "She looked me over like a judge inspecting a prize dog," said the flier, "even walked behind me to see the position of my tail. I saw a dollar sign twinkling in the pupil of each of her ferretlike eyes. Her husband had deserted her—deserted her, hell; he fled from her. There wasn't one single thing about her that even suggested that she was the mother of this beautiful, dainty, talented daughter that I had fallen head over heels in love with. She talked—oh how she talked, a never-ending babble of dull words. Her horn was stuck. Helene signed a new contract with the Goldwyn Studios, and I was within flying distance of her. We spent the weekends together, either in Hollywood or at the Del Coronado Hotel in San Diego."

It was early November of 1918, when Lieutenant Wellman invited Helene Chadwick to Rockwell Field. A special weekend had been planned by the Air Service to show off their facility, newest planes, and well-trained pursuit pilots. The Air Service wanted to be sure that the politicians from Washington stayed impassioned about the funding for the future of the Air Service program.

A Spad S.XIII in the colors of the U.S. 94th Aero Squadron. Wellman's plane was silver.

Banners fluttered, bands played, and the grandstand was filled to capacity, including a twelve-member inspection team of high-ranking officers—and two generals—politicians, VIP civilians, and Helene Chadwick, looking every bit the Hollywood movie star. The two generals, with their aides, stood just off the airfield, about fifty yards in front of the grandstand.

The air show was the final event of the weekend. After the political and military speeches, an energetic young officer speaking for Rockwell Field introduced the show over a loudspeaker. Against a backdrop of brilliant blue skies, dotted with white fleecy clouds, the young pilots took to the air in squadron order. They flew over the airfield, performing various types of simple stunts in perfect formation. Their landings were executed with precision, and they were greeted with vigorous applause and shouts of "bravo!" and "hip, hip, hurrah!"

The finale was announced by the inspired officer, his voice echoing over the loudspeaker, "Ladies and gentlemen, this is our best chase machine, the Spad S.XIII, flown by our top instructor, Lt. William Wellman, a decorated fighter pilot performing a series of spectacular stunts. I told him to show you something you hadn't seen before. Take it away, Wild Bill!"

Wellman, in his 235 hp Spad, taxied past the grandstand and heard the clamor from the spirited spectators. He looked over and saw the frantic waving from his Helene. He smiled and returned a salute. His Spad roared into the blue skies with all eyes on it. He executed the acrobatics—vrilles, loops, tourants, a Russian Mountain, and some stunts of his own.

Four times he passed the grandstand low enough to cause the throng to duck and grab for their hats. On his next pass, less than fifty feet off the ground, he barrel-rolled toward the officers (and generals). As the plane approached, the officers scattered and ran for cover. One of the generals tripped, fell, rolled over, got up, and raced toward the stands. Wild Bill figured he had given them enough show, but wanted one more showboat. His final stunt would be a close-to-the-ground renversement, a vertical virage, and then a wing-slip.

The Lafayette Flying Corps defines these terms as follows:

Renversements—a method of turning by pointing the machine up, flipping it over on its back, and then pulling up so that you come out in exactly the same line in which you came; vertical virages—another way of turning by snapping the machine around a 180° corner; and wing-slips—a way of losing altitude very quickly, by reducing the motor and turning the machine on its side.

Wellman's renversement went perfectly well, and the virage was proper, but when he went into his wing-slip—reducing his airspeed and turning the plane on its side—he was too close to the ground and crashed into the turf, somersaulting several revolutions before stopping in a heap. The wings and fuselage collapsed around him. Shock waves rippled through the crowd.

The stunned onlookers, and a tearful Helene, watched in horror as Rockwell Field's top instructor was carefully pulled from the wreckage and carried from the field. Wild Bill woke up in a hospital bed with Helene beside him. She smiled when she told him that he was lucky to have no serious injuries, just a few minor fractures and the loss of his front teeth. Wellman smiled back a toothless grin. He gummed out, "Well, I showed 'em somethin' they hadn't seen before."

Soon Billy was back on his feet and continuing the life of an instructor. His romance with Helene was continuing as well. The problem with Helene's mother was worsening, and the air show misadventure didn't help any. "I can just hear her," said Wellman. "Oh, he's a nice boy, but he's a flier, and they are all unreliable. You have a great future ahead of you. You are going to be a great star, but he can only be an aviator, and what good will they be after the war is over. He is just like Ralph [her late husband], attractive, impulsive, and treacherous, and he has killed men. I don't care if they were our enemy, it's a very unnatural thing to do, and it's bound to leave its mark."

When Billy presented to Helene his concerns about her mother, she shrugged them off. She told him not to worry, her mother would learn to love him just as she does—time cures all. About the last three words, Billy knew different. Time did cure one of Wellman's gnawing pains. A rumor became a fact: Tommy Hitchcock was alive and well. Billy immediately contacted the Hitchcock family in New York. It was true. Wellman heard a sketchy report that included hospital, prison camp, and escape. The Hitchcocks related that their son was still in Europe, but would be coming home soon. Billy could hardly speak.

Wellman went on a marathon celebration. The festivities spilled over to a big party at the Del Coronado—which included Helene, without her mother. Before this jubilee dwindled down, Billy had asked Helene to be his wife. She answered in the affirmative, and off they drove to the old Mission Inn in Riverside, on the outskirts of Los Angeles. It would be a secret wedding, so that Helene would have time to explain to her mother, and her studio boss, Sam Goldwyn. Wellman thought that telling Helene's mother was his responsibility; Helene would take care of Goldwyn.

"This was my job; and all the way from the Mission to my wife's apartment in Hollywood, I tried to figure a way to combat the multitude of objections that this frightful woman would expound. I had to be careful for my wife's sake . . . I asked her what I could expect. She changed it to 'you mean what we can expect. Anything; but don't let it bother you. It will quiet down in time. After all, she is not marrying you; I am. I am of age; I am very happy, and I am terribly in love.'"

That was good enough for the groom, so they drove up to the apartment and went in to meet the enemy.

"It was in the afternoon," said Wellman, "but she was still dressed for the morning. Slippers and a robe and a sort of nightcap on her head with ugly curls sticking out. Life had not been kind to her. She threw her arms around Helene and started to cry. This was even before she heard the bad news. She kept saying, 'Oh, my little girl, my little girl'; and there was nothing wrong with her little girl, she looked ravishing. Then

I thought there must be something wrong with me. I felt the same. I hadn't even said hello, but just in case, I looked down to see if maybe my fly was unbuttoned. It wasn't, and then she stopped her crying, looked at me, and snapped one word: 'Well!' I said, 'I just married your daughter.' 'You what?' 'Just married your daughter.' A funny sort of exhaling wheeze came out of her mouth, her eyes rolled over, and she fainted dead away. I didn't catch her."

Wellman's family never knew about his first wife, and now they had not been a part of his second marriage. Billy knew that sooner or later this marriage to a movie star would show up in newspapers and fan magazines. He would have to call home and make the announcement. Celia and Arthur took the news with great surprise and some disappointment. Their son's explanation that everything happened so quickly, there wasn't time to bring them all the way from Boston—didn't quite cut it. But Celia and Arthur realized that Billy had been through a great deal of conflict and depression in his young life, and they resigned themselves to meeting their daughter-in-law when possible. Celia, in an attempt to be supportive, commented to her son, "Your father and I sure do like the Pearl White serials."

Wellman's married life consisted of weekends together with his wife at the Del Coronado, or at Helene's apartment in Hollywood—with his mother-in-law. The time spent in the apartment was mostly silent, uncomfortable hours of being constantly screened. Wellman's mother-in-law never just looked at him, she audited him, over and over, up and down, inside and out, with never a change of expression. "The least I expected was a Mickey Finn," said Wellman. "It made Helene unhappy. I began to get worried."

Then came the two armistices. The first, a false alarm. The second, the real thing. Wellman received a short wire from his wife with but two words, "Thank God." "We—by we I mean the fliers," said Wellman, "celebrated the false alarm. We all got loaded, had a fight with the navy, made a shambles of the Coronado bar, and twelve of us goose-stepped off the long pier that extended out from the beach of the hotel."

It happened at night; there was a strong wind and the waves were high. Wellman's pilots were wearing their best uniforms, complete with officer's high boots. "It was great fun," said Lieutenant Wellman. "We did pretty well. We managed to reach the beach, half drowned, and then we found out the armistice was just a rumor. That sobered us up, but it was a little late. C'est La Guerre."

The real armistice was celebrated a few days later in a different manner:

quiet drinking, no fights, no laughter, little talking, no goose-stepping, just silent sorrow. The pilots went to bed early. Wellman didn't sleep much. "I asked for, and got, a complete divorce from the air corps," said Wellman. "During the time I waited for my discharge papers to come through, I became a member of the ever-growing group we called the Ruptured Penguins. There was no more flying. You reported in and then retired to the Coronado Hotel bar. You were forgotten. You drank a lot and did a lot of thinking, trying to decide what to do now. This was a new kind of war. A war that you had not been trained for. A lonesome war."

Wild Bill's spirits got a temporary boost. An invitation arrived for him to perform one more military operation before his final discharge. On Sunday, November 24, 1918, the *San Diego Union* printed a three-page story with banner headlines: "WAR-TIME FLYING BY AMERICAN DUELLISTS TO FEATURE PARADE OVER CITY." Page one was filled with biographical material and air combat experiences. The first page began, "War-time flying by a group of American air duellists who passed many strenuous months on the western battle front will be a feature of the aerial parade of 200 airplanes next Wednesday. . . . Lieut. Wellman has had the remarkable experience of falling 5800 meters, or 18,000 feet, in an airplane disabled by anti-aircraft gunfire and living to tell of it."

Large photos of a uniformed William Wellman and four other veteran pilots covered the top portion of pages one and three. More of Wild Bill's air battle experiences graced page two. Just above the photos on the third page was this caption:

Galaxy of Rockwell field airmen who will direct the great dawn of peace flight over San Diego next Wednesday. Top, left to right: Lieut. William Wellman, famous American ace, who has been decorated with the Croix de Guerre with two bronze palms and the distinguished service cross; Col. Harvey Burwell, commander of the flying academies at Rockwell, Ream and East fields; Maj. Carl Spaatz, veteran North Island flier, mentioned in army orders of the day for heroism in aerial battles. . . . Maj. Spaatz, Lieut. Wellman and Capt. Wilson [Francis Wilson, from San Jose, California, fought in the air at Château-Thierry, Verdun, and St. Mihiel] will execute next Wednesday every maneuver they employed on the battle front. It will be the first time in America that actual battle evolutions and tactics will be carried out by men who have participated in aerial engagements on the eastern or western battle fronts.

Colonel Burwell called attention to the fact that the coming flight will, of necessity, be the last of its kind probably held in this country for many years. Rockwell, Ream and East fields, now the largest permanent aeronautical institutions in the western hemisphere, will be reduced to peace strength within a short time. This means that, although there will be more than 170 airplanes in use, the number of qualified pilots will be materially reduced. There are now nearly 400 student officers and qualified fliers at the three aviation fields. . . . Extraordinary care will be taken to avoid mishap during the mass flight. Emergency landing fields are being plotted and will be guarded by troops during the flight. The massed planes probably will cross over the city at an altitude of 2500 feet. The acrobatic airmen, however, will perform their stunting at a height of 1500 feet. Each airman will be given a special "sector" over the city in which to perform his feats.

Unfortunately, Helene was unable to attend the awe-inspiring show, as she was in production on a new film. Billy and Helene's secret week-end marriage continued into the new year. A formal engagement was announced in January, with the nuptials reaching newspapers and magazines a few months later. When Wellman finally received his discharge papers, he also got a job offer from his brother and a letter from Helene.

The release papers officially ended his days at Rockwell Field, and his life as a military airman. Arch had also been discharged from the Air Service, and was back in the wool business. He offered his brother employment working with him in Boston, but Billy was married and Helene's life was in Hollywood. "I got a letter from my wife," said Wellman. "She was on location in Catalina and would be away for another two or three weeks. She said that she was so thankful that I was through with flying, that I could now come home and wait for her and concentrate on choosing a career. Whatever I wanted to become would make her happy. It sounded so simple. What if I wanted to become a bum? What if I didn't want to, but just became one?"

Wellman bought a couple of suits and became a civilian again. Even though he was in love, he felt empty and lost. "A Joe Doakes with a couple of little narrow, colored ribbons in my buttonhole," said Wellman. "You had to get real close to notice them, and then they didn't mean anything; probably just came with the suit. I threw away my limp and joined another war."

With Helene out of town on location, Wellman was in no hurry to take up residency in his bride's apartment with his mother-in-law. He took his time cleaning out and packing up his Rockwell Field quarters.

While doing this, he found something in his duffel bag: a worn cablegram sent by Douglas Fairbanks congratulating him on his Croix de Guerre. It said, "Great work boy we are proud of you when you get home there is a job waiting for you—Douglas Fairbanks." Wellman had met Hollywood people through Helene, and he now began calling them to find out where Fairbanks could be contacted. One told him about Fairbanks's lavish parties, and one was scheduled to take place next weekend. Wellman was up early the morning of the event. He dressed in full uniform, decorations, shined boots and all—a one-day reenlistment. He readied his silver Spad-S.XIII, and powered the 235 hp Hispano-Suiza engine into a cloudless blue sky on his way to Douglas Fairbanks and Mary Pickford.

Considered to be the world's first superstar, and the first female to found her own corporation, in 1915, Pickford was known to movie audiences as "America's Sweetheart." On February 5, 1919, she along with Fairbanks, Charlie Chaplin, and D. W. Griffith, formed United Artists Corporation. The company became official on April 17, 1919. Fairbanks, the swashbuckling action hero of such acclaimed films as *The Mark of Zorro* (1920), *Robin Hood* (1922), and *The Thief of Bagdad* (1924), and Mary Pickford, "the little girl with the curls," who had built her reputation playing delightful and lively youngsters in such classics as *Tess of the Storm Country* (1914), *Rebecca of Sunnybrook Farm* (1917), *The Poor Little Rich Girl* (1917), and later, *Pollyana* (1920), were in love. Insiders in Hollywood knew the truth, but since both were already married, their matrimony would not take place until 1920.

On this fateful day, Fairbanks and Pickford were cohosting a grand polo party. Dressed in white, they roamed through the fashionably dressed celebrities welcoming one and all. The guest's names and faces filled movie screens throughout the world: Theda Bara, John Barrymore, Cecil B. DeMille, D. W. Griffith, William S. Hart, Harold Lloyd, Tom Mix, Will Rogers, Mack Sennett, Gloria Swanson, Norma Talmadge, Rudolph Valentino, to name a few.

A hotly contested polo game, with eight players on horseback, was capturing much attention. The rest of the ruling class were involved in other pursuits like socializing, promoting, bargaining, negotiating, buying and selling, and, of course, feasting at the royal buffet. Some ambled through the crowd, while others were seated under the shade of the umbrella tables. Violinists played soft melodies while waiters and waitresses, in formal attire, strolled through the gathering serving the ritzy bill of fare—liquid as well as solid.

In the midst of all the action, the sound of a distant airplane engine caught no one's ear. The growing roar from Wild Bill's Spad, firing at 135 mph, began to raise the attention of some of the guests. Soon, the pursuit plane was on top of the polo party, zooming low over the heads of the chosen ones. They began to scatter in all directions, some fleeing away from the field, others diving under the umbrella tables. Some of the waiters and waitresses began scrambling behind the portable bars and under the buffet tables. Glasses, bottles, and culinary delights hit the ground. The polo ponies skittered, some rearing up, their riders holding on for dear life.

Wellman performed a few special stunts before disappearing, momentarily. He returned for another zoom-by, this time at a slower speed, but still low over the heads of the fleeing and hiding spectators. He disappeared for a second time. When he reappeared, he guided his aircraft in for a smooth landing at the far end of the field, away from the startled horses.

The silver Spad, with sunlight glinting off the wings, fuselage, and tail, taxied to a stop some sixty yards from the wide-eyed throng. Wellman unhooked his harness and stepped from the cockpit. He removed his goggles and helmet, tossing them back into the cockpit. He straightened his uniform, decorated with three different wings, ribbons, and medals, then limped toward the stunned luminaries. All eyes followed him to Douglas Fairbanks and Mary Pickford.

Wellman: Remember me, Mr. Fairbanks? You said if I ever came to Hollywood, to look you up.

Fairbanks: Mary, I'd like you to meet Wild Bill Wellman. He's a helluva hockey player and a war hero.

Fairbanks shook Wellman's hand, then passed it to Mary.

Pickford: We've read about you. You have an unusual way of dropping by.

Wellman: I hope I didn't cause any trouble.

Fairbanks: Can you ride a horse?

Wellman: No, but I could. I've ridden everything else.

Fairbanks: I've got a part for you in my new picture. Come with me, I'll introduce you to my director, Albert Parker.

Wellman: Thanks, Mr. Fairbanks.

Fairbanks: Call me, Doug. Excuse us, Mary. I'll be right back.

Wellman had traded his flier's helmet and goggles for a cowboy's hat and boots. Instead of flying a pursuit plane, he would be riding a horse,

The Knickerbocker Buckaroo (1919): Wellman is on the left, wearing a cowboy hat; Fairbanks is on the right, hatless.

playing the juvenile lead with Douglas Fairbanks in *The Knickerbocker Buckaroo* (1919) for $250 a week. The simple story was typical for a Fairbanks movie of the period. A man who doesn't fit in with high society selects a place on the map to make a new beginning. He arrives in a Southwestern town where he meets a beautiful young woman, played by Marjorie Daw, and her brother, played by Wellman, who are being terrorized by a dishonest sheriff and his gang in order to find their hidden treasure.

Fairbanks performed his many stunts, including leaping on and off a speeding train, running along the train's roof, then jumping off it, landing on the back of a racing horse. Three chases later, derring-do Doug saves the day, the money, and gets the girl. The film would have a long shooting schedule for that time. The releasing company proudly publicized the schedule of six months in production, seven reels, and the exorbitant cost—$264,000. Before production of *The Knickerbocker Buckaroo* began, Wellman took another journey—moving in with his mother-in-law.

"I didn't ring the bell," said Wellman. "I just walked in; after all it was really my home—now. She was in the kitchen getting dinner ready. I hoped, for me. She hadn't heard the front door close, so I Hi'ed my presence, but the Hi had a western twang to it. In she came. She had a dress on, and all her hair was showing. She looked very presentable. On her face, a struggling smile, which quickly changed to a look of puzzlement. I told her I had flown out of the air corps and onto the back of a horse, that I had landed a very important role with Douglas Fairbanks, who, thank God, was her idol. I was in. Within the short span of twenty-four hours, I had risen from a bum to a western Sir Galahad."

Dinner that night was in Wellman's honor. He sneaked out of the house and returned with a couple of bottles of wine. It was a good thing he got two. She finished the first one without batting an eye or dropping a syllable. On the second, things began to change and Wellman's mother-in-law pinned one on. "Her horn again became stuck," said Wellman, "and when at last she retired and weaved herself upstairs, I knew the whole history of her from childbirth. You can't go back further than that."

Sir Galahad was alone, exhausted, and bored to death. He had endured three hours of listening and struggling to pay attention. "During that interminable monologue," said Wellman, "my vocabulary had consisted of but three words: yes, no, and really, with all the inflections, modulations, and pitch of tone. When I heard her door close, I summed it up with one word: balls!"

Wellman started to read the script for *The Knickerbocker Buckaroo*. Upstairs was heard a discord of strange sounds. He stopped reading and played a game with himself. "On each sound, I would guess what she was doing. The shoes being tossed on the floor was easy, hanging something up and missing the hangars, throwing an empty bottle into the wastepaper basket that wasn't there, a dull thud. I hope she fell. Four-letter words. She did. The door opening, her door, unsure steps to the bathroom, that door opening but not closing, a moment of quiet, then—the game was over. There was no more guessing."

Wellman stopped reading and went up to bed quietly. He didn't want that horn to get stuck again. As he passed by her boudoir, the door was slightly ajar. He could see her sitting in front of her dressing table fiddling with her hair. "No, by God," he said, "she was taking it off. It was a wig, and when she got through peeling, she was as bald as an eagle. She looked like somebody from somewhere else as grotesque and eerie as a horror picture."

He stole into his room, undressed quietly, and slipped into bed. Then he realized he hadn't locked the door. He slipped out of bed, tiptoed to the door, locked it, crawled back to bed, and breathed a sigh of relief. "So help me, I was scared." He awakened in the morning with a bad taste in his mouth, and started downstairs to get breakfast. On the way past her room, he stopped momentarily and listened. "She was snoring, not an orderly snore, a convulsive snorting, like a pig rooting in a pile of wet mud. I ate a hurried breakfast and got out of there as fast as I could."

Wellman was missing his Helene, but the next few days were active and exciting. The assistant director took him out to the studio back lot, introduced him to an old cowboy who showed him his horse, saddle, and gave him his first riding lesson. Billy hung around the cowboys, listening to the way they talked, watched how they walked and rode. Fairbanks told him to wear his Western outfit as much as possible, even sleep in it, make it a part of him.

There were rehearsals, photographic tests, meetings with cast and crew members. There were also publicity photos. The photographer wanted to shoot Wild Bill in his flier's uniform, his American and French uniforms. Billy did not want to use his flying career as a crutch to get established as an actor. He allowed the taking of a few uniform photos, though, then said, "That's enough." When the picture taker asked for more, Wellman told him where he could stick the photos and in slow motion. When Fairbanks heard about the rift, he sided with his actor and a few more photos were taken with Billy as a civilian. Wellman took the military uniforms and filled up the duffel bag again, this time he hoped forever.

Filming began. Wellman stayed away from his mother-in-law as much as possible. Fairbanks asked him to dinner, also Victor Fleming, one of Fairbanks's cameramen and future director of *Gone with the Wind* (1939). Wellman took the cowboys out on his own. Then Billy got the idea to surprise his wife in the island paradise of Catalina, twenty-two miles off the Southern California coast. Fairbanks's company was not going to shoot on the weekend, and Billy, with the help of Doug's business manager, got passage on a water taxi to the island Friday night. After working all day and into the night, still dressed in his cowboy wardrobe, he barely made the last taxi to the island. He felt Helene wouldn't mind being surprised by her cowboy husband at such a late hour.

It was close to midnight when he arrived at the desk of the first-class Saint Catherine Hotel. He told the night clerk who he was and was given the key to her second-story suite. The elevator was too slow arriving, so he went up the stairs three at a time. He was so excited that his hands were perspiring. He didn't knock, just keyed open the door ready for the surprise. The living room was dark but he could see some light at the end of the hallway. He stole down the corridor to the dimly lit bedroom.

"The light came from the lamp on the nightstand," he said. "One bed was untouched; in the other were two figures entwined in sleep. Christ, I had the wrong room. One of the dim figures turned in its sleep. It was she. I never got so goddamned mad so quickly. I ran to the bed, he awoke and started up. He didn't get far. I hit him and he fell back with a groan. This awakened her, she sat up staring at me, not believing what she saw. She pulled the sheets around her to hide her nakedness. For the first time, she looked just like her mother. I did something I had never done before or since: I hit her. She let out a shriek like a little dog who's had its tail stepped on, and she crumbled up and fell back, naked. I left them the way they were when I came in, sound asleep."

Wellman spent the night in the water taxi with the skipper. He could

Douglas Fairbanks in *The Three Musketeers* (1921)

tell something had happened, but didn't ask any questions, just brought out a bottle and they drank themselves to sleep. "You meet the nicest guys in the strangest places," Wellman later said.

It was mid-morning when he arrived at what was his home. "When I came in," said Wellman, "the old shrew was as usual in the kitchen. When she came out to greet me, she was attired as usual, robe, slippers, and the nightcap with the fake curls sticking out like little angry black tongues. She greeted me, as usual, nastily. 'Where have you been? You might let me know when you're not going to be here.' I told her that I didn't think she would miss me. She said she didn't, but at least she could take care of me for her lovely daughter's sake. I told her that I was sure she would appreciate that now. Then she asked me the sixty-four-dollar question. 'Where will I tell her you've been? Oh, just tell her I have been to see an old whore I knew.' This unstuck the horn, and I went upstairs to pack and get the hell out of there for good. She went back into the kitchen and took it out on the pots and pans."

Wellman went into his room, packed quickly, and on the way out, as he passed by her boudoir, he got an idea. "I sneaked in to her dressing table, found her wig in one of the drawers, a pair of scissors in another, and I retired to the bathroom, gave it a butch haircut over the toilet, pulled the chain, and went out of that den of horrors as happy as a lark."

Wellman's "happy as a lark" feeling quickly dissipated into that lost feeling again. The old cliché, "a life of thrills and spills," could easily be attached to the young Wild Bill Wellman. By twenty-three years of age, he had already been a criminal on probation and expelled from high school; had survived six major air crashes and hundreds of enemy bullets; endured the tragic death of his first wife, and the losses of many of his friends; felt the pain of losing his flying career and his second wife.

Young Billy had been on many adventures and learned much. He knew that things don't always go your way. Pitfalls and tragedies are lurking around the corner. He believed that they were looking for him. He would have to move quickly to stay ahead of them. Somehow, some way, he was going to learn how to stay ahead of whatever was coming.

5

THE HOLLYWOOD LADDER

Welcome to Wild Bill's new world, Hollywoodland. Still wounded from the island episode, Wellman found an inexpensive room with a bath in a house on June Street in Hollywood. It was within walking distance of Doug's studio. Fairbanks had taken over the Clune Studio from William Clune in 1919. The studio was

The Knickerbocker Buckaroo: Fairbanks (center), Wellman (behind Fairbanks's left shoulder), and the cowboys

originally a farm, located on the southeast corner of Melrose and Bronson Avenues. Fairbanks would film the classics *The Mark of Zorro* (1920) and *The Three Musketeers* (1921) at this studio.

Wellman's June Street room was in a home owned by a nice, quiet, proper little lady, who was very careful about the tenants she took in. Wellman convinced her to rent to him by saying that he had been a flier in the war and was invalided home. Even though he was now an actor, he was still a normal young man and . . . didn't smoke in bed. Dropping the name of Douglas Fairbanks didn't hurt.

It was Sunday, of the same weekend that had brought Billy the broken-heartedness. Production on *Buckaroo* would continue on Monday. It was a constant battle not to think about Helene. His thoughts were filled with mixed-up notions like: Who could he blame? His wife? Her lover? The movie? Himself? The war? Should he go back to Catalina and apologize, beg her to take him back? Maybe have a friend intercede for him, plead his case. He thought about getting drunk. A bad idea. Then he might try to swim over to the island. Then he got angry, started feeling sorry for himself. Another bad idea. He had to get away somewhere, with someone he could talk to. The landlady? No. Fairbanks? No. It was Sunday and nobody was at the studio. He chose his movie horse. He rode and rode for hours. Then he walked and walked around Hollywood, climbed and climbed in the surrounding hills. He figured he would make himself so tired that he would fall into bed. He would be too tired to think about the Catalina caper. He would say his prayers while undressing, so that he would go to sleep as soon as he hit the pillow. It worked.

Monday morning. In makeup at 7:30, on set at 8:30, finish shooting at 6:00 p.m. or later. After work Billy would help the cowboys feed and bed down the horses, then drink beer and eat with them. He didn't get home until around ten. He was tired and went to bed. Wellman disliked putting on makeup, being the actor—he felt out of place in this arena. He liked the respect and the money. He was fascinated by the director, and when he wasn't in front of the camera, he watched Albert Parker at work. His mind was on the film and the work, not the other problem. Wellman was able to keep this plan going during the week throughout the shooting schedule. The weekends, however, were a different story. Then he was alone.

On one of those lonesome weekend evenings, Billy went walking and ended up at Helene's home. It was as if his legs wouldn't take him any-where else—he had to go there. He wouldn't go inside, just stood across the street and stared over at the house. Soon, a new sports car arrived on the scene, parking in front of the Chadwicks' home. Wellman recognized the driver as he walked to the door, knocked, was kissed by Helene, and entered. The invader was a bigger star than the Catalina cavalier.

Wellman figured that the star didn't know anything about him, unless of course the horn had become stuck. What should Billy do? Go over, knock on the door, deliver a solid right cross on the celeb's chin, then leave? Maybe go inside and start an argument with both of them, all three of them, including the mother-in-law? How about slitting his tires or scratching up the paint or messing with the engine? But what good would any of this do? Nothing, thought Wellman. It was all a lost cause. Billy decided to take the high road, show signs of growing up, and go on his way . . . after pissing on the car.

Before going home, Billy felt the need to confide in someone, so he went to the little bar the cowboys hung around. "I didn't recognize any of them, then I saw him, old Tex off in a corner getting lonesome loaded. I went over to him, asked him if I could buy him a drink. 'Never refused one in my life. Sit down, young fella, and have one with me.' We started from there. An hour later, we both were completely relaxed, and I asked the old boy if he would listen to a very sad tale and perhaps give me a little advice on how to lick myself. He said fire away, and I did, from start to finish. Old Tex never said a word, just drank and listened. When I finally finished my tale of woe, I ordered a couple of more drinks. Tex said, 'no, not for me. Gotta have a clear head.' A clear head? He had enough while I had been sitting there to put an ordinary guy under the table, but I guess he knew his capacity."

Old Tex: "I tell ya what ya do, young fella—it's very simple. There is only one cure for this brand of pizon that you're suffering with. Lots of fellas have had this sickness, you know. It's quite common. I've had it myself, a couple of times. Goddamned near drove me loco until I learned the secret."

"I started to say something, but he stopped me. 'Now you just sit there and listen, an' old Tex will straighten you out, by God. You're ridin' a wild horse now, so just listen carefully. You go get yourself a little willing filly. Tomorrow. Now you crawl right in there, boy, and pull the zipper right over you. You don't even come out for air. You get in there and hibernate. Yes siree, you get yourself a eager little filly and all that pizon will skedaddle right out of your system. It's that simple, boy, and it's very titillating. Now I'll have my drink.'"

Helene Chadwick

The romance between Helene Chadwick and Wellman ended, but the memory lived on.

Old Tex was right on. It didn't take Billy long before he found his willing filly, and they roamed the pasture together till the end of *Knickerbocker Buckaroo*'s shooting schedule. The thoughts of Helene disappeared into the past, and Wellman's weekends now belonged to him.

Wellman had mixed emotions about his life as an actor. To him, the bad features outweighed the good ones. He didn't like the fact that so many other people controlled your existence in front and away from the cameras. Even Douglas Fairbanks did not control his own life; it had to be shared with all kinds of people and obligations acquired when working for the public. Wellman said, "Doug was a servant, a well-paid one, but everything he did or said or thought had to be screened, carefully blueprinted to suit the tastes of the great American public." Since returning from the war, Billy had lived the life of a celebrity, and had tired of it. Now he was on a similar path as an actor and was already disgruntled.

When the final scene in *Knickerbocker Buckaroo* was completed, Wellman had but one more commitment—the company wrap party. There were laughs, tears, and farewells. The next morning, Wellman received a message from Helene's lawyer. He returned the phone call and spoke his first words to a big-time motion picture legal beagle. Billy was invited to Mr. X's office, where he was made to wait a long while in the reception area. When he had had enough waiting and started to leave, the secretary stopped him, ushering him into "Clarence Darrow's" emporium. Billy recounted, "Mr. X was immaculate and flashy, fleshy and smelly, sweet smelly. Mr. X didn't shave in a shower."

After a stream of underplayed compliments from Mr. X to the war hero, Billy said, "Listen, Mr. X, the war is over, so let's cut out this bullshit and just tell me what this is all about. What her highness wishes . . . how much of a patsy must I become to get you your fee, me my freedom, and how big a spread of publicity do you intend to brew?" Mr. X replied, "Now, Mr. Wellman, you are misjudging this and me completely. There are ways of doing things simply, aboveboard and quietly, provided the parties concerned understand and agree." Wellman answered, "What am I to be accused of?"

"Well, number one, you struck her."

"That's correct. Did she tell you why?"

"An ungovernable temper."

"Did she tell you what made it ungovernable?"

"No."

"Maybe you better ask her—just for your own curiosity—because it's out; and when you tell her I said it was out, she will agree. What's next?"

"You mistreated her mother."

"Not her mother, her mother's wig. Didn't they tell you about that?"

"No."

"Mr. X, if I were you, I would get together with your client and have a heart-to-heart talk. If you are telling me the truth, they are treating you very shabbily. The whole deal is liable to be most embarrassing, particularly to you. To cut this thing short, let me make a suggestion. Get it on desertion. This she won't like. It will offend her ego. A beautiful blossoming picture star deserted by a lousy ex-flier who has been unable to fit into the humdrum of everyday life, but this is what it's got to be as far as I am concerned. I refuse to have my lovely little mother think that her son goes around bopping beautiful women, and I don't want that nonsupport branded on me indelibly for the rest of my life. This is a give-and-take deal, as rugged for me as it is for her."

"Well," said Mr. X, "I will have to take it up with my client."

Wellman left Mr. X's lair feeling reasonably satisfied, but the story did not end there.

All Billy said was that he had just finished playing the juvenile lead in Douglas Fairbanks's *The Knickerbocker Buckaroo*, and he got another acting role, a raise to $400 a week, and a four-week guarantee. The film was *Evangeline* (1919) for the Fox Studios, and was written, produced, and directed by Raoul Walsh. Based on Longfellow's poem *Evangeline, A Tale of Acadie*, it starred Miriam Cooper. Wellman was to play the young British officer in the service of the queen of England.

"I was costumed, inspected, and okayed," said Wellman. "With a white wig, legginged feet, and red and white uniform, you can be sure they had fairies in George Washington's time. We opened the picture on the beach at Santa Monica. The first scene was mine, a very wet one."

Wellman had to wade out through the breakers, which were very small, and pluck the leading lady (Miriam Cooper) out of a boat and carry her safely to the shore. "She was very pretty and very tiny," said Wellman, "and you get paid for this?" The director called, 'Camera, action!'" Billy waded out, retrieved the star from the boat, and started in with the bundle in his arms that was as light as a feather. "Despite the closeness to the salt water and all the fishlike odors that go with it," said Wellman, "she had a boudoir sweetness about her that was very entrancing.

"I was young and strong and she felt it and liked it and showed it. This walk in the ocean might lead to something very interesting; and as I squeezed her a little tighter than was necessary and she cuddled up to me a little more than before, I kissed her and stepped into a hole and we both disappeared from view."

Wellman was a good swimmer; she couldn't swim at all, and she lost her head. "This lovely sweet-smelling little treasure became a maddened minx, a fighting, snarling minx under water and above. She made it so tough for me with my water-filled British uniform and my goddamned waterlogged leggings that, for her own good and mine, I had to subdue her, so I did; I cold-cocked her, swam in, and deposited her sleeping little body at the feet of the director."

Billy thought he had done the right thing. After all, he had cold-cocked the suicide-bent French woman at the Seine to save her life, why not a movie star in the Pacific Ocean? The problem was that this movie star was married to *Evangeline's* director, Raoul Walsh. Wellman was fired on the spot and this, historically speaking, ended his career as an actor. The one scene completed was eventually cut from the release print. Years later, Raoul Walsh and Miriam Cooper were divorced and Wellman and Walsh became great friends. Time cures some things.

On May 26, 1919, *The Knickerbocker Buckaroo* had its premiere at the Rivoli Theatre in New York. It was billed: "6 Months to Make— 7 Reels—Cost $264,000. That means 77 solid minutes of the Douglas Fairbanks brand of entertainment!"

The New York Times published this review: "The Photoplay bears out the reports of the cost of its production. It was elaborately staged, where elaborateness would count and Albert Parker, the director, must have used his good eye for scenic effects."

When *Knickerbocker Buckaroo* opened in Hollywood, Wellman was in the packed audience. He barely lasted through half the picture. He literally jumped from his seat, ran into the men's bathroom, and vomited. Then he ran from the theater to his home. He grabbed a shot glass and poured a stiff drink, then another and another. He took a shower, put out the lights, and crawled into bed. There in the dark and the quiet, he pillow-talked to himself and the young actor he had seen on the silver screen. This discussion would be the way old Tex would handle it— straight shootin' all the way.

"First of all, you looked like a sixteen-year-old boy from Fessenden [a very private school outside Boston], with an omelet for a face, a vertical omelet.

Secondly, you are undoubtedly the first actor in history that hoped the camera would stay off him.

Thirdly, the only reason they didn't laugh at you was because they weren't looking at you.

You made some pretty good mounts, but of course you have had plenty of practice climbing into Nieuports.

I have to say something for you, at least you walked like a man. Uh oh, here comes that limp. Christ, haven't you forgotten that yet?

The only acting that you did well, you should not have been doing. The leading lady was supposed to have been your sister, but the way you acted it looked like a little bit of incest, just a touch.

You have the most active face I've ever seen. Your ears are constantly wiggling, your nostrils dilating, your eyebrows teetering, you have a lip-licking tongue and the smile of a gargoyle, but there is one thing about your head that is good: the back of it.

In some of the long shots, you are not so bad; uh oh, look out, here it is again: a medium shot of you and Doug. Maybe you will get away with this one; it isn't too close, and they will be looking at Fairbanks anyway. Here comes the close-up. You're lucky, it's on Doug. If they will only keep it there and not pay attention to you. Too late—it's a big close-up, and it's on you, and it goes on and on—cut cut CUT. Oh God, I'm sick, and you are starting to laugh—a big silent silver screen crater-mouthed laugh. I got up and walked out on me."

"I threw the covers back. I was hot and sweating. I lay there for a few minutes and cooled off outside and inside. I had felt this way before in the air, in a dogfight with a son of a bitch on my tail. I had lost a lot of altitude and was too close to the ground, but I kept missing the trees and the little hills, and I lost him. I was safe and sound and alive. Tomorrow I would go to see Doug, ask him just one more favor. Get me a job, any job, in the production end of the business. I want to learn to be a director."

Fairbanks proved to be understanding. Although he couldn't make Wellman a director, he made sure that he was put on the path, the longest path—as a messenger boy, the lowest-rung job in the studio system. Billy went from a $400-a-week actor to a $22-a-week messenger carrier.

Wellman said goodbye to his proper little landlady, packed suitcase and duffel bag, and traveled west about a mile and a half to the Pickford-Fairbanks Studio on the corner of Formosa Avenue and Santa Monica Boulevard in West Hollywood. The studio was an eighteen-acre property originally owned by Jesse Durham Hampton called Hampton Studios. After Fairbanks, Pickford, Chaplin, and Griffith formed United Artists in 1919, Doug and Mary took over Hampton Studios and gave it their names.

For a while, Fairbanks had two studios bearing his name. By 1922, he had left his Melrose studio for Pickford-Fairbanks, later changed to United Artists Studios. When Samuel Goldwyn, the storied producer and future mogul, came on board as an independent producer, he and his partner, Joseph Schenck, expanded the facilities and called the studio Samuel Goldwyn Studios. Goldwyn became the owner of the facilities while Pickford and Fairbanks owned the deed to the land. With all the name changes of the 1920s, the studio was known as "the Lot."

The Lot served as Fairbanks and Pickford's dream of breaking away from the major studios' domination, bringing artists together, providing an independent distribution channel for the stars, who would have complete control over their pictures and subsequent profits. The two megastars, Mary Pickford and Douglas Fairbanks, upset the balance of power in Hollywood, beginning a new era of filmmaking, restructuring the star system of the day. This revolt brought about the famous Hollywood line from Metro Pictures president Richard A. Rowland, "The lunatics have taken charge of the asylum."

Throughout the 1920s and into the 1930s, United Artists continued with its concept of bringing stars and filmmakers together. In the beginning, the Lot and their pictures flourished: *Little Lord Fauntleroy* (1921, Pickford), *Robin Hood* (1922, Fairbanks), *The Thief of Bagdad* (1924, Fairbanks), *The Gold Rush* (1925, Chaplin). However, it was discovered that the lunatics could work in the asylum, but they could not run it. UA's problems were twofold: they could not release a consistent slate of films, and theater owners could not afford to wait while their theaters went dark; and the studio was never able to fully exploit their stars or develop new ones. Then, when the marquee value of the founders began to fade, UA was forced to bring in a series of independent producers, who were not always good.

In 1924, the UA founders hired Joseph Schenck to run the Lot. He was an excellent studio boss, and came with an insurance policy—his brother Nicholas at Loew's theater chain would support him and UA. Joe Schenck brought with him another valuable asset, his wife and major star, Norma Talmadge. Moving to increase the flow of films, Schenck signed A-list stars: Rudolph Valentino, Buster Keaton, Gloria Swanson, and producer Samuel Goldwyn.

It seemed that the insatiable appetite of the public's movie craze had made room for everyone to succeed, not only UA but the ever-expanding, thriving motion picture studios of Hollywood. On another level, a much lower level, we find William Wellman trying to become part of this booming film industry.

Because of Fairbanks wielding his influence, the studio manager was forced into hiring Billy. He was not at all pleased about this, and made the fact known to Wellman. The manager read Billy's résumé from the studio report out loud, mocking fliers, enjoying the salary and job demotion from actor to messenger, and . . . delighting in the fact that Billy's estranged wife, Helene Chadwick, would be receiving mail from him. The manager smiled when he said that Chadwick was in a position to fire him if she so desired. Before handing Wellman his route papers and first sack of mail, he warned Billy that he better toe the mark or his days at the Lot would be few and highly unpleasant.

As Wellman left the manager's office, he wondered how much of this abuse he was willing to take in order to achieve his goal. He decided that nothing or no one was going to keep him from becoming a director. As he walked along his mail route, he passed by the directors' board. This spelled out the names of all the directors and their current films. Billy paused and read these important names that were doing what he hoped to do someday: Reginald Barker, Clarence Badger, Harry Beaumont, Hobart Henley, E. Mason Hopper, T. Hayes Hunter, Frank Lloyd, William Parke, Victor Schertzinger, Wallace Worsley . . . he questioned whether he would ever be on a list like that. He thought, "How did those men get there? What made them so special? There was no school for directors, no particular education that was necessary, no college degrees, just the complete know-how of the making of a picture, great desire, unending work, and the great privilege of having lived unusual and exciting lives. I seemed to fit into that pattern: no college degree, great desire, willingness to work, and, for a kid, I had lived a couple of lives already."

Knowing Helene was on his route, Billy decided to take the bull by the horns and visit her first. After a deep breath, he knocked on the door. It opened, revealing the rising movie star, Helene Chadwick, wearing slippers, a dressing gown, a towel wrapped around her head with a few brown curls sticking out. "For the first time," said Wellman, "she looked like her mother . . . but her horn was not stuck. In fact, except for the strange, gasping sounds coming from her, she was speechless."

Wellman handed her the mail with the studio-approved line, "Red Arrow messenger bringing tidings from your growing public—congratulations." Still no words spilled forth from those beautiful lips. Billy continued with his own speech. "You don't have to say anything until the end of my small talk, and I hope you don't. I got sick of acting, or acting got sick of me, or I am just a sick actor, so I got Doug to get me a job in a production department and unfortunately it was here. I am starting, as you can see, at the bottom, way down. I am a messenger boy. My very personable boss is worried about what your attitude might be on seeing your outgoing husband grazing in your green pastures. This is his method of finding out, as it is mine. Of course your lawyer has described in detail my feelings on the demise of our bastard romance, and they will remain that way as long as we don't interfere with one another. Is that acceptable to you?" Three simple words finally emerged from Helene's lips, "Yes—of—course." Billy picked up his bag and continued on his way whistling "I Left My Love in Avalon" (Wellman's version of "I Found My Love in Avalon," Catalina).

A few blocks from the studio, Billy had rented a room that included two meals a day, breakfast and dinner. He could get by on his exorbitant salary if he didn't go out at night; maybe a movie Saturday nights, but no carousing. Billy remarked, "I sure as hell had been demoted, broken right back to a second-class soldier. C'est la guerre." In the following weeks he messengered himself to death. The directors' board seemed to disappear like a zoom shot in reverse. "I tried to hang around important places," Wellman said, "the sets, even when being constructed. The casting office, with the never-ending hordes of hopefuls. The cutting rooms, the heart of a picture. I stole scripts, new ones, old ones, and pored over them, always from a director's point of view."

Wellman went to as many movies as he could afford. He studied the best, the most artistic, the commercial successes. He saw D. W. Griffith's *The Birth of a Nation* (1915) and *Intolerance* (1916), Charlie Chaplin's *Sunnyside* (1919) and *A Day's Pleasure* (1919), Mary Pickford's *The Hoodlum* (1919) and *Suds* (1920), and Douglas Fairbanks's *His Majesty, The American* (1919), and *The Mark of Zorro* (1920).

Wild Bill's good luck came looking for him in the form of Will Rogers, one of the stars on Wellman's mail route. Rogers's multifaceted life and career were of legendary proportions. As a child, he learned to use a lasso to help work Texas longhorn cattle. As he grew older, his roping skills were so expert that he was listed in the *Guinness Book of Records*; his lariat feats were recorded in the classic movie *The Ropin' Fool* (1921); his trick roping earned him jobs in Wild West shows and on vaudeville stages. While on stage, he began telling jokes and humorous stories; soon, his wisecracks and homespun anecdotes became more popular than his roping. He blended a down-home humor, folksy wisdom, and political satire into major stardom. He became recognized as a very informed and intelligent philosopher—telling the truth in simple, understandable words. He was considered one of the best-known and best-loved men in the United States. He was America's folk hero.

Will Rogers mastered the worlds of vaudeville, journalism, publishing, radio, and movies. He wrote six books, his syndicated column appeared in four thousand newspapers, and he traveled around the globe three times covering wars, talking peace and family values. He met presidents, senators, kings and queens. His famous motto was, "I never met a man I didn't like." His film career lasted over fifteen years with seventy-one pictures to his credit. In his films, he was never the prototype hero, the para-

Wellman and Will Rogers on the set of *Wing*s, 1926

gon of virtue. His characters were always flawed but became role models. The underlying message of his films conveyed a generosity of spirit and help thy neighbor. His movie characters very much mirrored his life as a man of traditional values, a willingness to help the downtrodden, putting family first, and always with a sense of humor.

In August of 1935, while his career was still skyrocketing, he and the legendary one-eyed Oklahoma pilot Wiley Post were killed in a plane crash in Point Barrow, Alaska. Rogers left behind his beloved wife of twenty-seven years, Betty, three of his four children, Will Jr., Mary, and Jim . . . and a mourning nation. President Franklin Roosevelt, who had felt Rogers's satirical barbs, wrote, "There was something infectious about his humor. His appeal went straight to the heart of the nation. Above all things, in a time grown too solemn and somber, he brought his country-men back to a sense of proportion."

When Wellman met Rogers, they were not on a level field. Wellman knew Rogers only as a vaudeville star, but new to the movies. Rogers knew Billy as a decorated war hero, an actor in a Douglas Fairbanks film,

Helene Chadwick's about to be ex-husband, and a messenger boy. When Will asked Wellman why he was not still acting, Billy explained that he disliked the profession, and dreamed of being a director. Rogers took a liking to this young man and called his property master, James Flood, who was looking for an assistant. Flood and Wellman hit it off, and on Rogers's next picture, *Jubilo*, Billy was the assistant property man, with a slight raise in salary. This association led to four other Rogers films: *Jes' Call Me Jim, Cupid the Cowpuncher, Honest Hutch,* and *Guile of Women.* Wellman was promoted to head property man on *Guile.*

The year was 1920. It was the beginning of the Jazz Age and the Roaring Twenties.

Prohibition was in.

The Nineteenth Amendment had given women the vote.

Vaudeville was dead.

Nickelodeons were fast disappearing.

Opulent movie palaces with live orchestras were in.

America's entertainment craze was in full swing.

The Charleston, the fox-trot, and dance marathons swept the country.

"Mr. Vice-president" (Abraham Lehr, center), General Pershing to the right, Wellman, uniformed, lower right

The first radio broadcast was heard.

Warren G. Harding was elected president.

Babe Ruth was sold by the Boston Red Sox to the New York Yankees.

Jack Dempsey was the heavyweight champion of the world.

Belgium would host the summer Olympic Games.

Silent films were reaching their peak in popularity.

The king and queen of Hollywood, Douglas Fairbanks and Mary Pickford, were married March 28, 1920 . . . and William Wellman was working as a property man on Will Rogers pictures, but he wouldn't be doing this long. Another fortuitous event was on its way in the form of a studio directive and a famous general.

The directive stated that all ex-servicemen report at the front gate at twelve o'clock noon. They were all there at the prescribed time: grips, electricians, painters, construction men, assistant directors, property men, cutters, musicians, animal trainers, cowboys, messenger boys, but no actors. The employees were just milling around waiting for some kind of explanation.

"Suddenly Mr. Vice-president appeared," said Wellman. "This was important. He said that he would take but a few minutes of our lunch hour and then announced the arrival the next day of a very important general and that he wanted all of us in uniform." The employees, dressed in their wartime uniforms, were to form a long line and stand ready as the general reviewed the troops on his way to the stars at the end of the line.

"Nobody cheered this proclamation," said Wellman, "and the deadly silence angered Mr. Vice-president, who said, 'to put it in military terms, this is an order. All those who will be in line in uniform at twelve sharp tomorrow noon raise your right hand.'" Slowly and reluctantly hands were raised, all but Wellman's. "I was standing directly in front of him, and he singled me out for a blast. 'Wellman, we particularly want you, in the blue uniform of the French Flying Corps with the medals; gives the welcoming ceremony an international flavor. Why is your hand not raised?'"

All eyes were on Wellman. "This little pretentious derby-hatted vice-president of a motion picture company had suddenly become a monster of memories. He looked like a despicable little drill sergeant who made my life miserable at Avord. There was that about him that reminded me of four-letter Fleming of the Butterick Lumber Company, of the insufferable foreman that I scaled soles at in a shoe factory; and, by God, if he had nothing on his head, including hair, he would have looked like my ex-mother-in-law. In short, I didn't like him."

"Well, Wellman?" said the VP.

Billy needed a fast answer. He wanted to clip Mr. Vice-president on the chin, or at least knock the derby hat off his head, but this action would most certainly end Wellman's opportunity of becoming a director, and all his hard work and struggle would have been for nothing. So, in order to keep the directors' board in sight, Billy hoped that a reasonable excuse might do the trick. "I am sorry, sir, but my blue uniform has everything but a seat in the pants; it is so worn and torn that I can't wear it anymore." This answer didn't fly. Mr. Vice-president told him, "You go get your uniform, take it to the wardrobe, and they will rejuvenate the seat of your pants." Mr. Vice-president laughed out loud, dismissed the employees, and Wellman returned to his duffel bag one more time.

The following day, at exactly 12:00 everything and everybody was ready and in position inside the studio main gate: some sixty-five men in the uniforms of the army, navy, air force, marines, and coast guard—even a few officers. Wellman recalled, "All the uniforms looked as if they had just awakened, that is all but mine. Mine had a fresh press and I stood erect, very erect . . . with a half-soled ass, I stood erect because I didn't dare bend over." At the end of the line-up of ex-servicemen were the stars, directors, producers—and Samuel Goldwyn.

Sirens roared, the iron gates swung open, and in came a line of cars. Out of the first car stepped the general. Upon seeing him, Wellman and the other ex-servicemen snapped to attention. This general was *the* general, John J. "Black Jack" Pershing, commander of the Expeditionary Forces, and the only person to be promoted in his own lifetime to the highest rank in the United States Army—George Washington was granted his posthumously.

During the war, Wellman had encountered the general twice, the first time from a distance. As the new commander in chief of the American forces made his first visit to Paris, Billy stood in the frenzied crowd watching the motorcade arrival. Through a sea of waving arms and hands, over the deafening din of the French populace, Wellman got his first look at the hoped-for conquering hero.

Wellman's second encounter was much closer—face-to-face, in a Paris brothel. Dressed in their best uniforms, Billy and several flying pals had decided to inspect a high-class House of ill fame. In the reception area, like an over-elegantly decorated living room, they enjoyed cocktails, chose their partners, and proceeded up the stairs to the private quarters. Wellman stayed downstairs trying to decide if he wanted to partake. As he sipped his favorite Escadrille cocktail of champagne and brandy, he noticed a large uniformed soldier enter the front doors, peek into the living room, then quickly disappear up the stairs and away from inquisitive eyes. Wellman was shocked to recognize the soldier as the famous General Pershing.

When Billy made his decision to go upstairs, it was for a different reason than his original one. Maybe it was due to the alcohol, or his pleasure with practical jokes, but he climbed the stairs and began opening bedroom doors. Inside the first two doors were two of his flying buddies, the third door led to the prize. Even in the dimly lit room, Billy had no trouble identifying the big man at work. Quietly, he entered the bedroom, sank to his knees, and began a short journey. The sensual sounds emanating from the mademoiselle were just loud enough to cover the noise of Wellman's crawl across the floor to the trunk at the foot of the bed. Upon reaching said trunk, Wellman's hands felt around on top for a particular item of clothing known as trousers. With the aforementioned pantaloons firmly grasped in his fists, he made his return trip to the door and out into the hallway. After closing the door ever so gently, he stood, rolled up the uniform pants and marched back downstairs to wait for the result of the game.

Although only three years older than Wellman, Bernard Durning had a father-son relationship with his assistant director.

Shortly, a bellowing howl was heard from an upstairs bedroom. Then, a thundering, echoing phrase was heard throughout the parlor house, "Where's my damn britches?" In the living room, Wellman chuckled while the other men and their ladies of the night expressed a questioning fear. Wellman finished the last gulp of his drink, stood up, straightened his uniform, and began his walk back up the stairs. As he marched down the hallway, Pershing was standing outside the bedroom wearing only his army-issue undershorts. As Billy approached him, the general spied his britches held in Wellman's arms. Dumbfoundedly, Pershing stared at the youthful airman on his march to the general. Wellman came to a military halt in front of the flabbergasted commander and said, "Sir, I'm Corporal Wellman of Escadrille N. 87, and I had the honor of flying support for your Rainbow Division." He presented a snappy salute and the general's trousers. Pershing accepted the pants and raised his hand in salute while eyeballing the corporal. There was a long moment, then Pershing broke into hysterics, grabbing Billy in his arms and thrusting him about. They both laughed heartily and the general shouted, "You crazy son of a bitch airman!"

At the studio, General Pershing began his walk down the line of studio employees and ex-servicemen on his way to the promised land. He nodded and shook the callused hands of the hardworking employees. He gave a little more time to the men in uniform, but was in a hurry to grasp the sweet-smelling hands of the movie stars at the end of the line.

He shook Wellman's hand, then the next and the next before stopping and turning back. "Where have I seen you before?" "General," said Wellman. "I had better not say where, right here." He snapped his fingers and said, "That's it!" He came back to Wellman, started pumping his hand, saying, "How have you been, it's good to see you, been a long time." "Too long," said Wellman. Pershing asked how he was doing. "Not too good" was the answer. The general thought for a moment, then asked how he could help. The former flier told him, "By making me important in this hotbed of fakery." "You're damn right," said Pershing. "What do you suggest?" "Take me under the fig tree right behind us and talk to me for a few minutes." He did, and it worked like a charm.

The next day, Wellman was called into the vice president's palatial office and escorted into the president's super-palatial office, where he was properly introduced to Samuel Goldwyn, who stood up from his chair and shook his hand. The mogul said, "You are the type of young man that I want working for me." He turned to the vice president and said, "Make him an assistant director to start with," then he asked Will Rogers's prop man to sit down. "Sit down," recalled Wellman. "I goddamn near fell down. He started asking me about my life, but for a moment I didn't hear a word he was saying. I was thinking of the general: you meet the nicest guys in the strangest places."

Wellman's dream of becoming a member of the studio directors' board was beginning to take shape. He was now an assistant director, and for the next two and a half years he would work on at least twenty-two pictures—mostly Westerns—under quality directors like E. Mason Hopper, Alfred Green, Clarence Badger, Charles J. Brabin, Emmett J. Flynn, Harry Beaumont, Colin Campbell, and Bernard J. Durning.

Although he got along fine with the other directors, E. Mason Hopper was a different animal. Their personalities clashed. Wellman believed Hopper was talented but, in his words, "screwy and a real nut!" To make matters worse, Billy assisted Hopper on *From the Ground Up* (1921) starring Helene Chadwick. Wellman had already endured working with her on Will Rogers's *Cupid the Cowpuncher*, and any further continuation with her and Hopper was not on his agenda. He began looking elsewhere for assignments.

Wellman had heard great things about Bernard Durning at the Fox Film Corporation, at 1401 North Western Avenue in Hollywood, just a few miles from the Goldwyn Studio. Durning was looking for an assistant and he decided to give it a shot. "Durning was the top director of melodramas," said Wellman, "real blood-and-thunder action pictures, a big, handsome, hard-drinking, tough, lovable guy with a terrific temper. He was well over six feet, dressed immaculately, came from the actors' ranks, and was in love with and married to a little bitty gal named Shirley Mason, who was a star at the same studio."

Wellman did not know anybody who was acquainted with Durning, but he felt that if he could get in to see him, he might sell himself. Upon arrival at Fox, he sent in his name and the reason for being there, then sat in the reception room for three days, sending in his name in the morning when he arrived and later in the afternoon just before leaving.

When the appointment finally came, he raced to Durning's bungalow as quickly as he could. Breathing heavily, he arrived in front of the secretary, who said, "You may go right in, Mr. Durning is waiting for you." "How about that," said Billy, "waiting for me, what kind of a man is this? As I came into his office, he got up from behind his desk. He got up but never seemed to stop getting up: he was so tall that he breathed different air. . . . He stuck his big paw out, and we shook hands. I was nuts about him right then."

They talked about Billy's time at the front with Tommy Hitchcock, and his desire to be a film director. Durning picked up a script from his desk and motioned for Wellman to take it. Then the director called in his secretary and introduced her to his new assistant. "I almost fell on my face, acknowledged the introduction, and asked him when I start. He said you already have, slapped me on the back like a big bear, and started out." He opened the door for the secretary, then closed it behind her, saying, "By the way, there are two things I insist upon. One—loyalty, of which I

Assistant director Wellman on Durning's *The Devil Within* (1921), his first film with Durning

have no worry. Number two—dames in my pictures. No fooling around with any of them, at any time. On the set, on location, or in your stalking time." Durning's number two rang out like an order from a rugged sergeant, and Billy knew this wasn't a joke. Then in a more subdued tone of voice, he added a priceless piece of advice. "If you take my tip, you'd keep your chasing out of the business entirely. There are lots of happy hunting grounds all around, but you stay out of this fakey love nest."

Durning and Wellman would make eight pictures together. During that time, Billy's loyalty would never be questioned. The no fooling around with the dames in my pictures business would also be observed . . . after one mishap. She had beauty, talent, personality, and had graduated from Boston's Wellesley College, where Billy had roamed during his Newton High School days. The only thing she didn't have was opportunity and Wellman gave that to her. She, in turn, gave him gratitude and Durning caught them in the execution of such. She grabbed what was left of her dignity and fled from the scene of the crime. Bernie took off his coat and, in Wellman's words, "kicked the shit out of me."

It was a quick but vicious contest, with Durning losing the most blood, Wellman losing consciousness. Durning shook his assistant, saying, "You can't be like this. I'm going to need you soon." Next he told him to put some raw meat on his eye, and be on the set bright and early the next morning. Billy apologized and gave his word that it would never happen again. He kept his promise.

Strange Idols (1922) was Wellman's third picture with Durning. Like their other endeavors, it was a western starring Dustin Farnum. Born May 27, 1874, in Hampton Beach, New Hampshire, Dustin Lancy Farnum was a singer, dancer, and actor. He had great success on the stage before becoming one of the biggest Western stars of the silent era. In 1901, he starred on Broadway in the highly successful *The Squaw Man*. The story revolves around an Englishman who marries a Native American woman in the Wild West. The storied young filmmaker Cecil B. DeMille asked him to reprise his role in the movie version in 1914. It would be Hollywood's first feature-length film.

After reaching such a lofty position in the annals of filmdom, Farnum, called "Dusty," made a historic miscalculation when he rejected DeMille's offer to take a partnership in the latter's studio instead of his up-front salary for this eighteen-day, $15,450.25 picture. DeMille's studio became Paramount Pictures. However, in Dusty's defense, the low-budget film was a chancy venture and DeMille's studio was a barn shared with farm animals. Farnum went on to fashion an excellent career, starring in eleven Broadway plays and forty-two films from 1914 to 1926, until his passing July 3, 1929.

One of eight pictures assistant director Wellman worked on under Durning

Strange Idols locationed in Eureka, California. The simple plot was of a small-town lumberman who goes on a trip to the big city, where he falls in love with a New York cabaret dancer who gives up her career to become the lumberman's wife. She leaves the city and the young marrieds go to live in God's country. After a time, she can't take this life and goes back home, where she belongs. He, of course, is heartbroken but carries on nobly. After all, he still has his trees.

In the days of silent films, a movie company had with them a handful of musicians to play background music while scenes were being shot. Durning's company employed a fiddle, a cello, and a portable organ. It was their job to help bring the emotional element out of the actor's performance.

On one particular day, the leading lady, Doris Pawn, was playing one of her most dramatic scenes. In the scene, she realizes her mistake of leaving New York City and living in the forest with her lumberman. She stands beside a huge pine tree, gazing off into the timberland of God's country. Her heart is breaking, the tears will be flowing down her cheeks as she sinks to her knees, sobbing into her hands clasped in prayer.

The director called "Action!" Everything was going perfectly well. The fiddle, the cello, and the organ were doing their job playing melancholy music, but no tears streamed from Doris's eyes. Durning called "Cut!"

The music stopped, Bernie softly spoke his directions to his leading lady, describing the feelings she was to display, then signaled for the fiddle, cello, and organ to begin again. He called for "Action!" The music was sorrowful, the script girl was sniffling, the wardrobe mistress started crying softly, even Richard Tucker, an actor with a horrible hangover, looked as if he might break into a crying jag but . . . there were no tears from the leading lady, she was as dry as a parched throat. Durning yelled "Cut!" and the company fell silent.

Again, Durning spoke quietly to her, pleading, begging, beseeching, and . . . "Action!" The music was mournful, the script girl sniffled, the wardrobe mistress weeped, Tucker blew his nose as quietly as possible, but Miss Pawn was dry as a bone. Bernie began to lose it, his temper coming into play. "Goddamn it, cut!" He settled himself before trying again. This time, instead of the soft, caring approach, he showed his anger and yelled at her, trying to bring tears from his rage. This did not work either. She called to him in a very sweet, unaffected voice, "Mr. Durning, may I speak to you?" He went over to her and they shared a whispered conversation. After a moment, the director turned and walked away from her. He called Wellman over. The company waited with great anticipation as Wellman listened to his director's hushed tones. "You know what she said? She said call me dirty names and then hit me. How the hell am I going to hit her?" Then came a gleam in his eye, and he looked at his assistant saying, "Look, Bill, you do it." Wellman pleaded, "Now wait a minute, Bernie, I'm just the assistant director." Durning went on. "Bill, do it for me. You don't have to get along with her. You don't like her anyway." Bernie started to walk away and uttered three final words, "It's all yours."

"I walked over to our dehydrated heroine," said Wellman, "and asked her what she wanted me to call her, and she said anything." Wellman hadn't even thought of how to start, and then he realized how little he cared for this dame. What a lot of trouble she had caused him, late on the set, late to makeup, forgetting what she had worn the previous day, the works. Suddenly, this moment became a great opportunity to let her know what he really thought of her.

"In my loud and resonant voice, I let go right at the top. There was no build to my cursing. I threw her the roughest, dirtiest language that any dame ever heard anywhere. I was so convincing that Tucker blushed, and suddenly there appeared a faint mistiness in her eyes. I was about to run out of breath, and I knew that if I quit now, all would be lost, so I did the one thing I had wanted to do ever since I started working with her— I kicked her right in the ass. That pulled the finger out of the dike, and she cried and cried and cried, and the mascara got in her eyes and she cried some more, and the camera got it all. And when Bernie yelled cut, the troop applauded; the dumb dame thought it was for her and with bowed head took her curtain call."

This was the final scene in the picture. The company withdrew to Dusty's suite in the hotel for the wrap party. Farnum, who had finished earlier in the day, was told about the kick-ass adventure and the celebration commenced. The fiddle, the cello, and the organ played on and on, and the drinks were without end. Suddenly, when the party had reached its crowning point, a property man raced into the room shouting that the disliked movie heavy was being destroyed by the town bullies at the only bar in Eureka. Despised as he was, he was still a member of the company and, in those days, they all stuck together.

Led by the director, his assistant, the camera crew, Farnum, Tucker, the fiddle, the cello, and the organ, they raced to the rescue. Along the way, they were joined by other members of the company. In the group were an ex-prizefighter, two former ballplayers, a former pro football lineman, an old jockey, a couple of GIs—and a pilot from the Lafayette Flying Corps.

When the cavalry arrived at the bar, the movie heavy was on the floor, bleeding profusely and screaming for help. The bullies were lumberjacks from the town. There were more than a dozen of them and they were lit to the gills and mean. They had surrounded the actor and were teeing off on him individually. The movie boys charged in and the battle royal began. The loggers swung from above with wild roundhouse punches, while the movie pugilists worked from below with the lower-gut body punches.

Durning boxed with crisp jabs, short left hooks, and solid right crosses. Dusty performed a boxing-wrestling-judo routine that confused and bloodied several bullies. The Lafayette flier crowded in close to his assailant using lefts and rights to the body followed by uppercuts to the chin. This brought the taller logger down to his size and eventually to the floor. Tables, chairs, and lamps were thrown in all directions. The fiddle and the cello met their demise in splintered fashion over the heads of several big lumbermen. The organ played throughout.

The hostilities came to a crashing halt when the town sheriff and his posse arrived. The victorious cavalry spent the night behind bars, while the lumber bullies visited the hospital before returning to their lodgings. The movie producer paid for the damage and the release of the prisoners. Soon, the *Strange Idols* company went back to Hollywood where they belonged, while the wounded lumbermen carried on. After all, they still had their trees.

When Wellman found steady employment at the Fox Studios, he began looking for living quarters within walking distance. Buying a car was hardly in his budget. It was his desire to wait until he could afford the full price of a new vehicle. While he strolled the streets near the studio at Sunset and Western, he slept on couches in studio offices.

One day while walking down Sunset Boulevard, he spied two side-by-side rear ends. One belonged to a man, the other an animal. They were not connected by a leash or a rope, just walking together as companions. Wellman quickened his steps and introduced himself to Dan and Virgil. Dan Dix was the human, Virgil his well-trained and well-groomed movie mule. Virgil had more picture credits than many of the people Wellman was working with. His coat was shiny, his mane was tied in small perfect knots, and his ribs were not spare. Next to him, his master—only a partially correct term in this relationship—wore old blue jeans, a faded Western shirt, run-down boots, and the brim of his Western hat had holes in it. He looked like the half-breed that he was. As the threesome moved along the boulevard, he asked Billy where he was living. Wellman announced, "At the studio." Dix invited him to dinner at their home.

When they turned into the driveway, Billy could see two structures on an acre of level ground. There was an immaculate-looking, freshly painted white building next to an old shack. Dix lived in the shack. It had

Dan Dix, Virgil, and Wellman have a disagreement.

two rooms and a bathroom. One room served as the bedroom, the other housed the living room, dining room, and kitchen.

Virgil's residence was spotless with fresh straw on the floor and all the accessories a mule could ask for. Virgil was fed first with a big helping of oats and a binful of hay. The animal never looked at Billy because he never took his eyes off Dix. Wellman swore that Virgil was listening and understanding everything his master was saying. Every so often, the mule nodded his head in agreement. While Virgil ate, Dan brushed him down, changed his water, hugged his head. The humans then left for the shack. On the way, they passed a cluster of clean-cut apricot trees just in front of the building.

Once inside, Dix pointed to a chair and Wellman sat down. Dan went to the kitchen side of the room and came back with a couple of glass tumblers, went over to a beautifully carved oak desk, which was padlocked, pulled out a bunch of keys from his pocket, and unlocked it. "His back was to me," said Wellman, "so I couldn't see what he was getting. It must have been something of great value; when he turned around, I saw it: a jug half full of an orange-colored liquid! He filled both glasses and gave me mine, and we drank. My first mouthful damn near gagged me, but I didn't want to offend him, so I took another. This one wasn't so bad—in fact, it tasted pretty good, and it sure as hell warmed you up. He asked if I liked it, and I said yes after that first swallow. He told me that I would nuzzle up to it."

They sat there drinking, and the world started to get rosier. Dix said that it was apricot brandy. He made it himself from his own apricots, and it was the only liquor he drank. Billy saw his point. After another refill, Dix got up and busied himself making dinner. During the chefing, he told about Virgil. Starting from the day he found him standing over his dead mother and wondering why she didn't get up and give him his dinner. All through his bottle-feeding days, the training, the circuses, the rodeos when Virgil was a star. The kings and queens that had seen his performances. The money that they had made together—but not where it had gone. It was like a proud father telling about a famous son. "We got loaded," said Wellman, "had a great dinner, did a lot of talking, and when the evening was all over, two guys knew each other. I came to dinner and stayed for six months. Six of the happiest months of my life."

Dan never talked about his family or where he came from. Once he said, "It's all best forgotten and I've forgotten it." He didn't really talk much at all, except when it was the apricot's turn. He asked Wellman about his family, and Billy answered at length of his love of family and deep fondness for Celia, "a little bitty Irish gal, a beautiful woman who loves but one man and understands my rather unreliable father. She lives with him, loves with him, through every joy and sorrow, through every strength and through every weakness. I love her."

Although Billy had regularly phoned his family, he was disappointed that he hadn't seen them in a long time. He had planned a number of trips, but they had all fallen through due to marriage problems, work, or no work. His father didn't like to travel, Arch was busy climbing the ladder in the wool industry, and Celia was just waiting and hoping for her Billy.

Dan Dix never spoke about his age, but after hearing his stories, it was obvious to Wellman that his life had been filled with extraordinary events and unusual people. One night, during their apricot time, he told of his five loves—not counting Virgil, of course. He showed photos of the women.

Number One—a big muscular Amazon wearing dungarees and hip-high boots. She had a chair in her left hand, a whip and a revolver in her right. She was looking into the yawning mouth of a big tiger. Its white teeth were huge and sharp, but it was she who frightened Wellman. "They called her the Tiger Lady," said Dix, "whipped the livin' daylights out of me once. All the lions and tigers got mad as hell; I was stealin' their stuff. Damn near chewed the bars to bits, had bites all over her body and there wasn't a bare spot left for me." Billy believed this story.

Number Two—a smiling, jolly-looking lady with snakes curled around her neck. It made Wellman shiver. "A big mistake," said Dan, "especially in the winter. Her goddamned snakes used to get cold at night and crawl into bed with us. She liked me to call her Medusa, and I asked her who the hell was Medusa and she said she was the beautiful head of a headless Greek dame with snakes for hair. I took off for Phoenix." Wellman thought that was a good idea.

Number Three—an athletic-looking girl with a slim, boyish figure standing on the broad back of a galloping white horse. Billy said she looked exciting and Dan nodded his agreement. "The principal rider in the resin-back act, the one that runs and jumps up on the well-resined horse's back. The resin keeps her from slipping. I go to bed one night tired, and she ain't tired. She feels

Celia visits her son on the set of *Big Dan* (1923). Wellman is twenty-seven.

real frisky, so she gets ready for bed, and just as I'm going to sleep, she takes a run and a jump, stark naked, and lands on top of me, and I ain't got any resin on and I'm dead. Hits me in a place ladies ain't supposed to knock on—never could understand that girl, always hurtin' something she liked." Wellman inhaled, then exhaled.

Number Four—a gal way up high, hanging by her teeth to a whirling mouthpiece at the end of a leather and steel trap. Billy thought she looked like a pit bulldog with a death grip on a spinning Roto-Rooter. "My love name for that little gal was Little Spinner," said Dix. "She liked it. When I got mad at her, I called her swivel mouth. Once, just for a joke, I barbecued a shoe sole, covered it with my own special sauce. She ate it without battin' an eye. You know, she could have done me a serious injury if she ever clamped down. Lost my nerve, skedaddled." Billy thought this story might be exaggerated.

Number Five—a contortionist, looked like a corkscrew with a woman's head. Dan chuckled before explaining. "Funny thing about this little creature. Said she was a maenad. What's a maenad? Never found out, you know what 'tis?" "No," said Billy, "but I got a dictionary in the duffel-bag." He retrieved it and read the meaning: "A female who took part in the wild, orgiastic rites . . . a frenzied or raging woman." This left old Dan speechless for a moment and then, with a wicked little smile on his face. "Goddamn, she sure was." Wellman believed this story.

When Wellman received his director's stripes, the name of Dan Dix appeared on the production reports of many of his outdoor pictures—as an actor, extra, wrangler, stuntman, or friend.

In the late summer of 1922, Celia McCarthy Wellman decided to wait no longer for her son's return. She phoned and told him there was no stopping her, she would be riding the rails to California. Billy borrowed Dan Dix's jalopy, which towed Virgil's carrier whenever they went on location, and met her at the Los Angeles Union Station. He checked her into the Hollywood Hotel on Hollywood Boulevard. The hotel was built in February 1903 with wings and rooms added over the next two years. The 144-room grand hotel dominated the Hollywood landscape for decades. It was the social center of the growing community, featuring weddings, all sorts of social events, and business meetings. Many film industry luminaries frequented the elegant Mission-Moorish-style hotel.

Billy apologized for the state of the jalopy, and the condition of the shack, when he introduced his mother to his roommates. Celia's visit at the Dix estate was of short duration, and no apricots were in evidence except for those in the trees.

Mother and son's first dinner date took place at Frank's Francois Café, later called the Musso & Frank Grill on Hollywood Boulevard. The restaurant was crowded, but they were able to find a table away from the hubbub. Billy could hardly suppress his excitement and enthusiasm for the direction his career was heading. In only a year, he had worked as an assistant director on eleven pictures at Fox. He spoke glowingly about his mentor, Bernard Durning, and the five films they had done together. Number six, *Yosemite Trail,* starring Dustin Farnum, was already in preproduction.

Billy was sorry about having to leave Goldwyn Studios, but seeing and working with Helene Chadwick was just too much. Celia added, "Now, Billy. Just because the marriage wasn't successful, doesn't mean you couldn't have worked together. You have to get along with people. You shouldn't have jumped into the marriage in the first place. Why buy the cow when you can get the milk for free?" Billy responded that he thought he loved her and wanted a family. "Billy, listen to your mother. Slow down. You're very young and impulsive. Get settled in the pasture, and then look around for the cow."

Celia brought her son up to date on the family. Arthur was keeping his shoulder to the wheel in the investment banking business but, as usual, was falling down and then getting back up. Brother Arch was now married and finding great success in the wool business, and Celia was still happy working with wayward boys but missing her sons.

Yosemite Trail was nearing its start date. Mother and son spent as much time together as possible until Billy had to leave for location. He showed her many of the sights of 1922 Hollywood and its environs. In Dix's jalopy, they drove by the Hollywood studios and took a walking tour inside the Fox Studios. They picnicked in the sixty-five-acre Hollywood Bowl Park, later known as the Hollywood Bowl. They visited the orange groves of the San Fernando Valley, breathed the fresh salt air of the Pacific Ocean from the 1,600-foot, wooden Santa Monica Municipal Pier, opened to the public on September 9, 1909. Then strolled the Pleasure Pier next door, built by Charles Looff in 1916. Looff had built the first carousel at Coney Island, and Billy and Celia rode his carousel in the Pleasure Pier's Hippodrome building while listening to the accompanying Wurlitzer organs.

Billy took his mom to see a play at the Iris Theatre, the first legit theatre in Hollywood, which opened in 1916. It was originally called the Idle Hour Theatre in 1913. The name change happened when it moved across the street and expanded to over eight hundred seats. Celia loved movies and her son bought tickets to the Grauman's Egyptian Theatre to watch her favorite male star, Douglas Fairbanks, in *Robin Hood*. The time came for mother and son to part company. Billy put her back on the train, and before she rode out of town she promised to return every year for as long as she was able. She did so well into her eighties.

By May 1923, Wellman had completed eighteen films at Fox Studios. His nineteenth picture would be his eighth film with Bernard Durning. *The Eleventh Hour* was an action thriller starring Charles "Buck" Jones and Durning's wife, Shirley Mason.

One day, nearing the end of preproduction on *The Eleventh Hour*, Wellman was leaving the studio for home. As he walked out the front gate, he was stopped dead in his tracks by a familiar voice: "Wild Willy!" Across the street he saw a 1922 Rolls-Royce Silver Ghost touring car parked next to the curb. Leaning against the automobile was . . . Tommy Hitchcock, dressed in a silk sport coat and tie. The two men ran to each other, hugging and slapping one another on the back, leaping around in the middle of the street, hooting and hollering and calling each other every swear word in the book. "This was going to be a night of revived memories,"

said Wellman, "exciting, unusual, sad . . . back to the wonderful, unbelievable, often times grief-stricken days, of the Lafayette Flying Corps."
They ate dinner in a secluded café. The two forever pals, who had seen
and done many things together, began a question-and-answer period.
Tom started by inquiring about the picture business, what he called an
odd dreamworld, and his pal's participation in it. Billy explained that his
dream was to become a director and make every kind of film. When the
roles were switched, Tommy told about his life's love of polo and traveling
around the world playing.

Billy steered Tom away from polo and Hollywood, back to the time
when they devoured a Rumpler. They relived the whole fantastic battle
experience, and when they reached the climax, they were so excited it was
as if it had happened yesterday. They ordered a drink, drank silently, each
of them wrapped up in their recollection of the many dangerous times
they shared.

Then Billy asked the sixty-four-dollar question. "How did you make
your escape?" He had heard different versions and wanted to get it from
the horse's mouth. Tom told the remarkable story in such an unassuming
way he might have been describing a game of backgammon.

"I was on patrol when I spotted five Albatros beneath me, so I dove on
them. I got one, they got my controls and me, politely speaking, in the
rear end. I made a lousy landing, you could call it a crash-landing. That
is all I remembered until waking up in a prison hospital." Hitchcock
talked about a kind of depression he had never felt before. This attitude
remained buried inside him through all the interrogations, examinations,
physical and mental, the badgering and some very unnecessary abuse.
His captors believed that he was mentally unfit and left him alone. The
food was awful, the medical treatment nil, but they supplied him with
an assortment of so-called bandages and dressings. He became his own
practicing physician—the one difficulty, the location of the wound. "I
became a double-jointed contortionist," Tom said, "treating my awk-
wardly situated bullet hole.'" His great fear was infection but he was
lucky or, perhaps, a brilliant dresser of a shot-up ass.

Tommy began searching for a way to escape. He acted much weaker
than he was. "I did it so well," he told Billy, "had you seen my performance, you would have put me under contract to act in one of your pictures." What bothered Tom the most was the dreariness, the loneliness,
the helplessness, the frightful boredom. Then came the train trip.

Hitchcock was placed with two other very sick pilots, Whitmore
and McKee. He joked that they sounded like a legal firm—Whitmore,

McKee, and Hitchcock. Both had tried escapes before but now were too weak. "We were three miserable, half-dead-looking Americans," said Tommy. They were being transferred to another camp far away from the Swiss border and freedom.

The prisoners were boarded on the train in the middle of the day, which meant the whole afternoon would be spent piling up miles away from the haven, the Black Forest, which bordered on Switzerland. "If you were lucky," said Tommy, "you had a chance of dodging the three border patrols and slipping into freedom."

The train was filled to capacity with infantry. The unhealthy three were pushed and shoved into a separate compartment and, because of their weakened condition, had but one guard. "He was a big, hulking, ugly monster," said Tom, "who spent most of the time glowering at us with the most loathsome expression on his face I have ever seen. God how he hated us. He had a gun, bayonet and a map that he kept looking at. He acted as if he didn't know what the hell he was looking for or at, probably trying to find our destination. By the charming looks he threw at us, I knew where he wished he could put us, with a pile of native soil keeping us warm."

Tom figured that if he could get that map soon, he might have a chance to make the border. It started to get dark, but the infantrymen were wide awake and didn't seem at all interested in going to sleep. "Mile by mile kept whizzing by," said Tom. "I was crazy, acting half-dead waiting for my chance to pickpocket Mr. Ugly's map. Bit by bit it got quieter except for the welcome chorus of snoring in different tones, never in unison, a nightmare of discord."

Finally, Mr. Eyesore wrapped himself up in a blanket and trundled off to sleepy time. Tom was hardly a professional pickpocket but this guard had left his orders and the map under his head as a pillow. Tom tried sliding the map from under his noggin. No good. The second it started to move he awoke with a bellow of a bull, looked around sleepily, saw three sleeping Americans, and fell off to dreamland once again.

The miles were speeding by when Tom got a hunch. The Hulk smoked the foulest-smelling cigarettes, which were buried in a pack on the floor by his bunk. Tom snaked over, retrieved one, crumbled it up into tobacco dust, rained it down on his ugly beak, causing a seizure of God-given sneezes. "You can't sneeze without raising your head," Tom said to Bill. "I got the map, tore through two cars loaded with snoring Heinies, dove off the rear vestibule, went ass over teakettle down a steep grade, took off into the inviting darkness of a strange land. I had no idea where the hell

I was, but I had to keep going as long as I could, until it got light enough for me to find a hiding place to study the map. It was a bumping, stumbling, falling, exhausting trip in a moonless, pitch-dark, unfriendly night."

Dawn crept up through the darkness as Tom spotted a stack of hay in a field, and very carefully crawled to it. He unwound his puttees and wrapped them around his shivering body, burrowed into the hay, sneezed a couple of times, and fell into a half-starved asleep. When he awoke, it was at dusk with enough light left for him to crawl to the outer edge of the hay pile, stick his hands with the unfolded map outside, and peek at it while his head and body were well covered by the hay. "Bill," said Tom. "It wasn't as good as the map we had back in the pilotage. All those important miles gone by waiting for a jug head to go to sleep. C'est la guerre!"

For days it was a hide-and-seek of fear, hunger, and exhaustion, boring in its never-ending repetition. The days became weeks and there was one beautiful, unforgettable, tragic experience, which would always remain Tom's alone, to treasure the rest of his life. He ended his story with, "I made it to Switzerland. I was free again—but very sad."

Wellman realized that during his war-time buddy's flight to freedom, he had discovered ill-fated love—not fleeting romance but the staying power of true love followed by tragedy. Hitchcock and Wellman had shared many things during the war, now they would also share heartrending, never-to-be-forgotten love affairs.

The A-team, the Wild Bunch, the two

Hitchcock Expected to Go Back Into Aerial Combat

Tommy Hitchcock
The New York Times, 1939

By The United Press.

LONDON, Nov. 22—Ten-goal Tommy Hitchcock is picking up in a Warhawk where he left off twenty-five years ago in a Nieuport. According to information received here today, Lieut. Col. Hitchcock, now air attaché to the United States Embassy, is believed to be slated for command of a new fighter group.

If he gets such an assignment, he will be one of the very few First World War American fighter pilots flying in the present conflict, but age may not prove a formidable barrier in his case. In the First World War he was rejected by the United States Army because of his age—17. However, he made his way into the famed Lafayette Escadrille and, in company with such men as William Wellman, Raoul Lufbery, Quentin Roosevelt, Charles Nordhoff and James Hall, made that squadron immortal in the history of aerial combat.

Tommy Hitchcock,
newspaper clipping, 1939

pals talked deep into the night and when it was over, they were all caught up. Seven years later, they met again, in Hitchcock territory, for another long evening of revived memories, dreams fulfilled and those to come. That would be their final get-together as Lieutenant Colonel Thomas R. Hitchcock died testing a fighter plane at the outbreak of World War II. "I never saw Tom again," said Wellman. "He was killed while preparing his own unit for action at the front. He was doing a power dive and never came out of it. Tom's dogged determination was too much for his age." Many years later, Wellman admitted that from the time Hitchcock joined him at the front, he thought about him every day. He kept a photo of his Wild Bunch partner in his dressing room for the remainder of his life.

The Eleventh Hour company had moved location to San Diego. Like on their other seven pictures together, Durning and Wellman worked hard and played hard too. The films were loaded with excitement, the unexpected, and, for Wellman, learning. "Durning was a tough taskmaster," he said, "would excuse you a mistake, but never a repetitive one." When Durning was directing, he allowed his assistant to take care of everything else. If somebody else didn't like it, that somebody was the AD's responsibility to be handled the way he saw fit. Right or wrong, the AD was always right with Durning in front of anybody, from the head of the studio right down the whole parade: actors, extras, the troop, even the star. "But when he got you alone," said Wellman, "if you had been wrong, he let you have both barrels, loaded, and you never made that mistake again."

What amazed Wellman most was during all those pictures, under all the stress and emotion, Durning never gave in to that sickness that was supposed to possess him. On rare occasions, he imbibed a little, but nothing that ever caused him to lose a single minute of work. "The only drink he habitually overindulged in," said Wellman, "was chocolate ice-cream sodas. Three whoppers at a sitting and never bat an eye or add an inch to his waistline or a pound to his sit-down." Then came the explosion.

The company was filming air sequences on North Island, staying at the Grand Hotel. It was a special time for Wellman being back in his former world. Now, he was the teacher and Durning the pupil. Unlike on the earlier pictures, the director was now drinking steadily. With just over a week left on the shooting schedule, Wellman received a phone call to his room at 2:00 a.m. Durning's slightly intoxicated voice said, "Billy, this is Bernie. I need you." Wellman dressed quickly, ran down the hall to Durning's suite; the door was ajar, and he ended up at the foot of his director's bed.

"There wasn't much to say, so I said it: 'Hi, Bernie.' His head was bowed, and for a long moment he didn't answer me, he didn't even move . . . When finally he did raise his head, there was a look of remorse on his face that I will remember as long as I live . . . He didn't get words all screwed up. He knew what he wanted to say; it just sounded strange and bewildered."

"For the last two years, I have said my say," said Durning, "and there is nothing left. With great pride and complete confidence, it is yours, Mr. Wellman, and I don't want to see or hear from you until it is all wrapped up. Don't turn the light off on your way out. I don't want to be completely in the dark." The director lay back down and went soundly to sleep.

The new director yelled "Cut!" and "That's a wrap!" He had finished his five days of shooting with the fliers and the troupe, who were working their heads off to help him make a go of it. Wellman had even cut a full day off the schedule. It had been easy and exciting, and he didn't know how he could go back to the ranks of assistant director. Durning had said that he didn't want to see him until the film was wrapped up. So into Durning's suite he went, and there he was, fully dressed, clean-shaven, immaculate; and, believe it or not, he looked rested. His bags were packed, and he was ready to go home.

Sol Wurtzel and Winnie Sheehan were in charge of production at the Fox Studios, under the president and founder, William Fox. When Sol and Winnie saw the final cut of *The Eleventh Hour*, they were very pleased and complimentary to Durning. They picked out the final act as the best work. Durning could have accepted the credit and moved on to his next assignment, but he didn't. He told them that he had been on a full-blown bender and his assistant, Wellman, finished the picture and brought it in under budget, saving the studio money. As the production executives were considering this, Bernie gave them another. "Make him a director." As an addendum, he mentioned that their star, Dustin Farnum, was crazy about Wellman. The compliments worked and William Wellman saw his directors' board coming into perfect focus.

It had taken Wellman almost four years to reach this plateau: two pictures as an actor, some five months as a messenger boy, five films as a property man, and at least twenty-two pictures as an assistant director.

Wellman's first assignment was *The Man Who Won* (1923), a Western starring Dustin Farnum.

Wild Bill fights his way up the Hollywood ladder.

6

THE DIRECTORS' BOARD

For the first time, the name of William Wellman appeared on a directors' board at a Hollywood studio. Next to his name was his current project, *The Man Who Won*. An apt title for Wellman's first picture. He had worked hard and dreamed hard. For the time being, he had earned a place on that road to success, but it would prove a hazardous highway.

The Man Who Won was a remake of a 1920 Fox picture, *The Twins of Suffering Creek*, based on a 1912 novel by Ridgwell Cullum. Wellman received producer credit as well as director, and it seems clear that he was involved in the scriptwriting as well—the leading player, Dustin Farnum, plays a gambler by the name of Wild Bill.

The Western melodrama tells the story of Farnum and three friends caring for twin children whose mother, played by Jacqueline Gadsden, runs off with a gang of bandits. Her poor miner husband, Ralph Cloninger, chases down the outlaws and talks sense into her to return home. Farnum comes to the rescue and battles the bandits, killing all of them while sacrificing his life for the twins and the happiness of the family. The picture incorporates the themes of camaraderie, sacrifice, and family values that appear in so many of Wellman's films.

Wellman couldn't wait to tell Durning of his good fortune and thank him from the bottom of his heart. Bernie downplayed his involvement, stressing Wellman's work ethic, talent, and loyalty as the reasons for the promotion. "You have everything needed to become a fine director—everything but good luck, and that must be acquired by hard work." Those words of wisdom would become Wellman's maxim throughout his

Dustin Farnum, a star of the Broadway stage who became an icon in silent films, 1920s

career. Over time, he simplified the phraseology—"Do the work and the luck will come."

Durning offered another piece of advice concerning Wellman's *Man Who Won* star, Dustin Farnum. Dusty preferred playing his movie scenes with his cowboy hat firmly in place on his head, the reason being his pate was bald and he felt insecure with the toupee. "Never, but never, allow it to be dislodged," said Bernie. "When you hire your actors, their ability isn't as important as their allergy to that forelock, especially in fight scenes. One misdirected punch, one dusting off of Dusty's dustcloth, and you will be back assisting me and waiting for another battle of the Grand Hotel."

Wellman's picture began production at the studio. He hadn't seen Bernie for nearly a week when, one day, he showed up on the set. He wanted to know how his pupil was doing, if he needed any help. Billy assured him, "If, after two years with you, I can't handle a picture, then I better get back in the air." Durning patted Billy on the back and left with a big smile. The next week, Wellman spotted Durning, half hidden at the back of the set, just watching. The mentor still cared.

When Wellman's company was preparing to leave for location in Lone Pine, California, Billy went over to Bernie's office to say goodbye. It would be their final farewell. Wellman would never see his

Buck Jones and Silver, one of the greatest B Western stars of the era

mentor again, as Bernard J. Durning, only thirty years of age, died from typhoid fever, August 29, 1923, in New York City. Wellman was told on the location of his first directing job, the picture that Durning had made possible. Wellman was overcome with grief.

Between August 1923 and May 1924, Wellman directed seven Westerns at Fox Studios. Six of these oaters starred one of the best loved and most idolized of the series Western stars, Charles "Buck" Jones: *Second Hand Love* (1923), *Big Dan* (1923), *Cupid's Fireman* (1923), *Not a Drum Was Heard* (1924), *The Vagabond Trail* (1924), and *The Circus Cowboy* (1924). *Big Dan* is the only surviving Fox silent film. The Czech Film Archive discovered a complete nitrate print. The UCLA Film Archive has three nitrate reels.

The story of *Big Dan* deals with Buck's character, a World War I veteran, who returns home to find his wife has deserted him. He turns his home into a Big Brothers Camp for boys, trains boxers for the ring, meets and falls in love with Marian Nixon's character. He saves her from a loathsome suitor, and when his wife dies he is free to marry Marian. They live happily ever after.

Buck Jones was a hero and idol to millions of Americans. He starred in 168 movies. He was born Charles Frederick Gebhart, December 12, 1891, in Vincennes, Indiana. He came from a broken home and his school days ended when he reached the age of twelve. He taught himself to be an excellent horseman and, with his mother's help, joined the U.S. Cavalry at the age of sixteen. His mother had signed a consent form certifying that he was eighteen. After his army discharge, he worked as a trick rider in Wild West shows and the Ringling Brothers Circus. While performing in the Julia Allen Wild West Show, he met another performer, Odelle "Dell" Osborne and they were married August 11, 1915, in Lima, Ohio. In 1917, after the birth of his only child, Maxine, he became a movie extra and stunt double for some of the top Western film stars like William S. Hart, Tom Mix, and William Farnum. He received his first leading role in *The Last Straw* (1919), and soon became a top star at the Fox Studios. Over the following seventeen years, his annual salary rose to $143,000.

Jones's style was a compromise between the gaudy showmanship of Mix and the austere realism of Hart; the films followed the exciting Mix format in action and plot, but Jones dressed more soberly and played with more restraint. He also injected comedy and folksy humor, usually poking the fun at himself rather than at a comic sidekick.

Tom Mix was considered top dog at Fox in the silent era, but it was Buck, not Tom, who made a successful transition into talkies, achieving a twenty-five-year career that was still rising when he died tragically in 1942. "He wasn't as big as Tom Mix," said Wellman, "mainly because he didn't have a horse as well-known as Tony, who shared popularity honors with his master. Buck did it all on his own. He was very popular and a wonderful guy. My whole experience directing Buck was . . . one of the happiest hours of picture making I ever had. He was an ace."

After two enjoyable pictures together, *Second Hand Love* and *Big Dan*, Wellman and Jones were assigned *Cupid's Fireman*. Neither of them liked the script. In fact, they hated it and didn't want to make it. Buck and Billy squawked like hell to the front office and anyone they could find at the studio. Wellman said, "The title alone made you sick." Sol Wurtzel, production head, was the one who assigned the project. He wanted Buck to have a change of pace in a non-Western and he stood by his guns. Their contracts did not allow them to reject an assignment, so *Cupid's Fireman* went into production in the winter of 1923. "The big scene," said Wellman, "was the burning of a boarding house, well tricked with controlled fire on either side of the smoke-filled pathway through which Buck was to make three heroic rescues of a mother and her two children, plus a nine year old boy." The special effects and the director's unusual camera angles, combined with Buck's acting and speed, made it look real. The aftermath was Buck being decorated for bravery.

The front office liked the completed picture, the box office liked the picture, even the reviewers liked the picture. *Variety*, April 30, 1924: "It seems that every picture of Charles Jones' becomes better, and 'Cupid's Fireman' is no exception."

Always voted one of the country's favorite Western movie heroes, in 1936 he was number one. Boston was the final destination of a cross-country tour that had begun in California a few weeks earlier. It was a combination of war bond rallies and promotions for his *Rough Rider* series. Due to the grueling schedule, his wife decided to stay home.

On the morning of November 28, Buck had visited the children's hospital to cheer up the young patients before heading to the Boston Garden Arena where twelve thousand children and their parents were waiting to see their movie hero. That afternoon, in a drizzling rain, he was the guest of honor in Mayor Maurice Tobin's box at Fenway Park watching Holy Cross pummel Boston College in football. Next on his schedule was a party given by his film distributors at the Cocoanut Grove. Buck had a bad cold and was exhausted from the week's travel and activities. Even though he didn't want to attend the party, he didn't want to let down his distributors. Buck was the major celebrity at the club that evening.

When an accidental fire started, from a match struck by a sixteen-year-old busboy, it quickly spread throughout the block-long, one-and-a-half-story building. Nothing was fireproof; the decorations were highly flammable. Within a few minutes, the flames spread to the ceiling of the lower level, racing up and across the dance floor of the main level, exploding into a raging conflagration. The intense heat destroyed the electrical wiring and the building went dark. Pandemonium spread, many of the one thousand nightclubbers—more than twice the legal capacity—panicked in their attempt to flee. Exit doors were bolted shut to keep unticketed people from gaining access. Windows were locked and boarded up for the same reason. In the restaurant, many people died before leaving their seats due to asphyxiation from smoke and toxic gas. The revolving door at the main entrance became jammed with screaming, burning people. Smoke, flames, and darkness hindered the withdrawal of the terror-stricken crowd, as well as the entrance of the first-arriving fire crews.

It was the deadliest nightclub fire in U.S. history, killing 492 people, and leaving hundreds of others injured. Across the country, the morning papers bannered headlines with hundreds of stories filling their pages. World War II news was put on hold. Within days of the holocaust, more than a thousand stories of the horrific event and aftermath were written. Eyewitness reports of every kind and degree told amazing accounts of death, destruction, and heroism. An array of tales told of the demise of Buck Jones: that he never got out of the club and died at his table, that he managed to get outside before dying in the street, that he escaped through the roof and, after reaching safety, returned for rescue efforts.

"The newspapers told of the heroism of one unknown man," said Wellman, "who made four plunges through a wall of fire and came out with three doomed people who lived to remember their horror, and who never knew the giant of guts who saved them, all but one, the third, a kid whose movie star favorite was Buck Jones. With tears streaming down his face, he saw Buck go in a fourth time but never saw him come out."

The exact details concerning the death of Jones will never be known, but the records of Massachusetts General Hospital record that on November 30, 1942, Charles "Buck" Jones, age fifty-three, died from smoke inhalation, burned lungs, and third- and second-degree burns. His wife of twenty-seven years, Dell, arrived too late to say goodbye.

As a contract director at Fox Studios, Wellman earned $185 a week. After seven pictures, his salary was . . . $185 a week. The seventh film, *The Circus Cowboy*, premiered June 19, 1924, at the Loew's in New York City. This effort was also produced and directed by Wellman, and once again starred Buck Jones and Marian Nixon.

Variety, June 29, 1924: "Once in a while along comes a picture full of melodrama with high strung and far fetched situations which, nevertheless, gets over through the excellent direction and strength of the story. This is one of those rarities."

Now, at least, Wellman could afford his own place. Several months earlier, he had said goodbye to Dan Dix and Virgil, and moved into an apartment a few blocks from the studio. It had two rooms plus a bathroom with a shower. One room was a combination living room and bedroom, with a pull-down wall bed. The other was the kitchen. Fortunately, the apartment was large enough to accommodate Wellman's new roommate—a big chow dog.

Before *Cowboy* had gone into production, Wellman had found Chow, as he named him, walking the streets in much the same way as he had done looking for places to live near the studios where he was employed. Wellman put up notices around the area, then hoped nobody would respond. Nobody did, and the roommates became great pals. Wellman put together a large dog bed, placing it next to his pull-down.

The initial problem was Chow's eating. Dog food was expensive. Often they ate the same things, but Chow's portions were larger than his master's and he wanted to eat more often. In order to save food money, Wellman made a deal with his landlord that covered six months at a time. The second problem was what to do with the dog when Wellman was working. The landlord introduced him to an elderly female tenant in their building. She liked animals and took on the job of feeding Chow and letting him out once during the day. This worked quite well.

The whole business of working hard for almost a year, making seven quality pictures, but receiving no raise, was definitely wearing on Wellman. He was a big studio contract director. Why should he have to worry about feeding his dog? He had gotten nowhere with studio executives; his agent told him not to rock the boat, that he had a good deal and a bright future. Wellman was not convinced. He even discussed the matter with Chow.

"Chow and I went walking in the hills, Chow full of pep, me full of hatred that had been ripening in the last few Buck Jones pictures. My hatred was no raise in salary . . . I really got mad and explained the whole bloody business to Chow, there was nobody around except the squirrels who stopped their tree climbing the minute we came within ear shot. They didn't even move, just sat very quietly listening to a dumbwit talking business to a dog."

On Monday morning, the great mogul William Fox arrived at the studio. Since nobody would give Wellman a break, he decided to take things in his own hands and go see the big man. *Encyclopaedia Britannica*: "Wilhelm Fried Fuchs . . . motion picture executive who built a multimillion-dollar empire controlling a large portion of the exhibition, distribution, and production of film facilities during the era of silent film." At the tender age of nine months, his German-Jewish parents changed his name to the direct English translation, William Fox. Known as "W.F.," he was a publicity-shy individual whom the press called "a brilliant, excited, energetic, roughneck."

Wellman sat in the roughneck's office all day waiting for an audience. W.F. knew he was there and guessed for what reason. "Funny how flying could enter this problem but it did, and in a very understandable way. I was never afraid while flying fighting, some few times I couldn't breathe for a while, but it passed and the fear, such as it was, changed to a frightful anger, topped by a desire to kill. That's a hell of a topper. Being afraid of a man named Fox was as ridiculous as if I were going to have a fist fight with a nun."

It was getting late and the secretary was preparing to leave. She repeated the familiar phrase that had been used throughout the day, "Mr. Fox is too busy to see you today." Suddenly, W.F.'s door opened and out he came on his way home. He stopped, looked at Wellman, and said, "What do you want?" Wellman answered with two words, "A raise." He answered back with two words, "You're fired," and went out into the hallway. Wellman followed behind, reminding him that he had made seven pictures for the same salary. W.F. turned and restated, "You heard me, you're fired." With this, Wellman grabbed hold of his necktie at the throat and twisted it tight. He considered exploding a right fist in his startled face, then reconsidered after seeing the fright in the mogul's eyes. No more words were spoken. "I saw the fear of a coward on his face, so I did the thing a face like that deserved, I spit on it. I went out of the studio for good, he went back to his office to cleanse his face of the only sincere tribute he had received for a long time."

Wellman's name came down from the directors' board at the Fox Studios, and wouldn't appear on any other studio billboard for a long time. His agent was disappointed; however, he told the unemployed director that with his credits, jobs would come soon. Soon didn't happen. The rumor was out that Wild Bill had hit the saliva bull's-eye, and W.F. made sure the studio executives got the word—Wellman was blackballed. This state of exclusion would last for over a year.

As the weeks went by with no offers, Chow and his master began losing weight—the money was running out. Wellman had to make something happen. He did. He became a criminal. He got a job at a small grocery store as a delivery boy. The store was owned and run by an elderly couple with no children. Wellman did not mention his show business problems, just that he was a war veteran down on his luck, which, of course, was true. Wellman could see that when his small savings was depleted, his delivery boy wages were not going to cover his living expenses and hungry roommate. The job came with an old Maxwell delivery truck. He would pursue work at the studios between deliveries and . . . become a skillful pilferer.

"I became a thief, not a full-fledged one, just enough of one to live and support my hungry roommate, until some producer took a distinct dislike to my spit-upon producer target. It will happen, they all hated each other, it was just a matter of a not too hungry time of patience."

Billy's and Chow's diet changed from delivery to delivery. This was the easy part for man; Chow had the hard part, eating like a human. "He became so well adjusted that he downed fruit and his fur coat shined like gold." The pilfering plan went into effect: while filling out the orders, while delivering said orders, at homes where said orders were left, and while cleaning up the store at the end of the day. The best days were Fridays and Saturdays when everyone was preparing for the weekend.

Wellman would take one potato from a dozen delivery orders, which kept him in potatoes for quite a while. One pocketed can of salmon or tuna with rice or potatoes was good for a couple of days. Different broths with meat and potatoes on Saturday nights were fit for a king. If he had a little money left when he bought meat, dog bones were included. Saturday nights were like Christmas dinners to Chow and Billy. For desserts, he pocketed gelatin in all flavors. Both master and pet wanted milk. Wellman studied the routes the milk wagon was taking and when a large order was placed at a home, and the delivery person went back to the wagon for more, Wellman sneaked over and a couple of quarts vanished. The boys always had fresh oranges and avocados. By moonlight, they picked from the abundance of trees in their neighborhood. Chow had a soft mouth for holding and carrying the fruit. With Wellman's small savings, he occasionally bought eggs, bread, coffee, and sugar—their size and shape made them more difficult to pilfer.

When the roommates reached the end of their resources, a minor miracle took place. "The magic telephone rang. My agent had a hell of an important picture for me to make, a feature believe it or not, to be made in three and one half days and nights . . . He didn't need a director, he needed a voodoo."

The he who needed a voodoo was the infamous Harry Cohn of Columbia Pictures. The year 1925 was winding down as William Wellman, courtesy of this ruthlessly successful studio boss, was back on a directors' board . . . and that hazardous highway. "King" Cohn, as he was sarcastically called, was an outlaw in the industry, and hiring a blackballed director—who he believed would bring the results he wanted—was in perfect order.

Born July 23, 1891, to a working-class German Jewish family in New York's rough lower-class East 88th Street, Harry Cohn spent his youth in unheralded fashion. His education ended after grade school. He worked a variety of jobs: errand boy and shipping clerk, streetcar conductor, nickelodeon duo singer, song plugger, and producer of a series of silent shorts where popular songs were mimed by actors, inviting the audiences to join in. After riding the coattails of his more successful older brother, Jack,

Directors Frank Borzage (left) and Frank Capra (right) with
producer Harry Cohn (center), at Columbia Studio, 1930s

they began CBC Film Sales Corporation with Joe Brandt, a lawyer friend
of Jack's. Because of Cohn, Brandt, Cohn's propensity for low-budget,
low-class shorts and features, Hollywood pundits dubbed CBC "Corned
Beef and Cabbage."

On January 10, 1924, the three partners formed Columbia Pictures.
Jack stayed in New York to handle distribution; Harry went to Hollywood to run a small studio on Gower Street in what was called Hollywood's Poverty Row. Because of the hostility between the two brothers,
Brandt decided the whole business was too stressful and sold his share.
The brothers never had the resources to own a theater chain as did the 1925
majors: Fox, Loews/MGM, Paramount, Warners, and Universal. Without the support of their own theaters, Columbia struggled to survive. But
survive it did, concentrating on the production of modest-budgeted program pictures plus a few more expensive and ambitious films each year.
At the helm of this cost-conscious little ship was the brash, blunt, crude,
uneducated president and head of production, King Cohn. Unlike the
major studios of the day, Cohn did not have a list of stars and filmmakers
under contract. He rarely used A-list players—only occasionally borrowing them from the majors. He took flak from critics, studio executives,
and much of Hollywood about his way of doing business, but he never
had a losing year.

Into this bedlamized world entered William Wellman and the project, *When Husbands Flirt* (1925). Wellman was well aware of Cohn's outspoken, hot-tempered, take-no-prisoners style of negotiating, but he was in no position to play tough. Wild Bill needed the job. His interview in King Cohn's office was short and to the point. "He said hello, I said hello. He gave me the story and the script to read and talk to him about my objections, if any, and also a few hoped-for funny additions, but no dough." Wellman went right home and went to work. He liked the story, a humorous look at marital infidelity, written by Dorothy Arzner, who went on to become one of the first women directors of Hollywood's Golden Age.

Wellman interjected pieces of comedy into the script, hoping for a few belly laughs from Cohn. He got them and $250 right away. He would get the rest of his $500 salary—for preproduction, writing, producing, directing, editing, everything—when the picture was completed. "So I thanked him, that really surprised him, he smiled, so did I. We had apparently broken a Cohn record, two smiles in less than a minute."

It had been many weeks since Wellman and Chow had seen that much money. They celebrated at home over steak and a couple of big dog bones. Chow was happy, Wellman not completely—he felt guilty with a pilferer's conscience. He took out paper and pen and tried to figure how much he owed his kindly grocery boss. He hadn't kept records or done any bookkeeping. Through memory of the days and weeks of pilfering, he came to a figure of $100. He decided to tell the old gentleman and give him $50 now, the other $50 when the picture was finished and he had received his final $250.

"It is not an easy job to tell a helluva nice guy that you are a thief and have been keeping you and your dog alive at his expense . . . it is rugged and unusual things might happen, such as being confined for an indefinite period as a guest of the city." Wellman expected his boss to let loose and bawl the hell out of him. Instead, he said very quietly what an unworthy rascal Billy had been. His language was not like Wellman's, the four-letter kind, it had an old-fashioned ring to it, like calling him a rascal. "If he had called me a dirty lousy thief or even a son of a bitch, I would have felt more at home, but a bad boy made me think I was little Lord Fauntleroy. He said he never had a son and I fitted what he had dreamed about for a long time. He knew what I had been doing and didn't have the slightest doubt that I would pay it back."

The store owner said that $100 was too much to pay back. He would settle for $50 to teach Billy a lesson. Wellman apologized for his actions, but refused to leave it at only $50. He said that when he received his final payment, another $50 would be forthcoming. "So many small people that you meet," said Wellman, "are so much bigger than the big people that you meet. All over the world."

Production on *When Husbands Flirt* began in November of 1925. Wellman remembered the basic story, cast, production elements, and working conditions. "Old man takes dose of castor oil, leaves home for office, things start to move; and we got six reels out of that; by borrowing long shots of big scenes in other pictures, by building corners of the sets and cutting our close shots into them, by rewriting to fit what we had or could steal, to give the picture production, by working so long and so hard that you could sleep standing up or sitting down, or lying on the floor or in your car with your feet sticking out." This was making pictures the hard way, but learning how to make them quickly, cheaply, efficiently, and presentably.

During preproduction, production, and postproduction on *When Husbands Flirt*, Chow was once again under the direction of the elderly tenant in their building. At the end of one workday, Wellman came home to find no dog waiting for him. Chow was missing in action. The dog sitter apologized profusely, explaining that when she let the dog out, he never came back. Wellman searched everywhere. He knocked on doors, spread the word with neighbors, whistled down many streets and alleys, put up notices at local stores, in store windows, on telephone poles, trees, streetlamps, even trolley cars and delivery trucks. As time went by, he realized that he had lost his roommate. He believed that someone had noticed Chow's good looks and sunny disposition, then took him for a ride, a long ride.

As a celebration for the completion of *When Husbands Flirt* and Wellman's return to the directors' billboard, Ward Crane, an actor friend, and some acquaintances from Wellman's days at Fox gave him a dinner party at the Hollywood Hotel. Among the celebrators was Jacques "Jack" Chapin, who worked around Hollywood in various capacities as property man, stuntman, actor, assistant director. He and Wellman had worked together and become friends. At the table next to them was Jack's sister, Marjorie, who was visiting from New York. She was a former singer and dancer with the *Ziegfeld Follies*. Crane introduced Billy to Marjorie, and she joined their table, sitting between her brother and Wellman.

Miss Chapin's visit to Hollywood was extended by her tour guide, Wild Bill. As was his custom, they would get to know each other after they tied the knot in a small church in Riverside, California. Wellman presented his bride with a wedding ring purchased at a five-and-ten-cent store. *The Boston Globe Sunday Edition,* October 16, 1927, featured a Wellman interview with this comment: "It was a blazing hot day. We drove up to Riverside and were married by a one-armed minister. All four tires on my car were ready to blow out, and as I had no spare I was pretty worried about the heat. Our honeymoon consisted of listening to the pipe-organ recital in the Riverside Inn, and then when it got cool we came on back to Hollywood."

The Riverside church and Riverside Inn were the same locations where Billy and Helene Chadwick had said "I do" and spent a long weekend—at least, the Wellman-Chadwick minister could hold the Good Book in one hand while turning the page with the other. Their full weekend at the historic Mission Revival hotel, incorporating elements of the twenty-one California missions, was a lot more romantic than the Wellman-Chapin few hours of listening to a pipe organ while waiting for the temperature to cool.

For the time being, Wellman had a new roommate in his bachelor quarters. Times were tough but Marjorie Edinger Chapin, the golden-haired prima donna of the *Follies,* was making every effort to be the proper Mrs. William Wellman. Wellman said, "Margery [Marjorie] starved it through with me. She kept me going."

As in the past, marriage number three had taken place without the knowledge or presence of Wellman's family. When he called his mother, father, and brother, they were disapproving. Billy told Celia that he had bought the cow again, but this time it was different. Although Marjorie had been on stage and in the *Ziegfeld Follies,* she was not interested in being in the movies. She only wanted to be a wife and mother. Reluctantly, Celia gave her blessing and asked her son to bring his wife to Boston to meet friends and family. Wellman promised to do so when business improved.

Wellman and his agent believed that when *When Husbands Flirt* was released, offers would come. Columbia did not have an assignment for him at this time; so, in order to bring home a paycheck for him and his new bride, he took a step back and signed on as an assistant director at Metro-Goldwyn-Mayer Studios.

By 1925, MGM had already been formed by Marcus Loew, who had built a theatrical circuit empire, then purchased Metro Pictures, the Goldwyn moviemaking company, and Louis B. Mayer Pictures Corporation. Loew hired Mayer to oversee the picture-making colossus.

Born Lazar Meir, July 4, 1884, in Minsk, Belarus, Mayer, with his parents and four siblings, emigrated to Saint John, New Brunswick, Canada. He attended school there before beginning his rise to power in the entertainment industry. Through the acquisition of movie theaters, he eventually moved to Los Angeles, forming his own production company. Known as "L.B.," he believed in wholesome, family entertainment and "more stars than there are in heaven"—his phrase depicting the great stars in his films and under contract to his studio. L.B. built MGM into the most financially successful motion picture studio in the world.

While L.B. ran the studio, many of the production decisions belonged to a young, Brooklyn-born producer, Irving Thalberg. "The Boy Wonder," as he was called, was plagued with a bad heart and health issues throughout his relatively short life. After high school, he found employment at Universal Pictures' New York office. By age twenty-one, he had risen to executive in charge of production at Universal's California studio, then joined Mayer as head of production at MGM.

Some of Thalberg's triumphs would include: *Foolish Wives* (1922), *The Hunchback of Notre Dame* (1923), *The Big Parade* (1925), *Anna Christie* (1930), *Grand Hotel* (1932), *Mutiny on the Bounty* (1935), *China Seas* (1935), *A Night at the Opera* (1935), *Romeo and Juliet* (1936), *San Francisco* (1936), *Camille* (1936), and *The Good Earth* (1937).

Back to the more lowly assistant director, William Wellman. His first assignment at the rising MGM was *Sally, Irene and Mary*, to be directed by English-born Edmund Goulding. Goulding was an actor, playwright, and director on the London stage before coming to Hollywood. He began his studio career as a screenwriter and later directed thirty-seven films, including such classics as Best Picture Academy Award–winner *Grand Hotel* (1932), *The Dawn Patrol* (1938), and Best Picture nominees *Dark Victory* (1939) and *The Razor's Edge* (1946). Signed to a term contract, his second assignment was *Sally, Irene and Mary*. The film was based on a play by Edward Dowling and Cyrus Woodand and starred Constance Bennett and Joan Crawford.

The highly respected Goulding was so appreciative of Wellman's work on the film that he recommended him to the front office as a director. Unfortunately, the only directing work assigned Wellman was to fix (uncredited) problem-plagued pictures like the society melodrama *The Way of a Girl* (1925) starring Eleanor Boardman and Matt Moore, and *The Exquisite Sinner* (1926), toplining Conrad Nagel, Renée Adorée, and Paulette Duval. This story deals with the disillusionment of a French war veteran who leaves the business world for the life of an artist. The credited

Tony D'Algy playing Harry, the rum runner, with Gertrude
Olmstead as the "girl" in Wellman's *The Boob* (1926)

but fired director was Josef von Sternberg, who went on to great success
with his series of Marlene Dietrich films and other outstanding pictures.

After Wellman completed his work on *The Exquisite Sinner*, another
director, Phil Rosen, came on board for additional retakes. MGM's displeasure with the film grew and grew, and they kept it out of release for
months. From the *Photoplay* July 1926 review: "This is the production
directed by Joseph von Sternberg for Metro, that has been shelved for
many months. And we cannot understand why! For this is equally as
good as some of the pictures Metro has been tooting all over town." As
it turned out, *The Exquisite Sinner* made many of the best picture lists of
that year.

Wellman's next replacement job was *The Boob* (1926) starring Gertrude
Olmstead, George K. Arthur, and Joan Crawford. *The Boob*'s original
director was Robert Vignola, the same Robert Vignola that Wellman had
replaced on *The Way of a Girl*. Instead of doing a fix-it job, Wellman
directed almost the entire film and received full director's credit. When
the powers that be, the duo of L.B. and the Wonder Boy, saw the film,
Wellman was fired and the picture was left unreleased for almost a year.
Variety, June 2, 1926, declared *The Boob* "a terrible picture, the worst
made by Metro since its merger with Goldwyn and Mayer. . . . In places
where M-G-M means good pictures, this should never be shown."

B. P. Schulberg, head of
production at Paramount from
1925 to 1932

As word of Wellman's firing traveled
around the studios, King Cohn raised his
rebel head and came calling. He didn't care
about MGM or *The Boob*, was pleased
with Wellman's work on *When Husbands
Flirt*, and wanted to sign him to a contract at $200 a week. When *Flirt* finally
premiered July 14, 1926, two months after
Boob's opening, it was a success. *Variety*,
July 21, 1926, wrote, "Light and enjoyable
farce with plenty of hoke and snappy subtitles. Comedy all the way and handled as
comedy in a burlesque manner. Direction
by William Wellman is good. Attractive
title should bring them in and when in
they will laugh. An 8th Avenue audience
laughed heartily." After Cohn came a second caller who knew Wellman's work at
Fox and had seen a pre-release screening
of *Flirt*. He also would be vying for the
contract of the young director. He was an aspiring young producer by the
name of B. P. Schulberg.

Benjamin Percival Schulberg, known as B.P., was born on January 19,
1892, in Bridgeport, Connecticut. His education was cut short in order to
begin his career as a reporter on the *New York Mail*, editor of the magazine *Film Reports*, a scriptwriter for Rex Pictures, and as both screenwriter
and publicity man for Famous Players Film Company under Adolph
Zukor. Schulberg was responsible for the publicity campaign promoting
Zukor's very successful *Queen Elizabeth* feature. When Famous Players
merged with Jesse L. Lasky Feature Play Company, Schulberg continued
in the same dual capacity. Later, he formed his own company and produced a series of low-budget features.

B.P.'s publicity ingenuity made Clara Bow the "It" girl of the movies.
With this petite, dynamo superstar under contract, he rejoined Zukor
and Lasky at Paramount's Hollywood studio as vice president in charge
of production. In addition to Bow, he brought with him a small stable of
contract players including Wellman, a questionable asset, whom he had
signed after outbidding Harry Cohn by $25 a week.

The most important names on the signposts of William Wellman's
Hollywood highway to success were: Douglas Fairbanks, who had given

him his start; Will Rogers, who elevated the messenger boy to production level as a property man; General Pershing, who influenced Samuel Goldwyn to promote him to assistant director; Bernard Durning, who mentored and fought for him to become a director; Harry Cohn, who hired the blackballed director; and B.P. Schulberg, who was inspired to win the contract negotiation for a director of B Westerns and a three-day wonder called *When Husbands Flirt*.

7

THE ROAD TO A CLASSIC

Before the new year of 1926 was celebrated, William Wellman had arrived at his new studio under contract to B.P. Schulberg's Preferred Pictures. Although his $225 a week didn't change, the contract was rewritten to reflect the parent company title: Famous Players-Lasky, later Paramount Pictures Corporation.

A Hungarian-born furrier and a Jewish cornet player from San Francisco built a Hollywood studio into the number-one company in the film industry. Adolph Zukor was born on January 7, 1873, in a small, wine-growing village in Ricse, Hungary. Jesse Louis Lasky was born seven years later in San Francisco, California. The two future moguls would not meet for another thirty-four years. Their paths to the top sprang from humble beginnings that hardly anticipated fame and fortune.

By 1910, Zukor owned his own nickelodeon chain and was a partner in a theater circuit with Marcus Loew. In 1912, Zukor sold his shares in Loew's Consolidated Enterprises to finance the purchase of a French-made film, *Queen Elizabeth*, starring Sarah Bernhardt. The picture's success moved him to enter film production. His Famous Players company lived up to its name with the likes of James O'Neill, the father of Eugene O'Neill, starring in the role that had made him famous on the Broadway stage, *The Count of Monte Cristo;* Mrs. Fiske in *Tess of the d'Urbervilles;* John Barrymore in *An American Citizen;* Lily Langtry in *His Neighbor's Wife;* and Mary Pickford, becoming "America's Sweetheart" in Zukor's *In the Bishop's Carriage* (1913), *Caprice* (1913), *Hearts Adrift* (1914), and *A Good Little Devil* (1914).

Zukor was not the only person interested in starring famous stage players in movies. Jesse Lasky was another. In 1913, Lasky and Samuel

Moguls Lasky and Zukor join forces at Paramount Pictures.

Goldwyn teamed up with Cecil B. DeMille to form Jesse L. Lasky Feature Play Company. With limited funds, they rented a barn in the Los Angeles area where they made Hollywood's first feature film, *The Squaw Man* (1914), directed by DeMille and starring Dustin Farnum. Zukor's Famous Players Company had produced the first feature in New York, *The Prisoner of Zenda* (1914), starring James K. Hacket.

The two prized producers met in 1914 and on July 19, 1916, they agreed to merge. Zukor would devote his genius to the financial end and building a worldwide network of film exchanges and theaters. Lasky would be in charge of the studios and production of their films. During the 1920s, Famous Players-Lasky's annual profits rose from $5.2 million at the beginning of the decade to $15.5 million at the end. The company owned over a thousand theaters that played their smash hits *The Sheik* (1921), *Blood and Sand* (1922), *The Ten Commandments* (1923), *The Covered Wagon* (1923), *Beau Geste* (1926), and many others. Adolph Zukor and Jesse Lasky were the first moguls of the film industry; together they built the nation's largest movie company.

B.P. Schulberg handed Wellman his first assignment at Paramount Studios. It was, of all possible stories, a sex comedy entitled *The Cat's Pajamas*. Taken from a 1920s slang expression meaning something wonderful, the title could have been chosen from any number of popular slang expressions from the Roaring Twenties like bee's knees, cat's whiskers, cuckoo's chin, or bullfrog's beard.

The cast: Betty Bronson, Ricardo Cortez, Arlette Marchal, and Theodore "Daddy" Roberts. Bronson was Hollywood's first *Peter Pan* (1924). That film was a blockbuster and she became a major star. In order to continue her stardom, in the next few years the studio attempted to change her image, casting her as wholesome teenagers and as Mary, the mother of Jesus Christ, in the ultra-expensive *Ben-Hur: A Tale of the Christ* (1925).

In *The Cat's Pajamas*, Bronson plays a seamstress, often attired in pajamas, with an opera company who is secretly in love with its star, Ricardo Cortez. Bronson's character has a pet cat, Tommy, who gets loose and scurries backstage where the star is being interviewed by the press. Cortez is attracted to Tommy, telling the reporters that he will marry the first woman the cat leads him to. That woman turns out to be the boisterous dancer played by Arlette Marchal. Tommy the cat becomes a celebrity, causing Marchal to get jealous and refuse to try on her wedding dress. The dress is being modeled by Bronson and, with Tommy looking on, Cortez proposes to her and they are married. Instead of living happily ever after, Bronson wants to teach Cortez a lesson for his foolishness and leaves him. Following a series of complications, however, they are happily reconciled.

The finished picture had disaster written all over it, and the new studio bosses were unhappy with Schulberg and his protégé. Why B.P. would give this story to Wellman for his first assignment is hard to understand. Maybe because the director had turned the comedy *When Husbands Flirt* into a success, Schulberg believed he could do it again.

The studio casting of Betty Bronson as the pajama'd sexy seamstress is also questionable. Their attempt to find a different persona for their young star was failing and, by 1926, her star was shining less brightly—the innocent virginal types were being replaced by naughty flappers, who lifted their hemlines, smoked, and partied the night away.

"It was indescribably atrocious," said Wellman. "My defense had been a very honest one. The story called for the Peter Panish Miss Bronson to look and act like a woman of the world. She tried so hard, but all she succeeded in doing was to look like a little girl who had just wet her pants. They didn't need a director, they needed a magician."

The costar of *Cat's Pajamas* was one of the leading character actors of the day with over a hundred films to his credit, Theodore "Daddy" Roberts. "He died shortly after the picture," said Wellman, "and I often wondered if he had seen the finished product. It could have caused it."

Wellman believed that his days at Paramount were numbered. He also thought that *Cat's Pajamas* had put Schulberg in an awkward position, causing his days to be numbered. Instead of being defensive, B.P. went on the offense and bragged to Jesse Lasky that Wellman's next film would prove his merit. This time, Schulberg chose a European-style melodrama, a love story called *You Never Know Women* (1926), original title, *Love— The Magician*.

Since Wellman's marriage to Marjorie Chapin, he had been working steadily with little time for his bride. In the interest of togetherness, he schooled her as a script supervisor and hired her on *Cat's Pajamas*. With her at his side again, he began production on *You Never Know Women* in June of 1926 at Paramount's Vine Street studio. The cast: Florence Vidor, Lowell Sherman, and Clive Brook.

The story is a romantic triangle set against the colorful background of the Russian theatrical troupe Chauve-Souris. Clive Brook plays a Houdini-like illusionist secretly in love with a beautiful actress played by Florence Vidor. He thinks that she loves her wealthy suitor, played by Lowell Sherman, and concocts a faked death during one of his chained trunk routines in order to free her to marry Sherman. The stunt has the opposite effect and she pines for Brook. When she tells Sherman of her true love, he becomes enraged and attempts to rape her. Brook has discovered that Vidor loves him not Sherman, and returns to the theater in time to see her escape into his magic cabinet with Sherman in pursuit. She knows there is a trapdoor and disappears behind it, leaving Brook on stage in front of a confused but angry Sherman. The villain finds himself pinned to the wall by Brook's throwing knives. As the final blade is aimed at his throat, he breaks away, leaving Brook and Vidor alone and together.

The film was released September 22, 1926, and became an artistic and commercial success. *Variety*, July 28, 1926, reported, "Flawlessly acted, brilliantly directed and filled with novel situations. . . . Wellman at the megaphone, lifts himself into the ranks of the select directors by his handling of this story." The Paramount hierarchy was elated, B.P. Schulberg was vindicated, and the questionable asset was on a nonstop flight up that Hollywood highway to the top.

By 1927, silent films—an art form inspired by music, transmitted through light, and inviting dreams in the dark—were at the pinnacle of their artistic and commercial success. Eight hundred films a year were being produced for an audience of 100 million people, who attended 25,000 movie theaters every week. The box office receipts amounted to $1–1.2 billion a year; 42,000 people were employed in Hollywood, and the American film industry accounted for 82 percent of the world's movies. The American studios were valued at about $65 million.

During Lasky's time at Paramount, he was always searching for that one big winner each year. He believed that his Paramount Studio had the best directors, writers, and stars under contract, and expected to launch a film comparable to the studio's number one ranking in Hollywood. In February of 1926, his search took him to New York. At a banquet, publisher George Palmer Putnam, who later married Amelia Earhart, introduced him to a good-looking young man who was a graduate of the

Florence Vidor with writer Ernest Vajda (left) and
Wellman, 1926

University of Washington, a Rhodes scholar, a pilot in World War I, and
an aspiring screenwriter. His name was John Monk Saunders. The young
scholar proposed a story that excited the mogul. They set a meeting for
the following day.

How could Lasky have ever imagined that this chance encounter would
lead to an epic film of such grand proportions that it would involve gov-
ernments: the U.S. Senate would debate the issue, the president of the
United States would make his opinion known, the most important generals would plan a great war placing hundreds of lives at risk. The film
would skyrocket careers and set a lofty standard in the annals of motion
picture history. It would be a pioneering achievement, a masterpiece of
silent cinema, the last great silent picture, retaining its power for decades
to come.

John Monk Saunders later wrote, "The history of this film begins in
the library of Jesse L. Lasky's Fifth Avenue apartment in New York City
on a cold, gray afternoon in late February." The young writer outlined
his story of a young lad's dream of flight—leaving home and loved ones,
enlisting in the Air Corps, and becoming a World War I fighter pilot. It
was a story filled with action, romance, camaraderie, patriotism, tragedy,
hope, and love. The story was called *Wings*.

During the war years, Hollywood had turned out dozens of films extolling the patriotic, romanticized version of the war. After the Armistice in 1918, public sentiment turned against these films and they were taken out of release, out of production, out of Hollywood—they were considered box office poison. By 1925, however, the moviegoing public flocked to theaters to see King Vidor's saga of American soldiers on the Western Front in *The Big Parade*. This film and Raoul Walsh's *What Price Glory?* (1926) focused on the folly, the suffering, the tyranny, the waste of war.

With the success of these films, Lasky believed the public was now eager to see more stories about the Great War, and the story of that war fought in the air had never been told. Lasky's enthusiasm, however, was tempered by the many production problems facing a film of such magnitude—the cost, logistics, material, and manpower would be overwhelming. Early estimates placed the cost at $1.2 million. Lasky could well understand the production grandeur and commercial possibilities of *Wings*, but when he proposed the project to Adolph Zukor and the New York bankers, they believed it was ludicrous and hardly worth the cost. Over a million dollars sunk into a film about airplanes? Moving specks in the sky? The public couldn't be expected to show interest in something they could hardly see. How could they tell the good guys from the bad guys? Insert close-ups of the markings on the wings? Goggles made all pilots look alike—Hun, Yank, or Limey. How could you root for men you couldn't recognize? Worse, Lasky wanted to get sound effects into the silent film. Sound effects . . . ! Hadn't many exhibitors protested that sound in films would keep the audience awake? People, they said, went to movies to rest, relax, and yes—in many cases get some sleep!

Saunders had dreamed of this film for many years and was not ready to give it up. He presented the idea to Lasky that possibly he could persuade the federal government to become a partner. If not financially, at least they might provide troops, equipment, and military facilities. The country and the world were becoming plane-crazed. This film, he said, would help the War Department raise needed funds and volunteers. It would show the American people the activities of their American army in the air. And what better way than through the medium of a rip-roaring and extraordinary motion picture?

Lasky listened and his enthusiasm was reignited. He hired Saunders to write his story and go to Washington to make the pitch—as difficult a feat of salesmanship as one could imagine. Not only asking the government for a movie loan, but for the use of its army and air force for at least four months. How many official approvals would this require?

The Big Three of *Wings* (1927) inspect the war area of St. Mihiel at San Antonio, Texas, specially constructed for the great battle sequences of the Paramount road show. John Monk Saunders, author; William Wellman, director; and Lucien Hubbard, producer, on a tour of the area, which encompasses five square miles and is said to be perfect in every detail.

With a pocketful of letters of introduction, Saunders arrived in D.C. His film idea quickly became tied up in yards of red tape. He was passed from one VIP to another. His letters became worn, and as the days passed the War Department was still not persuaded that the loan of its generals, troops, aviators, and airplanes would popularize the army with the public.

Back in Hollywood, Lasky had appointed Lucien K. Hubbard, a bright young screenwriter-turned-producer, as supervisor and producer of the aerial epic. His successes included *The Vanishing American* (1925) and the Zane Grey Western series. Hubbard was sent to Washington to support Saunders. When Saunders met General C. M. Saltzman, chief signal officer of the army (the head of publicity), things took a turn for the better. The general heard that the film would be correct to the last uniform button, it would not make a villain out of an officer, or bring dishonor to the uniform. The writer presented an inspirational vision of the noble young men who would leave the theater after seeing *Wings* and hurry to the nearest enlisting depot.

General Saltzman was convinced. He went to Major General John L. Hines, chief of staff of the army, and Major General Mason M. Patrick, chief of staff of the air corps. They went to Secretary of War Lieutenant Colonel Dwight F. Davis, who visited the White House, where Calvin Coolidge gave a thumbs-up and, at last, permission for the cooperation of the War Department was given . . . but only on certain conditions: Paramount must pay for all damage to government property during filming, legitimate training must be provided for any of the troops who work on it, there must be a $10,000 insurance policy for each serviceman working on the film, the finished picture must be approved by the War Department before release, the government cooperation must be kept out of the papers so that foreign countries would not think it was being made to intimidate them. The War Department further suggested that due to the close proximity of the air and army services, the military aspects of the film could be shot in San Antonio, Texas.

Lasky again pleaded his case to Zukor and the bankers. They were still skeptical, but finally agreed and Paramount began preproduction. Lasky bought Saunders's story and gave him a contract to write the screenplay. He would also be the technical adviser during filming, and receive a percentage of the picture's profits. Because of the young writer's inexperience, top-grade screenwriters, Hope Loring and her husband, Louis D. Lighton, would work with him. The Loring-Lighton duo were considered Paramount's best writing team. One of their credits was the milestone accomplishment *It*, which rocketed Clara Bow into the heavens. Another first-rate scribe, Julian Johnson, would write the titles.

The story line for *Wings* eventually became a romantic triangle between small-town rivals Jack Powell (Buddy Rogers) and David Armstrong (Richard Arlen), both in love with beautiful aristocrat Sylvia Lewis (Jobyna Ralston). Mary Preston, played by Clara Bow, Jack's tomboy friend next door, has always loved him. War breaks out and the boys enlist, train at the same camp, and become pursuit pilots. After a training camp boxing match, they become friends and are sent to the front together. Mary joins the Red Cross to do her part in the war effort and find Jack. She encounters him in Paris on leave, but he's too drunk to recognize her. During combat, David is shot down and presumed dead. In a fit of revenge, Jack flies off after the enemy. Although wounded, David steals a German plane and attempts to return to his base. Thinking David is the enemy, Jack shoots down his plane. In an emotional moment, David dies in his best friend's arms. The war ends and Jack returns home a decorated hero. He apologizes to David's mother, father, and Sylvia. After discovering Mary's episode in Paris and her obvious devotion to him, he realizes that she is his true love.

Aside from hiring the aviation expert but unseasoned writer Saunders—who would be supported by first-class writers—Lasky's master plan was to attach the finest craftsmen to *Wings*. In every department, only the best of the best would have this film on their résumé. Soon, the studio artists would begin to design interiors of a French village set, Main Street of an American small town, and a Folies Bergère nightclub set. Special effects would experiment with harmless but effective bombs and explosives for the war scenes. Location scouts would be dispatched to San Antonio to begin the search for shooting sites, and . . . Lasky and Schulberg would begin discussions for casting the man who would direct this prodigious production.

The mogul boasted to his production head that the main reason Paramount was number one was because he had the best directors in Hollywood under contract, men like Cecil B. DeMille, Josef von Sternberg, Victor Fleming, Allan Dwan, Gregory LaCava, Eddie Sutherland, Clarence Badger, and Malcolm St. Clair, to name just a few of the fine veteran filmmakers. Lasky believed that the director was captain of the ship, but that he, Lasky, was commander of the fleet. The studio boss asked his VP which of his top-flight veteran directors should be chosen. B.P. answered with a name that astounded Lasky: William Wellman. Schulberg said that only a man with a history of war and aerial combat would understand the intricate characteristics of *Wings*. Wild Bill Wellman had been there. He had fought the enemy on the ground and in the air. He not only witnessed but experienced the terrifying experience of war, the bloodshed, the death of comrades. He was the only director under contract with frontline battle experience.

Jesse Lasky explained his position. He respected Wellman's background, but thought him too green, too untested for a film of this magnitude. After all, he was primarily a director of B Westerns. Of his four non-Westerns, *When Husbands Flirt* and *You Never Know Women* were good, but *The Boob* and *The Cat's Pajamas* were not. A fifty percent director was not good enough for *Wings*. B.P. countered that he had a good feeling about this young filmmaker who had paid his dues and was always on schedule and under budget. Schulberg begged his boss to meet with his protégé before making the final decision.

The intrepid young director met with the powerful mogul. When Lasky mentioned his dubious film credits, Wellman sparked, "I've directed eleven pictures. I took the scripts I was given and made the best pictures I could. Nobody at this studio could have done better. You said you liked *You Never Know Women*." "We all did," Lasky answered. Then he asked Wellman the sixty-four-dollar question: "What makes you think you can direct our big road show picture of the year better than my experienced directors?" The outspoken director shot back: "My war record does. I flew support for 'Black Jack' Pershing and his Rainbow Division when they went over the top. I know what those battles are about. You're worried about the damn budget. I never go over budget. This is a great story. I'll make it the best goddamn picture this studio's ever had!" Later, Lasky challenged Schulberg again. "What makes you think you can control this headstrong Wellman?" B.P.'s answer was straightforward. "He's my boy. I brought him here. I can control him." The studio boss said he would have to think about it.

Since Wellman's marriage to Marjorie, he had been steadily employed as an assistant at MGM, and a director at MGM and Paramount. Even though his wife worked with him on the last two pictures, there wasn't much time for their relationship to grow. Wellman had tried to fill in the separation blanks, even buying a nice home in the Hollywood Hills. It wasn't the kind of expenditure he wanted to make, as he couldn't afford to pay the full price. The down payment, however, was supplemented by a $25-a-week bonus for *You Never Know Women*, bringing his Paramount salary up to $250 a week.

Marjorie was not happy. She wanted to be a mother. When the doctors told her that she might never become pregnant, she talked of adoption. Wellman also wanted a family, but begged her to be patient and keep trying to have a child of their own. She would not wait and adopted a two-and-a-half-year-old daughter, Gloria. Wellman was disappointed and their marriage took a hit. He tried to make the best of it, but his work schedule did not allow him to be a proper father.

Wellman had been promising his wife a vacation, their first real vacation together. In July of 1926, Bill, Marjorie, and Gloria traveled to the Arrowhead Hot Springs Hotel in San Bernardino, California. During their stay, that magic telephone sprang into action. Wellman's spirits leaped high when the call came from Schulberg announcing his selection as the director of *Wings*. The vacation ended abruptly as Wellman returned to Paramount posthaste.

Before Wellman was hired, preproduction had been in progress for months. The producer had been signed, writers were developing the screenplay; the production team was being assembled without the knowledge or approval of their director. Even casting of the leading players was moving forward without a director on board. The first actor cast was superstar Clara Bow. Lasky wanted the biggest stars the studio had to offer as insurance against the huge financial risk. With a rewrite to improve her part, the cute, vivacious Clara was perfect for the role of Jack Powell's tomboy neighbor.

As in Bow's early family history, her *Wings* character must keep fighting in order to win the heart of Jack Powell, the love of her life. Her rise to the top resembled a street fight. Born in Brooklyn, New York, on July 29, 1905, to an impoverished and highly dysfunctional family of English, Scottish, and French descent, her early years were filled with conflict. At five feet, three and a half inches with bobbed, flaming red hair, nothing and nobody was going to stop her. At the age of seventeen, this 110 pounds of dynamite entered a *Fame and Fortune* fan magazine acting contest and won first prize. She received an evening gown, a silver trophy, and a screen test, which led to a screen contract. When her mother found out about the contest and her chosen career, she snuck into her daughter's bedroom and tried to slit her throat with a butcher knife. Clara awoke in time to defend herself and exit her wretched family life forever.

Her battles for stardom, however, did not end at home. In her screen debut in Metro's *Beyond the Rainbow* (1922), she suffered depression at being cut out of the picture. Her spirits were revived when a phone call from director Elmer Clifton, who had seen her photos, cast her in a small part in his *Down to the Sea in Ships* (1922). Her role called for her to be attacked, beaten, wrestled, and subjected to all sorts of physical abuse. Clifton liked her work so much that he built up the part, which led to a score of films and, eventually, a contract with B.P. Schulberg and Paramount Pictures. After 1927's *It*, she became a full-blown movie star.

In *It*, directed by Clarence Badger, Bow plays a high-energy, gold-digging department store salesgirl pursuing her attractive, high-class boss played by Antonio Moreno. Gary Cooper has an uncredited walk-on as a reporter. Before the film was produced, the word "it" and its meanings became a national conversation piece. The celebrated British author of erotic fiction, Elinor Glyn, had written a bestseller entitled *It*. Her book and the publicity campaign for the coming movie spread the phenomenon of *It* like a tsunami throughout the country—with Clara Bow riding the wave of popularity as the *It* girl.

Movie fans everywhere were discussing the term and the *It* girl. What exactly was *it*? What did *it* mean? How did Clara get *it*? Does anyone else have *it*? How long does *it* last?, etc., etc., etc. Everyone had their own ideas. *Webster's* wasn't much help: a term of reference to something indefinite but understood. When Madame Glyn explained that the use of *it* was a euphemism for sex appeal, people still thought that *it* meant much more than that. A feature article in *The Boston Post* for November 30, 1926, explained it all:

> The real meaning of "it," according to the English author, is that it is an invisible emanation which exudes from certain human beings rendering them irresistible to the opposite sex. . . . To make her explanation more clear, Madame Glyn has compiled a list of 10 things you must have to possess "it." Unless you score 100 per cent on each of them, you're definitely out of the running:
>
> 1. You must be free from all self-consciousness.
> 2. You must have that magnetic sex-appeal which is irresistible.
> 3. You must have complete self-confidence.
> 4. You must—if you are a man—give the impression unconsciously that you would be a masterful and passionate lover.
> 5. You must be indifferent to general opinion—but quite firm about your own.
> 6. You must give the impression that nothing on earth could influence or hold you unless you wished that it should.
> 7. You must have individuality.
> 8. You must be absolutely fearless.
> 9. You must be perfectly true to yourself, whether that self is good or bad, for no sham of any kind can have 'it.'
> 10. And last of all, you must be capable of deep and sincere love.

According to Madame Glyn, the quality of "it," is extremely rare among women—thousands of beautiful and physically attractive creatures who fascinate certain men, have no touch of "it." On the other hand, a girl considered homely by the usual standards of beauty may have "it," for it is a quality of mind as well as a magnetic emanation, and actual beauty has nothing to do with it. Among those who possess "it," Madame Glyn lists the following: Wallace Beery, John Gilbert, Douglas Fairbanks, the Prince of Wales, the King of Spain and Clara Bow.

Clara definitely had *it*, there were no dissenters. She represented the Roaring Twenties and was the model flapper of the Jazz Age.

Paramount Pictures announced that their marquee young stars Neil Hamilton and Charles Farrell would play the male leads in *Wings*. Hamilton's big break came in D. W. Griffith's *White Rose* (1923). By 1926, he was already an established star with seventeen features under his belt including Paramount's box office winner *Beau Geste* (1926). Farrell had made a big impact in *Clash of the Wolves* (1925), with dog star Rin Tin Tin, and *A Trip to Chinatown* (1926) before Paramount's high-budgeted *Old Ironsides* (1926).

Producer Lucien Hubbard wanted to replace Farrell with a well-praised youngster from their much publicized acting school at Astoria, New York, Charles "Buddy" Rogers. Next, the studio decided to cast Ralph Forbes, another star from *Beau Geste*, for the Farrell/Rogers role with Hamilton still clinging on to his part. The production team and studio executives continued to clash over casting. When Rogers heard that he was being dropped, he was so upset that he went to Lasky and asked out of his new contract. He told the studio boss that where he came from, Olathe, Kansas, things were different. "When a person says he's going to do something, he does it, and now, here I am, not making the picture." Lasky calmed him down by explaining the star system; the studio's huge investment; the cost of marketing, distribution, studio overhead; and how many theater tickets must be sold to return that investment. Lasky also mentioned the fact that Buddy was already set for another important picture.

The director arrived at Paramount Studios. As excited as he was at being the filmmaker of this monumental aviation epic, Wellman was not pleased with all the decisions made without his input. His first move was to throw out both Forbes and Hamilton, bringing back Buddy Rogers in the role of Jack Powell, the surviving hero of the movie. When Wellman met Rogers on the lot, Buddy's energetic, enthusiastic personality reminded him of his flying pals from the war. This casting event was not met with delight from the front office. "We not only gambled on an untried writer and an unknown director," said Lasky, "but parlayed the risk by starring a novice actor, Buddy Rogers, fresh out of our talent school."

Rogers grew up loving music. He learned to play many instruments, including piano, accordion, drums, trumpet, and trombone. His dream was to be the leader of his own band, and he did so in high school and at the University of Kansas. His father, publisher of a weekly newspaper, saw an advertisement by Paramount for an open audition for actors. He urged his good-looking, talented son to send photographs and a résumé. Rogers was six feet, one inch and 175 pounds, with brown eyes and black hair. Paramount answered right away and Buddy, as he was called, was on the train to New York and Paramount's acting school in Astoria, Queens.

He worked in two features produced at Paramount's New York studio, *Fascinating Youth* (1926) and Gregory LaCava's *So's Your Old Man* (1926) with W. C. Fields.

Because preproduction had been moving forward at such a rapid pace without a director, Wellman was far behind the *Wings* team. Having done two pictures at the studio, he already knew many of the crew. He wasted no time catching up in every area of the production process: writing, producers and production staff, assistant directors, photography, editors, art directors, set design and construction, script supervisors, stunts and stunt fliers, costuming and makeup, property managers, music, transportation, location, and so on.

The director and the writer hit it off from the opening bell. Wellman always believed that nothing was more important than the story and screenplay. The fact that he and Saunders spoke the same pilot's parlance was a plus. They spent much time together fashioning a story filled with Wild Bill's wartime experiences.

The producers, Hubbard and Schulberg, had been working on the picture for over four months, even handling normal director's chores. Now that Wellman was on board, friction began as to where to draw the line between the producers' and director's roles. The salient question was who had the last word. Even though Wellman was the new kid on the block, he wasn't going to back down to any producer, studio executive, to Lasky, or even to Adolph Zukor in New York. Wellman's attitude was quite simple: *Wings* was now his film, his big opportunity, and he wasn't going to do anything that wasn't in its best interests.

The producers accepted the reality that this youthful, undertested director was captain of their ship. They wanted to please him, but also expected that their more experienced voices would be heard and ratified. It was Wellman's contention that the producers would take care of the business and financial ends, making available enough resources for him to get the production values he needed on the screen . . . and stay out of his domain. The producers were responsible for keeping the budget in line. The major budgetary stumbling block to come would arise from the fact that since no aerial warfare on this scale had ever been produced, the costs were only guesstimates.

Before 1926, there had been some aerial warfare work in cheaply produced aviation dramas. Some flying footage was gathered from independent sources, government-financed films, and with the use of miniatures. Actors were never seen in actual flight. When an actor or stunt pilot was seen in the air, that footage was actually shot on the ground to simulate flight.

Throughout his career, Wellman talked and wrote about the chief cameraman being his right arm. Harry Perry took that important place on *Wings*. He had earned a reputation in Hollywood by photographing aerial sequences for such non–World War I flying films as *The Broken Wing* (1923) and *The Fighting American* (1924). Wellman and Perry had countless meetings to discuss the daunting task of creating a whole new dimension in aerial photography. They decided that at least a dozen cameramen, including Perry, would be needed to bring the story values to the screen. They set out to find as many cameramen as possible who had flight experience.

With all this intense preproduction, Wellman had little time for his wife and daughter. Because of Gloria, Marjorie would not be at her husband's side as script supervisor. It was hoped that the family would be united during the location shooting.

The War Department, with Paramount Pictures' approval, had named San Antonio, Texas, as the location site. Even though Wellman was not a party to this choice, he liked it. From his days as a pilot to his time in Hollywood, San Antonio had been talked about as "another Hollywood," and many films had been shot there. As early as 1910, Gaston Méliès and his Star Film Company went searching for a place where filming could be done all year long. He said goodbye to New York's harsh winters, settling in the Texas city on a twenty-acre parcel. The Star Film Ranch was the first movie studio in San Antonio. Star Films produced over 70 of the more than 110 pictures made there prior to 1926.

The city received much notice when King Vidor chose it to film some of the most important scenes for his *The Big Parade* (1925). Wellman remembered *Parade* as *the* picture of the year. "I saw it twenty-two times until I knew every cut and, I thought, every reason for it. I lay in bed and tried to figure out how I could have topped King Vidor in his direction. I had no success."

Wellman knew about San Antonio's pleasing climate, picturesque landscapes, close proximity to military bases, and immense property owned by the government. It was time to travel there and pick the exact locations so that construction could begin turning the Texas landscape into France with its airfields and battlefields. He put a stop to all further casting until his return. With Lucien Hubbard and John Monk Saunders, Wellman left for San Antonio. A local pilot flew the threesome and a location scout

St. Mihiel! The only difference is that this picture was taken some fifteen miles from San Antonio, Texas, where an exact duplicate of the famous original has been constructed for the mammoth battle sequences in *Wings* (1927), a Lucian Hubbard production, which William Wellman is directing for Paramount. The area covers five square miles. Members of the cast of *Wings* are Clara Bow, Charles Rogers, Richard Arlen, El Brendel, Richard Tucker, "Gunboat" Smith, and Gary Cooper.

Buddy Rogers, Clara Bow, Richard Arlen

over an eight-hundred-square-mile area of government land, researching sites for Allied and enemy airstrips, the French village and climactic battle re-creating the famous St. Mihiel offensive. Once the sites were found, hundreds of Mexican laborers, working with army artillery experts, tore great shell craters in the fields, dug a network of trenches, strung miles of barbed wire, creating a battlefield a mile and a half long. Many of the same workforce, along with studio art directors, set designers, and construction crew, fashioned an authentic French village. Army engineers laid miles of telephone wires connecting all parts of the field and village. Two one-hundred-foot towers were built over the field for the cameras. Flying over the finished work, Wellman was shocked and saddened. He was said to have uttered, "Goddamn, I'm back in France."

While Wellman was gone, his friend and assistant director on *Wings*, Charles Barton, secretly screen-tested Richard Arlen. Barton had previously suggested the actor, but Wellman didn't want another relative unknown in one of the leads, as he was already weathering the studio's resentment over the dismissal of their star for the newcomer Rogers. When Barton showed Arlen's test to his director, Wellman exclaimed, "Jesus Christ! Who's that good-looking son of a bitch?" When Barton owned up to his underhanded dealing, Wellman went from anger to gratitude. The director saw something special in the actor, and he cast Richard Arlen in the role of David Armstrong.

Arlen was born Sylvanus Richard Van Mattimore on September 1, 1899, in Charlottesville, Virginia. He began his film career as an extra before two acting roles in *Ladies Must Lie* (1921) and *Vengeance of the Deep* (1923). A big break came with an important role in *Volcano* (1926), but after only eight days in production he was fired. He persevered through a series of supporting roles until *Wings*. Arlen was five feet, ten inches and 150 pounds, with brown hair and blue eyes.

Although Wellman was satisfied with his three leads, Lasky and his executives were becoming more and more bitter toward this brash young director for accepting only one bona fide star, Clara Bow, in their ultra-expensive road show picture. Because no air picture of this magnitude—or anywhere close—had ever been attempted, the budget was difficult to nail down, and soon the preliminary budget of $1.2 million began climbing toward the biggest budget of all time.

There were fifteen supporting roles for Wellman to cast from the studio; the rest of the small parts, including pilots seen on screen, would be filled by locals, service personnel, and stunt fliers. The most important supporting player would take the role of the alluring, high-class Sylvia

Gary Cooper in *Wings*

Lewis, the centerpiece of the romantic triangle. Wellman chose Jobyna Ralston, who had captivated Harold Lloyd, becoming his leading lady in a series of films including *The Freshman* (1925). In *Wings*, she was so accomplished at playing the object of David Armstrong's fascination that she and Richard Arlen were married after the completion of the film.

During this frenetic period of casting, Wellman was on the lookout for a very special actor to play a very special small but important role, Cadet White. The young flier represents the film's first look at the tragedy of war. The recruits, played by Arlen and Rogers, are tent-mates of the more advanced Cadet White. On a simple training mission, White is killed and the recruits are stunned and grief-stricken. Wellman singled out this role, not only due to its story significance, but because it reminded him of his Avord pal Billy Meeker, who died in the same manner. This author believes that this is one of the scenes Wellman inserted into the film.

The actor receiving this role would have to be gifted with movie star charisma—the *it* man. He would need to make an instantaneous and permanent impression on the audience in just one scene. His only assistance would come from the on-screen words, "I've got to go up and do a flock of eights before chow" and "Luck or no luck, when your time comes, you're going to get it."

Wellman had met a tall, rangy, self-conscious actor on the lot who fit the director's idea for Cadet White. He was six feet, three inches, 175 pounds, with brown hair and light blue eyes. He may have reminded Wellman of Billy Meeker or even Wild Bill's wartime buddy Reginald "Duke" Sinclaire, who was well over six feet, gangly, and shy. The director cast Frank James Cooper, who became Gary Cooper.

"Coop" as he was often called, made his first appearance on May 7, 1901, in Helena, Montana. Cowboys and Indians still roamed the territory. Much of Gary's early childhood adventures occurred on the ranch his father, Charles, bought when Gary was five years old. He saw the likes of cattle rustlers, horse thieves, bordellos, and barroom brawls.

Coop's strict English parents suffered some years of poverty with the ranch, but Gary and his five-year-older brother, Arthur, found the outdoor life a paradise. However, their mother, Alice, never liked Montana or her sons' cowboy ways. In an attempt to refine their rough edges and broaden their culture, in the summer of 1909 Mom took her boys to England, enrolling them in a suitable school at Dunstable in Kent. Gary was homesick and endured three years of trying to become a proper young gentleman.

Back in Helena, Gary decided to pursue a dream—to become a commercial artist, as he admired the Western artists Frederic Remington and Charles M. Russell, the latter a friend of his father's.

In 1916, an automobile accident nearly took Cooper's life. He recovered and continued his career choice. He entered Grinnell College in Iowa as an art major, which led to a job as an illustrator and cartoonist in Helena. He was happy with his job, the ranch life, being at home in the small town, and . . . his pretty, curly-haired, strong-minded college heartthrob, Doris Virden. She was Coop's first love and dreamed of bigger things for her man and their life together. She encouraged Gary to leave his pleasant but humble existence for the chance of success in the big city. It was Coop's parents and his girlfriend who motivated him to take the plunge. On November 27, 1924, Cooper arrived in the City of Angels.

City editors, unfortunately, did not appreciate Coop's artistry. He struggled for acceptance with a string of unsuccessful jobs. Thinking himself a failure, he stopped writing Doris. As a last resort before going back to Helena, he went to the Hollywood studios and signed up as an extra in Westerns. He knew nothing about the film industry, but felt secure with his riding and cowboy skills. He was able to get work but the pay was only $5 a day. As his self-assurance grew, so did the quality of his jobs. He saved $65 for his own screen test—with his mother cranking the camera. In the test, he rode up on horseback, looked into the camera,

(Left to right): Maj. J. E. Cheney, commanding officer at Brooks Field; Wellman; Brig. Gen. Frank P. Lahm, commander, Air Service, Eighth Corps Area; John Monk Saunders; Maj. F. M. Andrews, commanding officer, Kelly Field; Lucien Hubbard, 1926

made a showy dismount, looked at the camera again, then ambled into a saloon. One day while sitting outside a casting director's office, he was noticed by director Henry King, who was preparing a Western, *The Winning of Barbara Worth* (1926) starring Ronald Colman and Vilma Banky. After viewing Coop's test, King signed him as one of the ten riders going on location for $50 a week.

Cooper's first acting role gave him renewed courage to start writing Doris again. His elation was short-lived as he discovered that his beloved had given up on him and married a local druggist. If it wasn't for *The Winning of Barbara Worth*, Gary Cooper might have given up Hollywood and returned to the placid life he had known in Montana. The film gave him the self-assurance to continue—and just around the corner came Wellman and *Wings*. Years later, after Coop became a star, one of his costars, Fay Wray, received a long letter from Doris explaining how much she had missed him and wanted him back. They never reunited, and Doris died of throat cancer in 1934.

We owe Gary's hometown sweetheart and his parents a debt of gratitude. If Charles and Alice Cooper had not moved to Los Angeles, and Doris Virden had not dreamed of greater goals for her lover, Gary Cooper

San Antonio welcomes the *Wings* company (left to right): Roscoe Karns and El Brendel, featured players; Lucien Hubbard, producer; Richard Arlen holding Gloria; Wellman; John Tobin, mayor; John Monk Saunders, author; Richard Tucker, actor; Buddy Rogers; Phil Wright, commissioner.

might never have crossed the Montana plains to the bright lights of Hollywood—and millions of fans over the many decades since would never have seen the tall, handsome, blue-eyed blending of an English gentleman and a rugged Montana cowboy, becoming a national icon symbolizing the American ideals of self-reliance, independence, courage, and integrity.

By the time the 1926 calendar pages had flipped over to the month of September, there had been six months of preproduction. The *Wings* company was now firmly entrenched in Texas. Paramount's construction team, army engineers, hundreds of local laborers, the various production departments, and Wellman on multiple trips had readied the location sites for filming. Preparations had been completed for all transportation, housing and production company facilities, food services, medical, entertainment, everything necessary for the many months of production.

The War Department had given their full support with $16 million worth of manpower and equipment, and the *Wings* budget would soon reach $2 million—the most expensive budget of all time! It was time for the massive assemblage in the "New Hollywood" of San Antonio, Texas.

8

BATTLEFIELD *WINGS*

Paramount Pictures' army of two hundred employees with their equipment was joined in San Antonio by some five thousand soldiers of the 2nd Division, who would be deployed in the re-creation of the St. Mihiel battle and other sequences. Additional troops came from the 15th Field Artillery and 2nd Engineers, the 12th Field Artillery, and the 3rd and 4th Brigades.

The film required so many men that the guardhouses on military bases were temporarily closed and the prisoners were released to serve in the epic conflicts. Pilots, mechanics, crews, ground administration, and aircraft came from Selfridge Field, Michigan; Crissy Field, California; Langley Field, Virginia, and Brooks Field, San Antonio. Balloon pilots, officers, crew, and equipment were imported from Scott Field, Illinois. Artillery, tanks, troops, wire, and high explosives came from Fort Sam Houston, in San Antonio.

The Paramount company stayed at the ten-story, 352-room St. Anthony Hotel, built in 1909 in the downtown section. "We were there for nine months," said Wellman. "I know that was the correct time because the elevator operators were girls and they all became pregnant. They were replaced by old men, and the company's hunting grounds were barren."

Another Paramount picture, *The Rough Riders* (1927), directed by Victor Fleming, was shooting in San Antonio at the same time, and their combatants were also at the St. Anthony. "San Antonio became the Armageddon of a magnificent sexual Donnybrook," said Wellman. "The town was lousy with movie people, and if you think that contributes to a state of tranquility, you don't know your motion picture ABC's. . . . We are monkeys in a weird cage. . . . A motion picture company lives hard and plays hard, and they better or they will all go nuts."

Clara Bow received twenty thousand fan letters a week. She was recognized wherever she went—in whatever country, state, city, or hamlet—and San Antonio was no exception. If Clara was there, crowds gathered to see the fetching, high-spirited, cute-as-a-button *It* girl. She was everybody's heart's desire. Extra security had to be hired for her: to and from the hotel including her favorite walks on the cobblestone path along the San Antonio River, at the various film locations . . . everywhere she went. Bow adored life. She loved the spotlight, her movie work, and, especially, men. Wellman described her: "To begin with, all the young actors in *The Rough Riders* and *Wings* fell in love with Clara Bow, and if you had known her, you could understand why. This presented a problem to both Vic Fleming and me, but a far greater problem to Miss Bow. She took care of it—how I will never know. She kept Cooper, Rogers, Arlen, Mack [*Rough Riders* star Charles Mack], and a few whose names I can't remember, plus a couple of pursuit pilots from Selfridge Field and a panting writer, all in line. They were handled like chessmen, never running into one another, never suspecting that there was any other man in the whole world that meant a thing to this gorgeous little sexpot—and all this expert maneuvering in a hotel where most of the flame was burning."

The time finally came when the *It* girl decided to end the cat-and-mice game, naming her *it* man as *Rough Rider* director Victor Fleming. She announced their engagement to the company. This revelation sent shock waves through the St. Anthony Hotel, but, of course, the show went on. There were other fires burning within the *Wings* production. Jealousies broke out between the army and the air force, the service personnel and the movie people. Wellman was there from the beginning, his very first night at the St. Anthony. A gala dinner party had been arranged by Paramount, via Lucien Hubbard, to introduce the director to the high-ranking military men and their wives. The top brass, wearing their military best, were seated at long tables waiting to inspect the boyish-looking former fighter pilot who was going to direct this masterpiece of military might. The generals, colonels, majors, and captains were suspicious of a sergeant in the army of France having the command of them and their troops. Word had spread that Wellman's age was under question, as was his branch of combat service in the Foreign Legion and Lafayette Flying Corps.

When Wellman made his entrance, he was not wearing a tie and his hair had not been cut for weeks—he had a superstition never to have

The maverick filmmaker and flier prepares for the battle of invention.

a haircut during production. Upon seeing Wellman, the officers began to stand up out of respect. The highest-ranking general took a look at Wild Bill and immediately sat down. The other officers followed suit and began eating their first course of fruit cocktails. Wellman, feeling the tension, seated himself between Hubbard and Saunders. He looked around the room, then lowered his head and clasped his hands in silent prayer. This display was noticed by all. Some of the wives whispered to their husbands. The first impression meter stopped dropping and started an upward move.

Lucien Hubbard introduced the young director, who stood and began a short speech.

Wellman reminisced:

> I started right out by telling them that the correct thing to say would be that I was very happy and honoured to be here. That is the correct way. The truthful way is that I am not happy and not honoured to be here, but since there seems to be great doubt of my ability because of my age, I would like to defend myself. . . . I was born on 29 February 1896, leap year, which makes me seven years old. For one so young I have lived a

tremendously interesting life. I have been married, not once but twice, I have flown at the front with some success, I have been in two armies, including the Foreign Legion, I have made moving pictures, and I know Clara Bow. . . . Perhaps the most prosperous producing company in the motion-picture business is the Paramount Pictures Corporation. The idiots that have been so successful in the development of a multimillion-dollar industry have appointed a seven-year-old to guide the destiny of this, their most important project. Quite naturally, one so young must be considered in the category of genius and because of his infancy must be given unending help and encouragement. I stand before you as that prodigy and in all humility request the decency and the support that is due him; and I sat down.

There was a long moment of silence in the dining room, then the ranking general's wife started the applause that spread through the room like a wave. It lasted for several minutes. The waiters were the last to stop. During the party afterward, Wellman was approached by the applauding wife of the commanding general. She asked, "Were you really saying grace, or better still, can you say grace?" Wellman looked her straight in the eye and said, "No." She continued, "You are an amazing young man, and I like you."

Because of Wellman's history as a pilot, he was accepted by the air force; the army was another matter. "In command was a general who had two monumental hatreds: fliers and movie people," said Wellman. "I could get nowhere with the old boy until I reminded him that whether he liked it or not, he was working for Paramount Pictures and that I, despite my age, was the director of the Paramount Picture called *Wings* and brought a copy of the orders as a convincer. It convinced. The old boy was still in the army."

Due to the lack of aerial footage shot for previous Hollywood films, Wellman and his cameraman, Harry Perry, had to write a new book, create a new technology for warfare shot in the skies. Experimentation and trial and error were the rule while Paramount dollars spilled over their budget.

During the first two months of *Wings* filming, Wellman threw away nearly all of the aerial footage. "It didn't look real. It looked like a lot of goddam flies up there!" In order to capture an airplane's true motion and speed, a backdrop of clouds was absolutely necessary. Many weeks of dull gray skies added to the unacceptable visuals. In addition, director and cameraman had not been able to develop a successful technique for

Harry Perry with camera mounted on wing, Wellman, and stunt pilot (unnamed)

shooting close-ups of the airborne actors in their cockpits. In previous films, actors were always shot on the ground to simulate being in the air. On numerous occasions, Wellman and Perry took to the skies to work out the problems.

As the weeks fluttered by, Paramount executives became more unhappy with Wellman's passion for realism. They didn't understand why their director could not shoot footage during the many days without rain. The long-distance phone calls became incessant, and Wellman began to lose patience with the executive interference. At first, he tried to explain the problems, then he handed it over to producer Hubbard. When the interruptions continued, Wellman stopped talking to the studio executives altogether. Hubbard, the link between the studio and the location, tried to support his director but, not being a flier, had trouble understanding the total situation. The producer believed some of the flying footage was acceptable, but Wellman would not back down. When the studio discussed firing Wellman, Hubbard fought for more time to work out the issues. Meanwhile, Wellman was shooting some of the nonflying scenes, but falling behind the schedule and over-budget.

Hand-cranked and battery-driven cameras were standard for the era. The newest motor-driven cameras were unveiled for *Wings*, but opera-

The *Wings* cameramen and their assistants

tors preferred the older method of turning by hand because they could control the speed of the action by cranking faster or slower. The motorized camera filmed at a constant speed. Early attempts found *Wings* cameramen hand-holding and cranking the cameras while flying next to the picture planes. The simultaneous camera and airplane movements distorted the image. The lightweight crafts shuddered and shook with the wind, up and down, side to side, to and fro, resulting in a shot that was unwatchable, even dizzying to the eye of the audience. Fastening the camera to the fuselage of the camera plane helped but did not solve the problem.

Wellman believed that one of Perry's operators saved the picture. E. Burton Steene was considered the best aerial photographer of the day. "He had a camera with an Akeley head," said Wellman, "which means that it had gears, a pan handle and a frightening whine to it as Burton panned up or down or from side to side. For 1926, it was unbelievable and Burton was so expert at it, he shot ninety percent of all the air scenes in *Wings*."

Another problem was how to film the actors as if they were flying the planes. When the camera plane got close to the picture plane, you could see that a stunt pilot, not the actor, was doing the flying. Wellman

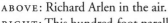

ABOVE: Richard Arlen in the air.
RIGHT: This hundred-foot parallel, one of the largest ever constructed, overlooks a battle area of five miles square

tried shooting close-ups on the ground to simulate being in the air, but they looked fake. Eventually, the director and his right-hand man, Harry Perry, made some formidable and precedent-setting decisions:

Camera mounts would be created and secured to the fuselages of the planes.

For close-ups, motor-driven cameras would be mounted in front of two-cockpit planes or behind the rear cockpit. The director would give his instructions on the ground. Once airborne, a safety pilot in the front cockpit would waggle the wings as a sign that all was ready, then duck down or hide behind a large headrest, and the actor would turn on the camera, pilot the plane, and perform.

During the camera take, while the camera was still running, the actor would hold up the proper number of fingers designating takes one, two, or three. If he thought the scene was bad, he would run a finger across his throat for a cut.

Platforms and up to one-hundred-foot towers would be constructed to photograph the low-flying aircraft and ground warfare.

Thirteen first cameramen and their assistants would be necessary to film the aerial and ground sequences.

There would be no fakery in filming actors flying. Buddy Rogers and Richard Arlen would learn to fly.

Richard Arlen had been in the Canadian Royal Flying Corps, with some actual flying experience. Buddy Rogers had none. "Rogers was a tough son of a bitch," said Wellman. "He hated flying, which made him sick. He logged over ninety-eight hours in the picture and every time he came down, he vomited. That's a man with guts. I love him." Both stars received but a few hours of instruction. Rogers reflected, "I was the photographer, the director, the actor, everything . . . for five hundred feet." The cameras held four-hundred-foot reels, which ran off at about ninety feet a minute, giving a little more than four minutes of picture.

When the studio found out that the actors were receiving flying instructions, they became irate—their "green" $250-a-week director was going to kill their stars. They sent an executive down to the location to demand that Wellman start shooting the aerial work—clouds or no clouds—and stop giving Arlen and Rogers flying lessons. Wild Bill listened to the studio executive's orders, then offered two choices: "A trip home or a trip to the hospital." The executive went home.

The director was still subservient to the weather. While waiting for clouds, Perry and his assistants tried to invent them. They placed white cotton balls on thin pieces of thread in front of the camera lens. Unfortunately, when the camera moved so did their cloud balls. Even when the camera was stationary, the effect looked unrealistic. They sent up skywriters in an attempt to create imitation clouds—their clouds disintegrated too quickly. None of these tricks worked.

During the weather waits, the Hollywood crew played tackle football on the concrete runways against army and air force teams. Wellman, as he had done in high school, was the quarterback. Arlen and Rogers were halfbacks, and the guy catching the passes was named Cooper. William Clothier, one of the cameramen, who went on to major cinematography status with Wellman as well as John Ford and John Wayne, played center. Clothier later boasted, "The movie company always won."

Paramount was now more upset than ever. If their director didn't kill the actors flying, he would certainly break their arms and legs playing football. Other pressing matters came Wellman's way that had nothing to do with directing a movie. He and Hubbard were continually working to settle problems and politics with the army and air corps. To keep the impatient service personnel happy and content during the downtime, the company also provided first-run movies, barbecues, and dances. The army and air force brass joined Paramount in displeasure. They did not send their troops to San Antonio to play football, attend beer parties, and step to the music.

Some crew problems surfaced. There was a steady stream of firings and hirings. The unit manager was skimming money off the top. He would purchase lumber for the construction of sets, then sell it back to the company at a higher price. Wellman's friend and assistant property man, Charlie Barton, was promoted at least three times, ending up as first assistant director.

The army, the air force, the War Department, Paramount were all lining up against the young director. It seemed just a question of time before he would be fired. Lucien Hubbard was still supporting him, and B.P. Schulberg, back in Hollywood, was caught in the middle. Studio bosses Lasky and Zukor, and the New York bankers, were questioning B.P.'s promise to control the defiant young director. Wellman badly needed their support, but made it unmistakably clear that this was his picture now and, whatever the cost, he would do what he thought best for *Wings*.

Gary Cooper presented another kind of over-budget and weather problem for Paramount. As usual, Wellman was at the heart of it—he wouldn't shoot Coop's one scene, keeping him on salary for many weeks. The scene was to take place inside an army tent. The tent could be assembled and the scene shot at any time, at any location, rain or shine, blue or gray skies, clouds or no clouds. "This was a travelling tent," said the director, "an emergency set to be used when all else failed or at my discretion. My discretion was influenced by a growing fondness for this awkward, lovable guy. He was broke, needed a break, and the longer his engagement on *Wings*, the more important his part looked to those back in Hollywood."

Wellman and his often-used sign

Charlie Barton, new assistant director, with signal flags for fliers
and crew

When the time to film Cooper's scene finally came, Wellman scheduled a rehearsal in his hotel suite the night before. The rehearsal went
well, the director remarked, "because he was very natural and very good."
When the scene was shot the next day, Coop was also very good. His
character, Cadet White, is admired by tent-mates Arlen's and Rogers's
characters as the more veteran flier. As he leaves the tent, he stops at the
entrance, turns back and salutes the new recruits, smiles, and exits. Cadet
White is killed on the training flight and the recruits feel the tragedy. "To
be remembered," said Wellman, "Coop not only must salute and smile,
but he must have something unusual about him, that indescribable thing
called motion-picture personality, to make it that effective that quickly.
Don't ask me what it is or how you get it, because I don't think you can
get it. If you have it, it came to you, and you're lucky as hell. . . . Cooper
had it."

That evening, Cooper came to his director's suite. Wellman thought to
say goodbye, but Coop was not finished. He was uncomfortable, embarrassed, shy. "You know I appreciate everything you have done for me, and
I'll never forget it, and, and, and I haven't any right to ask this but, but,
but couldn't I do that scene over again?" He relaxed as if a great burden
had been removed from him. Wellman was surprised and said that he was
the director and thought the scene was perfect. He asked what Coop did
not like about it. The actor said, "Well, you know right in the middle of

Wellman's wife, Marjorie, and daughter, Gloria, have roles in *Wings*.

the scene, I, I kinda picked my nose and, and—" "Just a minute, Coop," interrupted Wellman. "You keep right on picking your nose, and you will pick yourself into a fortune—and just one more thing, always back away from the problems, from the heavy, and, above all, from the girl. Make them pursue you. Never, but never be the aggressor." Wellman was show-ing early signs of his visionary talent as a star maker.

With all the activity, agitation, tension, and turmoil, Wellman had little time for his family. Marjorie and little Gloria made several trips to San Antonio but they were mostly on their own. Gloria was a big hit around the company and became a kind of mascot. In trying to keep his wife in the loop, Wellman found a role for her as a French peasant with a daughter who lives in the farmhouse where the climactic death scene between Arlen and Rogers takes place.

The central theme of *Wings* concerns the relationship between Arlen's David Armstrong and Rogers's Jack Powell. They are rivals before becom-ing buddies. In real life, they were competitors. They respected but only tolerated each other. They were the two male leads, the costars of the film. Off screen, they were adversaries for the affections of Clara Bow. In the *Wings* story, the turning point occurs as a result of a training camp boxing match when Rogers beats up Arlen but admires his courage.

Before the fisticuffs were shot, Arlen told Wellman, "I know how to box and Rogers doesn't. Tell him to be careful and I won't hurt him."

Stunt pilot Dick Grace and Wellman begin a successful friendship in *Wings*.

Instead, the director told Buddy that Arlen had it in for him and was going to pummel him. When Wellman called "Action!" the fight choreography soon turned into a battle royal, and Rogers, just as in the script, beat the hell out of Arlen on guts alone.

In spite of all the production problems, camaraderie flowed on the set. There were many days when the discord disappeared into an atmosphere of fun and frolic along with the hard work and long hours. There was a feeling of team spirit with the director, his crew, the cast, their producer, and, especially, the stuntmen. Their enthusiasm was contagious. The script was filled with stunts: boxing matches, fistfights, hand-to-hand combats; battle scenes with hundreds of soldiers walking, running, diving into trenches, being shot, burned, gassed, and blown up; parachute leaps from observation balloons; vehicle collisions and wrecks; every imaginable plane crash into houses, trees, rivers, other planes, and mother earth.

Seventeen stuntmen graced the payroll pages, and other less dangerous stunts would be performed by the service personnel. The stunt flier list included future generals: Hoyt Vandenberg, destined to become air force chief of staff in 1948; Frank Andrews, Hal George, Carl E. Partridge, Clarence "Bill" Irvine, Bill Taylor, and Rod Rogers. From Hollywood came Frank Tomick, a former army flier, who would be the chief pilot and aerial coordinator. Assisting him were Frank Clark, Ross Cooke, and the most celebrated stunt pilot of the silent era, Dick Grace. Other stunt fliers: Hal George; Al Wilson; Clinton Herberger; S. R. Stribling; Earl H. "Robbie" Robinson; Buddy Rogers's plane pilot, Thomas H. Chapman; and the soon-to-be-legendary Paul Mantz.

When World War I ended in November 1918, many young fliers left the air services to find other ways to use their skills and experience. At the same time, scores of military aircraft became available as surplus. Some of those ex-servicemen became famous as barnstorming pilots, performing their stunts in flying circuses, at carnivals and fairs, and joyriding throughout the country.

One of the best-known exhibition pilots who went from barnstorming to the movies was Ormer Locklear. He hit the national headlines with history's first midair transfer from one plane to another—without a parachute. His talents were the envy

Buddy Rogers and Richard Arlen

of the show business community and Hollywood came calling. In his own film, *The Great Air Robbery* (1919), he offered many of his best-known stunts including another history maker, a plane-to-car-to-plane transfer. On August 12, 1920, he and his fellow pilot, Milton Elliott, were killed doing a night dive in Locklear's second film, *The Skywayman*. Their plane, a Jenny, had ten magnesium flares totaling 30,000 candlepower attached to the canvas and wood wings. During the dive from two thousand feet, the flares were ignited by a "hot shot" battery. At the same time, five stationary sun-arc lights, totaling half a million candlepower, were turned on from the field and trained at the diving Jenny. They were to be extinguished when the craft reached five hundred feet from the ground. Instead, all five searchlight beams remained on, blinding the pilots. Like a flaming meteor, the plane crashed and burned.

No one did more to promote aviation in the period between 1918 and his air crash death in 1923 than Beverly Homer "Daredevil" DeLay. He established the first lighted airport in the United States, and initiated the

The plane that broke Dick Grace's neck

first aerial police. Some of his air show feats included the nosedive, ghost dive, Immelmann turn (defensive air battle maneuver), barrel rolls, tail spins, multiple loop-the-loops, mock battles, racing, flying fireworks, wing walking, and plane changing. DeLay is credited with the movies' first saddle-to-plane, auto-to-plane, and plane-to-train-to-plane transfers. In the process he compiled more than fifty movie credits.

Before 1926, wartime-filmed dramatizations of the air war were few and relied heavily on miniatures and simulations. The world of stunt fliers in feature motion pictures was small. It wasn't until 1924 that the first stunt fliers association was formed: The 13 Black Cats.

The noted aviation authority James H. Farmer, in his *Celluloid Wings,* writes: "The fact that not a single major feature-length American film dealing directly with wartime aviation was produced before 1926, suggests something of the dangers and technical problems, not to mention production costs, involved in flying and filming air-to-air any sizable number of period aircraft."

For *Wings,* Wellman had gathered up some of the best stunt fliers with motion picture experience and added his own personal expertise. He filled the tank of a German Fokker D.VII with only a small amount of gasoline to avoid setting himself on fire, strapped himself into the cockpit, and with the help of two crew members started the engine, was pushed out to the airstrip, and off he went. He flew around the field a couple of times before crashing the plane, flipping it over upside down. He unstrapped himself, dropped to the ground, and trotted over to his stunt fliers saying, "That's how you do it! And always remember to duck your head when you hit the ground. The goddamn plane will roll over on its own."

Even though the stunts were carefully prepared and carried out with precision, it is still amazing that the only serious injury to any of the stuntmen was to the fabled Dick Grace. He had performed such an array of difficult crashes in the film before his luck ran out on one of the less dangerous stunts. In the scene, he was to take off in his Fokker, then, pretending to be strafed by Richard Arlen in a stolen Fokker, crash-land back on the airstrip. Grace's Fokker had a ruggedly built steel tube fuselage. Mechanics had cut the structure in strategic places—the wings, fuselage, landing gear—so the aircraft would break apart on impact, thereby lessening the force of the crash on the pilot.

Unfortunately, while Grace's speed of 110 mph did not cause the plane to break apart, the force did cause his safety harness to separate, throwing him headfirst into the instrument panel. He crawled out of the wreck and waved to everyone that he was okay, even had photos taken with Wellman and Lucien Hubbard. Soon after, he collapsed and was taken to the hospital at Fort Sam Houston. His first and second cervical vertebrae were crushed together, as were the fourth and fifth. The sixth was dislocated. The large bone in his chest was fractured. A cast was placed around his neck and he was told to keep it on for a year.

"Six weeks later," said Wellman, "I walked into the dance hall at the Saint Anthony, to find the crazy son of a bitch on the dance floor, dancing up a storm." Grace had taken a hammer, broken the cast, and never wore it again.

Frank Tomick nearly lost his life in another accident when a series of small aerial bombs were dropped from a plane some three thousand feet above. The explosives were simulating an ack-ack (antiaircraft) attack and some of them exploded near his Fokker D.VII. His wing and aileron were badly damaged and he was barely able to land the aircraft. He was not injured.

Sadly, there was one fatality during the making of *Wings*. An army pilot, Cadet Charles M. Wiseley, was killed during a scene when he lost control of his plane and died on impact. He was listed as killed in the line of duty and was buried with full military honors on October 26, 1926. His parents received $10,000 from Paramount Pictures.

The two biggest war scenes were still left on the schedule: the re-creation of the battle of St. Mihiel and the great dogfight in the clouds. Paramount had reached the end of their patience and were again considering firing their director. Their problem was threefold: Who would be his replacement? Who would understand and be able to put it all together? How much more money would be lost in the turnaround? Zukor, Lasky, and Schulberg decided to send the three major financiers from New York with the power to dismiss the director if that was their decision. As if more drama was necessary, the air corps presented Paramount with an ultimatum. To date, there had been one fatality and two accidental crashes by air corps pilots. Neither flier was seriously hurt but the planes were destroyed. The ultimatum was that if there was one more wreck or serious injury to any of their pilots or troops, they would withdraw their personnel and equipment. Wellman remarked, "The whole damned picture would go down the drain."

St. Mihiel was up first, although inclement weather was causing further delays. History's four-day battle involved the American Expeditionary Force and 48,000 French troops under the command of General Pershing. The campaign was part of a plan by Pershing in which his troops would break through the German lines and capture the fortified city of Metz. It was one of the first U.S. offensives in World War I. St. Mihiel was also the greatest air combat of the Great War. Under the command of American colonel William "Billy" Mitchell, 1,476 Allied planes participated in the action—the largest mobilization to that time. They were opposed by some five hundred German aircraft.

The attack began on September 12, 1918. The U.S. troops captured St. Mihiel and cut off the retreating Germans on the first day. Pershing's detailed plan had two tank companies supporting the advancing infantry with a third tank company in reserve. The Americans reached their first day's objective before noon, and the second day's objective by late afternoon. Two American regiments took more than sixteen thousand prisoners, suffering fewer than 7,500 casualties. The battle of St. Mihiel was a crowning success. The German army was severely crippled, and the Allies took control of the skies.

Wellman could wait no longer for his St. Mihiel. For ten days, he had been rehearsing the 3,500 troops, 165 airplanes, and the demolition of dozens of preset explosive charges over a five-square-mile battlefield complete with miles of barbed wire, a network of trenches, and scores of authentic shell holes provided by the big artillery guns of the 2nd Division.

Wellman had spent $300,000 of the studio's money for this climactic sequence. He had constructed a hundred-foot tower with parallels built in a triangular setting. Camera positions were erected at the apex of the triangle and at various distances down either side. At the seventy-five-foot level, he would be operating the demolition buttons from an organlike board. He alone would be the button pusher that controlled and positioned the creeping barrage that preceded the advancing wave of doughboys.

There were seventeen first cameramen and their crews operating manual cameras while twenty-eight remote-controlled cameras would photograph individual pieces of action in the air and on the ground. The

Re-creation of the famous battle of St. Mihiel

filming of the entire scene would last but five minutes and . . . it would be a "onetime" take.

The day dawned solid overcast. The entire company gathered at the location site near old Camp Stanley to prepare and wait for a break in the weather. It would be a day of profound remembrance for many of the older members of the 2nd Division who had fought in the actual battle. Wellman would add his own tragic reminder of his hometown flying buddy, David Putnam, who was killed on the second day of that combat.

"The day had been set and arrived," said Wellman. "Everything was ready, everything but the weather. We needed sunshine, bright sunshine, because in those days we did not have the fast film of today. We were in the lap of the gods." Wellman considered himself a weatherman—"a sky-gazer," as he called it. During his days as a pursuit pilot, it could be the difference between life or death to predict how long a cloud layer might last so that he could find safety in its protective blanket and away from enemy planes and ground observation. The same kind of instinct was helpful to him in directing outdoor scenes, when a ray of sunlight was preferable over a veil of darkness.

The atmosphere on the set that day was filled with tension. "You can imagine my position and the condition of my not-to-be-trusted stomach," said the director. "I was sick, couldn't keep cooked cereal down. I was on the threshold of being a seven-year-old has-been." As a topper, the three financial giants of Paramount were expected momentarily. The railroad siding had been lengthened so that they would arrive within a hundred yards of the battle. The three bankers were, in order of importance, Otto Kahn, Sir William Wiseman, and a gentleman who owned among other things a leading cigarette company, William Stralem.

The three plutocrats arrived at the set while Wellman was seated at the seventy-five-foot level sky-gazing and waiting to push the first call button to start the war. Lucien Hubbard had joined the moneylenders and was explaining what was expected to happen. Suddenly, Wellman saw it . . . a thin shaft of light, narrow as an arrow, breaking through the cloud layer—undetectable to most. He ordered the planes into the air.

Knowing that full sunlight was necessary, Hubbard and some of the officers around the tower were shocked by the director's call. An infantry captain yelled up at Wellman, "What are you doing?" Wellman yelled back, "What the hell do you think I'm doing? I'm getting ready to shoot the scene." "But you need the sun," objected the officer. Wild Bill responded, "That's right. Get your big ass back and get ready."

Shortly, the skies darkened even more from the volume of fighter planes overhead in proper formations, at correct altitudes, in chosen positions, circling like hawks waiting to attack. That shaft of light was widening and the sun was breaking through. Wellman shouted for everybody to get ready. Even the moneymen were transfixed at this electrifying moment.

The director's fingers wiggled above the buttons. "I took my position with my fingers on the board," said Wellman, "readying myself to play the loudest, most exciting cacophonic solo of bedlam that has ever been wrapped up in five minutes. I yelled, Camera! They heard my voice in the lobby of the Saint Anthony Hotel fifty miles away."

Wellman's first button-push set off a signal for all the action to begin, on the ground and in the air. It was so loud that he said it nearly blew him off the parallel. All hell broke loose: thousands of doughboys advancing, enemy troops fleeing, diving planes, soldiers strafed from the air and shot at from the ground, Wellman pushing the buttons to keep the slow-moving barrage just ahead of the first wave of troops. The director's attention was solely on the first wave and his button board. The sun was still shining when he reached button eight, nine, and ten. "If it would shine for only one more minute," said the director, "we were in, eleven, twelve, only six more to go, and some son of a bitch spoke to me. I pushed the wrong button, and a couple of bodies flew through the air. They weren't dummies."

Wellman still kept his attention on the troops and the organboard, playing only the right notes—even when one of the pursuit pilots lost his head and was diving so low he almost hit the helmets of the running soldiers. "The bastard was going nuts," said Wellman. "He was slowing us down, screwing up the whole carefully planned advance, and then I saw him crash, and his plane rolled over and over, and I was almost glad."

Wellman, keeping his eyes on the action and the buttons, hollered to the son of a bitch behind him who had spoken. "Get down off this parallel, you goddamned idiot, or I'll break every bone in your body." The sunlight was beginning to fade with just two more buttons to push. Darkness arrived after numbers seventeen and eighteen—the scene was over.

Jubilation. The cameramen, the crew, the officers, even the generals were wildly shouting praises, running around and hugging each other. Many voices raised compliments up to the director. It was a scene of high exultation. "Generals were clustered around my parallel chattering like magpies," said Wellman, "and I was watching the ambulances picking their way to my big mistake." When Wellman reached the bottom of the ladder, Hubbard grabbed him in a big bear hug. Officers crowded around to shake his hand and slap him on the back. He broke away and ran across a shell-ravaged area of the battleground to an ambulance. The two soldiers who took the demolition charge were injured but alive. They would recover. Wellman's next race took him to another ambulance and another unscheduled occurrence. "When I got there," said Wellman, "the plane was demolished, but the pilot was leaning against an ambulance with a bandage around his head. He was dazed, but not from the crash, and I suddenly realized that in all my planning I had forgotten one terribly important factor, the human element. This pilot had flown at the front. He had been decorated. He had flown missions just like this one. For five minutes it was not 1926 to him; it was 1918. He just stuck out his hand and said, 'I'm sorry. C'est la guerre.'"

The *Wings* company, the twenty-one cameramen, the army, and the air corps were ecstatic, everyone believed that Hollywood and the armed services had won the war. The director, however, was played out, his emotions frayed. He was guilt-ridden and sick to his stomach about the injured men. He retired to his hotel suite. "To hell with everything and everybody," he thought. He told the telephone operator not to put through any calls and he locked the door behind him. The only one he wanted to spend time with was Jack Daniel's. After three drinks, his thoughts shifted to many places: the dead flier's family, the two wounded doughboys, the crashed pilot, the three New York bankers, and his many problems with the studio. He was way over budget, and still refusing to shoot the major dogfight until clouds were in the sky . . . and mad as hell at the wrong-button-pushing director. Then he remembered the son of a bitch who spoke to him after the twelfth button.

"Thirteen has always been an unlucky number for me," said Wellman. On the Friday the thirteenths that had come up during his life, he had made the effort never to leave the house, been careful how he walked downstairs, took the phone off the hook, sat down gingerly, nursed his way through the gruesome twenty-four hours, and had always uttered a prayer of relief on the dawn of the fourteenth. "As a matter of fact," he said, "why blame it on the thirteenth button? All my life, I have been coasting along under full sail and doing pretty well, when for no good reason I push the wrong button, and then pain. Already I have pushed wrong matrimonial buttons, wrong business buttons, wrong friendship buttons, and wrong sexual buttons. I am habitually a sometime wrong button-pusher . . ."

The director was in his cups, alone, tired, and in need of a good long shower in the hopes of changing his dark mood into something much brighter. After his hot and cold shower routine, he stepped out, felt better, even a bit sober. He sobered up a little more when he heard a loud knocking at his door. Bathrobed and slightly tipsy, he opened the door and there they stood: the Paramount bankers. He invited them in and poured them a drink. He did not take one himself. They sat down, all but Otto Kahn. "He started to pace the room," said Wellman, "and I knew I was in for it, but what a hell of a way to go out. I had just shown them five minutes of unbroken madness, and I don't think they will ever forget it as long as they live. I sat down and waited for the ultimatum. It came fast and concise."

Mr. Kahn: "Wellman, we like you . . . and furthermore you stay here as long as you think necessary to get what you believe is best for the picture. We have complete confidence in you, and the picture is in your capable young hands." "I excused myself," said Wellman, "and went into the bathroom to vomit . . .

"I did a good job, kneeling on the floor gazing into the relief bowl, when there was a very polite knock on the door and I heard Mr. Kahn asking: 'You all right, Wellman?' 'Yes, sir, all right and getting sober,' and he continued: 'I was that goddamned idiot who opened his big mouth at the wrong time. I am terribly sorry and I apologize.' I heard them go out," said Wellman, "and the door close. I lay down on the floor and cried."

Down the hall from the director's suite was the assistant director's room. After the wild day at war, Wellman's buddy Charlie Barton was enjoying his favorite libation in the quiet comfort of a stuffed easy chair. His thoughts were rudely interrupted by a steady stream of shouts com-

Wellman plays the role of a doomed soldier.

Myron Selznick, son of Lewis, brother of David O.—and
Wellman's agent

ing down the hallway to his room. Barton could hear, "Charlie! Charlie!"
He leaped to his feet, spilling his spirits down his bathrobe. Before he
could wobble to the door, a fusillade of fist pounding attacked it. When
it opened, director and assistant were face-to-face. A wide-eyed Wellman
roared, "We're going on, Charlie. We're going on." The director turned
and, with his assistant watching, charged back up the hallway. Barton
hollered from his doorway, "Yippee! Yippee!"

The weather improved and Wellman shot close-ups and several pieces
of business to cut into the St. Mihiel battle sequence. After finishing, he
released most of the army and air corps, keeping a small number of soldiers and fliers for additional work. These servicemen played both sides
of the battle—doughboys and U.S. pilots one day, enemy troops and
fliers the next. Some of the soldiers had earlier changed uniforms and
movie companies to fight in the Spanish-American War depiction from
The Rough Riders.

There was no more tension and suspense around the set. No Paramount executives arrived and the New York bankers left. The atmosphere was relaxed and enjoyable again now that they were gone. Wellman added stuntmen, soldiers, fliers, crew members, even himself, to the acting payroll. The director played a doughboy who is shot while advancing on a pillbox. After taking a burst of machine-gun fire, he twirls and falls to the ground. When Buddy Rogers's plane attacks the enemy troops, Wellman's doughboy looks to the sky and utters, "Atta boy, them buzzards are some good after all."

There was only one sequence left on the shooting schedule—the major dogfight. As it had for so many other days, the morning dawned overcast. This day, however, would be different. Soon, fingers of light began to poke holes through the dark layers until they spread into shafts of morning sun. The sky became radiant in blue, and white, billowy cumulus clouds filled the sky waiting for the airships to join them. "At long last," said Wellman, "we got the clouds, and I got a breathtaking dogfight." Wellman's battle in the clouds has been hailed as a masterpiece of aerial artistry that continues to gain fame.

Historian and filmmaker John Andrew Gallagher, in the May 1982 *Films in Review*, wrote, "The photography in *Wings* was full of breathtaking motion and classic imagery. Wellman takes the viewer on a graceful gliding ride in the sky, then creates dramatic tension with skillfully executed dogfights."

In the 1996 award-winning documentary *Wild Bill Hollywood Maverick*, Tony Scott, the A-list action director who helped make a star of Tom Cruise in the ever-popular aviation film *Top Gun*, said, "When I first started *Top Gun*, I said there's a master shot that I've got to get, which is the master shot in *Wings* which is the major dogfight . . . and I think they had eight aircraft all in the air, and they all felt like they were in touching distance of each other, and they're all twisting and swirling and ducking and diving. I was amazed at what they did in 1928 [1926] because of the lack of technology . . . because we had the state of the art in terms of technology . . . but what they got then with very simplistic cameras and equipment was brilliant."

Frank Thompson, historian, author, biographer, in his *Texas Hollywood*, 2002, wrote this about *Wings*: "Flying scenes remain unsurpassed even today."

Many different types of warplanes and postwar ships were used in the making of *Wings*. There were genuine Spad VIIs, Fokker D.VIIs, DeHavilland D.H.4s, and other World War I aircraft. Other planes were disguised non–World War I types: Boeing-built Thomas Morse M.B.3 Scouts served as Spads; Curtiss P-1s played the German Fokkers, and a postwar Martin bomber doubled as the German Gotha bomber. Harry Perry's camera plane was an army NBS-1, a Curtiss variant of the Martin M.B.2.

"It was the night before my home-going," said Wellman. "A small dinner with all my pilots, those from San Antonio and the boys from Selfridge Field. Contrary to what you might expect, there was but little drinking, no speeches, just a bunch of guys getting together to say good-bye."

When dinner was over and the coffee served, someone passed the director a simple, plain silver platter, with the lone letter "W" inscribed in the center. Around it, in their own handwriting, the pilots' nicknames. They were in no particular order, just sort of spotted here and there: Pop, Bill T., Bill P., Ris, Bill I., Burdie, Van, Whick, Robbie, Si, Barry, John I., Carl J., K.H., Rod, George, Buck. "They were the best," said Wellman, "and they are mine to treasure the rest of my life."

9

CONSEQUENCES AND
ACHIEVEMENTS

I f you think Wellman's homecoming was triumphant, think again. His defiant attitude and lack of respect for the Paramount hierarchy while on location had burned bridges that would never be repaired. "There was a very noticeable lack of enthusiasm at the studio," said Wellman, "and in my own home at the sight or sound of me."

Since the director was still on the picture, finishing the interior scenes and moving into postproduction, there was little time to patch up the domestic problems. As if he needed more points at issue, his paychecks stopped coming—he was off salary but still working. Nothing was going to stop him from finishing *Wings*, but he realized that he needed legal advice. He met a theatrical agent by the name of Myron Selznick. Myron had been a successful producer in New York before coming to Tinseltown. When no studio would hire him, he became an agent—at that time, agents inhabited one of the least respected positions in the film industry.

Myron had other chips on his shoulder. His father, Lewis J. Selznick, had been a pioneering producer in New York from 1912 to 1922. He was known as one rough, tough Russian Jew. One of eighteen children, he learned to fend for himself, emigrating from czarist Russia to England at twelve years of age. He worked in a factory until he could earn passage to America. He became a jeweler's apprentice before owning his own store, later a prosperous chain of stores and a national bank. By age twenty-four, he was married and soon fathered three sons. L.J. formed his own production company and produced a lengthy list of films. His hard-line approach and sometimes unethical business practices made him a long list of enemies, including Carl Laemmle, L. B. Mayer, Adolph Zukor, and Jesse Lasky, among others. By 1923, he was bankrupt and everyone turned against him. He never recovered and spent his remaining years living in retirement in California supported by two sons, Myron and David. David O. Selznick arrived in Hollywood after his older brother.

Myron listened to the young director's employment predicament, and couldn't wait to play financial havoc with two of the men who would not hire him and had helped ruin his father. Wellman's new agent told him to keep his mouth shut and keep working while he devised a plan of attack.

Wellman shot the final scenes at Paramount's Vine Street studio and local locations. The biggest interior scene was the Folies Bergère nightclub. One grandiose room crowded with five hundred extras dressed as soldiers of many nations, the French populace, the elite class, ladies of the evening—it was a red-hot time at the frenzied Folies. It would always be a trademark of Wellman films to witness so much of the action from one scene in just one shot. In this case, Wellman devised an overhead track with a platform for the camera crew, so that the audience could view all of the action within the scene as the camera moves from one end of the room to the other, skimming over the tops of the busy tables—one continuous dolly shot without a cut. Many film historians believe this was the first of its kind. Another Wellman trademark is the addition of humorous pieces of business, sometimes bizarre, sprinkled throughout his films no matter how serious or dramatically important the content. During the Folies Bergère sequence, the director inserted superimposed bubbles on screen to add humor and to magnify Buddy Rogers's champagne intoxication.

Burton Steene, the cameraman who shot most of the aerial work on the film, was on that Folies Bergère platform. Wellman said, "God knows what I would have done without him." Steene was a low-key, modest individual who did his job without fanfare. Wellman thought he resembled "a fakey, sorrowful undertaker with a glint in his eye."

One of the last scenes filmed in the picture was another long dolly shot. This one took place outside the studio on a tree-lined street. Buddy Rogers and Clara Bow were walking along the sidewalk with Burton and his noisy Akeley camera riding on a four-wheel cart, photographing their stroll. Wellman was also on that pushcart sitting behind Burton, peeking over his shoulder, when all of a sudden the cameraman fell backward, with Wellman catching him. His fall whipped the Akeley off Bow and Rogers and onto the sky above. Burton had a death grip on his pan handle, the gear head whining, the camera photographing the brilliant blue sky with magnificent pure white clouds. Burton had had a heart attack. "The next night," said Wellman, "when I ran the rushes [dailies], the fatalistic whining of the gear-headed Akeley had stopped and its last still photograph was Burton Steene's most beautiful, a sky so soft and ethereal, it had a face like heaven."

During postproduction, Wellman wanted to add a number of new or near-new dimensions to his *Wings*. In the movie when the dawn patrol takes off, Wellman wanted the screen to become larger in order to emphasize the magnitude of the moment. He gave the idea to Roy T. Pomeroy, the head of the special effects department and the man who had parted the Red Sea for Cecil B. DeMille in *The Ten Commandments* (1923). Using the Magnascope process, "invented by" Lorenzo del Riccio in 1924, and "discovered by" Glen Allvine in 1926, Pomeroy made it work for *Wings*. Basically, Magnascope was a zoom lens that, when the theater projectionist flipped the switch on another projector equipped with the Magnascope magnifying lens, the frame enlarged from the normal eighteen-by-twelve-foot size to forty by thirty feet.

The Wellman-Pomeroy team made other innovations as well. *Wings* was one of the first pictures to add sound effects to a silent movie. Pomeroy added the roar of the plane's engines, machine guns firing, bomb explosions, even the scream of a German pilot killed in a dogfight. The effects were synchronized from turntables behind the screen. Percussion instruments in the orchestra lent their sounds to the picture.

It was common to tint black-and-white prints with muted colors—red for battle scenes, blue for night scenes, and so forth. In addition to this norm, red-orange flames were seen coming from burning airplanes shot down in the *Wings* dogfights. On the first prints, these flames were colored by hand, frame by frame, in the special effects art department. Due to time constraints, on later prints the flame effects were created using Handschiegl color, an automated stenciling process that was a forerunner to the imbibition process used for Technicolor.

For the road show engagement of the picture, the film would be accompanied by an orchestra playing a specially written score by J. S. Zamecnik and a featured song, "Wings," by Zamecnik and Ballard MacDonald.

After almost a year on the film, Wellman finished his directing job. His film was ready for public consumption, and Myron Selznick was ready to seek vengeance upon Paramount Pictures. New York would be the site of a *Wings* preview to gauge audience reaction. The powers-that-be at the studio were twitching and wavering about the outcome. They argued about cutting scenes, shortening them, and other fixes. They were afraid that this expensive first-time air saga was on the road to financial doom.

Another Paramount big-budget war film, James Cruze's *Old Ironsides*, released December 6, 1926, had failed to perform up to expectations. Like *Wings*, it was a lavish epic, of sailing ships and pirates. Film historian Lewis Jacobs, thirteen years after *Ironsides*'s release, wrote in *The Rise of the American Film*, "The film on an American historical subject proved to be a dismal failure."

The average cost of a feature in 1926 and 1927 was $250,000. You can imagine the concern of the Paramount bosses considering the *Wings* cost of over $2 million. Before the preview, one of the Paramount executives bet Wellman a hundred dollars that the film wouldn't play for more than three weeks on Broadway. "After a very successful preview in New York (to which I was not invited)," said Wellman, "the front office began to suspect that they might have a pretty fair picture on their hands, so I was called into the head man's cave." The director's agent accompanied him to that office, then sat quietly in the waiting room.

B.P. Schulberg greeted Wellman as if he were a long-lost son. He apologized for their misunderstandings during and after the *Wings* location. He complimented the director on the excitement and beauty of the dog-fight, and finished his insincere speech by praising Wellman for his tenacity, which he pronounced "tenisity." The director responded with, "Let's cut this crap out right now. You've forgotten to take my option up, I'm not under contract with you. I've been working here for nothing the last six weeks." B.P. said that was ridiculous, probably some clerical oversight, and called Mike Levy, the business manager of the studio. Using one of the earliest interoffice communication boxes, Levy came on the line. Schulberg asked about the oversight and Levy, not knowing Wellman was in the room, reminded B.P. that he had said, "Tell the son of a"— Schulberg quickly shut the truth machine off: he remembered.

Schulberg apologized some more about being in a fit of anger at the time and didn't really mean it. He again mentioned Wellman being like a son to him, but he didn't say what kind of son. B.P. went on about their relationship and the young director's obligation to him and Paramount for his grand opportunity. Wellman had heard enough. He stood and spoke two words, "No dice," then started out of the cave. He stopped at the doorway, telling the head of production that if he was really serious about their association, his agent was waiting in the outer office. His name was Myron Selznick.

The Criterion Theatre of New York during the premiere engagement of *Wings*, 1927

Wellman winked at Myron as he passed by. The intercom on the secretary's desk came alive with Schulberg's voice, "Send Selznick in." He forgot to say "Mr." That was a mistake he would later regret. Myron stood, stretched, yawned, and told the secretary to tell God that he would call in the morning. He was now late for a very important meeting with the director of *Wings* at another studio. Wellman picks up the story: "When we got out in the corridor, I said to Myron: 'Jesus, do you think you did the right thing?' and Myron's answer was typical. 'If he wants you now, when he and that other nincompoop [Lasky] get through their dogfight, he will want you more; and when I finish talking to New York, he had better.'" New York meant Otto Kahn, the banker who had caused Wellman to push the wrong button during the re-creation of St. Mihiel. He greatly admired the young director and was only happy to add his recommendation to the negotiations.

Within a few days, Myron Selznick exacted a little of his revenge. After he and Schulberg consummated the deal, William Wellman went from $250 a week to $1,250 a week and a seven-year contract with yearly raises. For the six weeks without pay that he was owed, he received a check for $7,500—$1,250 times six instead of $250. Wellman had never seen so much money. "All I got out of it was a $1,000-a-week raise, a seven-year contract, at the end of which I was getting paid in figures I couldn't count. . . . Mr. Selznick had established himself at Paramount."

Before his next assignment, Wellman tried to heal the domestic wounds and enjoy a well-deserved vacation. Neither was successful. About his marriage, he believed the simple bottom line: "She fell out of love with me. I had been so busy, so completely wrapped up in my work when I found out, I didn't care." The director's new contract was well publicized—too well, and Mrs. Marjorie Wellman wanted her share . . . and more. Wellman asked around, talked to friends and experienced divorce travelers, until he came up with one of the best divorce attorneys in town. He and one of the best went to court to meet her and "the best."

When her legal crackerjack called him to the stand, he was asked but one question: "Mr. Wellman, what is your weekly salary?" He answered and was dismissed. "When I went back to sit by my perspiring legal beagle, everyone in the courtroom, including the judge, hated me. I was mistreating a beautiful, ex-*Follies* showgirl, clothed in a tight, but *tight*, fitting dark suit with a figure that made you wince." Wellman's perspiring mouthpiece made a horrible mistake of calling her to the witness stand. She didn't walk to it, she glided with just a little shimmer of the rudder. She sat down, crossed her legs at the judge, and the husband was penniless.

Three months after Charles Lindbergh's historic transatlantic flight, *Wings* premiered at the Criterion Theatre in New York City, August 12, 1927. The director's name was not on the invitation list. At a top ticket price of $2, the picture played at the 900-seat movie palace for sixty-three weeks before moving to the nearby Rialto, a 1,960-seat theater called "Temple of the Motion Picture." The New York first-run exhibition lasted for two solid years. From its opening through the spring of 1928, the film sold out almost every showing. Each performance was accompanied by an orchestra. Before its national run was completed, the picture was rereleased on January 5, 1929, with a sound effects track and synchronized musical score.

Millions of Americans crowded into movie houses from coast to coast. The film's praises were passed from lip to lip as rave reviews and stories about the picture, its stars, its director, the stunt fliers, the army and air corps, and Paramount filled the pages of magazines and newspapers everywhere. *Wings* became a high-and-mighty champion.

The New York Times, August 13, 1927: "Amazing air duels and an impressive study of aviators are depicted in 'Wings,' Paramount's epic of the flying fighters of the World War, which was launched last night in the Criterion Theatre. . . . This feature gives one the unforgettable idea of the existence of these daring fighters—how they were called upon at all hours of the day and night to soar into the skies and give battle to enemy planes; their light-hearted eagerness to enter the fray and also their reckless conduct once they set foot on earth for a time in the dazzling life of the French capital."

The Literary Digest, November 12, 1927: "Eagles strike and are stricken. The vanquished, blazing into meteors, topple, plunge and write their own epitaphs down the sky in serpentine trails of fire and smoke. Spiraling drunkenly earthward, they are dogged at each turn by relentlessly inquisitive cameras—now above, now below, now haply on the same level— intent on not missing the smallest pirouette in that dance of death. . . . The director, William A. Wellman, is given credit by most of the critics for a colossal achievement."

New York Morning Telegraph, October 19, 1927: "The picture ranks as the greatest long-run attraction ever to be presented on Broadway."

Variety, October 3, 1928: "*Wings*: Sound or silent, rolling up unheard of grosses wherever it plays. On its record, THE GREATEST PICTURE ATTRACTION EVER RELEASED."

The seemingly boundless success of the film continued to grow, and Wellman received his next Paramount assignment, *The Legion of the Condemned*. It was another aviation picture and a project that the director and his *Wings* writer, John Monk Saunders, had been proposing to the studio without interest. Now, after the New York triumph, Paramount thought that *Legion* might be another *Wings*. The studio urged Wellman to use outtakes and footage shot for *Wings* in order to keep the budget on the low side. Some of the advertisements would announce the film as "Another *Wings*," "A second *Wings*," and "The sequel to *Wings*"—which it was not. As the director would be working with Saunders and screen-writer Jean DeLimur from the early stages, the story would be even more personal, more of Wild Bill's experiences than in *Wings*.

Wellman received a call at his Paramount office from Howard Hughes. The young flier turned filmmaker was preparing *Hell's Angels* and wanted a meeting. He told Wellman that he had watched *Wings* over and over and wanted him to direct his aviation epic. Wellman explained that he was preparing *The Legion of the Condemned* and didn't want to do three air shows in a row. The two rebels had much in common and enjoyed each other's company. Wellman wanted to help the young filmmaker and offered advice and two lists containing the names of the stunt pilots and cameramen from *Wings*. Hughes, in turn, hired many of these men from both lists who had helped create the technology for aerial photography and warfare for the movies.

The Legion of the Condemned and *Hell's Angels* would only be two of a wave of pictures in the new film genre sparked by *Wings*. Some of the earliest stories of the chivalrous knights of the skies that filled movie screens for the next six years were *Hard Boiled Haggerty* (1927) with Milton Sills; a Rin Tin Tin adventure, *Dog of the Regiment* (1927); *Captain Swagger* (1928) with Rod La Rocque; *Lilac Time* (1928), starring Colleen Moore and Gary Cooper; Howard Hawks's *The Dawn Patrol* (1930) with Douglas Fairbanks, Jr., Richard Barthelmess, and Neil Hamilton; Wellman's *Young Eagles* (1930) with Jean Arthur and Buddy Rogers; *Sky Devils* (1932) with Spencer Tracy, William "Hopalong Cassidy" Boyd, and Ann Dvorak; John Ford's *Airmail* (1932) with Pat O'Brien, Ralph Bellamy, and Gloria Stuart; and *The Eagle and the Hawk* (1933), starring Fredric March, Cary Grant, and Carole Lombard.

Some of the other titles include *The Lone Eagle* (1927), *Air Circus* (1928), *Air Mail Pilot* (1928), *Air Patrol* (1928), *Sky Hawk* (1930), *Air Police* (1931), *Sky Raiders* (1931), *Men of the Sky* (1931), and *Air Eagles* (1931). None of these or any of the other air pictures of that time reached the artistry, technique, or epic quality of their parent, *Wings*.

Due to the fan mail and high praise from critics and exhibitors alike, the one-scene Gary Cooper was on the road to stardom. Wellman's visionary prowess had worked a miracle for the gentleman cowboy from Montana. Coop was given leading roles in two Paramount Westerns, *The Last Outlaw* and *Nevada*, both in 1927, and a starring role in *Beau Sabreur* (1928). *Beau Sabreur* was a low-budget follow-up to the big-budget winner *Beau Geste* (1926). Wellman was offered the directorship of *Sabreur* but declined, refusing to go from the major, *Wings*, to the minor, *Sabreur*.

He got his wish to continue developing *The Legion of the Condemned*. Fay Wray would be the female star after a career leap in Erich von Stroheim's *The Wedding March* (1928). As her leading man, Wellman cast . . . Gary Cooper.

Regrettably, *The Legion of the Condemned* is a lost film. What we do know is that production began October 10, 1927, on a budget of under $300,000 and a twenty-seven-day shooting schedule. They needed to film on a number of nights, but Wellman brought the picture in on schedule and under budget. As it had been before *Wings*, this would continue to be a trademark of Wellman films. He was prepared, and shot quickly with few takes. He believed in the spontaneity of the moment.

Legion was a World War I spy story with a twist. Cooper's character falls in love with a captivating socialite played by Fay Wray. When he discovers that she is a spy and sleeping with a German agent, he doesn't care if he lives or dies. He joins the Legion of the Condemned, a squadron of pilots whose desire is to die in combat. The twist comes when Cooper finds that Wray is actually an Allied spy, and he regains his will to live, joining in her mission. Both are caught behind enemy lines and sentenced to death by firing squad. Coop's squadron comes to the rescue and Cooper and Wray are together. After completion of the film, Fay Wray married *Legion*'s writer, John Saunders.

The Legion of the Condemned was released March 10, 1928, to excellent box office receipts. Paramount's advertisements shouted, "The thrilling story of a desperate band of war-fliers, whose only honorable discharge was a death certificate." From 1928 came the following reviews:

A. C. Findon, *Sunday Dispatch*: "One of the biggest thrillers Paramount has achieved. It is a picture packed with thrills—the flying episodes are full of realism."

News of the World: "No one should miss this film."

Daily Mirror: "The result is first-class aerial melodrama."

Monroe Lathrop, *Los Angeles Evening Express,* January 25, 1928: "Under similar circumstances I saw 'Wings' and have now seen its cinema blood-brother, 'The Legion of the Condemned' . . . it took no prescience to recognize in 'Wings' a great audience picture as experience has demonstrated. Nor can one fail to see in 'Legion of the Condemned' the same qualities. Indeed, my personal preference is for the latter. . . . Viewers will make two important discoveries—unsuspected dramatic talent in Gary Cooper and unusual beauty in Erich Von Stroheim's 'find,' Fay Wray. . . . War is hell, and this picture shows its satanic folly. But war has its humor, its heroism, its tender and beautiful emotion, and they are all in this story of its dare-devils."

Variety, February 29, 1928: "From its ingenious first flashes to its final whirlwind climax, the picture is superb in every department."

In Kevin Brownlow's *The Parade's Gone By*, David O. Selznick said about Wellman, "In his opening sequence of 'Legion of the Condemned,' I've many times quoted as one of the most brilliant uses of film to tell a story that I've ever seen. He told the whole story of four individual men in, I think, less than one minute each. He was really a remarkable talent."

Four days before *Legion* began production, October 6, 1927, motion picture history would be changed forever. Considered by many as the world's greatest entertainer, Al Jolson, on bended knee, sang "Mammy" to movie audiences in *The Jazz Singer*. This event signaled the end of the glorious reign of the silent movie, and the beginning of the revolutionary sound era. At the same time that *The Jazz Singer* marked the destruction of silent films, it was also creating a new form of film entertainment, the talkies.

Sound musical shorts had been produced during the silent era, but never a feature film that combined dialogue and musical numbers with a synchronized score. Soon movie theater marquees lit up with the advertising slogan "All Talking—All Singing—All Dancing!" Audiences could now hear the rhythmic tapping of dancing feet, the melodies and lyrics of enchanting songs, the crack of thunder, the clash of swords, the blast of gunfire, the voices of their favorite movie stars, and, of course, Al Jolson's catchphrase, "You ain't heard nothin' yet!"

The Hollywood studios were in a panic. Was sound a passing fad or here to stay? They struggled, challenged, debated, fought, wavered, and questioned whether to accept or reject this new phenomenon.

They would have to spend millions of dollars refitting their theaters with sound equipment, and more money would be needed to overhaul their facilities at the studios. In their quandary they wondered: silent films were so successful, so profitable, how could sound enhance these extraordinary pictures and their box office profits? Also, there were a number of sound systems out there, which one should be adopted? All these questions and more would have to be addressed by the studios before, one by one, they lined up and accepted sound in motion pictures.

When Paramount enlisted in the sound craze, Jesse Lasky called a meeting of his contract directors. Adolph Zukor brought some of the bankers from New York for the gathering. "He [Lasky] told us that pictures were going to start talking," said Wellman. "Those were his inspiring words. He added a few more that sucked the breath out of you." "We have hired the best stage directors in New York," said Lasky. "John Cromwell, George Cukor, George Abbott. These are the first that are coming, they will work with you and share credits."

The contract directors sank down in their seats, but Wellman grabbed at the chance for a fight with a man he was not particularly fond of. He got up and said nastily, "I have bad news for you, good for me. Have you forgotten I have a seven-year contract with you gentlemen of Paramount? It has nothing to say or do about any lousy stage director coming in and making half of my picture—furthermore, I won't accept one of them on my set, unless they are a better man than I am." He walked out of the office. The acclaimed New York stage directors did come, including George Cukor, who became an Academy Award winner. None ever worked with Wellman.

Still stinging from his conjugal collapse and the clouded atmosphere surrounding the studio, he immersed himself in his favorite pastime—making movies. A Wellman trademark: the way to survive life's imperfections is . . . make another film. He made seven pictures from December of 1927 to December of 1930. He continued his practice of producing as well as directing in order to stay as far from executive interference as possible. The films, however, were studio assignments, not of his choosing.

Ladies of the Mob, Wellman's first crime picture, was based on a fictionalized story by a convict, Ernest Booth, serving life at Folsom Prison. The story deals with Clara Bow, whose father dies in the electric chair, turning to crime at an early age. She becomes attached to a small-time crook, played by Richard Arlen, and together they follow a life of crime before attempting to go straight. They both end up in prison but look forward to their release when they can live together on the straight and narrow. *The New York Times*, May 18, 1928: "A gloomy, artificial and unedifying photoplay. . . . This so-called diversion, which yesterday attracted thousands of persons from the sunshine to the interior of the Paramount Theatre, begins with the depressing suggestion of a murderer expiating his crime in the electric chair and, although the unfortunate criminal is not seen, there is quite enough detail to satisfy morbid curiosity." *Time* magazine, July 2, 1928: "Now it can be told that Clara Bow can do other things than reveal her stimulating figure. She can act, tensely, convincingly."

Beggars of Life, based on the novel by "hobo author" Jim Tully, tells the story of a young woman, played by Louise Brooks, who kills her foster father when he attempts to rape her. She runs away with a young tramp, played by Richard Arlen, joining a group of hobos who hop rides on freight trains in search of a day's pay, a square meal, or a jolt of white lightning. The two eventually escape to Canada, having convinced the authorities that Louise is dead. *The New York Times*, September 24, 1928: "It is a rather dull and unimaginative piece of work." *Variety*, September 26, 1928: "Not an exceptionally good picture." Panned by many critics, the film's legacy, however, grew into a true classic of the silent cinema.

Chinatown Nights, another crime drama, based on "Tong War" by Samuel Ornitz, starred Wallace Beery. After his sixteenth birthday, Beery ran away from home, joining the Ringling Brothers Circus as an elephant trainer. Two years later, a losing battle with a leopard chased him to New York, where he found work in comic opera as a baritone. Soon Broadway called and eventually the movies. During a brief and abusive marriage to Gloria Swanson, his film career kicked into high gear. With his penchant for partying came fisticuffs and, in 1928, a new friend, Wild Bill Wellman.

Chinatown Nights deals with a society dame, played by Florence Vidor, who is riding a tourist bus through Chinatown and right into a gang war. Beery, one of the gang leaders, rescues her from the clutches of Warner Oland's rival gang. They fall in love and she works to reform Beery. *The New York Times*, April 1, 1929: "An absurd story from beginning to end." *Variety*, April 3, 1929: "So many glaring deficiencies in *Chinatown Nights* that a captious critic could devote paragraphs to itemize them . . . as a picture, it's nothing to brag about."

The Man I Love bears no relation to the popular torch song of the same name. It is a prizefight picture and comedy-drama. It is also Wellman's first full talking picture. The story is written by Herman J. Mankiewicz, who later coscripted *Citizen Kane*. Herman's brother, Joseph, wrote the titles for *The Man I Love* and became an Academy Award winner for writing and directing *A Letter to Three Wives* (1949) and *All About Eve* (1950).

Richard Arlen plays Dum Dum Brooks, an uneducated, unsophisticated, pompous waiter and boxer. Encouraged by his love for his wife, played by Mary Brian, he fights his way to the top of the game. When he allows the Countess Sonia, Olga Baclanova, to seduce him, Mary walks

Clara Bow and Richard Arlen in *Ladies of the Mob* (1928)

Louise Brooks and Richard Arlen in *Beggars of Life* (1928)

out of his life. In his depressed state, he is losing an important fight when he is told that Mary is listening on the radio. He recovers, wins the bout, and reconciles with his true love. *Variety*, May 29, 1929: "One of the best fight pictures yet released." *The New York Times*, May 28, 1929: "Herman J. Mankiewicz has some original incidents and a fair amount of good comedy. There are times, however, when his dialogue is foolish, or it makes the characters look idiotic."

Woman Trap, based on the play *Brothers* by Edwin Burke, is Wellman's third crime drama. The story concerns two brothers, played by Hal Skelly and Chester Morris, on opposite sides of the law. Their brotherhood deteriorates as Skelly, the police officer, and Morris, the bootlegger, fight over good guy/bad guy roles. Skelly has a stormy courtship with Evelyn Brent, but when he arrests her brother, played by Leslie Fenton—who dies on the gallows—Evelyn seeks revenge. Through betrayal, she causes Chester's demise. Since Skelly and Brent have caused the death of each other's brother, they can never find happiness together. *The New York Times*, August 31, 1929: "A talking film with extravagant and unconvincing action, verbose dialogue and patches of sentimentality. . . . There are a few interesting flashes, particularly a fight depicted between two men on an elevator and during which only their legs are seen." *Variety*, September 4, 1929: "Melodrama of average program quality. Generates enough suspense to pump up the balloon of an hour's engrossment. It's

Hal Skelly in *Woman Trap* (1929)

The Man I Love, starring Richard Arlen, Mary Brian, and
directed by William Wellman (1929)

Nancy Carroll and Richard Arlen on the set of
Dangerous Paradise, 1930

gangster and tough copper hodge-podge, seen before, but holding a primitive punch that will suffice to get it across."

Dangerous Paradise is based on incidents in *Victory* by Joseph Conrad. *Victory* was previously filmed in 1919, directed by Maurice Tourneur, and remade in 1940, directed by John Cromwell. *Dangerous Paradise* deals with an all-woman orchestra playing at a resort hotel. Nancy Carroll plays the singer and violinist. She gets it from all sides in an intense competition for her favors. She is verbally and physically abused by the men and their wives. She is only treated well by a hotel guest, played by Richard Arlen. They fall in love, escape from a multitude of villains aboard Arlen's boat to an island of safety. *The New York Times*, February 16, 1930: "It is an unusually good piece of work. . . . Wellman's direction is smooth and the scenes are magnificently photographed." William K. Everson, American archivist, author, historian, and film critic, wrote, "It's a comic-strip adaptation of Conrad."

Young Eagles, Wellman's third air picture, is based on the stories "Sky High" and "The One Who Was Clever" by Elliot White Springs. Although aerial footage from *Wings* is again on display, with Buddy Rogers in the starring role, the budget was too sparse to allow much original aviation work and the picture grinds along on a contrived spy story. *The New York Times*, March 22, 1930: "A highly incredible narrative with two good air-fighting episodes and a mass of wild and absurd incidents. . . . Jean Arthur seems to be somewhat afraid of the character she plays." Buddy Rogers later said, "The film was a cheater, strictly for promotion and cash-value." It is clear that this was not a film of Wellman's choosing. Even though *The Legion of the Condemned* is a lost film and we can't know how good or bad it is, *Young Eagles* is definitely the weakest of the director's three Paramount aviation dramas. It is interesting to note Wellman's penchant for loyalty to his previous cast members. Of his eight Paramount films after *Wings*, Richard Arlen, Buddy Rogers, Clara Bow, or Gary Cooper appear in six of them.

During the productions of these assigned films, Wellman was growing more and more dissatisfied with Paramount. The projects that he brought to the table were always rejected; only *The Legion of the Condemned* was green-lighted because the studio wanted a quick follow-up to *Wings*. Wellman's contention was that the major projects and better stories were being handed to the other directors, leaving him with the leftovers, the B picture material, the more "chancy" experiments. He felt that it was a continuing punishment from the front office for his behavior during *Wings* filming, and for winning the game of salary negotiation.

Wellman worked hard to improve the scripts and look of the films. He infused humor, added unusual and interesting camera angles and camera movement, shot scenes from different perspectives, whatever he could think of to make the pictures better. Favorable reviews for these films were harder to come by, but his pictures made money at the box office. He was also gaining the reputation as a director who could take any kind of story—aviation, boxing, crime and gangster, hobo, Western, action, adventure, comedy, or drama—get fine performances from both men and women, and . . . bring the films in on schedule and on budget.

One of the chancy ventures was Jim Tully's tale of hobos, *Beggars of Life*. Unlike Wellman's other assignments after *Wings* and *The Legion of the Condemned*, this project tapped into his visceral side. The story highlights two insignificant, downtrodden young people, played by Louise Brooks and Richard Arlen, who against great odds are trying desperately

Louise Brooks and Richard Arlen in *Beggars of Life* (1928)

to find a place for themselves in a defective world. Not unlike Wellman in his early existence, Brooks and Arlen are forced to endure many of life's struggles: social alienation, problems with authorities, life on the road without money, family, or friends. Their redemption comes through their love and devotion to each other as they find a way to escape to a new world.

This film would mark the beginning of a Wellman trend to find and film personal stories away from the mainstream studio-driven projects. Wellman later wrote, "This brings me to Paramount in 1928 where I was making perhaps the best silent picture I ever made, *Beggars of Life*." In this statement, he is passing over not only his personal story, *The Legion of the Condemned*, but the prodigious *Wings*.

Beggars of Life was thought to be a lost film until the 1960s, when the distinguished, Oscar-winning writer and filmmaker Kevin Brownlow, who saw a screening of a less-than-pristine, murky, 16mm print at the National Film Theatre in London, helped promote a revival of the *Beggars* legend. In his 1968 *The Parade's Gone By*, he wrote "the rich, highly polished surface of technique gleamed through, revealing a style of astonishing elegance—an elegance which seemed out of place in such a picture. . . . *Beggars of Life* is brilliantly thought out and superbly made." In the 1980s, there emerged an enormous interest in the life and films of Louise Brooks. Fan clubs burst on the scene in many countries. In 1995, the Louise Brooks Society became the largest and most popular website in the world devoted to any silent film star. Since its launch, this pioneering site has received more than three million visitors.

Louise "Lulu" Brooks, whose fame shined much brighter well after her retirement, made twenty-four pictures in a thirteen-year film career. With many lost films on her résumé, her legacy still stands tall primarily because of these four survivors: two German masterpieces, *Pandora's Box* (1929) and *Diary of a Lost Girl* (1929), both directed by Georg Wilhelm Pabst, the maestro of German cinema in the late 1920s; Howard Hawks's *A Girl in Every Port* (1928); and, arguably, her finest American film, *Beggars of Life*, in which she gives a brilliant and lasting portrayal of a woman on the run, masquerading as a young man, fighting for her very existence.

Of Brooks, David Thomson, British critic and author of *Hollywood: A Celebration!*, wrote: "One of the most mysterious and potent figures in the history of the cinema."

Ado Kyroit, French critic: "Louise is the perfect apparition, the dream woman, the being without whom the cinema would be a poor thing. She is much more than a myth, she is a magical presence, a real phantom, the magnetism of the cinema."

Sporting her signature short black hair and bangs in helmet style, she was a life's traveler: born in Kansas in 1906; a New York dance student at age fifteen; a touring professional dancer with the Denishawn Dance Troupe at sixteen; on the New York stage in *Scandals* at eighteen; at the Café de Paris in London at nineteen; back on Broadway in Florenz Ziegfeld's *Louis the 14th* at nineteen; her motion picture debut in *The Street of Forgotten Men* at Paramount's Astoria studio on Long Island also at nineteen; back to Ziegfeld's *Follies*, still nineteen; to Hollywood and a five-year contract with Paramount.

During her career, she never became attached to any place for very long. She was fiercely independent and a restless nonconformist. Much of her life was spent in a never-ending search for truth and some special discovery that she never seemed to find. She had many suitors who were constantly discovering Lulu, and moving her from one place to another. Her longest stay was in Hollywood and Paramount Pictures, a place of which she would later say, "The Astoria studio was closed and I was sent from its intimate friendliness to the factory coldness of the Hollywood studio."

Lulu made seven films at Paramount, including a loan-out to Fox and Howard Hawks for *A Girl in Every Port*. Then she hit the road again to Germany and her time-honored films *Pandora's Box* and *Diary of a Lost*

Girl. When she returned to chilly Hollywood, there were seven more films at different studios before she abruptly retired from the cinema.

In her memoir, *Lulu in Hollywood*, she wrote, "Someday, I thought, I would run away from Hollywood forever. Not just the temporary running away I did after making each of my films—but forever." For the ultra-beautiful, utterly captivating Lulu, with her seemingly blasé insolence and an outspoken critic of the Hollywood system, forever came too soon for her admiring public.

Throughout her career, her behavior on stage and in films was often labeled erratic, impatient, insolent. She would also work diligently to give her best performance. When she was assigned *Beggars*, the studio, as usual, had trouble finding her. They tracked her from Miami, to Havana, to Palm Beach, and, finally, to Washington, D.C., where she was visiting her suitor-of-the-time, George Preston Marshall, later to be owner of the Washington Redskins football team.

William Wellman and Louise Brooks were hardly a match made in heaven. Wild Bill was highly enthusiastic and crazy about making movies in Hollywood. Lulu, on the other hand, was admittedly bored with films, doing the same thing over and over. She couldn't wait to get away from movies and Hollywood. Her reputation preceded her. She had made five films during Wellman's tenure at the studio. He knew only too well that she could be trouble. He appreciated her talent but questioned her lack of interest in picture-making. Since both were assigned the same film, they would have to work together.

The director was pleased with his costar, Wallace Beery, in their first of three films together, but not happy having to delay the start of production while the studio located his leading lady. When they finally met, their relationship was guarded and restrained. Brooks wrote, "A coldness was set up between us which neither of us could dispel. . . . Billy greeted me with more suspicion than cordiality. . . . Bewitched by his own success in Hollywood, he could not imagine my hating the place."

When filming commenced, Wellman began to appreciate her work ethic and readiness to perform some of her own stunts. He was not pleased with her inability to "hang with the boys." The director always cared much for his company and their togetherness. "She was always trying to distance herself from the rest." Wellman and Brooks never became soul mates. Although she did her work in a responsible way, she was mostly quiet and introspective around the set. But there was a fighting spirit that seeped through and Wellman applauded that. He liked her independent nature, unafraid to speak her mind with total candor—as he

Wallace Beery and Florence Vidor in *Chinatown Nights* (1929)

always did. The director wanted to work with her again, but after one more Paramount film, *The Canary Murder Case*, Lulu left the country.

Fortunately, an excellent 35mm print made from 16mm preservation materials by George Eastman House exists today. The sound portion is lost. *Beggars of Life* was released September 22, 1928, as a silent film and a version with a musical score, sound effects, and a dialogue sequence . . . better said, a vocal sequence. The film was made as a silent, then Paramount, against the director's wishes, forced sound into it. Wellman believed that it was created as a silent and sound would unbalance the original vision. As a contract director, he was required to heed the instructions and make the best of it. As a result, gravel-throated Wallace Beery voices the first words in a Wellman picture.

During Beery's introductory scene as Oklahoma Red, the rewritten sequence has him entering a hobo camp and singing a drinking song, "Hark the Bells." Wellman preferred that his entrance be more theatrical; that he walk down the road leading to the jungle camp singing and swigging on his moonshine out of a jug before entering the camp. In the days of silent films cameras could be moved with the actors, but early sound was causing scenes to be more static. Microphones had to be hidden and steady. The actors had to stop and recite their dialogue close to the mics. Wellman hated this unnatural nonmovement of his players. Against the protests of his sound people, he grabbed hold of a broom, hung a microphone on it, and walked along with Wallace Beery just out of the frame.

David O. Selznick, brother of Wellman's agent, Myron, and future producer of classics like *Gone with the Wind* (1939), *Rebecca* (1940), *Since You Went Away* (1944), and *Spellbound* (1945), was on the set. He told Kevin Brownlow that it was the first tracking shot in a Paramount film, and the first dialogue scene and recorded vocal in a Paramount feature.

Wellman had met and liked the aspiring young producer. As payback to David's brother, Myron, for the work that he had done negotiating the Paramount contract, Wellman told the front office, "David O. Selznick is the only producer I can get along with!" They brought Selznick on board and, although he was not a producer on *Beggars*, he did produce Wellman's next two films, *Chinatown Nights* and *The Man I Love*. Their relationship would continue with two classic films of the future, *A Star Is Born* (the 1937 original) and *Nothing Sacred* (1937).

Wellman's next film was the crime story *Chinatown Nights*, with Wallace Beery, back for his second Wellman picture in a row. With the advent of talkies, the studios began to force sound into silent films. *Chinatown Nights* was originally silent but, encouraged by the success of part-talkies, the studio made the decision to put the picture back into production to add dialogue scenes.

In addition to the new sound scenes, Wellman dubbed in dialogue to already produced scenes, added sound effects and music. The result was quite interesting—having the novelty of sound while retaining the flow of silent cinema.

Although the reviews upon release swung in many directions, top-notch film critic William K. Everson later said, "*Chinatown Nights* is a perfect example of what Hollywood directors themselves envisioned as the talkies of the future. In pacing, mobile camerawork, and overall design, it is essentially a silent film, still using a constant musical score and narrative subtitles."

The film premiered March 30, 1929. Less than seven weeks later, the newly formed Academy of Motion Picture Arts and Sciences staged their first Academy Awards presentation. The Academy was the brainchild of mogul Louis B. Mayer, head of MGM. He and the reigning czars of the Hollywood studios were looking for a way to build their power structure in order to defeat the growing strength of the labor unions. In addition,

Poster created by Paramount Pictures for their
restoration of *Wings,* 2012

the new Academy could serve as its own censor before the church, activist
groups, and the government were able to intervene. As it turned out, they
could not stop the unions and censorship was just around the corner.

As an afterthought, an award ceremony would be good publicity for
their industry and give credence to their Academy. There were 230 members joining at a cost of $100 per. L.B. hired his studio's art director,
Cedric Gibbons, to design a proper trophy for the winners of the best of
the best. A gold-plated athletic figure fourteen inches tall and weighing
seven pounds was selected. The figure is plunging a sword into a reel of
film containing five notches denoting the branches of the Academy: producers, directors, writers, actors, and technicians. The nickname "Oscar"
arrived a few years later.

Films released between August 1, 1927, and July 31, 1928, were eligible
for nomination by a board of judges chaired by Mayer. Three months
before the ceremony, the winners were announced. One of the few sur-

prises of the night, in the adorned Blossom Room of the Hollywood Roosevelt Hotel, was the absence of the director of the winning Best Production, *Wings*—Wellman was not invited.

However, there were 270 well-coiffed guests paying $5 apiece for the sumptuous bill of fare. An abundance of seasoned waiters and waitresses in formal attire served the finest champagnes and wines. The food presentation included lobster Eugenie, filet of sole au beurre, jumbo squab, and, with a pinch of hometown sentiment, Los Angeles Salad. The guests wined and dined and danced until L.B. thought there had been enough merriment. He silenced the orchestra and got down to the real bread and butter of the evening.

How ironic it was that the master of ceremonies was Douglas Fairbanks, the man who had given birth to Wellman's film career. He presented the coveted Best Picture statuette, called Best Production for this year only, to Adolph Zukor, the president of Paramount Pictures. The film that had meant so much to Wellman, that he had fought so hard for, made so many sacrifices for, was receiving the industry's highest honor and . . . he was not allowed to share in its glory.

William Wellman's Academy snub has taken on some historic proportions since *Wings*. For the next eighty-four Academy Award presentations, there have been only three other times when the director of the Best Picture winner did not receive a Best Director nomination. Edmund Goulding was so dishonored for MGM's *Grand Hotel* in 1932, Bruce Beresford for his *Driving Miss Daisy* in 1989, and Ben Affleck for 2013's *Argo*. How is it possible for a film to be honored as the Best Picture of the year and yet not even a nomination for the individual whose vision created it and brought it to the screen? William Wellman is the *only* director whose film won for Best Picture and wasn't invited to the ceremony.

What did Wellman do the night of the awards? Did he host his own party? Did he go to another Academy Awards bash? Did he even accept his agent's invitation to join a small dinner party? No, none of the above. The director of the Academy Award winner for Best Picture of the year went home with an old friend, Jack Daniel's, and got stinking drunk.

Meanwhile, back in the Blossom Room, Fairbanks handed out all the awards in less than five minutes. The winners trotted to the podium, accepted their statuettes, made no speeches, and then sat at the head table. Losing nominees were handed honorable-mention certificates. *Wings* won just one other honor, a special award to Roy Pomeroy for Engineering Effects.

Producer Darryl F. Zanuck picked up another special award for the

The second anniversary of the Academy of Modern Picture Arts and Sciences
marked the first Academy Awards presentation, 1929

first talkie, Warner Brothers' *The Jazz Singer*. Its star, Al Jolson, ended
the evening with a song and two surprise remarks—they were the first
big laughs in Oscar history—when he said, "I notice they gave *The Jazz
Singer* a statuette. But they didn't give me one. I could use one; they look
heavy and I need a paperweight," and "For the life of me I can't see what
Jack Warner (head of Warner Brothers) can do with one of these awards.
It can't say yes."

10

PRANKS AND MISDEMEANORS

Regardless of the climate surrounding Paramount studio for William Wellman, within his film companies no clouded conditions existed. It was an all-for-one and one-for-all atmosphere. There was: hard work and long hours, frustration and disappointment at times, but also great enthusiasm, excitement, exhilaration, suspense, shenanigans, and madcap adventures.

The 1928 *Beggars of Life* was not filmed in Tahiti or the Hawaiian Islands, but Jacumba, California, on the U.S.-Mexican border. The small town was built in a valley at an altitude of 2,800 feet above sea level, below the Jacumba Mountains. The area is dry with little rainfall. Temperatures reach well above 100 degrees in the summer and Wellman's company shot there from May 31 through June as part of a thirty-nine-day shooting schedule.

In an attempt to reconcile with his wife, Wellman hired Marjorie as script girl and her brother, Jack Chapin, as an actor. Wellman's apricot-brandy-belting buddy, Dan Dix, was set to play one of the hobos—without his sidekick, Virgil, who had passed away.

The company was living in a broken-down old hotel with food that matched and nights so sizzling they moved their mattresses out on the second-floor porch that extended the length of the rear of the hotel. Sleeping under the stars were the director, actors, actresses, camera crew, grips, electricians, prop men, practically the whole sweltering company including a secretary and a scared script girl (Marjorie).

"In this Jacumba dream nest," said Wellman, "I was bivouacked between two of the actresses, one of whom slept like a baby, the other [Louise Brooks] talked in her sleep, in intervals of the most interesting

Wellman's "small oasis" on *Beggars of Life*

truths of different people of the motion picture industry, mostly men, producers, stars, actors, and one important director [Eddie Sutherland] whom she had recently divorced that I knew very well, at least I thought I did, but after a week of listening to her, I knew him much better than even his mother. It was all very racy and entertaining, but unfortunately I started to dislike her, she was so different when awake, so sweet and lovely, and such a bastard when asleep and the truth came mumbling out. I changed the location of my bed."

The reason the company was in this hotbed of discomfort was because there was a narrow gauge railroad that started and ended in Jacumba. "A little steam engine," said the director, "with a tiny passenger car and three little freight cars, it looked like and was a beautiful plaything."

A great deal of *Beggars of Life* was shot on this train, in the small freight cars, and in the jungles that the train passed by where the hobos assembled. There was a cluster of broken-down shanties, which was their main gathering spot; here Wallace Beery's character reigned as the king, and the company spent weeks in this deserted lifeless hot spot. There was one wonderful curative, a fresh, cool small stream that flowed close by. "Lunch time was spent by a naked motion picture company cooling off," said Wellman. "I found a spot where there was a mini waterfall and it was there that I sat for a half hour each day, letting the cool water splash down my head and shoulders, flowing over my body."

Wellman found this small oasis and kept it secret. Only once did a stranger try to take it away from him. He was a small-town, aggressive reporter and the director kicked the hell out of him. Soon after, the reporter struck back with a vicious newspaper column on what a son of a bitch the director was.

"I was very proud of it," said Wellman, "and one of my guys pasted it on the bulletin board in the town hall. It was very flattering."

In this kind of a location, there can be all kinds of problems, the most important of all the lack of decent food. There was one hotel and one café, and the director's four-letter complaints to the studio accomplished zero. So he had his unit manager send one of his helpers to San Diego to get good food and hire a chef. "This took some time," said Wellman, and, while they were waiting for the chef to arrive, "old Dan Dix saved our lives. He asked me for a rifle, a shot gun and beds for his two helpers, and a clean-up job in the most livable of the shanties." The director took care of it, assigning an assistant prop man to help him and providing an expense account for the cooking necessities. Dan promised a "feed"

The cast of *Beggars of Life* (1928): (front row) Richard Arlen, Louise Brooks, Wallace Beery, Wellman behind Brooks

Beggars of Life: Wellman, Brooks, writer Jim Tully, Arlen

on Saturday night, after the day's work was finished. This, of course, included beer, wine, and the hard stuff—unfortunately, there were no apricot trees in Jacumba.

Wellman had moved the whole company for a two-day stretch at another location a few miles down the track. The two-day stretch had become three and the director sent word to Dix that the whole company, plus those who ran the railroad, would arrive back in town late Saturday afternoon, in the toy train, just in time for cocktails and dinner.

It was a wondrous Dan Dix feast: a fresh lettuce and tomato salad with dressing à la Dix, venison steaks, quail, asparagus, and creamed potatoes, and Dan's hot biscuits that melted in your mouth. For dessert, his own apple pie with a slice of cheese and the topper of them all, Irish coffee, strong both ways! "How in God's name he did all this was unbelievable," said Wellman, "he fed and seated over a hundred starving people, it was pure magic, robbery and excellent marksmanship." Beery was so entranced that when he got back to Hollywood, he bought Dan the most beautiful Western boots and an expensive Stetson hat. Wellman added, "which Dan slept in, boots on and hat tipped over his forehead as if shielding his sleeping eyes from any spooky memories."

After the feast ended, the three-piece orchestra—organ, violin, and cello—played into the night. Wellman reminded, "We all had our little group to inspire joy or sorrow and believe me it helped the actors and actresses to let go and the performances were improved immeasurably." This little ensemble, inspired by many helpings of Irish coffee, played with such complete abandonment and skill that it sounded like an orchestra many times its size. "When the dancing started," said Wellman, "there were screwy bits of hilarious business by the stuntmen such as dancing upside down, a little rough on their noggins but the beat was right on time."

The entire company relaxed and let their hair down, it was like New Year's Eve. The skylarking went on and on and everybody began to feel no pain, when suddenly the long hard week's work crept up on them and the "good nights" took over. A people train began chugging back to the hotel. The director called for a cheer of thanks to Dix and came on board the train. Destination: his bed on the second-floor porch of the hotel. "I was sound asleep when awakened roughly by the owner of the hotel." "There is a big rumble in the pool hall," he said, "involving all your stuntmen and a tough gang of townspeople. I have called Mexicali and other towns and herds of police are on the way to diminish the size of your crew."

"You son of a bitch," said Wellman, "why did you do that? I could have handled it alone." He put on his shoes, fled down the stairs in his pajamas, and out into the street. An awesome sight greeted him. All the windows of the poolroom were broken, pool balls were lying in the gutter, and the war had reached its loudest, four-letter crescendo. "I have been met with a barrage of hatred," said Wild Bill, "which has happened to me many times by people who didn't care for me particularly, but this was going to be a little different, a barrage of hatred full of pool balls, so I grabbed two tops of trash cans and ran into the poolroom."

What a sight! It looked as if an earthquake had struck. Pool balls flew at him. Luckily, they bounced off his makeshift trash can shields, and in his most resonant voice he told them what the hotel owner had done and if they had any sense, they would get the hell out of there, or stay and end up in the can. He told his gang to get their mattresses out of the back porch, put them back on the beds in their rooms, lock the doors, and get in bed.

"I have never seen a battle end as quickly as did this one," said Wellman. "In no time at all, the joint was empty, with the exception of three of my stuntmen, Duke Green, Harvey Parry and Jack Holbrook, who was badly hurt. It looked as if one side of his face had disappeared." The company doctor arrived as Harvey, Duke, and the director carried Jack up to his room. Wellman volunteered to be the doctor's assistant. He explained that he had been bandaging himself for all kinds of cuts, bruises, sprains, and breaks for years. He got the job and after stitching up Holbrook, they looked after the other stuntmen.

"By God, we got away with it," said Wellman. "All the time we were patching up our wounded, siren after siren drew up and exhaled at the wrecked poolroom." Mike Donlin, an ex–baseball player, and one of the picture's fine character actors, witnessed the cops' complete bewilderment when they had nobody to arrest.

Wellman took care of the hotel owner by telling him that he would move the whole company out of his hotel if he said one goddamned word about who was who in the battle of the pool balls. The director added a little more to the budget of the picture to repair the owner's poolhall. The work was accomplished by the company grips, carpenters, painters, and prop men, and soon the stuntmen were playing pool again with the guys they had tried to dismantle. They were all laughing and joking about the escapade. Wellman even hired the battlers to be hobos for the big scenes that required extra bums. "Life makes strange friends in the eager race after happiness," said the director.

Wellman's attempted reconciliation with Marjorie had failed and soon the divorce became final. Marjorie got the house, the adopted daughter, and cash. Whatever was left in the loser's pocket went to the lawyers. Wellman didn't miss the house or the cash, he was used to being strapped and more green was on the way. He did not fight for custody of little Gloria since he believed that it was in her best interests to remain with her mother. What Wellman had was his movies, a few friends, and a secondhand automobile.

It was always Wellman's habit not to purchase anything without having the full amount on hand. Because his money had disappeared into pockets not his own, he was waiting for future considerations before getting an automobile. He didn't have to wait long.

On a double date with two beauties and an actor friend, Lefty Flynn, who was driving a 1920s Essex Roadster, both their attentions became fixed on the femme fatales and neither driver nor backseat lover noticed the line of red, lighted lanterns signifying "under construction." The roadster came to an abrupt, unscheduled halt in a torn-up ditch. The only injury from the crash was a wounded Essex.

Flynn never liked the car; his six-foot-six-inch frame had trouble squeezing into it. His overprotective father had gifted him with this undersized companion, and he was happy to offer the remains to his buddy. The new owner had enough money to fix it and surely enjoyed its ride. The Essex was not in a class with the cars the other stars, producers, and directors had, but he wouldn't have swapped it for any one of them. "If anybody or any dame was ashamed to ride in my car," said Wellman, "to hell with them." Director Josef von Sternberg made a disparaging remark and got a kick in the ass, with the promise to beat his brains out if he ever again said anything uncomplimentary about the Essex. He didn't.

The more Wellman drove around the studio, the more flak he encountered. He was even called into Jesse Lasky's office. Lasky, in a very cordial tone, discussed the director's image as a Paramount studio director and the man who made *Wings*. He said that an important man in Wellman's position should not be driving a lower-class Essex, but a Cadillac or Packard. The studio boss pointed out that one of his directors had a chauffeur. That did it. Wellman's temper flared. "It's none of your goddamned business what I do with my private life, as long as I don't rape dames or find some other nasty way to go to jail. As long as I make money for you by making good pictures, you sit right where you are and keep your loud mouth out of my affairs."

"To my dear pal 'Bill' for whom I'd go to the limit—best of health, good luck and success from 'Lefty.' " Maurice Bennett Flynn, called "Lefty" due to his kicking of footballs left-footed during his days as a star of the Yale team

The studio brass called Wellman's agent, telling him to intercede in this matter and prevail upon his client to purchase an automobile of stature. Myron called Wellman, who echoed some of the same remarks he had made to Lasky, "Oh, balls! I like my Essex and it's none of their goddamned business."

The Lasky meeting, the agent's call, and a few other bumps in the road all led to the final straw: Wellman was going to do something about his roadster problem. "I am a funny guy, I fall in love with odd people and odd things such as camouflaging. It helped me out of trouble in the air, it might do the same thing on the ground, so I had studio painters do a job on my Essex." Wellman's camouflaging job was similar to the way his French Nieuports were painted in World War I—with blotches of reddish brown and green.

"It was not only fantastic," said the director, "it was artistic, and my baby graduated into the top draw of unusual and very interesting looking automobiles." To top off the great job of camouflaging, they painted a black skull and crossbones on a front end unit you could open or close according to the weather, closed when cold, opened when hot. It helped to keep the motor cool or warm and it could be opened and closed slowly or quickly. Wellman chose the fast way because the artist had painted an eye on the skull and fast opening or closing gave it the effect of winking at you, always good for a laugh from those who saw it. "My humble Essex became famous, especially with the girls, which of course I did not take advantage of (hardy-har-har)."

Wellman wanted to show off his newly minted combat car, but only under the best circumstances. "Now was the time for me to display my baby to the biggies of the studio, especially the super biggy [Lasky], and I chose as the best time and place, their dining room as they came out from luncheon, unloosing their belts." Wellman positioned himself looking straight at the entrance, with the motor purring like a kitten, so they could get a good view of the camouflaging as he sped by.

The studio executives came out, Lasky first, unloosing his belt as anticipated, followed by the lesser lights unloosing theirs. Lasky scowled as he saw Wellman, who threw a wink at him. "It had as much effect," said the driver, "as if I had done it to George Washington at Mount Rushmore. I threw a quick couple more and one of the lesser lights laughed, he was from New York and probably on his way back. I gave it the gas and purred by them all, looking in my mirror I saw them watching me as I sped away . . . all but one had poker faces, the nice guy from New York was smiling."

In June of 1929, Wellman began work on *Woman Trap* starring Hal Skelly. "Hal Skelly," said Wellman, "was tall and skinny with an enormous appetite for fun and frolic, a very close relationship with whiskey and a rented estate in Beverly Hills." Wellman's buddy Charlie Barton said, "They were known as the unholy three—Wellman, Skelly, and John Barleycorn. They left their mark wherever they went." Skelly's greatest success was on Broadway and in *Burlesque* with Barbara Stanwyck. Paramount made the play into a movie, which was retitled *The Dance of Life*. They signed the stage star for three pictures, Wellman was assigned film number three. When *Woman Trap* was completed, the fun and frolic began.

Wellman and Skelly spent a great deal of time together, mostly in three places: the studio, south of the border in riotous Caliente, Mexico, and the actor's Beverly Hills mansion. Paramount had the work, Caliente had, in Wellman's words, "the hotel, the cottages, the pool, the gambling, the music, the food, the longest bar, the crookedest dog races, everybody from Hollywood . . . and women just waiting to take their hair down." More of their disorderly conduct happened at Skelly's two-story Mediterranean-style mansion on a two-acre lot in the heart of Beverly Hills. Those on the in called it Falstaff's Western Playhouse.

Hal Skelly and Nancy Carroll in *The Dance of Life* (1929)

It was never enough to invite guests for cocktails and dinner. Skelly loved game playing and was constantly devising new and unusual competitions to headline an evening's entertainment. When one of his devisings became popular, it would be repeated on a particular night of each month, sometimes sooner but always on the same day of the week. In this way, the regular guests could easily remember that "Pillow Polo" was a Friday-night event. Wellman introduced Charlie Barton to this popular contest. Charlie was short, strong as a bull, and could hold his liquor with the best of them. He would be a great contestant but not on this night . . . this was Ladies' Night. Charlie and Billy arrived in the camouflaged Essex. "I practically live here," the director told his assistant, "weekends, between pictures, when I get lonely."

The games always began after a fine dinner, comfortable conversation, and a lot of strong drinks. An Asian houseboy, who doubled as cook and bartender, took care of all nourishments, intoxicants, and cleanups. Since he spoke little English, he allowed the visitors to perform in their own languages without his interruption.

In the cavernous living room, sporting a very long bar, all the furnishings were pushed away from the center area. Most of the two dozen or so guests would be standing, sitting, or lying about on large pillows. During these festivities, a steady stream of couples went up the spiral staircase or came down from the many bedrooms. Every so often, the houseboy appeared with fresh beverages, then disappeared in a flash.

Falstaff stood in the middle of the room explaining the rules of the game. He was holding a pillow in one hand, a knee pad in the other. Wellman and Barton watched from bar stools. "Knee pads will be worn at all times," announced Skelly. "The pillow is dropped between the players lined up as in a football scrimmage." On this particular night, the two players were both female and movie stars. They were standing next to Skelly sizing each other up. One was blond, the other brunette. Both wore revealing dresses. Skelly continued. "Each player is on her knees with hands clasped behind her. With her head only, she will try to push the pillow through the goal. If a player unclasps her hands or rises above a kneel, she is disqualified. A player may unclasp her hands to chase the pillow, but when reaching it, clasp again. One hand, one foot on the ground at all times. Any questions?"

The two movie stars did not take their eyes off each other throughout the instructions. Skelly began to help the women put on their knee pads and get into position. The goals at either end of the living room were drawn with white paint about the depth of ice hockey nets. The playing surface was the highly polished pegged hardwood flooring. A thick white line in the center of the room was the starting point, the players on either side.

The secret of Pillow Polo was in the choosing of the contestants, finding people who disliked each other. The suppressed hatreds were the best because they would explode under pressure. Hal and Bill nosed around the studio, talking to their spies about possible choices. Tonight's fillies were two dillies. Blondie just lost her lover and had been drinking heavily. Brunette had questionable sexual desires. They had refused to work together. Much of the audience's fun derived from the unusual floor positions of the combatants in their skimpy dresses.

The pillow pushers were now ready and down in their starting positions, their eyes like two wildcats glaring at each other, their clasped hands clenched with knuckles pale white. Skelly took enough time to build the tension before the final signal. "Ready . . . Set . . ." He dropped the pillow between the two heads and the two heads hit the floor at the same time. It sounded like a cork being shot out of a popgun. Shouts and wild cheering were heard from the onlookers as the competitors rammed and butted like two billy goats.

The battle to push the pillow to the goal went on for many action-filled minutes. First, Blondie closed on the goal, then Brunette took over and the pillow flew in all directions. The races to the pillows were exceptionally rough with lots of head butting and dress tearing along the way. Sweat poured off their slippery bodies and muffled expletives leaped from their mouths. It was as noisy at ringside as the final round of a big fight. At one point, the two were locked in a corner, banging their bodies, fighting for the elusive puffery. From ringside, only two very active behinds were visible. It looked like a couple of hungry dogs fighting over a bone. When they turned around, Blondie's well-shaped right breast flopped out of her torn dress, matching the already visible left boob of Brunette. They looked like a match pair—the boobs, of course.

Finally, a lamp stand was knocked over, the shade tumbling down on Blondie's head. Brunette laughed loudly and Blondie crowned her with the shade. Brunette cried aloud, then fired the shade across the room and leveled a sharp left hook at Blondie's jaw. The Pillow Polo game came to a close. Skelly jumped in calling the contest a draw. The audience applauded with vigor.

Later that evening, most of the guests and both of the combatants

Charlie Barton and Wellman work on a "lousy" script, which the director never filmed, 1929.

had gone home. The only people who hadn't left the party were spending the night—including Wellman and Barton, but not in a bed. They were both feeling no pain, at least from this night of debauchery. Wellman's pain had been in progress for many months, Charlie's discomfort would begin at daylight. They were half sitting, half lying on Skelly's leather couch in the den. Their music was the light snoring from a passed-out couple on the floor. Barton was sipping a beer, Wellman's drinking was done. As they had done countless times, the two pals discussed the state of affairs in their lives or, in this case, Wild Bill's life.

This inebriated conversation was typical and has been gleaned from interviews with Barton in 1967 and 1971, in addition to Wellman's accounts told to this author.

> Barton: Billy, got a good place to go next weekend. Good food, good
>   drinks, good women. Wanna go with me?
> Wellman: No . . . gotta work on another lousy script. Charlie, people
>   I care about, they keep leaving me . . . even my wife . . .
> Barton: Which one?
> Wellman: The one you don't know about.
> Barton: Oh, I don't know about that one.
> Wellman: I know . . . I can't get it, damn it!

Barton gulps down some beer.

> Barton: Another drink?
> Wellman: I can't get what I want.
> Barton: They have ev'rything. The boyhouse, houseboy will get it.
>   What do you want?
> Wellman: I wanna family, goddamn it! That won't go away.

Barton: Do you want the drink first?

Wellman: No, I wanna wife and family first.

Barton: Oh . . . you've had two already . . . and the one I don't know about, three, I guess . . . jus' close your eyes, reach in, you're bound to pull out a good one eventually.

Wellman: Well, I'm gonna get out.

Barton: You are out. Your divorce is final.

Wellman: No, outta my contract with Paramount. Goddamn it! I directed *Wings* and they give me one bad script after another.

Barton: They pay you well.

Wellman: I don't care about the money. I wanna make good pictures, different ones, all kinds of pictures . . . every damn kind . . .

Barton: Well . . . you do make 'em kinda crazy. You don't need to yell foul words up to the executives' offices all the time. You never say hi, how are you to them . . . I understand you don't want 'em on your set, but if they're jus' visiting, you don't have to shoot out the lights with your air rifle or put an electric charge under their seats or punch 'em in the nose . . . You do all these things and they blame you for things you don't do . . .

Wellman: Like what?

Barton: Like somebody padlocked the executive restaurant door and they couldn't come outside. Somebody knocked paint off Lasky's new car. Mail was being misdelivered . . . stuff like that.

Wellman: Well . . . I didn't do the mail thing.

Barton: How 'bout . . . leave 'em alone a little.

Wellman: Goddammit, Charlie. I don't want those sons a bitches meddling in my pictures . . . they don't like my car, they don't like me, the hell with 'em. I've had it. I'm calling Myron to get me out of this damn studio.

Wellman dozed off, snoring louder than the passed-out couple. Barton talked on for a while before realizing that there was more snoring going on. He got up, brought Wellman's feet onto the couch in lying position. He found a blanket and covered him up. Since there was no more room on the couch, he wondered what he would do. He thought about walking all the way upstairs, searching for an empty room. He shrugged, then lay down on the floor next to the unconscious couple. In a few moments, there were four snoring guests in Hal Skelly's den.

During Wellman's years at Paramount, he had seen few extended vacation days. He took his final one in early 1930. Each day turned out to be special and memorable. He was with his family and old friends in the Boston area, his flying buddies, Tommy Hitchcock in Long Island and Duke Sinclaire in Denver, Colorado. When he returned, he set a meeting with his agent. He explained exactly how and why he felt the way he did about wanting to get out of his contract. Myron understood. "Don't worry, Bill, I'll make this right. Just keep doing your job and you will hear from me."

Myron set up an appointment at Warner Bros. with a very interested producer, Darryl F. Zanuck. Zanuck and Wellman hit it off and began a long and rewarding partnership. Before beginning that relationship, Wild Bill had one more mission to accomplish at Paramount. But he needed an accomplice.

Charlie Barton was sleeping peacefully in his bed in his apartment when the telephone rang at 4:00 a.m. It was Wellman calling with these words: "Meet me at the Sunset Ranch in twenty minutes. Bring a shovel." Charlie followed his director's orders. The Sunset Ranch was a horse ranch and much used film location in the San Fernando Valley. Both Barton and Wellman had worked there.

The luminous light from the full moon reflected off two shovels onto the dark horse manure being deposited into the bed of Wellman's rented pickup truck. The digging continued until there was a substantial pile of the fresh, organic fertilizer. There was no conversation until the two laborers were back in the truck and on their way to Paramount. Like a scene from one of his pictures, Wellman discussed it with his assistant. On this project, Charlie was not only the assistant director but an actor with a role to play. Wellman showed his pal a special prop for the scene, a small key that had taken the director two weeks to pilfer. There would be no dress rehearsal for this scene, just action.

Because of the late hour, the studio was dark and uninhabited. Wellman positioned his vehicle just outside the first-floor office of B.P. Schulberg, and Barton ran over to the drive-through gate to keep the night security guard occupied while Wild Bill carried out his assignment. Wellman thrust the aforementioned key into its lock and soon began to transfer manure from shovel to Schulberg. In less than fifteen minutes, a ponderous pile covered B.P.'s desk. After the final shovelful of horse shit, Wellman positioned his latest script on top of the foul-smelling mountain with a note that said, "Here's what I think of your lousy script!" After depositing his entrenching tool in the back of his truck, he whistled for his accomplice and off they drove into the semidarkness of the early morning.

This event signaled the final separation between William Wellman and Paramount Pictures, as well as the conclusion to his seven-year contract after less than three years. It is not clear whether Myron Selznick negotiated the termination, or the end came as a result of mutual agreement— both parties having had enough of each other. What is clear is that from 1925 to 1930, both parties had reaped great benefits. The eleven films directed by William A. Wellman had brought excellent profits to the studio; and one glorious picture, *Wings*, would stand for all time. In the words of John Andrew Gallagher, "*Wings*' impact on popular culture was comparable to that of George Lucas's *Star Wars* trilogy. *Wings* is a masterpiece of the silent cinema and Wellman's first great work, a legendary World War One aviation epic with dazzling cinematography and stunts, documentary-like realism, dynamic direction, and a warm, engaging cast. It stands as a pioneering achievement and a prototypical adventure movie, retaining its potency ever since its release."

Jesse Lasky's dream of finding the right road show picture of 1927 was certainly fulfilled. "We needn't have worried quite so much about whether it would make the grade. It turned out to be the last great silent picture and won the first Academy Award ever given for best production."

Paramount's main gate. B. P. Schulberg's first-floor office is to the right of entrance.

Darryl F. Zanuck, head of production at Warner Bros. and Wellman's new producer

As for William Wellman, even though he had acquired the reputation of "tough to control," his ability to make all kinds of films on schedule and within budget made him appealing to other studios and producers—especially if they left him alone. Charlie Barton later said, "I don't think Wellman ever made very many bad films. I really mean this . . . he always had some little thing in his films. He was real, he was honest. When the films were shaky in premise, underdeveloped, poorly motivated, the films still work. It's as if they are propelled forward on the strength of Wellman's convictions. Where the scripts provided no originality, when the actors brought no life to their roles, Wellman infused his own into the films until they whirred along with pace, energy, and enthusiasm."

Frank Thompson wrote, "No matter how slight the film seemed to be, no matter how trivial the subject matter, Wellman was able to leave his personal imprint on the finished product."

In March of 1930, Wellman exited the Paramount lot in Hollywood in his camouflaged Essex Roadster and sped over the hill to the Warner Brothers studio in Burbank. He signed a two-year contract: $2,500 per week for the first twenty-two weeks; $2,750 per week for the next forty weeks; and $3,000 per week for the remainder. This contract would be extended for another two years with continuing salary increases up to $5,000 a week. And the initial signing was taking place during the Great Depression. His executive producer, Darryl Zanuck, also promised that he could bring in his own projects and they would be green-lighted.

The milestone film and winner of the first Best Picture, *Wings*

11

I AIN'T SO TOUGH

After years of battles and retreats, from early nickelodeon to the launching of full-scale films, the Warner brothers, Harry, Sam, Albert, and Jack, finally achieved victory. After World War I, they had bought forty acres of a ranch on Sunset Boulevard in Hollywood and built a studio. They invested huge sums of money in the budding and highly competitive film industry. The years 1919 and 1920 were perilous times for them and they were pushed to the edge of bankruptcy.

Harry, the oldest brother, found a new source of investment capital with a Los Angeles banker, Motley H. Flint. Flint recognized the enormous potential of films and loaned the brothers $1 million. With the new funds, the studio could afford bigger and better films with John Barrymore as their star attraction. Barrymore, a distinguished stage performer, played the lead roles in the lavish *Beau Brummel* (1924) alongside Mary Astor, and as Captain Ahab in *The Sea Beast,* the 1926 adaptation of *Moby-Dick.*

Though business prospered for a time, escalating costs and the inability to buy a national theater circuit to assure first runs of their films brought about another financial crisis that threatened to close the studio. The Bell Telephone Company had developed a new sound-movie system called Vitaphone. Although the other major studios discounted it, Warners embraced it, believing this was the sound of the future.

Badly in need of financing to carry them through the experimental period of production and distribution, they searched for investors and found some who reluctantly agreed to furnish limited capital. The studio began to produce one- and two-reel films. The brothers were unable to convince the film industry that talking movies were not just a novelty but here to stay. Believing the experiment was only temporary, most theater owners refused to spend thousands of dollars on sound equipment. However, the ones who did soon found their audiences building as the film-going public began to embrace the new medium.

By 1927, the quality of sound reproduction, however expensive, was improving in leaps and bounds. The Vitaphone process was exceedingly costly, as specially trained personnel were required to operate the expensive machinery. Again, the Warner brothers' funds were dwindling rapidly but a big break was on the way—*The Jazz Singer.* In 1928, armed with the success of *The Jazz Singer*, the brothers Warner purchased a 110-acre lot in Burbank for their new and bigger studio. By the end of the year, the studio was thriving. The balance sheets showed a profit of several million dollars and the studio expanded its group of theaters. Nearing the end of 1929, Warners and their First National Pictures registered a gross profit of $19,700,000 over the $3,360,000 profit of the previous year. By the end of the decade, the studio was riding the crest of the wave. The title of one of Al Jolson's songs from his second film, *The Singing Fool* (1928), "I'm Sitting on Top of the World," describes the feeling at the Burbank studio at the time. And so Warners ended the 1920s and began what became their classic era of the 1930s. In a massive issue of *Variety*, June 25, 1930—celebrating the studio's twenty-fifth anniversary—it was written that Warner Brothers was "The Pacemakers of the Amusement World" and . . . "No other studio could match them."

Jack Warner later remarked, "I believe—and the box-office returns will confirm it—that the most profitable pictures are those made by men who understand every nerve and muscle and vein that make up the remarkable body of a motion picture film." His studio's young, ambitious, enthusiastic, and professional craftsmen—both in front of and behind the camera—began rolling out dozens of genre films: crime and social dramas, musicals, adventure stories, swashbucklers, comedies, mysteries, melodramas, Westerns, war films. Along with the other six major studios—MGM, RKO, Paramount, Columbia, Universal, and Fox—the high-octane glamour factories of Hollywood were beginning to flourish.

In the late 1920s and early 1930s, Warners was not known for artistry and awards, but for making films out of the day's headlines—the bread-and-butter movies that captured audiences in Depression times. A major contributor to the success of these films was . . . pre-Code Hollywood.

Until 1934, American movies were uncensored and left up to the morals and judgment of the studio moguls, writers, and filmmakers. Mick LaSalle, author, lecturer, and *San Francisco Chronicle* movie critic, wrote,

"If you think of old movies as corny, chances are you're thinking of the movies made after censorship took hold in the middle of 1934. Before then, movies were sexy. They were political. They were surprisingly feminist and they were adult. . . . Their appeal is that, through them, you get to hear a long-ago era speak with its own voice, unimpeded by censorship. That voice is surprisingly modern. . . . When you see pre-Code movies, you realize that this five-year period was no anomaly. The anomaly was the 34 years of censorship that followed it. This is how movies should always have been. These are the conversations movies should have been having with us, always. This is the past, without lies."

It wasn't until 1922 that the voices of church groups and concerned citizens began to make an impression on the Hollywood film studios about the overuse of sex, nudity, adultery, prostitution, and violence in their movies. When a trio of scandals startled Hollywood—the Roscoe "Fatty" Arbuckle rape/murder trial, the never-solved murder of director William Desmond Taylor, and the drug-related death of matinee idol Wallace Reid—the studios were forced to take action in an effort to protect against censorship and clean up their image. They formed an organization, the Motion Picture Producers and Distributors of America (MPPDA). With Will Hays, former postmaster general under President Warren Harding, at the controls, a set of guidelines was established to pressure the producers to eliminate the offensive content of their films and to include morals clauses in studio contracts. In doing this, they hoped that government censorship laws would be unnecessary. In 1930, a new version of the Production Code was drafted to standardize the censorship requirements of various states. In truth, the studios had only been paying lip service to the Code in order to find ways of luring audiences into theaters during the Depression. These MPPDA guidelines proved ineffective and Hays drafted stronger ones in 1927 and 1930, finally able to enforce a more rigid Production Code in 1934.

The pre-Code era came to an abrupt close July 1, 1934, when Catholic and other church groups threatened boycotts of all films, establishing their Legion of Decency to watchdog movies.

Studio heads bowed to the pressure and the era of censorship began, lasting until the establishment of the industries' rating system in 1968.

The sensational series of films from 1929 to 1934 helped Hollywood survive the economic crisis of the Depression, allowing moviegoers to enjoy the vicarious thrills the pictures provided. Into these exhilarating times of the classic period of the Hollywood studios rode Wild Bill Wellman. He joined a stable of quality young directors that included John

Adolfi, Lloyd Bacon, Michael Curtiz, Roy Del Ruth, Edmund Goulding, Howard Hawks, Mervyn LeRoy, Frank Lloyd, Archie Mayo, and William Seiter.

A list that Wellman cared more about contained the stars under contract that he could choose from for his pictures. These were some of the players who made up the famous Warners stock company from the late 1920s into the 1930s: George Arliss, Mary Astor, Richard Barthelmess, Joan Blondell, Humphrey Bogart, George Brent, Joe E. Brown, James Cagney, Ruth Chatterton, Ricardo Cortez, Bette Davis, Olivia De Havilland, Ann Dvorak, Douglas Fairbanks, Jr., Glenda Farrell, Errol Flynn, John Garfield, Bonita Granville, Walter Huston, Al Jolson, Ruby Keeler, Guy Kibbee, Paul Muni, Pat O'Brien, Dick Powell, Claude Rains, Ronald Reagan, Edward G. Robinson, May Robson, Barbara Stanwyck, Warren William, Jane Wyman, Loretta Young.

Star development was important to the major studios. They not only

Wife number four, Marjorie Crawford, with her dog, 1930

Wellman enjoys his new 1930 Packard.

built up their contractees' status through a series of carefully chosen roles, but provided lessons in acting, voice and elocution, personal grooming, physical fitness, singing, and dancing, as well as more specialized areas like fencing and archery. The new contract player was taught how to interact with the media: reporters, fan magazine writers, gossip columnists, even fans and fan clubs. The studio publicity staff took control of the neophyte's on- and off-screen life. When an unfortunate incident took place, the publicists minimized the damage.

Before starting his first Warners production, Wellman dismissed one favorite lady and took on two more. He later wrote, "My Essex lasted as long as I lasted at Paramount. I then signed at Warner Bros., said a sad good-bye to my first love, because of her age, long hours of work, and inability to get around, and bought a green Packard with a white convertible top." Soon there was a third favorite lady riding in the passenger seat of that stylish 1930 Packard 745 Roadster with rumble seat—wife number four, another Marjorie, with the last name of Crawford.

"I needed a wife," said Wellman, "and the quiet of a home. The love of one beautiful girl, so I married an aviatrix." Crawford also played polo and Wellman thought of her as a female Tommy Hitchcock. He described her as "rough and tough with the face of an angel—a beautiful blonde angel—and a figure, amen." She was one of the earliest female fliers to draw national criticism for entering air races and wanting to match Charles Lindbergh's transatlantic flight. Only men were expected to fill the airways with flying accomplishments.

Crawford was a compatriot of the more famous Ruth Elder and Amelia Earhart, who promoted flying for women. In 1928, Earhart became the first woman to span the Atlantic by air. She made her historic solo flight in 14 hours and 50 minutes, breaking the previous record of 16 hours and 12 minutes by a team of male pilots. Lindbergh was the only other pilot to make the solo flight until then. Earhart became the first person to fly it twice, and she set the distance record for women.

During the courtship of Bill and the new Marjorie, he received his first assignment. In the spring of 1930, he took off at a sprinter's pace, directing eighteen films in less than four years. *Maybe It's Love*, a football comedy about a college team saving their school, was a favorite project of Wellman's producer, Darryl Zanuck, who coauthored the story under the assumed name Mark Canfield. Until his departure from Warners in 1933, Zanuck made most of the production decisions.

Although the story had little appeal to the director, Zanuck's enthusiasm and Wellman's desire to please hastened his acceptance without argument. "I admired him for his guts and the quality he had of grabbing a headline and generating the speed and enthusiasm all down the line to make a good picture quickly—at this, he was a master and the hardest-working little guy you have ever seen in all your life. We had good moments and bad, but there was one thing you could count on. When you wanted an answer, you got it right then and there; if he shook hands on a deal, it was a deal, period."

Maybe It's Love stars Joan Bennett, James Hall, and comedian Joe E. Brown. As an additional publicity stunt, members of the 1929 All-American Football Team were hired as featured players. This film ranks as possibly Wellman's most trivial and uninspired made between 1930 and 1934 at Warner Brothers, although it proved to be a reasonable hit at the turnstiles. *Variety*, October 22, 1930: "The producers can thank the comedy for holding up a pretty poor football yarn. With the aid of funnyman Joe E. Brown and his elastic facial expressions and enormous mouth, Wellman gives a stale story some luster."

The story reveals that the president of Upton College is about to be fired unless the weak football team can rise up and defeat their archrival, Parsons University. Upton's team has only one good athlete, played by Brown. Joe E. and Joan B., playing the president's daughter, come up with a plan to bring home the trophy and save daddy's job—sexual recruitment of better football players.

In an amusing scene, Brown teaches Bennett how to flirt and she does the rest. One by one, she offers herself to the athletes, as long as they enroll at Upton. A calamity occurs when they all arrive at her bedroom at the same time to collect their recruiting prize. With Brown's help and comedics, the players forgive her ruse and go on to win the big game. Joan ends up with her rich boyfriend, played by James Hall, and Joe E. has his laughs.

Other funny scenes show Brown dealing with a honey-hungry bear he mistakes for a cow, and fighting off a belligerent millionaire in a basement during the big game. More laughs come from a scene with Bennett and one of the All-Americans when their canoe topples over, leaving them both underneath it, then back on shore soaking wet—the seductress showing everything she's got, pre-Code.

Wellman repeats a favorite long, slow dolly shot, this time through a water fountain to Bennett and her love interest, Hall, then back through the water as they disappear behind a pillar to kiss. Wellman also supplies vocal commentating to the climactic football contest. Studio advertising for the film's release said, "A College Education Minus the Classroom."

The director began his next film in the fall of 1930 and there would be four more to follow in 1931. The original title, *Romance on the Rails*, was changed to *The Steel Highway* when Warners had problems getting the title rights from an unrelated story with the same title. The picture was released as *Other Men's Women*; in Canada it was called *The Steel Highway*.

In the 1930s, titles were often changed for various reasons: to strengthen weak openings of films, to support better advertising campaigns, to respond to changes in audience attitudes, while taking advantage of current headlines of the day, authorship disputes, and so forth. The title changes could happen before release or even after weeks in distribution. The studios were committed to the success of each of their films—from start to finish to release and thereafter.

Other Men's Women stars Grant Withers, Mary Astor, and Regis Toomey, with Joan Blondell and James Cagney in supporting roles. The story deals with a romantic triangle in a tragicomedy about male camaraderie and sacrifice.

Two buddies, played by Withers and Toomey, work together as locomotive engineers. Withers is single and a skirt chaser. Toomey is happily married to a younger wife played by Astor. When the drunk Withers is thrown out of his apartment, he is invited to move into his pal's modest home. Soon, he and Astor fall in love, which is discussed but not consummated except for two kisses.

The friends become rivals and have a fight in the cab of a moving train, resulting in a disastrous crash that leaves Toomey blinded and Withers guilt-stricken. Withers attempts to make it up to his buddy, their relationship being more important than the love affair with Astor. In the climactic scene, the blinded Toomey staggers through a raging storm, and drives a train to a suicidal death, sacrificing his life for the happiness and togetherness of his friend and wife. Withers, Astor, and Toomey give fine performances, and Joan Blondell, as the wisecracking waitress, gives her early career a hike. James Cagney, in only a few brief scenes, shows why his star is ready to shine.

The director returned to his *Beggars of Life* location in Jacumba, California, for the railroad scenes. *Other Men's Women* features Wellman's fast-paced, documentary-style shooting of the train sequences. His dialogue is crisp and natural; the camerawork imaginative, particularly around the railroad yards, on top of trains, in diners, dance halls, and during the stormy nights. Much of the film is shot in rain—a Wellman trademark.

The film is full of humorous touches: Cagney meeting his date at the dance hall, peeling off his railman coveralls, revealing a formal suit underneath, then springing into a professional soft-shoe routine; Cagney with Withers on top of a moving train describing a boxing match, the two ducking their heads without looking as the train chugs under a low bridge; an elderly one-legged man, played by J. Farrell MacDonald, using his peg leg to poke a row of holes in the ground for Mary Astor to plant seeds in her garden; Withers counting passing trains behind him without looking as he orders breakfast and dialogues with the sassy Blondell; Withers being thrown out of his apartment by a stuttering landlady and responding with a stuttering retort.

The picture received mixed reviews, but mostly positive. One later assessment stands out. Gilbert Adair from *Flickers: An Illustrated Celebration of 100 Years of Cinema*: "Then there was William Wellman's *Other Men's Women*, not just the first indisputably great sound film but one of the greatest ever made in Hollywood." The illustrious, prize-winning Scottish novelist, film critic, and journalist goes on to compare *Other Men's Women* to such classics as Renoir's *La Bête humaine* and *La Chienne*, Jean Vigo's *L'Atalante*, and Godard's *Bande à part*. This critique from such a respected individual, for a film so seldom seen and rarely ever written or talked about, is simply amazing.

While waiting for his next assignment, Wellman went back to work on a favorite story rejected by Paramount in 1928. He and writer John Monk Saunders developed *Dirigible*, a World War I adventure story. As usual, the studio did not green-light the project, which contributed to Wellman's departure. But now he was at Warners and things might be different. Wellman believed Zanuck to be a master at selecting projects for his contract directors. "Sometimes if you got your own thing . . . brought it to Zanuck, and he liked it, he would let you make it. A lot of them I didn't choose, but a very few I didn't like."

While Wellman was working on the *Dirigible* story again after *Other Men's Women*, the title changed to *Jump* with a cast headlining two of his *Other Men's Women* players, Grant Withers and James Cagney. *All Quiet on the Western Front*'s Lew Ayres was to be another lead. When the director made his proposal to Zanuck, he received a warm reception and together they went to work with the title changed to *The Balloon Story*.

Marjorie Crawford flew Wellman to Arizona to be married.

It dealt with eight adventure seekers who joined the balloon school in St. Louis before America entered the war. The young airmen go into combat as "the eyes of the army" in their balloons. Wellman had shot down a number of these enemy balloons during his time in France, and certainly knew their importance in observing and reporting military activities. The balloon school comrades are killed off one by one, showing the horrors of war. The film ends with the balloon commander, now an old man, revisiting his fantasy of eight balloons with eight ghostlike figures bailing out with great white billowing parachutes to safety.

Clearly, this story material was Wellman's way of reliving his days of flight training and combat with his comrades who died in battle. Although their wings were folded about them forever, Wellman's ending saves them and brings them home. *The Balloon Story* was subsequently shelved, but Wellman was told it would be on the schedule at a later date. To his frustration, his film would never be produced. In its place, Zanuck preferred that his director begin production on *Night Nurse*, a story about the tribulations of a devoted nurse versus a sadistic chauffeur. As it turned out, *Night Nurse* would also be rescheduled.

Before his next film started, a different kind of project was put on the schedule—Wellman's marriage to his aviator-girlfriend Marjorie Crawford on December 22, 1930. As was Wellman's custom, no family members were invited to the affair.

In order to escape California's "gin marriage law," which required a three-day waiting period so couples could "sober up" before getting hitched, a flight to nearby Yuma, Arizona, answered the call to tie the Wellman knot. Before Las Vegas turned into a quickie marriage boomtown, Yuma, at the California and Mexico borders, required no waiting time for marriage licenses. The town was located next to the beautiful Colorado River, the climate was dry and pleasing, and there were historic hotels with nice spas. Wellman and Crawford took the plunge. Wild Bill didn't need to charter a flight—the pilot was his bride and the plane was hers.

When Wellman phoned home to report another nuptial, Celia was disappointed, Arthur was ho-hum, and Arch was exasperated. Their conversation went something like this:

Arch: What's her name?
Wellman: Marjorie.
Arch: I thought you two were divorced.
Wellman: This is another Marjorie, last name Crawford.
Arch: How long have you known her?
Wellman: Long enough. We have a lot in common. She's a flier and plays polo.
Arch: You don't play polo and you don't fly anymore.
Wellman: I know, but I saw Tommy Hitchcock play and we can talk about flying.
Arch: Well, you could have waited a while longer. You could have invited your mother to the wedding.
Wellman: I'm sorry about that, but I don't have time to wait.
Arch: But you have time for a wife? Oh, well. I hope it works out this time, Bill.

As usual, there was no stopping or even slowing down Wild Bill. He was choosing his own course of action. From the get-go, the marriage was stormy and the weather worsened from there. "How crazy can you be and not be confined?" said Wellman. "I knew fliers; I was one of them, not too reliable, on the goofy side, hard to handle, impossible to control, and not good to live with day in and day out, so I married one."

Wellman's next film project would become one of his classics and one of his own choosing. While on his way to lunch at the Warner Bros.

commissary, he was stopped by two well-dressed druggists from Chicago, Kubec Glasmon and John Bright. "They had written a story about some of their toughest and roughest customers, one gangster in particular. They called it *Beer and Blood*. They wanted me to please read it. Beer and Blood sounded like an unusual blending, they seemed like nice guys so I invited them to lunch. They were two men who came to lunch and stayed for many more. We finished eating, they left with full stomachs and high hopes."

The writers told the director that their project had been around the studio for many months, and they were afraid it was going to be dropped. Wellman went to his office to read the story. It begins in 1909 Chicago: clanging cable cars, honking automobiles, the clatter of horse-drawn buggies, the sounds of the crowded city streets and sidewalks; less noisy footage of the Union Stock Yards, a residential neighborhood with children playing on the sidewalk, riding bikes in the empty street, saloons, a beer wagon being pulled by two white horses. Now, a Salvation Army marching band passes revealing two youngsters coming out of a store.

The boys, Tom Powers and Matt Doyle, are already delinquents, stealing beer and drinking it. Powers is the tougher, meaner of the two. He has an older brother, Mike, who is intelligent and honorable. Their father is a policeman who beats Tommy for his troublemaking. Ma Powers is a dedicated wife and loving mother.

Time advances to 1917, and the grown-up Tom and Matt are further into the world of crime. Their attempted robbery turns sour as one of their juvenile accomplices is killed. Powers slips deeper into the underworld while his brother joins the Marines. Prohibition arrives. Powers and Doyle rise in the gangland ranks becoming enforcers of a bootlegging operation. They begin to live high, affording expensive cars, clothes, and women. They seek revenge on their former mob boss, Putty Nose, killing him in the process.

Mike returns from the war, a decorated hero. Tom and Matt attend his homecoming party, supplying bootleg beer. Mike, realizing his brother's crime connections, refuses the brew causing a rift. Mike remarks, "There's more than beer in that keg! There's blood! Beer and the blood of men!" Tom counters, "You killed and you liked it! You didn't get those medals for holding hands with those Germans!"

Powers's crime career takes a downturn as he fights with his brother and his woman, Kitty. His underworld boss, Nails Nathan, dies after being thrown from a horse. Tom, in turn, slaughters the animal. With the death of his mob leader, the rival gang, led by Schemer Burns, marks him for elimination. Powers hides out in an apartment with liquor and an overly aggressive prostitute. Soon, he emerges only to be attacked and his pal gunned down.

Seeking revenge on a rainy night, Powers marches into the rival gang's headquarters with guns blazing. In the shootout, he is seriously wounded, collapsing outside in the gutter. Before passing out he exclaims, "I ain't so tough."

While recovering in the hospital, Tom plans to go straight and return to his family. Unseen by the audience, Powers is kidnapped by the rival gang and murdered. His mother and brother get a phone call telling them that he is coming home. They happily prepare for his arrival. Ma straightens up her son's room, singing while she works. Tom's brother puts a record on the Victrola, "I'm Forever Blowing Bubbles."

There is a knock at the door followed by the sound of screeching tires. Mike opens the door and there is his brother, upright and wrapped in mummy cloth. Tom's corpse falls facedown on the floor with a thud, as the last strains of "Blowing Bubbles" fill the air.

"I finished without going to the bathroom," said Wellman, "and ran to Zanuck's office. He was about to close up shop and go home but my enthusiasm made him late for dinner, with a promise to read it despite his objections on doing another gangster story following the great success of *Little Caesar* and *Doorway to Hell*."

The next morning early, Zanuck called Wellman into his office. "He was nuts about the story," said Wellman, "had even changed the title to *The Public Enemy* but there was a big but to be answered. 'Give me one big reason why you think I should take the gamble and let you make the picture?'"

In Wellman's meeting with Jesse Lasky about *Wings*, the mogul had asked, "What makes you think you can direct our big road show picture better than my experienced directors?" Wellman answered, "It's a great story. I'll make it the best goddamn picture this studio's ever had!"

Now, five years later, in a meeting with Warner Brothers' Darryl Zanuck, Wellman answers a similar question with a similar response. "Because I'll make it the roughest, toughest, goddamn one of them all!" Zanuck's answer came quickly and to the point. "Get the two druggists in my office, I'll make a deal."

Veteran Warner Bros. scribe Harvey Thew was hired to adapt *Beer and Blood* for the screen. Among his recent credits were John Barrymore's *The Man from Blankley's* (1930), *Sinners Holiday* (1930) with Grant Withers and James Cagney, and *Illicit* (1931) starring Barbara Stanwyck.

Wellman dove into preproduction, working with Thew and casting the leading roles. No actors were more important than the ones who would play the two crime buddies, Tom Powers and Matt Doyle. Zanuck and Wellman chose Edward Woods as Powers, and Wellman's *Other Men's Women* supporting player, James Cagney, as Doyle. Zanuck thought it was a publicity coup casting Woods, who was engaged to Louella Parsons's daughter, Harriet. Louella was the most powerful Hollywood columnist at the time, the Queen of Celebrity Gossip. Woods had also received good notices for Hobart Henley's *Mothers Cry* (1930). Donald Cook was cast as Powers's brother, Mike. Zanuck and Wellman saw an uncanny resemblance in the two actors playing brothers.

The fact that the Cagney and Woods roles were switched has been fodder for the writings of many decades. From Jack Warner to Darryl Zanuck to Warner Bros. executives, to casting directors to the film's writers and on and on, many people wanted a share of *The Public Enemy* greatness and the role that made a star of James Cagney. Fortunately, Wellman receives most of the credit for the immaculate shift and well he should. Even Cagney always gave his director the honor.

Exactly how and when the flip-flop took place is another matter. Many historians have viewed Cagney's original contract and other production materials having Cagney in the role of Tom Powers before filming began. Wellman's version, which he never veered from:

No picture was prepared, well prepared as fast as this one, and in nothing flat I was making the picture. On the first day of shooting Zanuck came down on the set to see me. "I have to go to New York for a few days so it's all yours and I don't know anyone else I would rather leave it with than you, good luck" and he left.

I worked like hell for three days, so hard and so late that I didn't see any rushes. Then it happened, all alone with my cutter all Sunday long. The rushes were good, but something about them kept bothering me. Then I got it, asked my cutter to rerun a certain reel with Woods and Cagney. It hit me like a blow in the face, what a dumb bastard, me, carried away because Woods and Cook looked like brothers—I don't look like my brother, the brothers that look like brothers are twins. I had the wrong man in the wrong part, Jesus Christ!

I called Zanuck in New York, got him out of bed, to tell him what a dumb bastard this great director of his was. He didn't blow his top, didn't say, "Wait until I get home," "Ship the rushes to me," or "Shoot around the trouble," no, all he said was three magical words, *"Make the switch."*

Where does the truth lie? Why would the paperwork say the turn-around happened before filming when Wellman clearly maintains it was after shooting began? Here are some possible answers. Contracts and schedules are constantly changing. Even production reports are often revised. Cagney's original contract may have said that the actor was por-traying the role of Matt Doyle, then later revised to say Tom Powers—the old pages discarded. In that era, test scenes were often shot before actual production began. They were valuable to check costumes, period ward-robe, makeup, hairstyles, lighting effects, sound effects, dialogue changes, and casting choices.

Is it possible that Wellman made a test of Cagney and Woods that gave him the notion that their roles should be switched? Is it possible that when Wellman looked back on his vast career of over a hundred pictures, including seventy-six as director, that his memory told him that the test was a scene shot during the shooting schedule? The paperwork of the past aside, it probably all happened just as Wellman said it did. The bottom line, the director is the one who recognized and corrected his error in judgment all the way into motion picture history.

Another *Public Enemy* example of mistrust directed at old studio docu-ments is the curious case of Louise Brooks. She was Wellman's first choice to play the stunning and seductive role of Gwen Allen. Back in 1929, Brooks was offered a continuing contract at Paramount but instead left the studio for greener pastures in Europe. Her final Paramount picture had been *The Canary Murder Case* (1929). When she refused to do sound retakes on the silent film, she was "unofficially" blacklisted in Hollywood. Paramount also released the misinformation that her voice was not suit-able for sound pictures.

When she returned to Hollywood in 1931, good roles in good pictures did not come her way and her career was sliding. Regardless of Lulu's problems, Wellman, who never understood her apathy toward Holly-wood and the movies, wanted her for his leading lady. He always appre-ciated her *Beggars of Life* professionalism. He thought she was perfect for the Gwen Allen role. Back to those old parchments. By all accounts, Brooks rejected Wellman's offer.

Now that we have reached Wellman's career in the 1930s, a tremen-dously valuable and exciting resource comes into play—his shooting scripts. This author has most of his screenplays, leather-bound, including cast lists, shooting schedules, and other production materials. Between the rawhide covers of Wellman's *Public Enemy* script there is a cast list dated January 16, 1931, just nine days prior to the start date. Opposite the role of Gwen Allen is the name Louise Brooks. Even though we do not see the enchanting features of Lulu in the film, her name keeps popping up in the pages of the director's book and . . . what could be more up to date than the information contained in the director's shooting script?

Wellman was in the habit of writing notes in pencil on his script pages. They would be used as reminders for changes to scenes, dialogue, bits of special business, camera angles, and so forth. On page 100 of a three-and-one-eighth-page scene between Tom (Cagney) and Gwen seated on a couch kissing and ready to make love, the doorbell interrupts and Tom says "Aw nuts!" Wellman has written underneath the dialogue, "gets up so fast almost throws Brooks on her ass." This scene is checked off as being shot and finished.

From this, what are we to believe? Did Brooks do the scene? Was it unsatisfactory and she replaced? Did Wellman write the note earlier for Brooks, then when she departed forget to cross off her name and add the new actress's name? Hardly seems likely.

What about the film's reviews? Many contemporary critics such as Irene Thirer, Richard Watts, Jr., and Edwin Martin, who, after seeing the picture, listed the name of Louise Brooks in the cast and in their reviews. Were all these professional reviewers unable to identify such a recognizable star of over twenty pictures? Had Brooks been cut out of the film after release and replaced with a proviso that it was to be hushed up? Curious, isn't it?

In the *Monthly Film Bulletin*, July 1965, Brooks responded. "What happened was that William Wellman had offered me a part in *Public Enemy* and I turned it down to go to New York. But the advance publicity had gone out with my name in the cast, so when people see an extra girl walk through a scene with a black bob and bangs, they say: 'There is Brooks.'" One of her biographers, Barry Paris, wrote that Brooks rejected Wellman's offer in order to go to New York to be with her then lover, George Preston Marshall.

It is all memories and . . . paperwork from the long ago about an actress named Louise Brooks, who was very unpredictable and very special. She had a hypnotically beautiful face, a subtle and captivating style, one of the first naturalistic actors in film and way ahead of her time.

Henri Langlois, director of the Cinémathèque Française would say, "There is no Garbo! There is no Dietrich! There is only Louise Brooks!" Adoring fans would have loved to see her in Wellman's enduring classic. Barry Paris wrote, "Turning down *Public Enemy* marked the real end of Louise Brooks's film career." She said herself, "I must confess to a lifelong

WHY CONSIGN YOUR
MUSIC AND ENTERTAINMENT
MEMORABILIA TO HERITAGE?

Maybe you've decided to sell the collection you've spent
years putting together, or perhaps you've inherited
some stage or screen used costumes or wardrobe,
signed documents or photographs, stage or screen
used props or instruments, scripts, rare and vintage
vinyl, or other types of music and entertainment
memorabilia as part of an estate. Whatever your
reasons, you have one goal in mind: to realize the very
best prices for each and every piece. Only Heritage,
the unchallenged world leader in the sale of celebrity,
music, and Hollywood ephemera can help you do that.

Jean Harlow, costar of *The Public Enemy,* signed a page from a Heritage Auction Galleries catalogue to "Willie" Wellman

curse: My own failure as a social creature."

No matter how Louise Brooks left *The Public Enemy* company, her replacement was not too shabby. Borrowing from Howard Hughes's contract players at $1,000 a week, Wellman secured the services of the Platinum Bombshell, Jean Harlow. Already a star, *Public Enemy* would push her further into the stratosphere of stardom. Her on-screen and off-screen romances were legendary—as were her leading men. They went from the likes of Laurel and Hardy, Wallace Beery, and William Powell to Clark Gable and Howard Hughes. It seemed that everyone wanted Jean Harlow.

Wellman was shooting *Public Enemy,* working at night doing rain scenes. It was a Saturday night and the midnight luncheon was finished. Harlow's bungalow was at the head of the street, and a few of her late visitors disappeared like magic when the director yelled, "O.K., let's get going." The electricians were going to their positions on high and low rainmakers, getting ready to make things unpleasant again, when there appeared an apparition, an ivory-tinted naked phantom, coming out of the bungalow and starting to glide down the wet street. "It was like a beautiful statue," said Wellman, "that had suddenly come to life, from her toes to the tip of her head, it was carved ivory that tremored. Mad men were dancing in her head, you could have heard a pin drop, no whistles, no nothing, just a hushed, 'Jesus Christ!' "

The figure stopped, looked up and all around with a childlike expression on her face, then a sweeping kiss to everybody, turned like royalty and glided back to the bungalow, opened the door, and vanished. "The applause frightened you," said Wellman, "it was deadly and it would never be forgotten. 'O.K., turn on the rain!' "

One of the most powerful and memorable scenes in the picture belongs to Cagney's revenge on the rival gang and its leader, Schemer Burns. Written in the script, Cagney strides across the street and into the gang headquarters. A shootout occurs off screen. Nothing is seen, only the gunshots, screams, and groans are heard. Cagney reappears, badly wounded, staggering up the street trying to reach his automobile.

One of the Burns hoodlums runs out the door of the headquarters and fires back at him, then crumples up in the gutter. Pedestrians who have heard the shots run in all directions. A uniformed policeman blows his whistle and runs down the street to Cagney, who has dropped to his knees but is still trying to crawl to his car. A crowd surrounds him. FADE OUT.

Wellman's notes changed the scene:

> Rain is constant. No pedestrians or policemen are out in the rainstorm. Cagney strides into the building and the off-screen shootout occurs. More high velocity gunshots, screams and groans. Cagney reappears in wounded condition. He throws his two guns breaking the windows of the headquarters, then crumples up in the rain-swollen gutter. No hoodlum appears, Cagney is all alone. One line is spoken. Wellman's pencil writes, "I ain't so tough." FADE OUT.

The script is littered with special business notes for the actors. Two of the most consistent were directed to the crime pals, Cagney and Woods. Wellman wrote, "spits," "wipes," "spits and wipes," "wipes and spits" next to a number of their scenes together. These expressions become their signatures from their earliest hoodlum days to their later years. Eddie Woods wipes his nose with his sleeve, and James Cagney spits.

It is impossible to write about *Public Enemy* and not discuss one of the most celebrated scenes in cinematic history—the infamous "Grapefruit Squash," the scene in the kitchen when Cagney pushes a half grapefruit into the face of Mae Clarke. This clip became so famous that everyone connected with the picture wanted to take credit for the idea.

The writers said it was their idea from the start to the finish. Even Darryl Zanuck wanted the credit. He claimed, "It was my idea, the grapefruit. I think I thought of it in a script conference. When I made *The Public Enemy*, I was way ahead in thinking. No love story but loaded with sex and violence." Getting mad at Zanuck was not unusual for Wellman; in fact, it had long been a habit of his, but this one sizzled. "A man who had made as many pictures as he, picking one bit of business to claim as his own, typifies Zanuck, a good picker of other people's work."

"These acclaimed touches," said Wellman, "are oftentimes something

Mae Clarke and James Cagney in *The Public Enemy* (1931)

the director stole or had happened to him somewhere in his cross word life, and some few times, particles of a vivid imagination. My so-called touch came from none of these three, it came from beauty."

Here's the real story. Wellman's wife at the time was Marjorie Crawford, a beautiful polo-playing aviatrix, as graceful on horseback as in the air. His polo experiences were limited to spectatorship at a few Hollywood parties, and the few times he saw his pal Tommy Hitchcock play. Naturally she wasn't in the class of a ten-goal player but was very good. "Polo-wise," said Wellman, "we had no trouble but I made the mistake of going flying with her once as a guest, this followed a very strenuous argument, argument hell, it was a dogfight the evening before, but like a jerk I still climbed in the next morning and away we flew, she at the controls."

Wellman was sitting next to her, in the gunner's spot, with no gun, no controls, no nothing to help him if his charming wife got too crazy. "I was a good stunt pilot," he said, "could do every stunt there was, including a couple never before attempted, so what the hell, she can't show me anything I haven't done many times before."

On the takeoff, she kept it on the ground as long as the runway permitted, then pulled it up almost vertical, causing his gut to do strange new maneuvers. The gunner realized that this was not going to be an enjoyable flight.

Marjorie did all the stunts and some of the most dangerous. Her gunner was trying to figure out how he could knock her cold or choke her, and get her limp body where he was and his where she was. Much to his

Marjorie takes Celia for a comfortable flight. Her husband would get a different kind of ride.

disappointment, he couldn't work it out and settled for just sitting there, not making any remarks or showing any expression, as she could watch him in her mirror. Eventually, the nonreaction got to her and she brought the plane down, made a perfect landing, taxied into her spot. He jumped out, walked quickly to their car, and drove away. This fast exit did not please her, as the car was her ride home. A taxi got her home.

Wellman continued to maintain his silence when he got home that evening, late and loaded, a condition she detested. He slept in the guest room and arrived for breakfast, hungover and sick. Neither exchanged a "good morning," but the usual half a grapefruit was at his place. She had finished hers and was drinking coffee. She looked beautiful as usual, but she too was playing the game of silence, the only difference was that she looked stony beautiful, and he looked stoned ugly. He started on his grapefruit when, suddenly, a fantastic idea hit him, one that would show how he felt yesterday, weathering all her aerial acrobatics.

"I looked at her face, breathtaking, but absolutely expressionless, it was a statue. She looked at me but I out-looked her, as she turned her head

Bette Davis listens to mood music with her director, Wellman, on the set of *So Big* (1932).

slightly—this is your chance, you silly bastard, squash that grapefruit in her lovely face, and put some northern lights in it, at least it would break the monotony. I didn't do it—there must be something chaste about me."

Then came the scene in *Public Enemy*. Instead of shooting it the way it was originally written, the director changed it, had the two characters seated, and wrote a few new lines. "Instead of having Cagney throw the grapefruit at Mae Clarke, I had him do what I didn't do to the cold beautiful face of my then wife. I haven't the slightest idea who thought of throwing the grapefruit at the girl—for my money it was one of three, either Kubec Glasmon or John Bright, who wrote the original story, or Harvey Thew who did the screenplay—I with the most unexpected assistance from my wife conceived the dignified touch of squeezing a grapefruit in a lady's face, done with great fervor by a hell of an actor named Cagney."

Public Enemy wrapped production on February 21, 1931, after a twenty-nine-day shooting schedule. It cost $151,000 Depression-era dollars and made millions for Warner Brothers. It was one of the most successful films of the 1930s and helped write the gangster movie rulebook. It received an Academy Award nomination for Best Original Motion Picture Story, made a star out of James Cagney, and became an imperishable classic that lives as a genre milestone. In the words of a 1931 Warner Bros. advertisement, "WHEREVER YOU GO! WHEREVER YOU TURN! YOU HEAR ABOUT *THE PUBLIC ENEMY*!"

There was little time for patching up Wellman's rocky marriage, as the rescheduled *Night Nurse* came on the heels of *Public Enemy*. He was hoping for a break and was promising Marjorie a fine vacation. Her escape came in the clouds.

Borrowed from Columbia Pictures, where she had just starred in Frank

Capra's *The Miracle Woman*, Barbara Stanwyck entered Wellman's life. She was a Wellman woman: attractive, tough, strong, no-nonsense, independent, and liked to hang with the boys. She was also hardworking and professional. "Stanwyck not only knew her lines," said the director, "but everyone else's ... I love her." They did five pictures together.

In *Night Nurse*, Stanwyck portrays a dedicated night nurse who discovers a gruesome plot to starve two children in her care, keeping them from their inheritance. She demonstrates her strength by socking a drunken lecher, and her beauty by constantly showing off her 1931 lingerie while taking off and putting on her nurse uniform.

A 1946 publicity photo of Barbara Stanwyck

Cagney was supposed to play a supporting role as an intern, but after *Public Enemy*, he would be saved for bigger things. Joan Blondell, a Wellman favorite, was back for another top role as Stanwyck's nurse-partner. Here comes that name again ... Louise Brooks. When the project first came to Wellman before *Public Enemy*, he wanted her to play an important role. When *Night Nurse* was postponed, he tried to move Lulu over to *Public Enemy*.

There was a big surprise playing the sinister chauffeur, starving the children, beating up women and benevolent doctors: Clark Gable, only a supporting player at the time. "One of the most despicable heavies imaginable," said Wellman, "and he did it with such savoir faire that he became a star." The powers-that-be at Warner Brothers liked his performance but decided he was not worth a contract, not star material—his ears were too big. "They forgot to look at his dimples, listen to his voice, and see his smile," said Wellman.

A Wellman trademark: finding an important scene, even a climactic one, and shooting it in such a manner that the audience does not see all the action on screen—something is left to their imagination. As one example, in *Night Nurse*, the scene when Nick the chauffeur (Gable) punches Lora the nurse (Stanwyck), knocking her to the floor. The camera angle does not show the blow—it happens off screen—the camera panning down to Stanwyck falling to the floor.

In the first twelve months of Wellman's Warner Bros. contract, he directed four films. After *Night Nurse*, there would be twelve pictures made in the next twenty-two months. The stories covered a wide range—comedy, drama, adventure, romance, Western, aviation, crime, prostitution, drug addiction, even what became known as film noir.

The Star Witness (1931): Walter Huston, Frances Starr, Grant Mitchell, Sally Blane, and Charles "Chic" Sale. Crime melodrama. The Leeds family—Abby and George; their children Sue, Jackie, Donny, and Ned; and Abby's father, Private Summerill, a grizzled Civil War veteran—witness a gangland shooting, can identify the shooter, Maxey Campo, and are being terrorized to prevent them from testifying in court.

First, Pa Leeds, played by Grant Mitchell, is kidnapped and beaten.

Clark Gable as the sinister chauffeur and the two little girls he is attempting to starve to death in *Night Nurse* (1931)

Then, Donny, the middle son, Dickie Moore, is kidnapped and held hostage. The crooks threaten to kill him if the family does not keep quiet. Walter Huston plays the hard-boiled district attorney who is determined to bring down the mob boss, Campo.

When the family refuses to go to court, Summerill, played by Chic Sale, will not be intimidated and agrees to take the stand. Before doing so, however, he finds his hostage grandson and calls the police, who shoot it out with the gangsters. Donny is rescued, Summerill takes the stand, and Campo is convicted and executed. *Film Daily*, August 2, 1931: "Sure-fire box office smash." *The New York Times*, August 4, 1931: "Another underworld plum for Bill Wellman."

On July 28, 1931, in Harlem, New York, Vincent "Mad Dog" Coll unsuccessfully attempted to kidnap a rival gang member. In the shootout, a crowd of children were caught in the crossfire, a five-year-old was killed, and others were wounded. Family members were afraid to testify at the trial and, in December, Coll was acquitted. In order to take full advantage of the newspaper headlines, Warner Bros. rushed *The Star Witness* into release August 3, premiering it at New York's Winter Garden Theatre. The studio turned over the entire proceeds of the first two performances of the film to the families of the victims.

The picture became one of Warner Brothers' biggest hits that year, and the writer, Lucien Hubbard, Wellman's producer from *Wings*, was nominated for an Academy Award.

The Hatchet Man (1932): Edward G. Robinson, Loretta Young. Based on the play *The Honourable Mr. Wong* by Achmed Abdullah and David Belasco. Grim melodrama about the San Francisco Chinatown Tong Wars. Loretta Young, who ranks next to Barbara Stanwyck on Wellman's favorite actress list, plays an Americanized Chinese daughter of a dead Tong leader. In a Chinese custom, she becomes the ward and then the wife of the Tong hatchet man (enforcer), played by Edward G. Robinson, who, unbeknownst to her, had killed her father.

Robinson discovers Young in the arms of his bodyguard, Leslie Fenton, and at her insistence, spares his life but sends them both away. Eventually, Robinson and Young reunite and stay together as love conquers. Robinson, in his autobiography, *All My Yesterdays*, writes, "I'm able to say that . . . *The Hatchet Man* is one of my horrible memories." He called Wellman "a chilly, knowledgeable, 100-percent American." *Hatchet Man* was the first of four pictures Wellman would make starring the enthralling Loretta Young. In a meeting with this author in 1996, she said, "I loved your father and I loved working with him."

So Big (1932): Barbara Stanwyck, George Brent, Bette Davis. Third version of Edna Ferber novel. Youth-to-old-age melodrama as Stanwyck goes west, leaving Chicago's gambling world, becoming a schoolteacher and farmer's wife. *New York World-Telegram*, May 2, 1932: "a motion picture with moments of great beauty and simplicity, and some mighty fine acting and direction . . . but along about the middle it begins to flounder, and reaches its conclusion in a slow and heavy maze of uncertainty and sentiment."

Bette Davis, in one of her earliest memorable roles, always counted the picture as one of her favorites. In *Mother Goddam*, she is quoted as saying, "During all the years I found few roles that had the naturalness in the character, a naturalness similar to my own personality. This I often regretted."

Love Is a Racket (1932): Douglas Fairbanks, Jr., Ann Dvorak, Frances Dee. Comedy-drama set against a world behind the bright lights of Broadway. Fairbanks, playing a crusading reporter, becomes involved with murder and gangsters because of his nymphomaniac girlfriend, Frances Dee. *New York Sun*, June 10, 1932: "Full of wisecracks . . . light entertainment." Fairbanks called the director "reckless and wild," but also one of the best at Warners.

The Conquerors (1932) RKO-Radio: David Selznick had left Paramount for RKO and borrowed Wellman for this historical epic with Richard Dix and Ann Harding. The picture was a follow-up to *Cimarron*, the winner of the 1931 Oscar for Best Picture. Dix plays double roles as a Western pioneer and his grandson serving in the First World War. Much of Wellman's own life has been inserted into the picture: joining the Norton-Harjes Ambulance Corps, fighter pilot in the Lafayette Flying Corps, his parents reading about their son's exploits in the skies over Europe in the local newspapers.

The lavish production brings together the Old West, the Great War, and the Great Depression. *New York Daily Mirror*, November 19, 1932: "A dignified and stately film . . . a repetitious flavor which detracts from it as entertainment. But it is handsome and impressive, a meaty story of progress, spiced with comedy and sprinkled with sentiment." RKO ads clamored, "A man and a woman faced the future! In his eyes, the vision that had led a dauntless line of conquerors on to triumph. In her heart, the love and faith in this man who said, 'You can't stop America!'"

Central Airport (1933): Richard Barthelmess, Sally Eilers, Tom Brown, and John Wayne (bit). A romantic triangle in the aviation world. Barthelmess is cast as an ace flier, guilt-ridden from an accident that resulted in the death of several passengers. He leaves the commercial airlines for a life as a barnstormer with his brother, Tom Brown. They fall in love with the same girl, Sally Eilers. Barthelmess believes that due to their dangerous lifestyle, barnstormers should not marry. On the rebound, Eilers marries Brown. The resulting anxieties play havoc with their lives and careers. *Variety*, May 9, 1933: "There's a thrill in *Central Airport*'s flying moments, and just enough of those moments to cover up deficiencies in practically every other department, from story to cast."

John Wayne had reached stardom in Raoul Walsh's *The Big Trail* (1930). When the picture tanked at the box office, he was relegated to leads in B Westerns and small parts in A films. Wellman met and liked the ex-USC footballer, bringing him back later for *College Coach*. In *Central Airport*, the director cast him as a copilot on an ill-fated airliner that crashes in the ocean. There was so much protest at showing the crash of a commercial airliner that the scene was struck from the picture.

In the recut version, the audience hears about the crash and sees the aftermath. The surviving passengers crowd together on the wings of the downed aircraft in the storm-raging sea. Wayne attempts to save a passenger, J. Carroll Naish, who falls into the water. They both drown. Interesting to note that twenty-one years later, Wayne would be playing another copilot on an ill-fated flight in Wellman's aviation classic, *The High and the Mighty*—a starring role this trip.

Heroes for Sale (1933) is no glossy, feel-good picture. Nothing is sugarcoated. It is Warner Bros. at its best, taking real-life stories and events from the day's newspapers about ordinary people struggling to survive. The film is also Wellman's most powerful "message" picture of the 1930s.

A bright light in the silent era, New York–born Richard Barthelmess made a successful transition to talkies. He stars as Tom Holmes, who must endure drug addiction, rehabilitation, job loss, wealth to poverty, incarceration, political persecution, the death of loved ones, deep depression, homelessness.

The ever-glamorous Loretta Young stars as Ruth Loring, Holmes's adoring wife, killed in a labor riot. *Heroes for Sale* marks the second film for Wellman and Young together.

Holmes, a combat hero, barely survives the trenches of World War I. Wounded with shrapnel embedded in his back, he is captured and placed in a POW camp. He develops an addiction to morphine; prisoner exchanges bring him home. After a partly successful rehab, he takes a bank job with the father of the apologetic soldier, Roger Winston, played by Gordon Westcott, who, believing Tom was dead, stole the credit for his wartime bravery.

Tom's continuing addiction costs him his job and his mother dies from disgrace. Another turn at rehab cures him and he meets the love of his life, Ruth Loring. Life is good for a while as he climbs the ranks in the business world, happy with his marriage and pregnant wife. His business partner, Max, a socialist, invents a machine that takes the place of the company workers, who riot, and Ruth is killed in the fray. Even though Tom tries to prevent the rampage, as Max's partner he must suffer the consequences with a five-year prison sentence. After his release, he refuses to accept half of the invention money, calling it "blood money." He donates all of the funds to charity.

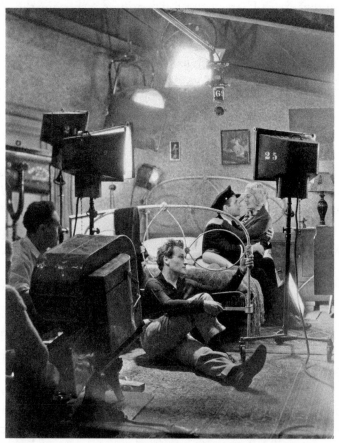

Safe in Hell (1931): Wellman listens to rehearsal with Donald Cook and Dorothy Mackaill.

Tom's world continues to spiral downward. Believing him to be a communist, the police drive him out of town. Unable to find a job, he becomes a homeless wanderer. With all his struggles, defeats, personal tragedies, neither the Great War nor the Great Depression can rob him of his positive, never-give-up attitude and his belief in the future of his country. When he meets up with Roger, whose father's bank had failed, he tells him, "It may be the end of us, but it's not the end of America. In a few years, it'll go on bigger and stronger than ever. That's not optimism. That's common horse sense. Did you read President Roosevelt's inaugural address? He's right. You know, it takes more than one sock on the jaw to lick a hundred and twenty million people." *New York World Telegram*, July 21, 1933: "It is hardly likely that the film will be popular and gross a lot of money." *New York Herald Tribune*, July 22, 1933: "Its grim bitterness will hardly please the cinema advocates of sweetness and light. Its occasional notes of good cheer will annoy those who might have been stirred by its frank facing of the unpleasant facts of recent life."

Wellman often remarked how pleased he was with the variety and quality of most of the eighteen films he directed under his Warner Bros. contract. But five of the films had similar story lines that caused him to strongly protest to the front office. Although 1933's *Midnight Mary* became a Wellman favorite, he grew tired of the popular "fallen woman" theme.

Safe in Hell (1931), *The Purchase Price* (1932), *Frisco Jenny* (1933), *Lilly Turner* (1933), and *Midnight Mary* (1933) had credible scripts but all focused on a woman in trouble. These members of the fair sex are floozies, prostitutes, a madam, even an immoral gangster moll.

Safe in Hell, written by Joseph Jackson and Maude Fulton, based on a play by Houston Branch, headlines silent screen star Dorothy Mackaill and *Public Enemy* costar Donald Cook. After stock footage of New Orleans, a fight breaks out between prostitute Gilda Karlson (Mackaill) and her ex-boyfriend (John Wray) in a hotel room. This results in an accidental fire that appears to cause his death. Her sailor lover (Cook) arrives on the scene, whisking her out of town as a stowaway on board his ship bound for a Caribbean island sanctuary safe from authorities and extradition. Before leaving on his tour of duty, Cook marries her and promises to send money in his letters. She is left under the constant scrutiny of a pack of unsavory scoundrels, including the island chief of police (Morgan Wallace), who withholds Cook's letters to her.

Gilda tries to keep her vow of faithfulness while waiting for her husband's return, but boredom and the habits of her past lifestyle cause her to join the lecherous males. She does keep a portion of the promise, not allowing the rogues to bed her. When her ex-boyfriend, who survived the flames, comes to the island to taunt her, she shoots him in self-defense and is sent to "island" trial. With the verdict comes two choices: six months as sex slave in the police chief's prison or the gallows.

When her husband returns for a brief encounter, she tells him nothing of her problems, not even the trial and the choice she must make. He tells her that he is willing to give up his love of the sea to meet her in New Orleans and live as man and wife. Not wanting to involve him in her sordid past or take away his seafaring life, she allows him to leave, believing that they would be together soon. Then she goes to the gallows rather than giving in to the villainous police chief's demands.

Michael Curtiz of future *Casablanca* fame was the original director, with the title of *The Lady from New Orleans*, starring newcomer Lillian Bond and David Manners, costar of the Bela Lugosi *Dracula*. Production chief Zanuck was so unhappy with the dailies and cast that he shut down production and brought in Wellman. The picture was recast and retitled *Safe in Hell*.

This picture was especially interesting to the director because of what later came to be known as the film noir concept—shooting the underbelly of society, the darker side of a prostitute's life, the shadowy characters and events that surround her. Wellman was pleased with his seductive, hardworking leading lady.

Dorothy Mackaill was born in Hull, Yorkshire, England. As a teenager, she ran away to London to pursue a stage career followed by the move to Broadway and the *Ziegfeld Follies*. She transitioned from a Follies girl to a film actress, reaching stardom in 1924 with *The Man Who Came Back*, starring George O'Brien. Just when she seemed to be making another transition, silents to talkies, her option with First National/Warner Bros. was not picked up and by 1937 her career was over. Wellman had appreciated her early struggles and was sorry to see her leave the studio.

Donald Cook was another bright spot in the cast. He and Wellman worked well together in *The Public Enemy* and again here. The director would hire him for two more films, *The Conquerors* (1932) and *Frisco Jenny* (1933). Three of the fine veteran character players deserve special attention. At a time when African Americans were rarely allowed to play real people, just stereotypes, Wellman cast three talented performers in major roles.

Nina Mae McKinney plays Leonie, the hotel manager. She was a dancer, singer, and actress, and the first African American to star in a

Hollywood musical, *Hallelujah* (1929), and be signed by a major studio (MGM). When few roles came her way, she took her talent abroad to Paris, London, Dublin, Budapest, and Athens, where she became known as the "Black Garbo" and the "Queen of Night Life." She possessed the talent and beauty to become one of America's enduring performers, but the doors were closed. Hollywood could accept black character actresses like Hattie McDaniel and Butterfly McQueen appearing with white cast members but not a beautiful black actress.

Wellman's lack of prejudice and desire to help the downtrodden allows McKinney to speak in normal language, not "Negro dialect," and sing a complete song, "When It's Sleepy Time Down South," where no song appears in the director's original shooting script.

Clarence Muse plays the porter, Newcastle. He was an opera singer, minstrel performer, vaudeville actor, composer, and playwright. He also earned a law degree from Dickinson College in Pennsylvania. He became the first African American to star in a nonmusical movie, *Way Down South* (1939), and one of the first black directors of a Broadway show, *Run, Little Chillun* (1943). Although most of his over one hundred film roles were stereotypes and often servants, he always took them seriously with a level of dignity. In *Safe in Hell*, he is able to use his natural, deep voice in a role with some dimension, and Wellman chose his written song for McKinney to sing.

Noble Mark Johnson, six feet, two inches, 215 pounds, played Bobo. His impressive physique and handsome features kept him in demand for over 140 films in a thirty-five-year career that began in the silent era and ended in 1950. He was able to rise above the stereotype, playing not only African Americans, but also Latinos, Arabs, and Native Americans. His devil character in *Dante's Inferno* (1924), Queequeg to John Barrymore's Captain Ahab in *Moby Dick* (1930), the tribal leader on Skull Island in *King Kong* (1933) and its sequel, *The Son of Kong* (1933), were standouts.

Johnson also formed his own studio, the Lincoln Motion Picture Company, producing films depicting African Americans as real people in everyday life. One of his last roles was Chief Red Shirt in John Ford's classic, *She Wore a Yellow Ribbon* (1949). He lived up to his Christian name: he was a noble and dignified presence who exhibited great power and substance. Noble Johnson lived ninety-six years.

As usual, Wellman made a number of notes in his *Safe in Hell* screenplay. When he first read the downbeat and tragic story, he felt the need to add lighter touches, slapstick humor, and interesting compositions and camera angles. The opening shot in the New Orleans hotel room shows a chest of drawers with a telephone on it, ringing. Into the shot come fancy high heel shoes and bare legs. When the phone is picked up, the camera pans the gams to their owner, the prostitute, Gilda (Dorothy Mackaill), as she talks to her female pimp while sitting in a chair with her legs up on the chest.

One of the director's signature shots shows Gilda conversing with her sailor lover, Carl (Donald Cook), while hiding in a storage bin below deck. He crawls in with her and, with their eyes and most of their faces hidden behind the wooden slats, only their mouths are visible while dialoguing.

Wellman decided that a slice of frivolity would play well against the dark, psychological drama. To *Safe in Hell*, the director brought a dose of comic opera. The five lechers living in the same hotel as Gilda become a choreographed burlesque. They follow each other around the hotel living room, bar, and dining areas, even up the stairs to the bedrooms. When one of them sits down, they all sit down. When one of them turns his chair to watch for Gilda's hoped-for appearance from her upstairs bedroom, they all turn their chairs. When one of them crouches down in his chair, they all sink down. This repeating burlesque does not let the atmosphere of boredom and claustrophobia take control of the film. The comedic touches and camera movement add amusement and excitement, depth and dimension on the way to Gilda's demise.

Safe in Hell was released December 22, 1931, to reasonable box office, but critical acclaim was harder to come by. *Variety*, December 22, 1931: "Picture's story is hardboiled and sordid. Too much so most of the time, which is *Safe in Hell*'s chief deficiency." *Time*, December 28, 1931, "*Safe in Hell* is crude, trite, sporadically exciting." A number of reviews echoed the Warner Bros. label—"Not recommended for children!" After the Code arrived in 1934, this picture was kept out of theaters.

The Purchase Price, from the story "The Mud Lark" by Arthur Stringer published in *The Saturday Evening Post*, was adapted by prolific, Oscar-winning, Warner Bros. scribe Robert Lord. This film finds Wellman and Stanwyck together for a third picture after *Night Nurse* and *So Big*. Her *So Big* costar, George Brent, also returns to try to cash in on their earlier success.

Instead of *So Big*'s woman in jeopardy going west to escape Chicago's gambling world, becoming a schoolteacher and a Dutch farmer's wife; in *The Purchase Price*, Stanwyck's troubled lady is a torch singer, becomes a mail-order bride to avoid the life of a mobster's woman, and eventually marries a farmer (George Brent) from North Dakota.

On location for *The Purchase Price* (1932): George Brent behind
Stanwyck and Wellman

The Purchase Price did not live up to *So Big* at the turnstiles nor with
the pundits. *New York Herald Tribune*, July 16, 1932: "An unprepossess-
ing tale . . . dull and ineffective." Stanwyck had received praise for *So
Big*. The *New York World-Telegram* echoed other reviews from 1932: "A
brilliant emotional actress . . . a fine and stirring performance." For *The
Purchase Price*, however, she and her costar were ill-treated by a number
of top reviewers. "Both Stanwyck and Brent are 100% miscast."

Due to *Public Enemy*'s aura still permeating throughout the industry,
Wellman escaped most of the negative criticism. *The New York Sun*, July
16, 1932: "Well done but very mild. . . . [Wellman] will long remain in
this generation's memory as the director of *The Public Enemy*."

Although it would be ten years until the director and his Wellman
woman, Barbara Stanwyck, would work together again, she continued to
stay on the top of his leading lady chart. As an example of her "ready to
work" attitude that Wellman loved, during the thrilling wheat-burning
sequence in *The Purchase Price*, she refused to allow her stand-in to take
her place. She told the director, "I don't like the way she's acting, I can
do it better!" It proved to be a thrilling scene, all caught on camera, with
Stanwyck receiving the director and crew's applause and . . . multiple
burns on both legs. She never complained to the concerned Wellman,
and the wounds eventually healed.

Frisco Jenny stars Ruth Chatterton and Donald Cook. A melodrama about the life of a San Francisco madam, it's based on a true story by Gerald Beaumont, Lillie Hayward, and John Francis Larkin. Robert Lord wrote the screenplay with help from renown playwright, raconteur, and entrepreneur Wilson Mizner.

Mizner's Warner Bros. career lasted a scant few years, until his death on April 3, 1933, at fifty-six years of age. But while he was on hand, he made his presence known. Because of first-rate films like *20,000 Years in Sing Sing* (1932) and Wellman's *Heroes for Sale* (1933), his reputation, which had preceded him, grew in size and shape. In his book *The Legendary Mizners*, Alva Johnston wrote: "[Wilson] Mizner had a vast firsthand criminal erudition, which he commercialized as a dramatist on Broadway and a screenwriter in Hollywood. . . . He was an idol of low society and a pet of high. He knew women, as his brother Addison said, from the best homes and houses."

Signed by Jack Warner in 1931, Mizner had little respect for the mogul or any other authority figure in Hollywood, which put him in good stead with Wild Bill. Some of his famous quotes: "I've spent several years in Hollywood, and I still think the movie heroes are in the audience." "Working for Warner Brothers is like fucking a porcupine: it's a hundred pricks against one." "Treat a whore like a lady—and a lady like a whore."

Frisco Jenny (1933) starring Ruth Chatterton and Donald Cook

You begin to get the idea why Wilson Mizner wrote stories about fallen women.

Frisco Jenny begins in San Francisco with a re-creation of the historic earthquake and fire of 1906, and ends with an emotional quake as the prostitute (Ruth Chatterton) is prosecuted by her own unknowing son (Donald Cook) for murdering the man who threatened to expose her secret motherhood.

After Chatterton is condemned to hang, Cook comes to her jail cell in an attempt to help her. She still refuses to divulge her secret in fear that her past might destroy her son's rising career. *New York Herald Tribune*, January 7, 1933: "Despite the frank hokum of the story and the film's plotty return to the days of Western blood and thunder, the director has kept it marching along its bizarre path with enough interest to hold on until the end, chiefly by use of colorful atmosphere, effective costuming and the logic with which he unfolds his episodic tale."

Ruth Chatterton was a star. She often displayed a temperamental attitude that made her difficult. Some directors refused to work with her, and she refused to work with them. Zanuck decided it would be a good move to put his high-strung leading lady and Wild Bill together. "Zanuck brought us into his office and before we could sit down, Chatterton took one look at me and said, 'I wouldn't work with that man.' I said, 'I wouldn't work with you.' Zanuck said, 'I've got news for you, you're both going to work with each other, or you're both out of work.'"

During preproduction, Wellman stayed clear of his star. His assistant took care of her needs until the first day of shooting. It was nine o'clock when the director asked, "Is Chatterton ready?" His assistant said yes. She came in. No good mornings, no nothing. They rehearsed, made the scene, a difficult one, which she did on the first take. The director said great and meant it, she thanked him, from then on they were the best of friends. "I don't know why," said Wellman, "it was just a couple of s.o.b.'s getting together, who suddenly liked each other."

Since the Wellman-Chatterton connection went so well, Zanuck assigned them another women's picture, *Lilly Turner*. This one costars the amiable George Brent. It is another melodrama relating the ups and downs of a wanton woman (Chatterton), traveling with a medicine show. She is exhibited as "the Perfect Body," but receives her walking papers from her dastardly magician husband (Gordon Westcott) when she becomes pregnant. She loses the child, discovers that Westcott is a bigamist, and marries the devoted alcoholic (Frank McHugh).

A frenzied romantic entanglement ensues, with Brent winning her love but not able to separate her from the kindly McHugh. The studio ads trumpeted, "It Will Make Frisco Jenny Blush." *New York American*, June 15, 1933: "First class entertainment, saved from banality by the engaging presence of Ruth Chatterton. . . . It has the advantages of good direction and good photography."

George Brent, top-flight leading man of the 1930s and 1940s, with nearly ninety films to his credit—three with Wellman—may have lost Chatterton's heart in *Lilly Turner*, but he had already won it in real life. They were married almost six months before production began, on August 13, 1932. The marriage lasted just over two years, until Chatterton's career hit the downswing in 1934. She came back to play one of her finest roles as Walter Huston's self-centered, self-dramatizing wife in William Wyler's much acclaimed adaptation of Sinclair Lewis's *Dodsworth* (1936). She made only two more films before retiring in 1938.

She was nominated for two Best Actress Academy Awards; wrote a Broadway play, *Monsieur Brotonneau* (1930); published several popular novels in the 1950s; was a licensed pilot owning her own plane, crisscrossing the country several times solo; and . . . had a positive relationship with a Warner Bros. director—just two s.o.b. pilots who made pictures together.

As soon as Wellman wrapped *Lilly Turner*, and before receiving his next assignment, he marched over to the front office and issued a loud protest with great gusto. He zeroed in on Zanuck and president Jack. He was not going to make any more distressed women stories. He threw in an additional spirited complaint—his *Dirigible/Balloon* project had not yet been scheduled.

The studio bosses were not pleased with his outburst. He was a contract studio director and was expected to make films from the scripts he was given without objection. As a consequence, they loaned him out—at $9,000 a week—to MGM and their B picture unit for *Midnight Mary*, the story, spiced with sex, of a female gangster, a kept woman who spends three years behind bars before trying the straight and narrow with wealthy playboy lawyer Franchot Tone. *Midnight Mary* is considered the only time MGM made a Warner Brothers picture.

Wellman was reunited with his *Wings* and *Star Witness* producer Lucien Hubbard and Loretta Young. In an interview with John Gallagher, the beautiful Miss Young recalled, "We were both being punished. . . . My part went from nine years old to what I thought old, 27. Because we were both mad at the thought of being punished, Bill was very easy and very fluid with the picture and so was I. It was their big moneymaker for two weeks and that put us right back into good graces with Warner Brothers. I thought he was a marvelous director." In a meeting with this author, eighty-three-year-old Loretta Young said that *Midnight Mary* was one of her favorite films.

Wellman returned to Warners with a very different attitude. After directing three of the highest-grossing Warner Bros. films of 1931—*The Public Enemy*, *Night Nurse*, and *The Star Witness*—as well as other popular pictures, he shouldn't have to plead for better product. This reality, the punishment of *Midnight Mary*, ten years and thirty-six films in the studio contract system, made him realize that it was time to go on his own. Although Warners rewarded him with an inspirational offering, a defining Depression saga, *Wild Boys of the Road*, soon he would become a freelance filmmaker as an auteur—having more control of stories and style.

Even though his career was in high gear, his private life was plummeting with another marriage headed for divorce court. The newspapers, trade publications, even Walter Winchell, the gossip voice of Hollywood, were all wondering who would be his next victim.

Midnight Mary (1933) starring Loretta Young

12

THE NEON VIOLIN

William Wellman had been married four times by 1931. In late 1932, he was rising from the financial ashes after paying off his latest divorce, which became official in 1933. But before even thinking about a fifth marriage, he would have to wait an additional twelve months—California's "cooling off" period—before tying a knot around another femme fatale. For the first time in his matrimonial mish-mashes, he was allowed to keep the house that he had purchased in the Whitley Heights district of the Hollywood Hills.

In his constant quest for a lasting soul mate, it was extremely difficult to endure the aftermath period from his transgressions. It wasn't about the money, more of that was on the way. It was about going home to an empty hearth. He liked the house, but needed a helpmate to fill the void between pictures. He found a playing partner in golf and a mentor in the legendary Bobby Jones.

Bobby Jones was the greatest golfer of the era. He and Wellman met at Warners where Jones was making a series of eighteen shorts between 1931 and 1933 called *How I Play Golf*. Some of the celebrities who appeared with the great one: Richard Arlen, Richard Barthelmess, Joe E. Brown, James Cagney, Douglas Fairbanks, Jr., W. C. Fields, Edward G. Robinson, and Loretta Young. The filmmaker was the prolific writer, actor, producer, and director George E. Marshall.

Wellman had received a letter from his brother challenging him to a game of golf. Arch Wellman had risen in the ranks from salesman to senior partner in Nichols and Company, Boston and New York commodities brokers. Arch was vice president from 1927 to 1939. He became a partner in 1935—and he played a good game of golf.

"He was coming to California," said Wellman, "on a business trip and would like to play golf with me for a hundred-dollar Nassau. He had a very wealthy millowner from the South with him, and they looked forward to seeing me, playing golf with me and taking my money."

The director had never played golf and didn't know what a Nassau was (a three-part bet: winner of the first nine holes; winner of the second nine holes; winner of the combined eighteen holes). He showed the letter to Bobby, who explained what the Nassau meant and asked him his handicap. Wellman told him a misspent youth. Jones said not that one, your golf handicap. "I told him I had never played the game but was going to learn how before my brother got here, which would be in almost three months."

Wellman with Bobby Jones on his Warner Bros. set, 1932

Wellman asked the pro if he could learn in that time. Jones shook his head. "You might learn how to hit a ball, but God knows where it will go." Wellman dug in his heels recounting his athletic past, assuring Bobby that he was dead serious and ready to meet the challenge. Realizing the determination of Wild Bill, the master proposed a course of action.

Jones made an appointment for Wellman with a golfing guru pal, Harry Bassler, who was a teaching pro at the Lakeside Golf Club. Fortunately, the golf course was across the street from Warner Bros. The beginner kept the appointment and explained the situation to Bassler. These were Bassler's rules: (1) he would choose all the equipment, even the golf bag and clothing; (2) Wellman would accept every instruction without objection; (3) lessons would be taken for three months without ever leaving the practice range; (4) no actual play on a golf course until the pro said so.

On the first lesson day, Wellman was handed one club, a 5-iron, and told to hit a bucket of balls. All Bassler did was place one ball at a time on the ground in front of the beginner, then step back and watch. When the pail was empty, the pro said, "I'll see you tomorrow." Wellman thought

Some of Wellman's golfing buddies at Lakeside Golf Club. Brother Arch (second from left) next to Robert Taylor, Wellman second from the right, 1930s

the lesson was ridiculous, but he had made a pact and returned the next morning for more of the same. Bassler kept him on the 5-iron for one month. For the novice, it was four weeks of sore hands, blisters, impatience, and frustration. When he uttered a squawk, Bassler would smile and say, "You want to beat your brother, don't you?"

As time went by, Wellman graduated from one club to another until he had used them all, except one. Nearing the end of the three months, Arch called saying that his trip was postponed for a while. The fledgling golfer drew a sigh of relief. The teacher announced that it was time to play a round of golf—and with the great Bobby Jones. Wellman broke into a cold sweat and said, "But Harry, I don't know how to putt." Bassler answered, "I'll show you on the way to the first tee." "He showed me," said Wellman. "It took five minutes and I was off to play my first game of golf, and with the champ. For the record, and because of Harry, I shot an 88, and I never shot higher than that for thirty years."

Arch had to postpone the trip for another four months, giving Wellman time to establish a fine handicap of four. Both Arch and his business friend had handicaps of twelve when they finally arrived for the big match. The weather was ideal and after watching his opponents drive off the first tee, Wellman made an additional hundred-dollar Nassau playing their best ball (his score against the best score of the two). They accepted the wager and watched the Bassler-Jones protégé out-drive them both by over sixty yards straight down the middle of the fairway.

Wellman won the three original bets—$300 each—an additional $100 apiece from the extra bet—and for the first time broke 70. The months of agonizing practice, lessons, frustrations, had paid off . . . and it didn't hurt the winner's chances that he was a highly competitive, fiercely driven individual, who had devoted himself to a renowned teacher and one of the greatest golfers ever. Wellman felt good about pocketing the $800 but, financially, he was well into the loss column. The expenses of his lessons, golf clubs, golf bag, wardrobe, and a full membership at the exclusive Lakeside Golf Club were far more costly than his winner's purse. The upside was: he had beaten his brother, he had found a hobby to carry him through non-working periods, and it was easier to go home alone.

The film that Dorothy Coonan, then eighteen years old, was working on when she met Wellman

In early 1933, Wellman was in preproduction on *Heroes for Sale*. He was walking along the studio street between soundstages on his way to the café/commissary. He passed a group of dancers on a break, standing and sitting outside the soundstage door. They were working on *Gold Diggers of 1933* starring Ruby Keeler, Dick Powell, Joan Blondell, and Ginger Rogers. The musical was being directed by Mervyn LeRoy with songs by Harry Warren and Al Dubin, staged and choreographed by the incomparable genius Busby Berkeley.

Born in New York, Berkeley brought his special brand of talent to Hollywood and the movies in 1930. At a time when the Depression had taken a great toll on the lives of Americans, they could relax in a movie theater and watch the amazing and unique artistry of Berkeley's brilliant staging and choreography in motion picture musicals. "In an era of breadlines, Depression and wars," said Berkeley, "I tried to help people get away from all the misery . . . to turn their minds to something else. I wanted to make people happy, if only for an hour."

The relaxing dancers were dressed in rehearsal garb, shorts and tops, chatting and smoking cigarettes. Wellman noticed a freckled-faced, non-smoking brunette, sitting on the ground, eyes shut, letting the sun warm her. Ruby Keeler, the dancing star, recognized Wellman from a previous meeting at the studio. She took a long drag, exhaled, and called out to him. He stepped over to her but his attention was riveted on the sun-bather. The freckled dancer opened her eyes and for a brief, electrical moment, their eyes met, then she closed them and they didn't reopen. "She looked at me," said Wellman, "no smile, no wink, no nothing, just looked, a long look. I got a hum in my head."

Wellman and Keeler chatted for a brief spell, then an assistant came out the stage door and called the dancers back from their break. Wellman went to his office, closed the door, and communed with himself. "This was so idiotic, so completely me. I didn't even know if she could speak English." He wondered if she was one of those kind of gals who talk and never listen. Maybe an other-people's-business watcher: What are the other girls wearing? Who are they going with? What kind of car are they driving and how did they get it? The sort of thing that Wellman did not like. The point is, he didn't know the first thing about her, but he couldn't get her out of his thoughts.

He didn't want to be like the other actors and directors who went on the Berkeley sets to meet the dancers and showgirls. He wanted to stay in the Bernie Durning system—"staying out of this fakey love nest." The problem was he couldn't stop thinking about her and had to do something about it. He considered asking his assistant to set up a meeting with her. Then, finally, "Oh, balls, I'll go on the Berkeley set and ask Buzz to introduce me."

So he wandered over to the *Gold Diggers* stage. It was the right time, as the troupe was returning from lunch and work had not started yet. "Buzz came in, and I went up and said hello. I didn't know him very well. Had a couple of drinks with him at different places, away from the studio. I liked him, he liked me, maybe because I never gave him any trouble, never fiddled around his sets."

"Well, Bill, this is an unexpected pleasure; don't tell me you're breaking down."

"Well, not quite—yes, by God, I am."

"Who is she?"

"I don't even know her name. I just saw her, and here I am."

Wellman looked around, and there she was, looking at him, not too eagerly, just sort of questioningly.

"She's that little freckled-face fella over there," continued Wellman.

"Dottie Coonan, huh? One of the nicest girls you'll ever know. Hey, Dottie!" and over she came.

"Dottie, I want you to meet Bill Wellman," and he walked away with a little smile on his face.

"How do you do?" said Wellman.

"How do you do. I have never seen you on a Berkeley set before."

"I've never had any reason to be on one of them before."

She got a little embarrassed, and he didn't feel too sure of himself. He was sure of one thing, though—the closer he got, the more lovely she became. This was not going to be easy, but he wasn't going to stop now.

"How do you say 'I would like to take you to dinner, sometime, anytime'?"

"You just said it, but unfortunately you are married."

"No, I'm not. I'm just waiting out the California dogma, the final decree."

The conversation was interrupted by the assistant director. "Come on, girls, find your places, let's get going!"

Wellman spent a lonely, restless night. That dainty little freckled face haunted him. He tried drinking to erase it, no dice. The last thing he remembered before passing out was the freckles. He dreamed of them, everything was freckled, every dream a freckled mass of disaster. "This sounds screwy," he said. "It was. A screwball in love with a cute little freckle-faced Irish gal named Coonan."

The next day, he planned a new approach. Directly across from Berkeley's stage was the one where sets were being built for his next picture, the Richard Barthelmess vehicle *Heroes for Sale*. The script was nearly completed, and he knew it by heart. He opened the big sliding stage door for light and air, and because it disclosed the Berkeley stage door, out of which poured the dancing girls when excused for lunch or for whatever reason. He sat there, feigning work, but waiting for Freckles to appear.

She did, about eleven o'clock, on roller skates. He pounced on her like a hawk diving on a lark. He called to her, but she skated faster. He chased her into the administration building and down a corridor and was stopped when she disappeared into the ladies' room. He couldn't go any further, so he sat down on the floor and waited. She had to come out sometime.

"I ran out of patience first, got up and went inside. She was standing alone, looking in the mirror. Her shyness gave way to controlled anger as she scolded me for this intrusion."

Dottie: How dare you come in here.

Wellman: Why are you afraid of me? I just want to talk to you. What is so distasteful about me? How can you tell what a bum I am after but a few embarrassed words? Can I take you out to dinner?

Dottie: You're married, Mr. Wellman.

Wellman: Stop calling me Mr. Wellman. I'm Bill and I'm not living with my wife, we're divorcing. You can bring your mother or sister, or sisters, bring the whole Coonan clan, but just give me the chance to make your life miserable.

Dottie started to laugh. It wasn't the giggle of an eighteen-year-old, it was a full-throated musical laugh.

Dottie: When your divorce is final, then I'll have a date with you.

Wellman: Okay. But can I at least talk with you?

Dottie: Not in here you can't.

Wellman: Okay, but on the outside?

Dottie: Yes. Now if you'll excuse me, Bill, I have to get back on set. Please leave.

"I left. The humming in my head began playing music, beautiful soft music."

On another occasion, Wellman was waiting outside the stage, leaning against his Packard, when Dottie, costumed in a white, wired skirt with a gold, sheer fitted top and skull cap, came outside with several other dancers dressed in the same fashion.

It was dress rehearsal day before the filming of "The Shadow Waltz" number, sung by Dick Powell and Ruby Keeler. It features a dance by Keeler, Ginger Rogers, and a host of female violinists—Busby Berkeley chorus girls—with neon-tubed violins that glow in the dark. In the blackness, the audience sees sixty neon-lighted violins waltzing on a huge curving staircase.

Seeing the director across the street caused Dottie to stop in her tracks and take a deep breath. Wellman broke into a wide grin, beckoned her over and, still in the dancing mood, she waltzed to him. Well-

Dottie Coonan costumed in her "Shadow Waltz" wardrobe for *Gold Diggers of 1933*

man complimented her on her outfit, showed her his divorce papers, and asked for a date of dinner and dancing at the Beverly Wilshire Hotel. Without a word, she continued her version of the Shadow Waltz around him and the Packard.

The next day during the filming of that number, an earthquake struck Burbank and surrounding area, causing a blackout and shortcircuiting some of the dancing violins. Berkeley was atop a camera boom at the time, losing his balance and dangling by one hand until he was able to pull himself back up. He yelled for the girls, many of whom were on a thirty-foot-high platform, to sit down until the sound-stage doors were opened allowing light to enter. Busby and his dancers were not injured.

On the first date, Wellman, dressed in his best sport coat and tie, arrived at the Coonan family home—a small house on Beechwood Drive in Hollywood. He rang the doorbell and soon met Dottie's mother, Florence. "Flossie," as she insisted on being called, was forty-nine years old. Her gray hair and gruff manner were a reminder of a burdensome life. Flossie's husband, Ray, had run off with his partner/secretary, leaving Flossie to raise six young children during the Depression. To make matters worse, Ray and partner lived in the same neighborhood but never visited the family and rarely sent money.

In an attempt to earn a living, Flossie took in laundry, sewing, and made clothes. The children went to school and took whatever part-time jobs they could find. When they couldn't pay their bills, they were forced to move but still tried to stay in the same school district. Dottie, age fourteen at the time, loved to dance and had taken a few classes. She took buses, streetcars, and trains to auditions and when Warner Bros. hired her

Dottie Coonan's family: (first row) Dottie, age three, baby Geraldine, Lucille; (back row) Maxine, Florence "Flossie," Josine, 1917

for *Show of Shows* (1929), she quit school and concentrated on a dancing career.

All the children's money was given to their mother to manage. She, in turn, paid the bills and gave them allowances. Dottie and the kids missed meals when their allowance ran out. If they needed more money, it was borrowed and had to be repaid. When a lawyer friend tried to get the courts to force Ray to pay regular child support, the judge ruled that because fifteen-year-old Dottie could earn $50 a week when she worked—which was not every week—Ray was not obligated to pay any support.

On this evening in 1933, Dottie's four sisters and brother, John, ranged from thirteen to twenty-eight years of age. Wellman was somewhat confused upon meeting the sisters, who all carried boy's nicknames: Gerry for Geraldine, Louie for Lucille, Joe for Josine, and Max for Maxine. Knowing Wild Bill's reputation, the women interrogated him while waiting for Dottie to make her appearance. When she arrived on the scene, she was wearing a flowing gown, made by Flossie, and rescued her date from further embarrassment.

Even though both Bill and Dottie were working constantly during their courtship days, they still found time for each other. There were occasional lunches in the studio commissary, a few dinner and danc-

Freckled-faced Dottie Coonan, 1933

ing evenings at the Beverly Wilshire and Wellman's favorite eateries—Romanoff's of Beverly Hills, Musso and Frank in Hollywood, and the Hollywood Brown Derby. Those dining places would be followed by one of Wellman's favorite pastimes—the Fights. When he wasn't shooting or on location, he took Dottie to the Grand Olympic Auditorium in downtown Los Angeles on Tuesday night, Jim Jeffries Barn in the San Fernando Valley on Thursday evening, and the Hollywood Legion on Friday.

Wellman always stayed away from John Barleycorn during filming, but with Dottie on his arm, he was also on his best behavior throughout the romancing days. He was constantly barraging her with questions and getting answers like:

Wellman: Don't you ever get tired of dancing?
Dottie: Never.
Wellman: How long have you been a dancer?
Dottie: Since I was fourteen.
Wellman: Would you rather be married and have kids or dance?
Dottie: Depends.
Wellman: Depends on what?
Dottie: Who I'd be married to.
Wellman: You've been to my favorite places. What are your favorites?
Dottie: I like them all.
Wellman: If you could live anywhere you wanted, where would it be?
Dottie: I don't know. I'd love to have my own house.
Wellman: Does it bother you that I'm thirty-seven and you're eighteen?
Dottie: No. Does it bother you?
Wellman: Not much I can do about it. Does it bother you that I've been married before?
Dottie: It bothers me that you're always asking questions.
Wellman: I don't want to make any mistakes this time.
Dottie: Good.
Wellman: Would you rather have a car or a ring?

Who's directing *Wild Boys of the Road* (1933)? Wellman
and Dottie

Dottie: What kind of ring?
Wellman: Engagement kind.
Dottie: I need to get to the studio. I can't drive a ring.

Instead of the standard engagement ring, Wellman purchased a secondhand but dependable automobile. Since Dottie had never owned a
car, he gave her a few driving lessons and off she went.

During the wooing period, Wellman completed *Heroes for Sale*, March
31, 1933, and *Midnight Mary*, May 4, 1933. Even though he had been reprimanded for objecting to the troubled women stories, the reward of *Wild
Boys of the Road* was significant. Instead of bolting from the studio right
then, he decided to stay around awhile. He loved the *Wild Boys* story of
America's young vagabonds during the Depression. It reminded him of
his own troubled youth.

From the beginning, this picture was going to be his. There would be no

Second from left: Dottie Coonan, Frankie Darro, Elwin Phillips (hand on ground), Sterling Holloway (hand on Phillips's shoulder)

interference of any kind from the front office, even from Jack Warner. Wild Bill would disregard their suggestions, objections, his contract stipulations, warnings of loan-outs or suspension. Only the director's stamp would be on *Wild Boys of the Road*. He began working on the screenplay and preproduction with renewed vigor.

In 1933, changes were taking place in the upper echelon at Warners. Darryl Zanuck was preparing to leave his post as head of production to set up his own operation at Twentieth Century Pictures with Joseph Schenck and William Goetz, releasing their films through United Artists. In 1935, they would buy out Fox Studios to become 20th Century-Fox.

In 1923, Harold Brent Wallis, better known as Hal Wallis, had entered Warner Bros. via the publicity department. In a few years, he became a producer under Zanuck and worked in that capacity on many Wellman films. When Zanuck left, Wallis became executive producer in charge of production.

On *Wild Boys,* Wallis shared executive producership with the outgoing Zanuck. As Zanuck had done in the past, Wallis figured he would be working closely with Wellman on the picture. The director had other ideas and they locked horns. It was Wallis's idea to cast rising young star

Arline Judge, or borrow the lovely Helen Mack from RKO or the beautiful Jean Parker from MGM. All three were fine actresses, very attractive, with star appeal. They weren't what Wellman wanted.

The role of Sally needed to be played by an actress who was or could look like a teenage tomboy. Wellman must have harked back to his *Beggars of Life* and Louise Brooks. As beautiful as Lulu is, in the right wardrobe she passes for a boy and plays the tomboy throughout the picture. Wellman listened to nobody else and cast freckled-faced Dottie Coonan, dressing her in Louise Brooks–type *Beggars of Life* wardrobe.

Dottie was a dancer and had no aspirations to be an actress. When Busby Berkeley had offered her speaking lines in his musicals, she had declined them. When Wellman suggested her playing an acting lead in *Wild Boys*, she declined again. Wellman told her that Wallis wanted him to use someone who was pretty, appealing, and an accomplished actress, and he was going to supply that actress for the role of Sally Clark.

Wellman said to Dottie, "I want you with your freckles and boyish charm. They're prettier than you but you are prettier to me. So that's it. You're playing Sally." The Warner Bros. publicity machine cranked out the news in *The New York Sun*, August 25, 1933: "GIRL TAKES OUT $100,000 FRECKLES INSURANCE. Dorothy Coonan has many freckles—182 in fact. Now in her teens, Dorothy earns her living by facing the cameras and exposing her good-looking but freckled countenance to the public gaze on movie screens. Her contract provides that she's out of a job if she loses her freckles. So yesterday she applied for $100,000 worth of freckle insurance."

It was rumored around the studio that Dottie and Bill were secretly married and living together before *Wild Boys* went into production. However, no documentation or official record of any kind ever surfaced until after Wild Bill had passed, and Dottie admitted to the hush-hush nuptials. The rumors couldn't have been very loud, as Frankie Darro, Dottie's costar, was trying to get a date with her. She always said no.

About the relationship between Wellman and Hal Wallis: In *Starmaker: The Autobiography of Hal Wallis*, written by Wallis and Charles Higham, not one of the thirteen pictures produced by Wallis and directed by Wellman is mentioned in his filmography and Wellman's name does not appear in the book. The name of Hal Wallis does not show up in Wellman's published book, *A Short Time for Insanity*. I guess it's safe to say that they didn't have a relationship worth acknowledging.

With a twenty-four-day shooting schedule, the teen drama began filming on June 17, 1933. Dottie Coonan (Sally) is teamed with young players

Frankie Darro (Eddie) and Edwin Phillips (Tommy). The three youths are forced to leave home and family to find work during the Depression. They hop freight trains, join gangs of dispossessed and desperate kids, live in hobo jungles, makeshift hovels, and in "sewer-pipe city." As their numbers grow, they band together to defend themselves against vicious railroad dicks and other authority figures in their search for work and a better life.

Along the way, Tommy loses a leg in a train accident and later all are involved in a full-blown riot against a horde of policemen. Sally, Eddie, and Tommy arrive in New York where they are nearly busted, find no work, and become panhandlers begging for food and money. Wellman added a scene with Dottie dancing for cash on the sidewalk. They are hunted by the authorities, finally captured, taken before a judge, and sentenced. Judge White (Robert Barrat) reads the charges: "vagrancy, suspected of murder in the second degree, petty theft, resisting police, breaking, and entering and hold-up. Not a very pretty record, is it?"

The bonded friends remain silent, answering no questions about their parents, where they came from, or where they might go. Finally, Eddie breaks, in a tearful emotional outburst, "Sure I've got something to say! . . . I'll tell you why we can't go home! Because our folks are poor! They can't get jobs! There isn't enough food to eat! . . . You're locking us up because you don't want to see us! You want to forget us! But you can't! I'm not the only one—there's thousands like me and more hitting the road every day! . . . I'm not a bad boy! Neither is Tommy! Us three kids have been only traveling around the country looking for work! You don't think we like the road, do you? . . . But what's the use? You're not going to believe me. . . . Go ahead! Put me in a cell—lock me up! I'm sick of being hungry and cold! Jail can't be any worse than the street—so give it to me!"

The judge reads the sentencing to the youngsters: "Sally Clark. House of Corrections. One year, ten months. Thomas Gordon. County Farm. Eligible for probation in one year. Edward, the law compels me to send you to the State Reformatory. You will be confined there until you reach your twenty-first birthday. I'm sorry to do this—but the law leaves me no other alternative."

The three kids are ushered by an attendant from the courtroom to a waiting police vehicle. As they drive away, the teenagers stare out the window at a world they won't be seeing for a long time. From an upper window of the court building, the judge watches their departure on the road to incarceration.

An alternate happy ending was also shot. Although Wellman disapproved of it, Jack Warner had the last word—he owned the film and believed the original ending too harsh, too downbeat for Depression audiences. In the more uplifting climax, Eddie gives the same tearful outpouring while the judge relents and announces that he is dismissing the case, and is going to help the kids find jobs and suitable places to live. They, in turn, think the judge is a great guy and New York a great town.

Saddled with the happy ending, *Wild Boys of the Road* found hard times at the box office. *The New York Times*, July 16, 1933: "the producers have robbed it of its value as a social challenge." *New York Evening Post*, September 22, 1933: "Theatrical, shallow and blubbering." There were also excellent reviews like the *New York American*, September 22, 1933: "A rousing, thoroughly exciting melodrama. . . . Director Wellman keeps the picture moving all the time." *Variety*, September 26, 1933: "Dorothy Coonan, described as a former chorus girl in screen musicals, shows much promise along the lines suggesting Katharine Hepburn."

To Wellman, the whole experience of *Wild Boys* was heartening and painful at the same time. Of all his 1930s shooting scripts, this one contained the most director's notes. He had worked long and hard at putting his fingerprints on a film that he believed was both entertaining and of social significance—a story exposing America's lack of response to its young people in Depression times.

Wild Boys of the Road is Wellman's morality play of the era. The picture is filled with hard-hitting, documentary-style footage, and touches of humor, presented in a realistic and dignified fashion. It is a harsh canvas of humanity as the director holds a mirror up to life in the Great Depression.

Although he loved making the picture and always counted it among his favorites, the studio's ending and scant box office returns were discouraging. Whether the ending was a contributing factor, making the story too grim for the times, we can never know. The fact remains that the film, released September 21, 1933, did not find an audience for decades to come. Since the award-winning documentary on the life and films of Wellman, *Wild Bill Hollywood Maverick* (1996), containing clips and stories of *Wild Boys*, the picture is continually being rediscovered on television (TCM), at film festivals and special screening events, in college film schools, and on its DVD release (2009). It is now considered a fine example of classic entertainment with enduring social value.

Before the theatrical release of *Wild Boys*, and still smarting from the Jack Warner ending, Wellman was assigned *Female,* starring flying buddy Ruth Chatterton and husband, George Brent. Although the title stirs

An autograph for Celia Wellman: Pat O'Brien stars in Wellman's *College Coach* (1933).

up notions of a woman-in-trouble theme, the story is about a woman who causes all the trouble. The romantic comedy has Chatterton playing a high-powered, hard-nosed CEO of a successful automobile company. Her good relations with employees hit a snag when she recruits one lover after another, discarding them when the lights go on. Only the independent executive Jim Thorne (Brent) refuses her advances to the bedroom. Finally he gives in, asking for her hand in marriage. She dumps him as well and he leaves the company and the town. Then she wants him back and goes to find him. Only when she admits that she was willing to risk bankruptcy for him does he accept her in marriage.

Female was already in production under the direction of William Dieterle. The director and Chatterton were at odds throughout the first ten days of interior shooting. The star was often late to the set and even rewrote some of the scenes, to the director's displeasure. The studio shut down production, announced that Dieterle was ill, and started up again with Wellman aboard. He shot all the exteriors while Zanuck and the producers, Robert Presnell and Henry Blanke, tried to work out the Dieterle-Chatterton interior scenes.

After Wellman had completed the exteriors, the film was shut down again. Wellman was assigned *College Coach,* and Michael Curtiz finished the picture. He directed ten days of retakes on the Dieterle material and became the director of record. *New York American*, November 4, 1933: "Although Director Mike Curtiz takes the official rap for this one, creditable word is circulated that both William Dieterle and Billy Wellman applied the torch of their talents to the wet powder in vain endeavor."

College Coach stars Dick Powell, Ann Dvorak, and Pat O'Brien. It is a lightweight football yarn about a Knute Rockne–type coach hired to save Calvert University from bankruptcy by building a winning team. O'Brien makes a mockery of a college sport by paying professionals to attend classes and play football against amateurs. The hard-driving coach goes to great lengths and low-down tactics to keep his athletes, who couldn't spell Knute Rockne, from failing courses and succeeding on the playing field.

The unmuscled Dick Powell, popular songster from musicals, is miscast, playing the only football player with an intellect. He is allowed one song in his attempt to play a rugged straight role. After the first fierce football practice, he is found in his room tinkling the ivories and singing about apple blossoms, summertime, and happy days.

Lyle Talbot plays Powell's rival on the field. He is the star player and chases after O'Brien's wife, Ann Dvorak. Coach O'Brien is so consumed with himself and his success that his wife is an afterthought. She rebels and goes off with Talbot.

In an important game, the opposing star player is killed because of O'Brien's methods. The team, the school, O'Brien's marriage are all falling apart until Dvorak, Powell, and Talbot band together to save the final big game and the movie audiences. *The New York Sun*, November 11, 1933: "It is done with certain down to earth quality by Mr. Wellman, but its satirical ideas are clumsily projected."

Wellman was put to the test with this script and assigned players: the amiable Pat O'Brien as a tyrannical teacher and uncaring husband; Dick Powell as a stalwart gridiron hero; Ann Dvorak, caught in the middle of an unconvincing cast and inconsistent script, doing her best to be believable as the tolerant wife of an egocentric husband.

John Wayne shows up as a football-playing student in his last bit part before starring in a string of B Westerns. He utters one line to Powell, "Hear you broke the rules, Phil, study during vacation."

Wellman works hard to add interest, humor, and excitement. He keeps it moving quickly. He films one of his trademark fight scenes between Powell and Talbot by keeping the camera focused on the movement of their legs rather than the punches and head action. The director finds a signature line to help O'Brien and Dvorak in their more intimate scenes. O'Brien: "Who am I doing this for? *Nobody but you.*" The nobody but you line is repeated during other scenes. In the beginning, Dvorak believes it but as time goes by, she realizes it is just a line . . . but the script says she must swallow it in the end.

One of the great pre-Code lines in the script comes from Talbot to Powell about one of Talbot's former flames seen in a provocative photo. "How'd you like to stick your finger in her coffee?" Powell responds, "I don't use coffee."

College Coach would be the final straw. The Warner Bros. gate was left open and Wellman fled from the barn to the outside world of freelance filmmaking.

The reasons for Wild Bill's getaway:

- Twelve years and thirty-eight pictures in the term contract studio system.
- Little or no control over film assignments.
- No control over final cut.
- Punishment if you refuse or kick up a fuss.
- In love and wanting to slow down his galloping pace.
- Hoping to become a family man.
- Tired of the Warner land baron's interference.
- Missed his contentious sidekick mentor, Darryl Zanuck, who had left for greener pastures.
- It was simply time to vamoose.

13

LOOKING FOR TROUBLE

More romance, more creative control, more brawling. Wellman's road ahead looked brighter but a glance in the rearview mirror showed sinister-looking clouds following.

Bill and Dottie were happy together, but their work schedules kept them apart. Wellman promised a slowdown of his film work soon, and suggested that Dottie retire from her dancing career. The impatient Wild Bill wanted to be officially and legally married to this eighteen-year-old, freckled chorus girl, but was forced by California law to wait a year.

It only took Wellman a few weeks to partner up with Darryl Zanuck and have a new script on his desk. It was titled *Trouble Shooter*. The release title became *Looking for Trouble* (1934) starring Spencer Tracy, Jack Oakie, Constance Cummings, and Arline Judge. Wellman had the right of refusal but was anxious to get back to work with Zanuck and away from Warners . . . he also liked the story being different from his Warner Bros. pictures.

Looking for Trouble is a crime/comedy/drama about two telephone repairmen, called "trouble-shooters," played by Tracy and wisecracking Jack Oakie. They become pals involved with racketeers and find themselves trapped in a romantic triangle with Tracy's girlfriend, Constance Cummings, and her boss, Morgan Conway.

While on duty, Tracy and Oakie discover a wiretapping robbery scheme. The trouble-shooters play detective. Tracy believes his rival, Conway, is part of the gang. There is much wit and excitement surrounding the uncovering of the criminal plot that proves Conway a crook. Tracy and Oakie quarrel with their women, discover a corpse, become trapped in a burning building, and survive an earthquake. Actual earthquake footage

Spencer Tracy and Wellman had a fighting feud that lasted for years.

was used in the making of the film, which became stock footage for a number of future films.

When Conway is murdered, Cummings is arrested for the shooting. Tracy finds the killer to be Conway's sometime girlfriend and partner, Judith Wood, who was double-crossed. Before she can be jailed, the earthquake nearly buries her alive. She lives long enough to give her confession to the police captain, Robert Elliot. Cummings is set free and thanks Tracy by finagling a marriage license from him while they are at city hall to witness the marriage of Oakie and his girl, Arline Judge. *Los Angeles Times*, April 7, 1934: "Well written, well directed and well acted. In some scenes, indeed, a new high for naturalness is set. . . . Wellman's gift for trenchant direction is admirably applied."

In *Looking for Trouble*, Spencer Tracy was able to break away from being typecast as a bad guy under his Fox contract. Being loaned out to Zanuck and 20th Century Pictures gave him the opportunity to play the good guy who gets the girl and wins the fights. He not only belted the bad guy in the picture but also the director, Wellman, on the set. A fighting feud erupted that lasted for several years with at least four encounters.

The Wellman-Tracy fistfight was not the first combat on the set of *Looking for Trouble*. Dolph M. Zimmer had become Wellman's most used assistant director during the Warner Bros. years. "Zimmy," as Wellman referred to him, would usually hire the second assistant under him. On *Midnight Mary*, Michael Lally had been awarded the position.

Mike Lally began his Hollywood career in the early 1930s. He was an assistant director first, then a stuntman and double for Warner Bros. stars like James Cagney and Pat O'Brien. He also played bit parts—mostly uncredited—as reporters, cops, gangsters, drivers, bartenders, gamblers, sailors, convicts, waiters, and the like. In a long career, his résumé shows over three hundred films. Some of his small roles were in big pictures like *Citizen Kane* (1941), *It's a Wonderful Life* (1946), and *Singin' in the Rain* (1952).

Wellman and Lally did not hit it off, and before *Midnight Mary* wrapped they had "words" and "blows." The crew broke up the fight and Lally left the picture. On *Looking for Trouble*, Lally appeared on the set as a visitor. When Wellman saw him, he ordered him off. They exchanged "pleasantries," then fists began to fly. The crew stepped in again. Wellman received an injured right hand; Lally a colorful black eye.

Two weeks later, Tracy and Wellman mixed it up. The reason for this encounter is not clear. A short time later, they battled again—probably to finish their first brawl—at a Hollywood club. The next round was held at the popular Trocadero nightclub on the Sunset Strip. This melee caused much chaos among the guests, as well as displaced tableware, broken glasses, and furniture. The combatants were told to leave the premises. It was reported that this duel was over Loretta Young, whom Tracy had been seeing. At that time, Wellman had become disenchanted with the beautiful Miss Young because of her affair with Clark Gable during the filming of Wellman's *The Call of the Wild*—the stars were more involved with each other than the film. The final round took place in the Hollywood Brown Derby restaurant. As usual, the pugilists were asked to vacate.

Over time, Wellman had developed a style or habit of drinking that meant: not a drop during production but periodic blasts between pictures. He had been on his best behavior around Dottie, but now began to slip. She was upset at this boozing business, and although she had not been present, when she heard about the Tracy fisticuffs she threatened to leave him. He asserted that it wasn't all his fault. He apologized and said he would try to stay closer to the straight and narrow.

A bomber pilot in World War I, an officer with the Flying Tigers in World War II, Merian C. Cooper was in charge of production at RKO-Radio in 1934. He had cowritten, codirected, and appeared in the classic *King Kong* (1933). He went on to producing chores for John Ford with *Fort Apache* (1948), *3 Godfathers* (1948), *She Wore a Yellow Ribbon* (1949), *Wagon Master* (1950), *Rio Grande* (1950), *The Quiet Man* (1952), and *The Searchers* (1956).

Cooper had been looking for a story to follow up on the studio's Academy Award winner *Cimarron* (1931). He found his story based on the novel *Stingaree* (1905) and stories by E. W. Hornung. After great difficulty sorting through a network of rights owners, he purchased the movie rights for $10,000 and hired the *Cimarron* stars, Richard Dix and Irene Dunne. When he approached Wellman to direct this lavish adventure tale, the director liked the story and was borrowed from Zanuck's 20th Century Pictures. Production began February 12, 1934, on a thirty-six-day shooting schedule.

Stingaree is a unique story combining an Australian Western with an opera-style musical. Dix, as the title character, plays a Down Under Robin Hood who is cultured, charming, good-humored, musically talented, and a bit of a rogue. When he meets an aspiring singer, Irene Dunne, he gives up some of his banditry to help her become an opera star.

With his sidekick, Andy Devine, providing lightheartedness, Dix masquerades as an importer, London composer, even as the governor general on his way to aiding Miss Dunne's rise to international stardom. Using his ill-gotten bounty, he sends her to Europe to receive special vocal training, then kidnaps a famous music critic, forcing him to listen to her sing. She becomes an important opera star but, in the end, gives up her career to live the unrestricted, excitement-filled life with her supportive lover, Stingaree.

RKO's publicity heralded "Great Romance Rides Again. . . . Love in the Arms of Danger . . . the stars of the immortal *Cimarron* unite in another glorious romance of life on earth's far frontiers." *New York World-Telegram*, May 18, 1934: "Fair-to-middling blend of romance and music. . . . Like most adventure stories it has a certain disarming simplicity and charm about it." *Los Angeles Times*, May 7, 1934: "Impossible but interesting."

Wellman made good on his promise to slow down. His next film project would not be for five months. During this downtime, he received the final divorce decree. His between-pictures time would be spent with Dottie and the kind of therapy needed to get rid of that humming in his head. "I have seen hound dogs nose-to-ground tracking a bear, and they remind me of me, always nose-to-ground, tracking a wife, never satisfied with a good-looking stray, had to go all the way. Must be some kind of a disease, and I had it bad. It was inoperable."

Unlike his previous marriage proposals, the secret one took many weeks to complete. It was a long line of hints like: "I think I'd like to get married again," "You'll make someone a good wife," "If we got married, we'd have a helluva good time." Dottie stayed noncommittal for a while, but now, with the final decree in hand, he proposed again in an unusual way. "Today I talked to Paul Mantz, the great stunt pilot. He wants to fly us to Vegas to get married officially. Do you want to go?" Dottie smiled in her crinkled-nose manner and responded, "I do." It was time to make it special for Dottie and completely legal.

In the 1930s, when flying work in pictures was slow, Mantz christened a Buhl CA-6 airplane *The Honeymoon Express*. Later he added a red Lockheed Vega to the small fleet. The title and charter service were not original, but Mantz made his little airline the most famous. Among his celebrity passengers were James Cagney, Cecil B. DeMille, Amelia Earhart, and Douglas Fairbanks, Sr. There were honeymoon couples like Carole Lombard and Clark Gable, Ann Dvorak and Leslie Fenton, Jean Harlow and Hal Rosson. Quickie marriages flew to Yuma, Arizona, or Las Vegas, Nevada. Quickie divorces to Reno, Nevada. Charter travelers would also be flown to fishing and hunting destinations, to movie previews and premieres as far away as New York.

Honeymoons were found in many places. The blissful-nuptialants were often kept as secret as possible, even from the pilot. Mantz would receive late-night phone calls from can't-wait individuals using fictitious names. They would arrive at the airport hiding behind an unusual wardrobe, then dive into the backseats of the plane. During the flight, they would partially disrobe and converse with their pilot.

This was Wellman's fifth marriage but, in the eyes of Hollywood and the rest of the world, the count was four. Only Tommy Hitchcock knew of Wellman's first wedding in Paris, and he had never divulged the secret.

In the case of Dottie and Bill, Mantz, who had befriended Wellman on *Central Airport*, provided special treatment. He said to the groom, "You bring the girl and the ring." Mantz did the rest, which included the flight in his red Vega, limo into Vegas, the wedding chapel, and the minister. And who was the best man? Paul Mantz, of course. After the ceremony, they flew west across Death Valley and the Sierra Nevada to San Francisco to cap off the weekend.

This flight of fancy on March 22, 1934, brought headlines to newspapers and trade publications. A Los Angeles newspaper even printed photos of Wellman's ex-wives and their settlement monies above the photos. Instead of a photo of Dottie, a big question mark with the caption "MOVIE DIRECTOR WILD BILL WELLMAN WEDS TEENAGE BUZZ BERKELEY CHORUS GIRL."

"All the warnings from friends? The snide quotes from the scandalmongers, the crucifying layout of pictures of my former wives, with the amount of settlement emblazoned above their pretty little heads like inscriptions of great courage, rewards for having lived with an imbecile for a certain length of moneyed time. Above my lovely little Dottie's head, a question mark."

Soon after returning from the wedding weekend, Mr. and Mrs. Wil-

Busby Berkeley dancers: Dottie Coonan Wellman (third from left), Ann Dvorak (fifth), Betty Grable (sixth)

liam Wellman went on an extended honeymoon—by automobile—to the Arrowhead Hot Springs Hotel in San Bernardino, California.

The newlyweds would live in Wellman's Country English–style house at 6747 Milner Road in Whitley Heights. Although Warner Bros. had offered Dottie a term contract, neither she nor her husband wanted it. Dottie gave up her successful career to be the wife of William A. Wellman—a daunting task to be sure. In *Gold Diggers of 1933*, Dottie Coonan had danced her final number of ten classic musicals from 1929 to 1933. She had also performed in dozens of musical shorts, plays, and prologues—musical stage numbers performed in theaters before the feature presentation.

Dottie had what she wanted most—a home of her own and a loving, supportive husband. She was hoping to become pregnant. This is what Wellman had always wanted—the love of a beautiful stay-at-home wife and mother. It was time to make that apologetic call to his family. The family, of course, were well rehearsed with their acceptance speeches.

Since Wellman did not bring his wives east, Celia had met the two Marjories on her yearly trips west. When she heard of her son's newest bride—a teenage chorus girl—she hopped on the first train west to see for herself.

In five minutes, Celia's fears disappeared. She fell in love with Dot-

tie and vice versa. There was ample room for all three in the Wellmans'
house, built in 1923, on three levels and eighteen hundred square feet.
The rooms were not large but there were three bedrooms and two and a
half tiled bathrooms. The living room had a beamed ceiling, built-in seating, fireplace, and bay window with treetop views of Hollywood. There
was a workable kitchen. The master bedroom had a fireplace and private
bathroom. Wellman used the lower-level bedroom as a den and office.

Celia had seen many of Dottie's musicals but wanted to go again to
catch the dancing numbers of her new daughter-in-law. Dottie's black
hair and prominent widow's peak made her easy to spot. While Wellman was preoccupied with his next picture, mother and wife went to the
movies.

Celia's choices were selected from the lavish revue film, *Show of Shows*
(1929) featuring many of the Warner Bros. stars; MGM's *The Broadway
Melody* (1929), the first sound film to win an Academy Award for Best
Picture; Samuel Goldwyn and Florenz Ziegfeld's *Whoopee!* (1930) star-
ring Eddie Cantor, Busby Berkeley's first Hollywood film; Mary Pickford in Sam Taylor's *Kiki* (1931); Samuel Goldwyn's *Palmy Days* (1931)
with Eddie Cantor, Charlotte Greenwood, and George Raft (Berkeley);
MGM's *Flying High* (1931) starring Bert Lahr, Charlotte Greenwood, and
Pat O'Brien (Berkeley); RKO's *Bird of Paradise* (1932) with Dolores Del
Rio and Joel McCrea, directed by King Vidor and produced by David
Selznick (Berkeley); Samuel Goldwyn's *The Kid from Spain* (1932) starring Eddie Cantor, Lyda Roberti, Robert Young, with Berkeley chorus
girls Lucille Ball, Betty Grable, Virginia Bruce; Warner Brothers' *42nd
Street* (1933) with Warner Baxter, Bebe Daniels, George Brent, Ruby Keeler, Dick Powell, Ginger Rogers (Berkeley); Warners' *Gold Diggers of 1933*
starring Warren William, Joan Blondell, Ruby Keeler, Dick Powell, Ginger Rogers, directed by Mervyn LeRoy (Berkeley).

It happened . . . and was Wellman happy. Dottie was with child. After
the initial outbursts of joy and subsequent celebrations, Wellman realized that his house was not a suitable family home—too many stairs,
three levels to climb for his pregnant wife and expectant child. So the
merry couple went house hunting. Two rented homes later, they were
at 722 Linden Drive in Beverly Hills. The Mediterranean Revival house
was filled with old dark furniture and paintings that matched. Dottie was
less than thrilled, but Bill explained that it was only a stepping-stone to a
residence she would love and own.

The switch of domiciles took place before producer Walter Wanger
called with a story that appealed to the director. The novel *The President*

Vanishes was a political thriller written by Rex Stout. His authorized biographer, John McAleer, wrote about the fictitious story being published anonymously to give the impression that it was truth written by someone high up in the nation's brain trust. As a result, sales were good and the movie rights were bought by important independent producer Wanger. Among his productions: *The Sheik* (1921) with Rudolph Valentino; Greta Garbo's *Queen Christina* (1931); John Ford's *Stagecoach* (1939), which finally made a star of John Wayne; Victor Fleming's *Joan of Arc* (1948) starring Ingrid Bergman; and *Cleopatra* (1963) with Elizabeth Taylor and Richard Burton.

In 1935, Wanger produced *Private Worlds* starring Claudette Colbert, Charles Boyer, Joel McCrea, and Joan Bennett. In 1940, Bennett became Mrs. Walter Wanger until their divorce in 1965. In 1950, Bennett signed with MCA agent Jennings Lang. When Wanger believed his wife was having an affair with her agent, he shot Lang twice, once in the groin. Lang recovered and returned to his 10 percenter world. Both he and Bennett maintained there was never a romantic involvement, that they were just friends and business partners. Wanger pleaded "temporary insanity" and threw himself on the mercy of the court. He served only a four-month sentence at an Honor Farm, then returned to his stellar career.

It was Joan Bennett who suffered the stain of the scandal and, virtually blacklisted, her movie career spiraled downward. She later said, "I might as well have pulled the trigger myself."

This event, and Wanger's imprisonment, made a powerful impression on him, and in 1954 he produced the prison film *Riot in Cell Block 11*. His production of *I Want to Live!* (1958) starring Oscar-nominated Susan Hayward in the anti–capital punishment picture became one of the most celebrated films on the subject. Wanger received an Honorary Academy Award in 1946 for his service as president of the Academy of Motion Picture Arts and Sciences.

Wellman was borrowed from 20th Century Pictures to direct *The President Vanishes* for a salary of $3,250 per week. He and Wanger cast Arthur Byron, Paul Kelly, Peggy Conklin, Edward Arnold, Andy Devine, and Rosalind Russell in the large cast. Production began September 30, 1934.

The story concerns the mysterious disappearance of the president of the United States, played by Byron. He is in a political crisis, facing impeachment over his handling of an impending war in Europe. While fascists, communists, and other radical militants fight to gain control of the White House and the country, Byron vanishes.

It turns out that the peace-loving, isolationist president pretended to be kidnapped in order to prove how false propaganda combined with media hype can mislead the public, stampeding the country into war.

The film opens with a series of montages: production shots, stock footage, newspaper headlines, bands, buglers, drummers, the playing of "The Star Spangled Banner," military personnel, a twenty-one-gun salute, the arrival of the president for the graduation ceremony at Annapolis, and the White House. We cut to a dinner party at the home of D. L. Voorman, an influential Washington lobbyist. His supportive wife, Sally, is prepared to introduce the dining elite. They consist of five men who are gathered for the purpose of masterminding America's entry into a world war.

The role of Sally was brief but pivotal as she sets the story in motion introducing the major players and plot. Wellman was looking for an actress with star quality: attractive, charismatic, quick-witted. He found her in a stage actress with only one supporting movie credit: Rosalind Russell.

There was one audition in the director's office. He liked her right away, she fit the role to a T, had a lovely, unusual voice—Wellman always paid close attention to the actor's voice. Because she was so new, he considered contacting the director of her only film, "but she impressed me so much I said to myself, the hell with it, so we made a picture."

The director's hunch turned out to be brilliant, so much so that a few days before the picture was finished, he went to Wanger and told him, "You have a star in the palm of your hand," and the producer asked "Who?" "I said one word, 'Russell,' and got the usual crappy reply, 'You're crazy.' 'Why am I crazy?' 'Because she is too tall.' That did it. I thanked God that I had two days left to finish the picture or I might have spilled over my temper and punched him right on the nose."

With films like *His Girl Friday* (1940), *Picnic* (1955), *Auntie Mame* (1958), and *Gypsy* (1962), Rosalind Russell would go on to receive four Academy Award nominations, a Life Achievement Oscar in 1972, five Golden Globes, and a Tony Award in 1953 for *Wonderful Town*.

Because of the controversial political issues in *The President Vanishes*, the picture was heavily criticized by the new and stronger version of the Production Code Administration. The film was banned in many countries, including Mussolini's Italy and Hitler's Germany. Paramount, the distribution company, was nervous about releasing the picture and toyed with the idea of shelving it. Some critics predicted public protests, even riots. As it turned out, the film caused no such disruptions, just good box office and matching reviews. *New York American*, December 8, 1934:

The Call of the Wild (1935): Loretta Young and Clark Gable

"A good melodrama . . . thrilling entertainment with a story that has the benefit of originality." *The New York Sun*, December 8, 1934: "combines all the excitements of a war, a kidnapping and a hotbed of political intrigue, and makes of them a smashing good melodrama."

So as not to repeat his previous mistake of being an absentee husband, Wellman took time off after *The President Vanishes* to be with his pregnant Dottie. During the next six years, the director made only eight pictures instead of his galloping pace of twenty-two between 1930 and 1934.

In August of 1934, Darryl Zanuck called with a magnificent project, Jack London's classic 1903 tale *The Call of the Wild*. The book centers on the adventurous life of a dog named Buck. The powerful half St. Bernard, half sheep dog perseveres from domesticated, coddled pet to abused sled dog in the frigid Yukon during the nineteenth-century Klondike Gold Rush to a true-blood creature living among the wolves.

The movie version would become something else. Written by Leonard Praskins and Wellman's soon-to-be friend and neighbor Gene Fowler, the screen story focuses on a reckless prospector's relationships with a savage dog, a devil-may-care buddy prospector, and a determined woman who captures his heart. Buck, a St. Bernard movie dog with the same name, stays important but the humans take center stage—the most prominent being Jack Thornton, the gold hunter Shorty Hoolihan, the sidekick, and Claire Blake, the object of Thornton's fascination. Although the dog is demoted to second-story status, his scenes with Thornton are emotional

Buck and Gable in *The Call of the Wild*

and memorable. Wellman's love of dogs is clearly on display. Zanuck's cast was Fredric March as Jack Thornton and Madeleine Carroll as Claire Blake. When Zanuck switched March over to *Les Misérables*, Wellman signed his *Night Nurse* costar Clark Gable. The director also picked *Looking for Trouble* costar Jack Oakie to play Hoolihan, supplying the comedy relief. To play the alluring Claire Blake, Wellman pushed for and got one of his Warner Bros. favorites, Loretta Young, who was under contract to Zanuck and 20th Century Pictures.

The director chose his major locations around Mount Baker, Washington. The company arrived on January 13, 1935, encountering extensive delays due to temperatures of 14 below, blizzards, cast and crew illness, and . . . the off-screen, on-screen love affair between Clark Gable and Loretta Young. The stars were late to the set, unprepared when they got there, and, in Wellman's words, "paying more attention to themselves than the damn picture." By the time the final location shot was taken, Wellman was only speaking to Gable when absolutely necessary—director to actor.

In addition to the tryst with Young, Gable had another affair of the heart with Buck. Clark Gable loved dogs and especially his four-legged costar. They spent weeks building their friendship.

When the company returned to Hollywood, an important scene was filmed at the RKO Ranch in the San Fernando Valley. It was Buck's race, where he was called upon to win a bet for his master, Gable, by pulling a thousand-pound sled over a hundred yards. The pooch refused. He had good reason. Unlike the bitterly cold Mount Baker, the San Fernando Valley in early spring can be hot as hell. This day was extra hot and in order to look like the cold of winter, fake snow was on the ground, the actors and extras wore fur coats, fur hats, wool socks, heavy shoes, the works. Some of the extras fainted and were taken to the hospital. Buck wouldn't budge. He just lay down in the heat, tongue hanging out, panting. The dog trainers tried to get him up, so did his buddy Gable. Nothing would work until Wellman got an idea.

The director called an early lunch and told his property man, Bob "Scotty" Lander, to scour the neighborhood for a female dog in heat. When Scotty returned, he had two ladies with fire, one a little Pomeranian, the other a saucy French poodle. Wellman said about the poodle, "You know, the bad girl of the dogs. She was ready, knew it, and flaunted it." The director kept them hidden from Buck and camera until the right moment. Wellman had Scotty and his helper put them on leashes, then he got the scene all ready. It was a long dolly shot. The director started the action with the two dames just out of camera prancing invitingly along, holding their heads and tails temptingly high. "The minute Buck saw them," said Wellman, "he leapt to his feet and started the goddamnedest mushing and pulling you have ever seen, he would have dragged that sled to San Francisco."

When the scene was completed, the girls were put back in the car, Buck watched it drive away as if his whole life were gone, and he blamed Gable because Clark was encouraging him all the time, shouting, "Come on, Buck, mush, Buck, mush—get going, Buck, mush." When Gable went over to see him and offered him a tidbit, Buck refused it and snapped at him.

The Call of the Wild completed production on March 23, 1935. Neither of Gable's affairs lasted longer than the shooting schedule. Hoping to win back his friendship, Gable tried to buy the $500-a-week Buck. He offered a sizable price but Carl Spitz, the owner-trainer who also trained Toto for *The Wizard of Oz* (1939), refused to sell his star dog. Spitz continued to find work for the St. Bernard in films like *The Country Beyond* (1936) and a fourteen-episode serial, *Robinson Crusoe of Clipper Island* (1936). The friendship and business relationship between trainer and man's best friend came to a tragic halt with Buck's poisoning by an unknown assailant.

Gable's love affair with Loretta Young was severed by the completion of filming. There was no time for togetherness between the end of principal photography and the stars' next commitments. Both were late arriving to their next pictures: Gable to *China Seas* and Young to *The Crusades*. Further complications ensued as Loretta became pregnant with Clark's child. With the emerging power of the Film Production Code heavily enforcing moral codes and condemning objectionable relationships, Miss Young felt forced to hide the coming of the child, even from the father.

In order to keep the secret, thereby protecting both their careers, a set of circumstances went into effect that kept the lovers apart and caused lasting discord between mother, father, and daughter (Judy Lewis).

The strife between the director and his stars throughout the production also caused rifts that lasted for many years. After four films, Wellman and Young would never make another picture together, but Wellman would always count her among his all-time favorite actresses. The director and Gable would stand apart for the next sixteen years before a reunion and another film.

The Call of the Wild once again showed Wellman's affinity for actors and crew from past pictures. Dolph Zimmer was again his assistant director. There were cast members like Frank Campeau, the crooked sheriff in actor Wellman's first film, *The Knickerbocker Buckaroo* (1919), assistant director Wellman's *Yosemite Trail* (1922), and others; Walter McGrail, in Wellman's first film as a director, *The Eleventh Hour* (1923), and in *Night Nurse* (1931) and more; Bob Perry, *Oath-Bound* (1922) and at least nine other pictures; Harvey Parry, stuntman who began with Wellman on *Iron to Gold* (1922) and worked on over a dozen other pictures, many long after his stunt days were over; Duke Green, another stuntman with the director on *Beggars of Life* (1928) and a host of others.

Even Wellman's second wife, Helene Chadwick, a star who had faded years before, appears briefly as one of the Dawson townspeople. In later years, Wellman remembered back to *Call of the Wild* as the first time he experienced the pain of arthritis, a disease that plagued him for the rest of his life.

In the end, *The Call of the Wild* was a smash hit. The ninety-one-minute film was rereleased twice, in 1945 and 1953, shortened to eighty-one minutes. To date, it has been remade three times plus a television series. By far, Wellman's version is the finest of the lot. The picture is filled with picturesque photography by Charles Rosher, two-time Academy Award–winning cinematographer. His and Wellman's composition of shots is outstanding. The look of the film is scenic and natural, full of breathtaking images, top-notch sound effects, first-rate performances, and dynamic direction. *Los Angeles Times*, June 25, 1935: "Wellman has imbued with poetry the love story between Gable and Miss Young. He also returns to the screen the old-time sweep of Frozen North scenic films."

It was still 1935, Wellman still owned the 1930 green Packard with white convertible top, and his car was traveling west on Sunset Boulevard to what would be his final residence, in the Brentwood area of West Los Angeles. The car was more crowded than usual with his first child, Patricia Luann. The bouncing baby had more freckles than mommy and just as much energy as her dad. Her hair was red, courtesy of Grandmother Celia. Her personality bubbled and her smile was constant.

For $26,000, Wellman had purchased Dottie's dream home on over three acres. By 1942, the original house would be demolished and a Roland E. Coate New England–style farmhouse built in its place. The home would contain a large living room, den, formal dining room and junior dining room, kitchen, breakfast room, butler's pantry, three-room basement, family room, sewing room, sitting areas, nine bathrooms, and seven bedrooms—enough for the large family that Bill and Dottie were planning.

The property would have a three-car garage, an orange orchard, gymnasium, pool, bathhouse, and two-story stables. The upper floor of the stables would be a playroom with Ping-Pong and pool tables, long bar, and bathroom with shower. A large bay window would look down on two horses in a roomy corral in front of their stalls and saddle rooms. Other residents of the Wellman Rancho: dogs, chickens, pigeons (squab), rabbits, even a goat.

With the success of *Call of the Wild* under his belt, Wellman moved to MGM, signing a lucrative contract under mogul Louis B. Mayer. The director was expecting to be reunited with his Paramount producer pal David Selznick, who had become one of Hollywood's most important producers. At MGM from 1933 to 1935, he produced classics like *Dinner at Eight*, *David Copperfield*, *Anna Karenina*, and *A Tale of Two Cities*.

Wellman's early days at the studio were disappointing; there was no picture for him, just uncredited work on films like *China Seas* starring Jean Harlow, Wallace Beery, Rosalind Russell, and Clark Gable. Wellman's second unit work did not involve the principals, so it was easy to stay away from Gable, but he did socialize with Harlow, Beery, and Russell. Additional disappointment came with Selznick's departure from MGM to form his own production company, Selznick International.

Wild Bill began hounding the hierarchy for a picture of his own. His outspoken manner and lack of respect for the studio bosses angered Mayer, but a picture was finally assigned the brash director. He took the

Dottie and first child Patricia

reins of only his second Western since his early days of the silent era. Well-man never rejected his beginnings as a Western director, and throughout his long career, he continually returned to the world of the West.

The story of Mexican outlaw Joaquin Murrieta, released as *The Robin Hood of El Dorado*, had been around the Hollywood studios for years without getting into production. Driven by MGM's success with *Viva Villa!* (1934), the project had found a home. The studio's romanticized version, with Wellman rewriting and adding punch at every opportunity, shows a kinder, more caring Joaquin as part bandit, part Robin Hood—a friend to some, an enemy to others. The screen story gives him reason for his outlaw ways as he and his mother are attacked and beaten, his wife raped and murdered by a band of Americans. Murrieta seeks revenge and gets it, killing the murderers one by one.

After an angry, drunken mob of Americans lynch Joaquin's brother, while he receives thirty-nine lashes, Murrieta takes over a notorious gang of outlaws led by Three-Fingered Jack, beginning a reign of terror against the Americans.

When Joaquin decides to give up his life of banditry, he and his men are attacked. A sensational battle sequence results in the death of Three-

Warner Baxter, hand raised, signed this photo on the figure of his director, Wellman: *The Robin Hood of El Dorado* (1936).

Fingered Jack and the massacre of Joaquin's men. A wounded Murrieta escapes only to die on the grave of his beloved wife. The real Murrieta was shot in the back by one of his own men, decapitated, and his head placed in a jar and carried about the territory that he had terrorized. Without the sadism and excessive violence of the true story, the director still imparts a potent, hard-hitting, and believable visualization but with feeling and redeeming values. Initially, Wellman was excited about the project. He wanted the young, handsome MGM contract player Robert Taylor as Joaquin. The powers-that-be at the studio rejected the idea and signed someone else. Wellman went to the producer's office and lost his temper.

The outburst set off a chain reaction of Wild Bill activity: emptying a full wastebasket over the producer's head, uttering a fusillade of unkind words to a mogul, and a wrestling match with his agent. To fill in the names, we have veteran producer John Considine, Jr., mogul L. B. Mayer, and longtime agent Myron Selznick. The studio-signed actor was Warner Baxter. In all fairness to the studio bosses, Baxter was a major star. He had won an Academy Award. He had even portrayed the Cisco Kid in two popular films, *In Old Arizona* (1929), the first all-talking Western, and *The Cisco Kid* (1930). Baxter seemed the perfect choice to play the fabled Mexican bandit—if it was still the 1920s. But it was the summer of 1935 and Baxter was in the winter of his discontent as an aging movie star with a staggering drinking problem.

During the get-acquainted meeting, Baxter said, "One thing, Bill, that unfortunately is a must for me—I drink a lot, for a lot of reasons which I will not bore you with. I can stick it out until five o'clock and then I'm lost. Please try to understand." Wellman did understand and the two veterans became friends . . . but there was still the problem of Baxter's age. Even when sober, he looked more like Murrieta's father than youthful warrior Joaquin.

The director discussed solutions with costume ideas—dressing in thinning black—hairdo changes, the casting of older, less attractive character actors, and a not too young leading lady. Baxter liked all the ideas and had one of his own—an on-screen double. Wellman did not have to cast this role, Baxter had already been using a double in his last films. This man, whom we will call "D" as he was never credited on screen and Wellman did not place a name with the story, had learned every move and mannerism of his master. He was so adept at it that Baxter rarely appears in the film except in close-ups. Legendary stuntman Yakima Canutt, who went on to double the likes of Roy Rogers and John Wayne, was Baxter's double for the more dangerous stunts. But it was D whom Canutt was really doubling. D was also Baxter's keeper, taking care of him during the drinking hours and fitful nights. The only problem was that D became hated by nearly every cast and crew member.

Wellman described Baxter's Mr. D: "His bosom pal, his day and night nurse, his manservant, drinking companion, his well paid double-crosser was despised by everyone in the company, especially the real stunt men, and by me, the director." Wellman was using all the patience he had, watching a guy take advantage of his position. D was the star's companion night and day and he let everybody know it. "He was," said the director, "insufferable but necessary, an uncomfortable mixture to have to take day after day."

D had but one friend, and that relationship may have been more business than friendship. The bartender at the company hotel on location was a good listener but a bad confidence keeper. He was also receiving a good deal of business from D on his treks to the watering hole for his master. On one occasion, the barkeep informed certain company members about a story of D's guardianship and a long rope.

During film locations and away from the friendly confines of his home, it was customary for Baxter—with D's assistance—to tie a rope from his bedpost to the nearest toilet. In this way, during the alcoholic confusion of a strange room in the dark, he would be able to grasp the hemp and follow it to the relief bowl. D liked this setup. He, in the other bed, would not have to wake and attend to his commander's deliverance.

Although the story had humorous touches for all who heard, it was more significant to the actor J. Carroll Naish, portraying Three-Fingered Jack, for Naish disliked D the most. One dark night, Three-Fingered Jack stole into Baxter's bedroom and retied the rope from the star's bed to the double's bed. During that right, cries and howls were heard throughout the hotel as D was introduced to a golden shower.

Regardless of *The Robin Hood of El Dorado*'s production problems, the film was successful. *Variety*, March 18, 1936: "Uncommonly exciting, colorful and well-balanced job." *Canadian Magazine*, May 1936: "A swashbuckling, somewhat overdone romantic melodrama, with Warner Baxter dragging out his broken English accent, which is pretty poor, but which everyone appears to love." *The New York Times*, March 14, 1936: "A brutally frank indictment of American injustice, greed and cowardice." This film continues the director's indictment of mob violence and injustice in his movies that would reach its fulfillment with one of filmdom's great Westerns, *The Ox-Bow Incident* (1943).

The conflict between Wild Bill and MGM had gone from simmering to boiling. The front office wanted to keep using him on problem-plagued pictures, taking advantage of his ability to add dimension and flavor to an unsatisfactory film. But there had been only one film for his full-time directorship. Wellman began to realize that he was back in the term contract studio world . . . a place where he no longer wanted to be.

It took four months for Wellman to get another picture, *Small Town Girl*. It wasn't a film of his choosing and there were loose ends dangling all over. The director had been assigned another Western, *3 Godfathers*, a remake of John Ford's 1919 version, which had been remade in 1929 as *Hell's Heroes*, directed by William Wyler. Before starting *3 Godfathers*, he was taken off and assigned *Small Town Girl*, which was already cast and ready to shoot. He liked the studio-cast stars, Janet Gaynor and Robert Taylor, whom he had wanted for Joaquin Murrieta. He did not like being brought in with all the preproduction work completed. He was able to bring in two former favorite actors, Andy Devine and Binnie Barnes, but the constant musical chairs of the MGM productions was maddening.

Small Town Girl is a romantic comedy. Tired of her small town and local boyfriend, played by James Stewart early in his career, a young girl (Gaynor) falls in love with a big-city doctor (Taylor), who is just passing through town on his way to the Yale-Harvard football game. After a night of drunken revelry, they end up married. Taylor wants out, Gaynor wants to stay in. Their wedding hits the newspapers.

In order to keep his surgeon's career alive, they decide to stay publicly married but privately at arm's length for six months, then divorce. Along the way, Taylor

David O. Selznick

falls for her and the two lovers drive off into the sunset. *Film Bulletin*, April 15, 1936: "There isn't a thing novel about the plot . . . but it is handled smartly by Director Wellman and acted to the hilt by the cast."

Small Town Girl was a box office hit, but still MGM did not assign the director a picture of his own but, instead, another uncredited work-in-progress—*Tarzan Returns*. The studio had made two popular Tarzan pictures but the third was in trouble. The original director, James McKay, was released during production and replaced by Richard Thorpe, then John Farrow. The film became so violent that preview audiences were horrified. Retakes began under director George B. Seitz but the studio was still dissatisfied and gave the job of making everything work to Wellman. The dejected director took over but knew the end of the road with MGM was just around the bend.

As it turned out, Wellman liked his work on the picture. The world of Tarzan was very different from any of his other films. Wellman was thrilled to grab the vines and swing through the trees on MGM's backlot jungle. He swam with Tarzan's Olympic gold medalist Johnny Weissmuller, played and laughed with Cheetah, the chimp. Similar to his early days as a director of low-budget films, he integrated shots from previous Tarzan pictures, cut out excess violence replacing it with action, and added humor in the form of Cheetah. The director so enjoyed the experience that he asked for directorship of the next Tarzan installment. The retitled *Tarzan Escapes* was successful and the series continued, but without Wellman.

The relationship between Mayer and Wellman was so strained that the director angrily told his agent that he wanted out of his contract at any cost. Myron Selznick, as he had done at Paramount and Warner Bros., made it happen. Wellman hit the road and the path to an Oscar was less than a mile from the MGM studio at Selznick International Pictures.

14

PASSIONS AND PRIZES

The best thing that happened to William Wellman during his time at MGM was meeting Robert Carson.

When the director was not being offered films of his own, he started developing projects that he hoped to direct. During the production of *The Robin Hood of El Dorado*, he asked to be assigned a writer. "I interviewed them all and chose Robert Carson," said Wellman. The twenty-five-year-old had little experience in the film industry but Mayer and the studio bosses felt that he had potential and signed him to a term contract in 1935. Little did they imagine that after granting his contractual release to leave with Wellman, he would become a much honored screenwriter, win an Academy Award, and work with the director on seven consecutive films.

After *The Robin Hood of El Dorado*, the duo worked on a number of projects that the vindictive L.B. either scrapped or gave to others to make. Wellman and Carson did retain story screen credit on *The Last Gangster* (1937), inspired by Wellman's *Public Enemy*. The film starred Edward G. Robinson and James Stewart and was directed by Edward Ludwig.

When Wellman signed with Selznick International, he proposed several of his and Carson's projects. One was called *It Happened in Hollywood*. Wellman had wanted to make a film about the triumph and tragedy, the rise and fall of movie stars. A story revealing Hollywood's inner workings: the magic and riches, the glamour and beauty, the meanness and backstabbing, the humor and cynicism, the heartbreak of the struggle to have and to hold Hollywood glory—life as it really exists in the tinsel capital. This picture had become a Wellman dream project. The film would be called *A Star Is Born*.

Fredric March and Janet Gaynor in *A Star Is Born* (1937)

It's the story of a young woman from Kansas, Esther Blodgett, who comes to Hollywood with dreams of stardom, but achieves them only with the help of an alcoholic screen star, Norman Maine, whose best days are behind him. They fall in love and are married but their happiness is short-lived. As the rechristened Vicki Lester's career rises, Maine's declines. His pictures cease to be popular and his career dribbles away. He tries to live in a world that no longer wants him but in the end, even though his wife is ready to give up her career for him, he ends his life so that her career can go on.

Wellman's movie models were chosen from the stars he knew personally: megastars like John Barrymore and John Gilbert, both suffering career and life endings through alcoholism. His ex-wife and faded star, Helene Chadwick, had a place in the scenario . . . and matinee idol of the silent screen, John Bowers, whose life was closest to the leading male character in the story.

John Bowers was one of the most popular leading men in the 1920s. In 1923, he married a rising star, Marguerite De La Motte. She starred in such popular films as Douglas Fairbanks's *The Mark of Zorro* (1920), *The Three Musketeers* (1921), and *The Iron Mask* (1929). She and her husband shared star billing in twelve pictures from 1923 to 1927. When talking pictures arrived, Bowers's career began arcing down and his alcoholism worsened. By 1932, he was a has-been with no picture offers, separated from his wife, looking at the end of the road. On November 17, 1936, he rented a boat in Santa Monica and sailed off. His body washed ashore on a Malibu beach the next day. Wellman chose to have Norman Maine swim out to sea instead of sailing.

Wellman presented the project to Selznick, who had produced a Hollywood story, *What Price Hollywood* (1932), to reasonable success. David O. rejected Wellman's dream, saying "stories of Hollywood are too much of a gamble." So, out the window went the director's baby . . . but not for long. "David was married to L.B.'s daughter, Irene," said Wellman, "a brilliant, fascinating, wonderful looking gal with no fear whatsoever of her titanic father, in fact I think it was in reverse. He was both scared and crazy about her, a dilemma."

Wellman went calling on Mrs. David O. Selznick while she was home alone. Without any oversell, he told her his story. She loved it and said not to worry, that she and her husband were going to Honolulu for a few weeks of vacation and there would be pillow talk. Ordinarily Wellman would be leery, as he always said that more films were ruined than helped as a result of pillow talk.

When the Selznicks returned, Wellman got a call from David. They met at his studio. "I heard the fakiest explanation of a change of attitude that I have ever listened to before or since," Wellman said. Then Selznick remarked, "It's a gamble but worth taking a chance on. We will make an epic of Hollywood—we'll tear down all the tinsel, people will know the gutty Hollywood, the tragedy, the humor, the real truth. We'll start tonight."

Wellman instructed his agent, David's brother, Myron, to put a clause in the contract allowing the producer to come on the set six times only. The director knew full well that Selznick was a hands-on filmmaker who wanted to make directorial decisions and was never satisfied with one script or the original writers. Wellman explained, "There will be other writers, great writers arriving in sets as if from department stores, young blossoming writer sons of famous dead writers who will get a crack at rewriting your script—idea men who talk fast, sometimes funny but who couldn't write a script to save their lives."

After Wellman and Carson finished their script, the parade of ink slingers began just the way Wellman had said. The names included Rowland Brown, Dorothy Parker, Alan Campbell, Budd Schulberg (son of B.P.), Ring Lardner, Jr., John Lee Mahin, Ben Hecht, Gene Fowler, and, of course, David O. "I spent most of my pre-production days putting back all the writing that had been replaced by the bevy of writers that came and as quickly seemed to go," said Wellman. The ones who advised Selznick to leave the script alone were fired.

Celia and her son at the *A Star Is Born* premiere. Dottie behind and upper left of Celia. Andy Devine's wife, Doagie, center, and Wellman

Selznick announced established star Merle Oberon for the Esther Blodgett role, but Wellman couldn't see his star-struck, small-town farm girl in the more mature and sophisticated foreign-born Oberon. The director fought for and got his Cinderella in his *Small Town Girl* costar Janet Gaynor. Selznick and Wellman had no disagreements over Fredric March, star of both stage and screen, and an Academy Award winner, as Norman Maine.

Shooting began October 31, 1936. Throughout the production, the rewrites and Selznick memos continued but the director kept his temper under control and his typewriter engaged rewriting the rewrites. Even a severe bout with the flu could only sideline him for a short period while directors Jack Conway and Victor Fleming substituted. Wellman refused to allow the steady stream of intrusions to deter him from the completion of his object of passion.

Wellman filled the frames of his film with the sights and sounds of Hollywood: Grauman's Chinese Theatre, the Hollywood Bowl, the Trocadero nightclub, the Brown Derby restaurant, Santa Anita racetrack, Hollywood Legion boxing arena, Beverly Hills, Central Casting Bureau, Malibu Beach homes, the Ambassador pool, and the Biltmore Bowl for the Academy Awards banquet.

Many of the director's oft-used favorite actors were also on display, most notably Adolphe Menjou, as pro-

A Star Is Born Oscar winners Robert Carson and Wellman

ducer Oliver Niles; Andy Devine, as Esther's friend Danny McGuire; "Big Boy" Williams, as the Posture Coach; Harvey Parry and Bob Perry, as the boxer and referee; and George Chandler, newcomer to Wellman's cast list, who would appear in twenty-two of the director's pictures. Screen extras picked to appear in the Santa Anita Bar were future stars Lana Turner and Carole Landis.

Giving the film some added realism, Wellman cast a number of has-beens: Tom Ricketts, a star in the director's *When Husbands Flirt* (1925), playing the butler at the Malibu home; Owen Moore, Mary Pickford's first husband and star of the silent era ruined by alcoholism; Marshall "Mickey" Neilan, an outstanding director also taken down by the bottle. There were two child stars of the 1920s, Buddy Messenger, playing a young man delivering fan mail, and his sister, Gertrude, seen at the climactic movie premiere. Gertie's one line was snipped from the final edition.

Other extra roles were filled by Charles King, a star of early musicals including *The Broadway Melody* (1929), and former leading lady Vera Steadman with over a hundred credits. Helene Chadwick shows up again doing background work still hoping to restart her career.

One of the most dramatic scenes in *A Star Is Born* happens at the Academy Awards presentation where Vicki Lester (Gaynor) wins a Best Actress Oscar. She has just received the coveted statuette when her inebriated husband, Norman Maine (March), bursts into the room to give his drunken acceptance speech for the worst performance of the year. In his present state, he makes fun of the Academy, the Oscar, the recipients, and the film industry.

The inspiration for this sequence goes back to the first Academy Awards of 1929 and Wellman's Oscar snub for *Wings*—not being nominated for Best Director and not being invited to the celebration of the first Best Picture Academy Award winner. He stayed home alone in his apartment drinking heavily and enacting his version of an acceptance speech, one designed to let the Academy members know what he thought of them.

Shooting ended on December 28, 1936. *A Star Is Born* was the first feature film with a contemporary setting shot in three-strip Technicolor. Unlike earlier attempts at color photography, the beautifully crafted muted tones do not intrude on the screen images or emotional moments of the highly romantic story.

The film became one of the biggest-grossing pictures of 1937 and won two Academy Awards with seven Oscar nominations: Best Picture, Best

Director, Best Actor (Fredric March), Best Actress (Janet Gaynor), Best Screenplay (Alan Campbell, Robert Carson, Dorothy Parker), Best Original Story, and Best Assistant Director (Eric Stacey).

Although Wellman lost out in the director category to Leo McCarey for *The Awful Truth*, he shared an Oscar with his protégé, Robert Carson, for Best Original Story. A special Oscar was given to Wellman's right-hand-man, W. Howard Greene, for color photography.

The 1937 Awards ceremony was held at the Biltmore Hotel. Wellman accepted his Oscar "stone sober," and strolled over to his producer's table. In "tongue and cheek" fashion, considering all the Selznick memos, he offered the statuette to David O., saying, "Here, you deserve this. You wrote more than I did."

In Wellman's shooting script, Selznick wrote,

> For Bill—who accepted the award!—but who should have had it for sweetness, for direction, and for insanity! With love from his ex-keeper,
> David

Much of the huge success of this picture must be credited to Selznick. He certainly orchestrated the grand production. In later years, Wellman acknowledged that he believed Selznick to be the greatest producer of all time. But Wellman's writing prowess, individualistic style of direction, and steadfast determination cannot be denied.

Whether *Star* should have won more Oscars, including Best Direction, is much debated. Taking nothing away from the excellence of the other Best Picture–nominated films of 1937—*The Awful Truth, Captains Courageous, Dead End, The Good Earth, In Old Chicago, Lost Horizon, 100 Men and a Girl, Stage Door,* and the winner, *The Life of Emile Zola—A Star Is Born*'s popularity exceeded all of these in the test of time.

The power of the film has resulted in two remakes: Judy Garland's musical version in 1954 and Barbra Streisand's in 1976. There is a continuing desire and discussion in the film industry for yet another version.

Wellman's father was proud of his son's achievements and boasted that he had seen each of his films at least twice. Sadly, Arthur missed seeing *A Star Is Born* and his son's Oscar, as he passed away in the summer of 1936. Celia, on the other hand, made her yearly trip west for the film's Hollywood premiere at Grauman's Chinese, the same legendary theater where the film's climactic line, "This is Mrs. Norman Maine!" took place. In 1949, Celia told this author that she felt like grabbing a microphone and calling out, "This is William Wellman's mother!"

Wellman's Oscar was not the only figure he received in 1937. Dottie presented him with a son, William Augustus Wellman, called Bill Jr., born January 20, 1937. There was great happiness at the Wellman house. Dottie loved her life taking care of the home and her two children.

At forty years of age, Wellman was on top of his game and now he had the wife and family he had always wanted.

The monumental success of *A Star Is Born* led to another Selznick-Wellman venture. David O., in his overly enthusiastic style—just like Wellman's—related a Ben Hecht story called *Nothing Sacred*. The director loved its dark humor and penetrating cynical satire of the media. Wellman decided to try another film with the gifted but domineering producer. The director's contract retained the clause of only six set visits by the mogul.

Wellman with his two children in his director's chair: Pat, not yet three, and Bill Jr., seventeen months

The screwball comedy deals with a young woman, Hazel Flagg, who believes she is dying from radium poisoning. When the press gets hold of her tragic tale, a savvy newspaperman, Wallace Cook, arranges a final, all-expenses-paid vacation to the Big Apple. The newspapers play up the story-grabbing headlines. When Hazel discovers she has been misdiagnosed and is not dying, she still goes through with the charade. She is treated to a ticker tape parade and the key to the city.

During the trip, Hazel and Wally fall in love. She tells him the truth and they must find a way out of the deception. After the hoax goes public, the lovers sneak off to Europe and, hopefully, happiness.

The bevy of credited and uncredited scribes began as customary in a Selznick production. Ben Hecht's acknowledged screenplay came from a story by James H. Street, "Letter to the Editor," published in Hearst's *International-Cosmopolitan* October 1937. Unacknowledged contributions were provided by Budd Schulberg, Ring Lardner, Jr., Dorothy Parker, Sidney Howard, Moss Hart, George S. Kaufman, Robert Carson, William Wellman, and as always, David O.

Carole Lombard and Fredric March with Wellman making
Nothing Sacred (1937)

Selznick announced that Ben Hecht was writing an original comedy
for Fredric March and Janet Gaynor to be directed by William Wellman. The picture would be a follow-up to *A Star Is Born*. Once in place,
the director preferred another leading lady instead of Gaynor—Carole
Lombard.

Lombard was the most beautiful comedienne during Hollywood's
golden era of the 1930s. Howard Hawks gave her the role that cemented
her stardom, *Twentieth Century* (1934), opposite John Barrymore. She
received an Academy Award nomination as Best Actress for *My Man Godfrey* (1936). When Wellman met her, he was struck by her beauty and
effervescent demeanor. He convinced Selznick to hire her.

Hecht was not so fortunate with his choice for the Wallace Cook role.
He had written the story for his friend John Barrymore, but Selznick
refused to hire the fading alcoholic star, leaving March in place. The producer and writer also fought over script changes causing Hecht to walk
off the picture.

On a $1 million budget, shooting began June 12, 1937. There was
plenty of Wellman slapstick in the film and on the set. Historian and
author Frank Thompson: "The set of *Nothing Sacred* was constant pandemonium, for Lombard had every bit the talent and enthusiasm for pranks
and mischief as Wellman. Lunch hours were spent driving a fire engine
around the lot at top speed, siren blaring, and the set was a place of
never-ending practical jokes, good-natured rough-housing, and continu-

The family enjoyed listening to their father play the piano, a favorite pastime of his.

ous uproar. That energy and enthusiasm somehow got onto the screen; it is what gives *Nothing Sacred* a rather hysterical edge over many other comedies. It is a frenzied film made by frenzied people. Hilarious and disturbing, *Nothing Sacred* is unique."

Nothing Sacred wrapped production in early August, five days under schedule. Reviews were mostly excellent and the film did holdover business. One uncomplimentary notice came from *Time* magazine, and Selznick wrote one of his memos to Henry Luce, the magazine's founder and editor:

> I was shocked by the very tepid, if not actually damning review of *Nothing Sacred* in this week's *Time*. I was particularly surprised because the reviewer seemed to miss the whole point of the picture, a point which has been commented upon by magazine and newspaper critics across the country, which is that the picture strikes some entirely new notes in adult entertainment. It is the first comedy in Technicolor; it has been termed a very daring satire that has come off successfully; and it has been hailed from coast to coast as one of the best pictures of the year. . . . It is gratifying to know that the public has supported the press opinion, as witness the picture's being held over a third week at (Radio City) Music Hall. . . . And the only reason for this squawk is to ask whether, for the sake of my stockholders and your readers, you won't ask someone to

cover my pictures who will not sense the news value in them, and have some fair conception of their entertainment values as well, and who has no scenario-writing ambitions.

The now classic picture became a Broadway play, *Hazel Flagg* (1953), and a movie version starring Dean Martin and Jerry Lewis, *Living It Up* (1954).

Wellman often remarked that if Carole Lombard had not died in the plane crash of January 16, 1942, near Las Vegas, they would have made other pictures together. Before that fateful day, she was a regular visitor at the Wellman household. She enjoyed playing with her director's young children and shared a wonderful friendship with Dottie.

A Star Is Born and *Nothing Sacred* were two of Wellman's finest films. He would always give credit to Selznick but they would never make another feature together. It wasn't because of David O's lack of ability or showmanship, but his egocentric, ball-busting style of producing that the director could not live with. For Selznick believed that collaboration meant the drawing out of special qualities from prime talent, then molding them to suit his vision while discarding those individuals for use at a future date.

Wellman and Selznick stayed friends. The director stepped in and helped the producer on future projects: uncredited direction on the features *The Adventures of Tom Sawyer* (1938), *Gone with the Wind* (1939), and *Duel in the Sun* (1946), and credited direction on a television special, *Light's Diamond Jubilee,* celebrating the seventy-fifth anniversary of Thomas Edison's invention of the incandescent lamp. Wellman directed the segment with President Dwight Eisenhower.

Dottie was well pleased that her Bill was spending more time at home with fewer pictures in production. Since *The Call of the Wild*'s wintry, out-of-town location, he had directed only four pictures in the next two and a half years and three of them, *Small Town Girl, A Star Is Born,* and *Nothing Sacred,* were studio-based. His uncredited work was also shot locally.

Wellman began a lifelong habit of finishing the day's shooting at five in the afternoon and being home with family for dinner at six. Before Dottie became pregnant with their third child, the contented couple hired a live-in nurse so that they could join Bel-Air Country Club to play golf together.

The time was right for Wellman to return to his favorite place in the cockpit of a plane in the cinema skies. He had been offered a script called

Wellman cooks a leg of lamb for the family in his favorite barbecue, 1950.

Men with Wings, a history of aviation from the Wright brothers to the present, Kitty Hawk to Howard Hughes's flight around the world. It would be the first Technicolor flying epic and the biggest air picture since *Hell's Angels* (1930). This would be Wellman's fifth story of flight and the men of the flying eagles.

The offer opened the door for the director to make his return to Para-

Wellman believed the family should eat together.

THE WHITE HOUSE

WASHINGTON

October 19, 1954.

Dear Mr. Wellman:

I am indeed grateful to you, both for remembering our conversation and for your kindness in
sending me the golf practice net.   It arrived
at the White House even before my return to
Washington.

Thank you, too, for your assistance in making
the film to commemorate the Diamond Jubilee
of the invention of the incandescent lamp.

With warm regard,

Sincerely,

Dwight Eisenhower

Mr. William A. Wellman,
The Selznick Studio,
Culver City,
California.

President Eisenhower's letter to his director, William Wellman

David Selznick, second from left, next to President Eisenhower. Wellman is
on Eisenhower's left. *Light's Diamond Jubilee* (1954)

Dogfight scene in *Men with Wings* shows Allied plane with Wellman's Black Cat insignia and number 7.

mount. Since he left, there had been changes at the top of the ladder. The Great Depression had thrown the studio into receivership forcing a bankrupt Jesse Lasky out of his vice presidency and into independent production in 1932. A further power struggle dismissed production chief B.P. Schulberg into the same independent situation. Left at the top was president Adolph Zukor.

Unlike Wellman's term contract with the studio in the 1920s, now he was given a choice of projects, and producer-director status with name above the title—"A William A. Wellman Production." He had cast and script approval. He brought along his own writer, Robert Carson, to develop the screenplay. It would be Paramount's first $2 million production since *Wings*.

Wellman had another reunion on this picture . . . Paul Mantz. The man who had established himself with the director for his outstanding stunt work on *Central Airport* (1933) and piloted the director and his fiancée to their Las Vegas wedding had earned rave reviews with his stunts in Hollywood. In films like Clark Gable's *Love on the Run* (1936), *Test Pilot* (1938), and *Too Hot to Handle* (1938), the flier had risen to the top of the stunt rankings. In *Too Hot to Handle*, he received extra kudos for his daring air work doubling costar Myrna Loy and crashing a light plane in front of the Gable character's newsreel truck.

Where Frank Clarke had been "King of the Air" and in charge of all pilots and airplanes on *Hell's Angels*, Wellman placed Mantz as his top technical adviser. It wasn't a slap in the face to Clarke, who went back to *Wings* with the director, just respect and friendship for Paul Mantz. Wellman held no grudges or jealousies against any pilots and hired all twenty-five members of the MPPA (pilots union).

Aside from Mantz's job of designing the stunts and aerial work for the high-budget picture, he needed to find and build the aircraft depicted in the historical drama. He built two power gliders from 1904 blueprints. He already owned a 1910 Curtiss pusher biplane replica; found a dilapidated Fokker D.VII German fighter in a Los Angeles garage; gathered up several Travel Air 3000s, which look like Fokkers on the screen; discovered a French Nieuport, British DeHavilland, a Moth, two Thomas Morse Scouts, and other vintage planes in different parts of the country. Many aircraft parts were located in Burbank at a place described as the world's first airplane junkyard.

A big surprise happened in the basement of a hotel in the Imperial Valley, California. Mantz found the fuselage and wings of a Spad with the initials WAW carved in the wood instrument panel. This aircraft turned out to be the one that Wellman flew to Douglas Fairbanks's polo field in 1918 to begin his career in the movies.

Wellman chose his stars from Paramount's young contract players. The triangle story centers on Patrick Falconer (Fred MacMurray) and Scott Barnes (Ray Milland), from childhood to adults, in love with Peggy Ranson (Louise Campbell), and flight. The barnstorming Pat and scientist Scott are contrasting archetypes. Scott works diligently to build an aviation company with his pal, but Pat, like Wellman at the same age, leaves to join the Lafayette Flying Corps and becomes a war hero.

Pat marries his childhood sweetheart, Peggy, but his reckless, adventurous ways drive her into the arms of the sincere scientist, who always loved her but had remained in the background not wanting to destroy the friendship with Pat. Scott is building a great bomber (like the later Flying Fortress) for the military while Pat finds another war to fight. He is shot down, captured, and killed by firing squad.

When the news of his death reaches Scott and Peggy, they are grief-stricken. Peggy speaks out against war and Scott's bomber. "Day by day, all over the world, airplanes are getting stronger—not to carry medicine or transport the sick, not to fly the mail or bring countries closer together, but to murder the innocent. . . . Once, a long time ago, they were going to make a new world. We believed that. It's what kept us going. Now we know the truth. They're going to destroy the world. And we're helping!"

Scott sympathizes with her pacifist stance and cancels the bomber plans, instead building a magnificent passenger liner.

Andy Devine supplies comic relief leading a squadron of Wellman favorites throughout 106 minutes.

Wellman hired his *A Star Is Born*, Academy Award–winning cinematographer on *Nothing Sacred*, W. Howard Greene. In addition to land-based duties, Greene would fly with Mantz while supervising aerial photography. Greene's two assistants, Charles Marshall and Wilford Cline, would fly and operate two huge Technicolor cameras, weighing 350 pounds each, from Mantz's Travel Air and Stearman camera ships. Special camera mounts developed for *Wings* and *Young Eagles* were built onto the planes to handle the weight and allow the actors to be photographed in the air. Their swivel design allowed the cameras to move in a 180-degree arc.

Wellman would gather the pilots and cameramen; using a blackboard and model planes, he would explain the scenes, illustrate the maneuvers and action needed. Then the pilots would take off, perform their stunts, land, and report the results to the director. Wellman would see their work at the studio rushes in the next day or two.

The director did not want weather delays as experienced in *Wings* and other aviation pictures. To protect against inclement conditions and cloudless skies, he employed sixteen cloud spotters stationed in various Los Angeles locations. When a cloud bank was spotted, the studio was notified and the pre-rehearsed pilots and camera crews took to the air. Each day, local radio stations, airports, and Mount Wilson Observatory were contacted regarding general weather and cloud formations.

The aerial production began in February and was completed in May of 1938. The weather delays were minor. There were as many as fifteen ships in the air at the same time. Although there were numerous close calls, no midair collisions or serious crashes took place. One mishap that could have turned grim happened when Mantz's plane burst into flames on takeoff and Wellman helped pull him from the wreckage. The pilot suffered only minor burns.

Over three months of aerial filming took its toll on the director. He was working fifteen hours a day and couldn't sleep when he got home. "I had developed a full head of gray hair. No matter where I was, I yelled at the top of my voice. . . . I could always hear those motors."

The work was difficult and exhausting but practical jokes were still on the schedule. One prank that backfired found the script girl wanting to fly from the location to Los Angeles with Frank Clarke. Mantz warned her to be careful because if Clarke was drinking, he might fall asleep at the wheel and would have to be awakened. Mantz explained that there were times when he had to fly alongside Clarke in preparation for waking him by "slapping his wing with my plane." She didn't believe him, saying, "Oh sure. Very funny!"

The two open-cockpit planes took off in formation and soon Mantz slid in close to Clarke's ship. When the girl wasn't looking, Mantz signaled to his partner, then began shouting and waving to the girl, who immediately unfastened her seat belt and crawled back along the fuselage to the second cockpit where Clarke was rolling his head back and forth, eyes closed. She grabbed him and shook him. Her action caused her to lose balance, nearly falling off the plane. Mantz and Clarke never played this gag again.

Principal photography began May 9 and finished July 16. Before the wrap, word came down from the front office for Wellman to change the ending. The director had a strong and binding contract with language benefiting him in many areas of filmmaking but, as was the standard in studio contracts of the day, no final-cut approval.

On May 28, 1938, *The New York Times* announced that "the army, the State Department and the Executive Division" had put pressure on Paramount to change the pacifist ending denouncing war and bombers. Since the studio required government cooperation on *Men with Wings* and other projects in development, changes would be implemented. Wellman and Carson fought against this but were told that it wasn't Paramount's decision and, furthermore, if they didn't make the changes, another writer and director would.

Frank Thompson reported that Wellman's assistant director, Joseph Youngerman, recalled that the director went to the studio bosses with a new ending—no tirade, no bomber, no plane at all . . . just a ramp upward with many people of all races and creeds climbing it and a voice announcing, "All aboard for China, England, places all over the world"— establishing the legacy of flight from its beginning to 1938 and into the future when people can fly all over the world.

The futuristic scene was rejected and never shot. The end of *Men with Wings* is at a banquet honoring the fallen war hero, Pat Falconer. There are no pacifist remarks, no ultra-airliner, just the military bomber . . . and World War II fast approaching.

The film received a reasonable welcome at the box office but failed to excite many critics and mainstream fans. As an example, the *New York Herald Tribune*, October 27, 1938, wrote: "There is enormous sweep and savage dramatic power. . . . Wellman, an ex-flier as well as a crack director, has tried to make the motion picture a cavalcade of man's conquest of the air. . . . To a large degree he has succeeded, but the very scope of his theme has premised an episodic narrative which is almost certain to leave one with a feeling of disappointment. . . . *Men with Wings* is so good that it is a pity it could not have had more dramatic unity."

There is a feeling that the director became so immersed in the aviation portion of the film that the human triangle story became almost an afterthought, the dynamics of the aerial work and history of flight overshadowing the standard human story line.

15

THE GOLDEN YEAR

The year was 1939, considered the greatest year in cinema history—and this author heartily concurs, but for a different reason than many film critics and historians have offered. The argument of which year had the best films usually comes down to the Academy Award nominees and winners. Considered champions in 1939: *The Wizard of Oz, Stagecoach, Ninotchka, Mr. Smith Goes to Washington, Love Affair, Wuthering Heights, Dark Victory, Goodbye, Mr. Chips, Of Mice and Men* . . . and the Best Picture winner, *Gone with the Wind*. All fabulous films.

Many other years had ten celebrated pictures as well. But to me, it's the 1939 losers that make the difference. Some of the non-nominees were: *Beau Geste, Gunga Din, Only Angels Have Wings, The Roaring Twenties, The Women, The Hunchback of Notre Dame, Golden Boy, Drums Along the Mohawk, Young Mr. Lincoln, Confessions of a Nazi Spy, The Old Maid, The Light That Failed*. These famed films of incredible variety could have made the top ten in other years.

So, where was Wellman in this mix of triumphant pictures? Right in the middle of it. He was finishing the 1930s in a flourish. He had three very special productions: Dottie produced his third child, Kathleen Kent, a blonde who would answer to Kitty, while he made two grand adventure stories, *Beau Geste* and Rudyard Kipling's *The Light That Failed*.

From a Percival Christopher Wren novel (1924), *Beau Geste* became an enormous success. It was first produced by Paramount as a silent film in 1926. There have been sequels and other versions; six movies in all, a Broadway play, and a television miniseries with stars like Ronald Colman, Gary Cooper twice, Laurence Olivier, Marty Feldman, and even

Another daughter: Kathleen "Kitty" (arm raised), sits on Dottie's lap next to Billy, Pat, and Tommy Scott, film editor of *The Great Man's Lady* (1941).

Laurel and Hardy. But Wellman's version is the most acclaimed and often considered one of the greatest adventure films of all time.

Wellman's stars are Gary Cooper (Michael "Beau" Geste), Ray Milland (John Geste), and Robert Preston (Digby Geste). They play separately adopted brothers raised by Heather Thatcher (Lady Patricia Brandon), the possessor of the Blue Water—one of the world's most valuable diamonds. Lady Brandon's husband, Sir Hector, is the owner of the Brandon Abbas estate and spends more time and the estate's money away from home. He is returning from a hunting trip and all expectations are that he plans to sell the Blue Water. When the gem is stolen, Beau disappears and joins the Foreign Legion. Not wanting their brother to suffer the blame, John and Digby follow him.

In flashback sequences, we see the Gestes as children—Donald O'Connor playing Beau—and learn of their brotherly love. Wearing cocked hats made of paper, brandishing wooden swords, they enact an emotional scene. With the use of model boats, toy soldiers and cannons, sticks, matchboxes, gunpowder, and a china dog, we see their version of a Viking funeral pyre. Susan Hayward (Isobel Rivers), another ward of Lady Brandon, adds her presence wearing a cocked hat with a red cross on it. She later becomes John's romantic interest.

The Gestes' dedication to each other is evident as they swear that if one of them dies, the others will give him the Viking funeral—wrapped in a flag on a burning deck with a dog at his feet. Digby fires up the small boat carrying a toy soldier on a bed of matchboxes, gunpowder, and the china dog at his feet. As the ship explodes and sinks, Digby raises his bugle and blows taps.

The story moves ahead to the reunion of the Gestes in the Foreign Legion. Brian Donlevy, as the sadistic Sergeant Markoff, is their leader and the villain of the piece. His brand of Legion toughness makes their lives and that of the rest of the legionnaires intolerable. In the climactic scenes, when Fort Zinderneuf is under siege from the charging hordes of Arab tribesmen (Touaregs), most of the legionnaires are killed. The Touaregs surge across the desert sands four times, leaving only Markoff and John alive with Beau mortally wounded. Beau had

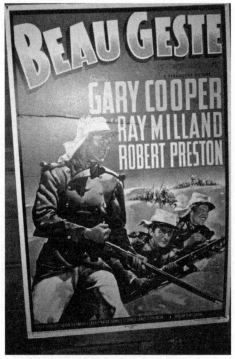

Beau Geste poster (1939)

stolen the gem, not for himself or financial gain but to keep it safe from the forced family sale. His secret became known among the legionnaires.

During the fierce battle, the dead legionnaires are systematically propped up in the fort embrasures, making the Arabs believe they are alive and ready to fight. The Touaregs leave and Markoff searches the dying Beau for the Blue Water. Enraged by this act, John thrusts his sword into the hated sergeant, killing him. John kisses his dead brother goodbye, and leaves the fort as Digby and the reinforcements arrive. Digby is commanded to go in first in case of an enemy trap. No one is left alive. Digby carries out the Viking funeral promise, wrapping Beau in kerosene-soaked barracks mattresses with the "dog" (Markoff) at his feet. He bugles taps after setting them ablaze.

This time there was no ending problem with the picture. The studio wanted no basic story changes from the original film, which suited the director just fine. Production commenced January 16, 1939, on the site of the 1926 location in Buttercup Valley, nineteen miles west of Yuma. Fort Zinderneuf had to be rebuilt with a single-lane plank road connecting the fort to the newly christened "Camp Wellman" over a mile away. At a cost of $50,000, a tent city was erected with 136 large tents holding a thousand men. There was a post office, mess halls, recreation facilities, a movie theater, and other conveniences. Live entertainment was brought in, including musicians, singers, and dancers—the female entertainers were the only women allowed in camp.

Wellman produced as well as directed, so the whole operation from beginning to end was in his hands. "The first big problem," said the producer-director, "I axed immediately—no dames in the camp, none, never—if the principals, including me had a wife or a girlfriend, they visited them in a cool hotel in Yuma . . . on Saturday nights and Sunday, back on the grind Sunday nights to prepare themselves for another tough week."

For the less fortunate, Wellman supplied a large comfortable bus that left the location after dinner on the weekends, bound for the only whorehouse in town. For three weekends, it was packed, every seat taken, guys sitting on the top, hardly enough room to breathe. But as the long hard days, from sunup to sundown, piled up, the bus became more and more forsaken, "with but one exception," said Wellman, "a crazy little stuntman actor, of whom I was very fond, and who in his loneliness finally went berserk and burned the house of ill fame down, to the ground."

As work continued, the desert heat took its toll on the company and several dozen members spent time in the Yuma hospital. Extreme weather conditions played havoc with the locations. The topography around Fort Zinderneuf changed as sandstorms shifted the landscape. Large dunes that were prominently featured in establishing shots disappeared. Tractors had to be trucked in to reproduce the dunes in order to match previously photographed scenes. The winds caused problems with sound transmission making the recorded tapes inaudible. The soundmen and actors were forced to continually move to other positions where the wind was less strong.

Wellman was always looking for ways to be economical with filming. Even when he wasn't both producer and director, he wanted to save time, money, and stay ahead of schedule. He never knew when delays would come as a result of weather or other conditions.

With the exception of *Wings*, he had built his reputation for being on schedule and under budget. His experience and personality would not allow him to be unprepared, to sit around pondering or just waiting for outside influences to settle or change. He loved the work and took great pleasure from his fast-paced, spontaneous, no-nonsense director's style. Even the Wild Bill moniker was a useful catalyst in getting results.

On *Beau Geste*, he had a unique solution for economizing—"simultaneous production." He mapped out a system with his stunt coordinator/second unit director, Richard Talmadge. While Wellman filmed the principals inside the fort, Talmadge rehearsed the action on the outside, waiting for a signal from Wellman. When the director completed a setup and began the move to the next position, he would blow his shrill whistle for Talmadge to commence the battle scenes. Most of the panoramic action scenes of the thundering hordes were shot utilizing this simultaneous method.

Right in the middle of the schedule—after a couple of sandstorms, hot and uncomfortable days and nights, long exhausting work hours—the director decided to veer from his taskmaster status. "I had a talk with the producer, a not too nice guy, me, and convinced him that it might be a good idea to take the whole company on a vacation to a town in Mexico . . . for three days, Friday, Saturday and Sunday, and there has never been a more welcome, unusual three days in the history of the Paramount Pictures Corp."

The holiday paid off. No one got drunk, no one went to jail, no fights, and the Mexicans loved the picture people. There was, literally, dancing in the streets with lively music from the townspeople and a few accomplished musicians from the company—"it was a gathering of two peoples," said Wellman, "speaking strange languages and having a hell of a good time together. They lionized Cooper and Milland who sang and danced with the big gals and little gals and Preston mesmerized them with his voice."

This weekend escape for the cast and crew sowed great contentment and better attitudes for the work ahead. It also contributed to marriage. One actor and one crew member tied the knot with their South of the Border lovers. When the picture wrapped, the happy couples returned to Hollywood.

The picture was progressing well. The producer-director had picked a horse out of the hundreds available for his own, to be ridden to and from the location and on many nights after shooting and before dinner. They would go for a workout in the desert and come home hungry, and mentally, as well as physically, relaxed. "It was my savior, and I fell in love with my new pal and changed his name from Chip to Beau and the wise old boy liked it."

Throughout the long days and nights, Wellman and his horse-pal were together. Beau seemed to realize that Wellman was the boss and he no longer had to work in the flaming sun with the rest of the herd—he was special. The master tethered him on a long rope outside his tent so that if Beau wanted, he could amble over and look in.

There were many nights when the horse did so, watching his master studying and writing in his script or just sleeping. When Wellman was awake, he could feel eyes watching him or hear a whinny outside the tent. He would get up, walk over and rub Beau's head, giving him lumps of sugar, patting him good night. Wellman said, "He could do everything but talk"—the master supplied the verbals with no four-letter accompaniments.

This relationship supplied enjoyment and relief for the producer-director from so much responsibility. It helped fill the void left by the missing Dottie, pregnant and unable to fly down to Yuma. Wellman had a Teletype machine installed in his Brentwood home so she could reach him immediately, if necessary. Dottie could not type, she just one-fingered her love notes to him.

The movie company was brimming with camaraderie. So many hard-working men had become a kind of family. There was one desert pothole in this scenario and it was filled by Sergeant Markoff—Brian Donlevy. "As a matter of fact, nobody liked the son of a bitch," said Wellman. "His

Wellman picked his horse to ride to location. Chip had a name change to Beau.

three tentmates left him. . . . Donlevy was even nasty when asleep." The director had a big reason for not taking part in any of the complications the actor was causing: "he was giving a sensational performance, so much so that it improved all the other performances."

Ray Milland hated Donlevy the most and on several occasions the director had to step in to stop him from slugging Donlevy. But Milland was waiting for a time and place to take care of the sergeant. He found it in the death scene at the end of the picture. The Welsh-born star had served in the cavalry, and was an expert marksman and swordsman. He had been doing some research and discovered that Donlevy suffered from a disease that caused him to faint at the sight of blood.

In the decisive scene, Sergeant Markoff—the actor safeguarded by a chest protector of steel and cushion—receives a bayonet piercing from the hand of John Geste, killing him instantly. "Milland had detected a pinch of flesh exposed just under his left armpit," said Wellman. As the fatal scene plays out, Geste's lightning-like thrust severs the flesh, causing a spurt of blood. As directed, Markoff falls to the deck of the fort. When the director yelled "Cut!" Donlevy stood up, saw his blood dripping, and fainted back to the same spot on the deck. The second fall was better than the first but, unfortunately, the camera was not rolling. "The company doctor stopped the bleeding and suggested we ambulance him to the hospital for shots and two lousy stitches," said Wellman.

Later that evening, Milland came to Wellman to apologize. "Bill, I couldn't help it, so help me God my hatred has been so savage. I knew there were only two shots left with him so it wouldn't inconvenience you. What are you going to do to me?" "Two things," said the director, "number one, thank God you are a skillful swordsman and hit the mark; number two, see if you can drink as much beer as I can. Let's go!"

Brian Donlevy nearly had the last laugh. He returned from the hospital the next day accompanied by a pretty young nurse—the only woman in the "no women allowed" camp. Dressed in nice street clothes thinking he wouldn't have to work so soon after the "accident," he gave her a guided tour of the tent city and the fort. He smiled widely as he passed the actors and crew members on the way to the upper deck of Zinderneuf.

While filming was in progress on the fort's ground level, Donlevy and helpmate, arm in arm, climbed the stairs. From the embrasures, the actor gave his account of the dramatic scenes of battle that had cost Paramount $250,000 to film. He pointed out the vast stretches of sand where the charging Arabs had made their relentless attacks. The eyes of the movie company watched every move of the beautiful, captivated nurse. The

Wellman's forty-third birthday party includes (left to right): Robert Preston, Ray Milland, Broderick Crawford, J. Carroll Naish, Wellman leaning over the piano, and Gary Cooper.

director noticed this display as well and with a quick change in shooting schedule ruined Donlevy's last laugh. Wellman shouted up to the actor, "Donlevy, go down to the dressing room and get on your uniform. I want your delightful little nurse to see how well you can act." The actor asked what scene he would be doing. The director announced, "Lying dead in your fainted position."

The calendar pages had flipped to February. Camp Wellman would be coming down on the twentieth with the main company returning to the studio on the twenty-first. Talmadge's second unit would stay behind for pickup shots. Principal location photography would be completed. Since it was not a leap year, the director would be celebrating his forty-third birthday back home on the twenty-eighth.

Joe Youngerman, Wellman's assistant director, was well aware of these dates and planned an early birthday—a company party in the main mess hall tent. To save time, money, and to help him stay on top of things, Wellman had his film editor with him on the location. Each day after shooting, they would look at the previous day's work before going to dinner. By the time Wellman arrived at the mess hall, it had been turned into a surprise party.

Wellman's buddy and former assistant director Charlie Barton, an actor in *Beau Geste*, had put together a raggedy orchestra. He was its leader and his baton was a brassiere tacked to a broomstick. As he waved it in the air, it would inflate itself. When the director entered the tent, the musicians piped up an off-key version of "Happy Birthday."

Ray Milland entered the rollicking festivities, leading a trotting Beau over to Wellman's table. Milland announced to all, "Bill, knowing how well you two animals get along together, we, your slaves, have purchased said four legged pal as a present to you from the whole company." Amid the following cheers, in strolled Gary Cooper carrying a wood tree rawhide–covered saddle with a silver plate in the saddle horn inscribed, "From the Beau Geste Company." The thirty-four-pound saddle was a duplicate of Coop's that Wellman had much admired. "This little goodie," said Coop, "has been acquired for you by the whole company because they felt very deeply the great sorrow and thankless job that is yours, directing Charlie Barton."

That brought laughs and a pratfall from Charlie that knocked over a table and signaled the entrance of buckets of beer. "It was a wonderful night," Wellman said. "A lot of guys had worked for me back in the Dustin Farnum and Buck Jones days, they remembered so many wonderful anecdotes that I had forgotten—it was a night of continuous laughter from all four corners of the tent, and I was a proud and very meek man." Wellman paid homage to his cast and crew that evening and later said, "I had Cooper, Milland and Preston, whom I loved, and dozens of character actors I had used in dozens of pictures, all of whom I was very fond of. As for my crew, they all loved me, as I did them . . . they were the guts of my success."

In a manner of speaking, Brian Donlevy did have the final grin. He was nominated for an Academy Award as Best Supporting Actor. *Beau Geste* received only one other Academy Award nomination in this glorious year of 1939. It was for Best Art Direction. Hans Dreier and Robert Odell were the key figures in planning the overall look of the film from design to construction of all the sets, including Fort Zinderneuf, authentic costumes, even the use of 1,200 Foreign Legion Lebel rifles.

The perennial favorite *Beau Geste* will always be remembered for fabled adventure, the romance of yesteryear, brotherly love, a vanishing code of honor, sweeping action, outstanding performances, exceptional photography, and an inspiring musical score by Alfred Newman. *Film Bulletin*, July 29, 1939: "Here is a flawless production, in which story, acting and direction rise to the great heights the screen is capable of achieving, but so rarely does."

Wellman was home for the birth of his third child, March 13, and *Beau*

Ronald Colman paints his *Woman of the Street* (Ida Lupino) in
The Light That Failed (1939).

Geste wrapped in mid-April. After two long and difficult big production
films, *Men with Wings* and *Beau Geste*, you might think the director
would take some time off or choose a studio-based picture . . . no way.

While *Geste* was still in postproduction, he jumped into the high-
adventure tale of Rudyard Kipling's *The Light That Failed*. After initial
location shooting, the script did allow for weeks of studio interior work
and Wellman could continue his routine of being home with Dottie and
his growing family at dinnertime.

Originally, the director was slated to do *Light* before *Geste*, but the
studio pushed the picture back. Now it was ready and Robert Carson had
finished a new screenplay. The film had two silent versions, both changing the novel to happy endings. Wellman stayed true to Kipling's vision.

It is the story of an artist, a painter of men and war, who creates his
true masterpiece, *Woman of the Street*, after being told he is losing his
sight. Facing total blindness, he discovers that his vengeful model has
destroyed his work of art. He commits suicide by riding horseback into
battle with the British army fighting the Fuzzy-Wuzzy warriors of Sudan.

Over time, Paramount had gone through a number of casting changes.
Wellman requested his *Beau Geste* star, Gary Cooper, but the studio
signed matinee idol Ronald Colman.

Born in Richmond, Surrey, England, on February 9, 1891, Ronald
Charles Colman discovered acting at an early age and soon was playing
a variety of roles on stage as a member of the West Middlesex Dramatic

Society. In 1909, he joined the London Scottish Regiment and fought in World War I. At the Battle of Messines in October of 1914, he was seriously wounded by shrapnel in his leg and invalided from service in 1916. This wound caused a permanent limp, which he attempted to conceal throughout his career. He went on to play leading stage and film roles in his native country until coming to America in 1920 where he continued to gain fame on the New York stage and soon the films of Hollywood.

Equally successful in romantic and adventure films, he was nominated for four Academy Awards, for *Bulldog Drummond* and *Condemned* (both in 1930), *Random Harvest* (1942), and *A Double Life* (1947), for which he finally won the Oscar.

From the beginning, it was clear that Colman, the sophisticated intellectual, and Wellman, the unpretentious common man, were not destined for kinship. "Ronald Colman and Wellman, an odd combination to say the least," said the director. "He didn't like me; I didn't like him—the only two things we agreed fully on." They did share a mutual respect but even that disappeared in the sands of New Mexico.

When the remainder of the film's casting began in the late spring of 1939, Colman raised his director's ire by continually campaigning for a young British star to play the pivotal role of the artist's model, Bessie Broke. At the time, the ingenue was in production on her American film debut but was expected to finish before the start of *Light*. Her film was *Gone with the Wind*. Her name was Vivien Leigh. Wellman had never met Leigh, who was relatively unknown to American audiences. He had nothing against her except for her countryman's constant pestering. Colman even attempted to persuade the front office into hiring her. When the director came to the end of his patience, he told his leading man that no matter her origin or experience, he was going to hire the next actress who came into his office.

This story got around. Soon, a young hopeful—who just happened to be English—heard it. Although her credits revealed a history of playing ordinary roles in an ordinary manner in ordinary films, she made her assault on immortality. "That crazy little English girl that tore into my office unannounced," said Wellman, "and demanded that I watch her play Bessie Broke in the big scene. . . . I did, right in my office, and I played Colman, and despite that, she was marvelous, and I gave her the part, and she became a star: Ida Lupino."

The fact that Colman didn't like Lupino and wanted her replaced, and the studio was shocked at this sudden turn of events, made Wellman all the happier about his casting.

Production began in mid-June on locations at Black Mesa, thirty-five miles northwest of Santa Fe. Paramount's public relations department issued this release:

William A. Wellman, who just can't seem to stay in Hollywood, went to New Mexico to film "The Light That Failed." Location scouts toured the Southwest for weeks before they found country that could aptly double for the Sudan.

The Rio Grande, which is a pretty small stream at the point 35 miles from Santa Fe which finally was chosen, was dammed so that it would broaden and more closely resemble the Nile.

The studio hired a company of the New Mexico National Guard to act as the British army, and hired about 200 Negroes to take the part of the Fuzzy-Wuzzies. Captain J. R. Durham-Matthews, of the Irish Guards, served as technical adviser on the battle sequences.

Wellman moved a narrow-gauge railroad down from Colorado to New Mexico to film the train sequence. When the smoke from the guns "blacked out" the action, he had an airplane flown in from Albuquerque, which was anchored down, and then run at top speed, so that the wash of the propeller would blow away the smoke.

Tractors, graders, Fresnos and other road-building equipment was put to work leveling a path from the main highway to the battle site. The noise of the conflict caused one tourist on the highway to telephone a frantic message into Santa Fe that the Indians had broken off their reservation and had gone on the warpath.

Following the filming of the desert scenes, the studio was billed for a mass hair-cutting job on the militia, and an item of $40.25 for sunburn lotion. The "Fuzzy-Wuzzies," unaccustomed to scanty attire, had been badly sunburned.

A ninety-foot steel tower, with cameras on three levels, was erected to shoot the battle scenes. Wellman and his production crew viewed rushes daily at a theatre in Santa Fe. The film was flown to Hollywood each night, developed, printed and returned in time to be shown the following day, traveling over 2,000 miles in less than twenty-four hours. Because no modern cloth resembles in style or pattern that worn by the top-ranking English Gentleman of the 1880's, the village of Glencraigie, Scotland, was put to work weaving enough cloth for suits for Colman, Huston [Walter] and other male members of the cast.

Huston and Dudley Digges had a narrow escape from injury on location when a cyclone blew down the portable dressing room in which they were conversing. A well to provide drinking water for the more than 500 men in the troupe was drilled at the location site. Ten gallons of spring water, however, were shipped to New Mexico for "Mr. Whiskers," the Scotty dog.

Just as had happened at the close of location filming on *Beau Geste*, Wellman and the main body of the company returned to the studio leaving a second unit behind. Joe Youngerman, Wellman's assistant for a third straight picture, directed the pickup shots that the director had carefully mapped out before leaving. The director's notes in his script detail the design of the shots for his assistant.

Back at the studio, the climate between Wellman, Colman, and Lupino grew darker. Although Colman continued to dislike his costar, Wellman was crazy about her. The Colman-Wellman relationship reached a climax during a highly dramatic scene where Lupino's Bessie Broke becomes hysterical. Ronald Colman was a perfectionist. He didn't like the director's method of one or two takes. He wanted to work at a higher level. He memorized every line in the script, not just his, but every actor's words. Wellman remarked, "He never blew a line."

In this particular scene, when Lupino reached the high point of her emotion, Colman kept blowing his line and the scene was cut. Finally, the director realized that the purist Colman was blowing his line on purpose. "Cut!" said the director. "I walked over to him and said, 'Let's you and I take a little walk.' We walked behind the set and I said, 'Look, Mr. Colman, once more and I will make a character man out of you. I will kick the hell out of you. That pretty face of yours is going to look awful funny.'"

They returned to the set, and the scene was shot with no dialogue miscues. The director later said, "They played it beautifully. Colman was wonderful. But he didn't talk to me again during the picture, except when necessary, and then it was 'Mr. Wellman' and 'Mr. Colman.'" Ronald Colman and his second wife, stage and screen actress Benita Hume, had their own radio show, *The Halls of Ivy*, from 1950 to 1952, which became a television program from 1954 to 1955. In those stories, the name of the villain was Wellman.

Los Angeles Times, December 20, 1939: "*The Light That Failed* wings its way to idealistic heights, and sounds psychological depths as one of the finest pictures of its type. . . . This is truly a worthy contribution to a banner season of the cinema . . . disclosing new powers for its director, William A. Wellman. . . . Colman proves his powers. . . . The work of Miss Lupino in any normal year might well be worthy of academy honors."

Los Angeles Examiner, December 20, 1939: "All the tragic drama, human emotion and morbidness which characterize Rudyard Kipling's famed book have been transferred to the screen with sympathetic fidelity. . . . It is blonde, diminutive Ida Lupino, in a dark wig and uncomplimentary makeup, who provides the most realistic acting. . . . There is only one word for her work—magnificent."

Variety, December 20, 1939: "No picture ever to flaunt Par's [Paramount's] banner before the theatre-going millions has surpassed it, while few have even approached it in greatness. . . . Ronald Colman's top characterizations of the past fade into memory's background when paraded alongside his brilliant portrayal in 'Light.' 'Light,' too, marks a broad forward step for William A. Wellman as a producer-director. . . . Victor Young's background music is another noteworthy factor."

Victor Young's music received much praise. When Wellman asked him for some authentic Hindu music, Young later responded by playing it on his piano. The director liked what he heard, as did many reviewers when the film opened the day before Christmas 1939. Years later, Young told his secret to Hollywood columnist Erskine Johnson, "I recorded 'Yankee Doodle Dandy' backwards."

It is difficult to find an uncomplimentary review of this film. It is a very special Wellman picture that has been sorely forgotten—partially due to the tremendous caliber of the other 1939 films. We leave *The Light That Failed* with this line from Ronald Colman's blinded character: "Painting is seeing—and then remembering better than you saw."

What better way to end Wellman's contributions to the golden year than with *Gone with the Wind*. The mighty Academy Award champion garnered thirteen nominations, and won eight Oscars including Best Picture, plus two special award statuettes and David Selznick's Irving G. Thalberg Memorial Award.

GWTW's actual production began January 26 and completed on July 1, 1939. The over five months of filming encountered halts in production and problems of every kind and nature. The original director, George Cukor, was fired after only three weeks of filming, as the picture's star, Clark Gable, did not like his personality or style of direction. Gable felt that the women, namely Vivien Leigh and Olivia de Havilland, received more attention and better direction while his role was being diminished.

Selznick was disappointed with Cukor's handling of the production scenes. So, out went George and in came Vic. Victor Fleming was a master craftsman, who had befriended Gable during their two successful films together, *Red Dust* (1932) and *Test Pilot* (1938). They were both rugged outdoorsmen, cut from the same cloth.

Well into the production schedule, Fleming was near exhaustion and suffered a nervous breakdown. He left the picture for four weeks before returning. To keep the project on track, Selznick hired a long list of talent to direct various scenes: Sam Wood, Sidney Franklin, B. Reeves Eason, Chester Franklin, also production designer William Menzies, editor Hal Kern, special effects supervisor Jack Cosgrove, and William Wellman.

All of the aforementioned individuals' names appear on daily production reports except the name of William Wellman. This omission is written about by noteworthy authors and historians claiming that Wellman did not work on *GWTW.*

Bob Thomas, in *Selznick*, writes, "Sam Wood was hired to take over for Vic Fleming. A versatile craftsman, he stepped in and began directing without delay. Sidney Franklin and William Wellman directed other dramatic scenes."

This author was present with his father at an afternoon party at David Selznick's Beverly Hills home in 1956. I remember the date. I was nineteen and had a crush on one of the guests after seeing her recent film, the science fiction thriller *Invasion of the Body Snatchers* . . . Dana Wynter.

The *Gone with the Wind* buggy holding Kitty, Pat, and Bill Jr., drawn by Beau with inspiration from Dottie, 1942

The Capras, Frank and Lu, dine with the Wellmans at
fashionable La Rue's on Sunset Strip, 1940s.

A small group including actor Louis Jourdan, my father, Miss Wynter,
me following close to her, and one or two others, had gathered in the
mogul's backyard. Selznick was pontificating on all the films that he and
my father had worked on together. When he finished, my dad piped up
with, "Don't forget, I burned down Culver City [the burning of Atlanta]
for your *Gone with the Wind*." Selznick responded immediately, "And
that too!"

On December 11, 1938, a month and a half before the actual start date,
the burning of Atlanta sequence was shot. Selznick planned to build
the set of Tara on the forty-acre back lot of the Pathé studio in Culver
City. Before he could do so, a huge amount of old movie sets had to be
removed. The decision was made to gather, shift, build a replica of 1864
Atlanta out of the old sets and . . . burn it all down. Seven Technicolor
cameras were positioned to cover every possible angle. It would have to
be shot in one take only.

Three sets of doubles were hired to pose as Rhett Butler and Scarlett
O'Hara as they ride a buckboard wagon past the holocaust. Selznick
gathered family, friends, associates, and the Culver City Fire Department
to watch the one-hour inferno.

George Cukor was reported to be on hand while Wellman worked
his technical skills. Rehearsals were performed and Wellman noticed an
old buggy piled into the debris waiting for the flames to end its days.

Wellman wondered in how many films had this single-seat runabout appeared? How many stars had sat in the black leather seat, now caked with dirt, as was the rear jump seat? The iron step was hanging off the sideboard and the yellow spoke wheels were filled with mud.

Wild Bill was doing a favor for a friend, for no pay, and decided to take something home to his family. He had a prop man pull the buggy aside for delivery to his home a few days later. When it arrived, he had it repaired, cleaned up, and repainted. There it sat, waiting patiently for the horses to arrive after the filming of *Beau Geste*.

Wellman's gift horse, Beau, arrived first but was too spirited for pulling the buggy with Dottie and his kids aboard. When he purchased for Dottie a gentler, dapple-gray saddle horse named Blue, excursions around the neighborhood and local hills became a joyous event. They lasted for many years, longer than old Blue and most of the other horses that followed. When the neighborhood became filled with houses, paved streets, and traffic, the buggy turned obsolete and was parked behind the pool house where it succumbed to old age and eventually disappeared.

In 2010, after a heavy rainstorm, part of the frame was sighted sticking out of the ground. The rusted metal frame and wheel covers were dug up. A family member, Al Anton, brother of Bill Jr.'s wife, Flossie, saw something special in the relics, much as Wellman did back in the old days, and asked for the remains of the once proud runabout buggy. It now resides at his home, displayed on a wall, looking down at adoring fans who look up, read the legend, imagine and appreciate its long and colorful life.

William Wellman's two meritorious pictures, *Beau Geste* and *The Light That Failed*, and his uncredited direction on *Gone with the Wind*, were significant contributors to the zenith year of Oscar's greatest glory . . . and a revitalized horse-drawn buggy was much appreciated by the Wellman family.

16

THE ROAD TO *OX-BOW*

Wellman was weary. The osteoarthritis that began during the filming of *The Call of the Wild* was worsening. From that glaciated location epic that began in January of 1935, he had directed eight films in four and a half years. Five of those pictures were rugged outdoor productions, and on the last three—*Men with Wings*, *Beau Geste*, and *The Light That Failed*—he was both producer and director. He needed a break. He told Paramount's production chief, William LeBaron, that he was taking some time off.

What better place to spend his retreat from Hollywood than his secluded, three-and-a-half-acre Brentwood estate. He would be with Dottie and play with his three young children. He could swim in the lagoon-style pool, work out in his gym, water his grove of orange trees, play Ping-Pong, shoot pool, and ride horseback. Dottie's Blue became an immediate pal with his *Beau Geste* present, Beau. The two active horses produced plenty of manure to fertilize his orange trees.

Since there were only a few houses in the seven-street, ten-block neighborhood of 1940, Bill and Dottie could ride horseback all over the environs including the hills and mountain range in their backyard. His passion for golf could be satisfied at Bel-Air Country Club just over two miles away.

Wellman was at the forefront of the Hollywood movement to West Los Angeles and Brentwood. Most of the film community was living near the studios in Hollywood and Beverly Hills. In the late 1930s and throughout the 1940s, the westward migration began as celebrities wanted more property, privacy, and distance from city life and their studios.

Homes were built and Wellman's neighborhood became filled with

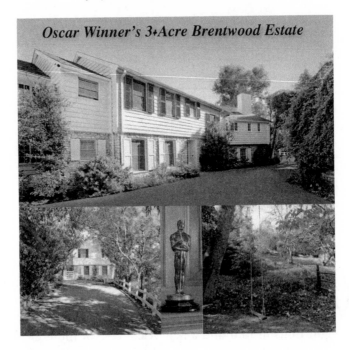

Oscar Winner's 3+Acre Brentwood Estate

such stars as William "Hopalong Cassidy" Boyd, Gary Cooper, Nelson Eddy, Henry Fonda, Van Johnson, Peter Lawford, Fred MacMurray, John Payne and Gloria DeHaven, Tyrone Power, Cesar Romero, Lana Turner, Robert Walker and Jennifer Jones; character actors Eddie Bracken and Keenan Wynn; bandleaders Xavier Cugat and Bob Crosby; comic star Red Skelton; singing stars the Andrews sisters; celebrated author and screenwriter Gene Fowler; filmmaker Frank Capra.

The Capras and their three children, Frank Jr., Lucille, and Tom, lived on a five-acre estate just down the street. "Lu [Frank's wife] and I had dinner with Bill and Dottie at least twice a week," said Capra. "We were as close as two families can be and not live under the same roof." Other family friends were the Coopers, MacMurrays, Paynes, and Fondas.

There were non-neighborhood, nonfamily sidekicks who darkened the Wellman's doorway like W. C. Fields, who was more interested in spirits and shooting pool. On more than one occasion, Dottie had to "put her foot down" after the gatherings got out of hand with the pie-eyed pool shooters. Wellman always apologized and finally stopped inviting his "bottoms up" buddies from the Wild Bill days. He was trying to break the habit.

Throughout his career, Wellman was never the social butterfly. He preferred the outskirts of sociality. He stayed away from the Hollywood grand parties and major galas. He favored the smaller, more intimate gatherings. What he most enjoyed now was being with his family and especially Dottie—they did everything together.

Wellman tolerated Dottie's four sisters but liked brother John, whom he helped get started as an actor in *Wild Boys of the Road* and *Stingaree,* production assistant on *The President Vanishes,* and assistant director on *Nothing Sacred* and *Reaching for the Sun.* Coonan went on to a fine thirty-three-year career as an assistant director, production manager, and producer.

Wellman was fond of Dottie's strong-minded mother, Flossie. He never forgot that after her husband departed, she raised six children during the Depression. He bought her a home in Westwood, a few miles from Brentwood, and sent her money every month.

Flossie was never afraid to speak her mind. Whether it was politics, economics, the weather, or the movies, she said what she thought. She even spoke up against Wellman's wild times. Mostly, the two of them saw eye to eye on things, but when they disagreed, Flossie was smart enough to stop talking and Wellman was smart enough to do the same. Fortunately for both, she liked his films and was pleased with the happiness of her daughter. Flossie was that strong independent woman that Wellman much admired.

Between *The Light That Failed* and his next picture, *Reaching for the Sun,* Wellman took six months away from the grind. "It was my first real vacation in fourteen years," said the director. Most of it was spent at his home and Bel-Air Country Club—golf was good exercise for his arthritic body and therapeutic for his overcrowded mind. He took Dottie to Boston. He hadn't been back in nine years. The New Englander enjoyed seeing family, old friends, and meeting some new ones. He visited childhood haunts and spent time with his mother and brother. Bill and Dottie stayed with Arch and Ruth, his wife of twenty years, and their children, Arthur Jr., John, and Marjorie. Now a successful wool merchant, Arch had a fine home at 75 Royce Road in Newton Center.

After the death of Wellman's father, Arthur, in 1936, Celia had stayed on at 22 Davis Avenue in West Newton. With Arch's help, she had purchased the small but comfortable green-shuttered, shingle house. She placed window boxes of pink geraniums in the front and kept her front lawn green and close cropped. On her Academy Award–winning son's first night in town, she cooked his favorite meal of beans, balls, clams, and nuts.

The family celebrated Bill's forty-fourth birthday on the leap year day of February 29, 1940. They dined at Boston's Statler Hotel, which opened

Joel McCrea, Wellman, and Ellen Drew enjoy the movie baby in *Reaching for the Sun* (1941).

on March 10, 1927, as part of the empire of E. M. Statler, one of the nation's most visionary businessmen and hoteliers. It was the first hotel in the world to have a radio in each of its thirteen hundred guest rooms, and for five decades was the largest independent hotel in New England and the eighth largest in the world.

A wonderful time was had by all but Wellman's creative juices began to boil and he yearned to get back behind the camera. One big decision needed to be made before reentering the production gates of Paramount Pictures—hiring a proper architect to build his new home on the Brentwood property. Dottie was pregnant again and the old-style house was too small for the growing family.

Roland E. Coate entered Wellman's life. Born in Indiana, on December 5, 1890, he came to California in 1919 after completing seventeen months as a first lieutenant in the American Expeditionary Force. He became a world-class architect with designs for such classic spaces as the All Saint's Episcopal churches in Pasadena and Beverly Hills, Saint Paul's Episcopal Cathedral in Los Angeles, and the Caltech Hale Solar Laboratory in Pasadena, as well as a long list of exquisite homes in the Los Angeles area. He was known as the designer for the Hollywood luminaries. His "art as architecture" was much appreciated by the likes of Howard Hughes, Robert Taylor and Barbara Stanwyck, David Selznick, Frank Capra, and Gary Cooper.

Coate loved versatility in style and his range covered English Tudor;

Italian Revival; American, Spanish, and Monterey Colonial; and more. Wellman, being a New Englander, asked for a Connecticut farmhouse and the architect delivered a tableau of perfectly framed shapes, lines, textures, and colors—it was art with at-home amenities. Plus, there were seven bedrooms and nine bathrooms—ample space for the future generation. The old house would be razed and the new one completed in 1942. For the next year, they would be enjoying seaside living in a comfortable beach house in the exclusive Malibu Colony.

Wellman would make only two more films for Paramount, *Reaching for the Sun* (1941) and *The Great Man's Lady* (1942). The studio that had provided the director with his flight to fame on *Wings*, and seventeen pictures in all, would no longer carry the "William A. Wellman Production" banner. This time, there was no Wellman-Paramount animosity, just the director's quest for more distinctive screen stories.

There was, however, hostility on the individual level. The highly rewarding Wellman-Carson duo was coming to an end. The writer-director pairing, which had traveled as a team from the turbulent times at MGM to the trumpet-blowing days at Selznick International to the prosperous pictures of Paramount that had placed them in the company of Hollywood's elite, would close its relationship after seven consecutive films.

The conflict between Wellman and Carson had been brewing for some time. It was a question of ego. Biographer Frank Thompson gave his thoughts: "Always one to espouse teamwork and to take pride in being a company man, in reality, Wellman possessed an enormous ego. Very possibly, he began to feel that Carson was claiming too much of the credit for the string of hits they had done together and felt that the only way to re-establish his reputation as the maverick director was to cut off the partnership."

The flip side says that the director was never concerned about a writer's credit on screen or off, and often took no credit for stories or writing that he had done. Carson, on the other hand, wanted more of his ideas incorporated in the choosing and writing of the scripts and more of his work celebrated. Wellman wanted everything to stay status quo.

Using the popular sport of football to draw an analogy: Wellman was the quarterback of a winning team. He was also a team player and supported by the team owner, who respected his track record as a winner. Carson was the star wide receiver with a much shorter track record who felt that the quarterback was not throwing the ball to him enough. He should be scoring more touchdowns for the team and himself. He became disgruntled, complaining and protesting to the quarterback and the owner, causing resentment and loss of team spirit. Thus, in the interests of keeping a winning record, the wide receiver was traded to another team.

The facts say: After the success of *The Light That Failed*, Carson wanted Wellman to do another Kipling adaptation, *The Man Who Would Be King* (made by John Huston in 1975). Wellman, staying true to his habit of changing genres as often as possible, refused his protégé's request. Instead, Wellman chose *F.O.B. Detroit*, from a novel by Wessel Smitter. A disappointed Carson began working with the novelist on the script. The two writers and the director clashed over ideas. Carson, who disliked the material from the start, fought with Wellman over script changes, leading to his firing.

Filmmaker and historian John Gallagher wrote, "After a productive relationship, Carson and Wellman parted ways, a decision that both men came to regret in later years." Although Wellman went on to direct twenty-seven more films, some of them classics, Carson's movie work produced only six screenplays and nine story contributions in less than outstanding films. The best of his offerings being *Western Union* (1941), a good Randolph Scott Western directed by Fritz Lang. The wide receiver had been traded and his skills depreciated while the quarterback of his former team went on to greater glory.

The novel *F.O.B. Detroit* became the movie *Reaching for the Sun*, which became . . . an enigma. When Wellman made a film based on a novel, he stayed true to that novel. When the novelist and/or screenwriter wrote the script, the director brought pressure to stick to the book. Wellman talked and wrote about this element of his filmmaking philosophy, yet *Reaching for the Sun* is a major departure from its original source.

F.O.B. Detroit, set in the automotive industry, is a story of social significance—man against machine, the factory workers against the motor magnates, employee versus employer, the underprivileged against the privileged. Oddly though, the picture turns out to be a romantic comedy devoid of social significance—a powerful story stripped down to a boy-and-girl tale with the capital-labor angle removed.

So, what happened? What was Wellman's thinking? Did his ego get in the way and deny another classic film from team Carson for his maverick march down the Hollywood highway?

This author believes that after such a long string of big, important, award-winning, major studio films, Wellman just wanted to retreat from the limelight and make a simple, uncomplicated, character-driven, studio-based picture. He threw out the portentous social and intellectual features of the book, retaining only the story material for one of the "little" pictures that dot his seventy-six-film landscape. He even sent his assistant, Joe Youngerman, to Detroit to film second unit and some principal business so that he could stay at the studio.

Youngerman filmed the climactic battle between the leading character, Russ Eliot, and the heavy, Herman. Their combat takes place in two huge factory machines—Herman in the high cabin of a gigantic traveling bridge crane, forty-five feet above the floor, Russ in the driver's seat of a massive manipulator looking like a battleship with enormous iron jaws (booms) for picking up chunks of white-hot steel.

Wellman and McCrea eye the outboard motor behind Eddie Bracken in *Reaching for the Sun.*

The conflict of man and machine ends with Herman the victor as Russ is pinned under his overturned manipulator. He loses a leg but achieves his destiny in the wilderness of a mountain lake community with his woman, son, and prized possession, an outboard motor.

Joel McCrea plays the outdoors enthusiast Russ Eliot, with Ellen Drew as Rita, his female interest. From Wellman's *Beau Geste*, Albert Dekker portrays the villain, Herman. The director had a hand in the making of a star, Eddie Bracken. The former child actor of vaudeville and Broadway was cast in only his third picture but first leading role as Benny Hogan, McCrea's comic sidekick. Preston Sturges would make Bracken a household name in *The Miracle of Morgan's Creek* and *Hail the Conquering Hero*, both released in 1944. As usual, Wellman the prankster was alive and well. Reminiscent of the now famous grapefruit scene from *Public Enemy* when Mae Clarke was not told that Cagney was going to crush the fruit in her face, Ellen Drew is unaware that there is a great hole in what appears to be a shallow stream as she wades, fully dressed but without

Wellman and McCrea team up again on *The Great Man's Lady* (1942), also starring Wellman's favorite actress, Barbara Stanwyck.

shoes, with McCrea through the cold, bubbling water. She reaches the hole and disappears from sight, then reappears coughing and sputtering. Joel picks her up in his arms and carries the still hacking Drew to the safety of the stream bank. The director was delighted and the movie received some surprise spontaneity.

Box office receipts were satisfactory while reviews swung in opposite directions. *The New York Times*, May 8, 1941: "Mr. Wellman and his facile scriptwriter have managed to smear a thick coat of goo over what was originally a harsh and decidedly unsweetened industrial story." *National Board of Review Magazine*, March 1941: "It is slow in keeping with the simple story, but full of quiet, honest humor and has some original touches to point up its development."

In spite of the fact that *Reaching for the Sun* is never seen on any Wellman best picture lists, excellent personal benefits resulted. Joel McCrea, from South Pasadena, California, the son of an executive with the L.A.

Gas & Electric Company, was already an established leading man and versatile enough to star in dramas as well as comedies. By 1942, he had worked in adventure films, musicals, mysteries, Westerns, and comedies with filmmakers such as Cecil B. DeMille, Alfred Hitchcock, George Stevens, Preston Sturges, and King Vidor.

When *Reaching for the Sun* wrapped production on November 16, 1940, Wellman and McCrea had become friends. They would work together on two more pictures and spend a lifetime of family friendship. Joel's wife, Frances Dee, had starred in Wellman's *Love Is a Racket* (1932) and the director liked her well enough to place her name on his favorite actress list. The McCreas had three sons, David, who became a rancher; Jody, an actor; and Peter, a real estate developer. Joel and Frances remained married for fifty-seven years until his death in 1990 at age eighty-four. Grandson Wyatt McCrea has been shining a light on the Joel McCrea legacy with the Joel and Frances McCrea Foundation and guest appearances at Western film festivals.

Another benefit came from the Joel McCrea character's affection for an outboard motor. This fondness soon spread to the director as well. Wellman had picked locations at Lake Arrowhead in the nearby San Bernardino Mountains. The spirit of the movie took him to the neighboring lake of Big Bear where the emphasis was on fishing and outboard motoring rather than the multi–water sports of Arrowhead.

In 1946, Wellman would buy an enchanting two-story log cabin in Fawnskin, on the north shore of Big Bear Lake. Made solely from logs and timber in 1910, the four-bedroom structure has two couch-beds in the large living room next to a separate dining room and kitchen. Most of the furniture is also crafted from logs. A wonderful smell of natural wood permeates the porches on both levels. The five-lot property boasts a small guest cabin with two beds, a second bathroom, and an attached garage. When not on the lake, Wellman's green outboard motorboat and his marvelous Martin motor were housed in that garage.

Since no roads had been built by 1910, the cabins were constructed from logs floated across the lake. Wellman heard about the property from movie star Lew Ayres, who had purchased it as a gift for his then wife, Ginger Rogers. She never set her dancing feet inside, their marriage failed, and the disconsolate matinee idol sold it. Years later, he attempted to buy it back but the director wouldn't sell.

The Wellman cabin remains a majestic piece of architecture, a partnership with nature, and an important part of the family heritage. The Martin motor has long since worn out but the garage still holds Wellman's boat, even if it's no longer seaworthy. You might say about this wondrous place that it belonged to a man in love with an outboard motor.

The Great Man's Lady would be Wellman's departing film from Paramount. It would also be a reunion film for the director and his three stars: Barbara Stanwyck, Brian Donlevy, and Joel McCrea.

Stanwyck would play Hannah Semplar, the woman behind the great man. It would be their fourth film together and first since 1932's *The Purchase Price*. The director had offered her *Reaching for the Sun* but she declined, citing exhaustion from the just completed *Meet John Doe* directed by Frank Capra. She also needed minor eye surgery, which required recuperation time.

Wellman had tried unsuccessfully to have her postpone the operation until after *Reaching for the Sun*'s conclusion. He told New York *Daily News* columnist John Chapman that he hoped *Reaching for the Sun* would be a big hit so he could go to Stanwyck and say, "See what you turned down?"

Wellman's dislike for his *Beau Geste* heavy, Brian Donlevy, did not keep him from casting him again. Neither man held a grudge. The Irish-born actor, son of a whiskey distiller, had run away from home, joining General Pershing's army against Mexico's Pancho Villa. He later became a major in the Army Signal Corps and fought in Europe. The actor's heritage, his outstanding work in *Geste,* and his war experiences all served as a bridge to the director and, although they would never be friends, there would be respect. Donlevy would fill the role of Steely Edwards, the gambler who loved the great man's lady.

It had only been three months since Wellman and McCrea had finished working together but the director wanted his pal back playing Ethan Hoyt, the great man.

Under the title *Pioneer Woman*, the story is a Western drama depicting over a century in the life of a frontier woman and the two men who love her. Based on a short story, "The Human Side" by Viña Delmar with story development by Adela Rogers St. John and Seena Gwen, the screenplay was written by *Reaching for the Sun*'s scribe, W. L. River.

Stanwyck's Hannah Semplar ages over a hundred years. Legendary makeup artist Wally Westmore and his team of Charles Gemora and Robert Ewing do a spectacular job showing Hannah at ages 16, 20, 28, 29, 30, 36, 74, and 109. She is everything a Wellman woman could be: strong, intelligent, honorable, creative, loyal, and quick-witted. She can fight, ride, cook, out-think, and out-do any man in the film. She is the compassionate and moral center of the picture.

Hannah's story begins in metropolitan Hoyt City, 1941, founded by her everlasting love, Ethan Hoyt. A giant statue of him riding a horse is unveiled in public tribute. She is 109 years of age and, at last, is persuaded by a young female biographer to tell her story. In flashback, we return to 1848 where a teenage Hannah flirts with the pioneer visionary Ethan. They fall in love and elope to his Western property where he unveils his dream of building a vast city. Hannah adapts well to the hard life of a homesteader and shares her husband's vision. The story weaves in and out of a century as the couple struggle through problems of wilderness, the Gold Rush, separations, jealousy, heartbreak, and peril.

Brian Donlevy's Steely Edwards is a gambler with a conscience and an enduring love for Hannah. For a long time, her feeling for him is platonic. One night, Ethan returns home from Virginia City and a gold-prospecting journey. After finding none of the "golden dust," he is a defeated man. He tells Hannah that the only color he found was blue in the mud and on his boots. She samples some of it and it turns out to be rich silver. She borrows money from Steely and sends Ethan back to Virginia City to buy up the mines.

Hannah is pregnant and cannot go with him. Fearing that her condition will deny him his dream, she keeps the secret. He misinterprets that her reason is an affair with Steely and leaves her forever. Hannah gives birth to twins. Again, Steely lends a helping hand buying a stagecoach ticket for Hannah and the babies to travel to Virginia City and Ethan. A flood washes the coach off a rain-battered bridge and the babies perish while Hannah survives.

Believing that Hannah also died, Steely travels to Virginia City to tell Ethan the news. Hoyt, now a wealthy man, shoots Steely and leaves Virginia City to build his empire. He eventually marries another woman and they have two children.

Steely recovers from the shooting, and discovers Hannah is alive but a changed woman after the loss of her Ethan and the death of her babies. She believes that it is best for Ethan, his family, and the building of his dream to think she is dead. Hannah and Steely live and work together in a grand casino in San Francisco. Refusing to end her one true love affair, she never marries the caring, supportive Steely. She savors the memory and the certificate of marriage to her Ethan.

Time passes. She hears that Ethan is running for senator and siding

Wellman's place in history was advertised in a popular comic strip just before *The Great Man's Lady* was released and only sixteen months after Pearl Harbor.

with deceitful politicians and railroad magnates against the people of the Hoyt City he built. Hannah returns to Ethan's side. Her support and their lasting love for each other rekindles his idealism, bringing him to the life of an honorable senator and leader of the masses—but without her.

Years later, now alone, the "great man" returns to Hannah and his Hoyt City home to die. His death coincides with Steely's in the historic San Francisco fire.

In Wellman's shooting script, his soft-leaded pencil adds a beautiful touch to their final scene together. Lying on his bed, near death, Ethan tries to raise himself for the last time. Hannah, age seventy-four, sits nearby with tears in her eyes. Ethan whispers for her to come closer. She does. Instead of a wordy death scene, Wellman writes Ethan's only line, "Just one more thing—a kiss." She leans over and kisses him tenderly. The director adds a stage note for camera, "Play his death on her face."

The film ends back at the Hoyt City statue with the 109-year-old Hannah and the biographer. Hannah dismisses the young woman without ever divulging the full story of her marriage to Ethan—keeping a sacred love trust. Now alone, the old lady turns back to the statue of Ethan on his horse, who seems to be looking down at her. She tucks her cane under her arm and reaches into a pocket drawing out a small folded paper. She unfolds the worn marriage certificate from long ago, tearing it into small bits and releasing them into the wind. She whispers to the statue, "Forever, Ethan. Now no one can change it. Forever." The bits of torn paper swirl around the base of the statue. The figure of Ethan Hoyt gleams like silver, triumphantly. FADE OUT.

Where *Reaching for the Sun* became a Wellman enigma—as he discarded nearly every original socially significant issue—*The Great Man's Lady* reverts to his standard approach. The film follows its primary sources and is filled with many societal values: American individualism, the never-give-up pioneer spirit and forging of a new frontier; poverty to riches, dreams can come true; freedom from oppression, the empowerment of the common man against the aristocratic class; all for one and one for all community support; honor, mutual respect, loyalty to your fellow man; the privilege of sacrifice and eternal love.

The Great Man's Lady did not fare well at the box office, disappointing both the director and leading lady. Even so, Stanwyck would always count the film among her favorites. Wellman didn't wait for public acceptance, he just made another film.

There is a saying, "timing is everything." When *The Great Man's Lady* entered the darkness of movie theaters, the country was also in a dark place. Only sixteen months had passed since the December 7, 1941, attack on Pearl Harbor, driving America into World War II. Even though *Lady's* star-crossed tale is upbeat at the finish, as Hannah Semplar has inspired Ethan Hoyt to greater glory, movie audiences of the day were looking for more escapism from the ravages of war and the grim aspects of a sad love story. This picture is on the director's near-forgotten list but holds up extremely well today.

NEWS FLASH: WILD BILL BECOMES BIKER BILL

Seven months passed between the completion of *The Great Man's Lady* and the start of Wellman's next film. During that period, he joined the Moraga Spit and Polish Motorcycle Club founded by directors Howard Hawks and Victor Fleming. The club grew out of World War II's gas rationing, which prevented Hollywood sailors and pilots from sailing their yachts or flying their planes.

Hawks and Fleming had been riding choppers for years but Wellman took it up on the spur of the moment. "Just for the hell of it," he said. The club grew in membership with the addition of stars Clark Gable, Robert Taylor and wife Barbara Stanwyck, Van Johnson, and Zeppo Marx; character actors Ward Bond, Keenan Wynn, and Andy Devine; as well as arguably Hollywood's greatest stunt driver, Carey Loftin, whose long career included *The Wild One* (1953), *Rebel Without a Cause* (1955), and *Bullitt* (1968); and a few other non-show-business riders.

The females in this macho-driven club were Barbara Stanwyck, who rode on the back of Taylor's bike, and Marion Marx, who did the same with Zeppo, while Devine's wife, Doagie, and Dottie Wellman were the only ladies to kick the starters of their own Harleys. Many of the club members' bikes were Harley-Davidsons, but there were also English and other foreign makes. Fleming owned a turquoise Harley, but his favorite was British, black with pinstripes, called the Ariel Square Four because of its unique engine design.

Dressed in sporting clothes of Levi's, nice shirts, sweaters, and jackets—not today's biker leathers—they looked and acted more like they were going on a picnic or to a ball game. The club would gather at one of their homes, usually Hawks's or Fleming's, sometimes Devine's or Wellman's because they had ranches and property to play on, have drinks and meals, and tinker with their bikes while waiting for the entire group to assemble. Dottie would comment, "They spent more time fussing with their bikes than riding." But, after all, it was all about fun and camaraderie.

Vroom! Off they went in a cloud of dust for a weekend or just a Sunday ride in the local hills and canyons, across the San Fernando Valley, or as far away as Malibu, Santa Barbara, Victorville, even Las Vegas. On one Vegas trip, the Wellmans and Devines sent their nightclubbing clothes ahead, then stopped along the way for a catered lunch served by formally attired Vegas waiters in the shade of a Mojave Desert billboard.

Motorbiking was another example of Bill and Dottie doing things together. Dottie joined the Spit and Polish Club later than her husband, as she was delivering their fourth child, Timothy Gouverneur—no blond or red hair here—April 29, 1941. The Wellman couple challenged the streets, roads, hills, and valleys of Los Angeles and beyond for over two years. When Dottie became pregnant with number five, they turned in their membership cards. Another reason for abandoning the Harleys was a growing number of accidents to other members. Andy Devine and Robert Taylor had minor mishaps, and Ward Bond and Keenan Wynn sustained injuries that were almost career-threatening. The Wellmans wondered if their turn was around the next corner, the next gravelly road, the next hill, the next trip. It was great fun while it lasted.

Wellman had been searching for a comedy to follow his *Nothing Sacred* success of 1937. Retooling *F.O.B. Detroit* into the comedy-drama *Reaching for the Sun* did not make the grade, but when the prolific writer-producer Nunnally Johnson pitched *Roxie Hart*, the director jumped.

Roxie was based first on a 1926 play, *Chicago*, by *Chicago Tribune* reporter Maurine Dallas Watkins about criminals and crimes she had reported on. The story next became a silent film in 1927, later a musical version as a Broadway play in 1975 choreographed by the legendary Bob Fosse. The musical play has been continually produced in the United States and other countries ever since, leading up to the 2002 milestone musical film directed by Rob Marshall, which won six Academy Awards including Best Picture.

Nunnally Johnson, who later added directing to his résumé with films like *The Man in the Gray Flannel Suit* (1956) starring Gregory Peck, wrote *Roxie*'s screenplay and produced. At this time in Wellman's career, he decided it was better for his health and happiness to forgo the producer's mantle on most of his films. "It's tough enough just to direct a picture," he said, "and the one thing I really hated was that I began to talk money. I didn't want to be in that class of people."

The title character, Roxie Hart, played by the incomparable Ginger Rogers, is a Roaring Twenties burlesque dancer who goes on trial for the murder of a suitor committed by her husband, Amos Hart (George Chandler). The conniving duo of newspaper reporter Jake Callahan (Lynne Overman) and theatrical agent E. Clay Benham (Nigel Bruce) conspire to build up the story for their own gain. They offer the publicity-wise performer a cabaret and vaudeville tour if she pretends to be the trigger puller. Believing that no jury in the city of Chicago would punish a woman defending herself, she takes the pledge and finds herself at the center of an outrageous trial.

Another reporter, Walter "Homer" Howard (George Montgomery), covers the trial, falls in love with Roxie, and tells the whole story in flashback.

Upon becoming a national celebrity, Roxie is motivated to continue the charade. Her unscrupulous lawyer, Billy Flynn (Adolphe Menjou), manipulates the courtroom antics delivering the promised acquittal. Just when Roxie's popularity reaches its zenith, the next sensational crime pulls the pack of press hounds away from her, leaving her celebrityism like yesterday's newspaper. In the end, we find that she has given up show-biz for marriage to Homer and a brood of kids.

Wellman is always striving for something different in every story. *Roxie*'s humor, when compared to *Nothing Sacred*, plays on the other side of subtlety. As such, it is remarkably hysterical and a savage satire of the press and justice system.

The director constantly adds short strokes and long splashes of comedy throughout the sprinting seventy-five minutes. Some examples are Roxie's continual gum chewing; her "billy goat" fighting method of head-butting her foe's stomach; a screeching soundtrack of a real cat fight over one of her battles with another female; her crossing her legs, pulling back her skirts to show more of her legs and knees to the gaping all-male jury. Other bits of business: during the trial, when newspaper photographers prepare to snap pictures, the judge leaving the bench to get into the shot; quirky camera angles like placing Billy Flynn in a chair and surrounding his face with huge flowers during a poignant dialogue scene; and everything to do with the character Amos Hart.

Beginning with his role in *A Star Is Born*, character actor George Chandler worked in twenty-two Wellman films. As Roxie's screwball husband, Amos, Chandler plays his biggest Wellman role. He was special to the director for a number of reasons: he was a competent performer adding slices of whimsy to every role; he was considered a good-luck charm; he was a caring friend; he carried a get-out-of-trouble card.

"He developed a second sight of my moments of uncertainty," said the director. "If he happened to be in the scene that was bothering me, he would find some way of buggering it up, forgetting his lines, sneezing, not once or twice, a seizure, or whispering while I was talking—then the roof blew off, and believe me I could blow it a mile. When I had put George and all his relatives and ancestors where they belonged, I called off work for ten minutes, stormed into my dressing-room office, slammed the door shut and sat down quietly, and always worked out my problem. It was like magic." If George was not on the picture, Wellman would make a deal with his most trusted crew member—a property man, an assistant, or a cameraman. "I gained the false reputation of always knowing what I wanted."

In the long pre-rehearsal of the interrogation scene between Amos Hart (George Chandler) and his defense attorney, Billy Flynn (Adolphe Menjou), George had an unusual way of learning his dialogue. He wrote the answers to the questions on slips of paper, hiding them in the pockets of his coat, shirt, pants, even his socks. When he couldn't remember the words, he would retrieve the notes from the proper place.

Just before shooting the scene, Wellman, who had been watching these antics, said to him, "George, I want you to play the scene exactly the way you have been rehearsing to yourself—when Menjou asks you the questions, get the slip from whatever pocket you have hidden it in and read it to him, always with that dumb expressionless face—if the question refers to one of the slips you have in your socks, lift your leg up for everyone to see, take it out, get comfortable again and read it."

The director explained the whole thing to Menjou, rehearsed the scene, shot it, and the laughs grew as the scene progressed. It was a howl. "What a magnificent director," said Wellman, "balls, just a guy who had sense enough to keep his eyes open, and saw a little magic." *Roxie Hart* received a generous share of magic at the box office and reestablished Wellman as a top comedy director.

Even though *Roxie* was a Darryl Zanuck, 20th Century-Fox presentation, it wasn't the project that brought the director-mogul friendship back from the ashes. The falling out between the two filmmakers had happened in Canada a few years before. Zanuck was a big-game hunter and invited the director on one of his safaris—it would be a onetime-only invitation.

"We were on our way to a hunting trip in true Zanuck fashion," said Wellman. "The correct guns, clothes, guides, booze, dames, and horses. Fifty of them; that is fifty of the horses." Wellman had a few drinks, Zanuck was ordering everybody around, Wild Bill got the feeling he was back in the army and said so. Soon fists began to fly. The director and producer were teeing off on each other while the other guests attempted to separate the pugilists. Most of the bodily damage was inflicted on the Good Samaritans, not the hothead director and pompous producer.

Order was temporarily restored but trouble later flared up again in the lobby of the hunter's hotel—same combatants, same helpmates trying to restore order. When the hotel manager called for the Mounties, the combat ceased and the hunting party escaped to the quiet of their rooms. Eventually, the two bullheads shook hands, the director laid off the booze, and the war of the hunters against the animals began with enough trophies of moose, caribou, mule deer, wolves, bear, Rocky Mountain sheep, and goats to make the riflemen happy—all save one, Wellman.

His pillage included a moose, a caribou, a Rocky Mountain goat, and a sheep. The moose was the last to fall. "I hit mine with four 30-30 slugs," said Wild Bill, "and that great giant of the wilderness took off and ran for two miles before he gave up and died." The hunting party followed his blood-soaked trail for the two exhausting, branch-slapping miles, and only the man-killing exertion made the prize seem worthwhile. After the dismembering of the head and cape, the trophy would eventually be worth hundreds of dollars. It would be mounted and hung in Wellman's playroom, "and gape down benignly at all the silly people, drinking and

Henry Fonda and Dana Andrews in *The Ox-Bow Incident* (1943)

hooting and babbling about nothing in particular, totally oblivious of this monarch of the wilds who once ruled his clean, carefree kingdom with no long-winded politicians, no two parties, no sex perverts, no delinquents, no Cosa Nostra, and no producers or agents or stars. Just a kingdom as uncontaminated as the snow on its towering mountaintops." Wellman never went big-game hunting again.

When the two-week bivouac ended, the soldiers saluted General Zanuck and took their plunder home. Even though Wellman and Zanuck shook hands and exchanged witticisms, they had no contact for many years. The project that finally brought them together would be a Western.

While Bill and Dottie were enjoying a weekend away from Hollywood at the Arrowhead Hot Springs Hotel, an out-of-work producer, Harold Hurley, approached them at the hotel pool. He owned the movie rights to a Western book and pitched the story to the sunbathing director. At first, Wellman tried to get rid of him but the story was so riveting that he listened intently, then read the novel over the weekend. Written by Walter Van Tilburg Clark, it was titled *The Ox-Bow Incident.*

The story was dark, it was real, it was terrifying: it dealt with mob violence and the hanging of three innocent men. The director met with Hurley, who began talking excitedly about making the movie in Technicolor starring Mae West. Somewhat shocked, Wellman answered, "You must have given me the wrong book." Hurley continued explaining that color and a star of the magnitude of Mae West would be a commercial addition to the downbeat theme. "When the posse and the tired cowboys gather in the saloon," said Hurley. "Mae will cheer them up with song and dance." The director ended the meeting with, "Sorry, that's not for me."

Wellman's fascination with the story grew and later he ran into the down-on-his-luck producer back in Hollywood. He asked Hurley if he still owned the rights and would he sell them. Wellman offered $500 more than the producer had originally paid and a deal was consummated for $6,500. He raced home and read the novel to Dottie from beginning to end.

Wellman had made many Westerns but never a story like this—so different, so unforgettable, a total departure from the standard Western. He had to make it. He took the project to all the studios that he had worked for: Paramount, MGM, UA, Selznick, and Warners—they all gave the same resounding response . . . NO!

Remember that timing is everything? Wellman picked the early 1940s to propose this kind of story when the nation was being devoured by one of its darkest hours in history: the world was at war; over 110,000 Japanese Americans were losing their citizenship rights and being placed behind guarded gates of internment camps; race riots raged in the North; dressed in their white costumes of robes, masks, and conical hats, the Ku Klux Klan was carrying out their acts of terror—including hangings—in the South and North. The Hollywood studios wanted escapist fare, not this melancholy Western with little action and no romance.

But William Wellman refused to take no for an answer. He had fought hard for *Wings, The Public Enemy,* and *A Star Is Born,* and he was not going to allow *Ox-Bow* to slip away. There was only one more place he could go, one more mogul to see . . . the big-game hunter, Darryl Francis Zanuck.

Armed with his hand-delivered novel, Wellman arrived, unannounced, at the studio head's outer office. He didn't ask, he told the secretary that he was there to see "the big man." She scurried into her boss's guarded domain and returned with an entrance pass. Inside the well-appointed space, there were no handshakes or verbal greetings. Zanuck spoke first. "Have you forgotten we aren't talking?" "No," said Wellman, "but I'd like to talk now because you are my last hope."

The director voiced the *Ox-Bow* story and the producer said he would read the book and get back to him. Within a few days, the filmmakers shook hands on a deal. "It won't make a dime," Zanuck said, "but I want my name on it."

The green light, however, came with conditions and caveats. Wellman would have to direct two sight-unseen pictures for Fox, and *Ox-Bow* would have to be low-budget. Translated that meant that the director would film whatever scripts he was handed without protest or changes. *Ox-Bow* would be shot entirely at the 20th Century-Fox studio, their soundstages, back lot, and Western town. The only location was second unit filming of the posse riding at night in the Alabama Hills of Lone Pine, California.

Regardless of the requirements, Wellman was flying high. He had been prepared to accept any deal offered for the privilege of making his passion Western and the only film he ever paid for the rights.

During preproduction, William Goetz, Zanuck's partner, Bill Koenig, production head, and the other executives tried to stop the making of what they believed to be a dreadfully depressing story, their excuse being that it was too costly. Zanuck was out of town when the stop order reached Wellman. The director cabled the mogul, "This is to remind you of our handshake; regards, Bill Wellman." Word came back to Goetz and company, "Let Wellman go ahead." Wellman said, "Zanuck was the only one with the guts to do an out-of-the-ordinary story for the prestige rather than the dough."

When the director began a new film, it was routine to check the studio's contract players list and hold some interviews. Rarely did Wellman ask for screen tests, see film from another picture, or hold readings—he went by his gut. When he met the gangly, thirty-seven-year-old pride of Grand Island, Nebraska, he stopped looking for his leading man.

Henry Fonda was already a star with pictures like *Jezebel* (1938), John Ford's *Young Mr. Lincoln* (1939) and *Drums Along the Mohawk* (1939), as well as Ford's filming of John Steinbeck's *The Grapes of Wrath* (1940). In order to do *The Grapes of Wrath*, however, Fonda had to sign a seven-year contract with 20th Century-Fox and Darryl Zanuck. This led to a string of routine, mostly forgettable assignments, and an unhappy contract actor—until Wellman arrived.

Fonda would always include *The Ox-Bow Incident* on his favorite-picture list, and stood alongside Wellman fighting to make the film when the top brass were trying to scuttle the production. The powers-that-be did not appreciate his insolence and wanted the director to hire someone else. They told Wellman that Henry Fonda would be miscast as Gil Carter. Wellman knew better. Fonda's natural qualities of simplicity, integrity, conscience had already endeared him to movie audiences who believed him the Everyman. He was far more than that—and he had his faults—but in films he was the Perfectman.

Two cowboys played by Fonda and Henry Morgan ride into the small cattleman's town of Bridger's Wells, Nevada, in 1885. A rancher named Larry Kinkaid is thought to have been murdered by rustlers while the sheriff was absent. A lynch-crazed posse is formed to find the guilty ones. Fonda and Morgan get swept up in the excitement and join the search party.

Three men, played by Dana Andrews, Anthony Quinn, and Francis Ford, are found, captured, and believed to be the killers. A mock trial takes place and despite Fonda's efforts to convince the posse to wait for the sheriff and more evidence, mob rule turns into mob violence as the three victims are hanged.

The sheriff returns with the news that Kinkaid is alive and the cattle thieves apprehended. When the sheriff hears what the posse has done, he tells them, "God better have mercy on you, you won't get any from me!"

Back in town, in Darby's saloon, Fonda reads a letter written by Andrews to his wife just before being strung up. Written by screenwriter and producer Lamar Trotti, this is a major departure from the novel. In the book, the contents of the letter are never revealed but Wellman believed it was of the utmost importance for the audience to hear those heartfelt words, to understand and feel the total tragedy, thereby bringing the full force of the story, and the moral of the movie, to the screen in just a few minutes.

The director used one of his insignia camera angles to bring even more attention to the reading. Fonda and Morgan stand together at the bar flanked by most of the posse members who have just hanged three innocent men. They all stand close together as if trying to draw strength in numbers, some drinking, no conversation, all thinking about what has transpired.

Now Fonda and Morgan share a few thoughtful lines of dialogue. Fonda turns sideways, positioning himself just behind Morgan, and takes the letter from his pocket. The camera pushes in on a two-shot of Morgan's face in profile, with the brim of his hat shielding Fonda's eyes. The frame is filled with the left side of Morgan's face while the brim of his hat completely covers Fonda's eyes, leaving his mouth and lips to quietly read the letter.

My dear Wife: Mr. Davies [one of the few posse members who tried to stop the lynching] will tell you what is happening here tonight. He's a good man and has done everything he can for me. I suppose there are some other good men here too, only they don't seem to realize what they're doing. They're the ones I feel sorry for, because it'll be over for me in a little while, but they'll have to go on remembering for the rest of their lives.

A man just naturally can't take the law into his own hands and hang people without hurting everybody in the world, because then he's not just breaking one law but all laws.

Law is a lot more than words you put in a book, or judges or lawyers or sheriffs you hire to carry it out. It's everything people have ever found out about justice and what's right and wrong. It's the very conscience of humanity. There can't be any such thing as civilization unless people have got a conscience, because if people touch God anywhere, where is it except through their conscience? And what is anybody's conscience except a little piece of the conscience of all men that ever lived?

I guess that's all I've got to say, except kiss the babies for me and God bless you. Your husband, Donald.

Fonda folds the letter, putting it back into his pocket, and walks out of the bar to the waiting horses. Morgan follows, asking where they're going. As Fonda mounts his horse he answers, "He said he wanted his wife to have this letter, didn't he? He said there wasn't anybody to look out for his kids." Morgan swings onto his horse and they ride out of town. After Zanuck saw the film, he cabled the director: "Congratulations on an excellent and efficient job of direction. You waded through it like a master and I have never seen any better quality or, as a matter of fact, quantity. Fonda was superb and I now am happy that when you cabled me in England, I made the decision to go ahead with *The Ox-Bow* and with him in the role. He has never been more effective."

On May 8, 1943, *The Ox-Bow Incident* premiered at the Rivoli Theatre in New York and became a box office failure. In Wellman's words, "It fell flat on its face. One of the important dailies, *The Hollywood Reporter*, had this to say in its criticism of the picture: 'not even a B-type Western.' Them's harsh words, and they can break your heart when everybody else seems to agree with them."

In the documentary *Wild Bill Hollywood Maverick* (1996), Henry Morgan tells the story of seeing a preview of the film where the audience reaction was very tepid. While leaving the theater, Orson Welles came up to him and said, "They don't realize what they just saw."

Although the picture did not find an audience in 1943, the Academy of Motion Picture Arts and Sciences could not dismiss excellence and bestowed a Best Picture nomination—no other nominations. The film was better received abroad and as time passed, it has grown in prestige and popularity. Today, the picture finds its way onto many of the best Western of all-time lists. The letter-reading scene has become one of the most famous in American cinema. Clint Eastwood told this author that his Best Picture Academy Award winner, *Unforgiven* (1992), was his *Ox-Bow Incident*.

Ox-Bow is Wellman at his best. Instead of having to infuse and force additional qualities into mediocre or poor material, now he had an outstanding story and an excellent screenplay. Having to work through and around low-budget studio restrictions gave him the opportunity to use his ability to improve the already fine story material.

A Wellman trademark: dogs. The opening of the film shows Fonda and Morgan riding down the street coming into town. An old hound dog crosses the dirt street—from left to right—just in front of them. Then, at the end of the picture, the same dog crosses behind the cowboys—right to left—as they leave the town. "I don't think anyone could tell me how it [*Ox-Bow*] survived," said Wellman, "except perhaps that very old, old mother hound dog that I had crossing the dusty road in the start of the picture and returning at the very end, she was the epitome of sorrow."

17

PICTURE PATCHWORK

After *The Ox-Bow Incident* and beginning with Wellman's first sight-unseen payoff to Zanuck, he would direct nine features in six years, all released by the end of 1948. Their success at the turnstiles ranged from moderate to mighty. Most were considered programmers—pictures made quickly and efficiently on a limited budget for the purpose of supplying a continuous stream of acceptable product, often as double feature material.

These nine pictures would represent many types: war films depicting the fighting men on the ground and in the air; the heroes and antiheroes of the Old West; a political thriller; pioneer aviation; a romantic comedy; and a musical murder mystery. The director would bring back stars of his previous films: Dana Andrews, Wallace Beery, Joel McCrea, Henry Morgan, Anthony Quinn, James Stewart, Barbara Stanwyck. There would be new stars: Anne Baxter, Glenn Ford, Robert Mitchum, Maureen O'Hara, Gregory Peck, Gene Tierney, Richard Widmark, Jane Wyman.

The first of Wellman's must-make pictures was *Thunder Birds: Soldiers of the Air*, released as *Thunder Birds* (1942). Although this sounds like a perfect fit for the ex-flier, the story centers on relationships during flight training with little action and no combat. And, contractually speaking, the director was not allowed to make changes or add more expensive action.

Shot before *Ox-Bow*, this was Wellman's first collaboration with screenwriter-turned-producer Lamar Trotti. Under the assumed name Melville Crossman, Darryl Zanuck wrote a flag-waving, propaganda story glorifying Arizona's Thunderbird Field and the American, British, and Chinese recruits who trained there. The director stayed on schedule

Thunder Birds (1942), Preston Foster, Gene Tierney, and John Sutton

and on budget as usual, with filming at the Fox studio and locations at the Thunderbird Field in Scottsdale.

The picture is another romantic triangle air story involving Preston Foster (Steve Britt) and John Sutton (Peter Stackhouse), both in love with the beautiful Gene Tierney (Kay Saunders). Foster, star of stage and screen in pictures like *I Am a Fugitive from a Chain Gang* (1932), *The Informer* (1935), and *Annie Oakley* (1935), plays the over-the-hill flight instructor with hero credentials. The dark, handsome Sutton, born of British parentage in Rawalpindi, India, appeared mostly in supporting roles in such movies as *Jane Eyre* (1943), *Captain from Castile* (1947), and *The Three Musketeers* (1948). His performance as Wing Commander Morley in 1941's *A Yank in the R.A.F.* vaulted him into a leading role in *Thunder Birds* portraying Foster's problem-plagued recruit.

Fox's contract star, Gene Tierney, takes top billing although Foster has the leading role. One of the great beauties of her day, she is best remembered for her performance in the title role of *Laura* (1944) and her Best Actress Academy Award–nominated achievement, *Leave Her to Heaven* (1945). In *Thunder Birds*, she is the archer of Cupid's arrow finding its mark in Foster and Sutton.

Sutton's Peter Stackhouse comes from a long line of family fliers but is afraid of heights. Foster's Steve Britt helps him overcome his fear in time to pass flight training and save his flight instructor from certain death.

In the end, the American is a hero at the flight school but loses the charmer to the Englishman.

The director works valiantly to keep the routine story flying through seventy-eight minutes. He adds a personal touch when Foster shows Sutton a photo of the Englishman's father—it is Wellman wearing a fur coat standing in front of his World War I fighter plane. Wellman's aerial photography is outstanding, but the lack of a more engaging story keeps the interest level on shaky ground.

Wellman's second and final obligatory operation for Zanuck was expected to be another programmer; however, it turned out to be . . . in Zanuck's declaration to Wellman, "our second biggest moneymaker of the year!" It was called *Buffalo Bill* (1944). For Wellman, this project began back in 1940, in his own neighborhood.

Joel McCrea and Maureen O'Hara in *Buffalo Bill* (1944)

Screenwriter-author Gene Fowler lived two blocks up the street from Wellman in a classic 1929 Spanish/Mediterranean-style home designed by the venerable Claude Knight Smithley. The director and the writer had become friends while working together on *The Call of the Wild*. One early morning, Gene phoned Bill about a story he had been investigating a long time. The neighbor was invited for breakfast of Irish coffee, mostly Irish blackened slightly by a small jigger of coffee. This early-morning libation becoming afternoon potation was not unusual for Fowler. It was out of Wellman's current norm, but there were times when he could be provoked into partaking. In this case, he partook. "It did one thing," said Wellman, "it awakened you, the second helping and you would gladly hit your mother-in-law, at least one of them."

The writer began the business of the day. "How would you like to make an epic about one of the fakiest heroes in the world?" "Which one?" answered the director. Fowler continued. "The one I have spent hours, days, nights, years researching, talking to old cronies, old Indians, old drunken cowboys, old whores, some loved him and a hell of a lot hated him. . . . The true story of William Frederick Cody nicknamed Buffalo Bill." The writer presented dozens of anecdotes, piles of notes, half and fully written pages as the two pickled pals read and chattered on and on about the project.

"Exhausted but happy, I left, talking to myself," said Wellman, "not because of the Irish coffee but of reading a whole day of Fowler, a style so unusual, happy, cruel, funny, poetic, so nobody else but Fowler; this is not only going to be fun, an education and a priceless unearthing of Gene's secret compilation on a fake."

The next day brought another gathering of the two neighbors, but this time a favorite Wellman breakfast of bacon and eggs, toast and coffee—no additives. Through many weeks, they worked on a script with no help from the Irish. A tall, unopened bottle of Irish whiskey looked down on the pair as they labored. "We needed but two more days to write fini on our three months of exhausting but wonderful days of arguments, almost fights, and a script that was so far superior to any that I had made pictures of that frankly there was no comparison—it made you cry, laugh and above all, wonder. It was a masterpiece."

While Fowler was putting the finishing touches on their script, Wellman was working with another scriptwriter on his next film. The director came home from the studio on a Friday prepared to work those final two days, Saturday and Sunday, with Fowler. Bill and Dottie had been invited out to dinner and dancing. They got home late and hit the sack. Wellman was in a deep sleep when the phone rang at seven in the morning. It was Fowler. He had already been with the Irish and sounded extremely troubled. The good neighbor raced up the street thinking that his partner had a heart attack or his wife, Agnes, had fallen down the stairs, something bad had happened. Wellman was right—but the trouble was not related to a health issue of Gene's or Agnes's but Buffalo Bill's.

The two pals sat down in front of a warm fire. For a few moments there was silence. Then Gene reached over and picked up the script that Wellman was to spend the weekend working on. He thumbed it through like a gambler riffling a pack of cards. When he looked at his friend, there was a trace of tears in his eyes. "I didn't know why they were there," said Wellman, "maybe he had a little too much and for some hidden reason felt sorry for himself—that always seems the why a drunk starts to cry, but I was dead wrong."

"Bill," said Fowler, "we can't go through with this blasphemy of the biggest hero the kids have, not necessarily our kids, but all kids, old kids and their grand kids. Christ, it's like shooting Babe Ruth or sticking a

Wellman watches Bill Jr., as Buffalo Bill, Jr., get the draw on
Thomas Mitchell in *Buffalo Bill* (1944).

knife in Jack Dempsey's heart. If it was ever made into a picture with our
names on it, we would be the worst sons of bitches of this or any other
generation. Our kids would disown us. You wouldn't want that, would
you? How about Agnes and Dottie? Jesus Christ, Bill, do I have to say
anything more?"

"Not another word, Gene. I have a hell of a suggestion, you get up
and brush off the thread-like castles the spiders have been weaving on
that inactive Irish bottle for three months, we will bottom it up together
and page by page feed our masterpiece to the very hungry fire." "You're
right, Bill—and incidentally, we are a couple of goddamned giants!" "No;
thanks to you, Gene, just good fathers."

Back to 1944 and 20th Century-Fox's Technicolor adventure story of
the Western legend: army scout, Pony Express rider, Indian fighter, bison
hunter, Medal of Honor winner, and circus performer. How sadly ironic
that Wellman's trade-off for the privilege of making the masterly *The Ox-
Bow Incident* would be this trumped-up heroic version rather than the
might-have-been classic, true story of William Frederick Cody.

Wellman thought that the only proper star to play the title role in this
romanticized account was Joel McCrea. He had starred in the large-scale
Westerns *Wells Fargo* (1937) and *Union Pacific* (1939), as well as Wellman's *The Great Man's Lady*. In the early 1930s, he began buying property,
which later became part of Thousand Oaks, California. He lived on a

2,600-acre spread with his wife, his kids, and his horses. He often listed his occupation as "rancher." This film would be McCrea's third and last with the director.

Wellman found his leading ladies in two Fox contract beauties, Maureen O'Hara and Linda Darnell. Born Maureen FitzSimons, on August 17, 1920, in Ranelagh, Ireland, Maureen found an early interest in dramatics moving from the Irish stage and films in Dublin to London where she was discovered by Oscar-winning film star and producer Charles Laughton. Under his tutelage, she changed her name to O'Hara and made her American film debut as Esmeralda opposite Laughton's Quasimodo in *The Hunchback of Notre Dame* (1939).

Under contract to RKO and 20th Century-Fox, she became known as the "Queen of Technicolor" with her flaming red hair, green eyes, and peaches-and-cream complexion. Displaying her strong-willed character with stars like Tyrone Power, Errol Flynn, Douglas Fairbanks, Jr., John Payne, Cornel Wilde, and John Wayne, she moved easily from the world of exploitation films to A-list productions with John Ford in *How Green Was My Valley* (1941), *Rio Grande* (1950), *The Quiet Man* (1952), *The Long Gray Line* (1955), and others. One of her best remembered performances was in the perennially popular, Academy Award–winning *Miracle on 34th Street* (1947), directed by George Seaton.

Linda Darnell, born Monetta Eloyse Darnell, October 16, 1923, in Dallas, Texas, made her film debut at sixteen in *Hotel for Women* (1939), becoming the youngest leading lady in Hollywood history. She remained a contract player at Fox for twelve years, appearing in a lengthy list of their pictures, her most remembered being John Ford's *My Darling Clementine* (1946). Her most coveted role was in Otto Preminger's *Forever Amber* (1947), where her character survives the famed London fire. Ironically, Linda Darnell died in a house fire, April 9, 1965, at age forty-one.

The supporting cast of Wellman's picture is filled with respected players. The top of the ladder belongs to the versatile Irishman Thomas Mitchell, portraying Ned Buntline, the newspaper journalist who painted the grand portrait of the Western hero. Mitchell is truly one of the greatest American character actors of Hollywood's Golden Age with an incredible list of classic pictures to his credit, some of which are *Lost Horizon* (1937), *The Hunchback of Notre Dame* (1939), *Mr. Smith Goes to Washington* (1939), *Only Angels Have Wings* (1939), *Gone with the Wind* (1939), *It's a Wonderful Life* (1946), *High Noon* (1952), and John Ford's *Stagecoach* (1939), for which he won a Best Supporting Oscar in 1940. Thomas Mitchell became the first performer to win the Triple Crown of acting awards: a Tony for the Broadway musical *Hazel Flagg* (1953), based on Wellman's *Nothing Sacred*, an Emmy, and his Oscar.

Production of *Buffalo Bill* began in February of 1944 with locations in Paria Canyon, Utah, the Navajo reservation near Houserock Valley, Arizona, and the Crow reservation east of Hardin, Montana. Filming concluded in April at the Fox studio.

The spectacular battle at War Bonnet Gorge covers nine minutes of screen time with hundreds of cavalry and Indian warriors. This sequence has been used as stock footage for many other Westerns. The climactic one-on-one combat between McCrea's Buffalo Bill and the Cheyenne leader, Yellow Hand, played by Anthony Quinn, was shot in typical Wellman style—much of the action hidden from the audience. The two warriors, with tomahawk and knife, plunge into a flowing river and, as the camera tracks them along the bank, their duel to the death is seen in and out of frame, behind and through trees and shoreline vegetation.

A closer angle shows the victor, Buffalo Bill Cody, rising from the surface of the water as Yellow Hand's body floats to the top. The final scenes show the carnage from the battle, the corpses of Indians and troopers scattered about the landscape. Cody picks up the dead Dawn Starlight (Linda Darnell), holding her gently in his arms. When asked if she was a friend, he replies, "They [Indians] were all friends of mine."

The exciting action sequence was not the only one-on-one duel that took place at War Bonnet Gorge. The other combat happened just before the cameras rolled. Anthony Quinn was not comfortable riding on his spirited animal and refused the director's request to lead his braves into battle. "Why not have my stunt double perform it?" exclaimed the actor. "I'd like the camera in close to see your courageous charge," said the director. Quinn still refused. Wellman asked for his war bonnet and wig so that he could do it for him. Angry words were spoken, then fists began to fly. This battle was terminated by the crew and, while the actor and director nursed minor injuries, a stuntman led the Cheyenne Indian charge against the U.S. Cavalry at War Bonnet Gorge.

Years later, in the 1960s at the Ojai Valley Inn and Country Club in Ojai, California, this author—knowing nothing of his father's rumpus with Quinn—approached the movie star wanting to shake his hand. When Quinn heard the young fan's last name, he turned quickly and walked away without so much as a hello. It was not the first encounter of this kind that William Wellman, Jr., was a party to, nor the last.

In Anthony Quinn's early film career, he portrayed mainly villains and ethnic types in supporting roles. After replacing Marlon Brando as Stanley Kowalski in Broadway's *A Streetcar Named Desire* (1951), his star began to shine. As Brando's brother and costar in Elia Kazan's *Viva Zapata!* (1952), he won the Best Supporting Actor Academy Award, becoming the first Mexican American to win an Oscar. As Paul Gauguin in *Lust for Life* (1956), he won a second Supporting Actor Oscar and went on to star in a long list of films, among them *Wild Is the Wind* (1957), *The Guns of Navarone* (1961), *Requiem for a Heavyweight* (1962), *Lawrence of Arabia* (1962), and, earning him his fourth Oscar nomination as Best Actor in his crowning performance of the title character, *Zorba the Greek* (1964). He somehow lost the Oscar to Rex Harrison in *My Fair Lady*.

Further disapproval of the director came from the lips of the lovely Maureen O'Hara. In an interview with this author in 1995 in preparation for *Wild Bill Hollywood Maverick*, she refused to participate in the Wellman documentary, citing problems of mastication and beautification. She explained, "He was always teasing me that I didn't eat much and he didn't like my wanting to look my best at all times." The translation is that Wellman preferred women and actresses that weren't afraid to eat a solid meal or appear in public casually dressed with little makeup and uncoiffed hair. In film work, he believed that the overly concerned with makeup, hair, and wardrobe were often late to the set and less prepared when they got there. Maureen O'Hara and Anthony Quinn did not make another picture with William Wellman.

To brush the final stroke on the saga of William F. Cody, we flip to the last two pages of the script and the last scene of the picture. Joel McCrea, dressed in his white buckskin best with long white hair beautifully combed, rides a handsome white stallion into the Wild West Show arena for the last time. He doffs his broad-brimmed Stetson in a sweeping gesture of gratitude to the cheering throng. He delivers an eloquent thanks and bids them a fond farewell.

The spirited crowd applauds, waving their handkerchiefs and shouting out to their retiring hero. The camera picks out a small, crippled boy who, with the help of his crutches, stands and calls out, "And God Bless you too, Buffalo Bill!" McCrea kisses his hat, motions another sweeping gesture of gratitude, sending the kiss to the boy, then turns and swiftly rides out of the scene and into the hearts of film audiences around the world.

For the rest of Wellman's life, he so disliked this overly sentimental line that he frequently used it in conversation as a joke, a compliment, or a negative comment—depending, of course, on who was at the receiving end of the remark.

Many a time, this author found himself chuckling or biting his lip to keep from guffawing when his father would finish a conversation with . . . "God Bless you, Buffalo Bill!" Depending on the way he said it, I could tell what he thought of the individual who was trying to figure out what the hell it meant.

NEWS FLASH: WILD BILL DIRECTS A MUSICAL

After an eighteen-year association, prized MGM producer Hunt Stromberg resigned from the Lion's Den wanting more creative control. He had become one of the biggest moneymaking executives in the film industry with over a hundred features to his credit, but at Metro he was under the rule of the Lion King, Louis B. Mayer.

In early 1942, he revived his independent company, Hunt Stromberg Productions, and signed a lucrative five-year distribution deal with United Artists. He launched his company with a project based on the novel *The G-String Murders* by burlesque queen Gypsy Rose Lee, thought to be ghostwritten by mystery writer Craig Rice. The screenplay was by James Gunn.

When Stromberg offered the picture to Wellman, the director was elated—of all the different kinds of films he had made, none was a musical. In this case, part musical, part whodunit, part comedy-drama.

Wellman brought back his favorite leading lady, Barbara Stanwyck, and she was as thrilled as her director to be playing the star burlesque stripper, sassy Dixie Daisy, in the renamed *Lady of Burlesque* (1943). The film gave Stanwyck another notch on her versatility belt proving that she could do almost anything.

The picture opens with a heart-fluttering dance number as a chorus of strippers are shaking their rear ends with large hearts embroidered on their panties. Stanwyck's scantily attired Dixie Daisy makes her entrance with a song and dance routine, "Take It Off the E-String, Play It on the G-String." Dixie bumps and grinds with the best of them. Later in the film, another number shows her doing the boogie woogie, high kicks, cartwheels, and some splits.

The story centers on Dixie's relationship with the show's lead comic, Biff Brannigan, well played by Michael O'Shea, and the whodunit murders of two strippers, both strangled with their G-strings. The film plays out amidst brawling backstage buffoonery, crossed love affairs, star rivalry, police intervention, the threat of murder, and many possible sus-

Pinky Lee, Michael O'Shea, and Barbara Stanwyck hoof it up in
Lady of Burlesque (1943).

pects. Dixie fends off Brannigan's constant advances while trying to solve the mystery.

The climax is a takeoff on "the butler did it" with the kindly seeming stagehand Stacchi Stacciaro, played by Frank Conroy—the major from *The Ox-Bow Incident*—apprehended in the act of attempting to kill Dixie when Brannigan arrives to save the day and win her heart. Stacchi's reason for murdering strippers? He hated vaudeville and burlesque, which had replaced the beauty and the glory of opera in this theater.

The cast is delightful, especially Pinky Lee (Mandy), a burlesque star of the past; Iris Adrian (Gee Gee), a chatterboxing brash blonde; and a host of irresistible players. George Chandler (Jake, the prop man) makes his eleventh appearance in a Wellman film and Dottie's sister, Gerry Coonan, is seen as one of the showgirls.

The ninety-one-minute film is highly entertaining, directed with style and pace, fitting neatly into the realm of dark comedy. The picture becomes a tribute to a dead art form. By 1942, burlesque was blackballed from society, from both cities and towns, by the relentless pursuit of moral crusaders. Hollywood's Production Code and the Church's Legion of Decency placed their "condemned" rating on the film until changes were made. They worked hard to subtract, from the final print, risqué dialogue, certain camera angles showing strippers too scantily clad, and sensual body movements.

Still, the dialogue remains provocative, the comic sketches ribald, and the strippers show their gams. Edith Head costumed Stanwyck with style and imagination. Some examples of the stimulating, double-entendre dialogue and sensuous sketches:

One stripper to another:

STRIPPER 1: Ever get the feeling that something was about to happen?
STRIPPER 2: It's been so long since it has that I wouldn't believe it if it did.

Man and Dixie converse:

MAN: Did I startle you?
DIXIE: Are you—kidding? I've been startled by experts.

A young man (Billy) talks to two strippers (Dixie and Gee Gee):

BILLY: (TO DIXIE) You look almost as good with your clothes on.

(She laughs.)

GEE GEE: What about me?

(He looks at her without response.)

GEE GEE: I know . . . I look almost as bad with my clothes off!

The comic (Biff) and Dixie converse:

BIFF: When we get around to that date, you'll have to wear your working clothes.
DIXIE: I'll wear a suit of armor, brass knuckles, and hobnailed boots! And where's that prop you swiped?
BIFF: The muff? I'm gonna have it stuffed and hang it over my mantelpiece.

A vaudeville routine:

The Cossack from Canarsie is seen with a bull whip, whipping the clothes off the stripper known as the Princess Nirvana (Stephanie Bachelor).

A comic skit between two men:

BIFF: How come you have all the luck with the girls?
RUSSELL: Because, m'boy, I've got something you haven't got.

(He takes from his pocket a long pickle tied to a short piece of string.)

RUSSELL: All I have to do is wave this little persuader under a woman's nose and she gives me anything I want.

(Biff tries to buy the pickle.)

Lady of Burlesque provided Hunt Stromberg's independent company and UA with a bona fide hit that grossed $1.85 million and received an Academy Award nomination for Best Musical Scoring of a Drama or Comedy Picture.

Wellman completed filming *Lady* in February of 1943. Dottie finished her production on March 13—another redheaded daughter, Celia McCarthy, named after the director's mother. The Wellman family now boasted five children: Pat, Bill Jr., Kitty, Tim, and Cissy. Life was good in their new Roland E. Coate Brentwood home. Dottie and Bill had no intention of stopping the family production at five.

Bad news hit the director three days after starting principal photography on MGM's *This Man's Navy* (1945). On March 23, 1944, Wellman lost the only agent he ever had. Myron Selznick died from chronic alcoholism at the early age of forty-five. Selznick was instrumental in orchestrating Wellman's career in and out of contracts, making him sought after by the studios, to become one of the highest-paid filmmakers in the business. Myron's client list included Constance Bennett, George Cukor, W. C. Fields, Paulette Goddard, Katharine Hepburn, Alfred Hitchcock, Vivien Leigh, Carole Lombard, Rouben Mamoulian, Laurence Olivier, and, for nineteen years, William A. Wellman.

This Man's Navy presented the director with another closure. It brought him back to his early Paramount days after *Wings*, to his time at Warners in the 1930s, to the triumphant tenure at Selznick International, to a pet project that had never received a green light. Back then it had been titled: *Dirigible, The Balloon Story, Blimp,* and *Jump.*

Celia visits with George Chandler on the set of *This Man's Navy* (1945).

This Man's Navy was a standard, predictable war film for the era—an MGM programmer. The picture Wellman had envisioned, written with John Monk Saunders, was unique, poetic, mythical, action-based, created from the experiences of both World War I pilots. It was Wellman's remembrances of the men he had stood beside and flown with in the war-torn skies over Europe, most of whom had been killed.

The two war projects had two things in common, pilots and the lighter-than-air blimp service. The director took solace in this fact and throughout the production felt a kind of satisfaction, even a relief . . . a closure.

Wallace Beery, now an international star at MGM, provided additional comfort and enjoyment to the director. Friends since Paramount's *Beggars of Life* (1928) and *Chinatown Nights* (1929), they worked well throughout filming.

Beery plays Chief Ned Trumpet, a navy blimp pilot referred to as "Old Gas Bag" because of his long-winded war tales. Verbal sparring mate Chief Jimmy Shannon (James Gleason) listens but has trouble believing—including the story of Trumpet's heroic son. Destiny saves Trumpet's made-up story in the form of Jess, a crippled young man (Tom Drake) and son of the chief's romantic desire. The blustery blimp pilot "adopts" the young man, persuades a navy doctor to successfully operate on his leg, helps him into the service, and eventually Jess becomes the hero of Trumpet's story. Before marrying his "son's" mother, Trumpet becomes a war hero in a dramatic, action-filled rescue sequence of Jess in a downed plane in the Indian jungle.

Wellman adds his voice to the narration and some comic interludes between exciting missions to give the familiar story comedic value, dramatic grit, and visual artistry. The director writes a slight change in the ending scene—adding the appearance of Trumpet's small white dog running out from the huge blimp hangar waiting for his master to arrive.

Few blimp stories were tried during the war and *This Man's Navy* pays homage to these unsung heroes of U.S. Navy and Marine Corps lighter-than-air aviation.

In August of 1944, the director had finished *This Man's Navy* and was looking for a change of pace in his next production. He was at home when the doorbell rang. It was producer Lester Cowan, whose credits included W. C. Fields's *You Can't Cheat an Honest Man* (1939) and *My Little Chickadee* (1940); *Commandos Strike at Dawn* (1942); and *Tomorrow the World* (1944). Wellman had never heard of him but when he mentioned Ernie Pyle's name and his storied books on the American combat soldier, *Here Is Your War* and *Brave Men*, he was allowed entrance.

The producer was a nonstop talker, filling the air with compliments about the director's work and how he and Pyle had decided that Wellman was the man to direct their picture. When Cowan finally ran out of breath, Wellman quickly interrupted. "I politely declined the great honor that they would bestow on me. It was like water off a duck's back. . . . He wouldn't take no and kept arguing until finally I shut him up and told him the truth. I was not interested in working my ass off for the infantry." The ex-pilot went on to tell about his war experiences, about being confined to close-to-the-ground tactics, shooting up airdromes, advancing infantry, front-line trenches, and, in the process, receiving hundreds of enemy bullets with many finding their mark in his aircraft. To say nothing of being shot from the skies by an infantry-manned antiaircraft gun. Wellman went on with "We fliers were not too popular. We led such an easy, clean life—my ass. In short, you know where you can stick the infantry, and in slow motion." The director continued. "There was such a fury behind this that I frightened him into getting the hell out of my house."

"That Cowan was a persistent bastard," said Wellman, and he had good reason for saying so. The producer came back on two more occasions; once with a letter from Pyle, and then with a load of presents for the director's kids. Wellman let him have it with a barrage of well-chosen four-letter words, to get out, stay away—or go to the hospital in an ambulance.

Next it was Pyle's turn to go on the attack. He called Wellman long-distance from his home in Albuquerque. The director respected the man and listened to his story of the thousands of young Americans fighting and dying in defense of our great country. "He damn near had me crying on the phone," said Wellman. Two days later, the ex-aviator flew to Albuquerque and shook hands with the doughboy storyteller. "He wasn't very big, maybe 125 pounds," recalled Wellman. "Not the kind of guy you would imagine fooling around the front lines, living the hard, brutal reality of personal participation in a war."

For two days, the men bonded. At their first evening dinner, Wellman witnessed an emotional gathering outside the restaurant. Two GIs had recognized Pyle and when he and Wellman came out, the group had grown to ten or eleven, some carrying books. There was no squealing of autograph hunters, no paparazzi, no shouting or running to be first in line, the group just stood together watching and waiting in the hope that their hero would recognize them. He did and went to them. Wellman felt uncomfortable trailing after Pyle, so he stayed a short distance away.

"I witnessed a pantomimic ritual that I will never forget. Ernie shook hands with them all. You could tell that they asked him to autograph the books. . . . He asked each of the boys their names, made a few more inquiries, held a brief little talk with each one, and then wrote something in each book. It was not the usual 'Best Regards—Ernie Pyle' stuff; he took time and wrote each a little note. When he had finished, he said good-bye to them with a funny half-wave, half-salutelike toss of his hand, joined me, and we went for the car." As they drove away, Wellman looked back and saw them gathered together looking over each inscription.

That evening, in Wellman's bedroom, he found a copy of *Brave Men* and read the prelude:

> In solemn salute to those thousands of our comrades—great, brave men that they were—for whom there will be no homecoming, ever.

Wellman read much of the book that night. In the morning, he and Pyle talked movie story. Finally, Ernie asked the director if he would make the picture. "I had always felt," said Wellman, "that to make a really fine picture, one must know all about the people. Fliers I know, I was one of them, from the beginning, right through to the end, with all the joys and sorrows and crazy living that went with it, but I didn't know one single foot soldier intimately. I was not in love with the infantry, and I didn't agree at all with their attitude toward a flier. I think they call them fly boys."

Without giving Pyle a yes-or-no answer, Wellman said that he was having trouble believing he was the right man for the job. With that, Ernie's living room fell silent. The outside noise of a single car, a jalopy, sounded loud as it lumbered by the front window. Before long, the once proud motorcar came back and stopped in front of the house, idled for a few moments, then drove off. It came back again and Ernie went outside to check it out. When he returned, there was a sadness on his face.

He looked at Wellman and said, "Do you know what that was? An old man and his wife. They had driven through three states just to thank me for a lousy little paragraph I had written about the death of their son. I asked them to come in, but they refused. They said they just wanted to thank me and drove away."

Wellman said to himself, "I knew I was going to make this picture."

Based on the writings of the Pulitzer Prize–winning, best-loved combat correspondent, with a screenplay by Leopold Atlas, Guy Endore, Philip Stevenson, and an uncredited William Wellman, *The Story of G.I. Joe* (1945) was no programmer. The film would be a brutally realistic portrait of war, a tribute to the battlefield GI, and a true classic. It would also be Wellman's seventh war film but first depicting the fighting men on the ground.

The picture opens on a dusty, windblown desert road in North Africa. The soldiers of Company C, 18th Infantry Regiment are loading into army trucks on the move to their next battle. This unit also represents the 34th and 36th Infantry Divisions—the three divisions that the forty-two-year-old Ernie Pyle accompanied into combat in Tunisia and Italy. We meet Ernest Taylor Pyle for the first time as he prepares to board one of the trucks. This troop carrier holds the major characters of the picture. A soldier cradles a small, white fluffy dog named Ayrab. The pup lets out a yip and the commanding officer, Lieutenant (later Captain) Bill Walker, standing behind the open-back truck, hears it and orders the dog out. Ayrab is passed lovingly from one GI to another and into the arms of the waiting reporter. It is obvious the men care for the mongrel dog for he is the company mascot.

Lieutenant Walker notices all this. He meets Pyle, still holding Ayrab, and says, "Correspondent, huh? Want to get up to the front don't you?" Then to the men: Make room for this guy." Pyle starts to set the dog on the ground but Walker orders him, "Get in, get in! Make it snappy!" As

The combat veterans and actors of *The Story of G.I. Joe:* Wellman, center (standing); Burgess Meredith, three to his left (hands clasped); Robert Mitchum, front row with beard; Wally Cassell (also beard and cigar), four to his left in second row

Pyle jumps in, he hands Ayrab to the closest soldiers and they pass him back to his master. The convoy moves out.

We come to know these fighting men from Company C—culled from GIs that Pyle knew well, even the company mascot. Their human-interest stories connect them to Pyle's readers back in the States. He is amazed at their will to survive after the loneliness, drudgery, distress, and horror of combat. He marvels at the friendships that grow out of their misery and sacrifice inherent in their dilemma and their heroic perseverance of it.

We follow Pyle, Walker, and Company C through the strife in the Tunisian desert, the battles of San Pietro and Monte Cassino. The scene at enemy-occupied fortress known as the Monastery at Cassino is the largest single episode of the picture. The monastery is historic, a national monument, and the American troops are not allowed to blow it up. Unable to advance, they must live in dug-out caves, enduring constant rain, mud, and ferocious artillery barrages. Their routine becomes one patrol after another. Finally, the ban is lifted, the air force arrives, and the troops take the fortress.

In the end, some of the major characters are killed while others survive, including the dog. The most tragic death is that of Captain Walker, who is brought down a hill, slumped over the back of a mule. We discover who the dead soldier is at the same time as the surviving members of Company C. One of them is Dondaro, a major character, and it was he who led the mule with its dead burden down the trail. He unlashes Walker's body, carefully laying it on the ground. Pyle and some of the men come over to look at their dead comrade. A few lines are spoken: "God damn it!" "God damn it to hell, anyways!" "I'm sorry, old man." "I sure am sorry, sir."

From Wellman's script:

> Dondaro takes Walker's dead hand in his and stares intently into his Captain's dead face. He says nothing. Pyle turns away to hide his emotion. Dondaro releases Walker's hand, then begins straightening his shirt collar. Pyle, fighting to control his emotion, walks away from the scene, toward the sunlight, leaving Dondaro and Walker in the shadowed background . . . FADE OUT.

The casting of the film is superb. Wellman did not want any stars or well-known actors. For the pivotal role of Ernie Pyle, he refused the producer's and studio's suggestions of top veteran character performers like James Gleason, who had done an excellent job in Wellman's *This Man's Navy*, and three-time Academy Award winner Walter Brennan. He chose the lesser known Burgess Meredith, who was a captain in the army and had to be released from service for the film. Meredith became best known for portraying Rocky Balboa's trainer in the *Rocky* films and the Penguin in the *Batman* television series.

The studio, United Artists, wanted a star to play Lieutenant/Captain Bill Walker for greater distribution success. They proposed several possibilities, including a Wellman favorite and friend, Gary Cooper. The director said no stars and saw an actor walking down the street near the studio. Wellman tested him and signed a great star of the future . . . Robert Mitchum.

Mitchum grew up the hard way. His railworker father was killed in a train accident when he was two. Raised on the move in Connecticut, New York, and Delaware by his mother and stepfather, a British army officer, he learned a distaste for authority. As a teenager, he took to the road, ending up on a Georgia chain gang, from which he escaped, and toiled in a variety of odd jobs. When he moved to California, he found employment with Lockheed Aircraft and began to work in small parts in films. After two years of supporting roles in mostly B Westerns and low-budget war films, he landed in Wellman's studio neighborhood.

In keeping with his desire for realism, there were no Hollywood extras. Wellman hired 150 combat veterans. They were training in California for deployment to the Pacific. These were not just used as extras, as the director picked some to be actors with dialogue. The few actors hired had to live and train with the GIs or they would not be signed.

Before the cameras rolled, Wellman gathered his troops together to dispel the rumor that he hated the infantry. He dispelled it . . . with the help of Pyle's earlier communication to the GIs that the director had received an awakening. "Not just a picture," said Wellman, "but something that you, Ernie, and I will be proud of. . . . I want to make this the goddamnedest most honest picture that has ever been made about the doughfoot."

The 150 American soldiers received screen credit: as themselves, the Combat Veterans of the Campaigns in Africa, Sicily, and Italy.

The Story of G.I. Joe: Jack Reilly and Dottie (center), playing the role of a nurse and Reilly's wife, takes lessons from Robert Mitchum on how to use a machine gun. Freddie Steele is behind Mitchum.

The signed actors did exemplary work. To pick a few: Wally Cassell, as Dondaro, could fight but couldn't stop thinking about women and conniving to be with them; Freddie Steele, an ex-prizefighter, as Sergeant Warnicki, was always searching for a Victrola to hear his son's recorded voice—losing his sanity in the process; Bill Murphy, Private Mew, who had no family back home in Brownsville, Texas, but found a family with his buddies in Company C; Jack Reilly, as Private Robert "Wingless" Murphy, was too tall for the Air Corps but just right for an army nurse played by Dottie Wellman. She had to be talked into playing the role by the director. Their "combat" wedding scene shows Murphy so fatigued that he falls asleep in his tent on his wedding night. The other soldiers watch, listen, and wish.

The grim and penetrating drama is not without the director's humorous snippets. Dondaro's remarks about his fondness for women are punctuated by the clicking of his tongue to teeth. In a scene with Pyle and several other GIs, Dondaro is asking about movie stars and their endowments, but shell blasts cover the significant words.

DONDARO: Hey Ernie, you been to Hollywood . . . ever know

(Blast drowns out words "Lana Turner.")

ERNIE: Well . . . I've met her . . .
DONDARO: Is it true she's got those great big

(Blast covers words.)

ERNIE: Well . . . I guess so . . .
DONDARO: Tell me something. Are they really on the

(Shell blasts over.)

DONDARO: Are they

(Two more blasts.)

ERNIE: Well . . . I forgot to ask. Probably.
DONDARO: Klk! Klk! (*his trademark clicking of teeth*).

The body of "Wingless" Murphy is too long to fit normal places. There are shots of this challenge, including his boots sticking out from the bottom of tents. The dog supplies his own comedic morsels as well.

James Agee, eminent journalist, critic, novelist, and screenwriter, wrote about the film: "It is an act of heroism, and I cannot suggest my regard for it without using words as veneration and love . . . it seems to me a tragic and eternal work of art."

Frank Thompson wrote, "*The Story of G.I. Joe* is Wellman's masterpiece; it is everything that has been attributed to *Wings* or *Public Enemy* or *The Ox-Bow Incident* in terms of quality, meaning, and beauty."

The film was nominated for four Academy Awards: Best Screenplay, Best Score, Best Original Song, and Best Supporting Actor—Robert Mitchum, his only career nomination. Sins of omission: no nomination for the film's director, and yet, the picture was, and remains, possibly the greatest fictional tribute to America's fighting men.

In 2009, it was named to the National Film Registry by the Library of Congress for being "culturally, historically or aesthetically" significant and will be preserved. "It's the one picture of mine that I refuse to look at," said Wellman. "All those kids [GIs] that were in it were great, and they all went to the South Pacific and none of them came home."

The film premiered June 18, 1945, two months to the day after Ernie Pyle was killed by a sniper's bullet on the tiny island of Ie Shima, off the coast of Okinawa in the Pacific. He was forty-four years old. He never saw his picture. His final words in *G.I. Joe* are heard in the narration at the conclusion. "For those beneath the wooden crosses, there is nothing we can do, except perhaps to pause and murmur, 'Thanks pal, thanks.'"

As was Wellman's habit in the 1940s, he took time off between pictures to be home with Dottie and the growing family. He often took this author and other members of the family to the studio. Soon after completion of his next production, Dottie announced her pregnancy with number six.

Wellman was approached by representatives of San Diego's Junior Chamber of Commerce to make a film commemorating pioneer aviator John J. Montgomery. His historic flight took place at Otay Mesa, seventeen miles from San Diego. The director sold the project to Columbia Pictures and the Chamber of Commerce received $25,000 to erect a monument at the site. Montgomery was a real-life inventor and flier who made America's first manned and controlled heavier-than-air flight in 1883. This man-powered glider event happened two decades before the Wright brothers accomplished their more conspicuous mark by fitting their plane with a gas-powered engine and propeller.

After the intense and tormenting drama of *G.I. Joe*, Wellman was happy to get back into the lighter air of *Gallant Journey* (1946), under the working title *The Great Highway*. The director felt so strongly about his eighth aviation picture and his control over it that he returned to the

Janet Blair and Glenn Ford in *Gallant Journey* (1946)

ranks of producer with screen credit: "Produced and Directed by William A. Wellman." He also coauthored the screenplay with Byron Morgan, veteran writer of aviation films.

After the death of Myron Selznick, Wellman took his neighbor and friend's advice and signed with Frank Capra's agency, Phil Berg–Bert Allenberg Inc. Bob Coryell was assigned the director and they became good friends. In 1949, Berg-Allenberg merged with the William Morris Agency, becoming the largest and most powerful in the industry. The first deal they made for Wellman included a 20 percent participation in the net profits of *The Story of G.I. Joe*. Wellman had never received a piece of the action, as the studios were committed against giving a director profit participation. On *Gallant Journey*, Wellman was not offered a percentage since he was receiving extra salary as writer, producer, and director. Coryell was still negotiating a share of profits when Wellman ended it with the statement to his agent, "They're paying me too goddamned much money as it is. Just let me get to work!"

Production began March 6, and filming completed in June of 1946. In the film, we follow Montgomery's dream from childhood to build and fly what he calls an "aeroplane." Against the odds he pursues an education, struggles as an inventor, searches for funding, defends and wins a lawsuit, survives an earthquake, suffers from vertigo, and always with resistance from family, neighbors, and some friends who believe he is just plain crazy. One of the people who support him and his vision is Regina

Haymaker. Director William A. Wellman throws a fake punch at Bobby Cooper as he shows the youngster exactly how he wants him to react for the next scene in Columbia's air epic, *Gallant Journey*, starring Glenn Ford with Janet Blair.

"Ginny" Cleary, his devoted love interest. Eventually, John marries Ginny and makes his historic glider flight but tragically perishes as it crashes.

In the leading role, Wellman cast Columbia contract player Glenn Ford, fresh from costarring with Rita Hayworth in *Gilda*. Born Gwyllyn Samuel Newton Ford in Quebec City, Canada, in 1916, he was the son of a railroad executive. The family moved to Santa Monica when he was eight. His thespian days began with high school plays and as a member of West Coast, a traveling theater company. His film debut came at Fox in *Heaven with a Barbed Wire Fence* (1939). A screen test brought him a contract at Columbia, which continued after time in the Marine Corps during the war. Some of his outstanding credits are: *The Big Heat* (1953), *Blackboard Jungle* (1955), *The Violent Men* (1955), *Ransom* (1956), *The Teahouse of the August Moon* (1956), *3:10 to Yuma* (1957), *Cowboy* (1958), and *The Courtship of Eddie's Father* (1963).

For the role of Montgomery's loyal love interest, Wellman's first choice, as usual, was Barbara Stanwyck, who, unfortunately, was already committed to another film. So was his second choice, Columbia contractee Evelyn Keyes, who had played the bit part of a nurse in the director's

Men with Wings. Wellman cast another contract player, the vivacious "strawberry blonde," Janet Blair. From Altoona, Pennsylvania, Martha Jane Lafferty took her acting surname from Blair County, Pennsylvania. Placed under contract in 1942, she appeared in a string of popular pictures, although she is most remembered for playing Rosalind Russell's sister in *My Sister Eileen* (1942) and Rita Hayworth's best friend in *Tonight and Every Night* (1945). In the late 1940s, she was dropped by Columbia and didn't return to film, television, or stage until the late 1950s when she took the lead role in a theatrical production of *South Pacific*, making 1,200 performances without missing a single one.

Some of the first-rate supporting cast members are Charles Ruggles, the storyteller in the park who turns out to be John J. Montgomery's brother; Henry Travers and Arthur Shields, the cooperative Jesuit priests; and Jimmy Lloyd, from *G.I. Joe*, as the flier who befriends Montgomery but dies in an early glider crash. Paul Mantz takes his fourth turn as Wellman's chief stunt pilot, and a host of the director's favorites climb on board: bit player Bob Perry; old friend Dan Dix; stuntmen Don House and Harvey Perry; and Dottie's sister Gerry Coonan, back after *Lady of Burlesque.*

The result of all Wellman's endeavors was disappointment at the box office and with the critics. *The Hollywood Reporter*, September 5, 1946: "Wellman's brainchild labors under too heavy a script handicap." *Commonweal*, October 18, 1946: "Wellman, who has made many good movies, must have gotten too involved in his subject." *New York Times* critic Bosley Crowther: "the work of a filmmaker quite as cuckoo as Montgomery was thought to be."

It is clear that Wellman admires and feels a communication with this innovator of flight. As a young teenager, Wellman was drawn to an airfield and watched the pilots and their planes in action, while he dreamed his dreams of flight. The picture certainly shows attention to detail. The audience is allowed to feel Montgomery's disappointments as well as his thrills and successes. They can see the beauty of his world when alone in Wellman's sky. But the film lacks the director's usual spirit and tempo. Even the action is minimal. The story soon becomes static. Never once do we believe Montgomery isn't going to achieve his goals. The conflict between characters and circumstance is mild compared with the grit and power of *Ox-Bow* and *G.I. Joe*. When a crisis presents itself, it is tempered by the help and support of Montgomery's devoted lover (Janet Blair), family members, and friends. He is never left on his own for long. There are no bad guys in this picture.

Montgomery does not appear to be an outcast from society or as crazy as some say he is. There is a line of dialogue, "They say he is a little touched, now complete." He is honest, hardworking, dedicated, friendly, and smarter than his detractors. He explains to Regina about a bird's flight:

JOHN: Uh-huh, exactly the same parabolic curve. Ever see a bird with a flat wing?

REGINA: No.

JOHN: That's why nobody's been able to fly . . . didn't figure out why their wings were curved.

REGINA: *(sewing cloth for glider wings)*
This part of the wing seems to bend a lot.

JOHN: Made it that way on purpose . . . so I can keep my equilibrium in the air . . . same way a bird does by twisting the outer ends of its wings.

After the death of his flying partner (Jimmy Lloyd) at an air show carnival, Montgomery concludes, "Science and exhibition, they don't mix."

As writer, producer, director, and lover of flight, maybe Wellman got too close, too immersed in his own childhood dreams to picture the hardships and disappointments of the inventor's plight. Aided by a lyrical, enchanting music score by Martin Skiles, the film becomes a feel-good, ethereal, romantic adventure biopic—lying on a sentimental bed but failing to rise higher than the ceiling, much less the clouds of John J. Montgomery's "great highway."

Wellman's next three pictures certainly provided variations in genre: a Capraesque social satire, a Cold War political thriller, and an offbeat Western. Although well made and interesting, none challenged the heights of *The OxBow Incident* or *The Story of G.I. Joe.*

Magic Town (1947) toplined major stars James Stewart, *Mr. Deeds Goes to Town* (1936), *Mr. Smith Goes to Washington* (1939), *It's a Wonderful Life* (1946); and Jane Wyman, *The Lost Weekend* (1945), *The Yearling* (1946). It was written and produced by Robert Riskin, Frank Capra's screenwriter from 1931 to 1941. Other Capra crew members were cameraman Joseph Biroc, assistant director Arthur Black, and editor William Hornbeck. Under the leadership of Riskin, the RKO Radio Production was behind schedule due to a trade union strike and the producer-writer's inability to move forward until Wellman was talked into taking over—even Capra put in a good word to his two pals.

The story traces the new science of public opinion polling. Lawrence "Rip" Smith (James Stewart) and partners Ike Sloan (Ned Sparks) and Mr. Twiddle (Donald Meek) believe that the middle-American town of Grandview is a "mathematical miracle," the perfect community where the sentiments of its citizens reflect the opinions of all Americans. Rip, Ike, and Twiddle journey there to gain the knowledge that will keep their jobs and save pollsters millions of dollars. There will be no more disasters like the 1936 presidential election predicting Governor Alf Landon of Kansas the victor over incumbent President Franklin Roosevelt—one of the biggest landslides in history.

The biggest obstacle to the success of their scheme is the crusading town newspaper editor, Mary Peterman (Jane Wyman). She wants to modernize her town and build a civic center that would reflect the simple, honest values of the citizenry being promoted by the pollsters. Rip and pals, who keep their occupation secret, manipulate the populace into accepting them as insurance salesmen and opposing Mary's plan. Along the way, romance blooms between Rip and Mary, but she discovers and exposes the conspiracy, which brings national notoriety, newshounds, and people wanting to live in Grandview. The citizens exchange their homespun values for inflated images, even selling their opinions. They answer polling questions with outlandish responses—for the time—like 79 percent of them would vote for a woman president. Their reputations crash and Grandview is disgraced. A disheartened Rip leaves the town but soon returns to be with Mary and help the township band together, restore their values, and build a better high school as well as the civic center.

Stewart, hemming and hawing at his likable best, and Wyman, exhibiting the Wellman woman style of smart, strong, attractive, and independent, give solid performances. There is excellent support from reliable character actors Kent Smith, Wallace Ford, E. J. Ballantine, Ann Shoemaker, Harry Holman, George Irving, and Regis Toomey. Extra kudos to Donald Meek and Ned Sparks, in their final film roles after long and successful careers. Wellman's direction is taut and stylish with his additions of slapstick and other humorous touches delivering more enjoyment. George Chandler brings cheer as the bus driver who meets Stewart at the train station, and a scruffy-looking dog comes out of nowhere to jump up the back of Stewart when he's attempting to climb a tree with a small boy on his shoulders.

The film is charming and whimsical with strong underlying morals and principles like honesty, being true to oneself, having pride and respect for your fellow man and community. The picture follows the ingredients of a Capra film with one glaring exception—no villains, only low hurdles to jump over.

Box office returns were moderate, reviews a mixed bag. *New York Herald Tribune*, October 8, 1947, summed it up: "It is a patchwork of all the things Riskin and Capra did together: the same people, the same situations, the same tricks. I think it all adds up to one thing: Mr. Deeds has reached the end of the line." What did Wellman think of this film? "It stinks. Frank should have made it."

In March of 1946, a powerful speech came over the radio that shocked the United States and much of the world. From Fulton, Missouri, Prime Minister Winston Churchill gave his message warning the world that the "Iron Curtain" was dropping across Europe. Only the United States had the resources to stop the advance of communism. Thereafter, Hollywood's first Cold War movie would be born—*The Iron Curtain* (1948), based on the memoirs of Igor Gouzenko with a screenplay by Milton Krims, who had authored *Confessions of a Nazi Spy* (1939). Back at Fox,

Wellman accepted the directorship of this compelling but inflammatory project.

It is the story of Igor Gouzenko, a devoted communist when he arrives in Ottawa, Canada, as a cipher clerk in the Russian embassy during World War II. He transmits Canada's top-secret nuclear documents to the USSR, stolen by a ring of communist spies in the highest levels of the Canadian government. As time passes, Gouzenko's wife, Anna, arrives from Russia and a son is born. Igor begins to realize the full impact of living under his government's fear and the knowledge that the Canadians are not enemies. He questions his own communist indoctrination and dreams of a better, safer life for Anna and their young son. In the climax, he puts it all on the line by exposing to the world documents taken from the Soviet embassy proving that the Russians are stealing atomic secrets and naming spies in high government positions. His official defection was September 5, 1945.

In the leading roles, Wellman cast his *Ox-Bow* star Dana Andrews and *ThunderBirds* star Gene Tierney, who had appeared together in *Belle Starr* (1941) and the classic *Laura* (1944).

Shooting began on November 28, 1947, on locations in Ottawa. Leftist demonstrations started immediately and continued throughout filming, even into the film's wide release beginning May of 1948. During the eighty-seven-minute film's first run at New York's Roxy Theatre, there was constant picketing, physical altercations, bomb threats, police intervention, and jailings as the film proved incendiary. Newspapers across the globe wrote about this political spy thriller. Many condemned it, some countries banned it, lawsuits were filed, but people streamed to the box office and 20th Century-Fox reaped the rewards. *Variety* had said, "a cinch b.o. leader." And for a time, the picture was either the highest- or second-highest-grossing film in the United States.

Wellman's documentary-style direction and the underplayed, strong portrayals from Dana Andrews and Gene Tierney were praised. Commendations went to June Havoc, Berry Kroeger, Edna Best, Stefan Schnabel, Nicholas Joy, and an exceptional Eduard Franz as Major Kulin. *Variety*, December 31, 1947: "Picture is a corking spy melodrama."

The Gouzenko affair and the Canadian spy scandal that followed were considered the starting points in what became known as the Cold War. These incidents foreshadowed the paranoia about espionage activities in North America. Gouzenko and his wife, Svetlana, had eight children, but were forced to live out their lives undercover. They resided somewhere in Ontario under the protection of the Canadian Mounted Police. There was constant fear of reprisals from the Russian KGB. During the ensuing McCarthy era, this film became "politically incorrect" and is rarely screened even today.

How did Wellman fare during all this paranoid political fever? He just made another picture, a Western titled *Yellow Sky* (1948). It was a 20th Century-Fox production, written and produced by *Ox-Bow*'s Lamar Trotti, based on the novel *Stretch Dawson* by W. R. Burnett. For the female lead, the studio wanted screen star Paulette Goddard, a Best Supporting Oscar nominee for *So Proudly We Hail* (1943). Wellman instead wanted and got Anne Baxter. This would be her twenty-third film. Born in Indiana, she was the daughter of a salesman and his wife, who was the daughter of world-renowned architect Frank Lloyd Wright. She moved to New York, and the stage was her first love when Hollywood called. Unable to crack Tinseltown, she returned to the New York stage. Her next try proved successful and, at only seventeen years of age, was signed to a seven-year contract at Fox. Her roles matured as she did. Her best early credit was as a supporting player in Orson Welles's *The Magnificent Ambersons* (1942). The next year, she received top billing in the successful *The North Star*, three years later a Best Supporting Oscar for *The Razor's Edge*, and in 1950, a Best Actress Oscar for *All About Eve*.

There were no dissenting votes for the starring role of Stretch Dawson . . . Gregory Peck. Born in La Jolla, California, son of a druggist, and whose parents divorced when he was five, Eldred Gregory Peck was raised by his grandmother. His premed studies at Berkeley were interrupted by the acting fever and he enrolled in New York's Neighborhood Playhouse after graduation. His Broadway debut was *The Morning Star* (1942). By 1943, he was in Hollywood with his film debut, RKO's *Days of Glory* (1944). His next picture was at Fox, *Keys to the Kingdom* (1945), which brought him an Academy Award nomination. *Spellbound* (1945), *The Yearling* (1946), *Duel in the Sun* (1946), and *Gentleman's Agreement* (1947) furthered his screen aura of nobility on the way to *Yellow Sky*.

Richard Widmark filled out the star roster. From Princeton, Illinois, he began in radio, then stage, before his big break in 1947 as Tommy Udo, a sadistic killer who pushes a wheelchair-bound old woman down a flight of stairs in *Kiss of Death*. His performance brought him an Academy Award nomination and a seven-year contract at Fox. He switched from playing heavies to leading-man status in a long and stellar career.

In 1867, a band of outlaws rob a bank and are chased by a posse of U.S. Cavalry into the blazing-hot desert. Believing the outlaws will perish in the waterless sands and extreme heat, the posse leaves but the gang

Anne Baxter and Gregory Peck in *Yellow Sky* (1948)

survives, barely. They collapse in a ghost town called Yellow Sky. The only inhabitants are an aging grandfather (James Barton) and his feisty grand-daughter, Mike (Anne Baxter), who supply water to the half-dead men, expecting them to leave—they don't. When they regain their strength, they discover that the old man and his granddaughter are mining gold and they want their share. A band of Indians appears while the outlaws are digging for gold. Grandpa is their friend and convinces them to leave. The gang leader, Stretch (Gregory Peck), is thankful and makes a bargain to share the treasure, not take it all. The other gang members disapprove and a gunfight leaves Bull Run (Robert Arthur) dead.

Stretch has fallen for granddaughter Mike, which sets off a showdown between the gang members. Stretch wants to keep the bargain but Dude (Richard Widmark) and Lengthy (John Russell) want all the gold. A deadly shootout in the ghost town's broken-down saloon follows. The director films the sequence in a dark, shadowy room and we do not see all the action, just hear the gunshots and see powder flashes. Stretch survives and is joined by Walrus (Charles Kemper) and Half Pint (Henry Morgan), who have switched sides. They return the money to the bank they robbed in the opening sequence. Afterward, the three reformed outlaws ride off with Grandpa and Mike.

Several days of filming began May 26, 1948, on the salt flats of Death Valley National Monument, three hundred miles from Los Angeles. Except for a few days shooting at the Fox studio and its Western town, most of the picture was made in picturesque Lone Pine, California, in the heart of the beautiful Eastern High Sierra. Lone Pine is home to spectacular panoramic views from the majestic Alabama Hills, with their rugged, high-desert rock faces and gigantic granite boulders surrounding the valley floor, and is the gateway to Mount Whitney, the tallest mountain in the contiguous United States at 14,496 feet. Hundreds of films have been shot in this magnificent place. Most of the company members lived at the historic Dow Hotel, built in the early 1920s. Wellman had slept in Dow beds in those early days, including while making his first picture as a director, *The Man Who Won* (1923). His Yellow Sky company was tight-knit and contented. Although there was little nightlife, they shared the hardworking bond of an exceptional movie company. On Sundays, they played softball, went hiking, trout fishing, and blue grouse and pheasant hunting. Those who hadn't spent enough time with the horses went horseback riding.

The director was fond of his cameraman, Joe MacDonald, who had photographed John Ford's *My Darling Clementine* (1946), his crew, and, for a change, all his actors throughout production. There was a slight problem, only in the beginning, with the handsome, intelligent, consummate actor, Greg Peck. From a story standpoint, Wellman was concerned about Peck's nobly heroic, well-educated, good-guy image playing against that of a rugged, unshaven, unsophisticated outlaw. The director kept adding bits of physical business to make Peck's Stretch more villainous, more dangerous, leading to this rugged scene: Stretch and the tall, strong Lengthy duke it out in a waterhole. After Stretch knocks him down, when Lengthy's head appears out of the water, Stretch kicks it like a football. After that, there was no question that Stretch was tough and not to be fooled with.

Anne Baxter played the Wellman woman to the hilt—on time, well prepared, ready to ride, shoot, or fight like one of the guys. She had a different problem with her costar. Although Peck treated everyone with courtesy and respect, he was more of an outsider, staying away from the fraternity-like camaraderie and the after-hours bar scene. Instead, he kept to himself working on his script and performance. Peck's individualism and slightly standoffish demeanor began to bother Baxter. During their knock-down, drag-out fight scene in the corral beside the ramshackle ranch house, she punched, kicked, wrestled, threw dirt in the face of her costar. Wellman later said, "She kicked hell outta him."

Gregory Peck accepted it as part of the job. He proved to be tough enough with the physical aspects of the outdoor spectacle, including the many scenes chasing around and over the giant boulders of Lone Pine—on foot with no double—even though he had broken his ankle from a fall off a horse prior to production. He asked for no special attention, never straying from the incredible actor and fine gentleman that he always was on his way to earning five Academy Award nominations, an Oscar for *To Kill a Mockingbird* (1962), and becoming a true icon of the film industry.

A substantial number of favorable reviews used the following descriptions: powerful performances, first-rate script, intriguing story line, well-paced and dramatic direction, masterful settings, a gritty sense of

The Wellman family is growing: (left to right) Bill Jr., Pat, Kitty, Tim, Wellman holding baby Mike, Dottie, and Cissy, 1948

the Old West. They went on with: terse, tough action, steel-spring tension, eye-filling cinematography and compositions, a skillful and satisfying movie, classy and exciting. A number of critics compared the story to Shakespeare's *The Tempest,* of which many versions have been filmed beginning in 1908. Wellman made a point of not reading reviews of his films. This *Tempest* business fascinated him and he wrote about it. One of the unnamed reviews he listed follows: "FILM: *Yellow Sky*; enjoy this excellent Western as a straight-forward yarn with Gregory Peck, Richard Widmark, Anne Baxter providing superior performances. But William Wellman provides enough clues for the literate to recognize it as a retelling of 'The Tempest,' as an old prospector and his daughter [actually granddaughter] guard their gold. Either way, it's superbly photographed, gripping stuff."

"I should feel very flattered," said Wellman, "but unfortunately I am not. Why? Because I have never read Shakespeare, and I am not going to start now. My reading has been very limited—stories for my pictures— Jim Murray every morning in the *Los Angeles Times,* Stewart Alsop in *Newsweek* and a few other sportswriters—fiction? No! . . . frankly I am very sorry that I am not as well educated as one who studied Shakespeare and read 'Tempest.'"

One of Wellman's favorite expressions was vocalized after his farting— "the voice of a critic!" While on the subject of wind, one of the most popular postproduction sources for the sound of wind in movies comes

John Hodiak, Denise Darcel, Van Johnson in *Battleground* (1949)

from *Yellow Sky* and is heard in hundreds of films. Premiered on February 1, 1949, at the Roxy in New York, the ninety-eight-minute *Yellow Sky* is one of Wellman's best films and one of his favorites. Although the picture was a moneymaker, it's somehow flown below the radar and, except for Western enthusiasts, lives in the world of underappreciated films.

18

BATTLEGROUND
SENDS A MESSAGE

After the completion of Wellman's *Magic Town*, Dottie performed a little magic of her own with a sixth child and another son for the filmmaker to come home to. Born August 24, 1947, Michael McCarthy made his entrance into the active Wellman farmhouse. With *Yellow Sky* in the can, the director took time off until a call came from MGM's new production chief, Dore Schary.

While head of production at RKO, Schary had been developing a World War II film with a battle-tested former GI, Robert Pirosh. The writer wanted to tell the story of the battle of Bastogne and the brave stand by the surrounded 101st Airborne Division known as the "Screaming Eagles" and after the conflict as "the battered bastards of Bastogne." The picture would be called *Battleground*.

Schary and Pirosh had been working on the project for nearly two years when it was announced as a September 1948 start date. The film was to star Robert Mitchum, Robert Ryan, and Bill Williams, and to be directed by Fred Zinnemann. So many war films had been produced in the 1940s that the studios no longer believed movie audiences wanted another one. Regardless of this industry antipathy, Schary poured his heart and soul into the pet project and it became known around Hollywood as "Schary's folly."

When Howard Hughes took over RKO, he canceled the film and Schary resigned to become vice president of production at MGM on July 1, 1948. The new chief brought several projects with him, including *Battleground*. MGM's president, Louis B. Mayer, was also against another war film but decided to allow his new VP to produce it, figuring that if it failed, it would be easier to keep him in line and under his control. The budget, however, would have to be lean. Although other directors had been considered before Wellman, Schary thought *The Story of G.I. Joe* one of the decade's best and the director's reputation for fighting the establishment might be a plus in getting him to sign on.

Wellman loved the script, liked the writer, Pirosh, and the savvy, confident, enthusiastic producer. The director was especially attracted to Schary's underdog status in Hollywood. Wellman signed a contract in February of 1949 and filming commenced April 4. To save money, the director shot most of the picture on two large MGM soundstages. He built a pine forest in one of them complete with artificial snow. He had shot an outdoor Western, *The Ox-Bow Incident*, on a soundstage, why not an outdoor war film? He also used the same set from *G.I. Joe* at RKO's Forty Acre Ranch in Culver City.

The main story line follows a platoon of the 101st Airborne who are trapped in the besieged town of Bastogne, Belgium, in December of 1944 during the battle of the Bulge. The film focuses on the psychology, morale, and camaraderie of these everyday Americans who fight, wait, and pray for a break in the snowy, foggy winter weather, so that Allied air support can deliver to them fuel, rations, ammunition—and to the enemy, bullets and bombs. There are no Hollywood heroics here, just battle-weary soldiers trying to survive one day at a time.

Wellman assembled the large cast filled with MGM contract players. Top billed were Van Johnson (Holley), John Hodiak (Jarvess), Ricardo Montalban (Rodriguez), and George Murphy (Pop). As Wellman had done with the actors in *G.I. Joe*, he put them through Spartan training prior to the start of production. He hired twenty veterans of the 101st who had fought in the Bastogne area, as instructors and extras.

The picture is highlighted by strong, convincing, and caring relationships among men. There are dominant character studies and well-developed performances. One of the best is James Whitmore (Sergeant Kinnie), who had served with the Marine Corps and patterned his bedraggled, tobacco-chewing character partly on Bill Mauldin's famous "Willie and Joe" cartoons.

What some thought was a typical Wellman comedic insertion, coming from the clicking of Douglas Fowley's (Kipp) false teeth, was authentically based on a toothless GI discovered during the writer's research. The director, of course, elaborated on the joke. Fowley served in the navy in

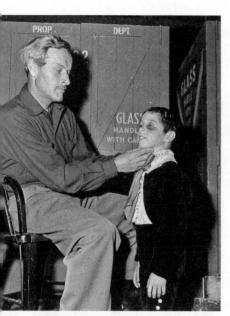

Wellman's son Tim plays the bell ringer with the black eyes in *The Happy Years* (1950).

the South Pacific during the war, losing his teeth in an aircraft carrier explosion.

An addition that Wellman did make during a rehearsal prior to a scene with a tent full of sleeping soldiers went like this: "I want you to make plenty of noise before being awakened by your sergeant [Whitmore]. I want to hear snoring, coughing, teeth clicking, even farting if possible." "If possible" turned up on the soundtrack but was covered over by the clicking of Kip's teeth.

James Arness (Garby) was the most decorated serviceman in the cast. Among other commendations, he was awarded the Bronze Star, the Purple Heart, and European-Mideast Campaign Medals. Arness went on to stardom as Matt Dillon in television's *Gunsmoke*. Of the few small female roles, French-born Denise Darcel shines. She was a Dore Schary discovery who would go on to star in a future Wellman Western.

Production was completed on June 3, 1949, at a cost of $1.6 million. The 118-minute film premiered November 11, 1949, at New York's Astor Theatre. Wellman had brought the picture in ahead of schedule and $100,000 under budget. *Battleground* took in $5 million in rentals, becoming the second-highest-grossing film released in 1949—second only to Cecil B. DeMille's *Samson and Delilah*.

Variety, September 23, 1949: "The first great picture to come out of Hollywood treating with World War II." Bosley Crowther, *The New York Times*: November 12, 1949, "The Big Parade of World War II." Christopher Wicking, *National Film Theatre London*, June/July 1972: "Wellman's scenes flow and blend like a grim kaleidoscope, before falling into breathtaking formal shape. . . . Compelling, compassionate emotional experience."

The picture received six Academy Award nominations: Best Picture, Best Director, Best Supporting Actor (James Whitmore), Best Story and Screenplay (Robert Pirosh), Best Black and White Cinematography (Paul C. Vogel), and Best Black and White Film Editing (John Dunning).

Oscars went to Pirosh and Dunning with Wellman bested by Joseph L. Mankiewicz for *A Letter to Three Wives*. Wellman did receive the prestigious *Look* award for Director of the Year. James Whitmore was shocked at his Oscar nomination, considering that he only spoke seventeen lines. He gave special credit to his director.

Dore Schary was vindicated. The picture was such a resounding hit that he was elected to the board of MGM parent Loews Inc., and soon after the great mogul L. B. Mayer was fired. A special friendship and respect was forged between Wellman and Schary that would bring family gatherings and six more films in the next three years . . . before politics reared its ugly head.

Wellman directs young star Dean Stockwell in *The Happy Years*.

Wellman "strongly" expressed to Schary his desire to continue his habit of making all kinds of pictures. Schary agreed and the director signed a three-year contract at MGM. After the battlefields of World War II, Wellman entertained the battlefields of prep school in the coming-of-age story *The Happy Years* (1950), based on Owen Johnson's *The Lawrenceville School Stories*, with a screenplay by Harry Ruskin. The director retained his *Battleground* Oscar-nominee cameraman, Paul C. Vogel, and Oscar-winning editor, John Dunning. The art directors were Daniel B. Cathcart and Cedric Gibbons, who had designed the statuette called "Oscar." Filming commenced September 12, 1949, at Lawrenceville School in New Jersey.

The story deals with an incorrigible youth, John Humperdink "Dink" Stover, expelled from public school and now at Lawrenceville Preparatory School for boys in 1896—the year of Wellman's birth. Dink is a prankster and teller of tall tales who has trouble with authority and his schoolmates' codes of behavior. His family, teachers, and classmates are ready to give up on him until he proves his bravery on the football field, in a fistfight with an older student, "Tough" McCarty, and allows a teacher, known as the Old Roman, to take him under his wing. Now his standing soars and life looks brighter—doesn't this sound a bit like the director's school days?

The picture was cast with young MGM contract stars Dean Stockwell, *Anchors Away* (1945), *Gentleman's Agreement* (1947), *The Boy with Green Hair* (1948), as Dink; Darryl Hickman, *The Grapes of Wrath* (1940), *Men of Boys Town* (1941), *Leave Her to Heaven* (1945), as Tough McCarty; Scotty Beckett, *The Jolson Story* (1946), *A Date with Judy* (1948), *Battleground* (1949), as Tennessee Shad.

Wellman liked the idea of casting MGM musical and comedy star Danny Kaye, *Wonder Man* (1945), *The Secret Life of Walter Mitty* (1947), *A Song Is Born* (1948), in a change-of-pace role as the teacher, Old Roman. Major star Kaye, however, didn't like this kind of role change, which included supporting the youngsters. This critical part went to respected character actor Leo G. Carroll, *Spellbound* (1945), *The Paradine Case* (1947), *Father of the Bride* (1950).

Darryl Hickman's brother, Dwayne, of television's *Dobie Gillis* fame, plays a small role as does future star of film and television Robert Wagner, in his movie debut. Another minor character is played by Mary Eleanor Donahue, later Elinor Donahue of TV's *Father Knows Best*. The director spices up the story with animal humor from a mouse and a barking dog to a herd of quacking ducks. He casts his eight-year-old son, Timmy, in a running gag of a schoolboy bell ringer who first appears with a black eye on his left eye, then the black eye moves to the right eye, and, finally, he is seen with both eyes blackened from unseen fistfights.

Filming was completed November 11, 1949, at a cost of $1.3 million. The 110-minute film is well crafted and entertaining, but the studio lost interest in it, as little advertising money was spent and its July 7, 1950, release found fewer theaters than a normal MGM release. Wellman always liked the picture but his nostalgic boyhood saga, in beautiful Technicolor, lived primarily as half of double-feature programming. *The New York Times* didn't bother to review it. The periodicals that opened their editorial spaces liked it.

Schary wanted Wellman to take part in his film philosophy—the making of message pictures. The producer explained that "together" they were going to provide movie audiences with learning experiences and important life lessons. Wellman, on the other hand, hated message movies. He was not against strong values and principles but the emphasis should be on entertainment. Mogul Samuel Goldwyn went a step further: "Pictures are for entertainment, messages should be delivered by Western Union."

The Schary "togetherness" that Wellman appreciated was the diversity in the stories that he would be directing. *The Next Voice You Hear* (1950) starred *Battleground*'s Best Supporting Actor nominee, James Whitmore, and future first lady Nancy Davis. The story of a typical 1950s suburban family who hear the voice of God on the radio—the world is also listening and reacting in various ways. For six days, the voice—which can't be recorded or heard by movie audiences—instructs people to perform miracles of kindness and peace.

Wellman was intrigued by the uniqueness of the story. It allowed his spiritual side to present itself in a tranquil setting. When Schary asked if he could make it within a small budget of $600,000 on a twenty-two-day schedule, the director boasted that he would beat it. He brought it in for $430,000 and eight days ahead of schedule. Surprisingly, when the eighty-two-minute picture premiered, June 29, 1950, at New York's Radio City Music Hall, it became a hit. *Film Bulletin*, April 24, 1950: "Here was a picture that made the most jaded reviewer proud to be a part of the industry that was responsible for it."

"A MIRACLE IN HOLLYWOOD: 14-DAY FILM COST $475,000." That was the headline in Lloyd Shearer's article in the *New York Herald Tribune*, Sunday, June 25, 1950.

The most inexpensive and most rapidly completed major production that Metro-Goldwyn-Mayer has turned out in the last twenty years. The director who engineered this speedup is William Wellman. . . . In Hollywood his direction of "The Next Voice You Hear" has already become a four-month-old legend and is now the standard at which all studio heads are aiming. . . . The man who says, "There were four reasons why I shot The Next Voice so rapidly: First, I had no front office geniuses tell me what to do. My producer was Dore Schary. He left me strictly alone. He's an angel to work with. . . . Number two: Charley Schnee took Dore's treatment and wrote a real tight script. . . . We shot the script exactly as it was written. Number three: I didn't have to spend two and a half hours waiting for Lana Turner to come out of the ladies' room. . . . I used two newcomers, James Whitmore and Nancy Davis. They're alert, intelligent, co-operative and they did what I told them to do. No tantrums, no temperament, no time out. Just good, solid acting. Also, I wouldn't have a makeup man on the picture. The only one on the picture who wears any makeup is Nancy Davis, and all she wears is lipstick which she put on herself. When you have a big-shot actress and a makeup man on the set, the actress sits down to powder her nose for a minute and the next

Wellman reads to James Whitmore, Nancy Davis, and
Gary Gray: *The Next Voice You Hear* (1950).

thing you know, they're giving her an all-day permanent. We had none
of that. Number four: The cast and I, as well as Bill Mellor, a great cameraman, had a number of dry runs before any one stepped in front of the
lens. We rehearsed the lines and setups in my office a week or so before
we got rolling. When we did, everything clicked. My crew was perfect.
We averaged one and a half takes per shot, which is very good. There
were an amazing number of first takes. . . . If anyone deserves credit, it's
my crew. Not an artistic genius in the whole lot. Just guys and gals who
knew their jobs."

Dore Schary and his "togetherness" partner had won another gamble.
Schary's next lecture was *American Anthology*, celebrating America as
the melting pot of the world. Released in 1952 as *It's a Big Country*, the
film consists of eight episodes; Wellman directed number seven, *The
Minister in Washington*. Schary wrote the story and screenplay starring
two *Battleground* thesps, Van Johnson and Leon Ames, with Lewis Stone.
Set in 1944, the short story depicts Johnson as a minister delivering a
sermon at St. Thomas Episcopal Church in the heart of Manhattan. In
the congregation sits President Roosevelt. The reverend speaks directly
to the president and forgets his flock. Afterward he is reprimanded for
leaving out the many for just the one. *It's a Big Country* performed poorly
with critics and patrons alike, all agreeing on a dull and uninspiring
movie.

Battleground, The Happy Years, episode seven of *It's a Big Country*, and
the fourteen-day wonder, *The Next Voice You Hear*, were all produced
within a seventeen-month period. Wellman needed a break. He was

Across the Wide Missouri (1951): William A. Wellman
and Dottie smile for the cameraman at MGM camp
headquarters for the 4 Technicolor outdoor film. (Left to
right): Bill (13), Cissy (7), Pat (15), Mrs. Wellman, Tim (9),
Kitty (11), with Wellman holding Mike (5).

promising Dottie and his six kids an extended vacation in the summer of
1950. They got it, but not what they had expected.

Dore Schary called for a meeting in his MGM office. "Here's the deal,
Billy," said the studio boss and friend. "I've got a great script by two-time
Academy Award nominee Talbot Jennings, an 1830's western called *Across
the Wide Missouri.* You can shoot it on location in Montana or Utah,
we've scouted beautiful locations there. I'll pay you ten percent above
your usual salary and . . . I've got Clark Cable for the lead. What do you
think?" Without a moment's hesitation, "Dore, I've made four pictures in
a row for you. I don't need the money, I need a vacation with my wife and
kids." Schary was silent for a moment, then, "You can have both. Take
your family to a lovely location and have a great time! And we'll pay for

it all!" "You've got another problem," said Wellman. "I don't think Gable will work with me again." He explained the Gable situation dating back to *The Call of the Wild* and Gable's love affair with Loretta Young. The director and "the King" had not been on good terms since.

A few days later, Schary called with the news that Gable had given his okay. Wellman had read the script and liked it. He saw it as an offbeat Western with an unusual love story. The Gable character (Flint Mitchell) is a rugged mountain man who leads a band of fur trappers into Blackfeet country, trading for an Indian wife, Maria Elena Marques, as security for this venture. He makes no emotional ties to her but she earns his love and respect through her courageous nature. There are battles with warring Indians and in the climactic combat she is killed by their leader, Ironshirt (Ricardo Montalban). Her horse, bearing Gable's son in a riding cradle secured to the saddle, is frightened and takes off at breakneck speed while the trappers battle the braves. Flint pursues the murdering Indian, who is chasing the horse, trying to kill the child. In a thrilling duel, Flint kills Ironshirt and saves his son.

By June of 1950, Wellman had chosen all of his locations within a seventy-five-mile radius of Durango, Colorado, with the company's camp based in a tent city fourteen miles north of Durango. Each and every location was set on or near a body of water—lake, pond, river, stream. Wellman told the unit manager, Ruby Rosenberg, and production manager, Walter Strohm, to hire a crew of fishermen. "Tell them to bring their fishing gear to work each day," said the director. "At five o'clock I wrap and go fishing. The actors can do the same."

At the end of July, the company began the move to Durango for a seven-week shoot. Dottie, with her youngest, Mike (five), and daughters Pat (fifteen), Kitty (eleven), and Cissy (seven), would arrive by train a few days later. This author, thirteen at the time, and brother Tim (nine) traveled with their father on a chartered plane. Although I had been a visitor on the sets and locations of eighteen of my father's films—some for the entire location—this was the first time the whole family was there for the complete shoot. The chartered aircraft was a DC-3 and there would be others onboard—Orville "Bunny" Dull, the location scout; Ruby Rosenberg; and other key company personnel. The plane would also carry location and company equipment. Dad wanted to see the finished construction at several location sites from the air before landing. This would save making a special automobile or plane trip at another time.

The studio limo arrived at our house before daylight. Dad, Timmy, and I were excited. We were driven to the San Fernando Valley Airport, now Van Nuys Airport, and right up to the waiting DC-3. It looked awfully big to me with its ninety-five-foot wing span and sixty-five-foot length. Dad told us they were the safest planes in the air. While he talked with the pilot, Bunny Dull, and Ruby Rosenberg, Timmy and I leaped up the stairway and into the plane.

We knew dad would be talking business, so Timmy and I sat in the back, on the left side. Timmy was at the window, peering out, with me next to him. I never felt comfortable in airplanes and never wanted to look out the window. Dad and his crew sat up front. Dad always wanted to be close to the pilot. It was still pretty dark when we took off. We went through a layer of clouds only to find the rising sun on the other side. There were colors of dark orange, grays, and deep blues, even a yellow flame, but the beauty lasted only a short time before the weather changed into a dark and turbulent storm.

Before long, rain began pelting our ship, and it rocked and rolled like a prizefighter, bobbing and weaving and ducking punches. I wasn't paying much attention to the men until dad came back to check on us. "Are you guys all right?" We nodded in the affirmative. He patted our heads and said, "This weather won't last much longer." He went back up front. I turned to Timmy, "Everything's going to be all right, Timmy." But I was scared. I saw dad disappear behind the door to the cockpit. He was with the pilot. The other men were hanging on like me.

The storm grew worse. Timmy said, "I feel sick!" I grabbed the barf bag from the seat pocket in front of Timmy. He barely got it opened before the "funnel job" started. I put my left arm around his shoulders, my right hand holding his head, helping his aim into the bag. I didn't think he ate that much for breakfast, but he vomited up two and a half bags worth.

At this point, the location-scout part of the trip was canceled, and the pilot was looking to set the plane down at the nearest airfield. In 1950, approaches and landings were handled not by the pilots, but by ground control radar. Our pilot had found a small private airfield and was attempting to land. Visibility was poor and before he touched down, the control tower was shouting that the DC-3 needed more landing area than this airfield permitted. The pilot really gunned it when he heard the warnings and saw the steep cliff looming up at the end of the runway. Dad told me later that ground control saw our landing gear touch the top of the cliff wall as we disappeared over it and into the gloom.

The weather began to clear. Another, larger airfield was found and soon we were on the ground. The men, including the pilot and me, were all shaken. Dad was mad mostly at himself for getting into this situation. The only one who wore a smile was Timmy. He felt much better and spent so much time in the barf bag that he didn't realize the seriousness of our dilemma.

I walked outside our cabin and looked around at the sparkling, sunny day, with temperatures in the mid-seventies. The few billowy clouds that floated lazily across the brilliant blue sky were the whitest of white, and the pinecones in the green trees moved to a gentle rhythm. I could hear the sounds of rushing water in the river nearby, and the engines of the few cars traveling the highway to Durango. The air was fresh and contained the smell of wood-burning fireplaces.

Clark Gable and Maria Elena Marques in *Across the Wide Missouri* (1951)

On our side of the highway, there were a dozen or more knotty pine rental cabins dotting the landscape. None of them was large, not even Clark Gable's. Our cabin had a small living room, smaller kitchen with dining area. There were three bedrooms and two bathrooms. Dad and mom had a bedroom, my two brothers and I another. The third bedroom housed my three sisters. After the first week, dad needed a bedroom to himself for quiet work, and he was a restless sleeper. Mother moved in with the girls; my sister Pat moved in with the boys, and I moved out into the living room. Dad got a cot for me. I didn't bother anyone since I got up early every day to go with him to location.

Across the highway was the headquarters for this small settlement known as El Encantado (The Enchanted). The few buildings housed the rental office, mini-market, and coffee shop. There were two gas pumps out front and a recreation center in the back next to the mineral water pool. I was told these waters had special powers, so I swam as much as possible.

Less than a hundred yards from El Encantado, and before the river, was the tent city. What a sight! Close to a hundred men and women living in white tents, with a large portable structure in the center for kitchen and dining complete with full-time chef. For entertainment, an outdoor movie theater was constructed, and the studio sent first-run films for the weekends. I continued with my belief that this movie business was something fabulous.

Many of the Hollywood movie companies had organized sports teams of one kind or another. Dad's companies loved baseball and often played on days off, usually Sunday; a field was cleared and a backstop inserted. The costume department brought uniforms—"Wellman's Wild Men" emblazoned across the front of the shirts, initials on the caps. They not only played against each other, but took on the local team. I suited up and played right field. The game was fast-pitch softball, and the rival team was Durango. We played a seven-inning game and Durango was ahead three to two in the bottom of the seventh.

Dad's arthritis was acting up, so he didn't play—but he was a very vocal coach. Another coach, even more vocal, was Adolphe Menjou. Menjou, playing a French trapper in the movie, was constantly yelling instructions and barbs at both teams. Our guys paid no attention to him, as they were familiar with his antics. The other team was unsure how to respond, even when Menjou started shouting in different languages—including one he made up.

I had gotten a base hit and our catcher, an electrician and former major league player, knocked me in with a double for our second run. But we were behind and it was our last at bat. We had runners at second and third with two outs. We needed one more hit to win the game. I was nervous because my turn at bat was coming up after the next hitter, and I didn't want to lose the game for our team and . . . my father. When I looked over to see who was coming to bat before me, I gave a sigh of relief. The crowd in the makeshift stands began shouting and clapping and cheering for "the King." Clark Gable stepped into the batter's box. He had already hit a home run over the fence earlier in the game. This would be a piece of cake, I thought to myself. He worked the count to three balls and two strikes. I thought to myself, "If the next pitch is a ball, he will walk and I will have to come to the plate with the game on the line!" I was more jittery than ever, thinking, "The Durango pitcher is not going to throw a strike to the King." But he did and Gable took a ferocious swing and . . . missed! The umpire called loudly, "STRIKE THREE. YOU'RE OUT!"

I couldn't believe it—Mighty Casey had struck out.

The next weekend, Clark Gable redeemed himself by winning the Fishing Derby, with a beautiful twelve-pound rainbow trout, caught at

Molas Lake, the Indian village location. Dad caught a ten-pounder for second place. Only two people didn't catch anything that day, and I was one of them . . . Adolphe Menjou was the other. I never saw or heard of him ever catching a fish. I surmised that all his chatter scared them away . . . or maybe they just didn't understand the language.

Frankie Darro, the former child star who had played the leading role in my father's *Wild Boys of the Road* (1933), was the company Ping-Pong champion—I couldn't get a point from him.

One day, while waiting for clouds to clear, dad challenged anyone in the company to a race. None of the crew took the challenge, for they had seen this in the past and knew dad's speed of foot. Two actors stepped up—Louis Nicoletti and Frankie Darro. I figured Frankie was fast, I wasn't sure about Nicoletti. The race was a hundred yards, stepped off by Howard W. Koch, the assistant director. Adolphe Menjou, of course, wanted to be a part of the action. He proclaimed himself the starter. His "On your mark, get set, go!" was cracking everybody up. He kept changing languages, coughing, sneezing, causing the runners to false start. Dad, who took the whole thing too seriously, fired Menjou, replacing him with the more serious John Hodiak.

The race was exciting and close between dad and Frankie. Nicoletti was clearly a distant third, claiming, "Menjou messed me up with all his nonsense!" Koch was at the finish line shouting, "It's a photo finish!" Then he signaled dad the winner. Frankie complained only slightly, while Nicoletti commented, "I want another race!" The clouds had cleared and everybody went back to work.

I never saw dad lose a race. I couldn't beat him until I turned eighteen and he was then sixty. Actually, he called our final race a tie and never raced me again.

When I think of all the movie stars whose laps I wrinkled, the ones I met on my dad's sets, Clark Gable rises to the top. As the director's son, everyone was nice to me, a few because they actually enjoyed my company. After all, I was quiet, seemed normal, stayed out of trouble, and was highly interested in their work and the wonderful world of movies.

Clark Gable had been denied the kind of family life he desired. The love of his life, Carole Lombard, had been killed in a plane crash, and he was now married to Lady Sylvia Ashley—who bore a physical resemblance to Lombard.

I remember thinking how strange it was that Gable, the consummate outdoorsman, would marry someone who not only wouldn't hunt or fish, but didn't like being outside at all and . . . didn't even like blue jeans! On this rugged, no-frills location, she wanted to have tea every day. I can still see her squinting behind dark glasses, batting flies away from her face, under large, brimmed hats. The few times she came out to the locations, she complained of the heat, or the wind, always something. Most of the time, she stayed in her small cabin with her nasty Chihuahua. The dog had a big wart on its back and didn't like anyone . . . except Lady Sylvia, of course. However, Gable was very attentive to her at all times. It seemed to me the only things they did together were drink, take short walks, and eat dinner. Since there were no restaurants around, I saw them most evenings at the company dining table—including that canine, who roamed around under the table, growling at everyone's feet. After a couple of weeks of this, some people, including my father, began to kick at the dog.

By this time, Gable's health was beginning to deteriorate. His heavy drinking was (at least partly) responsible for "the shake." In close-ups, my father had to station prop men in bushes and trees behind Gable out of sight of the camera. Their job was to move branches and twigs in synchronization with Gable's head movements. Although he still looked good, his body strength was fading.

Several times during the seven-week shoot, I went fishing with Gable. Now, fishing is a snobbery sort of sport. There are freshwater fishermen and saltwater fishermen. In the world of freshwater, which includes any body of water that doesn't contain salt, there are fly fishermen, bait fishermen, and lure fishermen. The fly fishermen, like Gable and my father, believe they sit above all other anglers, and they would never use bait or a lure. My father often voiced his uppishness, Gable kept his quiet and didn't mind me using homemade flies, self-painted lures, cheese, bread, salmon eggs, or anything else I thought might attract a fish.

After work one day, we walked quite a ways through woods and rough terrain, down a steep, brushy hill, to a shallow lake filled with tree trunks sticking out of the water. Gable had this idea that because the lake was difficult to get to, and didn't look inviting once you saw it, the fish were plentiful and just waiting to be caught. We talked all the way. He never spoke to me like parent to child or teacher to child or even adult to child. He had a way of getting down to my level and enjoying what I had to say . . . and I enjoyed what he had to say. He was right about the lake. We both caught our limit—as many fish as we could carry out—of cutthroat trout, distinctive due to their red, pink, or orange coloration on the underside of the lower jaw. All trout are fierce fighters on the line; cutthroats, although not the largest trout in size, seemed to us to be the most spirited.

On the way back to the location, and the waiting for transportation back to the tent city, he told me what he thought was a funny story concerning Lady Sylvia's dog and her brother-in-law, Basil Bleck, a British film producer. Gable never said anything negative about his wife or anybody else. He didn't even trash that disagreeable Chihuahua, and you just knew that Clark Gable should have a large hunting dog. Like everyone else, Basil didn't take to the pooch. Different from everybody else, he planned to do something about it. When he came over to the Gables' ranch house with his wife, Sylvia's sister, Lillian, the dog followed him everywhere he went—even to the bathroom. He never petted the little wretch for it always retreated out of reach. The little tyke just snarled, yipped, barked, and stepped lively after him.

The Englishman was consumed with evil thoughts of ridding himself and the world of "the beast." Would he dispense poison, back his car over it, take it for a walk and toss it off a bridge? All sorts of dastardly deeds were considered before settling on a very simple one, and no one would be the wiser. There were several swinging doors inside the Gable house, and since the dog followed him everywhere, he would simply slam the door behind him as the beast was passing through. On the fateful day, Basil and Lillian arrived by car and parked in front of the Clark Gable estate. As Basil stepped out, he looked up and saw the beast peering at him from the window of the living room. After knocking on the door, they let themselves in. The Blecks were welcomed by Clark and Sylvia on their way to the living room. Basil excused himself and began the trek to the bathroom. The beast followed closely behind. Basil cut through the dining room, which had two swinging doors. Upon reaching the second door, he looked back to make sure it was still right behind. Their gazes locked momentarily, then he grasped the door with his left hand and, at the right moment, slammed the door behind him.

In the living room, Lillian and the Gables were conversing, waiting for Basil's return. Suddenly, they heard a loud shriek followed by a softer whimper. The little Chihuahua trotted into the room and jumped up on Lady Sylvia's lap. She petted the pooch as the Englishman entered holding his left hand in his right hand and in obvious pain—he had broken three fingers on his left hand. Clark Gable laughed at the punch line to his story. I did, too, but I wasn't convinced it was funny. Then Gable commented, "Sylvia's brother-in-law thought it was a curse and never tried to hurt the dog again."

Timmy had already appeared in one of dad's pictures, *The Happy Years*. My turn came rather unexpectedly. Dad had been setting up a

Johnny Indrisano: from
1924 to 1934 he won
eighty pro fights, defeated
five world champions
in nontitle bouts,
and *The Ring* boxing
magazine called him
the "uncrowned world
champion."

big production shot all morning. He was wait-ing patiently for the right clouds to form over the 1830s fort, as fur trappers and traders, Indi-ans, horses, mules, move in and out of the huge entrance gate . . . with a shimmering lake visible in the background. Everything was now ready and my father called out—over a bullhorn—"Action!" The large gate slid open and the peo-ple and animals made their entrances and exits from the fort. The take was perfect, except for one thing. Visible through the open door of the fort, on the beautiful lake, was a 1950s rowboat with William Wellman Jr. fishing from it. My father's voice echoed forth from the bullhorn, "Bill, goddammit! Get the hell out of there!" I put down my fishing rod and started pad-dling as fast as I could. Knowing I had ruined a shot and made trouble for myself, I was afraid to come in for several hours. I decided that I wouldn't return until I caught a fish big enough to take the spotlight off my dimwitted deed.

I never wanted to catch a fish so badly. It seemed everything was against me. Even the wind picked up and the sky filled with dark clouds. At one point, a large eastern brook trout swam up near the surface and looked at me. I felt it was taunting me; it rolled over slowly and swam away. Finally, after more than two hours, I caught a big eastern brook—about four pounds—then paddled in to shore. When I docked, the company was on their meal break. As I got out of the boat, I held the trout up high, so everybody could see my trophy. I walked toward the lunching company, seated in card chairs at long portable tables. Some of the crew began to shout, "Hey, Bill Jr. caught a big one!" and "Look what the kid has!" The crew started clap-ping, even dad got swept up in the excitement. I deposited the fish with the chef for a future meal, and sat down to enjoy my meal. Nobody ever mentioned my faux pas . . . not even my dad.

There was an empty seat next to me, Johnny Indrisano filled it. During the first week of the location, dad had introduced Timmy and me to

Johnny. Dad's intro went like this: "I want you kids to learn how to fight. Johnny Indrisano is the best in the whole damn business. He stages my fights, he taught Dean Stockwell in *The Happy Years*. He'll be your teacher." Before coming to Hollywood, Johnny had been a world-class professional boxer. After a successful amateur career, he turned pro with eighty-three bouts in which he won eighty. He reversed those losses in subsequent fights. He defeated five world champions, all in nontitle fights. He never got a chance at a title because he wouldn't throw in with the gangsters who controlled much of the fight game at the time. He retired from the ring in 1934. The *Ring* boxing magazine called him the "uncrowned world champion."

Soon after arriving in the film capital, he became the number one fight technical adviser with credits like Robert Rossen's *Body and Soul* (1947) with John Garfield; Robert Wise's *The Set-Up* (1949) starring Robert Ryan and *Somebody Up There Likes Me* (1956) toplining Paul Newman; Mark Robson's *The Harder They Fall* (1956) with Humphrey Bogart; Ralph Nelson's *Requiem for a Heavyweight* (1962) starring Anthony Quinn and the then Cassius Clay (Muhammad Ali). Johnny worked with many filmmakers and stars before stuntmen took over the job of fight technical adviser. He played a variety of small roles and did some stunts but was never a true stuntman. His life ended tragically in suicide on July 9, 1968.

Indrisano became a personal friend of my father's, working in many of his films. In *Across the Wide Missouri*, Johnny choreographed the rough-and-tumble action and played an Indian brave. With his strong Italian and prizefighter features, dad kept him away from the camera, using him only in crowd and action scenes.

Even though Johnny was working most of the time, he still found time for Timmy and me. He showed us the fundamentals of boxing, and we shadow-boxed with him—a pretend kind of fighting where we squared off against him, moved around, throwing punches that never landed. Mostly, he talked to us about fighting and fighters. When I wasn't fishing or watching the movie being made, I was looking for Johnny and waiting for his wonderful stories.

One evening, around eight o'clock, I walked from my cabin down to tent city to find him. As I approached his tent, which had a flimsy screen door, his two roommates were approaching from another direction. Frank McGrath, one of Hollywood's finest stuntmen, who was short enough to stunt-double women in movies, and a much bigger stuntman, Terry Wilson, who later became an actor and a costar of the long-running television series *Wagon Train*, were coming back from an evening of playing cards and drinking in another stuntman's tent. They weren't drunk but feeling no pain as they entered their tent. Since it was dark, they hadn't seen me, and I walked closer to the doorway. Through the screen door, I could see Johnny in bed, with his backside to the door. The bedcovers were pulled up to his shoulders.

Ever since his boxing days, Johnny got up early and went to bed early. He didn't gamble, drink, or smoke. McGrath and Wilson did them all and often. They were hooting and hollering and talking loudly. Soon, they began directing barbs at the sleeping Indrisano. "Come on, Indrisano, get your dago-wop ass out of the rack. Have a drink with us, play some poker!" Johnny didn't move. They pranced over to his bed and began poking him, then kicking him lightly. "Come on, Indrisano, get up. Let's see you dance!" They were laughing and slapping each other on the back. There was a moment of silence; then Johnny reached back with his right hand, pulling the covers down. He turned over, got out of bed. Without a word, he stepped closer to the two men and, with five or six lightning-fast punches, knocked them out cold. Silently, he turned back, got into bed, pulling the covers over him. I turned and walked away, leaving the three "sleeping" men to themselves. The next day, I told Johnny what I had seen. He made one comment only. "They needed a lesson."

On another day, the company was working at an Indian village location, much smaller than the one at Molas Lake. We must have spent the better part of a week at this location. The lake was very small—more of a large pond. This location provided a company mascot—an old beaver. I was told that this beaver had been kicked out of the large lake nearby by the younger, stronger beavers. Our mascot had scars on his face and body and moved very slowly. He was tame enough to let us get near him, but not to pet him. I tried but there was no trust on his part. Some of us fed him, and nobody cared more about him than my father.

After this one scene in which the hostile Indian brave, played by Ricardo Montalban, comes riding up to the village, a commotion broke out. I walked closer to the group that had gathered around the disturbance near the pond. I pushed through the crowd to see my father charging up to George Robotham, Gable's good-looking double and stuntman. My father, at five foot nine and 145 pounds, was no match for the six-foot-two, 195-pound stuntman. The first thing I heard my father say was "Goddammit, you're fired! Get the hell off my set!"

There was shock, disbelief, and a loud murmur going through the company. I heard that Robotham had shot-putted a large rock, hitting and killing the old beaver. I could see the lifeless form of our company mascot, lying just out of the water, near where the stuntman and my father were jawing.

At this point, Robotham wasn't saying anything. I saw him pull his right hand back with his fist clenched. Since he had already been fired, he was considering hitting my father. After all, what did he have to lose? Just when I thought it was going to happen, he opened his fist and lowered his arm to his side. He was not looking at my father, but at someone else in the crowd. Something else had changed his mind. I looked over and saw that Johnny Indrisano had stepped into view. He stood there, with his arms folded across his chest, staring directly at Robotham. Howard Koch had not seen the action, but was now running over to intercede. Dad turned away, told Koch that the stuntman was fired, and walked disgustedly from the scene. Koch uttered a few low-toned words to Robotham. The next day, Clark Gable had another double and stuntman.

Timmy came out to the locations fairly often, but his activities differed from mine. He did some fishing and listening to Johnny's stories, but mostly hung around the animals. He rode the horses but the mules were his favorites. There were several dozen mules at every location, and they were a mixture of colors, sizes, and ages. My brother gave time to all of them. Another actor liked to go mule riding with Timmy. Imagine the vision of Timmy, little for his eight years, riding the smallest mule next to Brooklyn, six feet, four inches and 250 pounds or more, riding the largest mule. I remember looking up from my fishing to see the two of them riding off in the distance. It worried me. Three weeks into production, Brooklyn, who had heard that a film was being shot there, had hitchhiked from the East Coast to Colorado. He found our location and limped up to my father, who was sitting in his director's chair, working on the script. What a sight! This giant of a man, with shoulder-length, dirt-matted hair, full black beard, filthy old clothes, and burlap bags tied on his feet.

I was sitting near my father at the time, and heard this homeless-looking tramp introduce himself. In a very theatrical tone, he pitched his dream of hitchhiking out to Hollywood to become a movie star. About this time, Howard Koch hustled over thinking this might be some kind of deranged mountain man. My father assured him everything was okay, and continued listening to the story. Dad began thumbing through the script, stopping at a certain page. Brooklyn stood there waiting for my father's reply. Dad found him a small, one-day role, but to help him financially, he put him on the picture for a full week. His one scene was to play a trapper who walks down a slight embankment to a shallow lake. He removes his fur cap, leaning over to fill it with water and drinking.

An arrow, from an Indian's bow, is shot into his back. He falls dead into the shallow water.

I used to watch him, from a safe distance, preparing for his scene. He would go off by himself, into the woods, and gesture, shout Shakespearean phrases, jump up and down in a manner that had me convinced he was, indeed, a crazy man. This is why I was concerned that this lunatic would go mule riding with my brother. When I mentioned it to dad, he said it was okay and not to worry about it. But I worried just the same.

Finally, the day came to shoot the scene. My father explained to Brooklyn what he wanted. "Walk down the bank, take off your hat, lean over, scoop up some water, take a drink, the arrow hits you, fall over and lay dead." The effects people—prop men in this era—fixed a wire into a false, wooden back, and strapped it onto the actor's back. Brooklyn's coat had a small hole in the back with the wire attached. At the right moment, the arrow would slingshot down the wire into the hole in the false back. When "Action!" was called, the take was perfect, until Brooklyn fell dead in the water. Instead of lying there waiting for dad to yell "Cut!," Brooklyn stood up and began to groan and bellow out many of the same Shakespearean phrases I had heard during his preparations. He continued his outcries while falling and splashing around in the waist-high water, then rising again, shouting and falling all the way across the lake—some one hundred yards to the other side. It was the longest death scene I ever saw. Of course, dad had the scene cut where he wanted it, and just let Brooklyn have his moment.

Finally, Brooklyn splashed back to the applause of the crew and other actors. When he reached shore, he bowed, thanked my father, and left for Hollywood. It wasn't too long before Brooklyn, who became Timothy Carey, starred in many films including Stanley Kubrick's *The Killing* (1956) with Sterling Hayden and *Paths of Glory* (1957) with Kirk Douglas, and Marlon Brando's *One-Eyed Jacks* (1961).

While Timmy and I were on the locations, the rest of the family followed their own pursuits. Mother, the former Busby Berkeley dancer, and Kitty, who had studied ballet since age five, took dance lessons from Alex Romero. Romero was a top MGM choreographer and was assigned to work on several ensemble dance numbers in this film, most notably a rather silly dance number featuring Gable dancing with Adolphe Menjou and the fur trappers. Considering the big MGM musicals of the era, this job was a walk in the park. Both mother and Kitty took the work seriously and remembered it always. My youngest brother, Mike, and sister, Cissy, were too young to be involved with much of the movie company activities, but mother made sure they had a good time. The Silverton Railroad was of special interest to all of us.

A whistle blast, a hiss of steam, and suddenly we were aboard the last of the legendary steam trains ready to relive the frontier days railroading in the Rockies. With the chug-chug of the engine and the clickety-clack of the wheels, we were out of the station and on our way to a wilderness only rails could reach. From the windows of our gently rocking coach, we saw the wonderland of towering pines and peaks, steep canyons and gorges, plunging waterfalls, rushing streams, meadows filled with grass and wildflowers. We saw deer and elk, as the woodlands are home to more than seventy kinds of animals. There were remnants of old mining camps that saw their share of failures and fortunes. Our eyes were glued to the windows as we took in the incredible sights of the San Juan National Forest and heard the electrifying sounds made by the Silverton Narrow Gauge Train.

My oldest sister, Pat, a red-haired, freckled-faced, high-octane, boy-crazy teenager, was going to turn sixteen on the location. On the day of her birthday, over the tent city public address system, the record "Sweet Sixteen" was played throughout the day with birthday wishes to William Wellman's daughter Patricia. This was quite embarrassing to Pat because she had told everybody—including her crushes—that she was eighteen. It seemed to me that everybody was on her crush list. Her very favorites were Ricardo Montalban and Bill Smith, the location auditor.

Montalban was her object of affection from afar. The closest she got to him was in the mineral pool at the El Encantado headquarters. Ricardo had polio as a youngster and needed therapy on his degenerative leg muscles. This therapy condition became more extreme when he was thrown from his horse, landing on his back, on a rock, during an action sequence. He never complained about his physical problems, just did his job as a true professional. I saw his pain and always admired and respected him.

The good-looking Bill Smith was my sister's number one. As location auditor, it was his duty to take care of the company money. He spent most of his time in an office at the El Encantado company headquarters. Pat looked for reasons to visit there. When he came to the location, she would show up on horseback, parading in front of him. This was a strong flirtation on my sister's part, but Smith was older and wiser and kept it strictly platonic.

J. Carroll Naish, a veteran character actor playing an Indian chief, had brought his daughter, Elaine, to Durango. She was Pat's age and they hit it off, spending a great deal of time together. They rode horses and drove the company jeep around the area. Pat was an excellent rider and often rode Steel, Gable's horse in the film. Steely, as we called him, was one of the great movie horses and the most popular star mount of the 1940s and 1950s. He was a flashy sorrel with a wide blaze, flowing mane, long forelock, and three stockings. His striking good looks and gentle nature made him an ideal movie horse. This magnificent stallion had more film credits than most of the actors in the picture. Steely had felt the weight of such icons as Gary Cooper, Joel McCrea, Gregory Peck, Randolph Scott, John Wayne, and, of course, Clark Gable.

Production completed on September 20, 1950. The seven weeks had come and gone quickly. For us kids and mom, too, we would always remember that fabulous summer with dad on location in Durango, Colorado. By the way, Timmy and I went home on the train.

Many of the cast and crew members thought this film was going to be one of Wellman's best: in gorgeous Technicolor, dazzling scenery, superb action, historical accuracy, colorful characters, and a first-class performance by Clark Gable. Even the Indians are treated with respect in this epic tale of the pioneer spirit.

In spite of all this, the film turns out to be one of the director's weaker entries. Dore Schary and his MGM executives would not support this offbeat Western, and it became the most butchered of all Wellman's films up to this point. While the director was out of town on the location of his next picture, there were numerous reedits and much restructuring, including a second negative cutting. Film footage from other pictures and stock shots from Disney movies were added. This resulted in such a mixed bag that the powers-that-be hired contract star Howard Keel to narrate the entire film. It was kept out of release for nearly a year.

Before *Across the Wide Missouri* premiered November 5, 1951, at New York's Loews State, and before Wellman's anger surfaced at this carnage, he had hit the trail with another Western. This project did not begin as a Schary preachment but as a Frank Capra declamation.

The year was 1950 and Frank Capra's dinner bell tinkled another fine meal with his neighborhood friends, the Wellmans. Dottie and Lu enjoyed listening to their husbands' stories, even the rantings. There were reminiscences of togetherness: fishing trips, spirited Ping-Pong and pool matches, birthday parties, and their kids' growing years.

Frank Capra had been the president of the Academy of Motion Picture Arts and Sciences for five years (1935–1939). He had been the head of the Screen Directors Guild, now the Directors Guild of America. Wellman was a founding member of the Directors Guild but stayed at arm's length

Dottie and Bill fished with the Capras at their June
Lake cabin and on the Klamath River. Here they are
with a steelhead trout, 1940s.

thereafter. He did not like to practice politics, but Frank did and when he
became serious, he got Bill's full attention. On this evening, Capra was
serious and disturbed.

The Hollywood film industry was going through a major transformation, signaling the end of the Golden Age. The studio system monopoly
was crumbling. The American dream, as built by the great moguls, was
being shattered. Although the 1940s brought big box office success and
1946 was a record-breaking year, a tidal wave of change swept over the
studio kings.

There were union problems and labor strikes. The Hollywood agents
had gained stronger positions to support their actor clients, bringing an

end to the moguls' supreme power over them. For decades, the studio bosses had owned the stars, forcing seven-year contracts, six-day work-weeks with long hours and little time away from the cameras.

In 1945, star Olivia de Havilland challenged the moguls' power in the courts and won. Now the agents could write nonexclusive, short-term contracts with better working conditions, time off, and profit participa-tion. The writers and directors would soon follow.

World War II had brought a change in movie audience appetites. They wanted to see films with a harder edge; pictures revealing social injustice, bigotry, and racial prejudice. This attitude gave rise to a new type that became known as film noir—expressing the darker, seamier side of life.

In 1948, even the government took arms against the kingpins and their studio empires with an antitrust lawsuit known as the Paramount decree. The Supreme Court ruled that the studio chiefs must divest themselves of their theater chains, thereby releasing their stranglehold on distribution. The architects of the glamour factories were hard pressed to keep up with these rapid changes.

If all this wasn't enough, the country became gripped with a Red Scare. The House Committee on Un-American Activities became a federal gov-ernment witch hunt to find subversive forces in Hollywood. Congress pointed fingers at suspected communists and radical sympathizers and, with the help of the moguls, created the blacklisting of many in the Hol-lywood community.

The final curtain came down on the moguls' dreamworld with a small-ish, talking box known as television. TV audiences, who could watch entertainment in the comfort of their homes, began to stay away from movie theaters. The transformation of old Hollywood was complete; the once proud and prosperous Hollywood of the Golden Age was disappear-ing. The movies would find a way to live anew—but not with the great moguls.

Back to the Capra-Wellman dinner gathering. When Frank finished his after-dinner address of the past, present, and future of the film indus-try, he wanted to know what his friend was going to do about it. Wellman responded quickly, "I'm going to make another picture." The three-time Oscar-winning director was plenty irritated about a pet project rejected by the studios. "Billy, I've got a story for your next film. They won't let me do a Western," lamented Capra. "But they'll let you and I'll give you my story. I know you'll make a hell of a picture."

Wellman loved the story and sold it to Schary and MGM. Capra's *Pioneer Women* had a title change to *Westward the Women*, starring Robert

Westward the Women (1952): Robert Taylor and the women: (left to right) Lenore Lonergan, Renata Vanni, Marilyn Erskine, Denise Darcel, Julie Bishop, and Beverly Dennis

Taylor, *Battleground*'s Denise Darcel, and a hundred women. Wellman's constant pursuit of the offbeat brought this radical 1851 Western adventure to the screen, and it would be his tribute, his eulogy to the indomitable women who died blazing new trails.

Robert Taylor's Buck Wyatt leads a wagon train of mail-order brides two thousand miles to California and the men who helped settle the West. The women, from many ethnic backgrounds, must survive Indian attacks, flash floods, sandstorms, prairie fires, stampeding cattle—all manner of hazards in the hope of finding a better life. These courageous women, clutching the photos of their unknown husbands, must endure this perilous passage with the knowledge that one in three will never see the Promised Land.

In the opening sequence, John McIntire as Roy Whitman, the sponsor of the trip, realizes that only the strongest of the strong will arrive in his valley. He tells the men, "One thing I can and will promise. They'll be good women. Make sure you'll treat them with patience, understanding, and honesty. They will be your fortune." Buck, the wagon master, has no place for a "good" woman in his life and tells Whitman, "There's only two things in this world that scares me. And a good woman's both!" But by the end of the arduous journey, his respect for and appreciation of them leads him to take the hand of Denise Darcel's Fifi Danon, who had loved him from first sight.

Wellman had surely found a story that brought into focus his admiration of strong, independent women. In *Westward the Women*, these women are willing to sacrifice their lives for a man they have never met and a way of life they have never known.

Echoing Buck's warning speech to the mail-order brides at sign-up, Wellman told his movie women that they should reconsider signing on for this extremely difficult, no-frills production. "There will be no prima donnas on my picture," said the director.

Following the same plan assigned the actors on *The Story of G.I. Joe* and *Battleground*, Wellman put his actresses through a two-week training course. They were taught to ride, shoot, use bullwhips, handle mule teams and horse-drawn covered wagons. Their teachers were the few male stuntmen on the picture and the many stuntwomen. The director hired every working stuntwoman in Hollywood. He gave some of them acting roles. These were the trick riders, rodeo performers, and expert horsewomen who stunt-doubled the female stars of the day, from Shirley Temple and Esther Williams to Jane Russell, Maureen O'Hara, Lana Turner, and Marilyn Monroe.

These pioneering stuntwomen were Polly Burson, Opal Ernie, Evelyn Finley, Donna Hall, Edith Happy, Lucille House, Sharon and Shirley Lucas, Stevie Myers, and Ann Roberts. Evelyn Finley, a former equestrian rider, had doubled Maria Elena Marques in *Across the Wide Missouri*. She had a reputation for being a far better rider than most of the male cowboy actors.

Polly Burson, from a rodeo family and a renowned rodeo trick rider, accumulated hundreds of Western and adventure film credits during her long career. This slim and athletic horsewoman became an icon, stunt-doubling for Dale Evans, Betty Hutton, Sophia Loren, Barbara Stanwyck, Doris Day, and many others. Edith Happy's daughter, Bonnie, president of the United Stuntwomen's Association, told the *Los Angeles Times* on April 16, 2006, "She [Burson] had integrity. She never said she could do something that she couldn't do. But there was very little she couldn't do. . . . She was the first female stunt coordinator on William Wellman's 1951 film *Westward the Women*."

Historian and author Mollie Gregory, in her book *Guts and Grace: The Untold Story of Stuntwomen in the Movies*, writes about an interview with Bonnie, who said, "The director, Mr. Wellman, didn't choose her [Burson]. There were so many women on that show they decided to name her as their stunt coordinator, and he agreed. Polly took care of the women's stunts, and the few men on the show took care of theirs. So she was the first woman coordinator. Polly was a pistol."

Wellman liked telling the story of four of his stuntwomen in a bar during the film's location shooting. The long day's work was over, they had eaten and were enjoying a nightcap before retiring. A group of male locals noticed them, moved over next to them, and began mouthing off about their dislike of movie people.

One in particular started to tell everybody within earshot that the son of a bitch who was directing this all-female crap was a no-good fairy and ought to be kicked out of town on his ass. The nearest stuntwoman looked up at him and asked very politely if he would mind repeating that. "Sure, I'll do anything for you, little lady." He repeated it and just as he got to the word "fairy," a strange thing happened. He screamed and crumpled to the floor with an agonized groan. He cried and whimpered and rolled around on the floor, and after another loud-mouthed one screamed and hit the floor, and a third, and a fourth, the other two ran like hell out of that bar. The four ladies paid for their drinks and sauntered out to bed. "One would have thought nothing had happened," said Wellman, "except of course the writhing hicks tortured with pain, hanging on to their well belted testicles. Just a little word from one of the girls as they disappeared in the night, 'Doggone it, I broke a fingernail.'"

Production began April 9, 1951, in Surprise Valley, near Kanab, Utah. The picturesque desert landscape provided every sort of visual element written in the script—stretches of grassland, desert wasteland, deep canyons, a large river with streams connecting. The director asked his cinematographer, William Mellor, to refrain from using filters as much as possible in order to give the picture a more natural and parched appearance.

Robert Taylor and his director had an enduring friendship dating back to *Small Town Girl* (1936). "I was very fond of Bob on and off the screen," said Wellman. "He was the only man I ever knew who could drink scotch and sodas and eat chocolates at the same time." Their friendship continued to grow during the Moraga Spit and Polish motorcycle days of the 1940s.

On *Westward the Women,* Taylor arrived in his own plane with his own pilot at the small airport in Kanab. He wanted to fly to location each day with the director aboard. Regrettably, there was no airstrip at the Surprise Valley location. Wellman fixed that. "We found a very smooth area and I got the studio greensmen to get rid of the bushes and high grass," said the director, "and when they got through rolling and leveling it all up, we had a helluva runway. A desert airport unnamed." Wellman took care of that problem as well.

The small town of Kanab afforded little nightlife for the company. The star and the director shot pool on many of the evenings. They were equally proficient and little money changed hands. One particular evening, Henry Nakamura, the diminutive Japanese actor, was invited to partake. The star and the director warned him that he might be a little lighter money-wise at the end of the night's festivities. "Mr. Nakamura," said Wellman, "who had difficulty getting up to the table, making almost all his shots on tiptoe, beat the hell out of us, he was pure magic and wonderful to watch. He was so good that the few mistakes he made were punctuated by his version of 'Oh shit,' which was nothing like ours, it had the high oriental pitch and pleading tone to it that was almost a cry . . . it didn't sound dirty."

Wellman and Taylor were fascinated by the sound of Nakamura's "Oh shit," and waited for more of his mistakes, just to hear his vocalizing of the oft-used American expression. Later that evening, while the director was in bed, he tried to emulate the high-pitched sound but couldn't quite do it properly. Then it struck him. He conferred with Taylor and his pilot on their flight to location the next day. "Bob," enthused Wellman, "I got a name for the airport, sponsored by Henry Nakamura and named after a very old Indian chief—The Oshitawkwa Airport." They laughed their approval. Wellman put the company painters to work and on the edge of the runway, in large letters, for all planes in the area to see and on all the air maps of that sector, the name of an old, old Indian chief . . . *Oshitawkwa Airport*.

The film trumpeted many of the director's chosen ones: the great horse Steel carried Robert Taylor to one of his best performances; Johnny Indrisano's *Across the Wide Missouri* roommates, stuntmen Frank McGrath and Terry Wilson; George Chandler (Mackerel Face) in his seventeenth Wellman picture; Frankie Darro (Jean's Man), the director's *Wild Boys of the Road* star; cinematographer William Mellor, who shined on six of Wellman's films. Last, but not least, a small black-and-white mongrel dog successfully traverses the two-thousand-mile pilgrimage to the Promised Land.

Production was completed in May and the 116-minute film premiered December 31, 1951, at New York's Capitol Theatre to good box office returns and reviews. *New York Journal American*, January 2, 1952: "Striking outdoor settings and vigorous direction by William Wellman make it an interesting departure from the conventional Western." The director was well pleased with the picture and counted it among his favorites. It was one of his best Westerns and would be an excellent film to remake today.

After *Westward the Women*, Wellman took time off and was home for the christening of another daughter, Margaret, on September 7, 1951. The red hair of his mother continued to glow on three of his four daughters, including little Maggie. Her dad was still in the naming mood after Oshi-tawkwa. He and Dottie had always chosen family middle names for their children but this time the director made a different choice—born on the seventh day of the month and the seventh child, Maggie's middle name would be . . . lucky number "Seven."

19

GOODBYE MGM,
HELLO JOHN WAYNE

In January of 1952, at one of Dore Schary's family gatherings, he pitched another one of his "film intelligence reports." It was a story of interracial passion, prejudice, and patriotism. Wellman, who harbored no prejudices, saw the picture as an unconventional love story and a departure from his other films. What he didn't like was the growing suspicion that Schary was using him as a kind of studio tool for his message pictures.

The director's ability to make quality films from questionable material had been a part of his résumé for decades. No one at MGM could do more with less money, which reduced the studio boss's gambles and, in the case of *The Next Voice You Hear . . .*, brought profitability.

In the early 1950s, MGM was still developing and releasing some fine product. There were successful films bringing Academy Award consideration, even Oscars like *The Bad and the Beautiful, Father of the Bride, Ivanhoe, King Solomon's Mines, Pat and Mike, Singin' in the Rain, Quo Vadis . . .* but none of those important films was being offered to Wellman. The more he looked at the situation, the more disenchanted he became. Concealing his second thoughts, he accepted Schary's new assignment.

My Man and I, from the story "A Letter to the President" by John Fante and Jack Leonard, concerns the trouble and strife of a Mexican immigrant farmworker, Chu Chu Ramirez (Ricardo Montalban), who is proud of his new American citizenship and a congratulatory letter from the president of the United States. In an attempt to improve his lot in life,

Chu Chu battles intolerance and extreme hardship. During the ninety-eight-minute picture, he is:

- Cheated out of his paycheck.
- Jilted by his disillusioned, alcoholic girlfriend, Nancy (Shelley Winters).
- Jailed for trying to collect his money.
- Captured after escaping from jail to comfort Nancy, who had attempted suicide.
- Assaulted by his boss's vengeful wife (Claire Trevor).
- Framed for the attempted murder of his boss (Wendell Corey).
- Convicted in the courts.
- Imprisoned.

Through all the heartache and adversity, Chu Chu never gives up, never wavers from trying to do the right thing. Even after his release from prison, he goes to the hospital to see his sick, problem-plagued Nancy, who begs him to leave her. But he won't abandon her, saying, "We never say goodbye when both of us breathe in and out" and "You've got to get well. You've got to try." Then, she answers, "All right, I'll try. You won't be alone anymore, Chu Chu. Oh how I'll try."

Schary's message is strong. Chu Chu Ramirez embodies the best virtues in Americans and remains a working-class hero. Filming on the picture began March 24 and completed April 21. The premiere was held September 5, 1952, at New York's Palace Theatre.

Although the film is well made with fine performances by Ricardo Montalban, Shelley Winters, Claire Trevor, and Wendell Corey, it didn't rise to the profitable heights of *The Next Voice You Hear. . . .* Wellman felt the picture was an okay effort, nothing special. He did like working with Montalban again and Claire Trevor became a favorite. Shelley Winters, a student and teacher at the Actors Studio in New York, had trouble conforming to her director's one-take philosophy, wanting more time to perfect her performance—she didn't get it but delivers solid work just the same. She became a two-time Academy Award winner in a five-decade-plus career.

Wendell Corey and William Wellman had more serious problems. Corey, later known for his role as Jimmy Stewart's detective pal in *Rear Window* (1954), rubbed the director the wrong way. In an important dialogue scene with his wife, played by Claire Trevor, Corey kept blowing his lines. When the camera favored him, he was letter-perfect. When the camera favored her, he was anything but. This author, at fifteen years old, was present when his father exploded, and a hidden bystander to the following scene.

The director led the costar around behind the interior set and away from all but two prying eyes of the company. Corey was six feet, two inches. Wild Bill at five-nine shoved his forefinger into the actor's chest and said, "Listen, you son of a bitch. You better stop this bullshit or I'm gonna put you in the hospital. I'll recast your part if I have to." After a moment of consideration, Corey, in a surly voice, said, "All right." They went back to the set, the scene was shot, and there were no flubs. From then on, the actor and the director spoke sparingly to each other but Corey's performance on screen is first-rate.

During Wellman's more than four-decade career, there were few friendships with producers. Honorable mention goes to Lucien Hubbard, the director's producer on *Wings* (1927), *So Big* (1932), and *Midnight Mary* (1933); a writer on *The Star Witness* (1931); and a minor role actor on *The Story of G.I. Joe* (1945). This friendship was work-related only.

Darryl Zanuck's eighteen-year relationship saw congestion, blind alleys, and potholes, but was driven by mutual respect and admiration at their workplace. Brimming with respect, admiration, and family fellowship for thirty-seven years—until his passing—David O. Selznick wins Wellman's Life Achievement Award.

Dore Schary and Wellman's comradeship flourished for a scant three years and yet it was meaningful, inspirational, warm, and involved both families. In the fall of 1952, however, the benevolent river ran dry. After all the success of *Battleground*, which did so much to promote Dore Schary's comet-rise to the top of the MGM ladder, he, in turn, gave little support to the director's following film, *The Happy Years*, later destroyed *Across the Wide Missouri*, while pushing on his director three of his "educational" films, *The Next Voice You Hear . . .* , *It's a Big Country*, and *My Man and I*.

The closer their friendship became, the more Wellman was drawn into Schary's world of liberalism and politics. It was common knowledge around Hollywood that the MGM production chief was one of the industry's most liberal thinkers. During the war, he had given lectures on the causes of racial and religious tolerance. He was at the forefront of producing pictures with strong messages. He supported ultra-liberal causes.

Wellman, on the other hand, was not a cause person and, as we know, not in love with politics. He was a registered Republican who occasionally crossed the aisle if he saw a better man. He enjoyed pushing people's buttons by saying, "Hell, I voted for Harry Truman over Thomas Dewey."

In point of fact, he later wrote, "My politics are kind of eccentric. I am a Republican sometimes and a Democrat others. When Dewey and Truman were battling it out, I didn't cast a vote. I couldn't stand either one." He went on to say, "I abhor extreme rightists and leftists."

The final blow ending the Schary-Wellman togetherness came at a social gathering. What began as one of Miriam and Dore's fine dinner parties became a speechmaking, hand-clapping fund-raiser for the Democratic candidate for president, Adlai Stevenson. The former governor of Illinois was an accomplished politician, an intellectual, an eloquent orator, and nearly everybody's choice at the party. This affair was crowded with some of the most left-wing luminaries in Hollywood like Danny Kaye, Joseph Cotten, José Ferrer, Betty Garrett.

Bill and Dottie were the only Republicans and the only unmotivated political people. They sat quietly while one party guest after another stood, spoke about, and applauded the man they believed would enter the White House after Harry Truman packed his bags.

Negative remarks and jokes concerning the Republican choice filled the air. That candidate was one of America's heroes of World War II, the Supreme Commander Allied Expeditionary Force in Europe, with no political experience, Dwight D. Eisenhower. For a time during this election year, there was another war hero who might challenge Ike on the Republican side—five-star general Douglas MacArthur. After his "old soldiers never die; they just fade away" speech to Congress, there was massive public adulation and expectations that he would run for president. He claimed no political ambitions and when he gave the keynote address at the Republican convention, he endorsed the senator from Ohio, Robert Taft.

As the Schary convention-like atmosphere became more intense, Wild Bill exploded. He had heard enough politics for this or any evening. He leaped to his feet and began marching around the room shouting over the din, "MacArthur! MacArthur! MacArthur! General Douglas MacArthur for president!" He literally picked up a shocked Dottie and stomped out of the party, leaving the astonished Democrats behind. He never set foot in Dore Schary's home again or the MGM studio, even after being offered a new three-year contract with raises in salary.

History tells us that Adlai Stevenson, although an appealing and capable candidate, was no match for the popular Eisenhower, who became the thirty-fourth president of the United States and was reelected for a second term. Both Wellman and MacArthur faded away.

John Wayne in *Island in the Sky*

The Wellman children were not pleased with their father. The Schary association had been special. At least once a month, they were invited to the Schary home to see movies in Dore's private theater. Wellman never cared for such a room in his house. The Wellman brood and three Schary kids, Jill, Joy, and Jeb, got along just fine, and being able to go to a home theater that supplied popcorn, candy, cookies, soda pop, and ice cream at no charge and as much as you wanted was very appealing to the youngsters. Now that the producer-director togetherness had come to an end, the Wellman kids were unhappy with daddy.

Dore Schary was a good man. He was an elegant gentleman, hardworking, intelligent, well-dressed, and extremely personable. He was an exceptional writer and producer. His downfall was his message pictures, which meant more to him than to movie audiences. He always appreciated and gave credit to Wellman. In the director's *Westward the Women* script he wrote, "For William the man who I love very much and respect always and admire constantly—Dore." In Schary's book *The Case History of a Movie*, he signed, "For Bill, if it wasn't for Bill and all he did this book never would have been written. My thanks and my love always—Dore."

The Wellman clan was vacationing at one of their favorite spots, the picturesque resort of Ojai Valley Inn and Country Club. This legendary place resides in an atmosphere of casual elegance nestled in the peaceful, scenic Ojai Valley, just north of Ventura. Today it's a world-class spa, but in the 1940s and 1950s the favored activities were golf, on the still exquisite championship course, swimming, tennis, and horseback riding—the Wellman kids rode the hills and valleys, took hayrides to barbecues in the nearby meadows. In that era, the resort served as a hideaway for stars like Clark Gable, Irene Dunne, Judy Garland, Ronald Reagan, Lana Turner, and Loretta Young.

Although the inn afforded luxury accommodations, the Wellmans preferred the togetherness of one of the two-bedroom cabins that lined the fairway leading to the inn's main building. The two oldest daughters, Pat and Kitty, slept in one bedroom; mom, dad, and the youngest child at the time in the second bedroom. The other children slumbered in pull-outs and cots in the living room next to the kitchenette.

On this trip in the fall of 1952, an enterprising literary agent, Lester Linsk, heard about Wellman's departure from MGM and took the hour-and-fifteen-minute drive to Ojai with a client's book for the man he believed was best qualified to direct the movie version. He found his director having lunch on the patio after a round of golf. Wellman knew about the author of aviation stories Ernest K. Gann, and was immediately interested in his book, *Island in the Sky*. He read the book and wanted to make the picture. Linsk had some ideas about the casting for the lead role of Captain Dooley, the pilot of the transport plane that crash-lands in the frozen wastelands of Labrador, and struggles to keep his crew alive while waiting for rescue.

Based on a true incident from Gann's experiences as a pilot during World War II, the suspenseful story of the desperate battle for survival shifts back and forth from the search to the men on the glacial tundra with radio problems, little food, and barely any protective clothing.

In the early 1950s, a few of the major Hollywood stars began breaking from the still powerful studio system and forming their own production companies. Burt Lancaster, Kirk Douglas, and John Wayne were the vanguard of this movement. For the star role in the picture, Wellman wanted the young man he directed in small roles in *Central Airport* (1933) and *College Coach* (1933), Marion "Duke" Morrison, aka John Wayne. A meeting was set up at Wayne-Fellows Productions.

Robert Fellows, Wayne's producing partner, could not believe the reunion jubilation of these two grown men, jumping around, hugging each other, laughing, reminiscing, and joking like a couple of college fraternity brothers. "It was a sight to behold," said the producer. Wayne was as excited about the project as Wellman. Wayne-Fellows purchased the property and signed Wellman in November of 1952. Production began in December with locations at Donner Lake in Truckee, California. Shooting was completed on February 26, 1953, at the Warner Bros. studio in Burbank. Warners would be the distributor for *Island in the Sky* and all the Wayne-Wellman pictures to come.

The Wellman team put together a fine cast of featured players to support the Duke in one of his finest performances—seasoned veterans like Lloyd Nolan, Walter Abel, Sean McClory, Allyn Joslyn, Harry Carey, Jr., Gordon Jones, Regis Toomey, Paul Fix,

Writer Ernest K. Gann and Wellman on the location of *Island in the Sky* (1953)

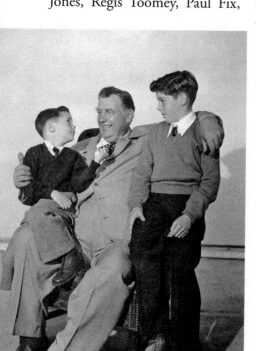

Wellman's sons Mike (left) and Tim play Andy Devine's sons in *Island in the Sky.*

Frank Fenton, and Fess Parker, later to be known as Davy Crockett and Daniel Boone.

They joined a group of Wellman favorites: Andy Devine, as rescue pilot Willie Moon with his two children played by Wellman sons Timmy and Mike; James Arness, from *Battleground,* in a much larger role as another rescue pilot, "Mac" McMullen; Darryl Hickman, *The Happy Years* star, as McMullen's radioman, Swanson; former cowboy star Bob Steele as Wilson; Wally Cassell, from *G.I. Joe,* again shining brightly as Dooley's radioman, D'Annunzia; *Our Gang* comedy star Carl "Alfalfa" Switzer as Hopper; George Chandler, in his twentieth Wellman film, as Rene; Johnny Indrisano, without roommates, as another radioman; and a major television star of the future.

Wellman had taken a liking to college basketball and picked out one of UCLA's players for future stardom, "Touch" Ohanian. The director helped him with a small role in the film. Not too many years later, the renamed Mike Connors became TV's *Mannix*.

Wellman was so married to this picture that he cast himself as narrator, and always counted the film among his best achievements. The 109-minute picture premiered September 3, 1953, in Los Angeles. *Variety*, December 31, 1952, wrote, "The Wayne-Fellows production was scripted with care by Gann for aviation aficionado William A. Wellman who gives it sock handling to make it a solid piece of drama." David Mamet, Pulitzer Prize–winning playwright and revered filmmaker, said, "*Island in the Sky* is one of the great flying films."

Ernest Gann was extremely pleased with his first movie experience from screenplay to technical adviser to finished production to critical and audience applause. He wrote about his director, "There was elegance and dash about Wellman and it seemed to me he might have fitted in very well as one of Napoleon's dragoons or as a Dumas musketeer. Wellman was an emotional child, mercurial in temper and unreasonable to the point of arrogance. But he was also exciting and inspiring and capable of true humility. Soon, his voice alternately booming and plaintive, he so captured my enthusiasm that I agreed 'we' were about to father a film masterpiece."

Island in the Sky was a hit and got the Wayne-Wellman association off to a flying start. It took little time for Gann to toss his next novel on the production table. It was called *The High and the Mighty*. The story details the experiences and interactions of the passengers and crew aboard a flight from Honolulu to San Francisco. Halfway across a turbulent ocean is the point of no return and one of the Trans-Orient-Pacific (TOBAC) DC-4 props catches fire, causing a fuel leak and hours of fear and trembling for all on board.

Before boarding and in flashbacks we learn the backgrounds, relationships, and personalities of the travelers and their crew. They act like a group of everyday people until the fireworks begin. Under the duress of the precarious predicament, they bare their imperfections.

The captain of the flight, John Sullivan, suffers from the fear of flight that sometimes strikes pilots after logging many hours in the air. When the engine fire occurs, he begins to prepare for what he believes will be the ditching of his aircraft in a stormy sea on a cold, dark night.

The seasoned copilot, "Whistling" Dan Roman, is haunted by a flight he piloted that crashed, killing the passengers, including his wife and son. When Sullivan loses his courage and dives for the deep blue, Roman slaps him around, taking control of the plane until the pilot regains his composure. The damaged airliner lands safely with only two of its four engines still running, and nearly empty of fuel.

Wellman heard Gann's story first and pitched it to Wayne and Fellows. Duke purchased the property on the spot paying the writer $55,000 for the story and screenplay plus 10 percent of the profits. Wayne agreed to give Wellman his $100,000 salary with an additional 30 percent of profits on the condition that the film be shot in CinemaScope—the new wide-screen projection process using an anamorphic lens to widen the frame of the regular 35mm film.

The director was concerned about the large and unwieldy Cinema-Scope camera, but felt comfortable with his *Island in the Sky* cinematographer, Archie Stout, a longtime Wayne favorite and Wellman's cameraman on *Young Eagles* (1930) and *Beau Geste* (1939). This would be Stout's final film. After a more than thirty-year career with over a hundred films, a heart attack ended the Oscar winner's life in 1954.

When Jack Warner was apprised of this project, he told Wayne and Wellman that it was insanity to think that movie audiences would sit for over a hundred minutes watching people talk inside an airplane. Wellman and Wayne begged to differ, and the mogul, not wanting to lose other John Wayne pictures, financed and distributed the film.

Gann and Wellman had no problems during the writing stage of *Island in the Sky*. Wellman made the ex-pilot the technical director and they worked well together. *The High and the Mighty* was a different situation. The two fought over the screenplay, nearly coming to blows. The novelist wanted to make changes and improve on his original material. Wellman, as was his custom, demanded he stay true to the book. The director told the writer, "Listen, I am going to get hold of Gann who wrote this novel and tell him what this silly son of a bitch who is writing the script is trying to do." The final screenplay mirrors the novel in story, character description, even much of the dialogue.

On *The High and the Mighty*, Gann was not allowed to be techni-cal adviser or involved in the actual production—except for the writ-ing. After the success of *Island*, Gann felt that he deserved to be part of the team in every aspect of production—casting, locations, flying, even postproduction. To Wellman, this meant having someone else sitting in a director's chair on his set. It was not going to happen.

This directorial problem later attached itself to John Wayne. Wild Bill and Duke had a serious confrontation on the set in front of the crew. The director told the interfering star, "Okay, we'll switch roles and you'll be just as silly back here directing this picture as I'll be in front of the camera with that screwy voice of yours and that fairy walk." Wayne accepted this harsh expression and both he and his director went about their own business. As for the writer, Gann later wrote, "Just before production began, I saw the covers of the newly typed script. I had labored hard and long on both the book and the scenario—not a word of either version was written by anyone else. The story, based on a true event, was part of my flying life. Now, in bold letters I read: William A. Wellman's *The High and the Mighty*. I knew then the chilling ways of Hollywood and left town immediately."

The High and the Mighty became one of the most difficult pictures for the director to cast. It started out rather well with both Wellman and Wayne wanting Spencer Tracy for the lead role of Dan Roman. Tracy accepted and casting moved on.

Although the film has an ensemble cast with at least nineteen other top roles and a dozen or more standout parts of shorter duration, the two best female characters are Sally McKee and May Holst. McKee is an aging beauty queen who fears rejection from a mail-order fiancé she has been courting with an eight-year-old photograph. Holst is a blond woman of the world trying desperately to appear young and exciting.

Wellman offered these choice characterizations to many leading ladies old enough to be convincing. Rejections came back from Joan Crawford (forty-eight years old), Dorothy McGuire (thirty-seven), *Roxie Hart*'s Ginger Rogers (forty-two), Wellman's find for *The Light That Failed*, Ida Lupino (thirty-six), even all-time favorites Barbara Stanwyck (forty-six) and Loretta Young (forty-one). Possibly, the roles did not appear "big" enough and/or the stars were not ready to bare their maturity for all to see.

Eventually, for the role of May Holst, Wellman chose his *My Man and I* costar Claire Trevor (forty-three), an Oscar winner for *Key Largo* (1948) and a Wayne costar in *Stagecoach* (1939); for the role of Sally McKee, Jan Sterling (thirty-two). She was best known for playing hard and determined characters but Wellman saw her sympathetic, nicer side. Casting the pivotal role of Captain Sullivan had its twists and turns as well. Scores of leading men were after this part like Richard Egan and Ronald Reagan,

Robert Stack wins the role of Captain Sullivan, the
pilot of the damaged aircraft, seen here with the welfare
teacher and Mike Wellman, who plays the youngster
caught up in the aviation drama, *The High and the
Mighty* (1954).

but John Wayne wanted his friend Bob Cummings, who was a pilot, a
star, and equally adept at comedies and dramas. Initially, Wellman okay'd
the choice. In Wellman's long career, he had never hired a leading man
that he had met and rejected . . . until now.

William Shiffrin, a persuasive Hollywood agent, talked the director
into meeting his client, Robert Stack. Stack was not a pilot. He was a
handsome leading man, well educated from a wealthy family, a polo
player and a national champion skeet shooter who had set two world
records. Wellman did not see the qualities he was looking for in Stack, so
he passed. Shiffrin, however, did not give up easily. He pressed for one
more meeting. He sent a constant stream of telegrams until the director
finally set one more get-together.

The agent told his client, "Stop being Mister Nice Guy. Dress down,
don't shave and act tougher—sell yourself to Wild Bill!" This second

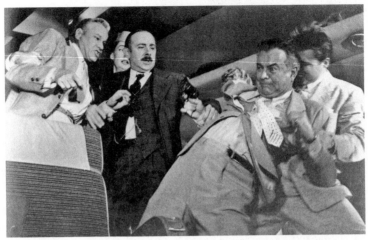

David Brian, John Qualen, and John Smith (behind Sidney Blackmer)
attempt to restrain the gunman in *The High and the Mighty* (1954).

encounter turned the tables on John Wayne and Bob Cummings. Wellman hired Stack, telling him, "You better do a helluva good job in this
picture or Wayne will kill both of us." When Stack first appeared on the
set, Duke walked over to greet him saying, "Mr. Cummings, I presume."

Wellman put together an impressive list of supporting players. For the
major roles: Laraine Day (Lydia Rice), John Howard (Howard Rice), Phil
Harris (Ed Joseph), Robert Newton (Gustav Pardee), Julie Bishop (Lillian Pardee), David Brian (Ken Childs), Paul Kelly (Flaherty), Sidney
Blackmer (Humphrey Agnew), John Qualen (Jose Locota), Doe Avedon
(Miss Spalding, stewardess), William Campbell (Hobie Wheeler), Joy
Kim (Dorothy Chen), Wally Brown (Lenny Wilby, navigator), newcomers Karen Sharpe and John Smith (the honeymooners). Also returning
were *Island in the Sky* alumni Paul Fix (Frank Briscoe), Ann Doran (Mrs.
Joseph), Regis Toomey (Garfield), Carl Switzer (Ensign Keim), Robert Keys (Lieutenant Mowbray), and, naturally, George Chandler (Ben
Sneed). Douglas Fowley (Alsop, the Hawaii ticket taker) stands out in his
fourth Wellman film.

There was one more *Island* alumnus. The director, with Gann's
approval, added another character to the story, a six-year-old boy who
sleeps through the ordeal, waking when safely on the ground. Wellman
cast his son Mike. The director called him "the best actor I ever had. He
went to sleep when I wanted, and woke up when we wanted it. He was
perfect."

On occasion, Wellman would discuss a role he was casting with the family and they would make suggestions. This author remembers the only time that he took their ideas to heart. They were sitting around the dinner table when he mentioned a casting problem for the lead heavy. Dottie and the older kids had recently seen a television show and were impressed with the bad guy, Sidney Blackmer. Wellman had used him in the small part of Teddy Roosevelt in *Buffalo Bill* and a larger role as Rosalind Russell's husband in *The President Vanishes* and immediately liked the idea. Sidney Blackmer never knew that it was Dottie and the kids who had cast him as Humphrey Agnew in *The High and the Mighty*.

Just when all the casting had fallen into place, Spencer Tracy backed out. A number of reasons circulated throughout the industry: his declining health problems were an issue; the ensemble nature of the cast might diminish his performance; he was an ardent Democrat and wanted nothing to do with the staunchly conservative John Wayne; friends told him it would be an ego-busting experience with Wellman and Wayne; maybe some of the Wellman-Tracy feud of the past still smoldered. Regardless, he was out and no one was playing the lead as the film's start date loomed nearer and nearer.

Jack Warner was ready to pull the plug at a moment's notice. He and many of Hollywood's ruling class believed this soap opera in the sky was destined for failure, but Wayne and Wellman would not back down. That being the case, Warner threw his candidate for the lead into the fray . . . Alan Ladd. He told Wellman that since the big success of *Shane*, audiences and the industry were seeing the mostly B picture star in a whole different light. "Of all the stars under studio contracts," said the mogul, "Alan Ladd is the only one who never made a picture that lost money."

Wellman was not impressed because he had another candidate in mind. After several get-togethers, the director talked his coproducer into playing "Whistling" Dan Roman—John Wayne rides again! But in this picture, he would not ride to the rescue as a Western action hero, but play an over-the-hill copilot commanding an endangered airliner. The iconic superhero John Wayne would become . . . a patriarch of the sky.

Filming took place from November 25, 1953, to January 11, 1954, on the Goldwyn lot in Hollywood and the Warner Bros. soundstages in Burbank. Many of the scenes showing the airliner in flight were filmed at Warner Bros. using a large-scale miniature. Other locations included Glendale Grand Central Air Terminal and Oakland International Airport. Second unit work was done in Hawaii and San Francisco.

Most of the large cast were forced to sit in cramped seats in the makeshift passenger cabin for hours at a time over many weeks. Even when they were not in the scene, the wide-angle CinemaScope lens would include them in the rows away from the camera. They were subjected to extreme temperature changes, as the soundstage was not heated until the hot lights were turned on for filming. The actors rarely complained but later admitted to a dismal experience.

It is a curious fact that many great films—*Gone with the Wind, Casablanca, Citizen Kane* to name a few—were burdened with serious troubles before, during, and after production. There were script dilemmas, rejections by actors, production shutdowns, multiple directors, even a fired director, and, in the case of *Citizen Kane*, the almost burning of its negative.

The High and the Mighty was loaded with complications on many levels, but overriding them was William Wellman's command of the material and the production that kept the show on course and arriving at its destination as a classic American film. The 147-minute picture premiered in Hollywood at Grauman's Egyptian Theatre on May 27, 1954, with general release on July 3, 1954. Although the CinemaScope format limited the number of theaters, it ranked number one at the box office and set a record for the "fastest return of negative cost," recouping its production cost of $1.47 million within two months. The film grossed $8.5 million.

Not all the pundits praised the picture, saying things like "an airplane soap opera," "the novel and the movie have the same weaknesses . . . every passenger is a character with a story," "All are fabricated characters," and "an unbelievably long trip!" Most of the reviews however were exceptionally favorable. Jack Moffitt of *The Hollywood Reporter*, May 26, 1954, wrote, "*THE HIGH AND THE MIGHTY* RANKS WITH ALL-TIME GREAT Productions: Wellman's Direction, Topnotch Acting, Tiomkin Score Key Wayne-Fellows Pic . . . high, wide and handsome in every sense of the word. This is one of the great pictures of our time. . . . For this is one of those films that the screen cannot live without. . . . John Wayne performs a masterpiece of restrained acting." Duke never thought much of his performance, but critics and audiences alike were applauding.

The film received six Academy Award nominations. Wellman was nominated for Best Director, receiving a nomination from the Directors Guild as well. He lost the Oscar to Elia Kazan (*On the Waterfront*). Both Jan Sterling and Claire Trevor, in their much passed-on roles, received Academy Award nominations, losing to Eva Marie Saint from *Waterfront*. A Best Film Editing nomination went to Ralph Dawson, Best Music/ Original Song to Dimitri Tiomkin and Ned Washington, and an Oscar was presented to Tiomkin for his musical score.

With all its many achievements, the film's greatest triumph was in its legacy. For it would be a CinemaScope bridge between 1932's Best Picture Academy Award–winning, all-star production *Grand Hotel*, and a new genre of all-star disaster-themed epics. It was the creation of fright films in the sky, in airport terminals, on cruise ships, and other confining venues. A seemingly never-ending cycle of pictures.

Wellman's good luck stood beside him, and he was on a roll with two winners in a row . . . make it three. Duke Wayne had given a filmmaking job to a writer friend, James Edward Grant, who had directed one film only. Wayne and Fellows did not like the first cut and were concerned that Warners would not distribute it. They asked Wellman to fix it. "I had made enough [money] for that year," said the director, "so I consented provided I didn't get paid and didn't get credit. That was agreeable to all, so I got me a couple of writers and went to work."

The picture was a low-budget circus murder-mystery written by Grant, Paul Fix, and Philip MacDonald. It starred popular circus performer Clyde Beatty, Pat O'Brien, mystery novelist Mickey Spillane, *Island in the Sky*'s Sean McClory, John Bromfield, Marian Carr, *High and Mighty*'s Pedro Gonzalez-Gonzalez, and Twelve Performing Acts of the Clyde Beatty Circus.

The contrived story deals with a homicidal Korean War veteran and former circus ringmaster (McClory) who escapes from a mental institution and goes on a killing spree while seeking revenge against his former bosses (Beatty and O'Brien) and their circus.

The maniac tries unsuccessfully to reunite with his past lover and trapeze artist (Marian Carr), who is now married and hanging with her partner (Bromfield). He blackmails a clown named Twitchy (Emmett Lynn) to sabotage the circus through a series of curious accidents. Unbelievably, he is rehired as ringmaster and enjoys torturing a caged tiger. A mystery novelist (Spillane) helps unravel the twisted plot, causing the maniac to drown the clown and flee, but not before setting the tiger free. He skedaddles to the train station, hiding in an empty freight car.

The vengeful tiger eludes his circus performing master and flies the coop to the train station, jumping into the same boxcar with the maniac. The master, in hot pursuit, shuts the freight car door so the cat can't make tracks. When the train takes flight, the anguished cries of the maniac fill the air as the furry one enjoys its sweet revenge.

"Most of my work was done in Phoenix," said Wellman, "where Clyde has his winter quarters. We changed the story here and there, added a bit of tiger action, such as breaking out of his cage at night and tracking down the heavy, and I mean tracking him down all the way through the city to the freight yards, and finally getting his quarry in an empty box car that was just pulling out." The director continued, "We cut here, added there, eliminated shot after shot of the Phoenixian debutants strolling through the scenes, and stuck with the atmosphere and the smell of a circus."

Wellman convinced Beatty to liven up his closing circus act with the addition of a "bad" lion in the cage with the others. The results were spine-tingling. Beatty, fortunately, came out of it with fewer scratches than the lions. "We had a little bit of lion pandemonium," said the director, "that kept you holding your breath. I don't know if you have ever seen and heard a lion gang fight, but that's what we had, and you have to see it to believe it."

After the film's preview, Warner Bros. agreed to release it and Wayne threw a celebration party at his home to which Wellman was invited. "Duke was happy and a little gay," said the director, "and in an unconscious moment sat down and wrote me a little gift, a small percentage of the profits, if any. There was, and still is, and I have often wondered what his true feelings are when he has to sign those checks to the half-wit that wanted to do it for nothing."

The ninety-three-minute *Ring of Fear* premiered in Phoenix, July 2, 1954. *The Hollywood Reporter*, July 2, 1954, wrote,

> *Ring of Fear* will be a treat for kid audiences and all who thrive in an atmosphere of peanuts, popcorn and Crackerjack. . . . But I am compelled to report that the story is a pretty Godawful mish-mash, one of the worst examples of movie construction that these old eyes have ever seen. . . . Bill Wellman, filled with a Samaritan's lust for self-sacrifice, volunteered to be the net. In three weeks of reshooting, he made it seem that the maniac was just one of the characters and not the spirit of the whole production. . . . He shot several wild animal sequences that, alone, are worth the price of admission. He enriches an impoverished script with many typical Wellman touches. Most important of all, Bill got the whole thing pasted together without getting his necktie caught in the splicer. The final result is far below the quality of any Wellman picture (and it should not be taken as such). But it serves as a demonstration of how much a talented man can drag out of the Slough of Despond if he has a loving heart.

As the success of *The High and the Mighty* continued to grow, John Wayne couldn't wait for Wellman to choose another project for his now thriving company. They discussed big productions but the director wanted to switch gears. For years, he had been looking for a project to make a black-and-white picture in color. Sounds crazy, but he always said, "Most motion picture directors are a little screwy. I know that fliers are, and I have been both, so draw your own conclusions."

Wellman needed an intimate story, small cast, with certain visual elements. He found it in Walter Van Tilburg Clark's psychological Western drama, *The Track of the Cat*—by the same author as the *The Ox-Bow Incident*. The screenplay, by A. I. Bezzerides, was personal, full of emotion and tension, a cast of only eight characters, and takes place in and around a ranch, out in the wilderness, in the winter with snow on the ground.

Cinematographer Bill Clothier and Wellman check the film strips of their hoped-for masterpiece, *Track of the Cat* (1954).

The director and his cinematographer, Bill Clothier, wanted to keep this movie vision a secret. Nobody else was in on their black-and-white dream in color. "The ranch house was painted off-white," Wellman recalled, "the snow was white, the cattle and horses black and white or a combination of the two. The big pine trees I shot from the shady side so they photographed black. The characters were all clothed in black and white. The only splash of color was the red mackinaw [worn by Robert Mitchum, the leading man] and a little flimsy yellow silk scarf [and pale yellow blouse worn by Diana Lynn, the young female lead]."

In the story, six of the eight characters belong to one dysfunctional family being terrorized by a killer black panther and their own personal demons. *G.I. Joe*'s Robert Mitchum plays Curt Bridges, the arrogant, bullying middle son of an alcoholic father (Philip Tonge) and a rigid, self-righteous mother (Beulah Bondi). The eldest son, Arthur (*High and Mighty*'s William Hopper), is the moral, caring one, and Harold (Tab Hunter), the youngest son, wants desperately to get family approval to marry his girlfriend (Diana Lynn), who is a visitor at the ranch. The only

Diana Lynn with Tim on
Track of the Cat

daughter, Grace (Teresa Wright), is unmarried and trying but failing to keep order and heal family wounds. The last character is a hundred-year-old Indian, Joe Sam (Alfalfa Switzer, in his third Wellman film in a row), who lives and works on the ranch. He believes the panther is a sacred myth.

Curt and Arthur track down the cat, which has killed many of their cattle. The family falls further apart while awaiting their return. The unseen beast kills Arthur, and Curt drapes his body over his horse, sending him back to the ranch. Then Curt dies from the panther's attack.

"Bill [Clothier] and I saw the first print back from the lab. We sat there together, drooling. We had it at last. It was a flower, a portrait, a vision, a dream come true—it was a flop artistically, financially, and Wellmanly." Neither the critics nor the audiences paid any attention to the unusual color, or rather the lack of color. "Most color pictures," said Wellman, "remind me of scrambled eggs, only they don't use eggs—just paints. All the colors of the rainbow, scrambled. *The Track of the Cat* had but four colors: black, white, a red mackinaw, and a yellow silk scarf and blouse."

The black panther was the symbol of the picture. It represented all that was bad in Mitchum and finally kills him. "In a fit of sophomoric thinking, I decided that we should never see said panther. . . . We would just hear it, and the audience could use their imagination, and the effect would be much more powerful." In this instance the director was wrong, as the audience's imagination failed to imagine. "My arthritis became my black panther," said Wellman, "and the son of a bitch has been prowling through my system ever since."

The 102-minute film premiered November 1, 1954, at New York's Paramount Theatre. Frank Thompson wrote, "*The Track of the Cat* is the most mannered film that Wellman ever made. The pace is slow and precise, the acting stylized and the atmosphere grim and depressing." Bosley Crowther in *The New York Times* called it, "A sort of Eugene O'Neill–ized western drama."

Joy Kim and Lauren Bacall costar with John Wayne in *Blood Alley* (1955)

The exterior scenes were shot at Mount Rainier National Park, Washington; interiors at Warner Bros. Although the production took place between mid-June and late July, the weather was anything but summery. Robert Mitchum recalled the film being the worst, most difficult conditions he ever experienced—bitterly cold, physically exhausting, all day sinking or falling over into the bottomless drifts.

The frigid temperatures and snowstorms kept the cast and crew inside whenever possible. One inside-out story was perpetrated by the cast prankster, Alfalfa Switzer. The company was housed in a hotel with the tourists or in cabins at the foot of Mount Rainier. Mitchum had a two-bedroom cabin he shared with his friend and stand-in. One dark, freezing night after work, Mitch was sitting in a chair next to a warming fire, sipping his beverage of choice, wrapped only in a towel, waiting for his turn to shower.

Alfalfa, affectionately called "Alfy," snuck over to Mitch's cabin with a wild, angry raccoon that he had caught earlier. He was holding the animal by the tail, shaking it often and hard to keep it from turning up and biting him, which it did anyway. He peeked through the window and saw the star sitting in his chair, drinking quietly. He flung the door open and released the infuriated coon into the room. Quickly, he slammed the door shut and made tracks to higher ground.

From a safe vantage point, he listened to the shouting, cursing, banging, and scuffling inside the cabin. Soon he heard the cries from two voices, then just one voice—the stand-in had retreated back into the bathroom, locking the door and leaving his buddy to deal with the uncontrollable, raging raccoon. All of a sudden, the cabin door burst open and out came the movie star running into the night and the deep snow . . . naked as the day he was born. The coon soon made his exit stage right.

On another occasion, in a soundstage back at the studio, Alfy leaned an open wooden casket—used in the film—against a wall. When visitors came to the set, he would get into the casket and pretend to be a corpse made up as a hundred-year-old Indian. The guests believed he was just a dummy. When the people walked by and looked in, he would snap open his eyes and step out or fall out onto the floor.

This, quite naturally, caused a great stir, with lots of yelling and shouting. Wellman enjoyed the prank but when the commotion interrupted a rehearsal, the director put a lid on the box.

Wellman brought his thirteen-year-old son to the location. Timmy, who had worked as an actor in *The Happy Years* and *Island in the Sky*, and as a riding double in *Across the Wide Missouri*, had another nonacting role in *Track of the Cat*. Due to his lightweight size, he was able to make the panther tracks in the deep snow without sinking down. The prop men fixed plaster of Paris paws on the bottom of his shoes and Timmy became the track of the cat.

"I started out like a racehorse with *Island in the Sky* and *The High and the Mighty*," said Wellman, "and then fell on my skinny butt with *Blood Alley*." When John Wayne read the novel by Albert Sidney Fleischman, he wanted to make the picture, and hired the novelist to write the screenplay. He was intrigued by the story of a merchant marine captain, Tom Wilder, who is held captive by the Chinese communists and, with the aid of strangers, breaks out of prison. Tom is taken by sampan to a small fishing village where he hides out in the home of an American, Dr. Grainger, and his beautiful daughter, Cathy. He discovers that it was the villagers who helped him escape, and when they ask for his assistance to break from the oppression in Red China to the freedom of Hong Kong, he accepts.

He commands their only large seaworthy vessel, *Blood Alley*, an old steam-powered ferryboat, down the Formosa Strait. They encounter enemy gunboats, sabotage, hand-to-hand combat, typhoons, and romance. When their safety is assured, Tom gives up his imaginary girlfriend, "Baby"—who helped him endure two years in prison camp—for Cathy.

Duke did not want to star in the film, just produce it for his new company. He paid off his producing partner, Robert Fellows, and created Batjac Productions. He offered the project to Wellman, who had chosen their last film, *The Track of the Cat*, and felt obliged to take his partner's choice this time. It wasn't that he disliked the story, but he had second thoughts. "An indelible question mark lodged in my screwy brain," he said. "There had been but one successful picture made about the . . . Chinese, *The Good Earth*. What the hell was I going to do with *Blood Alley?*"

For starters, the Wayne-Wellman team cast their *Track of the Cat* star Robert Mitchum as Tom Wilder and Lauren Bacall as Cathy. Shooting was scheduled for early January 1955, on a budget of $2 million. Locations were secured at China Camp in San Rafael, California; Point San Pablo in nearby Richmond; the San Francisco Bay; and other locations. Interiors at Goldwyn Studios. They received the cooperation of the Department of Defense and the Coast Guard.

In the early days of production, Wellman referred to himself as "a bitched, buggered and bewildered guy in Oakland . . . the bottom had fallen out, star trouble, bad weather, production headaches, and above all, my lack of confidence in a story concerning the Chinese." The director had nothing but good things to say about the Asians on the picture. "They were wonderful," he said, "always on time, never complaining, working like hell and loving it."

Before the first shot was in the can, the real trouble began. A few days before the start of principal photography, Wellman planned to shoot "run-bys"—filming of the ferryboat from different angles as it plows through the water—without the principal actors, using mostly extras. If Mitchum was piloting the boat, instead of a double, the camera could be closer and the shots more effective. So Wellman asked his star to come to location early. Even though Mitch didn't go on salary until the first day of principal photography, he said yes. He arrived, and all hell broke loose.

This story is gleaned from the mouths of the *Blood Alley* participants: John Wayne's son Michael; assistant director Andrew V. McLaglen; director Wellman; and the replaced star, Robert Mitchum.

The facts:

Robert Mitchum arrived at the location before the start date.
He was given a suite in the hotel above the director's suite.

John Wayne takes over for Robert Mitchum on *Blood Alley* (1955).

The first night he hosted a party in his room.

The director got little sleep that night.

The next day, Wellman asked the star to have pity on the restless sleeping
director.

The second evening was another pulsating party.

The director got little sleep that night.

The next day on the set, Mitchum was nursing a hangover.

The star went to lunch with members of the coast guard.

He came back late and "moody."

He took exception to the attitudes of some crew members.

He aired his displeasures to the director.

He left the location.

The director announced that he had been fired.

There was a slowdown in production.

John Wayne arrived at the location as the replacement.

Purported facts, opinions, and author conclusions:

> The first-night party was accompanied by loud noise, banging against the walls, breaking of furniture, even a broken window.
> The director got little sleep that night.
> The next day the director warned the star to knock off the bullshit.
> The second evening was another pulsating party.
> On the set the next day, the star was nursing an alcoholic and drug hangover.
> The star went to lunch with sailor admirers.
> He returned late and in no condition to work.
> He took exception with crew members trying to work.
> He pushed three-hundred-pound transportation captain George Coleman into San Francisco Bay.
> He aired his displeasures to the director, who supported his company members.
> He made disparaging remarks to the director, heard by the assistant director: "I wouldn't beat up an old, arthritic man like you."
> He left the location.
> The director announced that he had been fired.
> There was a slowdown in production.
> John Wayne, as Paul Revere, came to the rescue.

Robert Mitchum had his own story. He reported early as a favor to Wellman. His partying was much lower key than represented. His coast guard luncheon included very little drinking. He did not throw the transportation captain into the sea—just pushed him a bit for his poor attitude. Nate Edwards, production manager, was the worst offender and he told him so.

Mitch claimed that in conversation with Wellman the director apologized for having to fire him, but he had no choice—here is where the story gets real good. Mitchum said that John Wayne received orders from Jack Warner to get rid of him. Warner wanted a John Wayne–starring picture for his summer release schedule, and the only picture available was *Blood Alley*.

Mike Wayne was on the location as a production executive for Batjac. He said that his father never wanted to play the leading role and didn't relish having to do it. He tried but failed to get Gregory Peck or Humphrey Bogart to take over. Without the star, the picture was floundering, the budget increasing. To protect his company and its investment, Wayne became the replacement.

With John Wayne's reputation as a fair-minded player, a generous supporter of the people working with him, and a strong-minded individual not afraid to stand up to authority figures, it is difficult to believe that he would ever surrender to Jack Warner's demands and turn against his star player.

It is even harder to imagine that Wild Bill would accept this sort of underhanded behavior by a producer and, as a result, fire the man he discovered for *G.I. Joe* and had just cast and with whom he'd worked successfully in *Track of the Cat*. It seems fairly obvious that Robert Mitchum, for whatever reasons, was in no condition to perform his duties on this picture at this time. His director realized it and took the proper measures. As a replacement, maybe in the back of Wellman's mind, he believed that he could talk Duke into stepping up again as he had done in *The High and the Mighty*. "With the advent of Wayne," recalled Wellman, "everything started to straighten out and I began to make up some of the expensive time we had lost during the switchover."

"We were working on an old broken-down wharf," said the director, "when Bogie came up from Hollywood to visit the lovely, capable, unusual actress, Lauren Bacall of the fascinating voice, Mrs. Humphrey Bogart." The Wellman-Bogart relationship started back in 1933 with the director's *Central Airport*. He cast a couple in one scene only. Both actors came from the New York stage. Her name was Mayo Methot, his was Humphrey Bogart. The scene was cut from the final print but it began a lifelong Wellman-Bogart friendship. Bogie and Mayo were married five years later.

Before Bogart's first big success as Duke Mantee in 1936's *The Petrified Forest*, he came to Wellman with a problem. "His agent insisted," said the director, "that he have his teeth rearranged to get rid of his lisp—my reply was fast and colorful—tell the son of a bitch that he is so wrong, he should have his teeth rearranged for suggesting such a blooper, and not by a dentist." Wellman later said, "Mr. Bogart had a very unusual lisp—not the whistling kind that the microphone exaggerates and makes unbearable to listen to, an indescribable lishping sound that fascinated me, as it has millions of people since then."

During Bogie's visit to the *Blood Alley* location, he told Wellman about another problem. While watching his wife being readied for the next shot, Wellman noticed a worried look on his face. He asked, "How do you feel, Bogie?" He answered, "Lousy," then changed the subject for a while. When he came back to it, he said, "Bill, I got the big C, bad." Wellman felt sick to his stomach and told him so. There was a long, quiet moment before the director asked, "Does she know?" "Nope," answered the star. "When are you going to tell her?" "Goddamned if I know, what do you think?" "She's a wonderful woman, with more guts than you and I put together. Tell her some late night when the world seems quiet and you're all alone—she happens to be in love with you. You're lucky, Bogie, you have got a woman." Humphrey Bogart died two years later, January 14, 1957.

The location work was completed in mid-March, the interiors at the Goldwyn Studios, April 4. The 115-minute picture premiered in Hollywood, September 28, at Grauman's Chinese Theatre. *The New York Times* proclaimed, "a standard chase melodrama patterned on a familiar blueprint." Other reviews and box office receipts were unremarkable. *Blood Alley*, as Wellman had feared, was no *Good Earth*.

Wellman wasted no time getting back behind the camera with a novel by James Street, with a screenplay by *Blood Alley*'s A. S. Fleischman, *Goodbye, My Lady*. This film was a simple coming-of-age story of a young boy, an old man, and a dog.

"Skeeter" Claude (*Shane*'s Brandon deWilde) finds a dog (a Basenji) in the swamp that laughs but doesn't bark. He adopts and trains Lady not to hunt rats and the neighbor's chickens, but to be a fine hunting dog. Skeeter is an orphan who lives with his elderly, illiterate but caring Uncle Jesse Jackson (Walter Brennan). He loves the boy and teaches him important lessons of right and wrong. He wants Skeeter to be able to make his own decisions.

When it is discovered that Lady is a rare African breed and owned by a Northern sportsman, the boy must make a crucial decision—to keep "his" dog or give her back to its original owner. He shows his character, upbringing, and manhood by returning the dog to its rightful owner. He receives a reward and uses the money to buy his uncle what he always wanted, "roebuckers"—false teeth, so he could chew nuts. And for himself, a hunting rifle.

Three-time Oscar winner Walter Brennan is outstanding, and Brandon deWilde will break your heart. *High and Mighty*'s Phil Harris ("Cash" Evans) and William Hopper (Walter Grover, the dog's owner) also give fine performances. George Chandler (the newspaper editor) makes his final appearance in a Wellman film—number twenty-two. Sidney Poitier, in one of his early roles, shows the charm and talent that will help guide him on the road to great stardom. The director hired son Timmy again—on his summer vacation—to work as a dog wrangler and, with a blond wig, double deWilde.

Shooting began in early August of 1955. Wellman had left the cold, foggy, chaotic climate of *Blood Alley* for the heat, humidity, and racial seg-

...a picture to touch your heart!

A Mississippi boy, his devotion to a Yankee dog--and an old man who drew a Mason-Dixon line across his heart and dared you to cross it!

WARNER BROS. PRESENT

"Good-bye, My Lady"

WALTER BRENNAN · PHIL HARRIS · BRANDON de WILDE DIRECTED BY WILLIAM A. WELLMAN

regation of the bayou country in Albany, Georgia. Poitier was not allowed to room in the hotel with the company. He was billeted in a teacher's room at a nearby black college.

Wellman was upset by this arrangement. He told the hotel management of his unhappiness. Unfortunately, there were no other hotels in the area for the large company. The director would have to accept this discrimination, at least for a while. The matter accelerated when Sidney was not allowed to eat with the company in the hotel dining room. Wellman, exhibiting his best diplomacy, went to management. It was decided that Poitier could eat in the hotel, but only in the kitchen. Thereafter, Sidney and his director ate together in the hotel kitchen—but with all the trimmings. When the location wrapped, Wild Bill went back to management and offered a departing gift . . . his fists, which they declined.

Production was completed in late September of 1955 at the Goldwyn Studios. The ninety-four-minute picture had its world premiere in Albany, Georgia, on April 11, 1956. "*Good-bye, My Lady* was a financial fiasco," said Wellman. "I don't know why. The story was beautiful, the performance superb. . . . How could you miss? But I did. We went down in the swamps . . . all through the peanut fields, with the snakes and the heat, and worked like Trojans. For what? A plaque that reads:

> To William A. Wellman
> For his outstanding contribution to the
> Technique of Motion Picture Direction and for
> *Good-Bye, My Lady*
> The National Society, Daughters of the American
> Revolution, awards its CERTIFICATE OF HONOR for
> producing the Best Children's Picture of the Year 1956

"Now, don't misunderstand me . . . I am very proud and happy to receive such a certificate of honor . . . for the best children's picture of the year, but why didn't the kids go to see it? Why didn't they drag their mothers and fathers to the theater? I guess you can't make a good clean picture anymore and make any money. What am I talking about? Disney does it all the time. So it's as plain as the nose on your face, I am just not Disney."

In 1967, Walt Disney told this author that he loved the picture and wished that he had it for distribution. I think *Good-bye, My Lady* would have been a hit with the Disney banner above it.

Film critics of the day also liked the picture. *The Hollywood Reporter*, April 4, 1956: "Bill Wellman's direction gets a great deal of tenderness and human compassion into this story. . . . All I can say is that it deserves success." *Variety*, April 11, 1956: "Properly sentimental and thoroughly heart-warming." The London *Times*, June 25, 1956: "A folk-tale of heroic proportion."

John Gallagher wrote, "*Good-bye, My Lady* is one of the finest pictures about children and animals in the tradition of Stuart Heisler's *The Biscuit Eater* (1940), Fred Wilcox's *Lassie Come Home* (1943), and Clarence Brown's *The Yearling* (1946)."

Sidney Poitier excels in *Good-bye, My Lady* (1956), one of his early roles.

Humphrey Bogart arrives on the San Francisco location of *Blood Alley* (1955) to explain to Wellman the health problems that will deny him the starring role in the film in which his wife, Lauren Bacall, is the costar.

20

THE FINAL STRAW

Throughout Wellman's long career, he discovered projects that consumed his imagination and captivated his spirit. No matter what obstacles were thrown in his path, no matter how long the journey might take, these were the stories he had to make.

Unlike most filmmakers who never see all their favorite films produced, he did—a compliment to his stature in the industry, and his determination. Other pictures, other assignments were important, but they sometimes served as temporary distractions until he could return to those powerful plays that had possessed him.

With some of these films, he was able to attain the green light quickly: *Legion of the Condemned* (1928), a more personal aviation story than even his *Wings* (1927); the classic gangster film *The Public Enemy* (1931); his flying picture reunion with John Wayne, *Island in the Sky* (1953). His Oscar-winning *A Star Is Born* took months to secure that greenish gleaming. The timeless Western *The Ox-Bow Incident* was just a dream for several years before the verdant light shone down. Even the director's silent film project *Dirigible* experienced seventeen years of transformations before being produced as *This Man's Navy* (1945)—not the artistic version he had wanted, but a consolation prize nonetheless.

There were other "chosen ones" produced, but none of all these films compared to the odyssey of Wellman's pinnacle picture vision, *C'est la Guerre* (translation: That's life). This story was firmly implanted in his mind, in his very soul, and on his printed page—not for weeks, months, or years, but for decades. This was his story of the brave young heroes he knew, who died in defense of right and of liberty in the First World War. His narration in the film reveals, "They came with an air of adventure or a sense of impatience in the days before America entered the war. They wore French uniforms, they fought in French planes, and they fell in love with French women."

Wellman's ten previous films of aviation all carry a strong imprint of his days as a fighter pilot, and the fliers he knew in the Great War—some of the pictures were more defining than others, but *C'est la Guerre* was to be his crowning personal achievement.

The director first took the project to Darryl Zanuck at Warner Bros. in the early 1930s. He tried again in 1937 with David Selznick. He went back to Zanuck at Fox in the early 1940s. He proposed the film at MGM to Louis B. Mayer in the mid-1940s and Dore Schary in the early 1950s. There was some interest along the way, but no deals.

The year was 1955. After the huge success of *The High and the Mighty*, Wellman thought this would be the time to make it happen. Jack Warner had little interest in a First World War movie, but he wanted Wellman at the studio. He decided to take a chance, but only on certain conditions: the picture would be low-budget; Wellman would receive minimal salary but a third of profits, if any; the director would have to make another film "sight unseen"—whatever script he was given, he had to direct it without story changes. Wellman agreed to all the stipulations—he was finally getting a chance to make the film that was closest to his heart.

The director wrote the story, A. S. Fleischman the screenplay. The leading character is a rebellious young man trying to escape a troubled past—sound familiar? "The hero was part real, part fiction," said Wellman. "He was patterned after a pal of mine. We went to war together, and we had a great many of the experiences, good and bad, that I used in the story. It was a tragedy about a young American flier and a little fille de nuit [girl of the night]." The writer-director called her Renee, the name of his first wife, killed during the war.

The central theme of the love story had revolving around it the training, relationships, and experiences of adventurous American volunteers ready to fight and die for a country they hardly knew. The story is so personal that Bill Wellman is a main character and friend of Thad Walker.

While awaiting his official papers that will make him a member of the Lafayette Flying Corps, Thad falls in love with Renee, who speaks little English, and he speaks little French. They teach each other their written language, but the language of love doesn't need to be taught and they are in its grip. In the beginning, she thinks he will never be able to forget her sordid past. But he tells her the past is the past and only the present counts. Thad leaves for pilot training and Renee gives up her "trade" to become a streetcar conductress; clothed in black, working just enough to live while her man was preparing to fight for her country. It was a bitter existence for her, but she was respectable now and deeply in love.

While Thad was sweating it out at the Avord training center, he would get letters from her, and since Bill Wellman was his pal, he helped him translate them—from a pocket dictionary, sitting outside a hangar or in a deserted barracks or in the can. Thad missed her so much that finally his rebellious side kicked in and he hit a drill instructor, who happened to be a *sous-lieutenant*, and was put in the jug to await court-martial. His American friends knew what could happen—Devil's Island or worse for striking an officer in wartime. At night, keeping their identities secret, they overpowered the poilu guards and got him out. While they were at it, they released all the other prisoners. Over the wall, he was now on his own.

Thad was off to Paris and his Renee, but he was still in the uniform of the *élève pilote*—army shoes, puttees of blue, tan military trousers, leather coat, and the French blue cap. They would pick him up quickly; there were not many of those on the loose. On his way to the railroad station, he picked on a champion savateur, and it became a bloody battle. Thad knocked him out, but was seriously injured. He switched clothes and sneaked on a troop train destined for Paris.

After his arrival, he took a taxi to their garret hideaway and stumbled up the stairs, crashing through the locked door, collapsing on the floor. It was early afternoon, and she was still at work. When she came home, she found him there unconscious. With the help of an old *réforme* who was the concierge of the apartment building, they got him washed up and in bed, and the concierge brought a doctor friend who understood. They patched Thad up, got some hot soup down him, and he smiled again, this time into his loved one's face.

He was in pretty bad shape for a couple of weeks, but with the loving attention that he got from Renee at night and the old concierge in the daytime, he recovered with nothing to show for it but an ugly scar shooting out from his right eye—and a terrible loneliness. He couldn't go outside. Renee kept working during the day to support them. He was a prisoner of love.

Day in and day out, Thad studied French and read the Paris newspapers. At night, he had Renee and ecstasy. Some nights they would steal outside and sneak along the Seine, hand in hand. He had by now a heavy beard and looked just like a poilu. These wonderful moments were to be short-lived.

One day he kicked boredom in the butt, tossed the French grammar under the bed, threw caution to the winds, and sidestreeted his way to Renee's former house of employment.

Madam was glad to see him. Happy that Renee was happy, but a little puzzled; and when he explained his loneliness, how impossible it was to get a solution to their predicament, hiding in a room all day and all night, every day and every night, she gave him a job as a pimp, or as she said, a trumpeter of love. Made it sound kinda nice.

His territory was between the Folies Bergère and 23, rue X. You never spoke of them as houses of ill repute, just as a number on a street. A little more homey.

She explained to him that as long as he stayed within the confines of his territory, inside his new home, inside the Folies, or inside certain taxicabs, she could guarantee his safety. This meant that Renee would have to move back to her former home, this time as a beautiful young woman in love, employed elsewhere.

The shoe was on the other foot. Renee worked all day. Thad worked all night. Now she was the lonely one and even though they lived in the back of the house, the alley side, the sounds of revelry surrounded her. Sounds that she used to live by became part of her sentence. A punishment for what she had been before. A reminder of the greatness of her man and the fullness of their love, for neither one of them ever spoke of the old life.

To him this was a chance for them to get out. Maybe through the South Americans that played in the Folies Bergère orchestra. Maybe through some of his friends, like Wellman or Duke Sinclaire or Jim Hall. He was around now and active. He would find a way to get to South America, to get married, to get for them what he used to call the throw-out-your-chest kind of happiness. She understood and was patient.

Madam dressed her new protégé as a wealthy South American. The shave, the haircut, the clothes, and the false papers did the trick. From the left side, he looked like a handsome South American playboy, but when he turned and you saw the right side of his face, with its angry deep scar jutting down from the eye, the playboy was erased.

Thad did well as a procurer but failed in every attempt to get him and his loved one out of France. At one point he thought he had things arranged, but America's entrance into the war wiped that out completely. He was once more a prisoner. This time at a number on a street.

Came months of procuring, dodging the military police, living for the few wonderful hours he and Renee had together. An hour that came just before she went to work and after he had returned from work, and the hour when she returned from work and just before he went to work—two short hours spent with her and those long, never-ending ones spent waiting for her.

Then came an American general who wanted to be a playboy, and Thad spotted him and made contact.

On their way to the number on the street, Thad took the big gamble and told him everything. The general never said a word, just listened.

Thad begged him to give him another chance. Make him his driver, anything as a stepping-stone to becoming a flier again. Anything that would give him the chance to once more become a man.

When they arrived at 23, rue X, the general remained seated. Thad got out, came around, and opened the door to let him out. He still didn't move, just sat there thinking. Then very quietly told Thad to get back in, he wanted to go to his hotel.

All the way to the hotel not a word was spoken.

Thad began to figure what he would do if the general intended to turn him in. It wasn't his place to say anything more. He had declared himself. It was up to the general now.

They drew up to the hotel. The general got out, hesitated for a moment, and then turned to Thad, still inside the cab. He thanked him—for what, Thad didn't know. Then his manner changed, and in almost a command he ordered Thad to report to him at 10:30 in the morning, suite 302. Then he was gone.

Thad hurried home. It was early morning, and Renee was fast asleep. He wanted to awaken her to tell the big news, but she looked so peaceful, so beautiful, that he just sat there looking at her. She stirred a little, awakened slowly; and when she saw him gazing down at her, she reached for him and they kissed, a long, lingering, lovely kiss.

Then he told her about the general. This might well be their big chance. The chance to get away from "the number on the street."

Wherever he might go, she would follow him; others have done it. All over France, there were the camp followers. Women fighting to be with their men, sacrificing everything for a few precious moments. She would join this legion of the dedicated. Somehow they must always be together, forever.

Then he told her how the general had thanked him. Out of a clear sky he thanked me. For what?

Renee looked at him almost like a mother about to give her young son a little lesson in life.

"He thanked you because you made him think or maybe because you made him, how you say, remember?"

It suddenly became very quiet. For just a moment there was no noise. He took her in his arms. There were tears in her eyes.

Thad became the general's private driver. He was skillful and trustworthy. In a few months he got what he was after. He was sent to Issoudun and started his training to become a flier.

Months later he had received his wings and was commissioned a second lieutenant. Wellman was in Paris when he hit town, a full-fledged *pilote* and on his way to the front.

Renee never gave up her job, a job that in a small way helped her country. She worked and prayed and waited.

Wellman was there when they met. Words can't describe it. Neither one said a word, just melted into each other's arms. An immense sigh came from his lips; from hers, a little purr. They walked away arm in arm, oblivious of everything and everybody around them. Wellman watched them as they disappeared from view, a bright new knight and his lady fair, a conductress all in black. It seemed almost like gazing into a crystal ball.

Wellman was there when they were married, in a small church on the outskirts of Paris. The church organ played softly; and in the distance the music of war was playing its tune of madness. During the ceremony, Wellman saw her turn a frightened look at a faraway rumble and then saw her look at Thad, a look of love and worry and hope, and her faint "I do," a whispered two-word prayer.

They spent the afternoon in the Bois de Boulogne lying on the grass, with the sun on their faces, smiles on their lips, and the clouds in the sky. He gave her his identification bracelet and shortened the links so that it would fit her tiny wrist. Second Lieutenant Thad Walker, AEF Squadron 94—she read this aloud in her broken English, sealed by a kiss. Two lost souls in love. An ex-pimp and an ex-whore. The next morning, he flew out of Le Plessis-Belleville, bound for Squadron 94 in the Champagne sector. She was there all alone to watch her life fly away, never to return, for he became lost and strayed into Germany and was brought down by two Fokkers.

When she read of his death in the Paris paper, just a name in a too-long list of casualties, she jumped into the Seine and drowned her sorrow and her life, and only a friend and a general knew who it was that was dragged from the dirty waters clothed in black with an identification bracelet on her small, cold, chalk-white wrist that read: Second Lieutenant Thad Walker, AEF Squadron 94. Whom the gods love die young.

For the starring role of Thad Walker, the director wanted the twenty-five-year-old Warners contract player James Dean, who had received an Academy Award nomination for his first leading role, in *East of Eden* (1955). In his second starring vehicle, *Rebel Without a Cause* (1955), he brilliantly portrays a rebellious youth with a tormented past. James Dean was exactly what Wellman wanted. A meeting was to be scheduled when the director completed *Good-bye, My Lady*. The tragedy of Dean's death, September 30, 1955, continued the streak of bad luck that had been stalking Wellman for the past three pictures.

The director next turned to another Warners contract player, Paul Leonard Newman. He hailed from the New York stage, live television, and the Actors Studio. He was unhappy at Warner Bros., and not afraid to vent his dissatisfaction to the studio bosses over being cast, in his first starring feature, as a sword-and-sandals hero in the cheap production *The Silver Chalice* (1954), which featured as one of his love interests a fading Virginia Mayo, five years his senior.

The director and future icon sat down together and talked. When the meeting ended, Wellman remarked, "He tried to tell me how to direct my picture." Nonetheless he liked Newman's maverick attitude and felt they could work together. Jack Warner said they couldn't. "You can't use him," said the mogul. "He's causing trouble and I'm going to teach him a lesson. I'm putting him on suspension."

Warner began pushing his popular teenage heartthrob, born Arthur Andrew Kelm, Tab Hunter. The handsome golden boy of the era had

Screen lovers Tab Hunter and Etchika Choureau in *Lafayette Escadrille* (1958)

Wellman prepares Bill Jr. for pilot
training in *Lafayette Escadrille* (1958).

starred in successful Warner Bros. features, and the director's *Track of the Cat*. Due to the delays in casting and a start date looming, the director's impatience began to show, and so he set Hunter as his star and a French actress, Etchika Choureau, making her American film debut, as Renee. Next, he needed to add some younger players to support teen idol Hunter.

Since one of the top roles was Wellman's character, the heads of publicity and casting came up with the marketing idea of having the director's nineteen-year-old son, William Wellman, Jr., play his father. Wellman's other two sons, Tim and Mike, had worked in his films, and the thought of having his oldest boy, the same approximate age as he during the war, was appealing.

But there were problems. Wellman's other sons had appeared only in cameo roles—even little Mike had slept through most of *The High and the Mighty*—and this role was significant. Bill Jr. had never acted before. He had just finished his freshman year at Duke University, majoring in Business Administration. Dottie voiced her opposition to the scheme, wanting Billy to finish college. When his father posed the possibility, his son was hell-bent to give it a go. But first he would have to prove himself by testing live with Hunter in front of Jack Warner, second-in-command Steve Trilling, casting executive Solie Biano, and a host of other studio leaders . . . and his father.

After the test, in which Hunter appeared more nervous than the neophyte, Wellman broke the news to his son. "They all gave a thumbs-up, even Warner and me. But, you won't get any special treatment. Be on time, know your lines, and no fooling around." This sort of talk was nothing new to the youngster, as he had heard such directions all his life. When he asked his father how to be an actor, the answer came back, "Don't act, just be yourself." The director persuaded his wife that it would be a good learning experience, and that the boy could make some good money and take it back to college for the second semester. Dottie reluctantly agreed. The sons of Wellman favorites Joel McCrea (Jody) and Andy Devine (Dennis) were tapped to play fliers.

With time running out, Wellman called for a final casting session in the small parking lot next to his office. His assistant director, George Vieira, gathered a group of thirteen or fourteen hopefuls. Wellman displayed his amazing talent for choosing actors without live readings, watching film, or one-on-one meetings.

The prospective players were huddled together as the director approached carrying a clipboard. He was followed by the secretary, carrying her clipboard. The closer he got, the more uneasy they became, some pushing to get in front of the pack. He stood in front of them, looking them up and down. He asked questions like, "How long have you been waiting?" "How was the traffic getting here?" "Where are you from?" Answers were heard, "New York!" "Nebraska!" "Michigan!"

Wellman noticed a tall actor, looking very uncomfortable at the rear of the assemblage. He asked where he was from; the low-toned answer was "Universal." The director laughed, commenting "Universal what?" The thesp shot back, "Universal Pictures, they dropped my option." Wellman listened to his voice, noticed his six-foot-two frame, handsome face, then said, "Ever play football?" "Yeah," answered the young man. The director told him to give his name to the secretary, adding, "You're playing the part of George Moseley, the All-American Yale end." The secretary wrote down . . . Clint Eastwood.

Other actors that the director handpicked were Tom Laughlin (as Arthur Blumenthal), the Billy Jack counterculture hero of the late 1960s and 1970s; David Janssen (Duke Sinclaire), television star of *The Fugitive* (1963–1967); Will Hutchins (Dave Putnam), *Sugarfoot* (1957–1961); Maurice Elias (Alan Nichols) aka James Stacy, *Lancer* (1968–1970); Rad Fulton (Wally Winter), aka James Westmoreland, *The Monroes* (1966–1967), *Top Cops* (1991–1993), *Kung Fu: The Legend Continues* (1994–1995); Brett Halsey (Frank Baylies), *Follow the Sun* (1961–1962), soap opera star of *The Young and the Restless* (1980–1981), and . . . Bill Wellman, Jr., commencing an over fifty-five-year career with more than 180 movies and television shows—and never went back to college.

The director built his World War I location in Santa Maria, California. The airfield and hangars were a duplicate of Wellman's N. 87 field at Lunéville in southeastern France. Scenes were also filmed on the French street at 20th Century-Fox and the soundstages and back lot of Warner Bros.

For the important position of technical director and stunt pilot, the director called on his longtime friend and foe Paul Mantz—still considered number one in the business. He had been hard at work on two major films in the same year of 1956: Best Picture Oscar winner, Jules Verne's *Around the World in 80 Days*, directed by Michael Anderson; and John Ford's *The Wings of Eagles*, released in 1957 starring John Wayne.

In a letter to Warner Bros. executive Charles Greenlaw, Mantz explained his situation of not being available to work on the film, but was prepared to rent his planes to the studio. When Wellman heard the outrageous price quote, he met with his former stunt coordinator–pilot. Their meeting ended with the director socking Mantz.

For Wellman's second choice, he gave his first major film job to thirty-seven-year-old flier and collector of antique aircraft, Frank Gifford Tallman, who later became the number one stunt pilot in Hollywood. Just four years later, 1961, Tallman and Paul Mantz formed a partnership with Tallmantz Aviation. Tallman was lean and lanky with chiseled features and a neatly trimmed mustache. When wearing his helmet and goggles, he gave the dashing image of a World War I pilot. He brought aviation expertise and a flair for old planes. He also brought along stunt pilot and collector Dwight Woodward. They flew all the picture planes for the film: three Blériots, four Penguins, a Sopwith Camel, a Thomas Morse Scout, a Garland Lincoln Nieuport 28, a Travel Air disguised as a Fokker, a Curtiss Junior and Navion used as camera planes, and a Bonanza for production purposes.

The climactic dogfight was borrowed from the director's Paramount production *Men with Wings* (1938). The blue-screen process placed Tab Hunter and Bill Wellman, Jr., into the cockpits that Fred MacMurray and his compatriot had previously occupied.

Principal photography began October 19, 1956, in Santa Maria. The cast and crew exhibited fine esprit de corps and the production moved along smoothly. Even though the director was now sixty years old, with arthritis beating down upon his weakened body, he worked with enthusiasm and a special love of his craft.

Away from the set, however, there were some bumps in the road, or should I say, in the parking lot. On Halloween night, trick-or-treaters of all ages were coming to the Rick's Rancho Hotel lobby to claim their share of goodies. Bill Jr. and Jody McCrea had finished dinner in the hotel restaurant and cut a path through the costumed children to the outside parking area for some air. Here they would wait for Johnny Indrisano, handling the picture's rough stuff, for a walk around the long block. Johnny believed that a person should always take a brisk walk after the evening meal.

The hotel parking lot was dimly lit, but the two actors could see a group of a dozen or more ominous-looking forms gathering—they were a different kind of trick-or-treater—the town toughs. They began moving toward Billy and Jody, shouting, "Actors go home!" "Get the hell out of Santa Maria!" "Go back to Hollywood, you fairies!" and the like.

The youngsters stood their ground but were way outnumbered. Suddenly, out of the hotel side door came Indrisano. He saw the situation, and walked slowly through the mob toward the young actors. One of the leaders told him to take a hike and stepped in front of him. A lightning left hook to the

French actress Etchika Choureau in her American movie debut, as Renee in *Lafayette Escadrille*

body followed by a right cross to the jaw sent the bully to a Halloween nightmare. Johnny reached the boys and stood with them, staring at the murmuring mob, and watching several of them trying to revive their fallen friend. He yelled at them to disperse; they didn't and began moving toward the threesome. Now, a small group of actors, including Sam Boghosian, UCLA Hall of Fame football player and coach, stepped from the main lobby door. They quickly read the situation and joined their compatriots.

It is important to know that actors working together form a "camaraderie committee" that is all for one and one for all. Outnumbered two to one on this starlit, goblin-filled evening, they stood together waiting for the ghouls to make their decision. They did. Grumbling and calling out that they would return, they skulked away to their automobiles—and never came back.

Etchika Choureau had little to do with the Santa Maria location, as it dealt exclusively with the training and early combat of the fliers. When the company returned to Warner Bros., she was on call nearly every day.

Etchika was not fluent in English, but she was accomplished at being understood. She was high-spirited, constantly smiling and happy. Everybody on the picture loved her . . . except Tab Hunter.

In the 1950s, homosexual actors were in the closet. The studios protected them from the media; fans and film audiences knew only what was printed, and what was printed came from the studios' publicity engines. Poor little Etchika had no idea that her costar lover was gay. She had fallen madly in love with him. Tab Hunter was a star, a diligent worker, a caring individual who was personable and easy to work with. He conveyed this to her, but nothing more.

She began to appear disturbed and depressed. Eventually, her friend, translator, and stand-in came to the director for guidance. He was told that Etchika was in love with Tab, and couldn't understand why he was so loving on stage and during their love scenes, but disappeared after the wrap signal sounded.

The director cared about his leading lady and explained to her, as best he could, her predicament. This author was standing near enough to see her reaction but not hear the hushed dialogue. She was listening intently for a few minutes, then tears welled up and streamed down her cheeks. It was a thoroughly heart-wrenching scene, watching this beautiful little lady hear the tragic news of the death of her fantasy lover. She pulled herself together, surrendering a poignant performance.

Her director was not about to surrender anything that wasn't in the best interests of his film, or the comfort of his hardworking company—even the morning coffee. Tab Hunter was there when the coffee conflict came to a boil. "Jack Warner said I'm not giving free coffee out to these people anymore," remembered Hunter. "There's not gonna be a man making coffee on the set anymore. People are gonna have to pay for their coffee by the cup. So they brought in this big coffee machine, where people had to put money in to get a cup of coffee. And Bill—that's the first time I ever saw him blow. He said, 'I'll be damned if any one of my crew is gonna pay for coffee! Open the doors.' They rolled up the doors of the soundstage. He took the cart of coffee and pushed it right downhill where it smashed in the middle of the street and that was it."

"From then on," continued Hunter, "he had the special chef there brewing the coffee for the whole crew, and everything was great. That's the first time I saw him get upset. I thought, hey, I don't want to get this guy pissed."

Actor Tom Laughlin relates another incident told to him by one of the company electricians. "We were shooting a scene on the back lot, a night scene, rain coming down, and I was walking down the New York street set. And we set it up with the big Brute arc lamps and all of that. And just as we're ready to go, I noticed a diamond, a glare bouncing off one window, and I calculated how long it would take to realign the Brutes, and the cost of holding up shooting, and I went over with a hammer and I broke the window. And we shot it."

"The next day," the electrician told Laughlin, "as we come to shoot, there's a guy from the front office at Warner's down there just ripping me out, they're taking it out of my pay, et cetera, et cetera. And Wellman came over and said, 'What's going on here?' And the guy tells him. Without a word, Bill picks up a hammer and goes down and breaks every window on that set, on one side, come down the other side. He said, 'If you ever come down and interfere with my crew again, I'm gonna burn down Jack Warner's office.'"

Filming was completed in early December of 1956. The director's cut was previewed and the audience reaction seemed positive. Later, however, word came to Wellman that the studio felt the picture would not be successful with Tab Hunter dying—his teenage following would not accept it. A happy ending needed to be shot to replace the tragic one.

Wellman refused to make the change. Jack Warner said, "If you won't direct the new ending, I'll hire somebody who will." The director's contract did not allow him the final cut, and so, on April 26 and 29, an upbeat finish was filmed for Thad and Renee, which included a small church wedding shot on the 20th Century-Fox French street. Rather than have another director take over, Wellman filmed it himself. It was a truly sad time, one that the director would never forget.

Over time, this butchering business of his hoped-for masterpiece got uglier and more depressing. Not only was the ending changed, but the studio brass cut out some of the training, flying, and relationships of the men in order to focus more attention on the love story. Then they decided that the foreign title *C'est la Guerre* didn't fit with their vision, and substituted *With You in My Arms*. Eventually, they settled for *Lafayette Escadrille*, believing it more suitable and better known with older audiences. After all, they believed they already had the teenyboppers.

When Wellman began work on his contractual, sight-unseen picture, this additional scissoring had not taken place. The director's deal on the new film called for $5,000 a week for ten weeks and 20 percent of the net profits. The script he was handed was written by Guy Trosper, who had come into prominence as the result of two baseball films, *The Stratton Story* (1949) with James Stewart, and *The Pride of St. Louis* (1952), for which he received an Academy Award nomination. This story, however, had nothing to do with home runs and ballplayers. It dealt with the lives, loves, and battles of fictionalized characters in the U.S. Army's 1st Ranger Battalion of World War II.

Warner Bros. had had a critical and financial hit in Raoul Walsh's *Battle Cry* (1955), and hoped for another winner with Major James Altieri's biographical account of Darby's Rangers, as the unit was called. The story deals with the formation of the Rangers, under their leader, Major (later, Lieutenant Colonel) William Orlando Darby. The major and his master sergeant, Saul Rosen, who also narrates the film, choose from volunteers a select group of fighting men. They train in Scotland under British Commandos. Due to a shortage of housing, some of the Americans are billeted in Scottish homes, and find romance with Scottish lassies.

Youthful Rollo Burns hooks up with vivacious Peggy McTavish, whose father, Sergeant McTavish, is an imposing but humorous Commando instructor. Roguish Hank Bishop finds his maiden in Wendy Hollister, a daughter of royalty. The womanizing Tony Sutherland pursues the wife, Sheilah Andrews, of his host, John Andrews.

After a landing in French North Africa, two more Ranger units are formed, with Darby promoted to lieutenant colonel. Joining the Rangers is by-the-book Second Lieutenant Arnold Dittman, whose romantic attraction is Angelina De Lotta. When she becomes pregnant by her fiancé, who is killed in action, Dittman turns away from her. He later recants and does the right thing by marrying her.

Not all the Ranger battles are successful and there are many casualties in the invasions of North Africa, Sicily, and the amphibious landing at Anzio. The few who survive the battle of Cisterna are proud to know that they held off and escaped a fully mounted offensive by Hermann Göring's Panzer Division. The Rangers win the respect and admiration of the other fighting men.

The director viewed the script as mediocre material. He wasn't allowed to rewrite the story but, as he had done with many less than exceptional scripts during his term contract days, he set about infusing *Darby's Rangers* with additional action and extra layers of humor. With Bill Clothier back behind the camera, there would be room for out-of-the-ordinary camera angles and interesting compositions.

The budget was somewhat humbling—under a million dollars without studio overhead—and like *The Story of G.I. Joe* and *Battleground, Darby's Rangers* would be shot on soundstages and the back lot. To add realism and action, at a low cost, the director would cut army stock footage into

James Garner, before TV's *Maverick,* and Jack Warden in
Darby's Rangers (1958)

the black-and-white photography. Getting the most out of a low-budget
film was a Wellman strength but, unlike *G.I. Joe* and *Battleground,* the lack
of a strong, quality script made the prospects for *Darby's Rangers* limited.

In the past, Wellman had been able to put his last effort behind him—
whether a successful film or not—and pour himself into the next production. Unfortunately, this time he found it increasingly difficult to keep his
mind on *Darby's Rangers* while the sting of *C'est la Guerre's* ravagement
would not go away.

When casting for the picture began, Warner told Wellman that he
would cast the leading role of Major Orlando Darby, and the director
would fill all the other roles as he pleased. This did not sit well with Wellman but his hands were tied. Warner's first choice was Charlton Heston,
and it was announced in the trade papers that a deal was struck.

To thumb his nose at the mogul, Wellman had his assistant, George
Vieira, get a list of the actors who had been released from the studio's
talent program and contract system. The director began filling the roles
with these players. Just as he had done with *G.I. Joe* and *Battleground,* the
chosen actors began ranger training on the studio back lot—with a drill
instructor, Sergeant First Class Richard Sandlin, Ranger Department,
U.S. Army Infantry School. After two weeks of intense basic training, the
actors began thinking of themselves as soldiers—which, of course, was
Wellman's objective.

As the start date, April 22, 1957, was fast approaching, Jack Warner's
deal with Heston fell apart. The star wanted a piece of the profits and

Warner refused. Burt Lancaster came under consideration, so Wellman was told to delay the start of filming until a proper star was signed. Now Wellman refused.

The director sent Vieira to the back lot with a message for the cast. He stepped out of a black limousine and commanded Sergeant Sandlin to form his troops. When the actor-soldiers were standing at attention, in a straight line facing the assistant, Vieira announced the dispatch: "There's been a casting problem for the lead. Wellman says everybody move up one part!" The actors were shocked and confused. They began murmuring. James Garner, not yet TV's *Maverick* or an icon, and signed for the role of the roguish Hank Bishop, spoke first. "If I move up, I'm Darby. I'm the lead!" "That's right," said Vieira. "Get in the limo, Wellman wants to see you."

Stuart Whitman, who later starred in the extravagant aerial epic *Those Magnificent Men in Their Flying Machines* (1965), the television series *Cimarron Strip* (1967), and was expecting to play Sims Delancey, spoke next. "Do I move up to Garner's role?" "You got it," chuckled Vieira. Bill Wellman, Jr., was standing between Garner and Whitman. He was set for the role of the MP-turned-foot-soldier Eli Clatworthy. He called out to the AD, as he was about to step into the limo. "What about me? Do I move up to Whitman's role?" Vieira answered back, "No, you stay Eli Clatworthy." There were a few other move-ups before the start of production.

There were other newfledged talents: Edd Byrnes (Lieutenant Dittman), in his first major feature role, who later sparked the television screens as Kookie in *77 Sunset Strip*; Peter Brown (Rollo Burns), in his first feature before starring in television's *Lawman* (1958–1962) and *Laredo* (1965–1967); Venetia Stevenson (Peggy McTavish), a glamorous, blond, British-born starlet, active in both movies and television until her retirement in 1961; Corey Allen (Private Tony Sutherland), who had played James Dean's leather-clad nemesis in *Rebel Without a Cause* (1955) and later became an Emmy-winning director; Frank Gifford (squad member), Most Valuable Player during the team's 1956 championship, member of the New York Giants (1952–1964), and inducted into the Pro Football Hall of Fame (1977).

A host of fine character actors were headed by: Jack Warden (Master Sergeant Saul Rosen), whom Wellman had seen in his outstanding performance as Juror #7 in *12 Angry Men* (1957); Torin Thatcher (Sergeant McTavish); Murray Hamilton (Private/Sergeant Sims Delancy); Adam Williams (Corporal Heavy Hall); Andrea King (Mrs. Sheilah Andrews);

Frieda Inescort (Lady Hollister); Reginald Owen (Sir Arthur), who was in Wellman's *Stingaree* (1934); Philip Tonge (John Andrews), back with the director after *Track of the Cat* (1954).

The leading female role was that of Angelina De Lotta, Lieutenant Dittman's (Edd Byrnes) love interest. She is obviously of Italian ancestry, but Wellman went against type in order to cast his *C'est la Guerre* French star, Etchika Choureau. As in her first American film, her performance is exceptional. *Darby's Rangers* signaled the end of her American film career as she returned to her homeland, working in only three more films in the next eight years before retiring.

British actress Joan Elan, from Colombo, Ceylon (now Sri Lanka), was not Wellman's first choice for the role of Wendy Hollister, Hank Bishop's (Stuart Whitman) proper lady. The role was to be played by rising starlet Joanna Barnes, who was being groomed for stardom by Jack Warner via his special assistant, Richard Gully.

On her first day of shooting, Miss Barnes refused to play a love scene with Whitman the way the director wanted. The actors were seated on a couch in a living room set when an air raid takes place. They are so wrapped up in each other that they are oblivious to the ensuing danger. With sirens blaring, they kiss, and with the camera shooting from behind the couch, they slowly sink down going out of frame.

Wellman asked for a simple, closed-mouth kiss. Joanna gave an open-mouthed, French kiss to a surprised Whitman. The director called "Cut," and again requested the modest buss. The next take brought another salivating smooch, and the director blew sky high. "Cut! Goddammit, what the hell is wrong with you?" She answered, "Nothing. I just think this is a more appropriate kiss for the scene." "Well I don't," said Wellman, "and I'm the goddamned director. Either you do it my way or get the hell off my set." Indignantly, she stood up and said, "You can't fire me. Don't you know who I am?" Wellman shot back, "I don't care who you think you are. You're fired, now get the hell outta here." "I'll be back," she announced, then strutted like a peacock off the soundstage.

While the crew waited for further instructions, Wellman sat down in his director's chair. He began looking at the script, trying to figure out what to do next. Shortly, a messenger arrived with a note. Wellman read the contents that said, "Put her back on the picture at once." It was signed J.L. (Jack Warner). Wellman grabbed for a pencil and scribbled "Fuck you." He returned the note to the messenger and told him to deliver it to Mr. Big.

The director now told his assistant to call casting and get another

Daughter Pat, age fifteen, leans against Wellman's third car, a
1948 Oldsmobile. Bill Jr., thirteen, inspects the trunk.

actress over here right away. He was not going to halt filming. Word traveled quickly around the studio and within a half hour an agent with his
client arrived on the soundstage. Wellman met Joan Elan, a struggling
actress, who happened to be on the lot for an audition. The director and
the actress talked for a few minutes, and Wellman gave her the role. She
even fit Barnes's wardrobe. After several rehearsals, the scene was shot in
one take—with a simple, meaningful kiss.

Joanna Barnes was not the only actor fired from the picture. Stuart
Whitman remembered that Dennis Hopper, later of *Easy Rider* fame, also
was sent packing. He was doing a scene with Whitman while lying on
his back in an army pup tent. The director, looking for a slice of comedy,
asked him to leave his feet sticking out the back of the tent while dialoguing. The Actors Studio–trained thesp didn't see the humor in it, said it
didn't fit his "motivation," and he wasn't going to do it. Not very politely,
Wellman told him he was fired, and to shove his motivation where the
sun don't shine.

One exciting piece of action that the director added came from his *G.I.
Joe*. The enemy sniper in the church bell tower scene shot on the RKO
back lot was re-created for *Darby's Rangers* using the exact same Italian
street set.

Oftentimes, Wellman found his comedy on the set. One of the extras,
Norman Grabowski, had a habit of mimicking bird calls. It cracked up
the director and he added scenes with Grabowski and his warbling. In
one scene, a German rifleman hears a loud chirping and peeks his head
up to look for the bird. He is seen and the Rangers move forward, under
the cover of fog, and attack the enemy's position.

Wellman receives the keys to only his fourth (and final) automobile—
a 1955 Ford T-Bird.

Warner Bros. casting said that Wellman could not use an extra as an actor. So the director told them, "Make Grabowski an actor!" They did and, using his nickname, "Woo Woo" Grabowski, he went on to a long career as an actor and award-winning custom car designer. He built the custom car driven by Kookie (Edd Byrnes) in *77 Sunset Strip*. Production on the 121-minute *Darby's Rangers* was completed, June 21, 1957.

In that same year, Tab Hunter made his singing debut for Dot Records. He recorded "Young Love" and the single rocketed to the top of the charts, holding on to number one for six weeks. A follow-up, "Ninety-nine Ways," reached number eleven on the Billboard Hot 100 chart. Since Jack Warner had Hunter under contract as an actor, not as a singer, he reaped no financial rewards. Dot Records, however, was owned by rival Paramount Pictures, so the mogul was able to enforce his Warner Bros. contract to stop the release of Hunter's follow-up album.

To take advantage of Hunter's success, J.L. established his own Warner Bros. record company. This took time, and in a marketing ploy he held back the release of the now titled *Lafayette Escadrille* until his record company was open for business, March 19, 1958. The film lay unreleased for eleven months.

Darby's Rangers was released before *Escadrille* on February 12, 1958. As the director had guessed, and as hard as he had tried to improve the final edition, *Rangers* was far from the hard-hitting, gut-twisting, reality gems of *G.I. Joe* and *Battleground*. To give *Darby's Rangers* its due, the picture eventually became profitable, and presented Warner Bros. with at least three stars—James Garner, Edd Byrnes, and Peter Brown—for highly successful television series.

Released in March of 1958, *Lafayette Escadrille* failed with critics and at the box office. There was a multitude of possible reasons: Hunter's singing career did not materialize at Warner Bros. Records; his movie career was beginning to decline; in September of 1955 his fan base took a hit when the tabloid magazine *Confidential* reported his 1950 arrest for "disorderly conduct"; a second article again reported on his sexual orientation; Tab Hunter homosexual jokes began to spread throughout the film industry and movie audiences; the film itself suffered greatly from its straying from the original story.

The released version of this film brought reviews like: "Trussed up in surface moralities, this film is not artistically honest," *New York Herald Tribune*, April 9, 1958. "A maudlin and meaningless rehash of routine war-romance situations," *Christian Science Monitor*, March 4, 1958. Wellman added his own postmortem: "a made over happy ending that brought the hero back to his lady's ever-loving arms and fell flat on its ass, artistically, financially, and spiritually."

Wellman was devastated. He had certainly made unsuccessful pictures in the past, but this one carried with it a lifetime sentence of guilt and despair. "A bad picture," he said, "is like a frightful birthmark on your face—it never leaves you, first run, second run, TV prime time, late time, lousy time; it's always there for people to stare at unbelievingly or turn away from or worse still turn off, or should that be better still? It's your eternal badge of embarrassment."

If only Wellman had been allowed to exhibit his *C'est la Guerre* with James Dean or Paul Newman, even with Tab Hunter during his heyday of 1957, maybe everything would have been better—certainly, it would have been different.

Other questions come to mind. Had the director lost his touch? Become too old in mind and body? Or was it just bad timing? Or . . . bad luck? In any case, Wellman told his family that he was finished. "I'm not retiring," he said. "I'm quitting."

He asked Bill Jr. to go with him to Warner Bros. to pack up some personal items from his office. It would be his final trip there. They motored from Brentwood to Burbank in the fourth automobile that Wellman ever owned—from the infamous camouflaged Essex Roadster of his early Paramount days, to the green rumble-seated Packard 745 of his 1930s

Warner Bros. time, to the praline brown 1948 Oldsmobile Hydra-Matic convertible coupé, and now, the torch red 1955 Ford Thunderbird with removable hardtop. These four motor cars had a part in the last fifty years of his life.

The Wellmans boxed up photos of Dottie and the kids, Tommy Hitchcock, Duke Sinclaire, and other pilots; a few books and important papers; his favorite Eagle "chemi-sealed" draughting, soft-leaded pencils, and a few other desk items. They were placed in the smallish T-Bird trunk, then the two Wellmans walked along the studio street on their way to lunch in the commissary.

They walked past the soundstages where the director had made twenty-three of his films—personal favorites like *The Public Enemy*, *Heroes for Sale*, *Night Nurse*, *Wild Boys of the Road*, *Island in the Sky*, *The High and the Mighty,* and *Good-bye, My Lady*. He thought about the talented and hardworking men and women behind the cameras; the great stars that he had befriended: Humphrey Bogart, James Cagney, Bette Davis, Clark Gable, Barbara Stanwyck, Loretta Young, John Wayne; and the love of his life, Dottie Coonan.

There was not much conversation during the meal. When they finished and walked outside, Jack Warner drove up to the commissary curb in a studio golf cart. He was alone. He got out and Wellman approached him. The mogul uttered a low-toned, "Hiya, Bill." Wellman stepped up a few feet from J.L., with Bill Jr. a few steps behind. "I know this is your studio," said Wellman, "but if I ever catch you in a men's room or alone somewhere, I'm gonna put you in the hospital for six weeks." Wellman continued to stare at Warner, who couldn't hold his share of the stare, and quickly got back in his cart and drove away. The director's red T-Bird left Warner Bros. studio for the last time.

21

THE FLAME IS FLICKERING

It is hard to imagine that there would not be another picture directed by William A. Wellman. He was there in the glorious silent era. He transitioned into the classic period with the arrival of sound and talkies. He triumphed in the Depression days. He was a leader with the introduction of color and Technicolor. He succeeded with new technologies like widescreen. He starred in the Golden Age of Hollywood with popular film trends of the day: aviation, gangland, pre-Code melodrama, fallen women, screwball comedy, epic adventure, hero and antihero Western, political, patriotic, morale-boosting, war, coming-of-age.

He respected but fought with mighty moguls: Adolph Zukor and Jesse Lasky, Harry Cohn, William Fox, Samuel Goldwyn, Louis B. Mayer, David O. Selznick, Darryl F. Zanuck, Jack Warner—while their dream factories were at their most magical time. He watched those radiant kingdoms fracture and topple to the ground through corporate takeovers, real estate development, antitrust actions, and the departure of the men who built them.

His most respected mogul, David Selznick, later said, "Hollywood's like Egypt, full of crumbled pyramids. It'll never come back. It'll just keep on crumbling until finally the wind blows the last studio prop across the sands."

And now, the industry he helped to create had beaten him down and sent him packing. It had taken showbiz more than forty years and over a hundred credits to bring Wild Bill to his knees. But he would get up and simply go home. Home to his devoted wife and seven kids. To the New England–style farmhouse that he and Dottie had built. To the horses, dogs, chickens, rabbits, pigeons, and whatever other birds and animals

The Wellman family in the living room of their New England–style home: (left to right, top row) Bill Jr., Wellman, Pat, Kitty; (bottom row) Mike, Dottie, Maggie, Cissy, Tim, 1955

the kids brought home. He would shovel manure to fertilize his orange trees. He would hunt garden ants, trap gophers, clobber moles, direct the gardeners, swim laps, play Ping-Pong, shoot pool, strike the golf ball, and drink beer—hopefully, not too much.

Did he lose his enthusiasm for filmmaking? Did he mope around the house feeling sorry for himself? Not for a moment. Would he grumble and curse at his arthritis and Jack Warner? Many moments. But there would always be a scar, always a burning inside him to make another picture.

Wellman tried to keep his mind off moviemaking. He tried hard to stay "quitted." One day on the putting green at Bel-Air Country Club, James Aubrey, Jr., president of the CBS television network, approached him with a proposition. Aubrey, described by Academy Award–winning actor and producer John Houseman as "the smiling cobra," but better known as "Supersalesman," had heard about the director's so-called retirement.

Aubrey introduced himself and offered an amazing deal. If Wellman would direct a film for CBS, he could choose any story, have any cast, budget, and salary he desired. Wellman clearly stated, "Television is a different business and I'm too old to learn it. Thanks, but I've quit." The Supersalesman could not change his mind.

After several months of "vacationing," Wellman gave in to that inner desire. He found a story that excited him. Did he pick a safe project? A trend picture? A genre film that he had excelled with many times? No, he picked a comedy Western from popular Western novelist Max Evans called *The Rounders*.

In the past, the majority of successful Western comedies were those headlining star comedians like Laurel and Hardy, Buster Keaton, W. C. Fields, Mae West, and Bob Hope. Hope's *Son of Paleface* was a hit in 1952, but *Red Garters* (1954) starring singers Rosemary Clooney and Guy Mitchell, and *Many Rivers to Cross* (1955) with romantic leading man Robert Taylor and leading lady Eleanor Parker, failed. In 1959, Hollywood studios were not looking for fun in the West as a profitable venture.

Wellman was able to make a development deal at Paramount. The story revolves around two aging cowboys who bust broncos, drink heavily, and chase skirts with no intention of settling down. Their employer is a shrewd businessman who always outsmarts them. He talks them into taking an unremarkable horse in lieu of wages. The ornery roan can't be broken. They devise a plan to bet their bankroll that no cowboy at the big rodeo can stay on the maverick. Things go as planned as nobody can sit the horse. The animal, however, suddenly collapses and all the money they've won is spent on veterinary expenses. In the end, they are right back where they started, with only the nasty horse to show for their efforts.

During the development stage, Wellman contacted two actors who wanted the lead roles—Fess Parker, not yet Daniel Boone but already Davy Crockett, and Mickey Rooney, of Andy Hardy fame, and forty years old on his next birthday. After two months, Wellman and Tom Blackburn presented their script, but received a thumbs-down, with the final remark from the studio hierarchy, "You can't make fun of a Western." Very soon after, the genre took off with John Wayne's *North to Alaska* (1960) and *McLintock!* (1963), and among others, the hugely popular *Cat Ballou* (1965) with Jane Fonda and Lee Marvin, who won the Best Actor Oscar playing an alcoholic gunslinger riding a drunken horse.

It's very possible that the Wellman-Blackburn script about the two over-the-hill cowhands who know how to get themselves in trouble, played by six-foot-six Fess Parker and five-foot-two Mickey Rooney, might have been the picture to revitalize the genre. *The Rounders* was finally produced in 1965 by MGM, from a script by Burt Kennedy, who also directed, and starring the unlikely funnymen Glenn Ford and Henry Fonda. It proved to be a bland, box office failure.

This studio rejection caused some pain for Wellman but nothing like his radiculitis. A few months after the MGM turndown, he was working in the garden and leaned over to pick up a flower. A siren of despair sounded out as an ambulance, carrying the pain-racked gardener, sped through West Los Angeles on its way to St. John's Hospital. Radiculitis is the pain radiated along the nerve paths due to inflammation of the spinal nerve roots.

The Wellman family doctor, Richard W. Miller, told Bill Jr. at the hospital, "Plane crashes, war injuries, arthritis, his body's taken a pounding. Prepare Dottie and the kids, he might not survive this."

After four weeks in the hospital, he was allowed to go home but still in danger. "I went to the hospital in an ambulance," he recalled, "with the siren screaming like a ravished dame. I came home in an ambulance with the siren as silent as a little mouse. . . . The lovely little smile on Mommy's [Wellman's nickname for Dottie] face. All through the ride home, and now at home, that enchanting little smile said everything. How much she had missed me, how glad that I was home, how much she loved me. Even though I hurt like hell, life was still very sweet."

One by one, his seven children trooped in to tell him how much he was missed. There would be weeks of physiotherapy, traction, special exercises, and in Wellman's words, "bedsores, indigestion, slumbering bowels, faltering trips to the bathroom, agony, 'green hornets' [his name for codeine pills], and unending love and understanding."

No other visitors were allowed and rumors traveled around that he was in serious condition—which was true—and ready to meet his maker—not true. He did survive it and always joked about how this ailment was perfect for him—ra.dic.u.li.tis . . . ridiculous. Upon his return to mainstream life, those shadowy rumors disappeared.

On the morning of November 6, 1961, his world and that of his neighbors burst into the flames of the worst fire in the history of the city (to that time). According to the Los Angeles Fire Department's Historical Society, the Bel-Air/Brentwood fire destroyed 484 homes, 190 others were damaged, and 16,090 acres were burned. The cost of the devastation was in excess of $30 million (in 1961 dollars). The 2,500 firefighters saved 78 percent of the homes in the path of the fire. Lives were saved by the more than 300 police officers who made quick evacuations of 3,500 residents including Hollywood luminaries.

In a fifty-year-anniversary article in the *Los Angeles Times*, November 7, 2011, it was reported that Robert Taylor and Richard Nixon, then the former vice president, and his wife, Pat, were forced to flee their homes while the blaze consumed the mansions of Zsa Zsa Gabor and Burt Lancaster. The wildfire caused many injuries but no fatalities.

Not all residents of the fire area evacuated. William Wellman was one of those. He and Dottie were home with four of their children: Tim (age twenty), Cissy (eighteen), Mike (fourteen), and Maggie (ten). Bill Jr. (twenty-four) was married and living in an apartment in Santa Monica. When he and his pregnant wife, Flossie, heard the fire news, they came over to lend their support. A daughter, Kitty (twenty-two), also married and also pregnant, came over from nearby Studio City. The last Wellman child, Patricia (twenty-seven), was married and living in Colorado Springs, Colorado.

The accidental fire had started in ritzy Bel-Air. With the help of strong winds and the wood-shingled roofs of the 1950s-era homes, it jumped the 405 Freeway and burned a steady, leaping path west into wealthy Brentwood. Fortunately, there were no horses on the Wellman property at the time. The existing menagerie was: Alfy and Ruff (two hounds), Dinky (a Basenji), a few chickens (nameless), Boo and his brother Hector (owls), and Bismark (a duck).

The fire moved so rapidly that there was little time to gather many household items. The family collected some clothes, photo albums, jewelry, dad's Oscar, and the duck. All were packed into Dottie's station wagon and, following the director's instructions, on their way to the Miramar Hotel in Santa Monica. Flossie drove back to the safety of her apartment, Kitty, to her home in the San Fernando Valley. Wellman kept Bill Jr. and Tim with him to fight the fire, if necessary.

The sky became a billowing cloud of dark smoke filled with sparks and burning embers. The blaze was choosing the homes it wanted, while allowing others to go unscathed. A member of the LAPD drove down the Wellman driveway to give the evacuation order. Instead of Wellman saying something like, "Yes, sir. We'll just grab a few more things and leave right away," he marched up to the officer's patrol car, looked down at the seated cop, and said, "Goddammit, I'm not leaving my home. You'll have to shoot me to get me off my property." With that, he turned and walked over to the sport court next to the garage where he could watch the approaching fire on the next hill.

The officer called for backup and within minutes a second black-and-white arrived. The two cops stepped out of their vehicles, hands on their holstered pistols, telling the two visible Wellmans to get into their cars. Bill Jr., standing nearby, yelled to his father that they had to leave. Tim had hidden behind the garage. Wellman moved closer to his son and out of the cops' view. He whispered, "Take care of the animals, stay away from the fire, I'll be back." He turned and walked over, getting into the back of a police car next to Bill Jr.

Father and son were driven down Barrington and across Sunset to Brentwood Village. They were dropped off and the patrol cars sped away to continue the evacuations. Wellman said to his son, "We can run back up Layton Canyon. Let's go." Actor Richard Jaeckel, who had worked for Wellman in *Battleground*, was standing in a crowd watching the not-so-distant fire coming closer. He ran to the Wellmans offering his assistance. The three men crossed Sunset Boulevard and ran up Layton Canyon to the east side of the Wellman property.

By the time they got there, much of the property was on fire. The two-story barn and playroom structure, the horse stalls, corral, and gymnasium were engulfed in flames. Wellman yelled for Tim, who showed up quickly and pointed to the dog pen that had been spared. Wellman gave orders and handed a garden hose to Jaeckel, who leaped onto the garage roof. Another hose to Bill Jr., who climbed up on the two-story roof of the main house. Wellman worked the perimeter of both structures. Tim cared for the animals and observed the path of the fire, shouting out its movement.

Due to the many evacuations in the neighborhood, the Wellman team had water pressure for a while but then it disappeared. They were able to extinguish spot fires on the roofs and in the surrounding vegetation. Then, as if by some unseen force, the fire moved on across neighboring streets until the firemen with the aid of the LAPD had won the battle. The Wellman team had saved their home and the animals.

Wellman had released his last agent, Lester Linsk, but occasionally the phone rang with a producer on the other end. He usually gave the same comment, "Thanks, but I'm not interested. I've quit!" In early 1962, Merian C. Cooper called regarding a special project that Wellman could not turn away from.

He and Cooper had worked together successfully on *Stingaree* (1934), when Cooper was head of production at RKO Radio Pictures. They hooked up again in 1936 and 1937 with *A Star Is Born* and *Nothing Sacred*, when Cooper was vice president of Selznick International Pictures. Cooper's story about United States naval aviators in World War II was fact-based. During the heavy conflict, the navy was sorely in need of combat pilots, and couldn't wait for their student fliers to complete the flight training program. They decided to take their chances with young pilots who had received training but had washed out for various reasons before graduation.

The navy handed the leadership role to a rough-and-ready officer whose job it was to choose, quickly train, and turn mostly incorrigibles into combat-ready aviators. He is successful at bringing discipline and camaraderie into the lives of a dozen hard cases who become casualties, survivors, and heroes in the end. The story was titled *The S.O.B.'s* (no relation to the Blake Edwards's 1981 *S.O.B.*). Cooper had gotten the cooperation of the Naval War Department, which meant the use of outstanding aerial action footage.

A deal was struck at the only major studio where Wellman had never worked, Universal Pictures. The studio was the second oldest in Hollywood, beaten only by Paramount Pictures. In 1951, Universal International was acquired by Decca Records. In 1962, Decca was purchased by Music Corporation of American (MCA), leaving Edward Muhl in charge of production. Muhl came up through the Universal ranks from bookkeeper to accounting department to head of the legal department and, eventually, head of production—without any experience in film.

When Wellman believed the screenplay was ready, it was presented to head of production Edward Muhl, who had a problem with it. There were no females, no romance. He said to add women to the story. Wellman believed in the story and refused to change it. The deal died and the picture was never produced.

Again, Wellman was at the forefront of a developing genre but not allowed to participate. *The Magnificent Seven* (1960) was in the vanguard of this brand of storytelling about a group of male combatants (seven gunfighters), hired (by villagers) to get rid of evildoers (murderous bandits). *The Professionals* (1966) tells how a Texas millionaire hires four adventurers to rescue his kidnapped wife from Mexican outlaws. *The Dirty Dozen* (1967), closest to the Cooper-Wellman story, is about a dozen convicted murderers assigned to a U.S. Army major for training and leadership into a mass assassination mission of German officers in World War II.

There were only a few more possibles before Wellman finally hung it up for good. After the hospital episode, John Wayne, one of Hollywood's greatest loyalists, called to extend his sympathy and offer the directing job of a Western, *The Comancheros* (1961). Although Wayne was starring, Wellman read the script and decided to pass—it contained nothing that he hadn't already accomplished.

In 1964, Mike Frankovich called. He was the head of Columbia Pic-

The complete family gathers on Christmas of 1967: the seven children, grandchildren, wives, husbands, and Dottie's mother, Flossie, seated in center of living room couch

tures and was bidding on the movie rights to Elleston Trevor's novel *The Flight of the Phoenix* (1965), the story of a plane crash in the Sahara and how the survivors find a way to save themselves. Wellman was fascinated with the book and signed on—that is, if Columbia won the rights. Wellman always loved stories of men in peril and began his unofficial casting. He called his first-choice stars for the roles of the pilot and copilot, John Wayne and Joel McCrea, respectively. They both said, "Yes, I'll do it." James Franciscus, a popular leading man of the period and married to a Wellman daughter, Kitty, would play the aircraft designer who makes a flyable plane from the wreckage.

Unfortunately, director Robert Aldrich, Wellman's assistant director on *The Story of G.I. Joe*, outbid Columbia and made the film with a mostly foreign cast of Richard Attenborough, Peter Finch, Hardy Kruger, Ian Bannen, Christian Marquand, and James Stewart as the pilot. The film was remade in 2004, directed by John Moore and starring Dennis Quaid and foreign players.

The Aldrich picture had more than its share of problems with weather, planes, and a fatality. On July 8, 1965, on location in Buttercup Valley, Arizona, where Wellman had shot *Beau Geste*, the great stunt pilot Paul Mantz was killed while landing the put-together Phoenix aircraft. He and Wellman had had a storied history together, from the Las Vegas wedding flight with Dottie to a long list of films, fights, and friendship.

Mantz's partner in TallMantz Aviation, Frank Tallman, from Wellman's *Lafayette Escadrille*, was supposed to make that fatal flight, but a freak go-kart accident with his small son in the driveway of their home prevented him. He was hospitalized, infection set in, and his leg was amputated. He taught himself to fly with one leg, preferring to fly without the prosthetic he used for walking. He continued to perform stunts until 1978.

On Saturday, April 15, 1978, the fifty-nine-year-old Tallman was killed on a flight from Santa Monica to Phoenix, when poor weather conditions, heavy rainfall, caused his twin-engine Piper Aztec to crash into the side of Santiago Peak in the Santa Ana Mountains, near Trabuco Canyon. Frank Tallman and Paul Mantz were two of the greatest stunt pilots of all time.

In the disappointment over losing *Flight of the Phoenix*, Mike Frankovich offered Wellman a directing job at Columbia. Released as *The Trouble with Angels* (1966), it was an uplifting, coming-of-age story about life at a convent school where two mischief-makers make life difficult for the Mother Superior before seeing the light. Wellman had been willing to pour his arthritic body into the aviation world of *Phoenix*, but not the juvenile troubles of young convent girls and nuns. Ida Lupino, Wellman's discovery for *The Light That Failed* (1939), directed *Trouble with Angels* starring Rosalind Russell, whom Wellman had helped rise to stardom in *The President Vanishes*.

With nothing successful on his résumé since quitting, Wellman felt that his time as a movie director had truly passed, and he began searching for something else to keep the flame at least flickering. Several publishers had talked to him about writing an autobiography. He started to write and when a representative of Hawthorne Books flew out from New York to see how the work was going, Wellman showed him the wood-burning fireplace. "I don't understand," he quipped. "Where's your manuscript pages?" Wellman pointed to the burning embers in the fireplace, saying, "They're in there where they should be. I hate writing I did this and I did that. So, forget it. I'm not writing an autobiography."

Soon after, Wellman got an idea for his book. Being that he had spent so much time in hospitals, he would write stories about his life as if under the influence of hospital drugs, particularly green hornets. The many nurse's reports would be his guide. He called it *A Short Time for Insanity* and it was published by Hawthorne in 1974.

Mother Celia had been coming west to see her son for thirty-two years. She was eighty-five when she arrived in 1954 to be a participant in Ralph Edwards's popular TV show *This Is Your Life*. She was part of the surprise package that included, among other notables, James Cagney, John Wayne, Wellman's World War I flying buddy Reginald "Duke" Sinclaire, and his brother, Arch. Wayne had set up a bogus production meeting with the director to discuss the trailer for *Track of the Cat* when Ralph Edwards's voice boomed over the studio loudspeaker, "THIS IS YOUR LIFE: WILLIAM A. WELLMAN."

On the show, Celia told stories of her son's rebellious youth, and was very proud of his success in films and family life. She passed away on June 11, 1967—at ninety-seven years, ten months.

Wellman's brother and Celia spent their lives on the East Coast. Arch, before he retired in 1975, became the president and chairman of the board of Wellman Inc., of Boston (commodities brokers), Wellman Industries,

A scene from daughter Pat's wedding reception, 1959: (left to right) George Chandler, Cissy Wellman, age sixteen, Johnny Indrisano, Mrs. Fred MacMurray (June Haver), Fred MacMurray

June 16, 1972

On one of Miss Stanwyck's interviews she mentioned me as one of her favorite directors and ended with "I love that man." ___ needless to say I was very proud and had a lump in my throat which does not happen to me very often — Barbara Stanwyck- "I love that girl."

Bill Wellman

Wellman's return memo to the person who forwarded Barbara Stanwyck's letter to him

of Johnsonville, South Carolina (textile concerns), and Wellman Oil Corporation.

In 1981, Arch pledged $15 million to Massachusetts General Hospital to build a research building in his name and that of his third wife, the former Gullan Karlson.

Arch was always responsible for Celia's care and support. He didn't see the need for his West Coast brother to send money every month, but Wellman did it anyway, fulfilling his promise of paying her back for her support during the war.

Arthur "Arch" Ogden Wellman was ninety-two when he died of leukemia on March 7, 1987. He had three marriages and three children by his first wife, Ruth Kingman; two sons, Arthur O. Wellman, Jr., of Boston, and John, of Mount Gilead, South Carolina; a daughter, Marjorie Bullock, of Juno Beach, Florida, and Little Compton, Rhode Island; ten grandchildren and ten great-grandchildren.

Wellman and his brother never became close friends, although Arch tried harder to bridge the gap with more California trips in the 1950s and 1960s. They played golf, dined, told stories, but there was always an unspoken competition and a distance between them. When they weren't together, however, they talked and bragged about each other to anyone who might listen.

March 4, 1968, was the date of Wellman's eighteenth birthday celebration. He was actually seventy-two but his leap year birth allowed him only one birthday every four years. On those every-four-year celebrations, Dottie and Bill hosted major costume-themed parties at Chasen's Restaurant in Beverly Hills, the Bel-Air Country Club, or at their home. It was as if he was making up for the Hollywood parties he wasn't invited to or refused to attend.

Guests arrived in costumes representing Wellman's leap year age. For instance, 1968 was his eighteenth and the theme was "Hippies and Flower Children." Other party topics from his teenage years were "Surfers Only" and "Beatniks or Squares." The guest lists were crowded with family, friends, and celebrities. Robert Stack, who was invited after *The High and the Mighty*, remarked, "Everyone in Hollywood wanted to be on the guest list." With few exceptions, to be an invited celebrity one had to have worked in at least one of the director's films. Some of the movie dignitaries were (alphabetically): Charlie Barton, Anne Baxter, Julie Bishop, Ward Bond, James Cagney, Frank Capra, Hoagy Carmichael, George Chandler, Bill Clothier, Mike Connors, Bob Cummings, Nancy Davis, Frances Dee, Andy Devine, June Haver, Johnny Indrisano, David Janssen, Howard Keel, Ida Lupino, Fred MacMurray, Joel McCrea, Andrew McLaglen, Adolphe Menjou, Ricardo Montalban, John Payne, Ronald Reagan, and Jane Wyman.

Bill and Dottie's kids, plus a few of their friends, were in attendance at these gatherings. By 1968, five of the seven children were married and there were ten grandchildren.

Unlike today, with a superabundance of film industry awards, in the 1960s and 1970s there were few award presentations, film festivals, and retrospectives honoring the men and women who had made significant contributions to the art of film. By 1972, Wellman had never had a retrospective of his work, nor received an award of any kind for his achievements. Except for a handful of film scholars and historians who sought him out for interviews, he was a forgotten man in the film industry.

One of the men who made a change in this discrepancy was Kevin Brownlow, who interviewed Wellman for his celebrated 1968 book on the silent film world, *The Parade's Gone By*. The Honorary Academy Award–winning preservationist and filmmaker was also instrumental in organizing, with the British Film Institute, Wellman's first retrospective with the screening of thirty films in London. Wellman attended with Dottie, Bill Jr., and his wife, Flossie, from July 18 to 23, 1972.

The days and nights were filled with interviews, television appearances, Q and As after screenings, sightseeing, special luncheons, and dinner engagements. Even though he would never admit it, he was overwhelmed by the respect and admiration shown him by the English press, the people of the National Film Theatre—a division of the British Film Institute—and the audiences of his films. This homage, however, did not diminish his sense of humor.

When he was introduced with the naming of what they considered his finest films, he would counter with, "But I also directed *The Twins of Suffering Creek* (title of the novel that became *The Man Who Won*), *The Boob,* and *The Cat's Pajamas.*" Another favorite comment was "For every good picture, there were six stinkers."

Richard Schickel, author, film critic for *Life* and *Time* magazines, three-time Emmy nominee, and award-winning documentarian, chose Wellman to be a participant in *The Men Who Made the Movies* (PBS, 1972). Schickel also wrote the foreword for *A Short Time for Insanity.* Although Wellman never won an Oscar for directing, the Directors Guild of America bestowed on him their 1973 D. W. Griffith Lifetime Achievement Award. His friend Frank Capra presided at the gala awards banquet. From Capra's speech: "For Bill was born a rebel. And he lived, and still lives as a rebel. He never was and never will be anybody's boy, anybody's man; who pleads no special causes, except perhaps for the individual's freedom to do, think, and be any damn thing he pleases. As a director, he fought many a battle, some with his fists, for the right to make his films the way he thought he should make them."

Even with the well-received Schickel PBS film and the Directors Guild's highest award under his belt, no retrospectives came forth from his industry or his country until . . . Bill Jr. and Tom "Billy Jack" Laughlin organized a monthlong tribute and screening of thirty-eight films at the Royal Theatre in West Los Angeles, May 8 to 21, 1974. The tribute kicked off May 5 with an afternoon gathering of family and close friends at Wellman's home, followed by a more formal dinner party the next evening at his favorite restaurant, Chasen's.

The Chasen's celebrity guest list included Richard Arlen, James Cagney, Mike Connors, Mae Clarke, James Franciscus, Tom Laughlin, Ida Lupino, Fred MacMurray, Lloyd Nolan, Buddy Rogers, Robert Stack, Barbara Stanwyck, Regis Toomey. Also in attendance were director Tay

James Cagney and his wife, Billie, flew out from Martha's Vineyard to attend the 1974 tribute.

Garnett, George Chandler, and Johnny Indrisano. Madcap anecdotes and tall tales filled the room to the delight of everyone within earshot and, most of all, Wild Bill. The merriment and first-class cuisine lasted well into the late evening.

A highlight of the film festival was the screening of the winner of the First Academy Award for Best Picture, Wellman's *Wings*, with organ accompaniment by Chauncey Haines, who had performed his artistry at the Los Angeles premiere held at the Biltmore Theatre in 1927.

There were few sold-out screenings. Some of the newer pictures were playing on television, while others had not yet reached TV and were not known to movie audiences of the time. The people who came, however, were not disappointed and Wellman was gratified. All proceeds from this nonprofit event went to a William A. Wellman Scholarship in UCLA's Theatre Arts Department—Cinema Division.

The film festival date was set to coincide with the publication of his book, *A Short Time for Insanity*. Television appearances on Merv Griffin's and Tom Snyder's popular talk shows were also arranged to help promote the book. Wellman's tell-it-as-it-is style, caustic sense of humor, and sailor's slang were a hit and Griffin had him back for a repeat performance.

By this time, he had recounted further of his adventures in a book titled *Growing Old Disgracefully* (unpublished). It was in this edition that he decided to open the closed door that had protected his shining angel of the First World War. If only for a few pages, he would release the safe trance that had held beautiful Renee captive for fifty-five years.

His desire to set her free began in July 1972. With his wife, oldest son, and daughter-in-law, he traveled to London for the thirty-film retrospective given by the National Film Theatre. When the final frame of film passed through the projector, he took Dottie, Bill Jr., and Flossie to Paris for a last walk down memory lane.

On the morning of July 25, Wellman told Dottie and Flossie to enjoy a fine day shopping and sightseeing in Paris, while he and Bill Jr. would travel by taxi to the War Memorial, dedicated to American volunteer fliers who fought and died for France in World War I.

The Wellmans arrived at Parc de Villeneuve-L'Etang in Marnes-la-Coquette in less than thirty minutes. The eye-filling stone structure, built in 1928, consists principally of an Arch of Triumph and a semicircular Crypt or Sanctuary. The monument is half the size of the Arc de Triomphe in Paris. On the facade of the arch are inscribed the names of those American pilots of the Lafayette Escadrille and Lafayette Flying Corps who survived the conflict as well as those who made their final flights in that long-ago war.

While standing in front of that magnificent stone arch, Wellman read the names of the young knights of the air he had known and flown beside. He told his son, "They were not just names in 1917, they were headlines and they were the best."

The way back to their hotel took much longer than the arrival, as the former fighter pilot was trying to locate a piece of real estate from 1918. Bill Jr. and the cab driver were frustrated by the lack of information and proper directions. They drove up, down, and around many streets. Finally, Wellman told the driver to stop and pull over. He got out and stood there, entranced by something across the quiet street that was lined with time-worn and collapsed buildings. Bill Jr. followed suit, standing next to his father and asking, "What do you see, dad?"

After a long moment, Wellman pointed across the street to a small, crumbled building. Under his breath, "That building, what's left of it, was the church where I was married."

"To whom?" asked Bill Jr.

"Her name was Renee." Bill Jr. was speechless at the realization of another wife in his father's already crowded matrimonial history. His father had always talked freely about his ex-wives and anything else in his life and career. He never seemed to keep secrets. He would answer questions immediately and honestly. But this singular episode was never mentioned until now.

During the ride back, Wellman talked at length about Renee, their four months together, even her death. Bill Jr. listened intently, without questioning. He could feel his father's deep-seated pain. No words of this drama were spoken around Dottie, Flossie, or anyone else. After returning to the United States and home, Wellman wrote two-plus pages about his French angel who had captured a piece of his heart—a frozen love in a placid pool of dark blue, now stirring with ripples of sunlight.

Wellman started a third edition of memoirs, *Wrong Head on the Pillow,* but stopped suddenly. "I can't write another book," he told his family. "I'm out of stories and would have to make them up." The fact is, he had more stories to tell but was tired of the long process; his seemingly endless supply of energy and enthusiasm was vanishing.

At the end of *A Short Time for Insanity* he wrote, "That is all, and it is high time. Not the end of my troubles but the finish of this short piece of insanity. I have a new kind of pain, it hits like a hummingbird—whi-i-i-i-i-t and it's gone, and it leaves you with your mouth wide open! I have a corset that I should wear. I prefer to suffer. I broke the habit, and I feel lousy; I am growing a beard, and I look a little bit like Hemingway, but I can't write a little bit like him. My insides have been buffeted so hard and so long that everything inside me slumbers; I wish to high heaven I could sleep as soundly as some of my most important vitals."

In September of 1975, Wellman began complaining of something more than the pain and suffering he had been fighting. Tests at St. John's Hospital proved him right. The day he got the news, three doctors were in attendance: two cancer specialists and the family doctor, Dick Miller.

Specialist #1: "Mr. Wellman, I loved *The High and the Mighty.* I think your films are—"
Wellman (interrupting): "Cut the crap. What have I got?"
Specialist #2: "The medical term is acute myelogenous leukemia."
Wellman: "That's cancer, isn't it?"
Specialist #2: "Blood cancer, yes."
Wellman: "How long have I got?"
Nobody wants to answer.
Wellman: "Don't bullshit me."
Miller: "Bill, it's not that cut and dry. There are various treatments, radiation, chemotherapy—"
Wellman (interrupting): "Stop it, Dick. I want the truth."

Specialist #1: "Three months."

Dr. Miller and Specialist #2 are shocked at #1's candor.

Miller (to #1): "Wait a minute. You have no right to say that."

Specialist #2: "Let's all calm down. With proper treatment, there's no telling how long—"

Wellman (interrupting): "No, Goddammit! I don't want that. I'm not staying in the hospital. I'd rather die at home with my family."

Just as the St. John's cancer doctor had predicted, without any treatment other than the constant loving care from Dottie and his will to live, he deteriorated rapidly. He never cried, he never felt sorry for himself; he displayed a kind of

"Bill Darling—keep me with you always, because, as you know, I love you. Dottie"

understated dignity while his life was being taken from him. All the while, Dottie held fast to her belief that he would somehow make it through this dreadful torture. "He's gotten through everything else. He'll get through this, too," she would say. But it was obvious he would not.

On Thanksgiving Day 1975, he was conscious but barely able to walk. He hadn't shaved and his beard was white. All his children and grandchildren were present at his home, even Dottie's mother, Flossie, ninety-four years old. Dottie leaned over and kissed her husband, saying, "Bill, the photographer is here to take the family pictures. Do you feel up to sitting for one shot with all our kids and grandchildren?" "I'll try," he whispered.

In the Wellman living room, the photographer snapped photos of the seven children and six spouses—only Mike was unmarried. Shots were taken of Grandmother Flossie, the thirteen grandkids, and the Basenji pet, Dinky. With Dottie at his side, Bill Jr. half carried his father down the stairs, placing him in the center section of the couch. The family grouped around him and the camera flashed and the bulb popped the final picture.

With Wellman's permission, a priest was summoned to administer the Last Rites. His seven children were able to say their goodbyes. When Bill

Jr.'s turn came, he entered the master bedroom; his father was pale and weak, lying on his back in bed. His eyes moved sideways to see his oldest son standing beside him. He said, "I wrote something about my flying pals. It's in an envelope on my desk. See what you think." "Sure, dad," said Bill. Wellman continued, "Your mother is so wonderful. She has meant everything to me. Promise that you'll take care of my Mommy." Bill answered, "I promise, dad. Don't worry." After a pause, Wellman went on. "And I don't want some son of a bitch coming into my home." The emotions were getting the best of Bill and tears began to course down his cheeks. He tried to wipe them away quickly but his father was watching and said, "Bill, Goddammit, don't feel sorry for me. I've lived the life of a hundred men."

Exactly three months from the doctor's prediction, Wellman was gone. On the last page of *A Short Time for Insanity*, he wrote his own obituary:

> I'll die, but I will be around for a long time, with Mommy and all the kids and the grandchildren remembering the happy things about their old man, his love of flying, his pictures, his distaste for producers, his love of golf and the sometimes he played well; they wouldn't mention his temper or any of the nasty things, just laughs and maybe even his piano playing, not too good but quietly and softly, and Mommy used to like it, and his enormous appetite for beer and laughingly how Mommy could always tell how much the old boy had sneaked, by just looking at his eyes. Then something happens and his presence becomes embarrassing, maybe she falls in love again, so young, pretty, and attractive, or maybe there is just too much of him around. Then he dies, really dies, and he goes away forever.

Wellman added a footnote to the obituary:

> I want to be cremated and emptied high above the smog—high enough to join a beautiful cloud—not one that brings a storm, one that brings peace and contentment and beauty.

Dottie and the seven kids organized a funeral. Wellman hated funerals and rarely attended them. He was able to skip this one, too. Eight people stood together beside the runway of the small Santa Monica Airport. Dottie and the kids watched a single-engine Cessna taxi over. Pat, cradling a shoe box, climbed into the plane, sitting next to a pilot friend. She smiled at the family, pulled the door shut, and the Cessna taxied away. In a moment, the light aircraft left the runway and the solemn group behind.

Wellman, age twenty-two, in Lunéville, France,
in uniform for the Escadrille N.87, 1918

The flight plan was set for airspace between Hollywood and San Diego—the same corridor Wellman had navigated back in 1919, in his Spad, from Rockwell Field, San Diego, to Douglas Fairbanks's polo field in the movie capital. As per the director's instructions, the ashes would be distributed in the brilliant blue sky, high above white, billowy clouds.

As the sound of the Cessna engine faded away, the family listened to the words that Wellman had written and given to his son about the men who had meant the most to him in his lifetime:

Mine was a clean battlefield, young men died up there, they were never buried up there—but their bravery still drifts through the clouds, like ghostly headstones.

ADDENDUM

No son of a bitch ever came into Wellman's home.

For Dottie, there was but one man. After he was gone, her love and caring turned to her seven children, twenty-two grandchildren, and ten great-grandchildren. On September 9, 2009, she died from natural causes at ninety-five years, ten months.

Her husband of forty-two years was wounded in war and in life, but it never held him back. He was never the fragile American. Wild Bill never ran with the pack, he was never a part of the herd. He was more of the solitary figure, a maverick, never trailing behind, always pointing the way and sprinting forward. He was unconcerned about yesterday, always striving for tomorrow.

Many of his pictures came from dreams long dreamt, from talent long-proven. Dreams in the dark, some locked away in his soul like time capsules for a future event, while others filled the present-day screens with their wonder.

As a way of measuring a director's career, quantity, quality, and everlasting esteem, William Wellman achieved all three and should be included in the pantheon of filmmakers.

He did not care for glory or grandiose living, but for the realization of his films. William A. Wellman loved the art of making motion pictures. He did the work and the luck came. He and his films are forever woven into the fabric of moviedom.

The dark clouds begin to separate and the gray skies show signs of blue. A silver Spad finds a hole in the overcast and zooms up and away, disappearing from sight.

A voice on high shouts, "Here he comes! It's Wild Bill back from another mission! Send out the invitations to Tommy Hitchcock, Duke Sinclaire, and the other American fliers of the Great War. Add the French heroes from Escadrille N. 87. Don't forget Paul Mantz, Frank Tallman, Dick Grace, and the stunt pilots from his films. Chill the beer and prepare the Lafayette cocktails of champagne and brandy, we are going to hear stories and have a helluva good party!"

AFTERWORD

My father was one of the earliest film settlers to migrate west from the Hollywood studios and surrounding areas to West Los Angeles and exclusive Brentwood. Some of the other entertainment members that followed included William "Hopalong Cassidy" Boyd, Frank Capra, Gary Cooper, Joan Crawford, Bob Crosby, Xavier Cugat, Nelson Eddy, Henry Fonda, Gene Fowler, Van Johnson, Peter Lawford, Fred MacMurray, John Payne and wife Gloria DeHaven, Tyrone Power, Cesar Romero, Red Skelton, Lana Turner, Robert Walker and wife Jennifer Jones.

I grew up surrounded by these people. My father told me who they were and what they did. My childhood memories are filled with their comings and goings. If they didn't come to our house, I went to theirs. Their children were my friends. The first girl I kissed was Jane Fonda. For a long time, I thought movie people were in everybody's neighborhood.

These people colored my life and helped me develop my love for the movie industry. Since my nineteenth birthday, when I became a member of that community, I have worked with stars: Richard Arlen, James Arness, Richard Boone, Marlon Brando, Ellen Burstyn, James Caan, Rory Calhoun, Broderick Crawford, Phyllis Diller, Clint Eastwood, Richard Egan, James Garner, Greer Garson, Charlton Heston, William Holden, Bob Hope, David Janssen, Alan Ladd, Tom Laughlin, Jerry Lewis, Gina Lollobrigida, Julia Louis-Dreyfus, Fred MacMurray, Virginia Mayo, Audie Murphy, Pat O'Brien, Gregory Peck, Sean Penn, Walter Pidgeon, Ronald Reagan, Jane Russell, George C. Scott, John Wayne, Raquel Welch, Robert Young, and others. Also film directors: John Ford, Tay Garnett, Howard Hawks, Jerry Lewis, George Marshall, Lewis Milestone, William Wellman.

By mentioning all these names, I announce my deep-felt thanks for being a small part of their lives, while they provided a great inspiration in my career and the writing of this book. The creation of the book began many years ago. When I realized that my father's work was being forgotten, I vowed to do something about it.

During the period between 1965 and 2014, I proposed and worked on various projects that would shine a light on his legacy. In 1971, I wrote a television special called *Wild Bill*, which led to the award-winning feature documentary, *Wild Bill Hollywood Maverick* (1996). My profound gratitude goes to Michael Wayne, who financed the film, and my partners, Todd Robinson and Ken Carlson. Without their talent and tireless efforts, there would not be this film.

A major vote of gratitude must travel to Tom "Billy Jack" Laughlin, who sponsored the 1974 monthlong tribute and retrospective of thirty-eight Wellman films—the only U.S. film festival of my father's work during his lifetime.

A tip of the hat to the dozens of film festival organizers who accepted screenings of Wellman films. The same to the magazine editors who published my articles. A major bow to my book publishers: Greenwood/Praeger for *The Man and His Wings: William A. Wellman and the Making of the First Best Picture*, and Random House/Pantheon for this edition.

Although my endeavors were years in the making, as of this writing all have found a praiseworthy audience with only the movie version still in the wind.

With all the projects over all the years, I have interviewed countless numbers of celebrities, coworkers, family, and friends concerning their memories and recollections of the life and times of William "Wild Bill" Wellman. Some of the contributions were extensive, others fragmented, all are appreciated to the fullest.

Interviewed on film:

Mike Connors
Clint Eastwood
James Garner
Darryl Hickman
Arthur Hiller
Tab Hunter
Howard W. Koch
Tom Laughlin
Burgess Meredith
Robert Mitchum
Henry Morgan
Gregory Peck
Sidney Poitier
Nancy Davis Reagan
Robert Redford
Buddy Rogers
Martin Scorsese
Tony Scott
Robert Stack
Michael Wayne
Dorothy Wellman
James Whitmore
Richard Widmark
Robert Wise
Jane Wyman

Authors/Historians:

John Gallagher
Frank Thompson

Individuals interviewed in conversation and correspondence:

Richard Arlen
James Arness
Alec Baldwin
Charles Barton
Anne Baxter
Marjorie Bullock, daughter of Arthur O. Wellman
George Chandler
John Coonan, brother of Dorothy Wellman
Maria Cooper, daughter of Gary Cooper
Denise Darcel
Andy Devine
Henry Fonda
Johnny Indrisano
David Janssen
Fred MacMurray
Wyatt McCrea, grandson of Joel McCrea
Andrew V. McLaglen
Adolphe Menjou
Ricardo Montalban
Pat O'Brien
Donald O'Connor
Maureen O'Hara
Reginald "Duke" Sinclaire
James Stewart
John Wayne
Arthur O. Wellman, brother of William Wellman
Loretta Young

ACKNOWLEDGMENTS

It would be extremely difficult for me or anyone who takes pen in hand to write about William A. Wellman not to acknowledge the decades of research and writing by two very dedicated men, John Andrew Gallagher and Frank T. Thompson. In the production of *Wild Bill Hollywood Maverick*, I made use of their many talents as film historians.

I lift my glass to Kevin Brownlow and Richard Schickel, for when no one else seemed to care, they picked up the baton and carried my father's banner forward. My deepest gratitude goes to TCM (Turner Classic Movies). If it wasn't for their devoted network, the playing of more than forty Wellman films, the expertise of historian and film lover Robert Osborne, my father's work would be much less remembered.

Special consideration must go to the Bullocks, Bill and Marjorie Wellman, for their support and assistance with the Wellman family history. And, in the same regard, Mary K. Wellman, wife of Arthur O. Wellman, Jr., who passed down the memoirs and memorabilia treasures of Celia Wellman. Tender thanks goes to my wonderful mother, Dottie, for her many recollections of Wild Bill.

Hearty thanks must also travel to my literary agent, Mike Hamilburg, for his confidence in me and finding Greenwood/Praeger for my first book, which led to this edition. Gratitude must also shine on Sue Clamage, who typed hundreds of manuscript pages for this book and my first volume.

All of the following share my appreciation: (alphabetically) Barry Allen, Richard Arnold, A. Scott Berg, Daniel H. Blatt, Ben Burtt, Robert Byrne, Reno Carell, Mark Carlson, Lisa Close, Larry Cohen, Sky Conway, Craig Covner, Paul Cummins, Russell S. Doughten, Jr., Scott Eyman, George Feltenstein, James Franciscus, Thomas Gladysz, Randy Haberkamp, Mary Harris, Frederick Hodges, Leslie Jones, Andrea Kalas, Karen Kramer, Don Krim, Ronnie Leif, Jerry Lewis, Leonard Maltin, Mimi Mayer, Wyatt McCrea, Betsy Newman, Phillip Ney, Douglas Odney, Bruce Orriss, Marvin Paige, Jan Rofekamp, Jerry Rudes, Steven S. Spira, Connie Stevens, Frank Stewart, Lois Stewart, Donald Thompson, Jan Wahl, Stacey Wisnia, Linda Zaruches.

There is no way that I can properly acknowledge the contributions made by my editor, Victoria Wilson. Although she rejected my book several times, she pushed me forward, gave me confidence, pointed the way. Even in my frustration, I could always sense her caring for my father's legacy and my work. She gave me inspiration through the thick-and-thin days of the ever-long process leading to publication. I am forever in her debt.

FILMOGRAPHY

The Following Films Credit Direction to Wellman

THE MAN WHO WON (1923)

Fox. Copyright: August 23, 1923. New York Premiere: October 9, 1923, as part of a double bill. 5 reels.

Presented by William Fox. Produced and Directed by William A. Wellman. Screenplay: Ewart Adamson. Based on the novel *The Twins of Suffering Creek* by Ridgwell Cullum (1912, George Jacobs & Co.). Photography: Joseph H. August. Assistant Director: Edward Bernoudy. Originally released with color tints.

Cast: Dustin Farnum (Wild Bill), Jacqueline Gadsden (Jessie), Lloyd Whitlock ("Lord" James), Ralph Cloninger ("Zip" Scipio), Mary Warren (Birdie), Pee Wee Holmes (Toby Jenks), Harvey Clark (Sunny Oaks), Lon Poff (Sandy Joyce), Andy Waldron (Joe Minkie), Ken Maynard (Conroy), Muriel McCormack, Mickey McBan (The Twins), Bob Marks (The Drunkard), Pedre Leon (Farnum's Stuntman), Harvey Parry (Stunts).

SECOND HAND LOVE (1923)

Fox. Copyright: August 12, 1923. Released August 26, 1923. 5 reels.

Presented by William Fox. Produced and Directed by William A. Wellman. Screenplay: Charles Kenyon. Story: Shannon Fife. Photography: Dan Short. Originally released with color tints.

Cast: Charles "Buck" Jones (Andy Hanks), Ruth Dwyer (Angela Trent), Charles Coleman (Dugg), Harvey Clark (Scratch, the detective), Frank Weed (Deacon Seth Poggins), James Quinn (Dugg's Partner), Gus Leonard (Constable).

BIG DAN (1923)

Fox. Copyright: October 14, 1923. Released October 14, 1923. 6 reels.

Presented by William Fox. Produced and Directed by William A. Wellman. Story and Screenplay: Frederick and Fanny Hatton. Photography: Joseph H. August. Originally released with color tints.

Cast: Charles "Buck" Jones (Dan O'Hara, "Big Dan"), Marian Nixon (Dora Allen), Ben Hendricks (Cyclone Morgan), Charles Coleman (Doc Snyder), Lydia Yeamans Titus (Aunt Kate Walsh), Monte Collins (Tom Walsh), Charles Smiley (Father Quinn), Harry Lonsdale (Stephen Allen), Mattie Peters (Ophelia), J. P. Lockney (Pat Mayo), Jack Herrick (Muggs Murphy), Harvey Parry (Buck Jones Fight Double).

CUPID'S FIREMAN (1923)

Fox. Copyright: December 8, 1923. New York Premiere: Loew's New York, April 22, 1924, as part of a double bill. 5 reels.

Presented by William Fox. Produced and Directed by William A. Wellman. Screenplay: Eugene B. Lewis. Based on the story "Andy M'Gee's Chorus Girl" in *Van Bibber and Others* (New York, 1892) by Richard Harding Davis. Photography: Joseph H. August. Originally released with color tints. Working Title: *Andy M'Gee's Chorus Girl*.

Cast: Charles "Buck" Jones (Andy McGee), Marian Nixon (Agnes Evans), Brooks Benedict (Bill Evans), Eileen O'Malley (Elizabeth Stevens), Lucy Beaumont (Mother), Al Fremont (Fire Chief), Charles McHugh (Old Man Turner), Mary Warren (Molly Turner), L. H. King (Veteran), Harvey Parry (Stunts).

NOT A DRUM WAS HEARD (1924)

Fox. Copyright: January 27, 1924. New York Premiere: March 14, 1924, as part of a double bill. 5 reels.

Presented by William Fox. Produced and Directed by William A. Wellman. Screenplay: Doty Hobart (and uncredited, Ben Ames Williams). Based on a story by Ben Ames Williams. Photography: Joseph H. August. Originally released with color tints.

Cast: Charles "Buck" Jones (Jack Mills), Betty Bouton (Jean Ross), Frank Campeau (Banker Rand), Rhody Hathaway (James Ross), Al Fremont (The Sheriff), William Scott (Bud Loupel), Mickey McBan (Jack Loupel).

THE VAGABOND TRAIL (1924)

Fox. Copyright: March 9, 1924. Released March 9, 1924. 5 reels.

Presented by William Fox. Produced and Directed by William A. Wellman. Screenplay: Doty Hobart. Based on the novel *Donnegan* (1923) by George Owen Baxter. Photography: Joseph H. August. Working Title: *Donnegan*.

Cast: Charles "Buck" Jones (Donnegan), Marian Nixon (Lou Macon), Charles Coleman (Aces), L. C. Shumway (Lord Nick), Virginia Warwick (Nellie LeBrun), Harry Lonsdale (Colonel Macon), Frank Nelson (Slippy), George Reed (Deuces), George Romain (Man).

THE CIRCUS COWBOY (1924)

Fox. Copyright: May 6, 1924. New York Premiere: June 19, 1924, at Loew's New York as part of a double bill. 65 minutes.

Presented by William Fox. Produced and Directed by William A. Wellman. Screenplay: Doty Hobart (and uncredited, Louis Sherwin). Story: Louis Sherwin. Photography: Joseph Brotherton. Originally released with color tints. Working Titles: *The Circus Rider, Bucking the Tiger.*

Cast: Charles "Buck" Jones (Buck Saxon), Marian Nixon ("Bird" Taylor), Jack McDonald (Ezra Bagley), Ray Hallor (Paul Bagley), Marguerite Clayton (Norma Wallace), George Romain (Slovini), Harvey Parry (Stunts).

WHEN HUSBANDS FLIRT (1925)

Columbia. Copyright: November 23, 1925. New York Premiere: July 14, 1926, at the Columbus as part of a double bill. 61 minutes.

Presented by Harry Cohn. Directed by William A. Wellman. Story and Screenplay: Paul Gange Lin and Dorothy Arzner. Titles: Malcolm Stuart Boylan. Photography: Sam Landers.

Cast: Dorothy Revier (Violet Gilbert), Forrest Stanley (Henry Gilbert), Thomas Ricketts (Wilbur Belcher), Ethel Wales (Mrs. Belcher), Maude Wayne (Charlotte Germaine), Frank Weed (Percy Snodgrass), Erwin Connelly (Joe McCormick).

THE BOOB (1926)

Metro-Goldwyn-Mayer. Copyright: May 19, 1926. New York Premiere: May 26, 1926, at Loew's Theatre. 64 minutes.

Directed by William A. Wellman (and uncredited, Robert Vignola). Original Screen Story, "Don Quixote, Jr.," by George Scarborough and Annette Westbay (May 14, 1925). Screenplay: Kenneth B. Clarke. Treatment: Agnes Christine Johnston. Titles: Katherine Hilliker, H. H. Caldwell. Photography: William B. Daniels. Editor: Ben Lewis. Art Direction: Cedric Gibbons, Ben Carre. Asst. Director: Nick Grinde. Working Title: *I'll Tell the World.* British Title: *The Yokel.*

Cast: Gertrude Olmsted (Amy), George K. Arthur (Peter Good), Joan Crawford (Jane), Charles Murray (Cactus Jim), Antonio D'Algy (Harry Benson), Hank Mann (Village Soda Jerk), Babe London (Fat Girl).

THE CAT'S PAJAMAS (1926)

Famous Players-Lasky/Paramount. Copyright: November 17, 1926. Released August 29, 1926. 60 minutes.

Presented by Adolph Zukor and Jesse L. Lasky. Associate Producers: B. P. Schulberg and Hector Turnbull. Directed by William A. Wellman. Screenplay: Hope Loring and Louis D. Lighten. Story: Ernest Vajda. Photography: Victor Milner. Art Direction: Hans Dreier. Props: Charles Barton. Makeup: James Collins.

Cast: Betty Bronson (Sally Winton), Ricardo Cortez (Don Cesare Gracco), Arlette Marchal (Riza Dorina), Theodore Roberts (Sally's Father), Gordon Griffith (Jack), Tom Ricketts (Mr. Briggs).

YOU NEVER KNOW WOMEN (1926)

Famous Players-Lasky/Paramount. Copyright: September 22, 1926. Released September 22, 1926. 70 minutes.

Presented by Adolph Zukor and Jesse L. Lasky. Associate Producers: B. P. Schulberg and Hector Turnbull. Directed by William A. Wellman. Screenplay: Benjamin Glazer. Story: Ernest Vajda. Titles: Alfred W. Hustwick. Photography: Victor Milner. Art Direction: Hans Dreier. Props: Charles Barton. Makeup: James Collins. Working Titles: *Love—The Magician: Love's Magic.* French Title: *Masques d'Artistes.*

Cast: Florence Vidor (Vera Janova), Lowell Sherman (Eugene Foster), Clive Brook (Ivan Norodin), El Brendel (Toberchik), Roy Stewart (Dimitri), Sidney Bracy (The Manager), Joe Bonomo (The Strong Man), Irma Kornelia (Olga, his wife), Sidney Bracy (Manager), Eugene Pallette (Dinner Guest), Billy Seay (Little Boy), Fortunello and Cerellino (Acrobats), Louis and Freda Berkoff (Dancers), the Peccani Jugglers (Jugglers), Rue Enos (Frog Man Contortionist), The Russian Balalaika Orchestra (Orchestra), The Nelson Troupe of Aerial Performers (Aerialists), The Slayman-Ali Troupe of Blue Devils (Tumblers), The Melford Troupe of Risley Wonder Workers (Acrobats).

WINGS (1927)

Paramount Famous Lasky. Copyright: January 5, 1929. New York Premiere: August 12, 1927, at the Criterion. 140 minutes. National release (with Western Electric sound effects and synchronized musical score): January 5, 1929 (with four minutes of Clara Bow footage cut, but restored in current prints).

Presented by Adolph Zukor and Jesse L. Lasky. Produced by Lucien K. Hubbard. Associate Producer: B. P. Schulberg. Directed by William A. Wellman. Screenplay: Hope Loring and Louis D. Lighton. Story/Novelization/Technical Adviser: John Monk Saunders. Titles: Julian Johnson. Photography: Harry Perry. Engineering Effects: Roy Pomeroy. Editor: Lucien K. Hubbard. Editor-in-Chief: E. Lloyd Sheldon. Art Direction: Lawrence Hitt, Hans Dreier. Assistant Directors: Richard Johnston, Norman Z. McLeod, Charles Barton. Production Managers: Frank Blount, Richard Johnston. Supervision of Flying Sequences: Sterling C. Campbell, Ted Parson, Carl Von Hartmann, James A. Healy, Lt. Cdr. Harry Reynolds, Capt. Bill Taylor. Additional Photography: E. Burton Steene, William H. Clothier, Cliff Blackston, Russell Harlan, Bert Baldridge, Frank Cotner, Faxon M. Dean, Ray Olsen, Herman Schoop, L. Guy Wilky, Al Williams, Paul Perry, L. B. Abbott. Aerial Photography: Faxon M. Dean, William H. Clothier, Ernest Laszlo, Herman Schoop, Russell Harlan, Cliff Blackston, Bert Baldridge, Frank Cotner, L. Guy Wilky, Gene O'Donnell, Paul Perry, Art Lane, Harry Mason, Ray Olsen, Al Meyers, Guy Bennett. Photographic Effects: Paul Perry. Costumes: Travis Banton, Edith Head. Makeup: James Collins. Stunt Pilots: Dick Grace, Frank Clarke, Frank Tomick, Rod Rogers, Paul Mantz, Frank Andrews, Hoyt Vandenberg, Bill Taylor, Earl E. Partridge, Hal George, Al Wilson, Roy Wilson, Clinton Herberger, Clarence Irvine, S. R. Stribling, Earl H. "Robbie" Robinson. Buddy Rogers's Plane Pilot: Thomas H. Chapman. Supervisor of Troop Maneuvers: Major A. M. Jones. Technical Supervisor of Ground Operations: Capt. E. P. Ketchum. Ordnance Supervisor: Capt. Robert Mortimer. Communications Officer: Capt. Walter Ellis. Props: Charles Barton. Still Photographer: Otto Dyar. Musical Score: John S. Zamecnik. Song: "Wings" by Zamecnik and Ballard MacDonald. Sound Effects by Movietone. Originally released in color tints. French Title: *Les Ailes.*

Cast: Clara Bow (Mary Preston), Charles "Buddy" Rogers (Jack Powell), Richard Arlen (David Armstrong), Jobyna Ralston (Sylvia Lewis), Gary Cooper (Cadet White), Arlette Marchal (Celeste), El Brendel (Herman Schwimpf), Gunboat Smith (The Sergeant), Richard Tucker (Air Commander), Roscoe Karns (Lt. Cameron), Julia Swayne Gordon (Mrs. Armstrong), Henry B. Walthall (Mr. Armstrong), George Irving (Mr. Powell), Hedda Hopper (Mrs. Powell), Nigel De Brulier (Peasant), James Pierce (M.P.), Carl Von Hartmann (German Officer), Frank Clarke (Otto Kellermann), Dick Grace, Rod Rogers, Tommy Carr, Sterling Campbell (Aviators), Charles Barton (Doughboy Hit by Ambulance), Margery Chapin Wellman (Peasant Woman), Gloria Wellman (Peasant Child), John Monk Saunders (Bit Man), William A. Wellman (Dying Infantryman on Battlefield).

THE LEGION OF THE CONDEMNED (1928)

Paramount Famous Lasky. Copyright: March 10, 1928. New York Premiere: March 18, 1928, at the Rialto. 75 minutes.

Presented by Adolph Zukor and Jesse L. Lasky. Produced and Directed by William A. Wellman. Associate Producer: E. Lloyd Sheldon. Screenplay: John Monk Saunders and Jean DeLimur. Original Story: William A. Wellman and John Monk Saunders. Novelization: Eustace Hale Ball. Titles: George Marion. Photography: Henry Gerrard. Editors: Alyson Schaeffer, Carl Pearson. Editor-in-Chief: E. Lloyd Sheldon. Art Direction: Laurence Hitt, Hans Dreier. Unit Manager: Roger Manning. Assistant Director: Richard Johnston. Second Assistant Director: Charles Barton. Second Camera: Cliff Blackstone. Assistant Camera: Cliff Schwertzer, Loyal Griggs. Akeley Camera Assistant: Burton Steene. Stunt Pilots: Dick Grace, Frank Clarke, Frank Tomick, Earl H. "Robbie" Robinson. Costumes: Travis Banton, Edith Head. Men's Wardrobe: A. MacDonald. Makeup: James Collins. Props: John Richmond, Joseph Youngerman. Grip: Art Miller. Sound Effects: Western Electric. French Title: *Les Pilotes de la Morte*.

Cast: Fay Wray (Christine Charteris), Gary Cooper (Gale Price), Barry Norton (Byron Dashwood), Lane Chandler (Lane Holabird), Francis MacDonald (Gonzolo Vasquez), Albert Conti (Von Hohendorff), Charlotte Bird (Celeste, Tart in Café), Voya George (Robert Montagnal), Freeman Wood (Richard DeWitt, A Bored Man), E. H. Calvert (Commandant), Toto Guette (Mechanic).

LADIES OF THE MOB (1928)

Paramount Famous Lasky. Copyright: June 30, 1928. New York Premiere: May 17, 1928, at the Paramount. 66 minutes.

Presented by Adolph Zukor and Jesse L. Lasky. Produced and Directed by William A. Wellman. Screenplay: John Farrow. Adaptation: Oliver H. P. Garrett. Based on a story by Ernest Booth in *The American Mercury* (December 1927). Titles: George Marion. Photography: Henry Gerrard. Editorial Supervisor: E. Lloyd Sheldon. Editors: Alyson Schaefer, Edgar Adams. Art Direction: Hans Dreier. Unit Managers: Richard Johnston, Frank L. Newman, Jr. Assistant Directors: Otto Brower, Charles Barton. Second Camera: Cliff Blackstone. Assistant Camera: Cliff Schertzer, Loyal Griggs. Script Clerk: Ellsworth Hoagland. Technical Adviser: Captain Peoples. Costumes:

Travis Banton, Edith Head. Makeup: James Collins. Props: John Richmond. Grip: Art Miller. Assistant Grip: Jack Haring.

Cast: Clara Bow (Yvonne), Richard Arlen (Red), Helen Lunch (Marie), Mary Alden (Soft Annie), Carl Gerrard (Joe), Bodil Rosing (The Mother), Lorraine Rivero (Little Yvonne), James Pierce (The Officer).

BEGGARS OF LIFE (1928)

Paramount Famous Lasky. Copyright: September 21, 1928. Released with musical score, sound effects, and a dialogue sequence on September 22, 1928. New York Premiere: September 18, 1928, at the Paramount. Also released in a silent version. 80 minutes.

Presented by Adolph Zukor and Jesse L. Lasky. Produced and Directed by William A. Wellman. Associate Producer: Benjamin Glazer. Screenplay: Benjamin Glazer and Jim Tully. Based on the novel by Jim Tully (1924, Albert and Charles Boni). Titles: Julian Johnson. Photography: Henry Gerrard. Editor: Alyson Schaefer. Art Direction: Hans Dreier. Assistant Director: Charles Barton. Script Supervisor: Margery Chapin Wellman. Costumes: Travis Banton, Edith Head. Makeup: James Collins. Sound: Movietone. French Title: *Les Mendiants de la Vie*.

Cast: Wallace Beery (Oklahoma Red), Louise Brooks (Nancy), Richard Arlen (Jim), Edgar "Blue" Washington (Black Moose), H. A. "Kewpie" Morgan (Skinny), Andy Clark (Skelly), Mike Donlin (Bill), Roscoe Karns (Lame Hoppy), Bob Perry (The Arkansas Snake), Johnnie Morris (Rubin), George Kotsonaros (Baldy), Jacques "Jack" Chapin (Ukie), Robert Brower (Blind Sims), Frank Brownlee (Farmer), Guinn Williams (Bakery Cart Driver), Dan Dix (Hobo), Harvey Parry (Hobo/Stunt Double for Louise Brooks), Duke Green, Jack Holbrook (Stunts).

CHINATOWN NIGHTS (1929)

Paramount Famous Lasky. Copyright: March 23, 1929. New York Premiere: March 30, 1929, at the Paramount. Also released in a silent version. 88 minutes.

Presented by Adolph Zukor and Jesse L. Lasky. Produced and Directed by William A. Wellman. Associate Producer: David O. Selznick. Screenplay: Ben Grauman Kohn. Adaptation: Oliver H. P. Garrett. Dialogue: William B. Jutte. Based on the story "Tong War" by Samuel Ornitz. Titles: Julian Johnson. Photography: Henry Gerrard. Editor: Alyson Schaeffer. Art Direction: Hans Dreier, Wiard B. Ihnen. Technical Adviser: Tom Gubbins. Assistant Directors: Arthur Jacobson, Charles Barton. Costumes: Travis Banton, Edith Head. Makeup: James Collins. Props: Joseph Youngerman. Sound by Movietone. Musical Director: Nathaniel Finston.

Cast: Wallace Beery (Chuck Riley), Florence Vidor (Joan Fry), Warner Oland (Boston Charley), Jack McHugh (The Shadow), Jack Oakie (Reporter), Tetsu Komai (Woo Chung), Frank Chew (Gambler), Mrs. Wong Wing (Maid), Pete Morrison (The Bartender), Freeman Wood (Gerald), Bess Flowers (Bit Woman).

THE MAN I LOVE (1929)

Paramount Famous Lasky. Copyright: May 24, 1929. New York Premiere: May 27, 1929, at the Paramount. Also released in a silent version. 75 minutes.

Presented by Adolph Zukor and Jesse L. Lasky. Produced and Directed by William A. Wellman. Associate Producer: David O. Selznick. Story and Dialogue: Herman J. Mankiewicz. Adaptation: Percy Heath. Titles (for silent version): Joseph L. Mankiewicz. Photography: Henry Gerrard. Editor: Alyson Schaeffer. Art Direction: Hans Dreier. Assistant Director: Charles Barton. Costumes: Edith Head, Travis Banton. Makeup: James Collins. Props: Joseph Youngerman. Electrician: Pop Jones. Sound by Movietone. Musical Director: Nathaniel Finston.

Cast: Richard Arlen (Dum Dum Brooks), Mary Brian (Celia Fields), Olga Baclanova [billed as "Baclanova"] (Sonia Barondorff), Harry Green (Curly Bloom), Jack Oakie (Lew Layton), Pat O'Malley (D. J. McCarthy), Leslie Fenton (Carlo Vesper), Charles Sullivan (Champ Mahoney), William "Sailor Billy" Vincent (K.O. O'Hearn), Bob Perry (Gateman), William A. Wellman (Voice of Bill).

WOMAN TRAP (1929)

Paramount Famous Lasky. Copyright: September 27, 1929. New York Premiere: August 30, 1929, at the Paramount. Also released in a silent version. 82 minutes.

Presented by Adolph Zukor and Jesse L. Lasky. Produced and Directed by William A. Wellman. Screenplay: Bartlett Cormack. Adaptation: Louise Long. Based on the play *Brothers* by Edwin Burke. Titles (for silent version): Joseph L. Mankiewicz. Photography: Henry Gerrard. Editor: Alyson Schaeffer. Art Direction: Hans Dreier. Assistant Director: Charles Barton. Sound (Movietone): Earl Hayman. Costumes: Edith Head. Makeup: James Collins. Props: Joseph Youngerman. Electrician: Pop Jones. Musical Director: Nathaniel Finston.

Cast: Hal Skelly (Dan Malone), Chester Morris (Ray Malone), Evelyn Brent (Kitty Evans), William B. Davidson (Watts), Effie Ellsler (Mrs. Malone), Guy Oliver (Mr. Evans), Leslie Fenton (Eddie Evans), Charles Giblyn (Smith), Joseph L. Mankiewicz (Reporter), Wilson Hummell (Detective Captain), William "Sailor Billy" Vincent (Himself, a Boxer).

DANGEROUS PARADISE (1930)

Paramount Famous Lasky. Copyright: February 23, 1930. New York Premiere: February 15, 1930, at the Paramount. Also released in a silent version. 70 minutes.

Presented by Adolph Zukor and Jesse L. Lasky. Produced and Directed by William A. Wellman. Screenplay: William Slavens McNutt and Grover Jones. Based on incidents in *Victory* by Joseph Conrad. Photography: Archie J. Stout. Editor: Alyson Schaeffer. Art Direction: Hans Dreier. Assistant Director: Charles Barton. Costumes: Travis Banton, Edith Head. Makeup: James Collins. Props: Joseph Youngerman. Electrician: Pop Jones. Song: "Smiling Skies" by Leo Robin and Richard Whiting, sung by Nancy Carroll. Sound by Movietone. Musical Director: Nathaniel Finston. Working Title: *The Flesh of Eve.*

Cast: Nancy Carroll (Alma), Richard Arlen (Heyst), Warner Oland (Schonberg), Gustav von Seyffertitz (Mr. Jones), Francis MacDonald (Ricardo), George Kotsonaros (Pedro), Dorothea Wolbert (Mrs. Schomberg), Clarence H. Wilson (Zangiacomo),

Evelyn Selbie (His Wife), Willie Fung (Wang), Wong Wing (His Wife), Lillian Worth (Myrtle).

YOUNG EAGLES (1930)

Paramount Famous Lasky. Copyright: April 5, 1930. New York Premiere: March 21, 1930, at the Paramount. Also released in a silent version. 75 minutes.

Presented by Adolph Zuker and Jesse L. Lasky. Produced and Directed by William A. Wellman. Screenplay: William Slavens McNutt and Grover Jones. Based on the stories "Sky High" (*Redbook*, July 1929) and "The One Who Was Clever" (*Redbook*, August 1929) by Elliot White Springs. Photography: Archie J. Stout. Editor: Alyson Schaeffer. Art Direction: Hans Dreier. Assistant Director: Charles Barton. Aerial Stunts: Dick Grace, Leo Nomis. Technical Adviser: Earl H. "Robbie" Robinson. Costumes: Travis Banton, Edith Head. Makeup: James Collins. Sound (Movietone): Eugene Merritt. Props: Joseph Youngerman. Electrician: Pop Jones. Songs: "Love Here in My Heart" by Ross Adrian and Leo Silesew; "The Sunrise and You" by Arthur A. Penn. Musical Director: Nathaniel Finston.

Cast: Charles "Buddy" Rogers (Lt. Robert Banks), Jean Arthur (Mary Gordon), Paul Lukas (Von Baden), Stuart Erwin (Pudge Higgins), Virginia Bruce (Florence Welford), Gordon De Main (Major Lewis), James Finlayson (Scotty), Frank Ross (Lt. Graham), Jack Luden (Lt. Barker), Freeman Wood (Lt. Mason), George Irving (Col. Wilder), Stanley Blystone (Capt. Deming), Sterling C. Campbell (Aviator), Newell Chase, Lloyd Whitlock, Bodil Rosing, James Cunning.

MAYBE IT'S LOVE (1930)

Warner Brothers/Vitaphone. Copyright: September 12, 1930. New York Premiere: October 17, 1930, at the Strand. 71 minutes.

Executive Producer: Darryl F. Zanuck. Produced by Hal B. Wallis. Directed by William A. Wellman. Screenplay: Joseph Jackson. Original Screen Stories: "Footloose Widows" and "Maybe It's Love" by Mark Canfield (Darryl F. Zanuck). Photography: Robert Kurrle. Editor: Edward McDermott. Production Manager: William Koenig. Location Manager: W. L. Guthrie. Technical Adviser: Russell Saunders. Sound (Vitaphone): Bernard Brown. Costumes: Earl Luick. Makeup: Perc Westmore. Musical Director: Erno Rapee. Vitaphone Orchestra Conducted by Louis Silvers. Songs: "Maybe It's Love" and "All American" by Sidney Mitchell, Archie Gettler, George W. Meyer; both sung by Joan Bennett and James Hall. Theme: "Precious Little Thing" (Mitchell-Gottler-Meyer). Working Titles: *Freshman Love*; *Precious*; *Precious Little Thing*. Television Title: *Eleven Men and a Gift*.

Cast: Joan Bennett (Nan Sheffield), Joe E. Brown (Speed Hanson), James Hall (Tommy Nelson/Tommy Smith), Laura Lee (Betty), Sumner Getchell (Whiskers), George Irving (President Sheffield), George Bickell (Professor), Anders Randolph (Mr. Nelson), Stuart Erwin (Brown of Harvard), Toni Hanlon (Tony), Fred Lee, Harry Strathy (College Trustees), Donald MacKenzie (Stocky Trustee) and The All-American Football Team—Coach Howard Jones, USC (Coach Bob Brown), Russ Saunders (Himself, USC), Tim Moynihan (Himself, Notre Dame), Bill Banker (Himself, Tulane University), Howard Harpster (Himself, Carnegie Tech), Ray Montgomery (Himself, University of Pittsburgh), Otto Pommerening (Himself, Michigan), Elmer N. "Red" Sleight (Himself, Purdue), Kenneth Haycraft (Himself, Minnesota), George Gibson (Himself, Minnesota), Paul Scull (Himself, Pennsylvania), W. K. "Schoony" Schoonover (Himself, University of Arkansas), William A. Wellman (Voice of Game Commentator).

OTHER MEN'S WOMEN (1931)

Warner Brothers/Vitaphone. No copyright date registered. Release Date: January 17, 1931. New York Premiere: April 19, 1931, at the Strand. 70 minutes.

Executive Producer: Darryl F. Zanuck. Produced by Hal B. Wallis. Directed by William A. Wellman. Story and Adaptation: Maude Fulton. Dialogue: William K. Wells. Photography: Barney "Chick" McGill. Editor: Edward McDermott. Production Manager: William Koenig. Location Manager: W. L. Guthrie. Sound (Vitaphone): Bernard Brown. Costumes: Earl Luick. Makeup: Perc Westmore. Musical Directors: Erno Rapee, Leo F. Forbstein. Vitaphone Orchestra Conducted by Louis Silvers. Songs: "Leave a Little Smile" by Dubin and Burke, whistled by Withers, also sung by Withers, Mary Astor, and J. Farrell MacDonald; "Kiss Waltz" by Dubin and Burke, sung by Grant Withers; "On the 5:15" by Marshall and Murphy, sung by Regis Toomey and rail workers; "Tomorrow Is Another Day" by Green and Stept, performed by orchestra; "Cruiskeen Lawn" (traditional), sung by J. Farrell MacDonald. Working Titles: *Romance on the Rails; The Steel Highway.*

Cast: Grant Withers (Bill White), Mary Astor (Lily Culper), Regis Toomey (Jack Culper), James Cagney (Ed Bailey), Fred Kohler (Haley), J. Farrell MacDonald (Pegleg), Joan Blondell (Marie), Lillian Worth (Waitress), Walter Long (Bixby), Bob Perry, Lee Morgan, H. A. "Kewpie" Morgan, Pat Hartigan, Frank Hagney (Railroad Workers).

THE PUBLIC ENEMY (1931)

Warner Brothers-Vitaphone. Copyright: April 4, 1931. New York Premiere: April 23, 1931, at the Strand. Rereleased 1954. 83 minutes.

Executive Producer: Darryl F. Zanuck. Produced by Hal B. Wallis. Directed by William A. Wellman. Adaptation and Dialogue: Harvey Thew. Based on the story "Beer and Blood: The Story of a Couple o'Wrong Guys" by Kubec Glasmon and John Bright. Photography: Dev Jennings. Editor: Edward M. McDermott. Art Director: Max Parker. Assistant Directors: Frank Shaw, Dolph Zimmer. Second Assistant Director: Louis Marlowe. Production Manager: William Koenig. Location Manager: W. L. Guthrie. Costumes: Earl Luick, Edward Stevenson. Makeup: Perc Westmore. Props: Robert Priestley. Camera Crew: Willard Van Enger, William Schurr, Frank Kesson, Irving Glassberg, Bill Reinhold, Al Roberts, Sid Wagner, Harry Underwood, Nelson Larrabee. Stills: Scotty Welbourne. Sound (Vitaphone): Oliver S. Garretson. Sound Crew: Alf Burton, J. Thompson, Albin. Technical Adviser: Clem Peoples. Production Crew: Rule, Whitmore, Newitt, Dillingham. Casting: Rufus LeMaire. Vitaphone Orchestra Conducted by David Mendoza. Theme: "I'm Forever Blowing Bubbles," words by Jean Kenbrovin (pseudonym for James Kendis), James Brockman, Nat Vincent, music by William Kellette. Additional Theme: "Toot Toot Tootsie." Song: "Hesitation Blues" (traditional), sung by Murray Kinnell. British Title: *Enemy of the Public.* French Title: *L'Ennemi Public.*

Cast: James Cagney (Tom Powers), Jean Harlow (Gwen Allen), Eddie Woods (Matt Doyle), Joan Blondell (Mamie), Donald Cook (Mike Powers), Leslie Fenton (Samuel "Nails" Nathan), Beryl Mercer (Ma Powers), Robert Emmett O'Connor (Paddy Ryan), Murray Kinnell (Putty Nose), Mae Clarke (Kitty), Rita Flynn (Molly Doyle), Snitz Edwards (Hack Miller), Ben Hendricks, Jr. (Bugs Moran), Frank Coghlan, Jr. (Tommy as a boy), Frankie Darro (Matt as a boy), Ben Hendricks III (Bugs as a boy), Robert E. Homans (Officer Pat Burke), Dorothy Gee (Nails' Girl), Purnell Pratt (Officer Powers), Lee Phelps (Steve the Bartender), Mia Marvin (Jane), Clark Burroughs (Dutch), Adele Watson (Mrs. Doyle), Ronald Shannon (Limpy Larry), Marty O'Grady (Limpy as a boy), Helen Parrish, Dorothy Gray, Nancie Price (Little Girls), George Daly (Machine-Gunner), Eddie Kane (Joe, the headwaiter), Charles Sullivan (Mug), William H. Strauss (Pawnbroker), Frank Austin (Burns Hood), Sam McDaniel (Black Headwaiter), Landers Stevens (Doctor), Bob Reeves (Poolroom Customer), Douglas Gerrard (Assistant Tailor), Russ Powell (Bartender), Harvey Parry (Stunts).

NIGHT NURSE (1931)

Warner Brothers-Vitaphone. Copyright: July 10, 1931. New York Premiere: July 16, 1931, at the Strand. 73 minutes.

Executive Producer: Darryl F. Zanuck. Produced by Hal B. Wallis. Directed by William A. Wellman. Screenplay: Oliver H. P. Garrett. Additional Dialogue: Charles Kenyon. Based on the 1930 novel by Dora Macy (pseudonym for Grace Perkins Oursler). Photography: Barney "Chick" McGill. Editor: Edward McDermott. Art Director: Max Parker. Assistant Director: Frank Shaw. Second Assistant Director: Sylvan Karp. Production Manager: William Koenig. Technical Adviser: Dr. Harry Martin. Script Supervisor: Fred Applegate. Costumes: Earl Luick. Makeup: Perc Westmore, Ray Romero. Props: Robert Priestley, G. W. Berntsen. Gaffer: Claude Hutchinson. Grip: Owen Crompton. Camera Crew: Bill Whitley, Bobby Robinson, Kenneth Green, Harry Davis, Leo Hughes, Aaron Hower. Still Photographer: Homer Van Pelt. Sound (Vitaphone): Oliver S. Garretson. Sound Crew: Alf Burton, Burrell Kring, Frank Weixel, Merrick. Vitaphone Orchestra Conducted by Leo F. Forbstein. Production Crew: Sorenson, Hegarty, Hanlin. French Title: *L'Ange Blanc.*

Cast: Barbara Stanwyck (Lora Hart), Ben Lyon (Mortie), Joan Blondell (Maloney), Clark Gable (Nick), Blanche Frederici (Mrs. Maxwell), Charlotte Merriam (Mrs. Ritchey), Charles Winninger (Dr. Bell), Edward Nugent (Eagan), Vera Lewis (Miss Dillon), Ralf Harolde (Dr. Ranger), Walter McGrail (Drunk), Allan Lane (Intern), Martin Burton (Second Intern), Betty May (Surgery Room Nurse), Marcia Mae Jones (Nanny), Betty Jane Graham (Desney), Lucille Ward (Mother in Hospital), Bob Perry (Marty's Pal), Willie Fung (Chinese Man in Hospital Bed), Manuella Martinez, Prudie Johnson, Consuela Flores, Armando Murga, Ko Shimizu, Gilbert Fong, Angelita Ortega, Gloria Ulmer, Victor Gonzalez, Rosemarie Moore (Babies in Hospital), Jed Prouty, James Bradbury, Jr.

THE STAR WITNESS (1931)

Warner Brothers-Vitaphone. Copyright: August 8, 1931. New York Premiere: August 3, 1931, at the Winter Garden. 68 minutes.

Executive Producer: Darryl F. Zanuck. Produced by Hal B. Wallis. Directed by William A. Wellman. Story and Screenplay: Lucien K. Hubbard. Photography: James Van Trees. Editor: Harold McLernon. Art Director: John J. Hughes. Assistant Directors: Frank Shaw, Dolph M. Zimmer. Second Assistant Director: Sylvan Karp. Production Manager: William Koenig. Second Camera: Louis Jennings, Bobby Robinson, Irving Glassberg. Assistant Camera: Vernon Larson, Russell Simon. Additional Cameramen for exterior Leeds home: Willard Van Enger, Richard Towers, Wesley Anderson, Jerome Ash. Stills: Homer Van Pelt, Mac Julian. Sound (Vitaphone): Oliver S. Garretson. Sound Crew: Alf Burton, Frank Maher, J. Thompson. Gaffer: George Satterfield. Grip: Jim Carter. Props: Martin Hershey. Assistant Props: Lashus. Makeup: Perc Westmore. Hairstylist: Lucille D'Antoine. Technical Adviser: Clem Peoples. Vitaphone Orchestra Conducted by Leo F. Forbstein. Themes: "Yankee Doodle Dandy," "De Massa's in De Cold Cold Ground," played on flute by Chic Sale. Working Titles: *The Man Who Dared; This Is the Answer.*

Cast: Walter Huston (District Attorney Whitlock), Charles "Chic" Sale (Grandpa Summerill), Frances Starr (Abby Leeds), Grant Mitchell (George Leeds), Sally Blane (Sue Leeds), Ralph Ince (Maxey Campo), Edward J. Nugent (Jack Leeds), Dickie Moore (Ned Leeds), Nat Pendleton (Big Jack), George Ernest (Donny Leeds), Russell Hopton (Deputy Thorpe), Tom Dugan (Brown), Robert Elliott (Williams), Noel Madison (Horan), Mike Donlin (Mickey), Fletcher Norton (Dopey Al Allen), Guy d'Ennery (Dickie Short), Edgar Deering (Sackett), Allen Lane (Clerk), Robert Romans (Jim the Cop), Harvey Parry (Stunts), William A. Wellman (Voice of Lineman).

SAFE IN HELL (1931)

First National-Vitaphone. Copyright: December 9, 1931. New York Premiere: December 18, 1931, at the Strand. 68 minutes.

Executive Producer: Darryl F. Zanuck. Produced by Hal B. Wallis. Directed by William A. Wellman. Adaptation: Joseph Jackson and Maude Fulton (and uncredited, Raymond Griffith). Dialogue: Maude Fulton. Based on the play by Houston Branch (1930). Photography: Barney "Chick" McGill. Editor: Owen Marks. Assistant Editor: Steven Marks. Art Director: Jack Okey. Production Manager: William Koenig. Assistant Director: Frank Shaw. Second Assistant Director: Dolph M. Zimmer. Sound (Vitaphone): Oliver S. Garretson. Second Unit Photography (aerials of Tropical Island; fire sequence): Fred Jackman. Camera Plane Pilot: Ray Wilson. Makeup: Perc Westmore. Vitaphone Orchestra Conducted by Leo F. Forbstein. Theme: "Rumba (En blue)" by Harvey Brooks. Song: "When It's Sleepy Time Down South," by Clarence Muse, sung by Nina Mae McKinney; "Pagan Moon" by M. Witmalk and Sons. Working Titles: *How Long?, The Lady from New Orleans.* British Title: *The Lost Lady.*

Cast: Dorothy Mackaill (Gilda Karlson Erickson), Donald Cook (Carl Bergen), Ralf Harolde (Piet Van Siel), John Wray (Egan), Ivan Sampson (Crutch), Victor Varconi (Gomez), Morgan Wallace (Bruno), Nina Mae McKinney (Leonie), Charles

Middleton (Jones), Clarence Muse (Newcastle), Gustav von Seyfferititz (Larson), Noble Johnson (Bozo), Cecil Cunningham (Angle), Lionel Belmore (Judge), George Marlon, Sr. (Jack), Bob Perry (Sailor), Chris Pin-Martin (Juror), Kenneth MacDonald (Wireless Operator), Tom Gubbins (Man at Native Orchestra), The Cotton Club Band (Native Orchestra).

THE HATCHET MAN (1932)

First National-Vitaphone. Copyright: January 28, 1932. New York Premiere: February 3, 1932, at the Winter Garden. Rereleased in 1949 on a double bill with Frank Borzage's *A Farewell to Arms* (Paramount, 1932). 74 minutes.

Executive Producer: Darryl F. Zanuck. Produced by Hal B. Wallis. Directed by William A. Wellman. Screenplay: J. Grubb Alexander (and uncredited, Maude Fulton). Based on the play *The Honourable Mr. Wong* by David Belasco and Achmed Abdullah. Photography: Sid Hickox. Editor: Owen Marks. Art Director: Anton Grot. Assistant Director: Fred Fox. Second Assistant Director: Sylvan Karp. Production Manager: William Koenig. Script Supervisor: Jean Raymond. Technical Adviser: Louis Vincenot. Second Camera: Richard Towers. Assistant Camera: Wesley Anderson. Stills: Homer Van Pelt, John Ellis. Gaffer: Charles Ferguson. Grip: L. P. "Dude" Mashmeyer. Assistant Grip: Frank Wilkie. Sound (Vitaphone): Robert B. Lee. Costumes: Earl Luick. Hairstylist: Ruth Pershley. Makeup: Perc Westmore. Props: Martin Hershey, Howard Oggle. Vitaphone Orchestra Conducted by Leo F. Forbstein. Technical Adviser: Clem Peoples. Working Title: *The Honorable Mr. Wong*. British Title: *The Honourable Mr. Wong*.

Cast: Edward G. Robinson (Wong Low Get), Loretta Young (Toya Sun), Dudley Digges (Nag Hong Fah), Leslie Fenton (Harry En Hai), Edmund Breese (Yu Chang), Tully Marshall (Long Sen Yat), J. Carroll Naish (Sun Yat Ming), Charles Middleton (Lip Hot Fat), E. Allyn Warren (The Cobbler, Soo Lat), Eddie Peil (Bing Foo), Noel Madison (Charley Kee), Blanche Frederici (Madame Si-Si), Toshia Mori (Miss Ling), Ralph Ince (Big Jim Malone), Otto Yamaoka (Chung Ho), Evelyn Selbie (Wah Li), Anna Chang (Sing Girl), Gladys Lloyd Robinson (Fan Yi), James Leong (Tong Member), Willie Fung (The Notary, Fung Loo).

SO BIG (1932)

Warner Brothers-Vitaphone. Copyright: March 29, 1932. New York Premiere: April 29, 1932, at the Strand. 82 minutes.

Produced by Darryl F. Zanuck. Production Supervisor: Lucien K. Hubbard. Directed by William A. Wellman. Screenplay: J. Grubb Alexander and Robert Lord (and uncredited James C. Fagap, Joseph Jackson). Based on the novel by Edna Ferber (1924). Photography: Sid Hickox. Editor: William Holmes. Art Director: Jack Okey. Assistant Director: Dolph M. Zimmer. Second Assistant Director: Russell Saunders. Production Manager: William Koenig. Script Supervisor: Emily Moore. Second Camera: Richard Towers. Assistant Camera: Andy Anderson, Palmer Belmont. Stills: William Walling, Jr., Irving Lipman. Sound (Vitaphone): Robert B. Lee. Sound Crew: Francis E. Stahl, Frank Maher, White, Alphen. Grip: L. P. "Dude" Mashmeyer. Props:

John More, Gene Delaney. Costumes: Orry-Kelly. Makeup: Perc Westmore, Ray Romero. Hair: Helen Hunt. Production Crew: Hazen, Gilbert, Smith, Hogan, Ford. Musical Score: W. Franke Harling. Theme: "A Bicycle Built for Two." French Title: *Mon Grand*.

Cast: Barbara Stanwyck (Selina Peake), George Brent (Roelf), Dickie Moore (Dirk as a boy), Guy Kibbee (August Hemple), Bette Davis (Dallas O'Mara), Mae Madison (Julie Hernple), Hardie Albright (Dirk as a man), Robert Warwick (Simeon Peake), Arthur Stone (Jan Steen), Earle Foxe (Pervus DeJong), Alan Hale (Klaus Pool), Dorothy Peterson (Maartje Pool), Dawn O'Day [later Anne Shirley] (Selina as a girl), Dick Winslow (Roelf as a boy), Harry Beresford (Adam Ooms), Eulalie Jensen (Mrs. Hemple), Elizabeth Patterson (Mrs. Tepper), Rita LeRoy (Paula Storm), Blanche Frederici (Widow Parrlenburg), Willard Robertson (Doctor, Vermont Horne), Harry Holman (Country Doctor), Lionel Belmore (Reverend Dekker), Martha Mattox, Emma Ray (Maiden Aunts), Andre Cheron (General), Seesel Ann Johnson (Gertze), Olin Howland (Jakob), The Johnson Babies (Babies).

LOVE IS A RACKET (1932)

First National-Vitaphone. Copyright: June 8, 1932. New York Premiere: June 10, 1932, at the Strand. 74 minutes.

Executive Producer: Darryl F. Zanuck. Produced by Hal B. Wallis. Directed by William A. Wellman. Screenplay: Courtenay Terrett. Based on a novel by Rian James (1931, Alfred B. King). Camera: Sid Hickox. Editor: William Holmes. Assistant Editor: Jack Killifer. Art Director: Jack Okey. Assistant Directors: Dolph M. Zimmer. Second Assistant Director: Fred Karp. Script Supervisor: Maude Allen. Sound (Vitaphone): Robert B. Lee. Sound Crew: Francis E. Stahl, Swartz, Ryrnal. Props: John More, K. Malloy, Pinky Weiss, Gene Delaney, Harold Bowers. Assistant Camera: Wesley Anderson. Camera Crew: Frank Kesson, Ellsworth Fredericks, Lester Shorr, Fred Jackman (for Jimmy's apartment scenes). Stills: William Walling, Jr. Gaffer: Charles Ferguson. Grip: L. P. "Dude" Mashmeyer. Makeup: Perc Westmore. Hairstylist: Ruth Purshley. Vitaphone Orchestra Conducted by Leo F. Forbstein. British Title: *Such Things Happen*.

Cast: Douglas Fairbanks, Jr. (Jimmy Russell), Ann Dvorak (Sally Condon), Lee Tracy (Stanley Fiske), Frances Dee (Mary Wodehouse), Lyle Talbot (Shaw), Warren Hymer (Burney Olds), William Burress (Ollie), Andre Luquet (Max Boncour), Terence Ray (Seeley), Marjorie Peterson (Hat Check Girl), Edward Kane (Captain of Waiters), Cecil Cunningham (Aunt Hattie), John Marston (Curley), Charles O'Malley (Perkins), Lillian Worth (Tiny), Miss Terry (Smart Looking Girl), Gypsy Norman (Manicurist), George Ernest (Boy), Frank McHugh (Man at Speakeasy).

THE PURCHASE PRICE (1932)

Warner Brothers-Vitaphone. Copyright: July 28, 1932. New York Premiere: July 15, 1932, at the Strand. 68 minutes.

Executive Producer: Darryl F. Zanuck. Produced by Hal B. Wallis. Directed by William A. Wellman. Screenplay: Robert Lord. Based on the story "The Mud Lark" by Arthur Stringer, published serially in *The Saturday Evening Post* (October 1931) and in book form by Bobbs-Merrill (1932). Photography: Sid Hickox. Editor: William Holmes. Art Director: Jack Okey. Assistant Director: Dolph M. Zimmer. Second Assistant Director: Russell Saunders. Production Manager: William Koenig. Script Supervisor: Irva Ross. Assistant Camera: Wesley Anderson. Camera Crew: John Stumar, Tom Brannigan, Frank Kesson, Bobby Robinson, Perry Finnerman, William N. Williams, Harry Kauffman, Fred Young, Emmerick. Stills: Homer Van Pelt, William Walling, Jr., Irving Lipman. Electrician: Charles Ferguson. Grip: L. P. "Dude" Mashmeyer. Sound (Vitaphone): Robert B. Lee. Sound Crew: Charles Althouse, Francis E. Stahl, Spencer, Ryrnal, Monahan. Props: John More, K. Malloy. Makeup: Perc Westmore. Hairstylist: Alma Armstrong. Production Crew: Massbaum, Long. Vitaphone Orchestra Conducted by Leo F. Forbstein. Working Titles: *The Mud Lark, The Night Flower.*

Cast: Barbara Stanwyck (Joan Gordon), George Brent (Jim Gilson), Lyle Talbot (Ed Fields), David Landau (Bull McDowell), Leila Bennett (Emily), Murray Kinnell (Spike Forgan), Crauford Kent (Peters), Hardie Albright (Don Leslie), Matt McHugh (Waco), Clarence Wilson (Justice of the Peace), Lucille Ward (His Wife), Dawn O'Day [later Anne Shirley] (Farmer's Daughter), Victor Potel (Clyde), Adele Watson (Mrs. Tipton), Snub Pollard (Joe), Mae Busch (Woman on Train), John "Skins" Miller (Man on the Floor), Suzanne Talbot.

THE CONQUERORS (1932)

RKO-Radio. Copyright: November 18, 1932. New York Premiere: November 20, 1932, at the Mayfair. 88 minutes.

Executive Producer: David O. Selznick. Directed by William A. Wellman. Screenplay: Robert Lord (and uncredited, Howard Estabrook, Gene Fowler, Humphrey Pearson). Based on a story, "The March of a Nation," by Howard Estabrook. Photography: Edward Cronjager. Editor: William Hamilton. Art Direction: Carroll Clark, Sidney M. Ullman. Assistant Directors: Dolph M. Zimmer, James Anderson. Sound (RCA Photophone): John E. Tribby. Montage Effects: Slavko Vorkapich. Camera Operators: Robert DeGrasse, Burnett Guffey. Assistant Camera: George Diskant, Lestor Schorr. Special Photography: Vernon L. Walker. Aerial Photography: William H. Clothier. Stills: Fred Hendrickson. Stunt Pilot: Paul Mantz. Makeup: Ern Westmore. Wardrobe: Maxine Lockwood. Research: Bessie McGaffey and Dan McKinnon. Musical Director: Max Steiner. Themes: "Long Long Ago," "Tenting Tonight," "When Johnny Comes Marching Home," "Battle Cry of Freedom," "Bicycle Built for Two," "Stars and Stripes Forever." Working Titles: *Black Friday, The March of a Nation, March of Events.* French Title: *Les Conquerants.* Television Title: *Pioneer Builders.*

Cast: Richard Dix (Roger Standish/Roger Lennox), Ann Harding (Caroline Ogden Standish), Edna May Oliver (Matilda Blake), Guy Kibbee (Dr. Daniel Blake), Julie Haydon (Frances Standish), Donald Cook (Warren Lennox), Walter Walker (Mr. Ogden), Wally Albright, Jr., Marilyn Knowlden (Twins), Harry Holman (Stubby), Jason Robards (Lane), Richard "Skeets" Gallagher (Benson), Jed Prouty (Auctioneer), E. H. Calvert (Doctor), J. Carroll Naish (Agitator), Robert Greig (Mr. Downey), Elizabeth Patterson (Landlady), Bob Perry (Bartender/Flute Player), Harvey Parry (Stunts).

FRISCO JENNY (1933)

First National-Vitaphone. Copyright: January 11, 1933. World Premiere: December 30, 1932, Albany, Washington. New York Premiere: January 6, 1933, at the Roxy. 70 minutes.

Executive Producer: Darryl F. Zanuck. Produced by Raymond Griffith. Directed by William A. Wellman. Screenplay: Wilson Mizner and Robert Lord. Screen Story: John Francis Larkin and Lillie Hayward. Based on the story "Common Ground" by Gerald Paul Beaumont (*The Red Book*, January 1926). Photography: Sid Hickox. Editor: James Morley. Art Director: Robert Haas. Assistant Director: Dolph M. Zimmer. Second Assistant Director: Marshall Hageman. Script Supervisor: Maude Allen. Technical Adviser: Wilson Mizner. Second Camera: Wesley Anderson. Assistant Camera: Tom Brannigan, Frank Kesson. Additonal Camera Crew (10-10-32 for earthquake saloon interior): Ernest Haller, Willard Van Enger, Louis Jennings, Carl Guthrie, Bobby Robinson, William N. Williams, Vernon Larson, Harry Kauffman, William T. Cline, John Hoffman. Stills: Joe Hommel. Gaffers: Charles Ferguson, Leo Green. Grip: L. P. "Dude" Mashmeyer. Sound (Vitaphone): Francis Scheid. Sound Crew: Charles David Forrest, William Lynch, Lou Espinosa. Props: John More, Maurice Goldman, Gene Delaney, L. Hafley. Costume Design: Orry-Kelly. Wardrobe: Frank Beetson, Clem Harrington. Makeup: Perc Westmore. Hairstylist: Emily Moore. Vitaphone Orchestra Conducted by Leo F. Forbstein. Theme: "My Gal Sal" (Paul Dresser). Other Themes: "San Francisco Bay," "When Irish Eyes Are Smiling," "She Loved a Sailor," "The Ship Goes Sailing On," "Carry Me Back to Old Virginny." Working Title/British Title: *Common Ground*. French Title: *Jenny Frisco*.

Cast: Ruth Chatterton (Frisco Jenny Sandoval), Louis Calhern (Steve Dutton), Helen Jerome Eddy (Amah), Donald Cook (Dan Reynolds), James Murray (Dan McAllister), Hallam Cooley (Willie Gleason), Pat O'Malley (O'Hoolihan), Harold Huber (George Weaver), Robert Emmett O'Connor (Jim Sandoval), Willard Robertson (Capt. Tom Davis), Robert Warwick (Kelly), Edwin Maxwell (Tom Ford), Berton Churchill (Judge Thomas B. Reynolds), Nella Walker (Mrs. Janet Reynolds), Buster Phelps (Dan as a boy), Frank McGlynn, Sr. (Good Book Charlie), J. Carroll Naish (Ed Harris), Noel Francis (Rose), Sam Godfrey (Kilmer), Franklin Parker (Martel), Clarence Muse (Singer), Harry Holman (Eager Customer), Gertrude Astor (Miss Beulah), Fritzi Ridgeway (Miss Jessie), Claudia Coleman (Miss Tessie), Bob Perry (Bootlegger), Eulalie Jensen (Madam), Dorothy Granger (Girl), C. Heine Conklin (Waiter), Clarence Nordstrom (Young Man at Sandoval's), Wilson Mizner, Eddie Chandler, Syd Saylor (Barbary Coast Patrons), Harvey Parry (Drunk Sailor/Stunts), Mary Wiggins (Stunt Double for Chatterton), William A. Wellman (Reporter, close-up in telephone montage scene).

CENTRAL AIRPORT (1933)

First National-Vitaphone. Copyright: April 10, 1933. New York Premiere: May 3, 1933, at the Strand. 70 minutes.

Executive Producer: Darryl F. Zanuck. Produced by Hal B. Wallis. Directed by William A. Wellman (and uncredited, Alfred Green). Second Unit Director (for pickup shots): Ray Enright. Screenplay: Rian James and James Seymour (and uncredited, Jack Moffitt). Based on the story "Hawk's Mate" by John C. "Jack" Moffitt. Photography: Sid Hickox. Additional Photography: Tony Gaudio, Barney "Chick" McGill, Ernest Haller. Editor: James Morley. Art Director: Jack Okey. Assistant Director: Dolph M. Zimmer. Second Assistant Director: Marshall Hageman. Production Manager: William Koenig. Script Supervisor: Maude Allen. Stunt Coordinator: Dutch Pettit. Technical Effects, Process Photography, Miniatures: Fred Jackman. Assistants to Jackman: Fred Koenekamp, Frank Mattison, Ned Mann. Stunt Pilot: Paul Mantz. Aerial Cinematography: Elmer Dyer. Assistant Camera: Wesley Anderson. Second Camera: Tom Brannigan. Camera Crew: Frank Kesson, Ellsworth Fredericks, Fred Terzo, Bill Whitley, Vernon Larson, John Shepek, Olson, White. Stills: Scotty Welbourne, Bert Longworth. Camera Plane Pilots: Paul Mantz, Howard Batt. Photography for pickups: Sid Hickox, James Van Trees, Sol Polito. Camera Crew for pickups: James Van Trees, Jr., Louis Jennings, Lou DeAngelis, Michael Joyce, Evans. Gaffer: Leo Green. Grip: L. P. "Dude" Mashmeyer. Sound (Vitaphone): Robert B. Lee. Sound Crew: William Lynch, Francis E. Stahl. Properties: John More, K. Malloy. Costume Design: Orry-Kelly. Wardrobe: Frank Beetson. Makeup: Perc Westmore. Hairstylist: Emily Moore. Production Crew: William Dodson, Derry, Turner, Rogers. Circus Equipment: Hunsaker Exposition Company. Vitaphone Orchestra Conducted by Leo F. Forbstein. Working Titles: *Hawk's Mate, Grand Central Airport.*

Cast: Richard Barthelmess (Jim Blaine), Sally Eilers (Jill Collins), Tom Brown (Neil Blaine), Glenda Farrell (Girl in Wreck), Harold Huber (Swarthy Man), Grant Mitchell (Mr. Blaine), James Murray (Eddie Hughes), Claire McDowell (Mrs. Blaine), Willard Robertson (Havana Airport Manager), Arthur Vinton (Amarillo Airport Manager), Bradley Page (Scotty Armstrong), Harry Semels (Havana Airport Worker), Walter Miller (Havana Airport Official), Douglass Dumbrille (Field Manager), Irving Bacon (Weatherman), James Ellison (Pilot with Rabbit's Foot), Herman Brix [later Bruce Bennett] (Starter), Ben Hendricks (Checker), George Regas (Mechanic), Betty Jane Gordon (Little Girl in Wreck), Theodore Newton, Charles Levison [later Charles Lane] (Radio Operators), Harry Holman (First Farmer), William LeMaire, Milt Kibbee (Two Farmers), Jed Prouty, Lester Dorr (Desk Clerks), Sterling Holloway (Hotel Clerk, El Paso), Charles Williams (El Paso Desk Clerk), Phil Tead (Duke), Louise Beavers (Maid), Fred "Snowflake" Toones (El Paso Porter), Eleanor Holm (Cashier), Marilyn Knowlden (Little Girl), Lucille Ward (Waitress), George Pat Collins (Man in Plane), James Bell (Mexican on Plane Wing), Charles Sellon (Gray-haired Man in Wreck), John Wayne (Co-pilot in Wreck), J. Carroll Naish (Nervous Passenger), John Vosper (Man in Wreck), Robert Greig (Chef), Russ Powell (Chef), Dick Elliott (Man Looking for Driver), James Bush (Pilot), Sam McDaniel (Porter), Harry C. Bradley (Doctor), Toby Wing (Girl), William A. Wellman (Voice of Airport Flight Announcer).

LILLY TURNER (1933)

First National-Vitaphone. Copyright: May 15, 1933. New York Premiere: June 14, 1933, at the Rivoli. 65 minutes.

Executive Producer: Darryl F. Zanuck. Produced by Hal B. Wallis. Directed by

William A. Wellman. Screenplay: Gene Markey and Kathryn Scola (and uncredited, Sidney Sutherland, Robert Presnell). Based on the play by Philip Dunning and George Abbott, from a story by Frances Fox Dunning. Photography: James Van Trees. Photography (first four days of production): Sid Hickox. Editor: James Gibbon. Art Director: Jack Okey. Assistant Director: Dolph M. Zimmer. Second Assistant Director: Marshall Hageman. Production Manager: William Koenig. Script Supervisor: Jean McNaughton. Camera Crew: James Van Trees, Jr., Louis Jennings. Additional Camera: Rex Wimpy, Byron Haskin, Hans Koenekamp, Robert Burks, Frank Kesson, Henry Krause, Fred Terzo, Baxter, Landau. Stills: Bert Longworth. Camera Crew (first four days of production): Tom Brannigan, Wesley Anderson, Scotty Welbourne (stills). Gaffers: Charles Ferguson, George Satterfield. Best Boy: Bill Conger. Grips: L. P. "Dude" Mashmeyer, Harold Noyce. Sound (Vitaphone): Robert B. Lee. Sound Crew: Spencer, Lowe. Props: John Moore, K. Malloy. Costume Design: Orry-Kelly. Wardrobe: Ida Greenfield. Makeup: Perc Westmore. Hairstylist: Emily Moore. Production Assistant: Salzman. Magic Show and Tempts Supplied by Hunsaker Exposition Company. Vitaphone Orchestra Conducted by Leo F. Forbstein. Themes: "Apple Blossom Time," "Am I Blue?," "I Love You Truly," "My Wild Irish Rose."

Cast: Ruth Chatterton (Lilly Turner), George Brent (Bob Chandler), Frank McHugh (Dave Dixon), Guy Kibbee (Doc Peter McGill), Robert Barrat (Fritz), Ruth Donnelly (Edna), Marjorie Gateson (Mrs. McGill), Gordon Westcott (Rex Durkee), Arthur Vinton (Sam), Grant Mitchell (Dr. Halwey), Margaret Seddon (Mrs. Turner), Hobart Cavanaugh (Earle), Catherine Claire Ward (Mrs. Flint), Lucille Ward (Mother), Irving Bacon (Edna's Husband, Earle Yokum), William V. Mong (Druggist), Heinie Conklin (Counter Man), Tammany Young (Man in Carnival Tent), Dot Farley (Fat Woman), Ethel Wales (Mrs. Flint), Guy Usher, Gordon DeMain, Frank Darien. (Humprey Bogart and Mayo Methot, who played Mr. and Mrs. Durkee, and Mae Busch, who played Hazel, were cut from the final print, although Busch still received screen credit in the main title.)

MIDNIGHT MARY (1933)

Metro-Goldwyn-Mayer. Copyright: June 23, 1933. New York Premiere: July 14, 1933, at the Capitol and Loew's Metropolitan. 71 minutes.

A Cosmopolitan Production. Produced by Lucien K. Hubbard. Directed by William A. Wellman. Screenplay: Gene Markey and Kathryn Scola (and uncredited, Anita Loos, John Emerson, Robert Hopkins, William A. Grew, Lucian K. Hubbard [treatment]). Original Story: "Girl Delinquent, Age 16," by Anita Loos. Photography: James Van Trees. Editor: William S. Gray. Art Director: Stanley Rogers. Set Decorations: Hobe Erwin. Assistant Director: Dolph M. Zimmer. Second Assistant Director: Mike Lally. Production Manager: J. J. Cohn. Second Camera: Louis Jennings. Assistant Camera: Tom Dowling. Recording Director (Western Electric): Douglas Shearer. Sound Mixer: James Brock. Costumes: Adrian. Makeup: Jack Dawn. Musical Score: Dr. William Axt. Themes: "Sheltered by the Stars" (Fats Waller), "Please Mr. Hemingway" (Milton Drake), "Lullaby" (Emmett), "London Bridge" (Trad.), "Lazy Mary" (Trad.), "Christmas Bells" (Erno Rapee), "God Be with You" (Trad.), "Happy Times" (Jimmy McHugh), "When the Morning Rolls Around" (Woods),

"Remember Me" (O'Brien), "There's Danger in Your Eyes" (Wendling), "Hold Your Horses" (Jimmy Monaco), "Mighty Like a Rose" (Nevin), "I'm Through with Saying I'm Through" (Bert Kalmar), "Siboney" (Lecuona), "What Have We Got to Love" (Louis Alter), "Two Tickets to Georgia" (Coots), "Hello Gorgeous" (Walter Donaldson), "Hey Young Fella" (Jimmy McHugh), "Going Going Gone" (Baxter). Working Titles: *Girl Delinquent, Lady by Dawn, True Confession, Midnight Lady*. French Title: *Rose de Minuit*.

Cast: Loretta Young (Mary Martin), Ricardo Cortez (Leo Darcy), Franchot Tone (Tom Mannering, Jr.), Andy Devine (Sam Travers), Una Merkel (Bunny), Frank Conroy (District Attorney), Warren Hymer (Angelo Ricci), Ivan Simpson (Tindle), Harold Huber (Puggy), Sandy Roth (Blimp), Martha Sleeper (Barbara Loring Mannering), Charles Grapewin (Clerk), Halliwell Hobbes (Churchill), Robert Emmett O'Connor (Charlie the Cop), Louise Beavers (Anna), Robert Greig (Potter), Mike Donlin (Guard at Club Imperial), Otto Yamioka (Chinese Proprietor), Charles Sellon (Night Watchman), Bob Perry (Head Waiter at Club Saraband).

HEROES FOR SALE (1933)

First National-Vitaphone. Copyright: June 28, 1933. New York Premiere: July 21, 1933, at the Strand. 76 minutes.

Executive Producer: Darryl F. Zanuck. Produced by Hal B. Wallis. Directed by William A. Wellman. Story and Screenplay: Robert Lord and Wilson Mizner (uncredited, Darryl F. Zanuck). Photography: James Van Trees. Editor: Howard Brotherton. Art Director: Jack Okey. Assistant Director: Dolph M. Zimmer. Second Assistant Director: Marshall Hageman. Production Manager: William Koenig. Script Supervisor: Maude Allen. Second Camera: Louis Jennings. Assistant Camera: James Van Trees, Jr. Additional Camera: Ernest Haller, William Schurr, Wesley Anderson, Red Wimpy, Perry Finnerman, Henry Krause, Joe Dorris, Vernon Larson, Harry Davis, Ben White, Aaron Hower, John Shepek, William Thompson, Clifford Blackstone, Bill Reinhold, Ruler, Brigham, Emerick. Stills: Mac Julian, Gordon Head. Gaffer: George Satterfield. Grip: Jim Carter. Properties: John More. Assistant Props: K. Malloy. Sound Recording (Vitaphone): Charles Althouse. Sound Crew: Francis E. Stahl, Oren Haglund, Lou Espinosa, Jack Hart, Williams. Costumes: Orry-Kelly. Makeup: Perc Westmore. Hairstylist: Lucille D'Antoine. Vitaphone Orchestra Conducted by Leo F. Forbstein. Working Titles: *The Forgotten Man, Breadline, Mankiller*. French Title: *Heros a Vendre*.

Cast: Richard Barthelmess (Tom Holmes), Aline MacMahon (Mary Dennis), Loretta Young (Ruth Loring Holmes), Gordon Westcott (Roger Winston), Robert Barrat (Max Brinker), Grant Mitchell (George Gibson), Charles Grapewin (Pa Dennis), Robert McWade (Dr. Briggs), George Pat Collins (Leader of Agitators), James Murray (Blind Soldier), Edwin Maxwell (L.M., President of Laundry), Margaret Sadden (Mrs. Jeanette Holmes), Arthur Vinton (Mr. Joyce), Robert Elliott (Detective), John Marston (Judge), Willard Robertson (Sheriff), David Holt (Bill Holmes), Berton Churchill (Mr. Winston), Ward Bond (Red, hobo), Douglass Dumbrille (Jim, Chief Engineer), Lee Phelps (Ed Brady), Dewey Robinson (Arguer), Milton Kibbee (Teller), Guy Usher (Constable), Tammany Young (Dope Peddler), Hans Furberg (German

Prisoner), Jack Norton (Snorer), Mike Donlin, Bob Perry (Laundry Workers), Harvey Parry (Man in Mob/Stunts), Mary Wiggins, Gordon Carveth (Stunts).

WILD BOYS OF THE ROAD (1933)

First National-Vitaphone. Copyright: September 26, 1933. New York Premiere: September 21, 1933, at the Hollywood. 73 minutes.

Executive Producers: Darryl F. Zanuck, Hal B. Wallis. Produced by Robert Presnell. Directed by William A. Wellman. Second Unit Director (for pickup shot): William McGann. Screenplay: Earl Baldwin (and uncredited, Cyril Hume, Albert Wetzel, and Robert Presnell). Based on the story "Desperate Youth" by Danny Ahearn. Photography: Arthur Todd. Editor: Thomas Pratt. Art Director: Esdras Hartley. Assistant Director: Dolph M. Zimmer. Second Assistant Director: Marshall Hageman. Production Manager: William Koenig. Unit Manager: Al Alleborn. Script Supervisors: Jean McNaughton, Fred Applegate. Second Camera: William Schurr. Assistant Camera: Vernon Larson, Thad Brooks. Camera Crew: Perry Finnerman, Leo Green, Fred Terzo, Emilio Galori, Nelson Larrabee, John Shepek, Robert Mitchell, Fred Young. Process Photography: Fred Jackman, Fred Jackman, Jr., Fred Koenekamp, Robert Burks, Byron Haskin. Gaffer: Claude Hutchinson. Grip: Charles L. Davis. Stills: Mac Julian. Sound Recording (Vitaphone): Robert B. Lee. Sound Crew: Francis E. Stahl, Jack Brown, J. Jensen, Merrick, Oren Haglund, Williams, Jensen, Cooper, Larson. Props: John More. Assistant Props: K. Malloy. Wardrobe: Smoke Kring. Makeup: Perc Westmore. Hairstylists: Connie Conroy, Dot Carlson. Production Crew: McDonald. Vitaphone Orchestra Conducted by Leo Forbstein. Technical Adviser: Clem Peoples. Themes: "We're in the Money," "42nd Street" (Al Dubin-Harry Warren). British Title: *Dangerous Age*.

Cast: Frankie Darro (Eddie Smith), Dorothy Coonan (Sally), Edwin Phillips (Tommy Gordon), Rochelle Hudson (Grace), Ann Hovey (Lola), Arthur Hohl (Dr. Heckel), Grant Mitchell (Mr. Smith), Claire McDowell (Mrs. Smith), Sterling Holloway (Ollie), Robert Barrat (Judge White), Shirley Dunstead (Harriet Webster), Minna Gombell (Aunt Carrie), Ward Bond (Red), Willard Robertson (Captain of Detectives), Charles Grapewin (Mr. Cadmust), Adrian Morris (Buggie Haylin), Wilfred Lucas (Railroad Detective), Leon Holmes (Freckles), Carl Gross, Jr. (Black Boy), Raymond Borzage (Anemic Boy), George Offerman (Tough Boy), Alan Hale, Jr., Jack McHugh, Carlyle Blackwell, Jr., Bryant Washburn, Jr., Sidney Miller, John Coonan, Charles Cane, Buddy Messenger, Nestor Alber (Gang), Harvey Parry, Mary Wiggins, Gordon Carveth (Stunts).

COLLEGE COACH (1933)

Warner Brothers-Vitaphone. Copyright: November 18, 1933. New York Premiere: November 10, 1933, at the Strand. 75 minutes.

Executive Producer: Hal B. Wallis. Produced by Robert Lord. Directed by William A. Wellman (and uncredited, Dolph M. Zimmer). Story and Screenplay: Niven Busch and Manuel Seff. Photography: Arthur L. Todd. Editor: Thomas Pratt. Art Director: Jack Okey. Assistant Director: Dolph M. Zimmer. Second Assistant Director: Marshall Hageman. Production Manager: William Koenig. Unit Manager: Al Alleborn. Script Supervisor: Irva Ross. Technical Adviser: Ernie Nevers. Camera Crew: Warren Lynch, William Schurr; Frank Kesson, Emilio Galori, Vernon Larson, Al Roberts, Martin Glouner, Stuart Higgs, Harry Davis, Robert Mitchell. Insert Photography: Fred Jackman. Second Unit Director: Robert Lord. Second Unit Photography: Ernest Haller. Grips: C. L. Davis, Glen Harris. Sound (Vitaphone): Charles Lang. Sound Crew: Everett A. Brown, Francis E. Stahl, George Sweeney, McDonald, Buzzell, Lou Espinosa, Hendricks, Martin, J. Jensen, B. Berry, Cunningham. Props: Limey Plews, Martin Hershey, William B. Kuehl, Howard Oggle, William Kissell, Douglas Marshall, Edwards, Trusty. Costume Design: Orry-Kelly. Wardrobe: Smoke Kring. Women's Wardrobe: Mr. Riley. Makeup: Perc Westmore. Production Crew: Burkett, Thompson, Dexter, Dagel. Vitaphone Orchestra Conducted by Leo F. Forbstein. Songs: "Lonely Lane," sung by Dick Powell; "Men of Calvert," sung by students (Sammy Fain, Irving Kahal); "Just One More Chance" by Sam Coslow and Arthur Johnston; "Meet Me in the Gloaming" by Arthur Freed, Al Hoffman, and Al Goodhart; "What Will I Do Without You?" by Johnny Mercer and Hilda Gottlieb. British Title: *Football Coach.*

Cast: Dick Powell (Dick Sargent), Ann Dvorak (Claire Gore), Pat O'Brien (Coach Gore), Arthur Byron (Dr. Philip Sargent), Lyle Talbot (Herbert P. "Buck" Weaver), Hugh Herbert (J. Marvin Barnett), Arthur Hohl (Seymour Young), Charles C. Wilson (Charles Hauser), Guinn "Big Boy" Williams (Matthews), Nat Pendleton (Ladislaus Petrowski), Phillip Reed (Westerman), Donald Meek (Professor Spencer Trask), Berton Churchill (Otis), Harry Beresford (Professor), Herman Bing (Professor Glantz), Joseph Sawyer (Holcomb), Ward Bond (Assistant Coach), John Wayne (Football Player), Ernie Nevers (Coach), Lionel Belmore (Fan in Stands), Lynton Brent, Harry Seymour (Reporters), Harvey Parry (Stunts).

LOOKING FOR TROUBLE (1934)

Twentieth Century/United Artists. Copyright: March 9, 1934. New York Premiere: April 11, 1934, at the Rivoli. 77 minutes.

Presented by Joseph M. Schenck. Produced by Darryl F. Zanuck. Associate Producers: William Goetz and Raymond Griffith. Directed by William A. Wellman. Screenplay: Leonard Praskins and Elmer Harris. Based on an original story by J. R. Bren. Photography: James Van Trees. Editor: Hanson Fritch. Art Directors: Richard Day, Joseph Wright. Set Decorator: Julia Heron. Assistant Director: Dolph M. Zimmer. Production Manager: Edward Ebele. Technical Director: J. R. Bren. Assistant Camera: James Van Trees, Jr. Second Camera: Harry Davis. Assistant Editor: Richard Fritch. Sound (Western Electric): Frank Maher. Boom: Stan Cooley. Gaffer: Lou Johnson. Grip: Buzz Gibson. Props: Martin Hershey. Casting: Bobby Webb. Costume Design: Gwen Wakeling. Men's Wardrobe: William Bridgehouse. Women's Wardrobe: Peg O'Neil. Makeup: Guy Pearce. Hairstylist: Loretta Francel. Musical Director: Alfred Newman. Working Title: *Trouble Shooter.*

Cast: Spencer Tracy (Joe Graham), Jack Oakie (Casey), Constance Cummings (Ethel Greenwood), Arline Judge (Maizie), Judith Wood (Pearl LaTour), Morgan Conway (Dan Sutter), Paul Harvey (James Regan), Joseph Sawyer (Max Stanley),

Franklyn Ardell [later Robert Elliot] (Martin), Paul Porcasi (Cabaret Manager), Robert Homans (Cop), Charles Lane (Operator), Harvey Parry (Stunts).

STINGAREE (1934)

RKO-Radio. Copyright: May 24, 1934. New York Premiere: May 17, 1934, at Radio City Music Hall. 76 minutes.

Presented by Merian C. Cooper. Produced by Pandro S. Berman. Associate Producer: David Lewis. Directed by William A. Wellman. Screenplay: Becky Gardiner (and uncredited, Garrett Fort, Wells Root, Agnes Christine Johnston, Dwight Taylor). Adaptation: Lynn Riggs and Leonard Spigelgass. Based on the novel (1905) and stories by E. W. Hornung. Photography: James Van Trees. Editor: James B. Morley. Art Direction: Van Nest Polglase, Al Herman. Assistant Directors: Dolph M. Zimmer, Ivan Thomas. Production Manager: C. J. White. Unit Manager: Walter Daniels. Script Supervisor: Anita Speer. Special Photographic Effects: Vernon L. Walker. Assistant Camera: James Van Trees, Jr. Second Camera: Louis Jennings. Stills: Fred Hendrickson. Gaffer: Paul Bristow. Grip: Ralph Wildman. Best Boy: Slim Ackerman. Sound Recording (RCA): John E. Tribby; assistant: Jim Fields. Boom Operator: John C. Grubb. Sound Technician: J. O. Aalberg. Music and Sound Editor: Murray Spivack. Costume Design: Walter Plunkett. Wardrobe: Claire Cramer, Homer Watson. Makeup: Carl Axcelle. Hairstylist: Gwen Holden. Props: Thomas Little, John Sherwood. Musical Direction: Max Steiner. Songs: "Tonight Is Mine" and "Stingaree Ballad," music by W. Franke Harling, lyrics by Gus Kahn; "I Wish I Were a Fisherman" and "Once You're Mine" by Edward Eliscu and Max Steiner. Excerpts from the operas *Faust* by Charles Francois Gounod and *Martha: Oder der Markt von Richmond* by Friedrich Flotow, sung by Irene Dunne.

Cast: Irene Dunne (Hilda Bouverie), Richard Dix (Stingaree, aka Mr. Smithson), Mary Boland (Mrs. Clarkson), Conway Tearle (Sir Julian Kent), Andy Devine (Howie), Henry Stephenson (Mr. Hugh Clarkson), Una O'Connor (Annie), George Barraud (Inspector Radford), Reginald Owen (Governor General), Snub Pollard (Victor), Billy Bevan (Mac), Robert Greig (Innkeeper), Frank Dunn (Disraeli), Edgar Norton (Governor's First Aide), Lionel Belmore (Governor's Second Aide), Gordon DeMain (Prince of Wales), Rolfe Sedan (Salesman), Keith Kenneth (Sub-Inspector) Ralph Fitzsimmons, Allen Lee, Jack Kennedy, Jack Lendell, Hank Potts, Howard Hickey (Stagecoach Drivers), Earl Covert (Singer), Norma Adoree (Flower Girl), Adrienne D'Ambricourt (Mother), Georges Renavent (Marquis), Robert Adair (Doorman), Luis Alberni (Student), Alice Ardell, Patty James (Showgirls), Ben Hendricks, James Warwick, Carl Gordon, Frank Baker, Silver Harr, Roger Cluett, Harrington Reynolds, Arthur Clayton (Constables), Dan Dix, Sailor Billy Vincent, John Coonan, Joe Garion (Men with Beards), Ivan Simpson, Dick Lancaster, Harry Harris, Jack Ranier, May Beatty, Carol Tevis (Bits), Kenny Cooper, Cliff Lyons, Jack Lindall (Richard Dix's Doubles), Fred Gilman (George Barraud's Double), Mary Miner (Irene Dunne's Stand-in), George Lollier (Richard Dix's Stand-in), Gordon Jones (Andy Devine's Stand-in), Joe Bulch (Henry Stephenson's Stand-in), Dan Dix, Marcella Arnold (Stand-ins).

THE PRESIDENT VANISHES (1934)

Walter Wanger Productions/Paramount. Copyright: January 11, 1935. New York Premiere: December 7, 1934, at the Paramount. 83 minutes.

Produced by Walter Wanger. Executive Producer: Emanuel Cohen. Directed by William A. Wellman. Screenplay: Carey Wilson and Cedric Worth. Dialogue: Lynn Starling (and uncredited, Ben Hecht and Charles MacArthur). Based on the novel by Rex Stout (1934), published anonymously. Photography: Barney "Chick" McGill. Editor: Hanson Fritch. Art Director: Sydney M. Ullman. Assistant Director: Dolph M. Zimmer. Second Assistant Director: Tom Andre. Production Manager: Frederick Spencer. Script Supervisor: Corynn Keel. Assistant Producer: Judson Stevens. Special Photographic Effects: Slavko Vorkapich, John Hoffman. Additional Photography: Russell Cully, Paul Eagler. Second Camera: Kenneth Green. Assistant Camera: Bill Whittley, Don Green, Roy Tripp, J. Darrell, E. Liggett, G. Beckman. Stills: Madison Lacey, William Thomas. Sound (Western Electric): Hugo Grenzbach. Sound Crew: Mickey Myers, Wally Wallace, Leon Roberts, Bill Raab, Rube Morris, Robert Lohmeyer. Art Crew: Fred Stoos, Larry Eckes, A. L. Metcher, Harry Sherman. Gaffer: Robert Comer. Grip: Charles Rose. Props: Robert Lander. Location Manager: Harry Connolly. Technical Advisers: John F. Dockwieler, Lieutenant Walker. Assistant Editor: Richard Fritch. Apprentice Editor: Walter Reynolds. Special Effects Cutters: Thomas Persons, Zoe Edwards. Montage Assistants: Harold Gordon, Martin Zahn. Casting: William Forsyth. Assistant Casting: R. Cochrane. Makeup: Robert Stephanoff, Grace Boyd, Hugh Roman. Hairstylists: Helen Taylor, Regine DeMarsh, Rose Plancia. Production Assistants: John Coonan, J. Stevens. Musical Settings: Hugo Reisenfeld. British Title: *Strange Conspiracy*. French Title: *Le President Fantome*.

Cast: Arthur Byron (President Craig Stanley), Paul Kelly (Chick Moffat), Peggy Conklin (Alma Cronin), Edward Arnold (Lewis Wardell), Andy Devine (Val Orcott), Janet Beecher (Mrs. Stanley), Osgood Perkins (Harris Brownell), Sidney Blackmer (D. L. Voorman), Edward Ellis (Lincoln Lee), Irene Franklin (Mrs. Orcott), Charley Grapewin (Richard Norton), Rosalind Russell (Sally Voorman), Robert McWade (Vice President Bob Molleson), DeWitt Jennings (Edward Cullen), Walter Kingsford (Martin Drew), Douglas Wood (Roger Grant), Charles Richman (Judge Corcoran), Paul Harvey (Skinner), Jason Robards (Kilbourne), Harry Woods (Kramer), Tommy Dugan (Nolan), Martha Mayo (Mrs. Delling), J. Carroll Naish (Communist Agitator), Robert Romans (Pat the Cop), Clara Blandick (Woman), Charles K. French, William Worthington, William S. Holmes, Charles Meakin, Art Howard, Ed Lewis, Ed Mortimer, Emmett King, Edgar Sherrod, Henry Herbert (Senators and Congressman).

THE CALL OF THE WILD (1935)

Twentieth Century/United Artists. Copyright: June 13, 1935. New York Premiere: August 14, 1935, at the Rivoli. Rereleased in 1945 and 1953 in 81-minute versions. 91 minutes.

Presented by Joseph M. Schenck. Produced by Darryl F. Zanuck. Associate Producers: William Goetz and Raymond Griffith. Directed by William A. Wellman. Screenplay: Gene Fowler and Leonard Praskins. Based on the novel by Jack London

(1903). Photography: Charles Rosher. Editor: Hanson Fritch. Art Direction: Richard Day, Alexander Golitzen. Set Decorator: Julia Heron. Assistant Director: Dolph M. Zimmer. Second Assistant Director: Martin Zahn. Production Manager: Edward Ebele. Script Supervisor: Bobs Hoagland. Location Manager: Orville Stewart. Camera Operator: Carl Wester. Second Camera: Roy Clark. Process Photography: Roy Binger. Stills: Kenneth Alexander. Sound (Western Electric): Jack Noyes, Roger Heman. Gaffer: James Potevin. Grip: Freddie Williams. Props: Bob Lander. Construction: V. L. McFadden. Costumes: Omar Kiam. Men's Wardrobe: William Bridgehouse. Women's Wardrobe: Peg O'Neil. Set Wardrobe: Mickey Meyers, Nina Byron. Makeup: Guy Pearce. Set Makeup: Charles Garman. Hairstylist: Lucille D'Antoine. Assistant Editor: Richard Fritch. Casting: Bobby Webb. Research: Edward Lambert. Musical Director: Alfred Newman. Song: "It Ain't Goin' to Rain No More" by Wendall Hall. Buck trained by Carl Spitz. French Title: *L'Appel de la Foret.*

Cast: Clark Gable (Jack Thornton), Loretta Young (Claire Blake), Jack Oakie (Shorty Hoolihan), Frank Conroy (John Blake), Reginald Owen (Smith), Sidney Toler (Joe Groggins), Katherine DeMille (Marie), Lalo Encinas (Kali), Charles Stevens (Francois), James Burke (Ole), Duke Green (Frank), John T. Murray ("Heavy" on Stage), Mia Marvin ("Heroine" on Stage), Bob Perry (Stage Manager), Marie Wells (Hilda), Arthur Housman (Drunk in Skagway Saloon), Harry Woods (Soapy Smith), Sid Grauman, Philip G. Sleeman, Capt. C. E. Anderson, Frank Whitson (Poker Players), Thomas E. Jackson (Tex Rickard), Samuel T. Godfrey (Faro Dealer), William R. Arnold, Perry Ivins (Faro Players), Walter McGrail (Spectator), Russ Powell (Bartender in Skagway), Wong Chung, Lou Loy (Chinamen in Alley), LeRoy Mason (Pimp in Marie's Room), Frank Moran (Bartender in Dawson), Herman Bing (Sam, fat miner), Wade Boteler, Arthur Aylesworth, John Ince (Miners in Dawson), Jesse DeVorska ("Ike"), George MacQuarrie (Mounted Policeman), Joan Woodbury (Girl Crossing Street), Frank Campeau (Sourdough on Street), Pat Flaherty (Dandy on Street), Syd Saylor (Picolo Player), Larry McGrath, Jack Stoney, Leon Beaumont (Men Outside Hospital), Celia Marcel, Carol Mercer, Harriet King, Kay Johnson, Gladys Johnson, Kay Des Lys, Pearl Varvelle, Peggy Langton (Beef Trust Girls), Helene Chadwick, Mary MacLaren, Frank Mills, Bud Osborne, Jack Gray, Loretta Rush, Ted Lorch, Edwin Argus, Hazel Mills, Kay Howard (Dawson Townspeople), Harvey Parry, John Collins, Duke Green (Stunts), Frank Hotaling (Clark Gable Stand-in), Lowell Henderson (Jack Oakie Stand-in), Jessie Kenyon (Loretta Young Stand-in), I Grey Boy (Great Dane), King (Buck the Dog), Cappy (Buck's Double).

THE ROBIN HOOD OF EL DORADO (1936)

Metro-Goldwyn-Mayer. Copyright: March 4, 1936. New York Premiere: March 13, 1936, at the Capitol. 86 minutes.

Produced by John Considine, Jr. Directed by William A. Wellman. Screenplay: William A. Wellman, Joseph Calleia, and Melvin Levy (and uncredited, John Thomas Neville, James Kevin McGuinness, Rowland Brown [treatment], Howard Emmett Rogers, Dan Totheroh [dialogue]), C. Gardner Sullivan, Peter B. Kyne, Charles Arthur Powell, Leo B. Pride, Harvey Gates, Gladys Von Ettinghauser, Louis Paul, George Oppenheimer, Allan Garcia, Lynn Starling, John Farrow, and Robert Carson. Based on the book by Walter Noble Burns (1932). Novelization: Peter B. Kyne. Photography: Chester Lyons. Editor: Robert J. Kern. Assistant Director: Tom Andre. Production Manager: J. J. Cohn. Unit Manager: Horace Hough. Art Directors: David Townsend, Gabriel Scognamillo. Recording Director (Western Electric): Douglas Shearer. Makeup: Jack Dawn. Hairstylist: Agnes McMullen. Technical Adviser: H. O. Bombacher. Dialect Coach: Allan Garcia. Wranglers: Bob Roberts, Edgar "Pardner" Jones. Musical Score: Herbert Stothart. Additional Music: Edward Ward. Dance Number Staged by Chester Hale. Themes (all vocals): "Oh Susanna" (Stephen Foster); "Todo Para Ti" and "Baile de Bandidos" (Herbert Stothart and Rafael Sturm); Wedding March from *Lohengrin* (Richard Wagner); "La Golondrina" (traditional), arranged by Herbert Stothart. Working Titles: *Born to Die, In Old California, Murietta, I Am Joaquin*. French Title: *Robin des Bois d'El Dorado*.

Cast: Warner Baxter (Joaquin Murrieta), Ann Loring (Juanita de la Cuesta), Bruce Cabot (Bill Warren), Margo (Rosita Murrieta), J. Carroll Naish (Three-Fingered Jack), Soledad Jiménez (Madre Murrieta), Carlos de Valdez (José Murrieta), Eric Linden (Johnnie Warren), Edgar Kennedy (Sheriff Judd), Charles Trowbridge (Ramon de la Cuesta), Harvey Stephens (Captain Osborne), Ralph Remley (Judge Perkins), George Regas (Tomás), Harry Woods (Pete), Francis McDonald (Pedro the Spy), Kay Hughes (Louise), Paul Hurst (Wilson), Boothe Howard (Tabbard), G. Pat Collins (Doc), Harold Goodwin (Slocum), Ivan "Dusty" Miller (Marshall), Tom Moore (Sheriff Hannan), Richard Cramer (Bartender), Carlotta Monti (Dancer), Charles Stevens (Bandit), J. P. MacGowan (Danglong), Nick DeRuiz (Mexican Peon), Lew Harvey (Bill Young), Ben Taggart (Rancher), Cully Richards (Juan), Jason Robards (Pancho), Duke Green (Guerrera), Marc Lawrence (Manuel), Frank Campeau (Steve), Robert Perry (Miner at Grave), Frank Yaconelli (Peon), Lee Shumway (Deputy), Frank Hagney (Phil), Lee Phelps (Hank), George MacQuarrie (Smithers), Sam Ash (Arriga), Inez Falange (Nurse), Nigel DeBrulier (Padre), Mathilde Comont (Señorita Martínez), Lou Yaconelli (Julio Antón), Si Jenks (Man in Lynch Mob), Bill Steele (Rider), Murphy Alexandris, Robert Morse, Rene Sardello (Stunt Riders), Yakima Canutt (Stunt Double for Warner Baxter), Harvey Parry (Stunts).

SMALL TOWN GIRL (1936)

Metro-Goldwyn-Mayer. Copyright: April 6, 1936. New York Premiere: April 10, 1936, at the Capitol. Rereleased 1953. 90 minutes.

Produced by Hunt Stromberg. Directed by William A. Wellman (and uncredited, Robert Z. Leonard). Screenplay: John Lee Mahin, Frances Goodrich, Albert Hackett, Edith Fitzgerald (and uncredited, Horace Jackson, Lenore Coffee, Manuel Seff, Mildred Cram). Based on a novel by Ben Ames Williams (1935). Photography: Oliver T. Marsh, Charles Rosher. Editor: Blanche Sewell. Art Directors: Cedric Gibbons, A. Arnold Gillespie. Set Decorations: Edwin B. Willis. Assistant Director: Tom Andre. Production Manager: J. J. Cohn. Unit Manager: George Yohalem. Photographic Effects: John Hoffman. Recording Director (Western Electric): Douglas Shearer. Wardrobe: Dolly Tree. Makeup: Jack Dawn. Musical Score: Herbert Stothart, Edward Ward. Songs: "Small Town Girl," music by Herbert Stothart and Edward Ward, lyrics by Gus Kahn, sung in opening credits by Dick Webster; "Boola Boola" (Hirsch), vocals; "Harvardiana" (R. G. Williams), vocals; "Bingo" (unknown); "Solomon Levi" (unknown), vocal; "Up the Street" (R. G. Morse), vocals; "I'm in the Mood for Love" (Jimmy McHugh and Dorothy Fields), vocals. Other Themes: "Gridiron King" (R. K. Fletcher); "There's a Tavern in the Town" (Hills); "Wedding March" (Felix Mendelssohn); "Wedding March" from *Lohengrin* (Richard Wagner); "Sailing Sailing" (Geoffrey Marks). French Title: *La Petite Provenciale*. Television Title: *One Horse Town*.

Cast: Janet Gaynor (Kay Brannan), Robert Taylor (Bob Dakin), Binnie Barnes (Priscilla), Lewis Stone (Dr. Dakin), Andy Devine (George), Elizabeth Patterson (Ma Brannan), Frank Craven (Pa Brannan), James Stewart (Elmer), Douglas Fowley (Chick), Isabel Jewell (Emily), Charley Grapewin (Dr. Fabre), Nella Walker (Mrs. Dakin), Robert Greig (Childers), Edgar Kennedy (Captain Mack), Willie Fung (SoSo), Agnes Ayres (Catherine), Mary Forbes (Mrs. Hyde), John Harron (Pat), Nora Lane (Cissie), Walter Johnson (Jim), Drue Layton (Felicia), Joan Breslau (Martin Girl), Joan Russell (June Brannan), Adrian Rosley (Café Proprietor), Richard Carle (J.P.), James Donlan (First Attendant), Frank Sully (Bill), Claire McDowell (Bit in Bed), Buster Phelps (Boy), Grace Hale (Floor Nurse), Ethel Wales (Mrs. Johnson), Leonard Carey (Concierge), Helen Shipman, Ellen Lowe, Edna Bennett (Nurses), Thomas Braidon, Edward Cooper (Butlers), Earl Eby (Intern), Chester Gan (Cing), Ivan Simpson (Hyde Butler), Otto Fries (Cook), Jack Hatfield, William Wayne, Franklyn Parker (Reporters), Sherry Hall (Chauffeur), Claire DuBrey (Second Maid), Lillian Leighton (Mrs. Pruitt), Eddie Kane (Proprietor), Charles Wilson (Chief Engineer), Jimmy Grier (Orchestra Leader), Charles Irwin (Head Waiter), George Breakston (Little Jimmy), Robert Livingston (Man), Thelma "Pat" Ryan [Nixon] (Bit).

A STAR IS BORN (1937)

Selznick International/United Artists. Copyright: June 7, 1937. New York Premiere: April 22, 1937, at Radio City Music Hall. III minutes.

Produced by David O. Selznick. Directed by William A. Wellman (and uncredited, Jack Conway and Victor Fleming). Screenplay: Dorothy Parker, Alan Campbell, Robert Carson (and uncredited, Rowland Brown, Ben Hecht, Gene Fowler, John Lee Mahin, Ring Lardner, Jr., Budd Schulberg, David O. Selznick, William A. Wellman). Based on a story, "It Happened in Hollywood," by William A. Wellman and Robert Carson. Color by Technicolor. Photography: W. Howard Greene. Supervising Film Editor: Hal C. Kern. Editor: James E. Newcom. Associate Editor: Anson Stevenson. Art Director: Lyle R. Wheeler. Set Decorator: Edward G. Boyle. Color Design: Lansing Holden. Color Consultant: Natalie Kalmus. Assistant Director: Eric Stacey. Second Unit Director: Richard Rosson. Production Manager: Raymond Klune. Unit Manager: Ray Flynn. Location Manager: Mason Litson. Casting Director: Charles Richards. Camera Operator: Arthur Arling. Sound (Western Electric): Oscar Lagerstrom. Special Effects: Jack Cosgrove, Clarence Slifer. Costumes: Omar Kiam. Adolphe Menjou's Wardrobe Designed by Eddie Schmidt. Costume Supplier: Western Costume Company. Makeup: Paul Stanhope, Eddie Voight. Screen and Stage Makeup: Elizabeth Arden. Properties: Bob Lander. Head Grip: Fred Williams. Head Electrician: James Potevin. Construction Superintendent: Harold Fenton. Production Secretaries: Barbara Keon, Corynn Kiehl. Assistant to David Selzrtick: Marcella Rabwin. Editorial Assistant: Hal Lewton. Publicity: Russell Birdwell. Musical Score: Max Steiner. Musical Director: Louis Forbes. French Title: *Etoile Est Nee*.

Cast: Janet Gaynor (Esther Blodgett/Vickie Lester), Fredric March (Norman Maine/Alfred Henkel), Adolphe Menjou (Oliver Niles), Andy Devine (Danny McGuire), May Robson (Lettie), Lionel Stander (Libby), Owen Moore (Casey Burke), Edgar Kennedy (Pop Randall), Elizabeth Jenns (Anita Regis), J.C. Nugent (Theodore Smythe), Clara Blandick (Aunt Mattie), Albert Wayne Sweatt (Alex Blodgett), Peggy Wood (Miss Phillips, Central Casting Clerk), Clarence Wilson (Justice of the Peace), Adrian Rosley (Harris, makeup man), Arthur Hoyt (Ward, makeup man), Guinn "Big Boy" Williams (Posture Coach), Vince Barnett (Otto Fried, photographer), Paul Stanton (Academy Awards Speaker), Franklin Pangborn (Billy Moon), Jonathan Hale (George Barris, Night Court Judge), Pat Flaherty (Cuddles), Dr. Leonard Walker (Orchestra Leader in Hollywood Bowl), Edwin Maxwell (Voice Coach), Marshall Neilan (Bert), Jed Prouty (Artie Carver), Trixie Friganza (Mabel), Jane Barnes (Waitress in Commissary), Charles Williams (Assistant Cameraman), Robert Emmett O'Connor (Santa Anita Bartender), Olin Bowlin (Jud Baker), Carleton Griffin (Cameraman), Claude King, Eddie Kane, David Newell, Bud Flannigan, Dennis O'Keefe (Burke Party Guests), George Chandler (Delivery Boy), Francis Ford (William Gregory, First Night Court Drunk), Kenneth Howell (Milton Rails, Second Night Court Drunk), Chris Pin Martin (Jose Rodriguez, Third Night Court Drunk), Cecil Weston (Wardrobe Woman), Willy Morris (Niles's Secretary), Ferdinand Munier, Herbert Evans (Bartenders at Burke Home), Gayne Whitman (Announcer at Grauman's Chinese Theatre), Harvey Parry, Joe Grey (Boxers), Bob Perry (Referee), Irving Bacon (Station Agent), Sherry Hall (Clerk), Robert Homans (Bailiff), Eddie Hearn (Orderly), Willy Morris (Niles's Secretary), Eric Alden, Harry Bradley, Myra Marsh (Secretaries), Tom Ricketts (Butler at Malibu Home), Fred "Snowflake" Toones (Witness), Billy Dooley (Painter), Grace Hayle (Woman in Funeral Mob), Margaret Tallichet (Marion, Woman at Santa Anita Bar), Lana Turner, Carole Landis, David Newell (Extras in Santa Anita Bar), Charles King, Vera Stedman, Helene Chadwick (Extras), Jean Gale, Billy Coe, Rex Evans, Cynthia Westlake, Virginia Dabney, Blanche Bush, Harrison Greene, Sally Raynor, Renee Orsell, Leon Holmes, Buddy Messinger, Armand Kaliz, Dora Early, Kay Sutton, Luana Walters, Marla Shelton (Bits), Mary Jane Irving (Gaynor's Stand-in).

NOTHING SACRED (1937)

Selznick-International United Artists. Copyright: December 8, 1937. New York Premiere: November 25, 1937, at Radio City Music Hall. 75 minutes.

Produced by David O. Selznick. Directed by William A. Wellman. Screenplay: Ben Hecht (and uncredited, George Oppenheimer, Sidney Howard, Moss Hart, George Kaufman, John Lee Mahin, Ring Lardner, Jr., Budd Schulberg, Dorothy Parker, Robert Carson, David O. Selznick, William A. Wellman). Story by James H. Street, "A Letter to the Editor." Color by Technicolor. Photography: W. Howard Greene. Editor: James E. Newcom. Art Director: Lyle R. Wheeler. Set Decorator: Edward G. Boyle. Color Consultant: Natalie Kalmus; associate: Henri Jaffa. Assistant Directors: Frederick A. Spencer, John Coonan, Charles Samuels. Production Manager: Raymond

A. Klune. Camera Operator: Arthur Aring. Aerial Photography: Wilfrid M. Cline. Special Effects: Jack Cosgrove, Clarence Slifer. Sound (Western Electric): Fred J. Lau. Carole Lombard's Costumes: Travis Banton. Other Costumes: Walter Plunkett. Main Titles: Sam Berman. Production Secretary/Scenario Assistant: Barbara Keon. Assistant to David Selznick: Marcella Rabwin. Publicity: Russell Birdwell. Musical Score: Oscar Levant. Musical Director: Louis Forbes. Novelty Swing Music: Raymond Scott and His Quintet. Songs by Louis Alter and Walter Bullock. Dance Director: Dave Gould. French Title: *La Joyeuse Suicidee*. Remade as *Living It Up* (1954, director Norman Taurog).

Cast: Carole Lombard (Hazel Flagg), Fredric March (Wally Cook), Charles Winninger (Dr. Enoch Downer), Walter Connolly (Oliver Stone), Sig Rumann (Dr. Emile Egglehoffer), Frank Fay (Master of Ceremonies), "Slapsie" Maxie Rosenbloom (Max Levinsky), Margaret Hamilton (Drugstore Lady), Troy Brown (Ernest Walker), Hattie McDaniel (Mrs. Walker), Olin Howland (Baggage Man), George Chandler (Photographer), Claire DuBrey (Miss Rafferty, Nurse), John Qualen (Swedish Fireman), Charles Richman (Mayor), Art Lasky (Mug), Alex Schoenberg (Dr. Kerchinwasser), Monty Woolley (Dr. Vunch), Alex Novinsky (Dr. Marachuffsky), Katherine Shelton (Dr. Downer's Nurse), Ben Morgan, Hans Steinke (Wrestlers), Aileen Pringle (Mrs. Bullock), Hedda Hopper (Shipboard Dowager), Dick Rich (Moe), A. W. Sweatt (Office Boy), Clarence Wilson (Mr. Watson), Betty Douglas ("Helen of Troy"), Eleanor Troy ("Catherine of Russia"), Monica Bannister ("Pocahontas"), Jinx Falkenberg ("Katinka"), Margaret Lyman ("Salome"), Shirley Chambers ("Lady Godiva"), Ernest Whitman, Everett Brown (Policemen), Vera Lewis (Miss Sedgewick), Ann Doran (Telephone Girl), Bill Dunn, Lee Phelps (Electricians), Cyril Ring (Pilot), Mickey McMasters (Referee), Bobby Tracey (Announcer), Billy Barty (Little Boy), Nora Cecil (School Teacher), A. R. Hayzel (Copy Editor), John Wilson (City Editor), Louise Clark (Walker's Girl), Charles Lane (Rubinstein), Hilda Vaughan (Mrs. Cartwright), Bob Perry, Art Lasky (Mugs), Helen Brown (Secretary), Charles Sherlock (Printer), Tenen Holtz (Sad Waiter), Alex Mellish (D.S.C. Head), Walter Walker (E. J. Southern), Philippe Hurlie, Rudolph Chavers, Dolores Lilly (Walker's Kids), Sammy Stoller (Bit), Eddie Kane, Emily Fitzroy, Tom Ricketts, Allen Cavan, Mickey Morita, E. J. Hertz, Albert Conti, Eddie Dunn, Joe Cunningham, Chet deVito, Laurie Lane (Guests at Banquet), Wimpy (Dog), Raymond Scott and His Quintet (Themselves), "Pearl the Squirrel."

MEN WITH WINGS (1938)

Paramount. Copyright: October 20, 1938. New York Premiere: August 2, 1938, at the Paramount. 105 minutes.

A William A. Wellman Production. Executive Producer: William LeBaron. Presented by Adolph Zukor. Produced and Directed by William A. Wellman. Screenplay: Robert Carson (and uncredited, James Norman Hall, Cecil Lewis, Philip MacDonald, William A. Wellman). Color by Technicolor. Photography: W. Howard Greene. Editor: Thomas Scott. Art Direction: Hans Dreier, Robert Odell. Set Decorations: A. E. Freudeman. Assistant Director: Joseph Youngerman. Second Assistant Director: Eddie Salven. Assistant to William Wellman: Zoila Conan. Sound (Western Electric): Gene Merritt, John Cope. Aerial Photography: Wilfrid Cline, Charles Marshall, Elmer Dyer. Special Photographic Effects: Gordon Jennings. Process Photography: Farciot Edouart. Technical Adviser: Paul Mantz. Stunt Pilots: Frank Clarke, Paul Mantz, Frank Tomick, Tex Rankin, Eddie Angel, Dick Rinaldi, Garland Lincoln, Ace Brugunier, Herb White, Ray Crawford, Dick Randall, E. H. "Robbie" Robinson, Howard Bat, Jerry Phillips, Bob Blair, Chubby Gordon, Walter Quinton, Stanley Hicks. Mechanics: Todd Oviat, Jim Barton, Al Lary. Color Consultant: Natalie Kalmus; Associate: Henri Jaffa. Technicolor Technicians: Paul Hill, John Hamilton, Andrew J. "Duke" Callahan. Costumes: Edith Head. Makeup: Wally Westmore. Assistant Makeup: Glen Alden. Research: Gladys Percey. Musical Score: W. Franke Harling and Gerard Carbonara. Musical Director: Boris Morros. Music Conducted by Irvin Talbot. Music Recorded by Sam Wineland. Song: "Men with Wings," by Frank Loesser and Hoagy Carmichael. Theme: "I'm Forever Blowing Bubbles," words by Jean Kenbrovin (pseudonym for James Kendis, James Brockman, Nat Vincent), music by William Kellette. French Title: *Les Hommes Volants*.

Cast: Fred MacMurray (Patrick Falconer), Ray Milland (Scott Barnes), Louise Campbell (Peggy Ranson), Andy Devine (Joe Gibbs), Lynne Overman (Hank Rinebow), Porter Hall (Hiram F. Jenkins), Walter Abel (Nick Ranson), Kitty Kelly (Martha Ranson), Virginia Weidler (Peggy as a child), Donald O'Connor (Pat as a child), Billy Cook (Scott as a child), James Burke (J. A. Nolan), Willard Robertson (Major General Hadley), Richard Stanley [later Dennis Morgan] (Galton), Frank Clarke (Burke), Charles Trowbridge (Alcott), Jonathan Hale (Long), Juanita Quigley (Patricia Falconer, age 6), Joan Brodel (Patricia Falconer, age 11), Mary Brodel (Patricia, age 17), Archie Twitchell (Nelson), Dorothy Tennant (Mrs. Tennant), Helen Dickson (First Woman), Lillian West (Second Woman), Grace Goodall (Matron), Charles Williams (Telegraph Operator), Kitty McHugh (Nurse), Harry Woods (Baker), Jack Chapin (Sentry), Joe Whitehead (Cab Driver), Pat West, David Newell, Charles Hamilton, Lee Phelps (Photographers), Ronnie Randell, Frank Mills, Bobby Barber (Mechanics), Art Rowlands, Ralph McCullough, Garry Owen, Bobby Tracy, James Burtis, Paul Kruger, Jerry Storm (Reporters), Eddie Dunn (Field Employee), Edward Earle (Officer), John T. Murray (Jones), Dell Henderson (Chairman), Claire DuBrey (Edith), Willy Morris (Clerk), Billy Bletcher (Red Cross Man), Syd Saylor (Jimmy), Lu Miller (Norma), Al Hill (Mail Driver), George Chandler (Cody), Franklin Parker (Truck Driver), Sherry Hall (Field Official), Bob Perry (Waiter in Speakeasy), Russell Hicks (General Marlin), Ruth Rogers (Girl), Ethel Clayton (Woman), Jack Hubbard (Attendant), Norah Gale, Dorothy White, Dolores Casey, Sheila Darcy, Cheryl Walker, Jane Dewey, Jean Fenwick, Evelyn Keyes (Nurses), Paul Mantz (Pilot), Harvey Parry (Stunts).

BEAU GESTE (1939)

Paramount. Copyright: September 15, 1939. New York Premiere: August 2, 1939, at the Paramount. Rereleased 1950 on a double-bill with Henry Hathaway's *Lives of a Bengal Lancer* (1935). 120 minutes (six minutes were cut for rerelease and have never been restored).

A William A. Wellman Production. Executive Producer: William LeBaron. Produced and Directed by William A. Wellman. Screenplay: Robert Carson (and uncredited, Grover Jones, W. P. Lipscomb, Bertram Millhauser, William A. Wellman). Based on the novel by Percival Christopher Wren (1924). Photography: Theodor Sparkhul and Archie J. Stout. Editor: Thomas Scott. Art Direction: Hans Dreier, Robert Odell. Set Decorator: A. E. Freudeman. Assistant Director: Joseph Youngerman. Second Assistant Director: Eddie Salven. Unit Manager: Sidney Street. Assistant Unit Manager: Bill Wallace. Script Supervisors: Coleman, Busch. Second Unit Director: Richard Talmadge. Technical Advisers: Louis Van Der Ecker, Colonel H. Gerard (French Foreign Legion). Drillmaster: Carl Voss. Sound (Western Electric): Hugo Grenzbach, Walter Oberst. Location Mixer: Howard Fogette. Assistant Editor: Thomas Neff. Sound Editor: Reeve. Costumes: Edith Head. Makeup: Wally Westmore and Bud Westmore. Musical Score: Alfred Newman. Music Adviser: Troy Sanders. Orchestral Arrangements: Edward B. Powell.

Cast: Gary Cooper (Michael "Beau" Geste), Ray Milland (John Geste), Robert Preston (Digby Geste), Brian Donlevy (Sergeant Markoff), Susan Hayward (Isobel Rivers), J. Carroll Naish (Rasinoff), Albert Dekker (Schwartz), Broderick Crawford (Hank Miller), Charles T. Barton (Buddy McMonigle), James Stephenson (Major Henri de Beaujolais), Heather Thatcher (Lady Patricia Brandon), G. P. Huntley, Jr. (Augustus Brandon), James Burke (Lt. Dufour), Arthur Aylesworth (Renault, a deserter), Henry Brandon (Renour, another deserter), Harry Woods (Renoir), Harold Huber (Vousin), Donald O'Connor (Beau as a child), Billy Cook (John as a child), Martin Spellman (Digby as a child), Ann Gillis (Isobel as a child), David Holt (Augustus as a child), Harvey Stephens (Lt. Martin), Stanley Andrews (Maris), Barry McCollom (Krenke), Ronnie Rondell (Bugler), Frank Dawson (Burdon, the butler), George Chandler (Cordier), Duke Green (Glock), Thomas Jackson (Colonel in Recruiting Office), Jerome Storm (Sergeant-Major), Joseph Whitehead (Sergeant), Harry Worth (Corporal), Nestor Paiva (Corporal Golas), George Regas, Francis McDonald (Arab Scouts), Carl Voss (Legionaire S. Roberts), Joe Bernard (Legionnaire J. Williams), Bob Perry (Legionnaire L. Paul), Larry Lawson (Legionnaire N. Fenton), Henry Sylvester (Legionnaire T. Clements), Joseph William Cody (Legionnaire A. Virginia), Joe Colling (Trumpeter O. Leo), Gladys Jean (Girl in Port Said Café), Bob Kortman, Gino Corrado, Henry Lucenay, Nick Vehr, Alexis Davidoff, Bert Stevens [Barbara Stanwyck's brother], Otto Steiger, Charles Townsend, Tex Driscoll (Legionnaires), Otto Merete (Stuntman for J. Carroll Naish), Frank Henry (Donlevy's Stand-in).

THE LIGHT THAT FAILED (1939)

Paramount. Copyright: February 9, 1940. New York Premiere: December 24, 1939, at the Rivoli. 97 minutes.

Executive Producer: William LeBaron. A William A. Wellman Production. Produced and Directed by William A. Wellman. Screenplay: Robert Carson. Based on the novel by Rudyard Kipling (1890). Photography: Theodor Sparkhul. Editor: Thomas Scott. Art Direction: Hans Dreier, Robert Odell. Set Decorations: A. E. Freudeman. Second Unit Director: Joseph Youngerman. Assistant Directors: Stanley Goldsmith, Fritz Collings, Clem Jones. Second Assistant Director: Eddie Salven. Unit Manager: Sidney Street. Second Unit Camera: Guy Bennett. Stunt Coordinator: Yakima Canutt.

Technical Advisers: Capt. Jack R. Durham-Matthews, Alf Nicholson. Sound (Western Electric): Hugo Grenzbach, Walter Oberst. Costumes: Edith Head. Makeup: Wally Westmore. Musical Score: Victor Young. French Title: *La Lumiere que S'Eteint.*

Cast: Ronald Colman (Dick Heldar), Walter Huston (Torpenhow), Muriel Angelus (Maisie), Ida Lupino (Bessie Broke), Dudley Digges (The Nilghai), Ernest Cossart (Beeton), Ferike Boros (Madame Binat), Pedro de Cordoba (Monsieur Binat), Colin Tapley (Gardner), Fay Helm (Red Haired Girl), Ronald Sinclair (Dick as a child), Sarita Wooten (Maisie as a child), Halliwell Hobbes (Doctor), Francis McDonald (George), George Regas (Cassavetti), Charles Irwin (Soldier Model), Wilfred Roberts (Barton), George Chandler (Correspondent), Colin Kenny (Doctor), Clyde Cook, James Aubrey, Charles Bennett, David Thursby (Soldiers), Hanley Stafford (Officer), Joe Collings (Thackeray), Armbra Dandridge (Bull-Voiced Native), Ted Deputy (Johnnie, officer), Major Sam Harris (Wells), Larry Lawson (Andy, officer), Clive Morgan (Slim), Bob Perry (Hoke, officer), Carl Voss (Chaps, officer), Benjamin Watson (Manny), John G. Spacey (Policeman), Connie Leon (Flower Woman), Gerald Hamer (First Soldier), Harry Cording (Second Soldier), Harold Entwhistle (Old Man with Dark Glasses), Barry Downing (Little Boy), Leslie Francis (Man with Bandaged Eyes), Gerald Rogers (Sick Man), Bob Stevenson (Man with Thick Rimmed Glasses), Clara M. Blore (Mother), George Chandler (First Voice), George H. Melford (Second Voice), Cyril Ring, Hayden Stevenson (War Correspondents), William S. Hurley (Cab Driver), Pat O'Malley (Bullock), Barbara Denny (Waitress), New Mexico National Guard (British Soldiers).

REACHING FOR THE SUN (1941)

Paramount. Copyright: May 2, 1941. New York Premiere: May 7, 1941, at the Paramount. 90 minutes.

A William A. Wellman Production. Executive Producer: William LeBaron. Produced and Directed by William A. Wellman. Screenplay: W. L. River (and uncredited, Wessel Smitter, Robert Carson, Dwight Taylor). Based on the novel *F.O.B. Detroit* by Wessel Smitter. Photography: William C. Mellor. Editor: Thomas Scott. Art Direction: Hans Dreier, Earl Hedrick. Assistant Director: John Coonan. Second Assistant Director: Clem Jones. Second Unit Director: Joseph Youngerman. Second Unit Cameraman: Dewey Wrigley. Process Photography: Farciot Edouart. Sound (Western Electric): Harry Mills, Walter Oberst. Costumes: Edith Head. Makeup: Wally Westmore. Musical Score: Victor Young. Working Titles: *F. O.B. Detroit, The City That Never Sleeps.*

Cast: Joel McCrea (Russ Eliot), Ellen Drew (Rita), Eddie Bracken (Benny Hogan), Albert Dekker (Herman), Billy Gilbert (Amos), Bodil Ann Rosing (Rita's Mother), James Burke (Norm), Charles B. Brown (Johnson), Michael Duggan (Little Benny), Regis Toomey (Intern), Hobart Cavanaugh (Front Office Man), Charles Williams (Truck Driver), Nella Walker (Nurse), Warren Hymer (Percy Shelley), Billy Bletcher (Butch Svoboda), George Chandler (Jerry), Eily Malyon (Landlady), Anna Demetrio (Mrs. Amos), June Aileen Hedin, Jane Isbell (Amos's Children), Gordon Jones (Sailor), James Fiavin (First Guard), Larry Lawson (Second Guard), C. L. Sherwood (Assistant at Lunch Cart), Syd Saylor (First Man at Lunch Cart), Bobby Barber (Second Man at Lunch Cart), Bob Perry (Man in Line), Foy Van Dolsen (Tall Thin Man), John Kelly (Husky Man), Marshall Ruth (Man Type), Auguste Tollaire (Man on Street, Old Fluff), Douglas Gordon (Man in Assembly Line), Michael Morris (Rita's Partner, Dance Hall), Gerald Pierce (Special Delivery Boy).

ROXIE HART (1942)

20th Century-Fox. Copyright: February 20, 1942. New York Premiere: February 19, 1942, at the Roxy. 75 minutes.

Produced by Nunnally Johnson. Directed by William A. Wellman. Screenplay: Nunnally Johnson (and uncredited, Ben Hecht). Based on the play *Chicago* by Maurine Watkins, as produced on stage by Sam H. Harris and directed by George Abbott. Photography: Leon Shamroy. Editor: James B. Clark. Art Direction: Richard Day, Wiard B. Ihnen. Set Decorations: Thomas Little. Assistant Director: Ad Schaumer. Sound (Western Electric): Alfred Bruzlin, Roger Heman. Costumes: Gwen Wakeling. Makeup: Guy Pearce. Musical Score: Alfred Newman. Dance Director: Hermes Pan. Theme: "Chicago, Chicago."

Cast: Ginger Rogers (Roxie Hart), George Montgomery (Homer Howard), Adolphe Menjou (Billy Flynn), Lynne Overman (Jake Callahan), Nigel Bruce (E. Clay Benham), Phil Silvers (Babe), George Chandler (Amos Hart), Sara Allgood (Mrs. Morton), William Frawley (O'Malley), Spring Byington (Mary Sunshine), Ted North (Stuart Chapman), Helen Reynolds (Velma Wall), Charles D. Brown (Charles E. Murdock), Morris Ankrum (Martin S. Harrison), George Lessey (Judge), Iris Adrian (Two-Gun Gertie), Milton Parsons (Announcer), Billy Wayne (Court Clerk), Charles Williams (Photographer), Frank Darien (Finnegan), Jeff Corey (Orderly), Arthur Aylesworth (Mr. Wadsworth), Margaret Seddon (Mrs. Wadsworth), Leon Belasco (Walter), Lee Shumway, Jim Pierce, Philip Morris, Pat O'Malley, Stanley Blystone (Policemen), Frank Orth, Alec Craig, Edward Clark (Idlers), Larry Lawson, Harry Carter (Reporters), Jack Norton (Producer), Bob Perry (Prisoner's Bailiff), Leonard Kilbrick (Newsboy), Mary Treen (Secretary).

THE GREAT MAN'S LADY (1942)

Paramount. Copyright: March 26, 1942. New York Premiere: April 29, 1942, at the Paramount. 90 minutes.

A William A. Wellman Production. Produced and Directed by William A. Wellman. Screenplay: W. L. River. Original Story: Adela Rogers St. John and Seena Owen, from a short story, "The Human Side," by Vina Delmar. Photography: William C. Mellor. Editor: Thomas Scott. Art Direction: Hans Dreier, Earl Hedrick. Assistant Director: Joseph Youngerman. Special Photographic Effects: Gordon Jennings. Sound (Western Electric): Walter Oberst. Costumes: Edith Head. Makeup: Wally Westmore. Special Makeup: Charles Gemora, Robert Ewing. Musical Score: Victor Young. Working Title: *Pioneer Woman*. French Title: *L'Inspiratrice*.

Cast: Barbara Stanwyck (Hannah Semplar), Joel McCrea (Ethan Hoyt), Brian Donlevy (Steely Edwards), Katherine Stevens (Biographer), Thurston Hall (Mr. Semplar), Lloyd Corrigan (Mr. Cadwallader), Lillian Yarbo (Mandy), Damian O'Flynn

(Burns), Charles Lane (Pierce), George Chandler (Forbes), Anna Q. Nilsson (Paula Wales), George P. Huntley (Quentin), Milton Parsons (Froman), Etta McDaniels (Delilah), Mary Treen (Persis), Helen Lynd (Bettina), Lucien Littlefield (City Editor), Frank M. Thomas (Frisbee), William B. Davidson (Senator Knobs), Fred "Snowflake" Toones (Pogey), John Hamilton (Senator Grant), George Irving (Dr. Adams), Fern Emmett (Secretary of City Editor), David Clyde (Bartender), Eleanor Stewart (Daughter), Ottola Nesmith (Mrs. Frisbee), Pat O'Malley (Murphy, policeman), Irving Bacon (Parson), Hank Bell (First Man, Hoyt City), Monte Blue (Second Man, Hoyt City), Larry Lawson (Third Man, Hoyt City), Lee Phelps (Chairman), Theodore Von Eltz (Hank Allen), Lee Moore (Gambler), Buck Mack (Bartender), Charles Williams (Assayer), Bob Perry (Miner).

THUNDER BIRDS (1942)

20th Century-Fox. Copyright: November 20, 1942. New York Premiere: October 28, 1942, at the Roxy. 78 minutes.

Executive Producer: Darryl F. Zanuck. Produced by Lamar Trotti. Directed by William A. Wellman (and uncredited, Alfred Werker, Arthur Jacobson). Screenplay: Lamar Trotti (and uncredited, Laurence Stallings). Original Story by Melville Crossman (Darryl F. Zanuck). Color by Technicolor. Photography: Ernest Palmer; associate: Harry Jackson. Editor: Allen McNeil. Art Direction: Richard Day, James Basevi. Set Decorations: Thomas Little. Assistant Director: Ad Schaumer. Stunt Pilot: Paul Mantz. Sound (Western Electric): Alfred Bruzlin, Roger Heman. Costumes: Dolly Tree. Makeup: Guy Pearce. Color Consultant: Natalie Kalmus; associate: Henri Jaffa. Special Commentary: John Gunther. Musical Score: David Buttolph. Themes: "Wild Blue Yonder," "Deep in the Heart of Texas," "There'll Always Be an England." Working Title: *A Tommy in the U.S.A.* British Title: *Soldiers of the Air.*

Cast: Preston Foster (Steve Britt), Gene Tierney (Kay Saunders), John Sutton (Peter Stackhouse), Jack Holt (Colonel McDonald), Dame May Whitty (Lady Stackhouse), George Barbier (Grandpa), Richard Haydn (George Lockwood), Reginald Denny (Barrett), Ted North (Cadet Hackzell), Janis Carter (Blonde), Archie Got, Lawrence Ung (Chinese Cadets), Montague Shaw (Doctor), Nana Bryant (Mrs. Black), Viola Moore (Nurse), Connie Leon (Ellen), Walter Tetley (Messenger), Billy McGuire, Richard Woodruff, Robert Herrick, Anthony Marsh, Peter Lawford (British Cadets), Joyce Compton (Saleswoman), Kay Vallon (Large Woman), Bess Flowers (Nurse), Alan Baldwin, Marvin Jones, John Whitney, Herbert Patterson, Allan Nixon, Dick Hogan (American Cadets), George Ford (Johnnie), Selmar Jackson (Bit Man), Karen Palmer (Bit Woman), Charles Tannen (Recording), Harry Strang (Forest Ranger), Dorothy Deering, Vivian Mason, Mary Scott, Claire James, Elaine Fenwick (Nurses).

THE OX-BOW INCIDENT (1943)

20th Century-Fox. Copyright: November 19, 1942. New York Premiere: May 8, 1943, at the Rivoli. 75 minutes.

Executive Producer: Darryl F. Zanuck. Produced by Lamar Trotti. Directed by William A. Wellman. Screenplay: Lamar Trotti. Based on the novel by Walter Van Tilburg Clark (1940, New York: Random House). Photography: Arthur Miller. Camera Operator: Joseph LaShelle. Editor: Allen McNeil. Art Direction: Richard Day, James Basevi. Set Decoration: Thomas Little, Frank Hughes. Assistant Director: Ad Schaumer. Sound (Western Electric): Alfred Bruzlin, Roger Heman. Costumes: Earl Luick. Makeup: Guy Pearce. Musical Direction: Cyril J. Mockridge. Theme: "Red River Valley." British Title: *Strange Incident*. French Title: *L'Etrange Incident*.

Cast: Henry Fonda (Gil Carter), Dana Andrews (Donald Martin), Mary Beth Hughes (Rose Mapen), Anthony Quinn (Juan Martinez), William Eythe (Gerald Tetley), Henry Morgan (Art Croft), Jane Darwell (Ma Grier), Matt Briggs (Judge Tyler), Harry Davenport (Arthur Davies), Frank Conroy (Major Tetley), Marc Lawrence (Farnley), Paul Hurst (Monty Smith), Victor Kilian (Darby), Chris Pin-Martin (Poncho), Dick Rich (Mapes), Ted North (Joyce), George Meeker (Mr. Swanson), Almira Sessions (Mrs. Swanson), Margaret Hamilton (Mrs. Larch), Francis Ford (Old Man), Stanley Andrews (Bartlett), Billy Benedict (Greene), Rondo Hatton (Hart), Paul Burns (Winder), Leigh Whipper (Sparks), George Lloyd (Moore), George Chandler (Jimmy Cairnes), Hank Bell (Red), Forrest Dillon (Mark), George Flues (Alec Small), Willard Robertson (Sheriff), Tom London (Deputy), Donald House, Dan Dix, Ben Watson, Walter Robbins, Frank McGrath, Ed Richard, Cap Anderson, Tex Cooper, Clint Sharp, Larry Dads, Tex Driscoll (Posse).

LADY OF BURLESQUE (1943)

Hunt Stromberg Productions/United Artists. Copyright: March 30, 1943. New York Premiere: May 13, 1943, at the Capitol. Rereleased 1949. 91 minutes.

Presented and Produced by Hunt Stromberg. Directed by William A. Wellman. Screenplay: James Gunn (and uncredited, Ben Hecht, Craig Rice). Based on the novel *The G-String Murders* (1941, New York: Simon & Schuster) by Gypsy Rose Lee. Photography: Robert DeGrasse. Editor: James E. Newcom. Production Design: Joseph Platt. Art Direction: Bernard Herzbrun. Assistant Director: Sam Nelson. Production Manager: Joseph C. Gilpin. Sound (Western Electric): Charles Althouse. Casting: Robert Sterling. Art Titles: Elois Jenssen. Barbara Stanwyck's Costumes: Edith Head. Other Costumes: Natalie Visart. Stanwyck's Hairstylist: Hollis Barnes. Makeup: Robert Stephanoff. Hairstylist: Nina Roberts. Musical Score: Arthur Lange. Songs: "Take It Off the E-String, Play It on the G-String" (sung by Barbara Stanwyck), "So This Is You" by Sammy Cahn and Harry Akst (sung by Frank Fenton). Theme, "Temptation." Dance Direction: Danny Dare. Working Title: *The G-String Murders*. British Title: *Striptease Lady*. French Title: *L'Etrangleur*.

Cast: Barbara Stanwyck (Dixie Daisy/Debra Hoople), Michael O'Shea (Biff Brannigan), Iris Adrian (Gee Gee Graham), Charles Dingle (Inspector Harridan), J. Edward Bromberg (S. B. Foss), Frank Conroy (Stacchi Stacchiero), Virginia Faust (Lolita LaVerne), Gloria Dickson (Polly Baxter), Marion Martin (Alice Angel), Frank Fenton (Russell Rogers), Stephanie Bachelor (Princess Nirvena), Pinky Lee (Mandy), Eddie Gordon (Officer Pat Kelly), Janis Carter (Janine), Lou Lubin (Moey), Gerald Mohr (Louis Grindero), Bert Hanlon (Sammy), Claire Carleton (Sandra), George Chandler (Jake, prop man), Lee Trent (Lee, comic), Don Lynn (Don), Lew Kelly (Hermit), Beal Wong (Wong), Sid Marion (Joey), Florence Auer (Policewoman), David Kashner

(Cossack), Freddie Walburn (Messenger Boy), Isabel Withers (Teletype Operator), Virginia Gardner, Dallas Worth, Elinor Troy, Carol Carleton, Mary Gail, Barbara Slater (Show Girls), Jane Allen, Valmere Barman, Patti Brilhanti, Gerry Coonan, Joan Dale, Midgie Dare, June Eberling, Georgine LeMoine, Jean Longworth, Margaret Lee, Patricia Mace, Carmen Moreno, Gwynne Norys, Marjorie Raymond, Joette Robinson, Lynn Sterling, Melba Snowden, Pat Styles, Noel Neill (Dancing Ponies).

BUFFALO BILL (1944)

20th Century-Fox. Copyright: March 11, 1944. New York Premiere: April 19, 1944, at the Roxy. Rereleased 1956. 90 minutes.

Produced by Harry Sherman. Directed by William A. Wellman. Screenplay: Aeneas MacKenzie, Clements Ripley, and Cecile Kramer. Based on a story by Frank Winch. Color by Technicolor. Photography: Leon Shamroy. Editor: James B. Clark. Art Direction: James Basevi, Lewis Creber. Set Decorations: Thomas Little, Fred J. Rode. Second Unit Director: Otto Brower. Archery Adviser: Howard Hill. Special Photographic Effects: Fred Sersen. Sound (Western Electric): Alfred Bruzlin, Roger Hernan. Costumes: Rene Hubert. Makeup: Guy Pearce. Color Consultant: Natalie Kalmus; associate: Richard Mueller. Musical Score: David Buttolph. Musical Director: Emil Newman.

Cast: Joel McCrea (Buffalo Bill Cody), Maureen O'Hara (Louise Cody), Linda Darnell (Dawn Starlight), Thomas Mitchell (Ned Buntline), Edgar Buchanan (Sgt. Chips), Anthony Quinn (Yellow Hand), Moroni Olsen (Senator Frederici), Frank Fenton (Murdo Carvell), Matt Briggs (General Blazier), George Lessey (Mr. Vandervere), Frank Orth (Sherman), George Chandler (Trooper Clancy), Chief Many Treaties (Tall Bull), Nick Thompson (Medicine Man), Chief Thundercloud (Crazy Horse), Sidney Blackmer (Theodore Roosevelt), Evelyn Beresford (Queen Victoria), Cecil Weston (Maid), Larry Lawson (Adjutant), Vincent Graeff (Crippled Boy), Fred Graham (Editor), George Sherwood (Reporter), Harry Tyler, Arthur Loft, Syd Saylor (Barkers), Robert Homans (Muldoon, policeman), Cordell Hickman (Black Boy), Gerald Mackey, Eddie Nichols, Fred Chapman, George Nokes (Boys), John Reese (Tough Guy), John Dilson (President Rutherford B. Hayes), Edwin Stanley (Doctor), Tatzumbia Dupea (Old Indian Woman), Margaret Martin (Indian Servant), George Bronson (Strong Man), Billy Bletcher (Short Man), William Haade (Soldier), Merrill Rodin (Bell Boy), Charlie Teeth, Henry Little Coyote, Jeter Little Bird, Bert Two Moons, American Horse, Another Prairie Bear, Torn Flying Man, Chief Stands in Timber, Chief Plenty Coops, Frank Walks Last, White Man Runs Him, Henry Plain Feather (Crow Indians).

THIS MAN'S NAVY (1945)

Metro-Goldwyn-Mayer. Copyright: January 1, 1945. New York Premiere: April 15, 1945, at the Globe. 106 minutes.

Produced by Samuel Marx. Directed by William A. Wellman. Screenplay: Borden Chase (and uncredited, John Twist, Allen Rivkin, and Hugh Allen). Story: Borden Chase. Based on an idea by Commander Herman K. Halland, U.S.N., Ret., and a story, "They Also Wear Wings," by Samuel Marx. Photography: Sidney Wagner. Edited by Irvine Warburton. Art Direction: Cedric Gibbons, Howard Campbell. Set Decorations: Edwin B. Willis; associate: Glen Barner. Assistant Directors: Horace Hough, Leo Popin. Special Effects: A. Arnold Gillespie, Donald Jahraus. Montage Effects: Peter Ballbusch. Script Supervisor: John Banse. Recording Director (Western Electric): Douglas Shearer. Technical Advisers: Hugh Allen of Goodyear Aircraft; Lt. Cdr. Clyde E. Schetter, U.S.N.R.; Lt. Fred M. Lloyd, U.S.N.R.; Lt. Cdr. Richard Knopff; Lt. Cdr. F. A. Petrie; Admiral C. E. Rosendahl. Costumes: Irene; associate: Kay Dean. Makeup: Jack Dawn. Musical Score: Nathaniel Shilkret. Working Titles: *They Also Wear Wings*; *Air-Ship Squadron #4*.

Cast: Wallace Beery (Ned Trumpet), Tom Drake (Jess Weaver), James Gleason (Jimmy Shannon), Jan Clayton (Cathy Cortland), Selena Royle (Maude Weaver), Noah Beery, Sr. (Joe Hodum), Henry O'Neill (Lt. Cdr. Roger Graystone), Steve Brodie (Tim Shannon), George Chandler (Bert Bland), Donald Curtis (Operations Officer), Arthur Walsh (Cadet Rayshek), Will Fowler (David), Richard Crockett (Sparks), Frank Fenton (Captain Grant), Paul Cavanaugh (Sir Anthony Tivall), Carol Ann Beery (Nurse), Connie Weiler, Kathleen Williams (Waves), William Tannen (Red), Tom O'Grady (Co-Pilot), Jay Norris (Driver), Bob McCutchin (Helper), Dick Rich (Shore Patrolman), John Kellogg (Junior Pilot), Robert Sully (Lieutenant), Johnnie James (Station Radio Operator), Larry Thompson, Mel Schubert (Officers), Joe Sullivan (Fighter Pilot), Bruce Kellogg, George Ramsey, Eddie Hall, Douglas Cowan (NATS Pilots), James Warren (Bomber Pilot), Blake Edwards (Flier), Allen Ray (Radio Operator), Arthur Space (Station Commander), Key Chang (Chinese Officer), Ralph Brooke (Ensign), Stewart Garner (Ensign), Vernon Downing (English Officer), Crane Whitley (Commander Blain), Henry Daniels, Jr. (Crew Member), Jean Wong (Dark Skinned Nurse), Paul Singh (Maharajah), Kenneth Stewart, Don Shannon (Ground Crew Members), Carlyle Blackwell, Jr., Bob Lowell (Bit Mechanics), Richard Collin (Shore Patrolman), Will Walls (First Class Mechanic), Richard Crockett (Third Class Mechanic), Tom Trout (First Class Radio Man), Phil Hanna (Second Class Radio Man), Bob MacLean, Bill Dyer, Jack Mattis, Rad Towne (Naval Cadet), Bob Thorn, George Ryland, George Peters, Bob Miller (Officer Instructors).

ERNIE PYLE'S THE STORY OF G.I. JOE (1945)

Lester Cowan Productions/United Artists. Copyright: July 13, 1945. New York Premiere: October 5, 1945, at the Globe and Gotham Theatres. Rereleased 1949, retitled *War Correspondent* in some markets. 109 minutes.

A William A. Wellman Production. Presented and Produced by Lester Cowan. Associate Producer: David Hall. Directed by William A. Wellman. Screenplay: Leopold Atlas, Guy Endore, Phillip Stevenson (and uncredited, John Huston, Ernie Pyle, William A. Wellman). Based on the books *Here Is Your War* (1943, New York: Henry Holt & Co.) and *Brave Men* (1944, New York: Henry Holt & Co.) by Ernie Pyle. Photography: Russell Metty. Supervising Film Editor: Otho Lovering. Editor: Albrecht Joseph. Art Direction: James Sullivan. Set Decorations: Edward G. Boyle. Assistant Director: Robert Aldrich. Production Manager: Ray Heinz. Sound (Western Electric): Frank McWhorter. Makeup: Bud Westmore. Research: Paige Cavanaugh.

Technical Adviser for Documentary Footage: Jori Ivens. Technical Advisers for U.S. Army Ground Forces: Lt. Col. Roy A. Murray, Jr., Lt. Col. Edward H. Coffey, Lt. Col. Robert Miller, Major Walter Nye, Capt. Milton M. Thornton, Capt. Charles Shunstrom. Technical Advisers for the Combat Correspondents: Lucien Hubbard [*Reader's Digest*], Don Whitehead [Associated Press], George Lait [International News Service], Chris Cunningham [United Press], Hal Boyle [Associated Press], Sgt. Jack Foisie [*Stars and Stripes*], Bob Landry [*Life*], Clete Roberts [Blue Network], Robert Reuben [Reuters]. Musical Score: Ann Ronell and Louis Applebaum. Musical Director: Louis Forbes. Songs: "Linda" by Jack Lawrence and Ann Ronell; "I'm Coming Back" and "Infantry March" by Ann Ronell. Working Titles: *Here Is Your War*, *G.I. Joe.* French Title: *Les Forcats de la Goire.*

Cast: Burgess Meredith (Ernie Pyle), Robert Mitchum (Lieutenant/Captain Bill Walker), Freddie Steele (Sergeant Steve Warnicki), Wally Cassell (Private Dondaro), Bill Murphy (Private Mew), William Self (Gawky Henderson), Dick Rich (Sergeant at Showers), Billy Benedict (Whitey), Jimmy Lloyd (Private Spencer), Jack Reilly (Private Murphy), Tito Renaldo (Lopez), Yolanda Lacca (Amelia), Michael Browne (Sergeant), Dorothy Coonan Wellman (Nurse), and Combat Veterans of the African, Sicilian, and Italian Campaigns.

GALLANT JOURNEY (1946)

Columbia. Copyright: September 24, 1946. New York Premiere: October 9, 1946, at Loew's Criterion. 86 minutes.

A William A. Wellman Production. Produced and Directed by William A. Wellman. Original Screenplay: Byron Morgan and William A. Wellman. Photography: Burnett Guffey. Editor: Al Clark. Art Direction: Stephen Goossen, Carl Anderson. Set Decorations: Louis Diage. Assistant Director: Sam Nelson. Second Unit Director: Otho Lovering. Second Unit Photography: George B. Meehan, Jr. Aerial Photography: Elmer Dyer. Technical Adviser: Colonel C. A. Shoop. Sound (Western Electric): Frank Goodwin. Chief Pilot: Paul Mantz. Stunt Pilots: Don C. Stevens, Paul Tuntland. Glider Design: Lloyd Ruocco, Don Driese, Gordon Wiggins. Costumes: Jean Louis. Musical Score: Marlin Skiles. Musical Director: Morris W. Stoloff. Songs: "Man on the Flying Trapeze," sung by Jimmy Lloyd; "Bicycle Built for Two," sung by Glenn Ford and Janet Blair. Working Title: *The Great Highway.*

Cast: Glenn Ford (John Montgomery), Janet Blair (Regina "Ginny" Cleary), Charles Ruggles (Jim Montgomery), Henry Travers (Thomas Logan), Arthur Shields (Father Kenton), Willard Robertson (Zachary Montgomery), Selena Royle (Mrs. Montgomery), Robert DeHaven (Jim Montgomery as a young man), George Tyne (Pendleton), Jimmy Lloyd (Dan Mahoney, "The Great LaSalle"), Charles Kemper (Father Dickie Ball), Loren Tindall (Jim Logan), Byron Morgan (John Logan), Eula Guy Morgan (Mrs. Logan), Michael Towne (Raymond Walker), Paul Marion (Tony Dondaro), Henry Rowland (Cornelius Rheinlander), Paul E. Burns (Peacock Fox), Robert Hoover (Dickie Ball as a boy), Chris Pin-Martin (Pedro Lopez), Fernando Alvarado (Juan Morales), Bobby Cooper (Tom), Rudy Wissler (Hep), Tommy Cook (Cutty), Buddy Swan (Sharkey), Conrad Binyon (Snort), Crystal Reeves (Margarette), Kathleen O'Malley (Mary), Helene Nielsen (Jane), Frank Darien (Doctor), Gil

LaCava (Bit Student), Emory Parnell (Car Driver), Billy Bletcher (Mahoney's Valet), Robert Dudley (Process Server), Joseph Palma (Waiter), Hugh Hooker (Mahoney's Coachman), Frank Dae (Judge), June Bryde (Fat Woman), Ernie Adams (Husband), Lou Davis, John Kascier, Cy Shindell, Earl Hodgins, Fred Amsel, Bob Perry, Jack Frack (Barkers), Gerry Coonan, Dessie Arnohf, Wanda Perry (Bit Women), Hurley Breen, Dan Dix, Charles Perry, Cy Malis, E. L. Dale, William Kahn, Victor Travers, Bob Ryan, Bill Wallace, Tim Wallace, Don House, Pat Moran, Mike Lally (Bit Men), Harvey Parry (Stunts), William A. Wellman (Glider Pilot).

MAGIC TOWN (1947)

RKO-Radio. Copyright: September 26, 1947. New York Premiere: October 7, 1947, at the RKO Palace. 103 minutes.

A William A. Wellman Production. Presented by Robert Riskin. Written and Produced by Robert Riskin. Directed by William A. Wellman. Story: Robert Riskin and Joseph Krumgold. Photography: Joseph F. Biroc. Edited by Sherman Todd, Richard G. Wray. Montage: William K. Hornbeck. Production Design: Lionel Banks. Set Decorations: George Sawley. Assistant Director: Arthur Black. Production Manager: William S. Holmes. Sound (RCA): John Tribby, Terry Kellum. Jane Wyman's costumes: Milo Anderson. Musical Score: Roy Webb. Musical Director: Constantin Bakaleinikoff. Songs: "Magic Town" by Mel Tormé and Bob Wells; "My Book of Memory," lyrics by Edward Heyman. Working Title: *The Magic City*.

Cast: James Stewart (Rip Smith), Jane Wyman (Mary Peterman), Kent Smith (Hoopendecker), Ned Sparks (Ike Sloan), Wallace Ford (Lou Dicketts), Regis Toomey (Ed Weaver), Ann Doran (Mrs. Weaver), Donald Meek (Mr. Twiddle), E. J. Ballantine (Moody), Ann Shoemaker (Ma Peterman), Mickey Kuhn (Hank Nickleby), Howard Freeman (Nickleby), Harry Holman (Mayor), Mary Currier (Mrs. Frisby), Mickey Roth (Bob Peterman), Frank Fenton (Birch), George Irving (Senator Wilson), Selmar Jackson (Stringer), Robert Dudley (Dickey), Julia Dean (Mrs. Wilson), George Chandler (Bus Driver from Moody's Mansion House), Frank Darien (Quincy), Larry Wheat (Sam Fuller), Jimmy Crane (Shorty), Dick Elliott (Man Being Interviewed), Joel Friedkin (Dingle), Paul Scardon (Hodges), Richard Belding (Junior Dicketts), Danny Mummert (Benny), Griff Barnett (Henry), John Ince (Postman), Edgar Dearing (Gray-Haired Man), Snub Pollard (Townsman), Edna Holland (Secretary), Eddie Parks (Bookkeeper), Paul Maxey (Fat Man), Lee "Lasses" White (Old Timer), Wheaton Chambers (Electrician), Emmett Vogan (Reverend), Eddy Waller (Newcomer), Tom Kennedy, William Haade, Frank Marlowe, Dick Wessel (Moving Men).

THE IRON CURTAIN (1948)

20th Century-Fox. Copyright: March 11, 1948. New York Premiere: May 12, 1948, at the Roxy. 87 minutes.

Produced by Sol C. Siegel. Directed by William A. Wellman. Screenplay: Milton Krims (and uncredited, Martin Berkeley). Based on the memoirs of Igor Gouzenko. Photography: Charles C. Clarke. Edited by Louis Loeffler. Art Direction: Lyle Wheeler, Mark Lee Kirk. Set Decorations: Thomas B. Little. Assistant Director: William Eckhardt. Special Photographic Effects: Fred Sersen. Sound (Western Electric): Bernard Freericks, Harry M. Leonard. Costumes: Bonnie Cashin. Makeup: Ben Nye. Music: Dimitri Shostakovich, Serge Prokofieff, Aram Khachaturian, Nicholas Miakovsky. Musical Director: Alfred Newman. French Title: *Le Rideau de Fer*. Television Title: *Behind the Iron Curtain*.

Cast: Dana Andrews (Igor Gouzenko), Gene Tierney (Anna Gouzenko), June Havoc (Karanova), Berry Kroeger (Grubb), Edna Best (Mrs. Foster), Stefan Schnabel (Ranev), Nicholas Joy (Dr. Norman), Eduard Franz (Major Kulin), Frederick Tozere (Colonel Trigorin), Noel Cravat (Bushkin), Christopher Robin Olsen (Andrei), Peter Whitney (Winikov), Leslie Barrie (Editor), Mauritz Hugo (Leonard Loetz), John Shay (Sergeyev), Victor Wood (Captain Class), Anne Curson (Helen Tweedy), Helena Dare (Mrs. Kulin), Eula Morgan (Mrs. Tregorun), John Ridgeley (Policeman Murphy), John Davidson (Secretary), Joe Whitehead (William Hollis), Michael J. Dugan (Policeman), Harry Carter (Fairfield), Robert Adler (Wilson), Arthur E. Gould-Porter (Mrs. Foster), Matthew Boulton (Inspector Burns), Reed Hadley (Commentator).

YELLOW SKY (1948)

20th Century-Fox. Copyright: December 21, 1948. New York Premiere: February 1, 1949, at the Roxy. 98 minutes.

Produced by Lamar Trotti. Directed by William A. Wellman. Screenplay: Lamar Trotti. Based on the novel *Stretch Dawson* by W. R. Burnett. Photography: Joe MacDonald. Editor: Harman Jones. Art Direction: Lyle Wheeler, Albert Hogsett. Set Decorations: Thomas Little, Ernest Lansing. Special Photographic Effects: Fred Sersen. Sound (Western Electric): Bernard Freericks, Harry M. Leonard. Costumes: Charles LeMaire. Makeup: Ben Nye. Musical Direction: Alfred Newman. Orchestral Arrangements: Edward B. Powell. Music originally used in main title of Henry Hathaway's *Brigham Young: Frontiersman* (1940, 20th Century-Fox), scored by Alfred Newman. Theme: "Oh Susanna" (Stephen Foster). French Title: *La Ville Aba*.

Cast: Gregory Peck (Stretch Dawson), Anne Baxter (Mike), Richard Widmark (Dude), Robert Arthur (Bull Run), John Russell (Lengthy), Henry Morgan (Half Pint), James Barton (Grandpa), Charles Kemper (Walrus), Robert Adler (Jed), Victor Kilian (Bartender), Paul Hurst (Drunk), William Gould (Banker), Norman Leavitt (Bank Teller), Chief Yowlachie (Colorado), Eula Guy Morgan (Woman), Harry Carter (Lieutenant), Hank Worden (Rancher in Bank), Jay Silverheels (Indian).

BATTLEGROUND (1949)

Metro-Goldwyn-Mayer. Copyright: October 19, 1949. New York Premiere: November 11, 1949, at the Astor. 118 minutes.

Produced by Dore Schary. Associate Producer: Robert Pirosh. Directed by William A. Wellman. Story and Screenplay: Robert Pirosh. Photography: Paul C. Vogel. Editor: John Dunning. Supervising Editor: Margaret Booth. Art Direction: Cedric Gibbons, Hans Peters. Set Decorations: Edwin B. Willis; associate: Alfred E. Spencer. Assistant Director: Sid Sidman. Production Manager: William Kaplan. Unit Manager: Walter Strohm. Location Manager: Howard "Dutch" Horton. Script Supervisor: John Banse. Special Photographic Effects: Peter Ballbusch. Camera Crew: Dale Deverman,

Harold Baldwin, Matt Cluznik, Emilio J. Galori. Electricians: Fred Peterson, Hal Wynn, G. Leider, Harold Bowers, Pat Fennell. Grips: Art Spang, Mel Anderson, C. H. "Hank" Forrester, Lloyd Taylor. Recording Supervisor (Western Electric): Douglas Shearer. Sound: Spurgeon Marsh, Carroll Pratt, Fred Faust. Stills: Eddie Hubbell. Technical Adviser: Lt. Col. H. W. O. Kinnard. Unit Publicist: James W. Merrick. Makeup: Jack Dawn. Musical Score: Lennie Hayton. Songs: "Jodie's Chant (Sound Off)" by Willie Lee Duckworth; "Milkman Keep Those Bottles Quiet" by Don Raye and Gene DePaul; "Sweet and Lovely" by Gus Arnheim; "I Surrender Dear" by Harry Barris and Gordon Clifford; "White Christmas" by Irving Berlin; "Santa Claus Is Coming to Town" by Coots and Gillespie; "There Is a Boarding House" (unknown); "Abner's Song" (unknown). Working Title: *Prelude to Love*. French Title: *Bastogne*.

Cast: Van Johnson (Holley), John Hodiak (Jarvess), Ricardo Montalban (Rodriguez), George Murphy (Ernest "Pop" Stazak), Marshall Thompson (Jim Layton), Jerome Courtland (Abner Spudler), Don Taylor (Standiferd), Bruce Cowling (Wolowicz), James Whitmore (Kinnie), Douglas Fowley ("Kipp" Kippton), Leon Ames (Chaplain), Guy Anderson (Hansan), Thomas E. Breen ("Doc," Medic), Denise Darcel (Denise), Richard Jaeckel (Bettis), James Arness (Garby), Scotty Beckett (William J. Hooper), Brett King (Lt. Tiess), Roland Varno (German Lieutenant), Edmon Ryan (Major), Michael Browne (Levinstein), William Erwin (Warrant Officer), Jim Drum (Supply Sergeant), Nadine Ashdown, Janine Perreau (Little Girls), Dewey Martin, Tom Noonan, David Holt (G.I. Stragglers), Arthur Walsh, George Offerman, Jr., William Self (G.I.'s), Steve Pendleton (Sergeant), William R. Murphy, Philip Pine, Sam Resnick (Non Coms), Jerry Paris (German Sergeant), Tommy Bond (Runner), Nan Boardman (Belgian Woman Volunteer), Ivan Triesault (German Captain), Henry Rowland (German), John Mylong (German Major), Ian MacDonald (American Colonel), William Leicester (Tank Destroyer Man), George Chandler (Mess Sergeant), Charles B. Smith (Clerk), Tommy Walker (Mechanic), Dan Foster (Gunner), Roger McGee, Dick Jones (Tankers), Joel Allen, James Horne (Transportation Captains), George Dee (Frenchman), Bert Davidson, Carl Saxe (Lost Battalion Officers), Irene Seidner, Martha Bamattre, Gertl Dupont, Louise Columbet (French Peasant Women), Jean Del Val, Albert Pollet (French Peasant Men), Lilian Clayes (Old Woman), Chris Drake (Medic Private), Tommy Kelly, Raymond C. Browsher, Harry Mackin, John Mansfield, Richard Bartlett, Peter Rankin (Casualties), Norman Budd (Crying Casualty), John Gardner (Bit Soldier), Gene Coogan (G.I. Scout), Otto Reichow (German Platoon Leader), John Royce, Peter Michael, Robert Boon, Fred Zender, Tommy Christian, Eugene Gericke (German Soldiers), John Piffel, Robert N. Porter, Ted Eckelberry, Martin Lowell, Victor Paul, Nelson Scott, John Dutra (G.I.'s), Billy Lechner (Runner), Robert Ward Wood (Replacement), Jim Martin (G.I. from the South), Edmond Glover (G.I. from Maine), Richard Irving (G.I. from New York), and 20 original "Screaming Eagles" of the 101st Airborne Division, including Sgt. Paul Burnett, Corpl. Edward Hunt, and Sgt. Max Trujillo.

THE HAPPY YEARS (1950)

Metro-Goldwyn-Mayer. Copyright: April 24, 1950. New York Premiere: May 24, 1950, at the Loew's State Theatre. 110 minutes.

Executive Producer: Dore Schary. Produced by Carey Wilson. Directed by William A. Wellman. Screenplay: Harry Ruskin (and uncredited, John Meehan). Based on *The Lawrenceville School Stories* by Owen Johnson. Color by Technicolor. Photography: Paul C. Vogel. Edited by John Dunning. Supervising Editor: Margaret Booth. Art Direction: Cedric Gibbons, Daniel B. Cathcart. Set Decorations: Edwin B. Willis; associate: Henry W. Grace. Assistant Director: Bert Glazer. Production Manager: Walter Strohm. Unit Manager: William Kaplan. Assistant Unit Manager: Charles Hunt. Special Effects: Warren Newcombe. Color Consultants: Henri Jaffa, James Gooch. Recording Director (Western Electric): Douglas Shearer. Location Sound: Francis Scheid. Costumes: Walter Plunkett. Makeup: Jack Dawri. Hairstylist: Sidney Guilaroff. Musical Score: Leigh Harline. Themes: "Out on the Esplanade" (traditional), "Ewing" (traditional), "All Saint's New" (Cutler), "On Memorial Steps" (Gow and Eno), "In Olden Days" (Trench and Raymond). Fight Technical Adviser: Johnny Indrisano. Working Titles: *Dirk Stover: The Lawrencevile Stories, You're Only Young Once*. Re-released as *The Adventure of Young Dirk Stover*.

Cast: Dean Stockwell (John Humperdink "Dink" Stover), Darryl Hickman (George "Tough" McCarty), Scotty Beckett (Tennessee Shad), Leon Ames (Samuel H. Stover, Jr.), Margalo Gilmore (Mrs. Stover), Leo G. Carroll (Mr. Hopkins, "The Old Roman"), Donn Gift (Joshua Montgomery Smead, "The Great Big Man"), Peter Thompson (Sambo Stover), Jerry Mickelsen (Cheyenne Baxter), Alan Dinehart III (Coffee Colored Angel), David Blair (White Mountain Canary), Danny Mummert (Butsey White), Eddie LeRoy (Poler Beekstein), George Chandler (Johnny), Claudia Barrett (Miss Dolly Travers), Mary Eleanor Donahue [later Elinor Donahue] (Miss Connie Brown), Jeralyn Altyn (Tootsie Stover), Robert Board (Burt, Reporter), Jacqueline deWit (Mrs. Cameron), Wheaton Chambers (Baggage Man), Arthur Space (Al), Dwayne Hickman (Happy Mather), Ralph Votrian (Tacks Brooker), Henry Blair (Joe Crocker), Freddie Chapman (Skippy Burns), Leon Tyler (Puffy Ellis), Robin Camp (Butch Sidney), Lisa Golm (Maid), Georgianna Wolff (Jane Tupper), Matt Moore (Butler), Frank Reicher (Headmaster), Irving Bacon (Mr. Conover), Phyllis Morris (Mrs. Conover), Bob Valentine (Fatty Harris), Sandy Oster (Pitcher), Roger McGee (Referee), Robert J. Wagner, Jr. (Catcher, Bit in Classroom), Timothy Wellman (Bell Ringer), Clifton Powers (Double for Dean Stockwell). Charles B. Smith as Sock Mazula was filmed but cut from the release print.

THE NEXT VOICE YOU HEAR (1950)

Metro-Goldwyn-Mayer. Copyright: April 7, 1950. New York Premiere: June 29, 1950, at Radio City Music Hall. 82 minutes.

Produced by Dore Schary. Directed by William A. Wellman. Screenplay: Charles Schnee (and uncredited, Dore Schary). Suggested by a story by George Sumner Albee. Photography: William C. Mellor. Editor: John Dunning. Supervising Editor: Margaret Booth. Art Direction: Cedric Gibbons, Eddie Imazu. Set Decorations: Edwin B. Willis, Ralph S. Hurst; assistant: William Skamnes. Assistant Director: Joel Freeman. Second Assistant Director: Fletcher Clark. Unit Manager: Ruby Rosenberg. Location Managers: Howard "Dutch" Horton, Charles Coleman. Script Supervisor: Bill Hole. Camera Operator: Neal Beckner. Assistant Camera: Matt Kluznick, King Baggot, Jr.

Stills: Eddie Hubbell. Gaffer: Chester Philbrick. Best Boy: Howard Roberts. Electricians: Eugene W. Stout, Frank Huszar, Zeb Bojarsky, William McConnell, J. Toney, Lee Cannon. Key Grip: Leo Monlon. Second Grip: Les Coleman. Grips: Don Larson, Art Spang. Props: James Luttrell. Assistant Props: Dick Hendrickson. Recording Supervisor (Western Electric): Douglas Shearer. Sound Mixer: Conrad Kahn. Sound Crew: Fred Faust, Bill Edmondson. Assistant Editor: Greydon Gilmer. Wardrobe: Bob Streeter, Florance Hackett. Casting Director: Leonard Murphy. Assistant Casting: James Broderick. Second Unit Director: John S. Waters. Second Unit Photography: Harold Lipstine, Max Fabian (Process). Second Unit Camera Crew: John Nickolaus, A. C. Riley, Bert Spurlin. Second Unit Gaffer: Bill Allen. Second Unit Best Boy: George Lasher. Second Unit Script Supervisor: William Orr. Second Unit Grips: Harold Constable, Roy Strickland. Process Photography: Hal Marzorati. Process Assistants: Dan Powers, Carroll Shepphird. Process Grip: Joe Gabourie. Standby Painter: Frank Wesselhoff. Laborer: Al Simpson. Unit Publicist: James W. Merrick. Musical Score: David Raksin. French Title: *La Voix que Vous Allez Entendre*.

Cast: James Whitmore (Joe Smith), Nancy Davis (Mrs. Joe Smith), Gary Gray (Johnny Smith), Lillian Bronson (Aunt Ethel), Art Smith (Mr. Brannan), Tom D'Andrea (Hap Magee), Jeff Corey (Freddie), Douglas Kennedy (Mitch), Tim Hawkins (Red), Eula Guy (Woman), Jim Hayward (Arthur), Thomas Brown Henry (Doctor), Marjorie Hoshelle (Sweetie), Milton Ackorey, Sr. (Bishop), Mary Bear (Nurse), Donald Kerr (Hot Dog Man), George Chandler (Traffic Cop), Frankie Darro, Mickey Little (Newsboys), Grace Lord (Elderly Woman in Church), Tommy Myers (Boy), Douglas Carter (Father), Bob Alden (Soda Jerk), Jack Sterling, Billy Bletcher, Jim Pierce, Frank Gerstle, John McKee, Rush Williams, Dwight Martin (Men), Fred Hoose, William H. Vedder, Helen Eby-Rock, Rhea Mitchell, Howard Mitchell, Michael Barret, Donna Lee Boswell, Sherry Jackson (People in Church), Louis Merrill, Chester Huntley, Cecil Brown, Wilson Wood, Lyle Clark (Radio Announcers), Jack Semple, Harry Wollman (Stunt Doubles), Jack Harris, Phoebe Campbell, Dorothy Whalen, Henry Stone, Billy Cartledge, Venita Murdock, Ike Isaacs, Ben Watson, Bill Scully, Dick Ames (Stand-ins).

ACROSS THE WIDE MISSOURI (1951)

Metro-Goldwyn-Mayer. Copyright: September 17, 1951. New York premiere: November 6, 1951, at the Loew's State. 78 minutes.

Executive Producer: Dore Schary. Produced by Robert Sisk. Directed by William A. Wellman. Screenplay: Talbot Jennings (and uncredited, Albert Lewin and Chief Nipo T. Strongheart [Indian translations]). Story: Talbot Jennings and Frank Cavett. Suggested by the book by Bernard DeVoto. Color by Technicolor. Photography: William C. Mellor. Editor: John Dunning. Supervising Editor: Margaret Booth. Art Direction: Cedric Gibbons, James Basevi. Set Decorations: Edwin B. Willis, Ralph S. Hurst. Assistant Director: Howard Koch. Production Manager: Walter Strohm. Unit Manager: Ruby Rosenberg. Location Scout: Orville O. "Bunny" Dull. Second Unit Director: John Waters. Second Unit Photography: Harold Lipstine. Special Effects: Warren Newcombe. Color Consultants: Henri Jaffa, James Gooch. Technical Adviser: Chief Nipo T. Strongheart. Archery Adviser: Howard Hill. Recording

Director (Western Electric): Douglas Shearer. Location Sound: J. N. Woltz. Location Auditor: Bill Smith. Costumes: Walter Plunkett. Makeup: William Tuttle. Hairstylist: Sidney Guilaroff. Musical Score: David Raksin. Main Title Music: David Raksin and Al Sondroy. Themes: "Highland Fling" (traditional), "Skip to My Lou" (traditional), "Square Dance" (arranged by Al Columbo), "Indian Lament" (Al Columbo), "Indian Lullaby" (Al Columbo), "Flowers of the Forest" (traditional), "Alouette" (traditional), "The Bibroch of Donald Dhu" (traditional).

Cast: Clark Gable (Flint Mitchell), Maria Elena Marques (Kamiah), Ricardo Montalban (Ironshirt), John Hodiak (Brecan), Adolphe Menjou (Pierre), J. Carroll Naish (Looking Glass), Jack Holt (Bear Ghost), Alan Napier (Captain Humberstone Lyon), George Chandler (Gowie), Richard Anderson (Dick Richardson), Henry Letondal (Lucien Chennault), Douglas Fowley (Tin Cup Owens), Louis Nicoletti (Roy DuNord), Ben Watson (Markhead), Russell Simpson (Hoback), Frankie Darro (Cadet), James Whitmore (Old Bill), Frank Richards (Tige Shannon), Michael Dugan (Gordon), John McKee (Killbuck), Bert LeBaron (LeBonte), Elmer Napier (Shad Skeggs), Tex Holden (Peg Leg Smith), Elaine Naish (Indian Girl), Edith Mills, Talzumbie Dupea (Indian Women), Bobby Barber (Gardipe), Gene Coogan (Marcelline), Fred Graham (Brown), Fred Gillman (Harris), Chief Nipo T. Strongheart (Indian Crier), Andrew Knife (Yellow Plume), Frank McGrath (St. Leger), Donald House (Luke), Jack Sterling (Davis), Albert Pollet, Albert Pettit, Manuel Paris, Maurice Brierre (French Trappers), Ed Juarequi, Slim Talbot, Rocky Shahan, Fred McDougall, Ray Thomas, Henry Wills, Jimmy Van Horn, Clint Sharpe, Archie Butler, Johnny Indrisano, Fred Kennedy (Stuntmen), Evelyn Finley (Stunt Double for Maria Elena Marques), Howard Keel (Narration).

WESTWARD THE WOMEN (1951)

Metro-Goldwyn-Mayer. Copyright: November 12, 1951. New York Premiere: December 31, 1951, at the Capitol. 116 minutes.

Produced by Dore Schary. Directed by William A. Wellman. Screenplay: Charles Schnee. Based on a story, "Pioneer Women," by Frank Capra. Photography: William C. Mellor. Editor: James E. Newcom. Supervising Editor: Margaret Booth. Art Direction: Cedric Gibbons, Daniel B. Cathcart. Set Decorations: Edwin B. Willis, Ralph S. Hurst. Technical Advisers: Jim Louch, Chief Nipo T. Strongheart. Fight Technical Adviser: Johnny Indrisano. Recording Director (Western Electric): Douglas Shearer. Costumes: Walter Plunkett. Makeup: William Tuttle. Musical Score: Jeff Alexander. Song: "To the West! To the West!," melody by Harry Russell. Working Title: *Pioneer Women*. French Title: *Convoi des Femmes*.

Cast: Robert Taylor (Buck Wyatt), Denise Darcel (Fifi Danon), Hope Emerson (Patience Hawley), John McIntire (Roy E. Whitman), Julie Bishop (Laurie Smith), Beverly Dennis (Rose Meyers), Marilyn Erskine (Jean Johnson), Lenore Lonergan (Maggie O'Malley), Guido Martufi (Antonio Moroni), Henry Nakamura (Ito), Renata Vanni (Mrs. Moroni), Bruce Cowling (Cat), Patrick Conway (Sid Cutler), Chubby Johnson (Jim Stacey), Mary Alan Hokanson (Cora), Raymond Bond (Preacher), Terry Wilson (Lon), Michael Dugan (Outrider), Edith Mills (Sadie), John Cason (Margaret's Man), Mikel Conrad (Rose's Man), Lou Nova (Blacksmith), Frankie Darro

(Jean's Man), Z. Yaconelli (Mrs. Moroni's Man), Ted Adams, Gene Roth (Bartenders), George Chandler (Mackerel Face), Earl Hodgins (Drunk), Stan Jolley (Gambler), John War Eagle (Indian Chief), Bert LeBaron (Ken), Elmer Napier (Walt), Tom Greenway (Bart), Fiona O'Shiel (First Woman), Kathleen O'Malley (Second Woman), Tom Monroe (First Man), Tennessee Jim (Second Man), Claire Carleton, Dorothy Granger, Mil Patrick, Joan Valerie (Flashy Girls), Henry Wills, Ed Juarequi, Archie Butler, Bill Cartledge, Carl Pitti, Pat Ford, Frank McGrath, Don House, Ray Thomas, Clem Fuller, Clint Sharp, Gene Coogan (Outriders), Ann Roberts, Lucille House, Shirley Lucas, Pat Paul, Donna Hall, Opal Erne, Norma Santillo, Norma Young, Jody Smith, Mary Murphy, Sharon Lucas, Mary Casiday, Cornelia Flores, Stevie Myers, Alice Wills, Edith Happy, Karen Hale, Claire Andre, Maxine Garrett, Marilyn Lindsey, Marlyn Gladstone, Alice Markham, Polly Burson, Evelyn Finley, Doris Lee Cole (Pioneer Women).

IT'S A BIG COUNTRY: AN AMERICAN ANTHOLOGY (1951)

Metro-Goldwyn-Mayer. Copyright: November 16, 1951. New York Premiere: January 8, 1952, at the Trans-Lux 52nd Street Theatre. 89 minutes. Wellman episode, 9 minutes.

Executive Producer: Dore Schary. Produced by Robert Sisk. Story for Episode One: "Interruptions, Interruptions." Directed by Richard Thorpe. Screenplay: William Ludwig. Story: Edgar Brooke.

Cast: William Powell (Professor), James Whitmore (Mr. Stacey).

Episode Two: "The Lady and the Census Taker." Directed by John Sturges. Screenplay: Helen Deutsch.

Cast: Ethel Barrymore (Mrs. Brian Patrick Riordan), George Murphy (Callaghan), Keenan Wynn (Michael Fisher).

Episode Three: "American Montage." Written by Ray Chordes. Consists of documentary stock footage.

Episode Four: "Rosika the Rose." Directed by Charles Vidor. Screenplay: Isobel Lennart. Story: Claudia Cranston.

Cast: Gene Kelly (Icarus Xenophon), Janet Leigh (Rosa Szabo), S. Z. Sakall (Stefan Szabo), Sharon McManus (Sam Szabo), Luana Mehlberg (Lenka), Jeralyn Alston (Yolande), Jacqueline Kenley (Margit), Benny Burt (Soda Jerk), George Economides (Theodore), Hal Hatfield, Richard Grindle, Anthony Lappas, Tom Nickols, Costas Orfis, David Alpert (Greek Athletes).

Episode Five: "Letter from Korea." Directed by Don Weis. Screenplay: Allen Rivkin. Story: Lucille Schlossberg. Cast: Marjorie Main (Mrs. Wrenley), Keefe Brasselle (Sgt. Maxie Klein).

Episode Six: "Lone Star." Directed by Clarence Brown. Story and Screenplay: Dorothy Kingsley.

Cast: Gary Cooper (Texas).

Episode Seven: "The Minister in Washington." Directed by William A. Wellman. Story and Screenplay: Dore Schary. Photography: William C. Mellor.

Cast: Van Johnson (Adam Burch), Lewis Stone (The Sexton), Leon Ames (Secret Service Man).

Episode Eight: "Four Eyes." Directed by Don Hartman. Screenplay: George Wells. Story: Joseph Petracca.

Cast: Fredric March (Papa Esposito), Nancy Davis (Miss Coleman), Bobby Hyatt (Joseph Esposito), Angela Clarke (Mama Esposito), Dolly Arriage (Concetta Esposito), Elena Savonarola (Amelia Esposito), Carol Nugent (Girl), George Mac-Donald, Charles Myers, David Wyatt, Mickey Little (Boys), Tiny Francone (Girl in Classroom), Rhea Mitchell (School Teacher).

Photography: John Alton, Ray June, Joseph Ruttenberg. Editors: Ben Lewis, Frederick Y. Smith. Supervising Editor: Margaret Booth. Art Direction: Cedric Gibbons and Malcolm Brown, William Ferrari, Eddie Imazu, Arthur Lonergan, Gabriel Scognamillo. Set Decorations: Edwin B. Willis, Jack Bonar, Ralph S. Hurst, Arthur Krams, Fred MacLean, Alfred E. Spencer. Special Effects: A. Arnold Gillespie, Warren Newcombe. Recording Director (Western Electric): Douglas Shearer. Hairstyles: Sydney Guilaroff. Makeup: William Tuttle. Musical Supervisor: Johnny Green. Musical Adaptation: Alberto Colombo, Adolph Deutsch, Lennie Hayton, Bronislau Kaper, Rudolph G. Kopp, David Raksin, David Rose, Charles Wolcott.

MY MAN AND I (1952)

Metro-Goldwyn-Mayer. Copyright: August 14, 1952. New York Premiere: September 5, 1952, at the Palace. 99 minutes.

Executive Producer: Dore Schary. Produced by Stephen Ames. Directed by William A. Wellman. Screenplay: John Fante and Jack Leonard (and uncredited, Marguerite Roberts, Millard Kaufman). Story, "Letter to the President," by John Fante and Jack Leonard. Photography: William C. Mellor. Editor: John Dunning. Supervising Editor: Margaret Booth. Art Direction: Cedric Gibbons, James Basevi. Set Decorations: Edwin B. Willis, Fred MacLean. Assistant Director: George Rhein. Unit Manager: William Kaplan. Location Managers: Howard "Dutch" Horton, Charles Coleman. Second Unit Director: James C. Havens. Special Effects: Warren Newcombe. Montage Sequences: Peter Ballbusch. Recording Director (Western Electric): Douglas Shearer. Makeup: William Tuttle. Hairstylist: Sidney Guilaroff. Musical Score: David Buttolph. Themes: "Stormy Weather" (Harold Arlen and Ted Koehler), "Jukebox" (Leith Stevens), "Noche de Ronda" (Maria Teresa Lara), "Swimming Pool" (Lennie Hayton), "Jump Right In" (Jeff Alexander), "Looking for Joe" (Al Columbo), "I Wanna Be a Dancin' Man" (Harry Warren and Johnny Mercer). Working Titles: *This Night Forever, Shameless.*

Cast: Shelley Winters (Nancy), Ricardo Montalban (Chu Chu Ramirez), Wendell Corey (Ansel Ames/Floyd Hawkson), Claire Trevor (Mrs. Ansel Ames/Louise Hawkson), Jose Torvay (Manuel Ramirez), Jack Elam (Celestino Garcia), Pascual Garcia Pena (Willie Chung), George Chandler (Frankie), Robert Burton (Sheriff), Juan Torena (Vincente Aguilar), Carlos Conde (Joe Mendacio), Dabbs Greer (Bailiff), Alec Benson (Truck Driver), Martha Wentworth (Landlady), Lee Phelps, Fred Coby (Plainclothesmen), James H. Harrison (Clerk), Billie Bird (Waitress), Jay Adler (Bartender), Jack Daly (Bank Teller), Joe Mell (Deputy Commissioner), Ralph Moody (Rogers), Edward Hearn (Deputy), Tom Greenway, John McKee (Patrolmen), Dennis Fraser (Sailor), Tristram Coffin (Fingerprint Man), Philip Van Zandt (Doctor),

Alan Dreeben (Prosecutor), Earl Lee (Judge), Jim Hayward (Foreman), Rhea Mitchell (Nurse), Lillian Molieri (Bride), Tyler McVey (Defense Attorney), John Indrisano (Foreman), George Lynn, Peter Leeds, Cliff Clark (Men).

ISLAND IN THE SKY (1953)

Warner Brothers. Copyright: September 17, 1953. New York Premiere: September 9, 1953, at the Paramount. 109 minutes.

A Wayne-Fellows Production. Executive Producers: Robert Fellows and John Wayne. Produced and Directed by William A. Wellman. Screenplay: Ernest K. Gann (and uncredited, Seton I. Miller), based on Gann's novel (1944). Photography: Archie J. Stout. Editor: Ralph Dawson. Art Director: James Basevi. Set Decorations: Ralph Hurst. Assistant Director: Andrew V. McLaglen. Production Manager: Nate H. Edwards. Aerial Photography: William H. Clothier. Camera Plane Pilot: Loren Riebe. Picture Plane Pilot: William H. Benge. Special Effects: Alex Weldon. Script Supervisor: Sam Freedle. Warner Phonic Sound (RCA): William Mueller. Dialogue Recording: Earl Crain, Sr., Ed Borschell. Properties: Joseph LaBella. Costumes: Carl Walker. Makeup: Web Overlander. Stills: Don Christy. Musical Score: Emil Newman. French Title: *Adventure dans le Grand Nord.*

Cast: John Wayne (Captain Dooley), Lloyd Nolan (Stutz), Walter Abel (Colonel Fuller), James Arness (McMullen), Andy Devine (Willie Moon), Allan Joslyn (J. H. Handy), James Lydon (Murray, navigator), Harry Carey, Jr. (Hunt), Hal Baylor (Stankowski, engineer), Sean McClory (Frank Lovatt, copilot), Wally Cassell (D'Annunzia, radio man), Regis Toomey (Sgt. Harper), Louis Jean Heydt (Fitch), Bob Steele (Wilson), Darryl Hickman (Swanson), Mike "Touch" Connors (Gainer), Gordon Jones (Walrus), Frank Fenton (Captain Turner), Robert Keys (Major Ditson), Sumner Getchell (Lt. Cord), Paul Fix (Miller), Jim Dugan (Gidley), George Chandler (Rene), Carl Switzer (Hopper), Cass Gidley (Stannish), Guy Anderson (Breezy), Tony DeMario (Ogden), Dawn Bender (Murray's Wife), Phyllis Winger (Margaret, Girl in Flashback), Ann Doran (Moon's Wife), Tim Wellman, Mike Wellman (Moon's Kids), Tom Irish, Richard Walsh, Gene Coogan, Johnny Indrisano. William A. Wellman (Narration).

THE HIGH AND THE MIGHTY (1954)

Warner Brothers. Copyright: July 3, 1954. New York Premiere: June 31, 1954, at the Paramount. 147 minutes.

A Wayne-Fellows Production. Executive Producers: Robert Fellows and John Wayne. Produced and Directed by William A. Wellman. Screenplay: Ernest K. Gann, based on his novel. Color by Warnercolor. Filmed in CinemaScope. Photography: Archie J. Stout. Editor: Ralph Dawson. Art Direction: Alfred Ybarra. Set Decorations: Ralph Hurst. Assistant Director: Andrew V. McLaglen. Production Manager: Nate H. Edwards. Aerial Photography: William H. Clothier. Camera Plane Pilot: Loren Riebe. Special Effects: Robert Mattey. Technical Adviser: William H. Benge. Technical Adviser for United States Coast Guard: Lt. Cdr. Robert M. Cannom, U.S.C.G. Script Supervisor: Sam Freedle. Sound (RCA): John K. Kean. Properties: Joseph LaBella.

Costumes: Gwen Wakeling. Makeup: Web Overlander, Loren Cosand. Hairstylist: Margaret Donovan. Music Composed and Conducted by Dimitri Tiomkin. Song: "The High and the Mighty," music by Dimitri Tiomkin, lyrics by Ned Washington, also whistled by John Wayne. French Title: *Ecrit dans le Ciel.*

Cast: John Wayne (Dan Roman), Claire Trevor (May Holst), Laraine Day (Lydia Rice), Robert Stack (Sullivan), Jan Sterling (Sally McKee), Phil Harris (Ed Joseph), Robert Newton (Gustav Pardee), David Brian (Ken Childs), Paul Kelly (Flaherty), Sidney Blackmer (Humphrey Agnew), Doe Avedon (Miss Spalding, stewardess), Karen Sharpe (Nell Buck), John Smith (Milo Buck), Julie Bishop (Lillian Pardee), Pedro Gonzalez-Gonzalez (Gonzalez), John Howard (Howard Rice), Wally Brown (Lenny Wilby, navigator), William Campbell (Robie Wheeler), Ann Doran (Mrs. Joseph), John Qualen (Jose Locota), Paul Fix (Frank Briscoe), George Chandler (Ben Sneed), Joy Kim (Dorothy Chen), Michael Wellman (Toby Field), Douglas Fowley (Alsop), Regis Toomey (Garfield), Carl Switzer (Ensign Keim), Robert Keys (Lt. Mowbray), Walter Reed (Mr. Field), William DeWolf Hopper (Roy), William Schallert (Dispatcher), Julie Mitchum (Susie), Dorothy Ford (Mrs. Wilson), Robert Easton (Clerk), Philip Van Zandt (Mr. Wilson), John Indrisano (Radar Operator).

TRACK OF THE CAT (1954)

Warner Brothers. Copyright: November 27, 1954. New York Premiere: December 1, 1954, at the Paramount. 102 minutes.

A Wayne-Fellows Production. Executive Producers: Robert Fellows and John Wayne. Produced and Directed by William A. Wellman. Screenplay: A. I. Bezzerides. From the novel by Walter Van Tilburg Clark (1949). Color by Warnercolor. Filmed in CinemaScope. Photography: William H. Clothier. Editor: Fred MacDowell. Art Direction: Alfred Ybarra. Set Decorations: Ralph Hurst. Assistant Director: Andrew V. McLaglen. Production Manager: Nate H. Edwards. Script Supervisor: Sam Freedle. Properties: Joseph LaBella. Sound (RCA): Earl Crain, Sr. Properties: Joseph LaBella. Costumes: Gwen Wakeling. Makeup: Gordon Bau, George Bau. Hairstylist: Margaret Donovan. Musical Score: Roy Webb. Orchestrations: Maurice de Packh.

Cast: Robert Mitchum. (Curt Bridges), Teresa Wright (Grace Bridges), Diana Lynn (Gwen Williams), Tab Hunter (Harold "Hal" Bridges), Beulah Bondi (Ma Bridges), Philip Tonge (Pa Bridges), William Hopper (Arthur Bridges), Carl Switzer (Joe Sam).

BLOOD ALLEY (1955)

Warner Brothers. Copyright: November 1, 1955. New York Premiere: October 5, 1955, at the Paramount. 115 minutes.

A Batjac Production. Executive Producers: John Wayne and Robert Fellows. Produced and directed by William A. Wellman (and uncredited, John Wayne). Screenplay: Albert Sidney Fleischman, based on his novel. Color by Warnercolor. Filmed in CinemaScope. Photography: William H. Clothier. Editor: Fred MacDowell. Production Design: Alfred Ybarra. Set Decorations: Victor Gangelin. Assistant Director: Andrew V. McLaglen. Production Manager: Nate H. Edwards. Unit Manager: Tom Andre. Second Unit Photography: Archie J. Stout. Apprentice Editor: Sam O'Steen.

Script Supervisor: Sam Freedle. Technical Adviser: W. F. Hsueh. Properties: Joseph LaBella. Sound (RCA): Earl Crain, Sr. Costumes: Gwen Wakeling. Men's Costumes: Carl Walker. Makeup: Web Overlander, Norman Pringle. Hairstylist: Margaret Donovan. Transportation Manager: George Coleman. Unit Publicist: Lee Ferrero. Musical Score: Roy Webb. Orchestrations: Maurice de Packh, Gus Levene. Song: "Chinese Song," music by Roy Webb, lyrics by W. F. Hsueh. French Title: *L'Allee Sanglate*.

Cast: John Wayne (Captain Tom Wilder), Lauren Bacall (Cathy Grainger), Paul Fix (Mr. Tso), Joy Kim (Susu, Cathy's maid), Mike Mazurki (Big Han), Berry Kroeger (Old Feng), Anita Ekberg (Wei Long), Henry Nakamura (Tack, engineer), W. T. Chang (Mr. Han), George Chan (Mr. Sing), Victor Sen Yung (Corporal Wang), Walter Soohoo (Feng's #1 Nephew), Eddie Luke (Feng's #2 Nephew), Lowell Gilmore (British Officer), James Hong (Communist Soldier), Harvey Parry (Stunts).

GOOD-BYE, MY LADY (1956)

Warner Brothers. Copyright: May 12, 1956. No New York Premiere. 94 minutes.

A Batjac Production. Executive Producer: John Wayne. Produced and Directed by William A. William. Screenplay: Albert Sidney Fleischman. From the novel by James Street. Photography: William H. Clothier. Editor: Fred MacDowell. Art Director: Donald A. Peters; assistant: Gordon Gurnee. Set Decorations; Edward G. Boyle. Assistant Director: Al Murphy. Production Manager: Nate H. Edwards. Unit Manager: Gordon B. Forbes. Script Supervisor: Hazel Hall. Camera Operator: Bob Johannas. Second Unit Photography: Archie J. Stout. Sound (RCA): Earl Crain Sr. Properties: Joseph LaBella. Costumes: Carl Walker. Makeup: Web Overlander. Assistant Editor: Sam O'Steen. Music Composed and Conducted by Laurindo Almeida (guitar) and George Fields (harmonica). Song: "When Your Boy Becomes a Man," music by Don Powell, lyrics by Moris Erby. Working Title: *The Boy and the Laughing Dog*.

Cast: Walter Brennan (Uncle Jesse Jackson), Phil Harris (Cash Evans), Brandon deWilde ("Skeeter," Claude), Sidney Poitier (Gates), William Hopper (Walden Grover), Louise Beavers (Bonnie Dew), George Chandler (Newspaper Editor), William A. Wellman (Narration).

DARBY'S RANGERS (1958)

Warner Brothers. Copyright: February 22, 1958. New York Premiere: February 12, 1958, at neighborhood theaters. 121 minutes.

Produced by Martin Rackin. Directed by William A. Wellman. Screenplay: Guy Trosper. Suggested by the book by Major James Altieri. Photography: William H. Clothier. Editor: Owen Marks. Art Director: William Campbell. Set Decorator: William L. Kuehl. Assistant Director/Second Unit Director: George D. Vieira. Technical Adviser: Col. Roy A. Murray, U.S. Army, Fourth Ranger Battalion. Project Training Instructors: Second Lt. Lee Mize and Sgt. First Class Richard Sandlin, Ranger Dept., U.S. Army Infantry School. Camera Operator: Andy Anderson. Sound (RCA): Robert B. Lee. Costumes: Marjorie Best. Makeup: Gordon Bau. Musical Score: Max Steiner. Orchestrations: Murray Cutter. French Title: *Les Commandos Passant a L'Attaque*.

Cast: James Garner (Major William Orlando Darby), Etchika Choureau (Angelina De Lotta), Jack Warden (Master Sgt. Saul Rosen/Narration), Edward Byrnes (Lt. Arnold Dittman), Venetia Stevenson (Peggy McTavish), Torin Thatcher (Sgt. McTavish), Peter Brown (Rollo Burns), Joan Elan (Wendy Hollister), Corey Allen (Tony Sutherland), Stuart Whitman (Hank Bishop), Murray Hamilton (Sims Delancey), Bill Wellman, Jr. (Eli Clatworthy), Andrea King (Sheilah Andrews), Adam Williams (Heavy Hall), Frieda Inescort (Lady Hollister), Reginald Owen (Sir Arthur), Philip Tonge (John Andrews), Edward Ashley (Lt. Manson), Raymond Bailey (Maj. Gen. Wise), Willis Bouchey (Brig. Gen. Truscott), Tom Brown Henry (Major), Hilda Plowright, Allegra Vernon (Women), Reggie Dvorak (Waiter), John Marlin (Italian Machine Gunner), Joel Smith (Corporal), Mike Ragon (Sergeant), Julie Reding (Sexy Girl), Tom McKee (Sgt. Slim Rathburn), Edward Colmans (Italian Doctor), Francis DeSales (Captain), Miguel Landa (Priest), William Hudson (Operator), Jerry May (Medic), Sean Garrison (Young Soldier), Isabella Rhye (Tall English Girl), Marion Collier (English Girl), Michael Gibson (Cockney), Tom Watson, Jim DeCloss, John McKee, Michael Pierce, Frank Gifford (Squad Members).

LAFAYETTE ESCADRILLE (1958)

Warner Brothers. Copyright: March 22, 1958. New York Premiere: April 18, 1958, at neighborhood theaters. 93 minutes.

A William A. Wellman Production. Produced and Directed by William A. Wellman. Screenplay: Albert Sidney Fleischman (and uncredited, William A. Wellman). Based on a story, "C'est La Guerre," by William A. Wellman. Photography: William H. Clothier. Editor: Owen Marks. Production Design: Donald A. Peters. Art Director: John Beckman. Set Decorator: Ralph Hurst. Assistant Director: George D. Vieira. Camera Operator: George Nogel. Stunt Pilot: Frank Tallman. Sound (RCA): John Kean. Costumes: Marjorie Best. Makeup: Gordon Bau. Musical Score: Leonard Rosenman. Orchestrations: Maurice de Packh. Theme: "Pretty Baby." Working Title: *C'est Le Guerre, With You in My Arms*. British Title: *Hell Bent for Glory*.

Cast: Tab Hunter (Thad Walker), Etchika Choureau (Renee Beaulieu), Bill Wellman, Jr. (Bill Wellman), Jody McCrea (Tom Hitchcock), Dennis Devine (Red Scanlon), Marcel Dalio (Drillmaster), David Janssen (Duke Sinclaire), Paul Fix (American General), Veola Vonn (The Madam), Will Hutchins (Dave Putnam), Clint Eastwood (George Mosley), Bob Hover (Dave Judd), Tom Laughlin (Arthur Blumenthal), Brett Halsey (Frank Baylies), Henry Nakamura (Jimmy), Maurice Marsac (Sgt. Parris), Raymond Bailey (Mr. Walker), George Nardelli (Concierge), Louis Mercier (Captain Honore), Cain Mason (Charlie), Roger Til (Le Capitaine), Warren Coley (Rankin Drew), Les Johnson (Jim Connelly), Rad Fulton (Wally Winter), Buck Roberts (Stuart Edgar), Gus Thaxter (Austen B. Crehore), Tom Watson (Chuck Kerwood), Bart Mattson (George Dock), Robert Berry (Alan Winslow), Sam Boghosian (Vernon Booth), Phil Adams (Landram Covington), Ralph Guldahl (Dudley Tucker), Ray Smith (Cy Chamberlain), Maurice Elias (Alan Nichols), Dick Rich (Policeman), Lomax Study (Recruiting Officer), Craig Hill (Lufbery), Norman DuPont (Guynemer), Richard Gray (Englishman), Louise Columbet (Old Hag), Edward Manouk (French Sergeant), Francis Ravel (Gate Guard), H. W. Gim (Annamite), Peter Camlin

(Poilu), Al Cavens (Poilu Sergeant), Tom Cound (First R.A.F. Flier), Louis Gasnier (French Bartender), Tony Millard (First Canadian), Roy Dean (Second Canadian), John Barton (French Blesse), Richard LaMarr (Taxi Driver), Frank Arnold (Photographer), Robert Bourne, Robert Hoy (German Pilots), Jacques Gallo, Charles Bastin (French Gendarmes), William A. Wellman (Narration).

The Following Are Wellman Films with Uncredited Direction

THE ELEVENTH HOUR (1923, FOX)

Presented by William Fox. Directed by Bernard J. Durning. Screenplay: Louis Sherwin. Photography: Dan Short. Assistant Director: William A. Wellman. Cast: Shirley Mason, Charles "Buck" Jones, Richard Tucker, Alan Hale, Walter McGrail.

THE WAY OF A GIRL (1925, MGM)

Presented by Louis B. Mayer. Directed by Robert G. Vignola. Screenplay: Albert Shelby LeVina. Based on the story "Summoned" in *Ainslee's* (February 1923) by Katherine Newlin Burt. Photography: John Arnold. Art Direction: Cedric Gibbons. Assistant Director: John Carle. Cast: Eleanor Boardman, Matt Moore, William Russell, Matthew Betz, Charles K. French.

THE EXQUISITE SINNER (1926, MGM)

Presented by Louis B. Mayer. Directed by Josef von Sternberg. Screenplay: Josef von Sternberg and Alice Miller. Based on the novel *Escape* (1924) by Alden Brooks. Titles: Joe Farnham. Photography: Max Fabian. Editor: John W. English. Art Direction: Cedric Gibbons, Joseph Wright. Assistant Director: Robert Florey. Wardrobe: Andreani. Cast: Conrad Nagel, Renee Adoree, Paulette Duval, Frank Currier, George K. Arthur, Matthew Betz, Helen D'Aigy, Claire Dubrey, Myrna Loy.

FEMALE (1933, FIRST NATIONAL-VITAPHONE/WARNERS)

Executive Producer: Darryl F. Zanuck. Produced by Robert Presnell and Henry Blanke. Directed by Michael Curtiz. Screenplay: Gene Markey and Kathryn Scola. Photography: Ernest Haller, George Barnes, John Mescall. Editor: Jack Killifer. Art Direction: Jack Okey. Cast: Ruth Chatterton, George Brent, Lois Wilson, Johnny Mack Brown, Ruth Donnelly.

VIVA VILLA! (1934, MGM)

Produced by David O. Selznick. Directed by Jack Conway, Howard Hawks. Authors: Edgcumb Pinchon, O. B. Stade. Screenplay: Ben Hecht, Charles MacArthur. Photography: James Wong Howe, Charles G. Clarke. Cast: Wallace Beery, Fay Wray, Leo Carrillo, Stuart Erwin, Henry B. Walthall, Donald Cook.

CHINA SEAS (1935, MGM)

Directed by Tay Garnett. Screenplay: Jules Furthman, James Kevin McGuinness. Cast: Clark Gable, Jean Harlow, Wallace Beery, Lewis Stone, Robert Benchley, Rosalind Russell.

TARZAN ESCAPES (1936, MGM)

Produced by Bernie Hyman. Associate Producer: Sam Zimbalist. Directed by Richard Thorpe. Screenplay: Cyril Hume, Louis Mosher, John Farrow, Wyndham Gittens, Otis Garrett, Edwin H. Knopf. Based on characters created by Edgar Rice Burroughs. Photography: Leonard Smith. Editor: W. Donn Hayes, Basil Wrangell. Art Directors: Cedric Gibbons, Elmer Sheeley. Set Decorations: Edwin B. Willis. Special Effects Photography: Max Fabian, Thomas Tutwiler. Special Effects: A. Arnold Gillespie, Thomas Tutwiler, James Basevi, Warren Newcombe. Cast: Johnny Weissmuller, Maureen O'Sullivan, John Buckler, Benita Hume, William Henry, Herbert Mundin, Cheetah the Chimp.

THE GARDEN OF ALLAH (1936, UNITED ARTISTS)

Produced by David O. Selznick. Directed by Richard Boleslawski. Screenplay: W. P. Lipscomb, Lynn Riggs. Novel by Robert Hichens. Photography: W. Howard Greene, Harold G. Rosson. Cast: Marlene Dietrich, Charles Boyer, Basil Rathbone, C. Aubrey Smith, Tilly Losch, Joseph Schildkraut, John Carradine.

THE ADVENTURES OF TOM SAWYER (1938, UNITED ARTISTS)

Produced by David O. Selznick. Directed by Norman Taurog. From the Mark Twain classic. Screenplay: John V. A. Weaver. Photography: James Wong Howe. Cast: Tommy Kelly, Jackie Moran, Ann Gillis, May Rosson, Walter Brennan, Victor Jory, David Holt, Victor Kilian, Nana Bryant, Olin Howland, Donald Meek, Charles Richman, Margaret Hamilton, Marcia Mae Jones, Mickey Rentschler, Cora Sue Collins, Spring Byington.

GONE WITH THE WIND (1939, MGM)

Produced by David O. Selznick. Directed by Victor Fleming. Author: Margaret Mitchell. Screenplay: Sidney Howard. Photography: Ernest Haller. Cast: Clark Gable, Vivien Leigh, Leslie Howard, Olivia de Havilland, George Reeves, Fred Crane, Hattie McDaniel, Everett Brown, Zack Williams, Thomas Mitchell, Oscar Polk, Barbara O'Neil, Victor Jory, Evelyn Keyes, Ann Rutherford, Butterfly McQueen, Howard Hickman, Alicia Rhett, Rand Brooks.

DUEL IN THE SUN (1946, SELZNICK RELEASING ORGANIZATION)

Produced by David O. Selznick. Directed by King Vidor. Author: Niven Busch. Screenplay: David O. Selznick. Adaptation: Oliver H. P. Garrett. Photography: Lee Garmes, Hal Rosson, Ray Rannahan. Cast: Jennifer Jones, Joseph Cotten, Gregory Peck, Lionel Barrymore, Herbert Marshall, Lillian Gish, Walter Huston, Charles

Bickford, Harry Carey, Butterfly McQueen, Otto Kruger, Charles Dingle, Tilly Losch, Scott McKay.

RING OF FEAR (1954, WARNER BROS.)

Produced by Robert Fellows and John Wayne. Directed by James Edward Grant. Story and Screenplay: Paul Fix, Philip MacDonald, and James Edward Grant. Photography: Edwin B. DuPar. Editor: Fred MacDowell. Art Direction: Alfred Ybarra. Set Decoration: Ralph Hurst. Musical Score: Emil Newman, Arthur Lange. Cast: Clyde Beatty, Pat O'Brien, Mickey Spillane, Sean McClory, Marian Carr, John Bromfield, and Twelve Performing Acts of the Clyde Beatty Circus.

ACADEMY AWARD RECOGNITION

Wellman films earned a total of thirty-two nominations, including seven Oscars.

WINGS (1927)
Academy Award for Best Picture and Best Engineering Effects (Roy Pomeroy).

THE PUBLIC ENEMY (1931)
Nominated for Best Writing-Original Motion Picture Story (Kubec Glasmon and John Bright).

THE STAR WITNESS (1931)
Nominated for Best Writing-Original Motion Picture Story (Lucien Hubbard).

A STAR IS BORN (1937)
Academy Awards for Best Writing-Original Story (William A. Wellman and Robert Carson) and a Special Award for Color Photography (W. Howard Greene). Nominated for Best Picture, Best Actor (Fredric March), Best Actress (Janet Gaynor), Best Direction (William A. Wellman), Best Screenplay (Dorothy Parker, Alan Campbell, Robert Carson), and Best Assistant Director (Eric Stacey).

BEAU GESTE (1939)
Nominated for Best Supporting Actor (Brian Donlevy) and Best Interior Decoration (Hans Dreier and Robert Odell).

THE OX-BOW INCIDENT (1943)
Nominated for Best Picture.

LADY OF BURLESQUE (1943)
Nominated for Best Music-Scoring of a Dramatic or Comedy Picture (Arthur Lange).

THE STORY OF G.I. JOE (1945)

Nominated for Best Supporting Actor (Robert Mitchum), Best Screenplay (Leopold Atlas, Guy Endore, Philip Stevenson), Best Music-Scoring of a Dramatic or Comedy Picture (Louis Applebaum, Ann Ronell), Best Song ("Linda," music and lyrics by Ann Ronell).

BATTLEGROUND (1949)

Academy Awards for Best Writing (Robert Pirosh) and Best Black-and-White Cinematography (Paul Vogel). Nominated for Best Picture, Best Direction (William A. Wellman), Best Supporting Actor (James Whitmore), Best Editing (John Dunning).

THE HIGH AND THE MIGHTY (1954)

Academy Award for Best Music-Scoring of a Dramatic or Comedy Picture (Dimitri Tiomkin). Nominated for Best Direction (William A. Wellman), Best Supporting Actress (Claire Trevor, Jan Sterling), Best Editing (Ralph Dawson), Best Song ("The High and the Mighty" by Dimitri Tiomkin and Ned Washington).

NOTES

1. *The Rebel*

3   "Bill, goddammit": Wellman to author, December, 1975.

3   "Wellman was a true Jack London character": Kevin Brownlow, *The Parade's Gone By* (New York: Alfred A. Knopf, 1968), 169.

3   "He was a bully": Frank Thompson, "Making Movies with Both Fists," publicity book article for *Wild Bill Hollywood Maverick* (1996).

3   "He used to stand outside": Scott Eyman, *The Speed of Sound* (Baltimore: Johns Hopkins University Press, 1999), 227.

3   "Bill was a born rebel": Frank Capra, "Capra on Wellman," *Action Magazine* (DGA), March/April 1973.

3   "He didn't waste a lot of time": *Wild Bill Hollywood Maverick* (1996).

4   "The eternal rebel": Ibid.

4   "He has humor and guts": *Wild Bill Hollywood Maverick* publicity booklet (1996).

4   "Bill Wellman was a man's director": *Wild Bill Hollywood Maverick* (1996).

4   "He could be very intimidating": Ibid.

4   "A slim, handsome young man": Louise Brooks, *Lulu in Hollywood* (New York: Alfred A. Knopf, 1982), 25.

4   "You were always my favorite": Clara Bow letter to Wellman, December 1963.

4   "I miss you": Barbara Stanwyck letter to Wellman, June 1972.

4   On February 29, 1896: Boston Birth Index, Book No. 1894–1900, Entry 70, p. 20, Brookline Preservation Commission, Brookline, Massachusetts, *Wellman Family History*.

4   Cecilia Lee was a member: Henry Seymour Guinness, *The Family of Guinness* (Dublin: privately printed, 1924); letter to Celia McCarthy Wellman from Lord Iveagh, July 23, 1935.

4   When the young Cecilia declared: Ibid.

6   Arthur's parents: *Wellman Family History*; Historic Neighborhood brochure, *The Lindens*, Brookline Preservation Commission, Massachusetts, 1996.

6   Arthur's sister: Samuel Williston, *Harvard Law School Bulletin*, Vol. 2, No. 4 (October 1951).

6   After a brief courtship: *Wellman Family History*; Historic Neighborhood

brochure, *The Lindens*, Brookline Preservation Commission, Massachusetts, 1996.

6   On the property: Ibid.

7   For the next eight years: Ibid.

7   Knowing Billy was born on a leap year: *Morning Telegraph* (Boston), July 21, 1918, 2.

7   Celia was the all-caring mother: *Wellman Family History*; Historic Neighborhood brochure, *The Lindens*, Brookline Preservation Commission, Massachusetts, 1996; Project for Public Spaces, Boston Common and Public Garden Historical and Pictorial History, Boston.

8   Celia and the boys: William A. Wellman, *A Short Time for Insanity* (New York: Hawthorne, 1974), 10; Museum of Fine Arts, Historical History, Boston, Massachusetts.

8   Crystal Lake was a block from: Wellman, *Short Time for Insanity*, 8, 9.

8   "In the winter we skated": Ibid.

8   "Have you ever tasted": Ibid.

8   "Boston baked beans": Ibid.

9   Wellman wrote about his dad: Ibid.

9   Soon after the move: Ibid., 11.

9   Arch loved to tinker: Ibid., 12.

10   On Sundays: *Morning Telegraph* (Boston), July 21, 1918; *Boston Evening Globe*, October 26, 1938, front page.

10   At Newton High School: Newton High School yearbook, *The Newtonian* (Newton, MA: Andover Press, 1914).

10   Boys began to ask Celia: *Morning Telegraph* (Boston), July 21, 1918.

10   as a probation officer: Wellman, *Short Time for Insanity*, 10; William A. Wellman, *Growing Old Disgracefully*, 7, 8.

10   Beginning in grammar school: "Director's Mother Producing Show," *Boston Globe*, November 9, 1937.

12   "My first call of the wild": Wellman, *Growing Old Disgracefully*, 7–9.

13   Jesseppi Shinicerella: Ibid., 10

13   High school brought no changes: Wellman, *Short Time for Insanity*, 10.

13   "I have fought with Irishers": Wellman, *Growing Old Disgracefully*, 294.

13   Even the law: *Boston Evening Globe*, October 26, 1938, front page.

15   One sunny summer morning: *Bear Island Reflections*, Storey Communications, Inc., 1989, Bear Island Conservation Association, Lake Winnipesaukee, New Hampshire.

15   For a time: Wellman, *Short Time for Insanity*, 14.

15   Campers were not allowed: Ibid., 15.

16   On the next crossing: Ibid., 15, 16.

16   "There was a big fat guy": Wellman, *Growing Old Disgracefully*, 295.

17   This perpetual distraction: Ibid., 296.

17   In order to graduate: Wellman, *Short Time for Insanity*, 13; Wellman, *Growing Old Disgracefully*, 88; *Boston Post*, January 20, 1914.

18   "I didn't have to use my brain": Wellman, *Short Time for Insanity*, 17.

18   Billy was a piler: Ibid., 24.

18   The old-timers ignored: Ibid., 24, 25.

18   The poor kid: Ibid., 25.

19   Billy's passion: Ibid., 122.

19   Douglas Fairbanks: Ibid., 122, 123.

19   The star even invited Billy: Ibid., 123; William A. Wellman, Jr., *The Man and His Wings: William A. Wellman and the Making of the First Best Picture* (Westport, CT: Praeger, 2006), 3.

19   On another day: Woburn Historical Society, *History of Woburn, Massachusetts*.

20   Billy's acquaintance: James H. Farmer, *Celluloid Wings: The Impact of Movies on Aviation* (Blue Ridge Summit, PA: TAB Books, 1984), 3, 6, 7.

21   On the ground: Wellman, *Growing Old Disgracefully*, 88; Wellman Jr., *Man and His Wings*, 3.

21   Before sentencing: Wellman, *Short Time for Insanity*, 10.

22   Celia was so successful: "Newton Woman to Be at World Parley," *Boston Globe*, September 1923.

23   Billy suited up: *Morning Telegraph* (Boston), July 21, 1918, feature article.

23   "For me": Wellman, *Growing Old Disgracefully*, 88, 176.

2. The Recruit

25   Billy neglected to mention: Wellman, *Growing Old Disgracefully*, 88.

25   The C&G bosses believed: Wellman Jr., *Man and His Wings*, 15: Wellman letters to brother and father, September 20, 1917, Avord, France.

25   On May 19: *Wellman Family History*.

25   Taffy was getting old: Wellman, *Growing Old Disgracefully*, 176.

26   On May 20: Ibid., 304.

26   "My beloved son": Ibid.

26   Billy suddenly felt heartsick: Ibid., 305, 306.

26   This letter would become: Ibid., 306.

27   The *Rochambeau*: *New York Times*, March 9, 1917, 2; Albert Durfee McJoynt, *Rochambeau* (*Journal of Early Modern Warfare*, Gorget & Sash, III: 4, 1990), Part III; Melvin Maddocks, *The Great Liners: The Seafarers* (Alexandria, VA: Time-Life Books, 1978), 136, 137.

27   In World War I: Albert Durfee McJoynt, *Rochambeau* (*Journal of Early Modern Warfare*, Gorget & Sash, III: 4, 1990), Part III.

28   The *Rochambeau* was not: *New York Times*, March 9, 1917, 2.

28   Billy's trip: Wellman Jr., *Man and His Wings*, 6, 7: Wellman letter, June 4, 1917, Hôtel De Bayonne, Bordeaux, France; James Norman Hall and Charles Bernard Nordhoff, *The Lafayette Flying Corps*, Vol. I (Boston: Houghton Mifflin, 1920), 48, 49.

28   With so many American adventure seekers: Hall and Nordhoff, *Lafayette Flying Corps*, Vol. I, 48, 49, 66.

28   On October 9, 1918: Ibid., Vol. I, 68.

28   Wellman was in fine company: Wellman Jr., *Man and His Wings*, 13, 14: Wellman letter, September 15, 1917, Avord, France.

28   There was great passion: Wellman, *Growing Old Disgracefully*, 88, 89.

32   "The reception given Pershing": Wellman Jr., *Man and His Wings*, 8, 9: Wellman letter, June 14, 1917, Paris, France.

33   For the next week: Wellman Jr., *Man and His Wings*, 9, 10: Wellman letters, June 22, 26, 1917, American Hospital, Paris, France.

33   Billy stripped off his boots: Wellman Jr., *Man and His Wings*, 9, 10: Wellman letter, June 26, 1917, American Hospital, Paris, France. Note: Story censored in this letter for Wellman's mother. Actual story: Wellman, *Growing Old Disgracefully*, 308.

33   Two French policemen: Wellman, *Growing Old Disgracefully*, 309.

34   On the morning of June 27: Wellman Jr., *Man and His Wings*, 10; William A. Wellman, *Go, Get 'Em!* (Boston: The Page Company, 1918), 36, 37.

34   Wellman's circle of friends: Wellman, *Go, Get 'Em!*, 37–43; Wellman, *Short Time for Insanity*, 22.

35   There were five basic steps: Wellman Jr., *Man and His Wings*, 11, 12: Wellman letter, July 30, 1917, Avord, France; Arch Whitehouse, *Legion of the Lafayette* (Garden City: Doubleday, 1962), 26–29.

35   For the final two steps: Whitehouse, *Legion of the Lafayette*, 26–29; Wellman Jr., *Man and His Wings*, 15, 16: Wellman letter, September 30, 1917, Avord, France.

35   Those who survived: Whitehouse, *Legion of the Lafayette*, 26–29; Wellman Jr., *Man and His Wings*, 17: Wellman letter, October 25, 1917, Avord, France.

35   Quite often: Wellman Jr., *Man and His Wings*, 12, 13; Wellman, *Go, Get 'Em!*, 51.

43   On September 29, 1917: Hall and Nordhoff, *Lafayette Flying Corps*, Vol. I, 483; Wellman, *Go, Get 'Em!*, 93.

43   After seven days' furlough: Wellman Jr., *Man and His Wings*, 18: Wellman letter, October 30, 1917, Pau, France.

43   Before the war: Ibid.; Wellman, *Go, Get 'Em!*, 99, 100; Whitehouse, *Legion of the Lafayette*, 16; Herbert Molloy Mason, Jr., *High Flew the Falcons* (New York: J. B. Lippincott, 1965), 57.

44   During Wellman's time there: Ibid.

44   Some of Wellman's Avord pals: Wellman, *Go, Get 'Em!*, 99, 110; Wellman, *Short Time for Insanity*, 117. Note: These six recruits received the same training at Avord, Pau, and Le Plessis-Belleville (G.D.E.) but advanced through aviation school at different periods between May 26 and December 10, 1917. Hall and Nordhoff, *Lafayette Flying Corps*: 116 (Baylies), 268 (Hitchcock), 296 (Judd), 395 (Putnam), 431 (Sinclaire), 483 (Wellman). Sidney Drew trained with the aforementioned recruits at Avord only and arrived at Pau after they had left, ibid., 220.

44   Staff Brown: Wellman, *Short Time for Insanity*, 22.

44   The first casualty: Hall and Nordhoff, *Lafayette Flying Corps*, 357; Wellman, *Go, Get 'Em!*, 84, 85.

45   At Pau: Wellman, *Go, Get 'Em!*, 100–3.

45   Wellman and the other pilots: Ibid., 105–8; Whitehouse, *Legion of the Lafa-yette*, 28.

46   One bright and sunny day: Wellman, *Go, Get 'Em!*, 102.

46   After that incident: Ibid., 102, 103, 114; Wellman Jr., *Man and His Wings*, 20: Wellman letter, November 4, 1917, Pau, France.

46   He was recommended: Wellman Jr., *Man and His Wings*, 20: Wellman letter, November 14, 1917, Pau, France.

47   The finished pilots were sent: Whitehouse, *Legion of the Lafayette*, 28, 29.

47   "I had finished": Wellman Jr., *Man and His Wings*, 20: Wellman letter, November 11, 1917, Pau, France; Wellman, *Go, Get 'Em!*, 184.

47   "Your time in Plessis": Wellman Jr., *Man and His Wings*, 21: Wellman letter, November 14, 1917, Chatham Bar & Grillroom, Paris, France; Wellman, *Go, Get 'Em*, 185.

48   It was at Plessis: Wellman Jr., *Man and His Wings*, 20: Wellman letter, November 4, 1917, p. 2, Pau, France.

48   On a cold: Wellman, *Go, Get 'Em!*, 118–22.

49   Wellman's second shining: Whitehouse, *Legion of the Lafayette*, 29; Wellman, *Go, Get 'Em!*, 115, 116.

50   Near the hotel: Personal audiotapes of William Wellman, unpublished, 1973; Wellman, *Growing Old Disgracefully*, 313, 314; Wellman conversations with author during trip to Paris, France, July 25, 26, 1972.

50   The next few weeks: Ibid.

50   On December 3, 1917: Wellman, *Go, Get 'Em!*, 136.

50   By December 12, 1917: Hall and Nordhoff, *Lafayette Flying Corps*, Vol. I, 116 (Baylies), 268 (Hitchcock), 296 (Judd), 395 (Putnam), 431 (Sinclair), 220 (Drew); Whitehouse, *Legion of the Lafayette*, 324 (Stafford Brown).

51   Wellman's departure: Personal audiotapes of William Wellman; Wellman, *Growing Old Disgracefully*, 313, 314; Wellman conversations with author during trip to Paris, France, July 25 and 26, 1972.

3. The Pilot

53   After a long, slow ride: Wellman, *Go, Get 'Em!*, 136, 137; Wellman Jr., *Man and His Wings*, 25, 26: Wellman letter, December 3, 1917, N. 87, Sector 44, Lunéville, France.

53   The pilots lived: Wellman, *Go, Get 'Em!*, 138, 139, 140.

53   There were not enough bedrooms: Ibid., 139, 140.

54   The pilots of N. 87: Lawrence L. Smart, *The Hawks That Guided the Guns* (Privately printed, 1968), 66; Wellman Jr., *Man and His Wings*, 27.

54   Early on the morning: Wellman, *Go, Get 'Em!*, 142, 143; Wellman Jr., *Man and His Wings*, 28.

55   Wellman was assigned: Wellman, *Go, Get 'Em!*, 143.

55   Depending on the surprise factor: Personal audiotapes of William Well-

man; Wellman conversations with author; Wellman Jr., *Man and His Wings*, 28–30.

55 Back at N. 87: Ibid.

56 That evening: Ibid.; Wellman Jr., *Man and His Wings*, 35, 36.

56 When the dinner was ready: Ibid.; Wellman, *Go, Get 'Em!*, 140.

58 The weather forecast: Personal audiotapes of William Wellman; Wellman conversations with author.

58 "She was older than I": Wellman, *Growing Old Disgracefully*, 313, 314; Wellman Jr., *Man and His Wings*, 33.

59 It was standard procedure: Wellman, *Go, Get 'Em!*, 145; Wellman Jr., *Man and His Wings*, 34.

59 Wellman's first patrol: Wellman, *Go, Get 'Em!*, 158–60.

59 The disappointed American: Ibid., 161.

59 That evening: Wellman, *Growing Old Disgracefully*, 294, 295; personal audiotapes of William Wellman; Wellman conversations with author.

62 On December 10: Hall and Nordhoff, *Lafayette Flying Corps*, Vol. I, 268, 269; Whitehouse, *Legion of the Lafayette*, 303.

62 Hitchcock and Wellman: Lonnie Raidor, *Cross & Cockade* (Manhattan Beach, CA: The Society of World War I Aero Historians, Vol. 17, No. 3, Autumn 1976), 206, 209.

63 Of Wellman's friends and fliers: Wellman, *Growing Old Disgracefully*, 313, 314; Wellman conversations with author.

64 Darkness drifted away: Wellman, *Go, Get 'Em!*, 163, 164.

64 Six escorting Nieuports: Ibid., 165, 166.

64 After completion: Ibid., 166–69.

64 windstorm: Ibid., 169, 170.

65 "On one occasion": Whitehouse, *Legion of the Lafayette*, 303, 304.

66 The A-team was part: Wellman, *Growing Old Disgracefully*, 310–12.

67 On January 19, 1918: Wellman, *Go, Get 'Em!*, 172.

67 The mission was successful: Ibid., 173, 174.

68 Wellman turned back: Ibid.; Wellman letter, January 19, 1918.

68 *Celia III:* Wellman, *Go, Get 'Em!*, 179–85.

69 Billy and Renee: Wellman, *Growing Old Disgracefully*, 313, 314; Wellman conversations with author.

71 When Hitchcock and Wellman: Wellman, *Go, Get 'Em!*, 191–200; Wellman, *Short Time for Insanity*, 221–24.

74 It started to rain: Wellman, *Growing Old Disgracefully*, 314–16; Wellman conversations with author.

76 Wellman returned to Lunéville: Wellman conversations with author during trip to Paris, France, July 25–26, 1972.

76 Wellman's former friend: Whitehouse, *Legion of the Lafayette*, 304; Hall and Nordhoff, *Lafayette Flying Corps*, Vol. I, 258.

76 Hitchcock didn't return: Whitehouse, *Legion of the Lafayette*, 303–6.

77 After repeated attempts: Hall and Nordhoff, *Lafayette Flying Corps*, Vol. I,

269, 270; Whitehouse, *Legion of the Lafayette*, 304, 305; Wellman, *Growing Old Disgracefully*, 56–60.

77   Hitchcock and Wellman: Wellman, *Short Time for Insanity*, 22; Wellman, *Growing Old Disgracefully*, 313, 314.

77   On March 9: Lonnie Raidor, *Cross & Cockade* (Manhattan Beach, CA: The Society of World War I Aero Historians, Vol. 17, No. 3, Autumn 1976), 223; Wellman, *Go, Get 'Em!*, 209, 226; Jewish Virtual Library, *World War II: History of the 42nd Infantry "Rainbow" Division* (American-Israeli Cooperative Enterprise, 2014).

77   The Rainbow Division: Ibid.

77   The government created: Ibid.

78   Captain Azire explained: Wellman, *Go, Get 'Em!*, 238, 239.

78   Wellman was chosen: Ibid.

78   *Celia V:* Ibid., 242.

78   Below, he could make out: Ibid., 243.

78   Wellman could not distinguish: Ibid., 244.

78   Suddenly, the wait was over: Ibid., 244, 245.

79   Random thoughts: Ibid., 245.

79   The unordered thoughts: Ibid., 246, 247.

79   Before the dogfight ended: Ibid., 250, 251.

79   Military observers had reported: Ibid., 252.

79   On March 21, 1918: Ibid., 266–72; Lonnie Raidor, *Cross & Cockade* (Manhattan Beach, CA: The Society of World War I Aero Historians, Vol. 17, No. 3, Autumn 1976), 224, 225; Wellman Jr., *Man and His Wings*, 46; Wellman conversations with author.

80   Wellman dropped down: Ibid.

81   William Wellman's days: Hall and Nordhoff, *Lafayette Flying Corps*, Vol. II, 317 (Brown), 320 (Meeker, Drew), 321 (Baylies, Putnam), 323 (Hitchcock).

82   Of Wellman's closest friends: Ibid., Vol. I, 296 (Judd), 431 (Sinclaire), 483 (Wellman).

82   Wild Bill's Croix de Guerre: Wellman, *Go, Get 'Em!*, 252, 254, 264; "American Airman Home with Record of 4 Boche Victims," *New York Tribune*, May 3, 1918.

82   Two hundred ten Americans: Hall and Nordhoff, *Lafayette Flying Corps*, Vol. II, Appendix, 320–27, 340.

4. The War Hero

83   The French ocean liner: Duncan Haws, *Merchant Fleets: French Line*, No. 30, *Espagne* (TCL Publications, 1996); "Modest Air Hero Back from France," *Evening Telegraph* (Boston), May 2, 1918; "Eager to Get Back in Fight," *Boston Globe*, May 3, 1918.

83   During Wellman's rehab: "At Cambridge with William A. Wellman," *Morning Telegraph* (Boston), July 21, 1918.

84 Before returning home: "Eager to Get Back in Fight," *Boston Globe*, May 3, 1918; "At Cambridge with William A. Wellman," *Morning Telegraph* (Boston), July 21, 1918.

86 Wellman explained: Ibid.

86 Now it was time: "At Cambridge with William A. Wellman," *Morning Telegraph* (Boston), July 21, 1918; Wellman, *Growing Old Disgracefully*, 177.

86 "Taffy was there": Wellman, *Growing Old Disgracefully*, 177.

87 "Taffy tried to jump": Ibid.

87 Soon, the two walkers: Wellman Jr., *Man and His Wings*, 49–51; Wellman conversations with author.

88 Realizing his son: Ibid.

88 Arthur entered the chug-a-lug: Ibid.

88 The morning after: Ibid.

89 With the morning headlines: "Modest Air Hero Back from France," *Evening Telegraph* (Boston), May 2, 1918; "A Twenty-Five-Mile Fight on Wings," *Boston Sunday Post*, February 24, 1918; "Buy Thrift Stamps to Win War, Says Airman Wellman," *Boston Post*, May 14, 1918.

89 Newton mayor Edwin O. Childs: "At Cambridge with William A. Wellman," *Morning Telegraph* (Boston), July 21, 1918; "Buy Thrift Stamps to Win War, Says Airman Wellman," *Boston Post*, May 14, 1918.

90 For the next several months: Ibid.

91 The former president: John Durant and Alice Durant, *Pictorial History of American Presidents* (New York: A. S. Barnes, 1955), 206, 209, 217.

91 Wellman figured: Wellman, *Short Time for Insanity*, 210, 211; "Aviators, Quentin Roosevelt," *Aviation History*, October 29, 2007; Theodore Roosevelt Association, family tree.

92 In 1919: Ibid.; Hall and Nordhoff, *Lafayette Flying Corps*, Vol. II, 194.

92 Roosevelt sent a driver: Wellman, *Short Time for Insanity*, 210, 211.

92 The two veterans: Ibid.

92 Roosevelt turned to Wellman: Ibid.

92 "How do you feel, boy?": Ibid.

93 A short time later: Whitehouse, *Legion of the Lafayette*, 24, 25, 77, 82, 83; Wellman, *Growing Old Disgracefully*, 181–84, 187, 190–93.

93 Seriously wounded: Ibid.

95 Balsley's system had worked: Ibid.; Wellman, *Short Time for Insanity*, 117.

96 "Good-looking tailored uniform": Wellman, *Short Time for Insanity*, 117–19.

97 "She looked me over": Ibid.

97 It was early November: Wellman Jr., *Man and His Wings*, 57, 58; Wellman conversations with author.

99 Soon Billy was back: Wellman, *Short Time for Insanity*, 119.

100 Wellman went on a marathon celebration: Ibid., 118.

100 "This was my job": Ibid.

100 "It was in the afternoon": Ibid., 119.

101 Wellman's married life: Ibid., 120.

101 Then came the two armistices: Ibid.

103   Unfortunately, Helene was unable: Ibid., 121.

103   The release papers: Ibid.

103   Wellman bought a couple: Ibid.

103   With Helene out of town: Ibid., 122.

104   On this fateful day: Richard Schickel, *His Pictures in the Papers* (New York: Charterhouse, 1973), 108; Wellman Jr., *Man and His Wings*, 61–63; *Wild Bill Hollywood Maverick* (1996).

105   "Wellman: Remember me": Wellman, *Short Time for Insanity*, 123.

105   Wellman had traded: Ibid., 123–28.

5. The Hollywood Ladder

111   Welcome to Wild Bill's new world: Wellman, *Short Time for Insanity*, 128; Marc Wanamaker and Robert W. Nudelman, *Early Hollywood* (Charleston, SC: Arcadia, 2007), 35.

112   Wellman's June Street room: Wellman, *Short Time for Insanity*, 128.

112   It was Sunday: Ibid., 129.

112   Monday morning: Ibid., 130, 132.

112   On one of those: Ibid., 132.

113   Wellman figured: Ibid.

113   Before going home: Ibid., 133.

113   Old Tex: Ibid.

113   "I started to say": Ibid.

114   Old Tex was right on: Ibid.

114   Wellman had mixed emotions: Ibid., 134.

115   When the final scene: Ibid., 135.

115   After a stream: Ibid., 136, 137.

116   All Billy said: Ibid., 138–40; Leonard Maltin, *Classic Movie Guide* (New York: Penguin, 2014), *Evangeline*.

117   On May 26, 1919: Frank Thompson, *Lost Films* (New York: Citadel, 1996), 90.

117   When *Knickerbocker Buckaroo* opened: Wellman, *Short Time for Insanity*, 140–42; Wellman conversations with author.

118   Fairbanks proved to be: Wellman, *Short Time for Insanity*, 142, 143.

118   Wellman said goodbye: Ibid., 142; J. A. Aberdeen, *Classic Hollywood and the Independent Filmmakers* (Hollywood Renegades Archive, 2005); Gomery, *Hollywood Studio System*, 61, 62; Wanamaker and Nudelman, *Early Hollywood*, 39.

118   For a while: Ibid.; Jeffrey Vance, *Chaplin: Genius of the Cinema* (New York: Harry N. Abrams, 2003), 136.

118   The Lot served: Ibid.

119   Throughout the 1920s: Ibid.

119   In 1924: Ibid.

119   Because of Fairbanks: Wellman, *Short Time for Insanity*, 142, 143.

120   As Wellman left: Ibid., 142. Some names of directors were changed. Research
       showed that a few of these directors were not at the Goldwyn Studio at this
       time. Wellman met them at MGM or other studios at a later date.

120   "How did those men": Ibid., 144.

120   Knowing Helene: Ibid., 145.

120   Wellman handed her: Ibid.

121   A few blocks from the studio: Ibid.

121   Wellman went to as many movies: Ibid.; Wellman conversations with author.

121   Wild Bill's good luck: Wellman, *Short Time for Insanity*, 146; Estate of Will
       Rogers, Official Site: Biography; Richard B. Jewell, *The Golden Age of Cin-
       ema: Hollywood, 1929–1945* (Malden, MA: Blackwell, 2007), 277–79.

121   Will Rogers mastered: Ibid.

122   In August of 1935: Ibid.

122   When Wellman met Rogers: Ibid.

123   The year was 1920: *New York Times* headlines, 1920; Jennifer Rosenberg,
       Timeline of the 20th Century (website), 1920s; Annie Gertrude Gilliam,
       Headlines of the 1920s (History Orb.com), 1920 Historical Events.

124   The directive stated: Wellman, *Short Time for Insanity*, 146, 147.

124   "Suddenly Mr. Vice-president appeared": Ibid.

124   "Nobody cheered": Ibid.

124   All eyes were on Wellman: Ibid.

125   "Well, Wellman?": Ibid., 147, 148.

125   The following day: Ibid., 148.

125   Sirens roared: Ibid.; Whitehouse, *Legion of the Lafayette*, 202.

125   During the war: Letter home, June 14, 1917, Paris.

125   Wellman's second encounter: Wellman, *Short Time for Insanity*, 149; Well-
       man Jr., *Man and His Wings*, 72.

126   When Billy made his decision: Ibid.

126   Shortly, a bellowing howl: Ibid.

127   At the studio: Wellman, *Short Time for Insanity*, 148, 149.

127   He shook Wellman's hand: Ibid.

127   The next day: Ibid.

127   Wellman's dream: Wellman Jr., *Man and His Wings*, 74; Wellman conversa-
       tions with author.

128   Although he got along: Frank T. Thompson, *William A. Wellman* (Metuchen,
       NJ: Scarecrow Press, 1983), 36.

128   Wellman had heard: Wellman, *Short Time for Insanity*, 55.

128   Wellman did not know: Ibid.

128   When the appointment finally came: Ibid., 56, 57.

128   They talked about: Ibid.

129   Durning and Wellman: Ibid., 57, 58.

129   It was a quick but vicious contest: Ibid., 58, 59.

130   *Strange Idols* (1922): Samantha Hart, *The Hollywood Walk of Fame* (La Cañada
       Flintridge, CA: Crybaby Books, 1987, 2000), 70; Jesse L. Lasky, *I Blow My*

Own Horn (New York: Doubleday, 1957), 92; Bret Wood, *The Squaw Man*, 1914, Internet article.

130   After reaching such a lofty position: Ibid.; Wanamaker and Nudelman, *Early Hollywood*, 31, 33.

130   *Strange Idols* locationed in Eureka: Wellman, *Short Time for Insanity*, 60–64.

133   One day while walking: Ibid., 53–55.

135   Dan never talked: Ibid., 154–56.

137   In the late summer: *Celia Wellman Family History*; Wellman, *Short Time for Insanity*, 55, 202; Wanamaker and Nudelman, *Early Hollywood*, 55, 56; Wellman Jr., *Man and His Wings*, 78.

137   Mother and son's: *Celia Wellman Family History*; Wanamaker and Nudelman, *Early Hollywood*, 114; Wellman Jr., *Man and His Wings*, 74.

137   Billy was sorry: Wellman conversations with author; Wellman Jr., *Man and His Wings*, 78.

138   Celia brought her son: Ibid.; *Celia Wellman Family History*.

138   *Yosemite Trail:* Ibid.; Wanamaker and Nudelman, *Early Hollywood*, 37, 47; Jeffrey Stanton, *Santa Monica Pier: A History from 1875 to 1990* (Donahue Publishing, 1990).

138   Billy took his mom: Wanamaker and Nudelman, *Early Hollywood*, 45, 48.

138   By May 1923: Wellman, *Short Time for Insanity*, 215.

138   One day: Wellman Jr., *Man and His Wings*, 79–82; Wellman, *Growing Old Disgracefully*, 55–60; Wellman conversations with author.

141   The A-team: Wellman, *Growing Old Disgracefully*, 60, 61; Wellman conversations with author regarding meetings with Hitchcock after the war. There were two meetings, not just one as written in *Growing Old Disgracefully*, 54, 60.

142   Many years later: Wellman, *Short Time for Insanity*, 22: "I don't think I ever passed through my dressing room that I didn't look at Tom's picture."

142   *The Eleventh Hour* company: Ibid., 215.

142   What amazed Wellman: Ibid.

142   The company was filming: Ibid., 216.

143   "There wasn't much to say": Ibid.

143   "For the last two years": Ibid.

143   The new director: Ibid., 217.

143   Sol Wurtzel and Winnie Sheehan: Ibid., 218.

6. The Directors' Board

145   For the first time: Wellman Jr., *Man and His Wings*, 84.

145   *The Man Who Won:* Thompson, *William A. Wellman*, 40, 41; Wellman, *Short Time for Insanity*, 218.

145   The Western melodrama: Larry Langman, *A Guide to Silent Westerns* (Westport, CT: Greenwood, 1992), 281.

145   Wellman couldn't wait: Wellman, *Short Time for Insanity*, 218, 219.

146   Durning offered another piece of advice: Ibid.

147   Wellman's picture began: Ibid.

147   When Wellman's company: Ibid.

147   Between August 1923 and May 1924: Wellman, *Growing Old Disgracefully*, 263.

148   Buck Jones: Edwin Schallert, *Los Angeles Times*, December 1, 1942; Hart, *Hollywood Walk of Fame*, 468; Wellman, *Growing Old Disgracefully*, 263.

148   After two enjoyable pictures: Wellman, *Growing Old Disgracefully*, 264, 265.

150   "The newspapers told": Ibid., 263.

150   As a contract director: Ibid., 275–80. Wellman remembered his salary as $200 a week (p. 275). Studio records say $185 per week.

153   Born July 23, 1891: Bernard F. Dick, *The Merchant Prince of Poverty Row* (Lexington: University Press of Kentucky, 1993), Chapter 1; TCM Archive: Harry Cohn.

155   Into this bedlamized world: Wellman, *Growing Old Disgracefully*, 281–83.

155   "It is not an easy": Ibid.

156   "Old man takes": Ibid.

156   As a celebration: Wellman Jr., *Man and His Wings*, 94, 95; Thompson, *William A. Wellman*, 48.

157   By 1925: Gomery, *Hollywood Studio System*, 30, 33; Hart, *Hollywood Walk of Fame*, 355, 508; Kevin Thomas, "Louis B. Mayer," *Los Angeles Times*, December 25, 2005.

158   Back to the more lowly: Thompson, *William A. Wellman*, 49, 50; Wellman Jr., *Man and His Wings*, 95, 96; Matthew Kennedy, mini-biography for "Silents Are Golden," from *Edmund Goulding's Dark Victory: Hollywood's Genius Bad Boy* (Madison: University of Wisconsin Press, 2004).

159   Wellman's next replacement job: Ibid.; Wellman, *Short Time for Insanity*, 52, 53.

160   As word of Wellman's firing: Wellman, *Short Time for Insanity*, 161, 162; Brownlow, *Parade's Gone By*, 168.

160   Benjamin Percival Schulberg: Ibid.; Hart, *Hollywood Walk of Fame*, 312; Mary Melton, "Hollywood Star Walk: B.P. Schulberg," *Los Angeles Times*, February 27, 1957.

7. The Road to a Classic

163   Before the new year: Wellman, *Short Time for Insanity*, 162.

163   A Hungarian-born furrier and a Jewish cornet player: Bernard F. Dick, *Engulfed: The Death of Paramount Pictures* (Lexington: University Press of Kentucky, 2001), 1–8; Wellman Jr., *Man and His Wings*, 98–102.

164   B.P. Schulberg handed Wellman: Wellman, *Short Time for Insanity*, 162; Brownlow, *Parade's Gone By*, 168; Thompson, *William A. Wellman*, 53.

166   The story is a romantic triangle: Maltin, *Classic Movie Guide*, *You Never Know Women*.

166   By 1927: Eyman, *Speed of Sound*, 16, 17.

166   During Laskey's time: Wellman, *Short Time for Insanity*, 162, 163; Frank Thompson and John Gallagher, *Wings* program article celebrating Paramount's 100th Anniversary, produced for the Academy of Motion Picture Arts & Sciences by Randy Haberkamp, January 17 and 18, 2012; Brownlow, *Parade's Gone By*, 168, 174, 176, 177; Farmer, *Celluloid Wings*, 29–38; Wellman Jr., *Man and His Wings*, 103–6.

167   "The history of this": Saunders writings; Dick, *Engulfed*.

168   Over a million dollars sunk: Jesse Lasky Jr., *Whatever Happened to Hollywood?* (New York: Funk & Wagnalls, 1973, 1975), 23.

8. *Battlefield* Wings

185   Paramount Pictures' army: Wellman, *Short Time for Insanity*, 163–77; Wellman Jr., *Man and His Wings*, 107–36; Bruce W. Orriss, *When Hollywood Ruled the Skies* (Los Angeles: Aero Associates, 2013), 2–15; Frank Thompson, *Texas Hollywood* (San Antonio: Maverick, 2002), 20–25.

185   five thousand soldiers: Frank Thompson, *Texas Hollywood* (San Antonio: Maverick, 2002) 24, 25.

185   The film required: Ibid., 22, 23.

185   "We were there": Wellman, *Short Time for Insanity*, 162, 163.

185   Another Paramount picture: Ibid.

186   Clara Bow: Wellman Jr., *Man and His Wings*, 115.

186   "To begin with": Wellman, *Short Time for Insanity*, 164.

186   The time finally came: Wellman Jr., *Man and His Wings*, 115.

186   There were other fires: Wellman, *Short Time for Insanity*, 164–68.

186   When Wellman: Ibid.

187   Wellman reminisced: Ibid.

188   There was a long: Ibid.

188   Because of Wellman's history: Ibid.

188   Due to the lack: Wellman Jr., *Man and His Wings*, 118–20.

188   During the first: Ibid.

189   As the weeks: Ibid.

189   Hand-cranked: Ibid.

190   Wellman believed: Wellman, *Growing Old Disgracefully*, 272.

190   Another problem: Wellman Jr., *Man and His Wings*, 118–24.

192   Richard Arlen: Ibid.

192   When the studio: Ibid.

192   The director: Ibid.

192   During the weather: Ibid.

192   Paramount was now: Ibid.

193   Some crew problems: Ibid.

193   The army: Ibid.

193   Gary Cooper: Wellman, *Short Time for Insanity*, 168–70.

194   When the time: Ibid.
194   That evening: Ibid.
195   With all the activity: Wellman Jr., *Man and His Wings*, 126.
195   The central theme: Ibid.
195   Before the fisticuffs: Ibid.
196   In spite of: Ibid.
196   Seventeen stuntmen: Ibid.; Orriss, *When Hollywood Ruled the Skies* (Los Angeles: Aero Associates, 2013), 5–7.
197   When World War I: Mark Carlson, *Flying on Film: A Century of Aviation in the Movies, 1912–2012* (Albany, GA: BearManor Media, 2013), 3, 6, 7.
197   One of the best-known: Ibid.; Orriss, *When Hollywood Ruled the Skies*, Introduction, vi, vii; Farmer, *Celluloid Wings*, 12–24.
197   No one did more: Shawna Kelly, *Aviation in Early Hollywood* (Dover, NH: Arcadia, 2008), B. H. "Daredevil" Delay chapter.
198   The world of stunt fliers: Farmer, *Celluloid Wings*, 24.
198   "The fact that not a single": Ibid., 28.
198   For *Wings*: Wellman Jr., *Man and His Wings*, 126, 127.
199   Even though: Ibid.; Orriss, *When Hollywood Ruled the Skies*, 10, 11.
199   Unfortunately: Ibid.
199   "Six weeks later": Wellman Jr., *Man and His Wings*, 27.
199   Frank Tomick: Orriss, *When Hollywood Ruled the Skies*, 10, 11.
199   Sadly: Thompson, *Texas Hollywood*, 23.
199   The two biggest: Wellman Jr., *Man and His Wings*, 127–29.
200   St. Mihiel was up: Lt. Col. George M. Lauderbaugh, *The Air Battle of St. Mihiel*, Airpower Research Institute (website); *Battle of Saint-Mihiel*, Summer of Monuments (website).
200   The attack began: Ibid.
200   Wellman could wait: Wellman Jr., *Man and His Wings*, 128, 129.
200   Wellman had spent: Ibid.
201   There were seventeen: Ibid.
201   The day dawned: Wellman, *Short Time for Insanity*, 170–77.
206   The weather improved: Wellman Jr., *Man and His Wings*, 135.
207   There was no more: Ibid.; Wellman, *Short Time for Insanity*, 176.
207   Frank Thompson: Thompson, *Texas Hollywood*, 23.
207   Many different: Orriss, *When Hollywood Ruled the Skies*, 8, 9; Carlson, *Flying on Film*, 19.
208   "It was the night": Wellman, *Short Time for Insanity*, 176, 177.

9. Consequences and Achievements

209   If you think: Wellman, *Short Time for Insanity*, 177.
209   Since the director: Ibid.
209   Myron had other chips: Bob Thomas, *Selznick* (New York: Doubleday, 1970), 18–20, 22, 23, 35.

210   Myron listened: Wellman, *Short Time for Insanity*, 177.

210   Wellman shot the final scenes: Brownlow, *Parade's Gone By*, 168, 170; Wellman Jr., *Man and His Wings*, 138, 139.

210   Burton Steene: Wellman, *Growing Old Disgracefully*, 272, 273.

210   One of the last scenes: Ibid., 274. Wellman wrote, "Burton had a heart attack from which he did not recover." Wellman remembered the heart attack correctly, but Steene made a recovery and continued working for two more years before passing away, April 21, 1929. His last picture was *Hell's Angels*, released in 1930.

211   During postproduction: Eyman, *Speed of Sound*, 335; Wellman, *Short Time for Insanity*, 178; Wellman Jr., *Man and His Wings*, 140.

211   The Wellman-Pomeroy team: Ibid.

211   It was common: Ibid.; Andrea Kalas, Paramount Archives, Restoration Notes, 100th Anniversary of Paramount Pictures booklet, Academy of Motion Picture Arts & Sciences, Randy Haberkamp, January 17 and 18, 2012.

211   After almost a year: Thomas, *Selznick*, 60; Wellman, *Short Time for Insanity*, 178, 179; Lasky, *I Blow My Own Horn*, 210.

214   Before his next assignment: Wellman, *Short Time for Insanity*, 177, 180.

215   The seemingly boundless success: Ibid., 178, 147.

216   Wellman received a call: Wellman Jr., *Man and His Wings*, 156; Wellman conversations with author.

216   *The Legion of the Condemned:* Ibid.; Frank Thompson and John Gallagher, *Wings* program article, 100th Anniversary of Paramount Pictures booklet, Academy of Motion Picture Arts & Sciences, Randy Haberkamp, January 17 and 18, 2012, 3.

216   Due to the fan mail: David Shipman, *The Great Movie Stars: The Golden Years* (New York: Bonanza, 1970), 120, 121; Thompson, *William A. Wellman*, 73.

217   Regrettably: Thompson, *Lost Films*, 218–21, 226.

218   Four days before: Eyman, *Speed of Sound*, 11; Brownlow, *Parade's Gone By*, 570.

218   Sound musical shorts: Brownlow, *Parade's Gone By*, 570; Eyman, *Speed of Sound*, 25; Daniel Blum, *A Pictorial History of the Silent Screen* (New York: G. P. Putnam's Sons, 1953), 323; Ted Sennett, *Warner Brothers Presents* (New Rochelle, NY: Arlington House, 1971), 24.

218   The Hollywood studios were in a panic: Ibid.; Eyman, *Speed of Sound*, 229.

218   They would have to spend: Eyman, *Speed of Sound*, 16, 17; Brownlow, *Parade's Gone By*, 568, 569; Jewell, *Golden Age of Cinema*, 3.

219   When Paramount enlisted: Wellman, *Growing Old Disgracefully*, 111.

219   The contract directors: Ibid.

225   "The film was": Interview with Buddy Rogers for *Wild Bill Hollywood Maverick* (1996).

225   One of the chancy ventures: *Variety*, September 26, 1928.

226   This film would mark: Wellman, *Growing Old Disgracefully*, 297.

226   *Beggars of Life* was thought to be: Brownlow, *Parade's Gone By*, 169, 356, 358.

227   Louise "Lulu" Brooks: Ibid.; Shipman, *Great Movie Stars*, 81–83; Brooks, *Lulu in Hollywood*, 21, 22.

228   When she was assigned *Beggars:* Brooks, *Lulu in Hollywood*, 21.

228   When filming commenced: Ibid.

229   Fortunately, an excellent: Brownlow, *Parade's Gone By*, 432; Thompson, *William A. Wellman*, 82, 83; Wellman Jr., *Man and His Wings*, 145, 146.

230   Wellman had met: Wellman, *Short Time for Insanity*, 107; Wellman, *Growing Old Disgracefully*, 18, 19; Wellman Jr., *Man and His Wings*, 74, 75.

230   Wellman's next film: Eyman, *Speed of Sound*, 227–29; Thompson, *William A. Wellman*, 82, 83.

230   The film premiered: Gail Kinn and Jim Piazza, *The Academy Awards: The Complete Unofficial History* (New York: Black Dog & Leventhal, 2002), 11; David Sheward, *The Big Book of Show Business Awards* (New York: Billboard, 1997), 4–6; Academy of Motion Picture Arts & Sciences.com: History of the First Academy Awards.

232   What did Wellman do: Wellman Jr., *Man and His Wings*, 153; Wellman conversations with author.

10. Pranks and Misdemeanors

235   The 1928 *Beggars of Life:* Jacumba Arts Council, Jacumba Hot Springs, California, U.S. Geological Survey, 1997; Wellman, *Growing Old Disgracefully*, 297–303.

240   Wellman's attempted reconciliation: Wellman, *Short Time for Insanity*, 180.

240   It was always Wellman's habit: Wellman, *Growing Old Disgracefully*, 255.

240   On a double date: Ibid., 256–61.

242   In June of 1929: Wellman, *Short Time for Insanity*, 184, 188, 194.

245   Later that evening: Author interviews with Charlie Barton in 1967 and 1971; Wellman conversations with author.

248   Myron set up an appointment: Wellman, *Growing Old Disgracefully*, 108.

248   Charlie Barton was sleeping: Author interviews with Charlie Barton in 1967 and 1971; Wellman conversations with author; Barton interview with John Gallagher, February 27, 1989.

249   In the words of John Andrew Gallagher: Interviews for *Wild Bill Hollywood Maverick* publicity booklet (1995/96).

249   Jesse Lasky's dream: Lasky, *I Blow My Own Horn*, 210.

250   Charlie Barton later said: Barton interview with John Gallagher.

250   Frank Thompson wrote: Thompson, *William A. Wellman*, 88.

250   In March of 1930: Wellman Jr., *Man and His Wings*, 156, 157; Victoria Wilson, *A Life of Barbara Stanwyck: Steel-True, 1907–1940* (New York: Simon & Schuster, 2013), 230.

11. I Ain't So Tough

253 After years of battles: Sennett, *Warner Brothers Presents*, 14–25.

254 Jack Warner later remarked: Jack Warner, *My First Hundred Years in Hollywood* (New York: Random House, 1965), 101, 102.

254 His studio's young, ambitious: Jewell, *Golden Age of Cinema*, 55, 56; Sennett, *Warner Brothers Presents*, 21.

254 In the late 1920s: Jewell, *Golden Age of Cinema*, 121; Thomas Doherty, *Hollywood's Censor* (New York: Columbia University Press, 2007), 52, 53, 56.

255 When a trio of scandals: Doherty, *Hollywood's Censor*, 33; Brownlow, *Parade's Gone By*, 39.

255 The sensational series of films: Sennett, *Warner Brothers Presents*, 21, 26.

256 A list that Wellman: Ibid., 27–55; Jewell, *Golden Age of Cinema*, 55.

256 Star development: Jewell, *Golden Age of Cinema*, 258.

257 Before starting: Wellman, *Growing Old Disgracefully*, 261.

257 "I needed a wife": Wellman, *Short Time for Insanity*, 180; Wellman, *Growing Old Disgracefully*, 15.

257 Crawford was a compatriot: Forney Museum of Transportation, Denver, Colorado, Amelia Earhart newsletter, biography, photos (1929 Women's Air Derby photo with Earhart, Ruth Elder, Florence "Pancho" Barnes, and Marjorie Crawford).

258 Although the story: Wellman, *Short Time for Insanity*, 28.

259 The director began: Gilbert Adair, *Flickers: An Illustrated Celebration of 100 Years of Cinema* (London: Faber & Faber, 1995), 72, 73.

260 While waiting: Wellman, *Growing Old Disgracefully*, 108; Thompson, *William A. Wellman*, 76, 77; Wellman conversations with author concerning the *Dirigible/Jump/Balloon Story* project.

261 Before his next film started: Wellman, *Growing Old Disgracefully*, 15; Celia Wellman Family History; Wellman conversations with author.

262 As usual: Wellman, *Short Time for Insanity*, 180.

262 Wellman's next film project: Wellman, *Growing Old Disgracefully*, 98–100.

266 Another *Public Enemy* example: Wellman's *Public Enemy* script notes regarding Louise Brooks playing Gwen Allen; Shipman, *Great Movie Stars*, 81–83.

266 When she returned: Ibid.; Brooks, *Lulu in Hollywood*, 21.

266 Now that we have reached: Wellman shooting scripts.

267 One of her biographers: *Monthly Film Bulletin*, July 1965.

267 Henri Langlois: R. Dixon Smith, "The Miracle of Louise Brooks," 1955.

268 No matter how: Shipman, *Great Movie Stars*, 263–67.

268 Wellman was shooting: Wellman, *Growing Old Disgracefully*, 177, 178.

268 One of the most powerful: Wellman, *Public Enemy* script.

269 It is impossible: Wellman, *Growing Old Disgracefully*, 14–18.

272 *Public Enemy* wrapped: Sennett, *Warner Brothers Presents*, 56; Jewell, *Golden Age of Cinema*, 203; Wellman, photo album with stories and advertisements.

272 Borrowed from Columbia Pictures: Wilson, *Life of Barbara Stanwyck*, 238,

240, 241, 292; Wellman quote during Q&A at London Film Festival, July 1972, and numerous other audience events.

273   In *Night Nurse:* Wellman, *Short Time for Insanity,* 229; Wellman, *Growing Old Disgracefully,* 290, 291; Wilson, *Life of Barbara Stanwyck,* 238.

273   Here comes that name again: Wellman script pages for *Night Nurse;* Brooks, *Lulu in Hollywood,* 21.

275   On July 28, 1931: "Mad Dog Coll," *New York Times,* July 28, 1931; Maltin, *Classic Movie Guide;* TCM Notes: *Star Witness* (1931).

276   Bette Davis: Whitney Stine, *Mother Goddam: The Story of the Career of Bette Davis* (New York: Hawthorne, 1974).

276   "reckless and wild": "Billy Wellman was reckless and wild . . . one of the three or four best": Fairbanks letter to John Gallagher, March 13, 1978.

276   *The Conquerors* (1932): Thompson, *William A. Wellman,* 128.

277   John Wayne had reached stardom: Shipman, *Great Movie Stars,* 149.

277   There was so much protest: Carlson, *Flying on Film,* 55, 56.

277   A bright light: Shipman, *Great Movie Stars,* 46–48.

280   Michael Curtiz: According to *Film Daily;* TCM Notes: *Safe in Hell* (1931).

280   Dorothy Mackaill: Dave Kehr, "A Short Career in Lurid Hollywood," *New York Times,* January 6, 2012; Wellman conversations with author.

280   Three of the fine: African American Registry, Minneapolis, Minnesota, newsletter issues: Biographies of Nina Mae McKinney, Clarence Muse, and Noble Mark Johnson.

283   As an example: Wilson, *Life of Barbara Stanwyck,* 304.

284   Mizner's Warner Bros. career: Edward Dean Sullivan, *The Fabulous Wilson Mizner* (New York: Henkle, 1935); Alva Johnston, *The Legendary Mizners* (New York: Farrar, Straus & Young, 1953).

285   Ruth Chatterton was a star: Wellman, *Growing Old Disgracefully,* 109–11.

286   George Brent: Shipman, *Great Movie Stars,* 106–9.

286   The studio bosses were not pleased: Wellman conversations with author; author's meeting with Loretta Young, November 10, 1996; John Gallagher, "Rediscovering *Midnight Mary,*" *Films in Review,* March/April 1995.

12. The Neon Violin

289   William Wellman had been married: Wellman, *Growing Old Disgracefully,* 315, 316; Wellman, *Short Time for Insanity,* 180, 181.

289   Bobby Jones: Wellman, *Short Time for Insanity,* 74–77; *Bobby Jones: The Complete Warner Bros. Shorts Collection* (1931): Warner Bros. Archive with editorial reviews and list of WB stars on film.

292   In early 1933: John Kobal, *Gotta Sing Gotta Dance: A Pictorial History of Film Musicals* (London: Hamlyn, 1971), 120–23, 128; Wellman, *Short Time for Insanity,* 257–60.

293   "In an era of breadlines": Tony Thomas and Tim Terry, *The Busby Berkeley Book* (New York: New York Graphic Society, 1973), 9.

293   "She looked at me": Wellman, *Short Time for Insanity*.

295   "I ran out of patience first": Wellman wrote that he didn't go into the ladies' room. He later recanted. Dottie always remembered that he did come into the ladies' room.

295   Seeing the director across the street: Dottie recalled the incident in later years.

296   The next day: Frank Miller, TCM newsletter, *Gold Diggers of 1933*.

296   On the first date: Dottie's recollections to author and family members.

298   When he wasn't shooting: Ibid.; Wellman conversations with author; "Boxing Venue Had Heavyweight in Its Corner," *Los Angeles Times*, February 10, 2008, B2.

298   Wellman always: Wellman conversations with author.

300   In 1933: Wilson, *Life of Barbara Stanwyck*, 353, 354.

301   The role of Sally: Dottie's recollections; Wellman, *Growing Old Disgracefully*, 70, 71.

301   Dottie was a dancer: Ibid.

301   Wellman said to Dottie: Ibid.; Thompson, *William A. Wellman*, 140.

301   It was rumored around: Dottie's recollections.

301   With a twenty-four-day: Production schedule in shooting script.

304   *Female* was already in production: *Film Daily*, August 8, 1933; Brian Cady, TCM article on *Female* (1933); daily production reports from the Warner Brothers Collection, Cinema & Television Archives, University of Southern California.

304   *College Coach:* Script notes.

13. Looking for Trouble

307   Bill and Dottie: Dottie's recollections; Wellman conversations with author.

308   In *Looking for Trouble*: Shipman, *Great Movie Stars*, 526, 527; Dorothy Townsend, obituary of William Wellman, *Los Angeles Times*, December 10, 1975: "[Wellman] referred to animosity between himself and Spencer Tracy saying that when we got together, there was usually a fistfight." In *Spencer Tracy: A Biography*, James Curtis wrote that after punches were thrown and the two were separated: "Wellman later said, [Tracy] and I just didn't like each other . . . we had a lot of fistfights, and I always beat him because he'd start talking and I didn't talk"; *San Francisco Chronicle*, Datebook section, May 17, 2013; Thompson, *William A. Wellman*, 147.

308   Mike Lally: TCM Overview: Mike Lally.

309   Two weeks later: Classic Images (website), "Films of the Golden Age," "Hollywood Hotspots," "Trocadero Nightclub": "While drinking at the Troc . . . [Wellman] made a disparaging remark about Loretta Young and was promptly flattened by her pal, Spencer Tracy."

310   "I have seen hound dogs": Wellman, *Short Time for Insanity*, 180.

310   Unlike his previous marriage proposals: Wellman conversations with author; Dottie's recollections.

311   In the 1930s: Don Dwiggins, *Hollywood Pilot: The Biography of Paul Mantz* (New York: Doubleday, 1967), 60, 77; Wellman, *Short Time for Insanity*, 256; Wellman marriage certificate; Dottie's recollections of wedding and honeymoon.

311   This flight of fancy: Richard Schickel, *The Men Who Made the Movies* (New York: Atheneum, 1975), 211.

312   The newlyweds: *Wellman Family History*; two visits by author—one with Dottie—to 6747 Milner Road, Whitley Heights, Hollywood.

312   Since Wellman did not: *Celia Wellman Family History*; author visits to Milner Road house.

313   Celia's choices: Kobal, *Gotta Sing Gotta Dance.*

313   It happened: *Wellman Family History*; author visit to house at 722 Linden Drive, Beverly Hills.

313   The novel: Wellman, *Growing Old Disgracefully*, 289, 290; John Douglas Eames, *The Paramount Story* (New York: Crown, 1985), 100; Andre Sennwold, "The Mysterious Disappearance of President Stanley in *The President Vanishes*, at the Paramount," *New York Times*, December 8, 1934; Shipman, *Great Movie Stars*, 58–60; J. A. Aberdeen, The Society of Independent Motion Picture Producers: Walter Wanger biography and film history.

315   With films like: Shipman, *Great Movie Stars*, 482–84.

316   In August of 1934: TCM Overview (in association with Leonard Maltin, *Classic Movie Guide*, 2014): cast, synopsis, notes, trivia, *Variety* review; Wellman, *Short Time for Insanity*, 229–32.

320   For $26,000: *Wellman Family History*; Pacific Coast Architecture Database (PCAD): Roland Coate.

320   With the success: Thomas, *Selznick*, 73, 95, 351–53.

321   The story of Mexican outlaw: Wellman, *Growing Old Disgracefully*, 153, 154: "I wanted Bob Taylor who had just finished . . . *Small Town Girl*." Wellman had met and liked Taylor but *Small Town Girl* came after *The Robin Hood of El Dorado*, 155–59, 163, 168–73.

324   It took four months: Thompson, *William A. Wellman*, 155, 156.

325   *Tarzan Returns:* Ibid., 161; Wellman conversations with author and Johnny Weissmuller (1950s).

14. Passions and Prizes

327   "I interviewed them all": Wellman, *Growing Old Disgracefully*, 19, 20.

327   When Wellman signed with Selznick: Ibid., 20–22; TCM Overview: *A Star Is Born.*

328   Wellman's movie models: TCM Overview: *A Star Is Born;* Wellman, *Growing Old Disgracefully*, 32.

331   The inspiration for this sequence: Wellman conversations with author.

332   Wellman's father: Ibid.; *Wellman Family History*.

333   The screwball comedy: Thomas, *Selznick*, 118–20; Wellman, *Growing Old Disgracefully*, 37, 39.

334   On a $1 million budget: Thompson, *William A. Wellman*, 173.

335   *Nothing Sacred* wrapped production: Rudy Behlmer, *Memo from David O. Selznick* (New York: Viking, 1972): letter to Henry Luce.

336   The now classic picture: TCM Overview: *The Adventures of Tom Sawyer*, director credits; Thomas, *Selznick*, 164.

336   Wellman began a lifelong habit: *Wellman Family History*.

336   The time was right: Carlson, *Flying on Film*, 59; Farmer, *Celluloid Wings*, 121–24.

337   The offer opened the door: Jewell, *Golden Age of Cinema*, 53, 54; Gomery, *Hollywood Studio System*, 87–89.

339   Unlike Wellman's term contract: Farmer, *Celluloid Wings*, 122, 123; Dwiggins, *Hollywood Pilot*, 62–66; Thompson, *William A. Wellman*, 179–81.

341   The director did not want: TCM Overview: *Men with Wings*; Wellman conversations with author.

341   Over three months: Ibid.

341   The work was difficult: Dwiggins, *Hollywood Pilot*, 82.

342   Frank Thompson reported: Thompson, *William A. Wellman*, 181.

15. The Golden Year

345   The year was 1939: Sheward, *Big Book of Show Business Awards*: 1939; Kinn and Piazza, *Complete History of Oscar*: 1939; Jack Mathews, *Los Angeles Times*, January 1, 1989: 1939; Mark A. Vieira, *Majestic Hollywood: The Greatest Films of 1939* (Philadelphia: Running Press, 2013).

345   So, where was Wellman: *Wellman Family History*.

345   From a Percival Christopher Wren novel: B.R.C., "Remake of "Beau Geste" with Gary Cooper Has Premiere at the Paramount," *New York Times*, August 3, 1939; TCM Overview: *Beau Geste* (1939), synopsis, notes, articles, reviews.

348   Wellman produced: Wellman, *Growing Old Disgracefully*, 240–55.

353   In a manner of speaking: Ibid.; Kinn and Piazza, *Complete History of Oscar*: 1939.

354   Originally, the director: Thompson, *William A. Wellman*, 189.

354   Born in Richmond, Surrey, England: Shipman, *Great Movie Stars*, 117–20.

355   From the beginning: Wellman, *Short Time for Insanity*, 203.

355   When the remainder: Ibid.; Patrick McGilligan, *Film Crazy* (New York: St. Martin's/Griffin, 2000), 246.

355   This story got around: Ibid.

356   Production began: Paramount World Premiere booklet, *The Light That Failed* (1939): complete cast, crew, story and vital statistics (production notes).

357   Just as had happened: Wellman script notes.

357   Back at the studio: Schickel, *Men Who Made the Movies*, 222, 223.

357 In this particular scene: Ibid.

357 They returned to the set: Ibid., 223.

358 "I recorded": Thompson, *William A. Wellman*, 194.

358 What better way: Kinn and Piazza, *Complete History of Oscar*: 1939; Thomas, *Selznick*, 155, 156, 164.

359 Bob Thomas: Thomas, *Selznick*, 164.

360 On December 11, 1938: Ibid., 150, 151.

360 George Cukor was reported: *Wellman Family History* with notes, photos; Wellman conversations with author.

16. The Road to Ox-Bow

363 What better place: *Wellman Family History* with notes, photos; Wellman conversations with author; Wellman, *Short Time for Insanity*, 92.

363 Since they were only: *Wellman Family History*, photos of neighborhood—1935 and 1942.

363 Wellman was at the forefront: Wanamaker and Nudelman, *Early Hollywood*, 85; Robert J. Wagner with Scott Eyman, *You Must Remember This* (New York: Viking, 2014), 63, 66.

363 Homes were built: *Wellman Family History*.

364 The Capras: Frank Capra, *The Name Above the Title* (New York: Macmillan, 1971), 424.

364 There were non-neighborhood: *Wellman Family History*.

365 Between *The Light That Failed*: Ibid.

365 They dined at Boston's Statler Hotel: *Celia Wellman Family History* with photos and restaurant menus; "The Boston Park Plaza Hotel History," Boston Park Plaza Hotel website.

366 Roland E. Coate: *Architecture in Los Angeles: A Complete Guide, 1985*, 195; *Wellman Family History*.

367 Wellman would make: Thompson, *William A. Wellman*, 194, 195.

368 The facts say: Ibid.; John Gallagher and Frank Thompson, *Nothing Sacred: The Cinema of William Wellman* (unpublished, Men with Wings Press); *Reaching for the Sun* (1941).

368 This author believes: *Reaching for the Sun* script and production notes.

369 As usual: Wellman script notes.

370 In spite of the fact: Shipman, *Great Movie Stars*, 384–87; TCM Overview: Joel McCrea family biography.

371 When *Reaching for the Sun*: *Wellman Family History*.

372 Stanwyck would play: Wellman script notes for *Reaching for the Sun* and *The Great Man's Lady*; Wellman conversations with author; John Chapman, New York *Daily News*, December 6, 1940.

372 Wellman's dislike: Wellman, *Growing Old Disgracefully*, 249; TCM Biography: Brian Donlevy; Wellman shooting script for *Pioneer Woman* (retitled *The Great Man's Lady*).

375   *NEWS FLASH:* Dwiggins, *Hollywood Pilot*, 146; Michael Sragow, *Victor Fleming: An American Movie Master* (New York: Pantheon, 2008), 388–90; Wellman, *Growing Old Disgracefully*, 90, 228, 229; Slim Keith with Annette Tapert, *Slim* (New York: Simon & Schuster, 1990), 83, 99; Wellman and Dottie conversations with author.

376   Dressed in sporting clothes: Involved people viewed the dress code differently. Some saw the casual dress as mostly leather clothing. Wellman and Dottie remembered wearing more sporty wear without the leather of future motorcycle clubs.

376   When Dottie became pregnant: *Wellman Family History.*

377   *Roxie* was based: TCM Overview: *Roxie Hart* (1942), cast and crew, synopsis, notes, articles, reviews.

377   "It's tough enough just to direct": National Film Institute retrospective, London, July, 1972: Q&A with audience; Wellman conversations with author.

378   "He developed a second sight": Wellman, *Short Time for Insanity*, 51; Wellman, *Growing Old Disgracefully*, 142–44.

379   Even though *Roxie:* Wellman, *Short Time for Insanity*, 27, 28, 41–47.

380   While Bill and Dottie: Ibid., 28, 29, 205, 206; Wellman, *Growing Old Disgracefully*, 81–84, 112–14, 307; Wellman conversations with author.

382   Henry Fonda: Shipman, *Great Movie Stars*, 202–5.

384   "Congratulations on an excellent": Wellman, *Growing Old Disgracefully*, 307.

384   "It fell flat": Wellman, *Short Time for Insanity*, 29.

384   Although the picture: Kinn and Piazza, *Complete History of Oscar.* 1943.

385   Clint Eastwood told this author: From an event in Carmel Valley, California, May 1992.

385   "I don't think": Wellman, *Growing Old Disgracefully*, 114.

17. Picture Patchwork

387   After *The Ox-Bow Incident:* Vincent LoBrutto, *Becoming Film Literate: The Art and Craft of Motion Pictures* (Westport, CT: Praeger, 2005), 292.

387   The first of Wellman's must-make: Curtis Lee Hanson, interview with Wellman, *Cinema*, July 1966, 22, 24; John Gallagher, "William Wellman (Part Two)," *Films in Review*, June/July 1982, 324, 326; Carlson, *Flying on Film*, 103; Farmer, *Celluloid Wings*, 178.

388   The picture is another romantic triangle: TCM Overview: *Thunder Birds*, cast, notes, articles; Thompson, *William A. Wellman*, 217.

389   Screenwriter-author Gene Fowler: Denver Press Club, Historical Archive: Gene Fowler; *Architecture in Los Angeles: A Complete Guide*, Claude Knight Smithley (472 N. Barrington Avenue, Los Angeles, CA, 90049); Wellman, *Growing Old Disgracefully*, 134–40.

391   Wellman thought: Wyatt McCrea, the Joel and Frances McCrea Ranch Foundation.

392   Wellman found his leading ladies: TCM Overview: Maureen O'Hara and

Thomas Mitchell; *Linda Darnell: Hollywood's Fallen Angel* (1999), documentary film directed by Hillary Atkin, written by Monica Regal.

393   Production of *Buffalo Bill:* TCM Overview: production notes; 20th Century-Fox production reports.

393   The exciting action sequence: Personal audiotapes of William Wellman; Wellman conversations with author.

393   In Anthony Quinn's early film career: TCM Overview: biography, filmography.

394   Further disapproval: Maureen O'Hara interview with author at the home of her brother, Charles FitzSimons, in Brentwood, California (1995).

394   To brush the final stroke: Wellman's *Buffalo Bill* shooting script and the film.

395   After an eighteen-year association: The Society of Independent Motion Picture Producers: Hunt Stromberg, by J. A. Aberdeen; Jeff Stafford, TCM Overview: *Lady of Burlesque.*

396   The cast is delightful: Hart, *Hollywood Walk of Fame*, 212.

396   The picture becomes a tribute: Gary F. Taylor review, "An Almost Forgotten Gem," *The Guardian*, January 1, 2004.

397   Still, the dialogue remains provocative: Wellman script and film.

398   *Lady of Burlesque* provided: Kinn and Piazza, *Complete History of Oscar.* 1943.

398   Wellman completed filming: *Wellman Family History.*

398   Bad news hit: Thomas, *Selznick*, 208, 209; *The Memoirs of William Wellman*: list of Myron Selznick clients.

398   It had been titled: Written by Wellman and John Monk Saunders but their story was never produced.

399   Wallace Beery: Shipman, *Great Movie Stars*, 53–56; Wellman, *Growing Old Disgracefully*, 325.

400   In August of 1944: Wellman, *Short Time for Insanity*, 81–94, 232–35.

400   It was producer Lester Cowan: Ibid.; Burt A. Folkart, obituary of Lester Cowan, *Los Angeles Times*, October 25, 1990.

404   The casting of the film: TCM Overview: *The Story of G.I. Joe*, notes.

406   She had to be talked into: Ibid.; Wellman conversations with author; Dottie's recollections.

406   James Agee: TCM Overview: notes, reviews.

407   Frank Thompson: Thompson, *William A. Wellman*, 215.

407   The film was nominated: Kinn and Piazza, *Complete History of Oscar.* 1945; Sheward, *Big Book of Show Business Awards*, 1945: National Board of Review's Ten Best Films.

407   In 2009: Wellman, *Short Time for Insanity*, 234.

407   The film premiered: Ibid., 235; review summary by Hal Erickson, *New York Times*, May 5, 2014; *This Day in History*, April 18, 1945: Obituary of Journalist Ernie Pyle; NBC News report, from New York, updated February 3, 2008, provided photo of Ernie Pyle shortly after he was killed by a Japanese machine-gun bullet on the island of Ie Shima, April 18, 1945.

407   Wellman was approached: *Hollywood Reporter*, April 1946; Roland W. Hoagland, *The Blue Book of Aviation: A Biographical History of American Aviation*

(Los Angeles: Hoagland Company, 1932), 234; Farmer, *Celluloid Wings*, 238–41; "Wellman's Gallant Journey," San Diego Historical Society: Montgomery Memorial at Otay Mesa.

408   After the death: *The Memoirs of William Wellman*; *Wellman Family History*; letters between Wellman and Coryell, Wellman files.

408   Production began: Wellman script notes.

409   In the leading role: TCM Overviews: Glenn Ford, Evelyn Keyes, Janet Blair; Wellman script notes; Wellman conversations with author.

410   It is clear: *Wellman Family History*; Wellman shooting script and film info.

412   *Magic Town*: Shipman, *Great Movie Stars*, 506–9; TCM Overviews: *Magic Town*, Jane Wyman, Robert Riskin; Capra, *Name Above the Title*, 378; McGilligan, *Film Crazy*, 254, 255; Jane Wyman interview with author for *Wild Bill Hollywood Maverick* (1996).

413   "It stinks": Thompson, *William A. Wellman*, 219.

413   In March of 1946: *New York Times*, March 5, 1946; TCM Overviews: Dana Andrews and Gene Tierney.

414   Leftist demonstrations started: TCM Overview: *The Iron Curtain* (1948), notes, articles, reviews.

414   The Gouzenko affair: *The Defection of Igor Gouzenko: Report of the Canadian Royal Commission* (Intelligence Series, Vol. 3, No. 6), Aegean Park, 1996.

417   Several days of filming: Wellman script notes and production report; Lone Pine Chamber of Commerce (lonepinechamber.org) and Lone Pine Film History Museum: *Yellow Sky*.

417   Anne Baxter played: Wellman conversations with author. Author present during the fight scene; Thompson, *William A. Wellman*, 223.

418   Gregory Peck accepted it: Peck conversation with author on location of *MacArthur* (1976); Michael Freeland, *Gregory Peck* (New York: William Morrow, 1980), 92, 93.

418   A substantial number of favorable reviews: *Variety*, December 31, 1947: "Lamar Trotti has put together an ace screenplay . . . then proceeded with showmanly production guidance to make *Sky* a winner. The direction by William A. Wellman is vigorous, potently emphasizing every element of suspense and action, and displaying the cast to the utmost advantage. There's never a faltering scene as sequence after sequence is unfolded at a swift pace."; Bosley Crowther, *New York Times*, February 2, 1949: "in the best realistic Western style. . . . And William Wellman has directed for steel-spring tension from beginning to end . . . they have made it tough, taut and good."

419   A number of critics compared: Wellman, *Growing Old Disgracefully*, 174, 175.

419   "I should feel very flattered": Ibid.

419   While on the subject of wind: Story told at Sony Pictures Studio during postproduction for *Wild Bill Hollywood Maverick* (1996).

18. Battleground *Sends a Message*

421   After the completion: *Wellman Family History.*

421   Dore Schary: *Variety: 75 Year Anniversary of Metro-Goldwyn-Mayer,* November 19, 1999, 6, 10.

421   While head of production at RKO: Ibid.; Lawrence H. Suid, *Guts & Glory: Great American War Movies* (Reading, MA: Addison-Wesley, 1978), 74–81.

421   Schary and Pirosh: Ibid.; TCM Overview: notes, articles.

423   An addition: Wellman script notes.

423   James Arness: James E. Wise, Jr., and Paul W. Wilderson III, *Stars in Khaki* (Annapolis, MD: Naval Institute Press, 2000), 184, 185.

423   Denise Darcel: Suid, *Guts & Glory,* 78.

423   Production was completed: MGM production reports; Wellman's script.

424   James Whitmore: Tells story of nomination in *Wild Bill Hollywood Maverick* (1996).

424   Dore Schary was vindicated: *Variety: 75 Year Anniversary of Metro-Goldwyn-Mayer,* November 19, 1999, 10.

424   Wellman "strongly" expressed: Wellman, *Growing Old Disgracefully,* 80; personal audiotapes of William Wellman; Wellman conversations with author.

424   *The Happy Years* (1950): TCM Overview: notes, articles.

425   Wellman liked the idea: Wellman script notes.

425   Darryl Hickman's brother: TCM Articles: Dwayne Hickman and Robert Wagner; Wellman script notes.

425   Filming was completed: TCM Overview: *The Happy Years* (1950), original print information.

425   Schary wanted Wellman: Curtis Lee Hanson, interview with Wellman, *Cinema,* July 1966, 28.

426   *The Next Voice You Hear . . .* (1950): Wellman script notes; TCM Overview: production details.

427   Schary's next lecture: TCM Overview: *It's a Big Country* (1952), articles.

428   Dore Schary called: Wellman, *Short Time for Insanity,* 230, 229; TCM Overview: *Across the Wide Missouri* (1951).

429   By June of 1950: Wellman conversations with author, who was present on the *Missouri* flight and locations for the run of the picture.

433   Clark Gable: Wellman, *Growing Old Disgracefully,* 90, 91; author's conversations with Clark Gable.

436   There was an empty seat: Author's story; Wellman, *Growing Old Disgracefully,* 42, 43.

437   Indrisano became a personal friend: Johnny Indrisano: TCM Filmography; *IMDb* biography; Wellman, *Growing Old Disgracefully,* 42.

438   Ever since his boxing days: Johnny Indrisano: TCM Filmography; *IMDb* biography; Wellman, *Growing Old Disgracefully,* 198–201.

440   Finally, Brooklyn: TCM Biography: Timothy Carey.

442   Pat was an excellent rider: Petrine Day Mitchum with Audrey Pavia, *Hollywood Hoofbeats* (Irvine, CA: Bowtie Press, 2005), 89–92.

442   Production completed: TCM Articles: *Across the Wide Missouri.*

442   The year was 1950: Capra, *Name Above the Title,* 424, 266, 267; Gomery, *Hollywood Studio System,* 193.

443   The Hollywood film industry: Gomery, *Hollywood Studio System,* 193–95, 198–200.

444   World War II had brought a change: Doherty, *Hollywood's Censor,* 248; Jake Hinkson, *Noir City* (Film Noir Foundation, 2013), 15; LoBrutto, *Becoming Film Literate,* 122, 123.

444   In 1948: Doherty, *Hollywood's Censor,* 228.

444   If all this wasn't enough: Ibid.

444   The final curtain: Ibid: Television.

444   Back to the Capra-Wellman dinner: Capra, *Name Above the Title,* 404, 424; Wellman conversations with author and audiences at Q&As.

445   Robert Taylor's Bucky Wyatt: Wellman script; Wellman conversations with author.

446   Following the same plan: Ibid.; Molly Gregory, "Guts and Grace: The Untold Story of Stuntwomen in the Movies" (excerpt from unpublished manuscript); Dennis McLellan, obituary of Polly Burson, *Los Angeles Times,* April 16, 2006.

447   Wellman liked telling: Wellman, *Growing Old Disgracefully,* 203–6.

447   Production began: Thompson, *William A. Wellman,* 237.

447   Robert Taylor: Wellman, *Growing Old Disgracefully,* 203, 205, 206.

448   The film trumpeted: Wellman script notes; *Wellman Family History.*

19. Goodbye MGM, Hello John Wayne

451   In January of 1952: Author present at Schary gathering.

451   *My Man and I:* TCM Articles.

452   Wendell Corey and William Wellman: TCM Overview: Wendell Corey; Wellman conversations with author.

453   Darryl Zanuck's: *The Memoirs of William Wellman*; Wellman conversations with author; *Wellman Family History.*

453   Dore Schary and Wellman's comradeship: Ibid.

453   The closer their friendship became: Doherty, *Hollywood's Censor,* 297; Lee Server, *Robert Mitchum: Baby, I Don't Care* (New York: St. Martin's, 2001), 131, 133.

453   Wellman, on the other hand: Wellman, *Growing Old Disgracefully,* 81; Wellman, *Short Time for Insanity,* 205.

454   The final blow: Durant and Durant, *Pictorial History of American Presidents,* 288: Adlai Stevenson; Wellman, *Short Time for Insanity,* 206–8; Wellman's and Dottie's recollections of dinner guests.

454   Bill and Dottie: Wellman, *Short Time for Insanity*; Wellman's and Dottie's recollections of dinner guests.

454   As the Schary convention-like atmosphere: Ibid.

455   The Wellman children: *Wellman Family History.*

455   The Wellman clan: Ojai Valley Inn & Spa: Resort history; *Wellman Family History.*

456   On this trip: Author present at lunch meeting; Marvine Howe, obituary of Ernest K. Gann, *New York Times*, December 21, 1991.

456   Based on a true incident: Ibid.

456   In the early 1950s: TCM Biography: Burt Lancaster; TCM Biography: Kirk Douglas; Randy Roberts and James S. Olson, *John Wayne: American* (London: Bison, 1997), 406–9.

456   Robert Fellows: "It was a sight to behold," story quote told by Michael Wayne, son of John Wayne, during interview (1995) for *Wild Bill Hollywood Maverick* (1996).

458   Wellman had taken a liking: Author with Wellman at the initial meeting with Mike "Touch" Connors.

458   Wellman was so married: Wellman, *Growing Old Disgracefully*, 226; TCM guest programmer David Mamet, March 22, 2007: "*Island in the Sky* is one of the great flying films." He had also made the same statement in his play (the Afterword) *David Mamet: A Life in the Theatre*, produced in 1977.

458   Ernest Gann: Gann conversations with author (1953); "Wild Bill," *AMC Magazine* (September 1999), 9; "There was elegance . . . masterpiece," quote from Gann, also in *Wild Bill Hollywood Maverick* (1996).

458   *Island in the Sky* was a hit: "The Top Box Office Hits of 1953," *Variety*, January 13, 1954; Curtis Lee Hanson, interview with Wellman, *Cinema*, July 1966, 24.

459   Duke purchased the property: TCM Articles: *The High and the Mighty*; Michael Wayne conversation with author (1995).

459   The director was concerned: *The Memoirs of William Wellman*; Forest Lawn Memorial Park Obituary: Archie Stout, March 10, 1973; Curtis Lee Hanson, interview with Wellman, *Cinema*, July 1966, 25.

459   When Jack Warner: Wellman, *Growing Old Disgracefully*, 225, 226; Wellman conversations with author and audiences at Q&As.

459   Gann and Wellman: Wellman, *Growing Old Disgracefully*, 74; TCM Articles: *The High and the Mighty*; McGilligan, *Film Crazy*, 242.

459   On *The High and the Mighty:* Thompson, *William A. Wellman*, 245.

460   This directorial problem: Ibid.; Wellman quote from *Merv Griffin Show*, taping on March 21, 1975; Schickel, *Men Who Made the Movies*, 200.

460   "Just before production": Thompson, *William A. Wellman*, 246.

460   *The High and the Mighty* became: TCM Articles; Richard Egan, friend and neighbor, conversations with author; Michael Wayne conversations with author regarding Ronald Reagan.

461   William Shiffrin: TCM Articles ("Stack gave the approval for his agent to pester Wellman"); TCM Biography: Robert Stack; Robert Stack interview with author for *Wild Bill Hollywood Maverick* (1996).

462   There was one more: Wellman, *Growing Old Disgracefully*, 74, 75.

462   On occasion: *Wellman Family History.*

463   Just when all the casting: Michael Wayne interview with author for *Wild Bill Hollywood Maverick* (1996); TCM Notes: *The High and the Mighty*.

463   Jack Warner was ready: Author was present at meeting with Warner.

463   Wellman was not impressed: TCM Notes: *The High and the Mighty*; TCM Articles: production details.

463   Most of the large cast: Ibid.

464   It is a curious fact: Thomas, *Selznick*, 140–54, 156, 158, 159.

464   *The High and the Mighty* was loaded: TCM Articles; Michael Wayne interview with author regarding box office record, "fastest return of negative cost."

464   Not all the pundits: Reviews in *Commonweal*, July 16, 1954 ("the novel and the movie"); *New York Times*, July 1, 1954 ("All are fabricated characters"); Richard Griffin, *Los Angeles Times*, July 1954 ("an unbelievably long trip").

465   With all its many achievements: A short list of all-star "disaster" epics since *The High and the Mighty*: *Zero Hour* (1957), *A Night to Remember* (1958), *Voyage to the Bottom of the Sea* (1961), *Airport* (1970), *The Poseidon Adventure* (1972), *Skyjacked* (1972), *Earthquake* (1974), *The Towering Inferno* (1974), *Airport 1975* (1974), *Airport 77* (1977), *Avalanche* (1978), *Executive Decision* (1996), *Titanic* (1997), *Air Force One* (1997), *The Perfect Storm* (2000), *Poseidon* (2006), *United 93* (2006), *Snakes on a Plane* (2006), *Nonstop* (2014).

465   Wellman's good luck: Author interview with Michael Wayne (1995); Wellman, *Short Time for Insanity*, 96, 97; TCM notes, article, print information: *The Ring of Fear*.

466   As the success: Wellman, *Short Time for Insanity*, 98, 99; Curtis Lee Hanson, interview with Wellman, *Cinema*, July 1966, 30; Schickel, *Men Who Made the Movies*, 237, 238.

467   *The Track of the Cat*: Thompson, *William A. Wellman*, 248.

469   Robert Mitchum recalled: Server, *Robert Mitchum*, 259.

469   The frigid temperatures: Author interview with Robert Mitchum (1995) for *Wild Bill Hollywood Maverick* (1996); Tim Wellman, friend of Alfalfa Switzer and witness to the prank, conversation with author.

470   On another occasion: Author present on the set and witness to Alfalfa's wooden casket prank.

470   Wellman brought: *Wellman Family History*.

470   "I started out like a racehorse": *Short Time for Insanity*, 96; Wellman, *Growing Old Disgracefully*, 317, 318; Wellman script notes.

471   In the early days: *Growing Old Disgracefully*, 318.

471   This story is gleaned: Ibid.; Wellman conversations with author; author phone conversation with Andrew McLaglen (1995); author interview with Michael Wayne (1995); author interview with Robert Mitchum (1995); Server, *Robert Mitchum*, 281–84.

474   "We were working": Wellman quote from *Growing Old Disgracefully*, 92.

474   The Wellman-Bogart relationship: Ibid., 91.

474   During Bogie's visit: Ibid., 92, 93; TCM Overview: *Blood Alley*, production details.

475   Wellman wasted no time: TCM Overview, notes, articles: *Good-Bye, My Lady*; author interview (1995) with Sidney Poitier for *Wild Bill Hollywood Maverick* (1996); author interview with Michael Wayne (1995); conversations with Tim Wellman, who was on the location for the run of the picture; Wellman conversations with author; Wellman, *Short Time for Insanity*, 97, 98.

477   "Now, don't misunderstand me": Ibid.

477   John Gallagher wrote: Thompson and Gallagher, *Nothing Sacred: The Cinema of William A. Wellman*; *Good-bye, My Lady*.

20. The Final Straw

480   The director first took: *The Memoirs of William Wellman*; Wellman conversations with author.

480   The year was 1955: *C'est la Guerre* script, notes, production report; Wellman conversations with author; author present throughout filming.

480   The director wrote the story: Wellman, *Short Time for Insanity*, 29, 30–36.

485   For the starring role: Richard Griffith and Arthur Mayer, *The Movies* (New York: Bonanza, 1957), 423; Wellman conversations with author; author present throughout preproduction and production.

485   The director next turned to: Wellman conversations with author; author present through preproduction and production; TCM Biography: Paul Newman: "The picture [*The Silver Chalice*, 1955] was critically dismissed. Newman considered it such a personal embarrassment that he took out a full page ad . . . apologizing."

485   The director and future icon: Wellman conversations with author and family.

485   Warner began pushing: Hart, *Hollywood Walk of Fame*, 368; TCM filmography: Etchika Choureau.

486   Since one of the top roles: Wellman conversations with author; author conversations with Warner Bros. executives (September 1956).

487   With time running out: Author present at casting session.

487   The director built: Wellman conversations with author; shooting script notes, production reports; author present on location.

488   For the important position: Orriss, *When Hollywood Ruled the Skies*, 114.

488   In a letter to Warner Bros. executive: Letter on file, Warner Bros. Archives at the USC Cinema-Television Library; author conversation with executive Charles Greenlaw.

488   For Wellman's second choice: Orriss, *When Hollywood Ruled the Skies*, 112–15; Dwiggins, *Hollywood Pilot*, 240.

488   Principal photography began: Author present.

490   Tab Hunter was there: *Wild Bill Hollywood Maverick*.

490   Actor Tom Laughlin: Ibid.

491   Filming was completed: Author present; Wellman conversations with author.

491   Wellman refused: Ibid.; McGilligan, *Film Crazy*, 243.

491   Over time: Wellman shooting script TCM Notes: *Lafayette Escadrille* (1958).

491   When Wellman began work: Warner Bros. financial reports in Wellman file; TCM Articles; Poem Hunter biography of Guy Trosper.

492   Warner Bros. had had: TCM Articles: *Battle Cry* (1955); Wellman script notes.

492   The director viewed: Wellman conversations with author; Wellman script notes, production reports, financial reports.

493   When casting for the picture: TCM Articles.

493   To thumb his nose: Author present throughout production.

495   "Put her back on the picture, at once": Wellman conversation with author re: note; author present on set.

495   The director now told his assisstant: Author present.

496   Stuart Whitman remembered: Author phone conversation with Whitman (2013).

496   One exciting piece of action: Author present.

496   Oftentimes: Ibid.

497   Warner Bros. casting: Ibid.

497   In that same year: Hart, *Hollywood Walk of Fame*, 368; author conversation with Hunter on set of documentary taping in 2013, *Tab Hunter Confidential* (2015).

497   To take advantage: Ibid.

497   *Darby's Rangers* was released: Warner Bros. financial reports in Wellman file.

498   Released in March of 1958: Ibid.

498   Wellman was devastated: Wellman, *Growing Old Disgracefully*, 132, 133: "It caused my abdication from the moving picture business"; "it developed in me a hatred . . . as long as I live"; Wellman, *Short Time for Insanity*, 36: "a bad picture . . . your eternal badge of embarrassment"; Curtis Lee Hanson, interview with Wellman, *Cinema*, July 1966, 25: "The thing that broke my heart."

498   He asked Bill Jr.: Wellman and author drove to Warner Bros. Studio.

499   They walked past the soundstages: Wellman conversations with author.

499   There was not much conversation: Wellman and author together; Warner and Wellman exchange heard by author.

21. The Flame Is Flickering

501   His most respected mogul: Selznick quote from TCM's invitation card for the seven-part original documentary series (Episode 1), *Moguls and Movie Stars: A History of Hollywood* (2010).

501   And now: *Wellman Family History.*

502   Did he lose his enthusiasm?: Ibid.

502   Wellman tried to keep: "quitted"—term Wellman used for his retirement. In 1958, he told his family, "I quit. I'm not retired, I'm quitting"; obituary of James Aubrey, Jr., *Los Angeles Times*, September 11, 1994; author present during Wellman-Aubrey meeting.

503   After several months: Max Evans, *The Rounders* (New York: Macmillan, 1960).

503   Wellman was able: Paramount movie deal with Wellman as producer-director, from the Max Evans novel, *The Rounders*, screenplay by Tom Blackburn; deal memo, May 26, 1961, in Wellman file with other contractual info signed by Paramount story editor, Curtis Kenyon; synopsis from Wellman-Blackburn script, in Wellman file.

503   During the development stage: *The Memoirs of William Wellman*; Wellman conversations with author.

503   *The Rounders* was finally produced: TCM article.

504   This studio rejection: *Wellman Family History*.

504   The Wellman family doctor: Author present at hospital.

504   "I went to the hospital": Wellman, *Short Time for Insanity*, 48–50; *Wellman Family History*.

504   No other visitors: Ibid.

504   On the morning of November 6, 1961: According to the Los Angeles Fire Department's Historical Society, and *Los Angeles Times*, November 7, 2011.

505   Not all residents: *Wellman Family History*; author a participant during fire.

506   Wellman had released: Lester Linsk letter, Wellman files; TCM Overview: Merian C. Cooper biography, filmography.

506   Cooper's story about: Author present at initial meeting of Wellman and Cooper; Wellman script, notes.

507   A deal was struck: Memo contract and studio letters, one signed by Eduard Muhl, studio head, Wellman files.

507   When Wellman believed: *The Memoirs of William Wellman*; Wellman conversations with author.

507   There were only: Wellman conversations with author

507   In 1964: Wellman conversations with author; author present for initial Columbia Studio meeting with Wellman and Frankovich.

508   Unfortunately: Carlson, *Flying on Film*, 283–87; Dwiggins, *Hollywood Pilot*, 244–46, 42–48.

509   On Saturday, April 15, 1978: Aero Vintage Books website, Scott A. Thompson, Frank Tallman biography; obituary of Tallman, *Los Angeles Times*, May 11, 1978.

509   In the disappointment: Wellman conversations with author; author present at the Frankovich studio meeting; TCM Articles: *The Trouble with Angels* (1966).

509   With nothing successful: Wellman conversations, memoirs, and Hawthorne Books letters, Wellman files.

510   Soon after: Hospital nurse's records on file, Wellman files.

510   Mother Celia: *This Is Your Life*: William A. Wellman tape, Wellman files; author and family present at taping (1954); *Wellman Family History*.

512   March 4, 1968: *Wellman Family History*; events pictured in photo albums, written material, Wellman files.

512 "Everyone in Hollywood wanted": Robert Stack, *Wild Bill Hollywood Maverick.*

512 One of the men: Brownlow came to Wellman's home in 1964 for the book interview, *The Parade's Gone By* (1968); author present at film retrospective in 1972; Wellman, *Growing Old Disgracefully*, 69–118.

513 Even with the well-received: Author (producer) organized and was present at all events during monthlong festival. Tom Laughlin funded and executive-produced the event.

514 A highlight of the film festival: 1927 *Wings* photo album and playbook with biography of Chauncey Haines.

514 There were few sold-out: Author present at Royal Theatre in West Los Angeles.

514 The film festival date: Publication date for *A Short Time for Insanity* (Hawthorne Books), January 1, 1974; author present at television show taping.

514 By this time: Wellman, *Growing Old Disgracefully*, 313–16.

515 On the morning of July 25: Wellman left this part of the story out of his book.

515 The Wellmans arrived: Wellman and author, father and son; "Memorial De L'Escadrille Lafayette" report, 31 July 1926, Herbert Clarke Printer, 338 Rue St. Honore, Paris, France.

516 Wellman started a third edition: *Wellman Family History.*

516 At the end of: Wellman, *Short Time for Insanity*, 260, 26: his own obituary.

516 In September of 1975: Author present at hospital when news was announced.

517 "He's gotten through": Dottie's recollections and conversations with author.

517 On Thanksgiving Day: Gathering of the family; author present in Wellman's bedroom.

517 With Wellman's permission: A priest came from St. Martin of Tours in Brentwood; author was alone with Wellman for the last time; Wellman's words written down later.

518 Exactly three months from: Wellman, *Short Time for Insanity*, 262.

518 Dottie and the seven kids: The funeral was organized at the Santa Monica Airport with Dottie, the seven children, a pilot friend, and a Cessna.

519 The flight plan was set: As per Wellman's cremation instructions.

519 As the sound of the Cessna: Author read aloud the words that Wellman had written. From *Growing Old Disgracefully*, 153.

519 Addendum: From Wellman's last remarks; family history.

SELECTED BIBLIOGRAPHY

Adair, Gilbert. *Flickers: An Illustrated Celebration of 100 Years of Cinema*. London: Faber & Faber, 1995.

Alicoate, John W. *Film Daily Year Book*. 10th ed. New York: Film Daily, 1928.

Bogdanovich, Peter. *Who the Devil Made It*. New York: Alfred A. Knopf, 1997.

Brooks, Louise. *Lulu in Hollywood*. New York: Alfred A. Knopf, 1982.

Brownlow, Kevin. *Mary Pickford Rediscovered*. New York: Abrams, 1999.

———. *The Parade's Gone By*. New York: Alfred A. Knopf, 1968.

Cannom, Robert C. *Van Dyke and the Mythical City, Hollywood*. Culver City, CA: Murray & Gee, 1948.

Capra, Frank. *The Name Above the Title*. New York: Macmillan, 1971.

Carlson, Mark. *Flying on Film: A Century of Aviation in the Movies, 1912–2012*. Albany, GA: BearManor Media, 2012.

Cohen, Henry. *The Public Enemy*. Madison: University of Wisconsin Press, 1981.

Dene, Shafto. *Trail Blazing in the Skies*. Chicago: Lakeside Press, 1943.

Dick, Bernard F. *Engulfed: The Death of Paramount Pictures and the Birth of Corporate Hollywood*. Lexington: University Press of Kentucky, 2001.

Doherty. Thomas. *Hollywood's Censor*. New York: Columbia University Press, 2007.

Durant, John, and Alice Durant. *Pictorial History of American Presidents*. New York: A. S. Barnes, 1955.

Dwiggins, Don. *Hollywood Pilot: The Biography of Paul Mantz*. New York: Doubleday, 1967.

Eames, John Douglas. *The Paramount Story*. New York: Crown, 1985.

Eliot, Marc. *Cary Grant*. New York: Harmony/Random House, 2004.

Eyman, Scott. *The Speed of Sound*. Baltimore: Johns Hopkins University Press, 1999.

Farmer, James H. *America's Pioneer Aces*. California: BAC Publishers, 2003.

———. *Celluloid Wings: The Impact of Movies on Aviation*. Blue Ridge Summit, PA: TAB Books, 1984.

Freedland, Michael. *Gregory Peck*. New York: William Morrow, 1980.

Goldman, William. *Tinsel*. New York: Delacorte, 1979.

Gomery, Douglas. *The Hollywood Studio System*. London: British Film Institute, 2005.

Grace, Dick. *I Am Still Alive*. New York: Rand McNally, 1931.

Griffin, Richard, and Arthur Mayer. *The Movies*. New York: Bonanza, 1957.

Hall, James Norman, and Charles Bernard Nordhoff. *The Lafayette Flying Corps*, Vols. I & II. Boston: Houghton Mifflin, 1920.

Hart, Samantha. *Hollywood Walk of Fame*. La Cañada Flintridge, CA: Crybaby Books, 1987, 2000.

Higham, Charles. *Cecil B. DeMille*. New York: Scribner's, 1973.

Hirsch, Foster. *Otto Preminger: The Man Who Would Be King*. New York: Alfred A. Knopf, 2007.

Jeavons, Clyde. *A Pictorial History of War Films*. Secaucus, NJ: Citadel, 1974.

Jewell, Richard B. *The Golden Age of Cinema: Hollywood, 1929–1945*. Malden, MA: Blackwell, 2007.

Keith, Slim. *Slim*. New York: Simon & Schuster, 1990.

Kinn, Gail, and Jim Piazza. *The Academy Awards: The Complete Unofficial History*. New York: Black Dog & Leventhal, 2002.

Lasky, Jesse L. *I Blow My Own Horn*. New York: Doubleday, 1957.

Lasky, Jesse, Jr. *Whatever Happened to Hollywood?* New York: Funk & Wagnalls, 1973, 1975.

Leaming, Barbara. *Marilyn Monroe*. New York: Crown, 1998.

LoBrutto, Vincent. *Becoming Film Literate: The Art and Craft of Motion Pictures*. Westport, CT: Praeger, 2005.

Maltin, Leonard. *Classic Movie Guide*. New York: Penguin, 2014.

Marquis, Albert N. *Who's Who in America*. Vol. 15. Chicago: Marquis, 1928, 1929.

Mason, Herbert Molloy, Jr. *High Flew the Falcons*. New York: J. B. Lippincott, 1965.

McGilligan, Patrick. *Film Crazy*. New York: St. Martin's/Griffin, 2000.

Mosley, Leonard. *Lindbergh, a Biography*. New York: Doubleday, 1976.

Orrison, Katherine. *Lionheart in Hollywood*. Metuchen, NJ: Scarecrow Press, 1991.

Orriss, Bruce W. *When Hollywood Ruled the Skies*. Los Angeles: Aero Associates, 2013.

Paramount Produced Properties and Releases. Los Angeles: AMPAS, 1920–27.

Paris, Barry. *Louise Brooks*. New York: Alfred A. Knopf, 1989.

Parish, James R. *The Paramount Pretties*. New York: Random House, 1972.

Parkinson, Michael, and Clyde Jeavons. *A Pictorial History of Westerns*. London: Hamlyn, 1972.

Rickenbacker, Edward V. *Rickenbacker*. Engelewood Cliffs, NJ: Prentice Hall, 1967.

Riva, Maria. *Marlene Dietrich*. New York: Alfred A. Knopf, 1993.

Rollins, Peter C. *Hollywood as Historian*. Lexington: University Press of Kentucky, 1983.

Rubin, Steven J. *Combat Films: American Realism, 1945–2010*. Jefferson, NC: McFarland, 2011.

Schickel, Richard. *His Pictures in the Papers*. New York: Charterhouse, 1973.

———. *The Men Who Made the Movies*. New York: Atheneum, 1975

Sennett, Ted. *Warner Brothers Presents*. New Rochelle, NY: Arlington House, 1971.

Server, Lee. *Robert Mitchum: "Baby, I Don't Care."* New York: St. Martin's, 2001.

Seydor, Paul. *Peckinpah, the Western Films: A Reconsideration*. Chicago: University of Illinois Press, 1980, 1997.

Sheward, David. *The Big Book of Show Business Awards*. New York: Billboard, 1997.

Shipman, David. *The Great Movie Stars: The Golden Years.* New York: Bonanza, 1970.

Smart, Lawrence L. *The Hawks That Guided the Guns.* Privately printed, 1968.

Sragow, Michael. *Victor Fleming: An American Movie Master.* New York: Pantheon, 2008.

Suid, Lawrence H. *Guts and Glory: Great American War Movies.* Reading, MA: Addison-Wesley, 1978.

Teichmann, Howard. *Fonda: My Life.* New York: New American Library, 1981.

Thomas, Bob. *Golden Boy: The Untold Story of William Holden.* New York: St. Martin's, 1983.

———. *Selznick.* New York: Doubleday, 1970.

Thompson, Frank. *Lost Films.* New York: Citadel, 1996.

———. *Texas Hollywood.* San Antonio: Maverick, 2002.

———. *William A. Wellman.* Metuchen, NJ: Scarecrow Press, 1983.

Variety Film Reviews. Vol. 3. Los Angeles: Variety, 1926–1929.

Wanamaker, Marc, and Robert W. Nudelman. *Early Hollywood.* Charleston, SC: Arcadia, 2007.

Wellman, William A., Jr. *The Man and His Wings: William A. Wellman and the Making of the First Best Picture.* Westport, CT: Praeger, 2006.

Whitehouse, Arch. *Legion of the Lafayette.* Garden City: Doubleday, 1962.

Wilson, Victoria. *A Life of Barbara Stanwyck: Steel-True, 1907–1940.* New York: Simon & Schuster, 2013.

Wingart, Earl W. *Biographies of Paramount Players, 1930–1931.* New York: Paramount Publicity, 1931.

Wise, James E., and Anne Collier Rehill. *Stars in Blue, Stars in the Corps, Stars in Khaki.* Annapolis: Naval Institute Press, 1997–2000.

Documentary Film

Wild Bill Hollywood Maverick. Created and Executive Produced by William Wellman Jr. Produced by Kenneth Carlson. Directed by Todd Robinson. Wild Bill Pictures, 1996.

Wellman Sources

Wellman, William A. *A Short Time for Insanity.* New York: Hawthorne, 1974.

Wellman, William A. *Go, Get 'Em!* Boston: The Page Company, 1918.

Wellman, William A. *Growing Old Disgracefully.* Unpublished, 1974.

Wellman, William A. *Wrong Head on the Pillow.* Uncompleted, 1975.

Personal audiotapes of William Wellman, unpublished. Wellman spent countless hours telling his stories and remembrances into a tape recorder before making selections and writing them down.

The Memoirs of William Wellman, unpublished. Typed and pencil-written pages, letters, notes, photo albums with publicity, magazine and newspaper clippings, self-written labels, among other items of personal memorabilia.

Wellman Family History, unpublished. Conversations and written accounts from family members. *Celia Wellman Family History*, part of *Wellman Family History*.

INDEX

Page numbers in *italics* refer to illustrations.

A Note on the Type

This book was set in Adobe Garamond. Designed for the Adobe Corporation by Robert Slimbach, the fonts are based on types first cut by Claude Garamond (c. 1480–1561). Garamond was a pupil of Geoffroy Tory and is believed to have followed the Venetian models, although he introduced a number of important differences, and it is to him that we owe the letter we now know as "old style." He gave to his letters a certain elegance and feeling of movement that won their creator an immediate reputation and the patronage of Francis I of France.

Composed by North Market Street Graphics, Lancaster, Pennsylvania

Printed and bound by Berryville Graphics, Berryville, Virginia

Designed by Iris Weinstein